Sheer Joy

ALSO BY MATTHEW FOX

SHEER JOY

*Conversations with Thomas Aquinas
on Creation Spirituality*

MATTHEW FOX

Foreword by Rupert Sheldrake
Afterword by Bede Griffiths

Jeremy P. Tarcher/Putnam
a member of Penguin Group (USA) Inc.
New York

Most Tarcher/Putnam books are available at special quantity discounts for bulk purchase for sales promotions, premiums, fund-raising, and educational needs. Special books or book excerpts also can be created to fit specific needs. For details, write Penguin Group (USA) Inc. Special Markets, 375 Hudson Street, New York, NY 10014.

Jeremy P. Tarcher/Putnam
a member of
Penguin Group (USA) Inc.
375 Hudson Street
New York, NY 10014
www.penguin.com

First published in 1992 by HarperSanFrancisco

First Jeremy P. Tarcher/Putnam Edition 2003

Library of Congress Cataloging-in-Publication Data
Fox, Matthew, date.
Sheer joy : conversations with Thomas Aquinas on creation spirituality / Matthew Fox ; foreword by Rupert Sheldrake ; afterword by Bede Griffiths.
p. cm.
Originally published: San Francisco : HarperSanFrancisco, 1992.
Includes bibliographical references and index.
ISBN 1-58542-234-7
1. Spirituality—Catholic Church. 2. Catholic Church—Doctrines. 3. Thomas, Aquinas, Saint, 1225?–1274. I. Title.
BX2350.65 .F693   2003   2002075097
248.4'82—dc21

Printed in the United States of America
1   3   5   7   9   10   8   6   4   2

*Sheer joy is God's,
and this demands companionship.*

(In 1 Sent 2.1.4)

To Père M. D. Chenu, O.P.,
my mentor and brother in communion of thought,
who, like his brother Aquinas,
never shrank from studying the signs of his times.

And to Doris and George Carland,
for their never-failing encouragement.

CONTENTS

KEY TO ABBREVIATIONS USED IN FOOTNOTES

(with most likely dates of authorship)

AC	*Sermon on the Apostles Creed* (1273)
BCC	*Breviary Lessons for Corpus Christi* (1264)
CBH	*Commentary on Boethius's* De Hebdomadibus (1256–1259)
C et M	*De caelo et mundo (On Heaven and Earth)* (1272–1273)
CG	*Summa contra Gentiles (Summa Against the Gentiles)* (1259–1264)
CI	*Contra impugnantes Dei cultum et religionem (Against Those Attacking the Worship and Religion of God)* (1256)
CT	*Compendium theologiae (A Compendium of Theology)* (1269–1273)
DA	*De anima (On the Soul)* (1270)
DC	*De caritate (On Love)* (1269–1272)
DCC	*Commentary on Proclus's* De causis (1271–1272)
DDN	*Commentary on Dionysius's* De divinis nominibus (1261?)
DEE	*De ente et essentia (On Being and Essence)* (1252–1256)
De malo	*On Evil* (1266–1267)
De perf	*De perfectione vitae spiritualis (On the Perfection of the Spiritual Life)* (1269)
DP	*De potentia (On Power)* (1265–1266)
DRP	*De regimine principum (On the Ruling of Princes)* (1265–1267)
DT	*Commentary on Boethius's* De Trinitate (1258–1259)

DV	*De veritate (On Truth)* (1256–1259)
DVC	*Questiones de virtutibus cardinalibus (Questions about the Cardinal Virtues)* (1269–1272)
DVV	*De virtutibus (On the Virtues)* (1269–1272)
DS	*De spe (On Hope)* (1269–1272)
DSS	*De substantiis separatis (On Separated Substances)* (1271–1273)
DVI	*De unione verbi incarnati (On the Union of the Word Incarnate)* (1272)
IL	*Inaugural Lecture (1256)*
In Dec I	*In Decretalem I. Expositio ad Archdiaconum Tridentium (First Decretal. Letter to the Archdeacon of Trent)*
In Dec II	*In Decretalem II. Expositio ad Archdiaconum Tridentium de errore Abbatis Joachim contra Magistrum Petrum Lombardum. (Second Decretal. Letter to the Archdeacon of Trent concerning the error of Abbot Joachim in his polemic against Peter Lombard)*
In Col	*Commentary on the Letter to the Colossians* (1259–1265; 1272–1273)
In Cor	*Commentary on the Letter to the Corinthians* (1259–1265; 1272–1273)
In DA	*Commentary on Aristotle's* De anima (1269–1270)
In Eph	*Commentary on the Letter to the Ephesians* (1259–1265; 1272–1273)
In Ethics	*Commentary on Aristotle's* Ethics (1271)
In Heb	*Commentary on the Letter to the Hebrews* (1259–1265; 1272–1273)
In Is	*Commentary on Isaiah* (1256–1257?)
In Jer	*Commentary on Jeremiah* (1268?)
In Jn	*Commentary on the Gospel of John* (1269–1272)
In Job	*Commentary on Job* (1261)
In Lam	*Commentary on the Book of Lamentations* (1268?)

In Meta   *Commentary on Aristotle's* Metaphysics
           (1269–1272)

In Mt   *Commentary on the Gospel of Matthew*
           (1256–1259)

In Phil   *Commentary on the Letter to the Philippians*
           (1259–1265; 1272–1273)

In Pol   *Commentary on Aristotle's* Politics (1269–1272)

In Pss   *Commentary on the Psalms* (1273)

In Rom   *Commentary on the Letter to the Romans*
           (1259–1265; 1272–1273)

In Sent   *Commentary on Peter Lombard's* Books of
           Sentences (1252–1256)

In Thess   *Commentary on the Letter to the Thessalonians*
           (1259–1265; 1272–1273)

In Tim   *Commentary on the Letter to Timothy*
           (1259–1265; 1272–1273)

LAP   *Letter to the Archbishop of Palermo* (1261–1262?)

OF   *Sermon on the Our Father* (1273)

QQ   *Questiones quodlibetales (Questions on Any
           Subject)* (1271)

SC   *On Spiritual Creatures* (1267–1268)

Sermo   *Sermons on the Two Precepts of Charity and the
           Ten Precepts of the Law* (1273)

ST   *Summa theologiae (A Summa of Theology)*
           (1266–1273)

It is an honor to contribute to this marvelous book. And I write with the enthusiasm of a convert. In my education as a biologist I had hardly heard of St. Thomas Aquinas, except when he was dismissed as a medieval scholastic, one of those who whiled away their time disputing over how many angels could stand on the head of a pin. He belonged to the dark age of superstition that prevailed until the dawn of modern scientific consciousness.

This is still the predominant prejudice. From the conventional modern point of view, nature is inanimate and mechanical. This attitude was born in the scientific revolution of the seventeenth century. It arose in reaction against the organic, animistic worldview of the later Middle Ages. With the shift of metaphor from organism to machine, the world of Aquinas, pervaded by invisible souls and intelligences, seemed unscientific and incredible and was increasingly dismissed as an elaborate form of superstition.

It was not until 1978 that I came to know more about this great and visionary thinker, after more than twenty years' scientific research in universities and research institutes. By then, I had become convinced that mechanistic science was too limited. I was developing a new hypothesis, called the hypothesis of formative causation, involving the idea of an inherent memory in nature. At the age of thirty-five, I went to live in Dom Bede Griffiths's ashram on the bank of the Cauvery River near the small Tamil village of Tannirpalli, in South India. I was writing a book on this hypothesis called *A New Science of Life*. In the course of my stay, Father Bede introduced me to aspects of the Western philosophical and mystical traditions of which I was largely ignorant.

Under the palm trees of the ashram, I found that European culture contained a depth and wisdom to which I had been blind. And I found that St. Thomas's writings in particular were full of ideas relevant to the problems I was thinking about. He was writing about a living world pervaded by formative influences, by kinds of causation that went far beyond the limited conceptions of mechanistic science. He was what we would now call a holistic thinker, but he went much further than most modern holists in recognizing the all-pervasive influence of the spiritual realm.

Yet, although what I learned in India about the Western philosophical and mystical tradition was new to me, I realized that I had always known something about this great vision, not through books, but through my direct experience of Gothic cathedrals and churches. I was born and brought up in the English Midlands, only fifteen miles from Lincoln and eight from Southwell, and I often visited their cathedrals with my father. They are still among the most inspiring places I know. I now see that they are aspects of a great synthesis in which the Christian faith was brought together with pre-Christian animism. This took place through the assimilation of pre-Christian philosophies of the ancient world, the absorption of local beliefs and practices, and the spread of the cults of the Holy Mother and the saints. I had to go to India to appreciate the cultural and spiritual flowering of medieval Europe, and the part played in it by St. Thomas Aquinas. And in him I found a breadth of approach, a true catholicity, more commonly encountered today among Hindus than Christians: "Every truth without exception—and whoever may utter it—is from the Holy Spirit."

The triumph of the mechanistic worldview has given us the characteristic features of the modern world, including the ecological crisis. As the humanist dream of endless technological and economic progress turns into a nightmare, many are now searching for a new philosophy and way of life. In this process it is important for Westerners not only to learn from other cultures but also to recognize that there are major sources of inspiration within the Western tradition, including the writings of Aquinas.

Until now, Aquinas's insights have been buried in dusty tomes, some still only in Latin. They have also been hidden behind a fog of scholastic and neoscholastic commentary and interpretation, surviving him in very restricted habitats, such as

Roman Catholic seminaries. This book changes all that. Matthew Fox allows Aquinas to speak for himself, and at the same time the dialogue form enables the relevance of what he says to come across with great clarity. After more than seven centuries, we can meet Aquinas again and hear what he has to say to us.

I find that he has a lot to say to me. As a biologist, I especially like his strong sense of the spontaneity of life. But he goes far further and leads into an amazing realm of creative synthesis. For the life of nature and the life of the mind are not independent of the life of God; they are an expression of God's life and creative power:

> "Divine life" is supereminently living and the active and preserving cause of life per se, that is, of common life. Consequently, all particular life and all vital motion and every beginning of every life proceeds from divine life, which is above all life. . . . God is the cause of all life. Whether you call it the intellectual life in the case of the angels or rational as in the case of humans or sensible in the case of plants or whatever kind of life.

In the realm of biology, the animating principles are the souls of plants, animals, and man. They are the life-principles of the vitalist tradition. In a sense they have reemerged into modern science in the guise of fields, such as the morphogenetic fields that shape the development of embryos, plants, and animals. I have generalized this field idea, well-established in developmental biology, in the concept of morphic fields. These fields, according to the hypothesis of formative causation, contain an inherent memory, a kind of pooled or collective memory of the species. They organize not only bodily development but also instinctive behavior and mental activity.[1] Whether or not empirical research supports the idea of morphic fields, there is no doubt that much of the medieval conception of the soul as an invisible animating principle has been carried over into the field concept.[2] This is particularly clear in the case of magnets, which were believed from ancient times until the seventeenth century to have magnetic souls within and around them. Today we would say that the properties of magnets depend on the magnetic fields within and around them. In the context of electromagnetic fields, and particularly the properties of such fields expressed in holograms, I find Aquinas opens up an amazing vista of thought by inviting us to compare the pervasive nature of the soul with that of God: "The whole human soul is in the whole body and also in every part of the body, just as God is present to the entire universe."

This suggests to me a need to look for a connection between modern conceptions of fields and energy and aspects of God's being:

> Every creature participates in some way in the likeness of the Divine essence. All creatures are images of God, who is the first agent. . . . In all creatures there is a footprint of the Trinity.

I myself find it helpful to compare the field aspect of physical reality to the Logos, the Word, the formative principle. The energy aspect of reality, with energy as the principle of flow, change, and activity, is like an aspect of the Spirit. Both come from and relate back to a unifying source.

And if we are tempted to form too simple a conception of human nature, Aquinas reminds us

> When it is written, "The Creator made him to the image of God," the sense is not that the Father made the human to the image of the Son only, who is God, as some explained it, but that the Divine Trinity made the human to its image, that is, of the whole Trinity.

I am finding this book a source of joy and inspiration. I am sure that many others will do so.

RUPERT SHELDRAKE

NOTES

1. See Rupert Sheldrake, *A New Science of Life* (Los Angeles: Tarcher, 1982) and *The Presence of the Past* (New York: Vintage, 1989).
2. See Sheldrake, *The Rebirth of Nature* (New York: Bantam, 1991).

Thomas Aquinas's Spirituality and the Emerging Renaissance

The experience of God should not be restricted to the few or to the old.

(CG I, ch. 4 n. 4)

Psychologist Carl Jung once confessed that he "took a dive into St. Thomas but did not feel refreshed afterwards."[1] I suspect that Jung is not the only twentieth-century reader who has had that experience. Having attempted over many years to teach Aquinas in various forums and classrooms, I have been struck by what a stumbling block his scholastic methodology is to the twentieth-century mind. And yet much of his worldview is also shared by Hildegard of Bingen, Francis of Assisi, Mechtild of Magdeburg, Meister Eckhart, Dante, Julian of Norwich, Nicolas of Cusa, and other great spiritual thinkers of the medieval period, either because they influenced him (Hildegard and Francis) or because he influenced them (the others mentioned above).

For many years I have asked myself: Is Aquinas's spiritual genius in effect lost to us forever? Is he to be remembered solely by an academic elite who specialize in obscure rationalistic nitpicking? Is there any way to resurrect Aquinas from the dead? Is he worth resurrecting? Aquinas himself had an opinion about the questions I am asking when he said: "All of us have a natural desire to know God, and success in this quest should not be restricted to the few or to the old."[2] If Aquinas himself can assist us in our "desire to know God," then it is time to allow him a hearing that is not restricted to the elite few academic specialists or to those living out memories of a bygone era.

How This Book Attempts to Revision Our Understanding of Thomas Aquinas

In this book I attempt a way of making Aquinas accessible, giving him a forum so that he can be heard in our time. I present Thomas Aquinas entirely in his own words but in a form that I believe allows late twentieth-century minds and hearts to hear him in a fresh way. The structure of the book provides an essential basis for this revisioning of Thomas Aquinas. There are four aspects to it.

1. I descholasticize Aquinas by interviewing him. By interviewing Aquinas I am able to ask him *our* questions and allow him access to *our* pressing issues in spirituality. This is important because the questions that preoccupied his thirteenth-century contemporaries are of course not always the issues that concern us. As Aquinas himself put it, "even teachers in matters of faith are not bound to believe everything explicitly in every age. For there is a gradual progress in faith for the whole human race just as there is for individual persons."[3] There is something fitting about this interview form as well vis-à-vis medieval scholasticism: the very heart of scholasticism is the art of asking questions, so it should come as no shock to Thomas Aquinas to put our questions to him as I do in this book.

The interview method is also useful because among the source books that exist on Thomas Aquinas,[4] there is a supposition that such general philosophical categories as "God," "Man,"[5] "Moral Life," and so on will suffice for today's reader. Presuming that these categories interest the minds of our age leads to a critical deadness and often bores contemporary readers. The result is often a collection of Aquinas's sayings that is only partially useful and only partially vital. The dissection of Aquinas's thought that results leaves the reader looking for the juice, the vitality, the person behind the analytic mind. It is my experience that many students are not excited by such presentations. The interview method that I have used separates him from a scholastic methodology that is cumbersome to the twentieth-century mind, allowing him to speak freshly again.[6] His personal side, his passionate and mystical personality come through, especially in his biblical commentaries.

2. The second approach to Aquinas I've taken here is to translate many of his biblical commentaries as well as his *Commentary on Dionysius* into English for the first time. It is remarkable how few of Aquinas's biblical commentaries have been translated, especially in light of how important scripture was to Aquinas, to the Dominicans of his day, and to the entire intellectual awakening of the twelfth and thirteenth centuries. As Pere Chenu says of Aquinas's work in Scripture: It "must certainly have extended over the whole of his teaching career since commenting on the Bible was the prime task of the master in theology."[7] How conveniently Thomists lost sight of Chenu's observation that "in XIIIth century theological teaching the Bible was the basic book. . . . In the XIIIth century, the university institution produced disputed questions and *summas* only within the framework of scriptural teaching."[8]

To recover Aquinas's whole spirituality we must get back to his scriptural works.[9] This is of great significance for correctly regrounding our understanding of Aquinas—not in an exclusively philosophical tradition, but in a biblical, theological one. Aquinas knew the Bible thoroughly, and it is sad to note how uninterested many Thomists have been in his biblical theology over the centuries. Weisheipl comments that "there are ten distinct works that must be ascribed to Thomas as the fruit of his mature years as master: the commentary on Job, that on the prophecies and lamentations of Jeremiah, that on the Psalms, that on the Canticle of Canticles, and those on Matthew, John, and the letters of Paul respectively."[10] This being the case—that his biblical commentaries represent the "fruit of his mature years as master—," it is even more surprising that they have so often been ignored. These works are fully employed in the Conversations that follow.

One reason why Aquinas's biblical commentaries are so important to a complete treatment of his spirituality is that in them he is less restricted by a scholastic methodology than in his other works. Following the inner logic of the biblical text, he is free to make connections, let his creative genius work, and allow his heart as well as his head to speak. Here his passion often comes tumbling out—especially when he is speaking of his favorite love, Wisdom.

As for his *Commentary on Dionysius,* Aquinas found in the sixth-century Syrian monk (who, until the fourteenth century, was believed to be St. Paul's companion, as mentioned in the *Acts of the Apostles*) a cosmological thinker, an alternative to the introspective conscience of Augustine that so dominated Western thought. Aquinas wrote his *Commentary on Dionysius* early in his career, and in many ways it should be considered an underlying source work to all his subsequent works. He was led through it by his mentor, Albert the Great, when he was in his twenties. It was supplemented late in his life by his series of commentaries on Aristotle, the scientific cosmologist who was being newly discovered by way of Islam in Aquinas's time.

All his life Aquinas had a passion for cosmology, which attracted him to both Dionysius and Aristotle.[11] The latter attraction cost him a great deal of support in the Christian community when he accepted the "pagan" Aristotle's science in order to return a cosmological perspective to the Christian faith. Indeed, it could be said that this attraction cost him his life and certainly his sanity; during his last year he was rendered mute, and it is said that he died of burnout and intense fighting, a breakdown—a loss of anima, as Louise von Franz puts it.[12] During those last years he fought with both the Christian "fundamentalists" on the right, who abhorred the idea of science and cosmology, and with the "secularized" followers of Siger of Brabant, who increasingly claimed authority for interpreting Aristotle and stripped him of any overtones about the Divine. Aquinas found himself increasingly isolated, yet in the middle between these two extremes. He felt you could "have it both ways": science and knowledge of nature and therefore of the God of nature through whatever tradition (for grace does not eradicate nature but complements it), and revelation of God through Scripture and church traditions. As he puts it in our "First Conversation," "Revelation comes in two volumes—that of nature and that of the Bible."

Protestants in particular have been left out in the cold by the scant attention paid to Aquinas's biblical bases, beginning with Martin Luther himself, who never read Aquinas's scriptural works but reacted angrily to the exclusively "summa-oriented" Thomists of his day. I hope that this reclamation of Aquinas's scriptural insights might invite Protestants into the amazing cosmological and mystical world of Aquinas, who, after all, was a Christian protester himself, deeply in touch with his prophetic vocation.

3. A third feature of my treatment of Aquinas is an attempt to center our conversations on the themes of spirituality and around the Four Paths of creation spirituality in particular. I know no other source book or reader on Aquinas that has attempted to map out his spirituality. One reason for this is that, in the words of my former professor of the history of Christian spirituality at the Institut catholique de Paris, l'abbé Louis Cognet, "Aquinas does not have even one question in his *Summa theologiae* about spirituality because his spirituality is everywhere throughout his work."[13] For Aquinas—as for any creation-based thinker—all of life, existence itself, the universe, all history, is mysterious and holy. Or, as Rabbi Heschel puts it, "Just to be is a blessing; just to live is holy."[14] The reader will see this theology amply laid out in our "First Conversation," on what the creation spirituality tradition calls the Via Positiva. There it becomes abundantly clear that cosmology is the key to Aquinas's spirituality being "everywhere." The lack of cosmology on the part of Western interpreters of Aquinas for centuries is also key to our misuse of Aquinas and misunderstanding of his spiritual genius over the ages.

What this book offers is not only an exploration of the spirituality implicit in all of Aquinas's work but also a *hermeneutic* applied to that work. That hermeneutic or interpretation is one of the gifts of creation spirituality in our time.[15] Without the critical hermeneutic that creation spirituality affords, studies on spirituality lack depth and run the extreme danger of falling into pious ideologies and sentimental thoughts that, among other things, serve to sacralize the status quo. Invariably the dialectic of mysticism/prophecy is ignored and creativity and justice are relegated to forgetfulness.[16]

Specifically, the hermeneutic in this book consists of the Four Paths of the Via Positiva (experiencing the God of delight and joy); the Via Negativa (experiencing the God of darkness, letting go, and suffering); the Via Creativa (experiencing the God with whom we cocreate); and the Via Transformativa (experiencing God by doing justice, celebration, and compassion in society). These Four Paths serve as the outline of this source book on Aquinas. They allow us to gather his wisdom from *all* his writings—biblical as well as Aristotelian commentaries, both his summas as well as his philosophical questions—into a coherent "conversation" on the issues in spirituality that interest us most keenly.

Curious to tell, there are passages in Aquinas that come very close to naming the Four Paths as I have named them above and elsewhere. Says Aquinas:

> Now order is related to reason in a fourfold way. There is one order that reason does not establish but only beholds, such is the order of things in nature. [I see this act of "beholding" as commensurate to Paths I and II, which are paths of nonaction or beholding of awe and darkness.] There is a second order that reason establishes in its own act of consideration, for example, when it arranges its concepts among themselves, and the signs of concepts as well, because words express the meanings of the concepts. There is a third order that reason establishes in the operations of the will. [I see these two "orders" as commensurate with the Via Creativa, which gives birth to both words and will or heart.] There is a fourth order that reason in planning establishes in the external things that it causes, such as a chest and a house. [This fourth order can be seen as the Via Transformativa.][17]

One might also approach the Four Paths in Aquinas's work by way of the four causes that he and Aristotle develop so fully. In some ways the Via Positiva is the efficient cause, the beginning of things and of our spiritual journeys (our delight and awe); the Via Negativa somewhat parallels the material cause since it is the source of the journey in the sense of a return to the source or nothingness by letting go (also, matter as privation and emptiness); the Via Creativa certainly corresponds to the formal cause, because it is in our creativity that we give birth to the form that expresses our imagination; and the Via Transformativa corresponds to the final cause, the "cause of causes," which in the creation spiritual tradition is compassion. But this also takes us back to Path 1 and the efficient cause, just as celebration (an integral part of compassion) takes us back to increased delight and awe (the Via Positiva). For compassion for Aquinas is the beginning and the end of all beings.

Aquinas also speaks of a fourfold path on another occasion when he says:

> The soul is elevated toward God in four ways: namely, for the purpose of admiring the height of God's power, as in Isaiah 40: "Lift your eyes on high, and see who created these things." And in Psalm 103: "How wonderful are your works, O Lord." And this is the elevation of faith. Second, the mind is raised for the purpose of extending toward the excellence of eternal Beauty, as in Job 2: "You can lift your face without stain, you will be stable and you will not fear. You will also forget misery, and as it were the noontime brightness will rise for you." And this is the elevation of hope. Third, the mind is raised for clinging to divine good and sanctity, as Isaiah puts it (51): "Lift, rise up Jerusalem, etc." And this is the elevation of charity. Fourth, the mind is lifted in work for the imitating of divine justice as in Lamentations 5: "We will lift up our hearts with our hands to God in the heavens." And this is the elevation of justice.[18]

It is evident that these "four ways" or "four movements" correspond strikingly to the Four Paths of creation spirituality.[19]

4. My treatment of Aquinas also attempts to take us beyond the modern era's interpretation and use of Aquinas. The era that began with the Enlightenment in the eighteenth century is referred to as the "modern era" and is often characterized as being mechanistic and literalistic. Enlightenment prejudices have often been employed in interpreting Aquinas over the centuries.

Creation spirituality has been called a "postmodern theology,"[20] a name I don't mind as long as the term "premodern" is used as well. In our yearning for cosmology today, a yearning made critical in light of our ecological crises, youth crises, poverty crises in so-called third world countries, and various ecofeminist movements, we need to look not only at moving out of the modern era but also at the wisdom that preceded the modern era. When Voltaire, one of the champions of the modern era's "Enlightenment," declared that he wanted to "exterminate Aphrodite," he was talking about killing the principle of eros (love of life) that characterized much of the wisdom spirituality of pagan and biblical peoples previous to the modern era. As Chartres Cathedral as well as Francis of Assisi's devotion to "Lady Poverty" can attest, Aphrodite was by no means absent from the medieval spiritual renaissance. But Voltaire and company have pretty much achieved their goal for Western culture. The goddess appears dead. Mother Earth is dying everywhere.[21] With the banishment of eros from society and religion we have a growth in pornography of many stripes, including militarism, the great art form developed by twentieth-century humanity.

Is Western culture what Carl Jung calls "an error outlived"? Is our society so devoid of imagination, as Henry Adams declared at the beginning of this century, that we can construct neither "an art nor a faith"? I agree with psychologist James Hillman that a time of cultural breakdown is a time for "going back" to retrieve some of the wisdom of our ancestors. While he chooses to go back to the sixteenth century, I prefer going back to the twelfth and thirteenth centuries, when there was a renaissance that the great historian Pere Chenu has called "the only renaissance that succeeded in the Western world." It worked because it caught the imaginations and elicited the labor of freed serfs, women, and the young. It was a grassroots renaissance ushered in by a recovery of the goddess, the symbol of cosmic creativity and divine beauty within all beings. (In 125 years, five hundred churches the size of Chartres Cathedral were built in France, all dedicated to Mary, the mother goddess of Christianity.) With the recovery of the goddess there appeared the archetype of the green man, also found in and on these cathedrals.[22] The Cosmic Christ was in the air—as well as in the sculpture of twelfth-century cathedrals. This renaissance worked because a cosmology underlined it. It involved, as Chenu puts it, "new birth, new existence in all the changed conditions of times, places, and persons."[23] It was not mere imitation, which is what fueled so much of the elitist and excessively anthropocentric renaissance of the sixteenth century.[24]

In many ways Thomas Aquinas embodies the story of the twelfth- and thirteenth-century renaissance. He was an important figure in the liberation movements of his day, ranging from university to church, from the city life that displaced feudalism to the preaching and poverty movement. As Josef Pieper puts it:

The intellectual dynamics of the early thirteenth century was
. . . determined chiefly by two forces, both revolutionary and
both of tremendous vitality: on the one hand the radical evan-
gelism of the voluntary poverty movement, which rediscov-
ered the Bible and made it the guide to Christian doctrine and
Christian life; and on the other hand the no less fierce urge to
investigate, on the plane of pure natural philosophy, the reality that lay before men's eyes. . . . The remarkable thing
about St. Thomas, who was exposed to these two intellectual
currents while he was still a student at Naples, is that he recognized and accepted the rightness of both approaches; that he
identified himself with both; that he affirmed both, although
they seemed mutually opposed to one another; and that he
attempted to incorporate both in his own spiritual and intellectual life.[25]

From an intellectual point of view, Aquinas's efforts achieved
a kind of architecture of the mind no less impressive than the
newly invented architecture of the Gothic Cathedral proved to
be for churches. Aquinas's work furnishes a kind of conduit for
the microcosm/macrocosm spiritual psychology of Hildegard
of Bingen and Francis of Assisi, who preceded him. And it furnishes a launching pad for the spirituality of Mechtild, Eckhart,
Dante (one of whose teachers, Remigio de' Girolomi, studied
under Aquinas), and Julian of Norwich and Nicholas of Cusa,
who look back on Aquinas, incorporating his creation theology
into living praxis. Each of these persons, not unlike Aquinas,
underwent opposition reminiscent of all prophets.

My perspective in this book, then, is both premodern and
postmodern, because only by consciously leaving the modern
era of mechanism and dualism, patriarchy and anthropocentrism, control and rationalism, can we recover our hearts and
well as our minds.

It is equally true that, in terms of our efforts to appreciate
Aquinas, we need to leave Thomism behind. Thomism is, like
so many "isms," a reductionistic movement ossified and ide-
ologized, lacking in Thomas Aquinas's breadth and depth of
spirit. It is little wonder that Thomists have brought us so little
of Aquinas's spirituality—they cannot possibly be aware of it
when they ignore, for example, the Bible. Or social justice. Or
the mystical. Or cosmology and science's story of the universe.

Or the apophatic God of the Via Negativa. Or creativity. Or the theological tradition of original blessing.

Just as Jung was not a Jungian and Jesus was not a Christian and Buddha was not a Buddhist, so Aquinas was not a Thomist. I believe that the Four Paths of creation spirituality employed herein as a basic hermeneutic along with a conscious effort to leave the modern, Enlightenment era behind us can assist us in leaving Thomism behind us as well. Josef Pieper writes: "It seems to me highly questionable to treat the teaching of St. Thomas as an 'ism,' and . . . we should use the term 'Thomism' only with important reservations."[26]

Let me make myself perfectly clear. I have not written this book in order to restore Thomism in any shape or form whatsoever. I am not a Thomist, nor a neo-Thomist, nor a crypto-Thomist. I am a late twentieth-century citizen deeply concerned about the way our species is treating the Earth, our young, women, the poor, other creatures, our bodies, and our souls. I am a student of Western spirituality for the purpose of learning what wisdom lies hidden in the recesses of our tradition that will help us to change our ways of living, relating, celebrating, and healing. It has been my privilege to dig in to the treasures of Meister Eckhart (who was deeply indebted to Aquinas), Hildegard of Bingen, Julian of Norwich, Nicolas of Cusa, and others from the Middle Ages.[27] But Thomas Aquinas belongs with these others as a spiritual writer in his own right. Indeed, in writing this book I have come to admire Aquinas as a genius who is as imposing as Albert Einstein, Wolfgang Mozart, or Hildegard of Bingen. I find much power and wisdom in Thomas Aquinas, and the purpose of this book is to make available to others some of that wisdom and some of that empowerment.

To do this, however, the reader cannot approach Aquinas with the left brain alone. To comprehend Aquinas's spirituality one must read this book with right *and* left brain, with heart *and* head. Aquinas has suffered long enough from persons interpreting him without heart, without cosmology, without wisdom, without mysticism. A rationalist ideology does an injustice to Aquinas's lifework. I was amazed in writing this book to see Aquinas say that the bodily organ corresponding to the intellect is the heart and indeed to see how much emphasis he puts on the heart throughout his writing.

While this book may be understood as an "Aquinas Reader," and I hope it inspires persons in that fashion, still it is more than that. It is a treatise on spirituality in Aquinas's own words. Recently I lectured on Aquinas using some of his own words found in this text, and three responses to the lecture remain vividly with me. One person said: "I have been a Catholic all my life. This presentation shows me how vulnerable truth is." Another student expressed "grief" over the way she had been taught Aquinas in the past and how distorted a view of him she had received. A third person said he had studied Aquinas in Catholic universities on several occasions and had never once heard the exciting things Aquinas had said in the citations I had put forward. Aquinas's truth has often been distorted by his interpreters during the modern, rationalist era, interpreters whose souls were seldom the size of his own. To use one of Aquinas's favorite terms, pusillanimous souls were not capable of receiving his magnanimous ideas. Often, in a "procrustean bed" kind of process, Aquinas's soul was reduced to the size of that of his interpreters.

Aquinas himself addresses one of the problems I have with Thomists in the very beginning of his *Summa theologiae* when he says he is writing the book because students he has known are frequently hampered on account of "the multiplication of useless questions, articles, and arguments" and because what is necessary for students to learn is "not taught according to the order of the subject matter, but according to the plan of the book."[28] Many persons teaching Aquinas have not been treating the important questions and have not followed any order proper to the subject matter because they have not known the history of Western spirituality. Ignorant of creation theology and deprived of an appreciation of the origin of wisdom literature in goddess history, they lack a deep and critical hermeneutic that would allow the issues of spirituality to emerge from Aquinas's thought. I hope that this book does what Aquinas attempted when he says that in his *Summa theologiae* he endeavors "to avoid these and other like faults."[29]

The modernist era is a rationalist era. Descartes, one of its philosophical founders, said, "I think, therefore I am." Aquinas is prerationalist just as he is premodernist. Yet some Thomists, while frequently rejecting much of Descartes and modern philosophy in argumentation, in fact have often succumbed to rationalist tendencies in vigorous attempts to prove Aquinas was "scientific" and respectably rational. In doing so they have often limited themselves to the scholastic texts of Aquinas and the linear thinking of scholasticism. I believe Aquinas deserves—and we today require from Aquinas—a nonlinear celebration of his amazingly mystical *and* intellectual thought. This book attempts to provide a first step in that process of revisioning this deep and mystical thinker. (The "Second Conversation" on the Via Negativa provides his own arguments for a nonlinear naming of the divine experience.) The form of a dialogue provides Aquinas an outlet for his amazingly dialectical and dynamic and even passionate cosmic spirituality. Yet the words in this book attributed to him *are all his own.*

The Second Vatican Council held from 1962 to 1965 resulted in the de-emphasis of Thomism, and with good reason. But now it is time to look again—not at Thomism, but at Aquinas; and not through Thomist lenses but through the larger lenses of creation spirituality, the new cosmology, and the hermeneutic it can offer us.

My own personal encounter with Aquinas goes back to my high school days when, attending public high school and engaging many friends in philosophical debates, at the suggestion of my parish priest I read some Aquinas and some of G. K. Chesterton on Aquinas. Then, when I joined the Dominican Order, we studied an immense amount of Aquinas in our philosophy training (in particular his commentaries on Aristotle's *Ethics* and *Physics* and *Posterior Analytics* and *Metaphysics*). And later, in theology, we studied his *Summa theologiae.* But how much of Aquinas we never studied! We never studied his biblical works nor his *Commentary on Dionysius,* nor did the words "mysticism" or "prophecy" ever come up in connection with Aquinas. I hope an attempt to ask some new questions of this medieval "master" may assist us in appreciating him as the mystic and prophet that he was. It may also assist a new generation of young seekers after spirituality to find some wisdom from their Western heritage.

Even though the expressed method of this book is to allow Aquinas to speak in his own words, it is of course an interpretative work. (Einstein and Heisenburg have demonstrated that all human knowledge is interpretative and relative—one of the principles that moves us beyond the modern era's obsession with supposed "objectivity.") This book is interpretative by the questions I ask, the order in which I ask them, the texts I have chosen in composing Aquinas's "answers," and the texts I leave out. In this first postmodern interpretation of Aquinas, my hope is that we can recover some of his spiritual genius. Aquinas has often been the victim of a reductionism that has practically managed to stifle him. The abuse of Aquinas perpetrated by reducing his thought to a comfortable ideology had already occurred as early as the sixteenth century, when, as Pere Chenu comments, Thomists had lost the spirit of discovery that was so important to Aquinas and offered nothing new to the issues raised by the Renaissance in that era.[30]

One reason for my methodology is aptly put by Aquinas himself when he writes that "we accept from certain of our predecessors whatever views about the truth of things we think true and disregard the rest."[31] In other words, not everything from the past is of equal value to us today. I hope that the methodology employed in this book will allow to come forward some of what is truly valuable from Aquinas. And we can let go of what is not. (I will elaborate on both these areas later in this introduction.) Let those who complain about my choices being selective meditate on how selective most topics are that Thomists have brought forth from Aquinas and especially how thoroughly they have left out the cosmic vision, the lifelong struggle to bring matter and spirit together, the political consciousness of the rights of the poor, the commitment to intellectual and religious ecumenism that so inspired this mystical genius and intellectual prophet.

I hope this book and the four points briefly enunciated in this introduction assist the process of making Aquinas available to more students of spirituality. I envision this book as a source book from which new insights can be derived concerning our Western spiritual heritage, a heritage that is by no means one-sidedly psychological, introspective, anthropocentric, guilt-ridden, shame-based, and politically right wing. When we read the shocking denigration of nature and human nature, of body and sexuality, that professor Jean Delumeau collects in his *Sin and Fear: The Emergence of a Western Guilt Culture 13th—18th*

Centuries, we understand anew the radical alternative that Aquinas stood for. As Delumeau puts it, Aquinas "spurned the macabre" that so dominated European fall/redemption spirituality;[32] he also honored human intelligence. In short, Aquinas is indeed part of the "family tree" of creation spirituality mystic/prophets, even if his interpreters have not always been of the same tradition.[33]

Aquinas's Story: His Life and Writings

Born in 1225 in a castle named Roccasecca near Naples, Thomas Aquinas practically embodied controversy his entire life and beyond. He was born of a family of lower nobility whose intentions were that he would one day be abbot of the famed Monte Casino Abbey, thereby uplifting the fallen family fortunes. They put him in that abbey's school as a Benedictine oblate at the age of five. Nine years later he left the abbey to pursue undergraduate arts studies at the University of Naples, a state university independent of the pope. It was there that he heard the Irish lecturer Peter of Hibernia lecture on Aristotle, whose thought was considered so revolutionary that the pope had forbidden Christians to study it.

In 1244 Aquinas received the Dominican habit at Naples. This new and "upstart" movement had been launched in 1215 by Dominic, a contemporary of Francis of Assisi. The order, among other things, dared to teach in the newly invented universities, and it rejected outright the feudal/monastic political/religious establishment. Chesterton reports that for a person of Aquinas's pedigree to join this group was comparable in our time to "running away and marrying a gypsy." This especially for one whose family had their sights on the establishment's place of honor at Monte Casino. So upset was his family with his decision to join this upstart religious order that on the way to study with the Dominicans in Paris he was kidnapped by his brothers at the instigation of his mother and imprisoned at Roccasecca. He resisted temptations to give up his vocation, including, we are told, sexual enticements.[34]

With the help of his sister, Aquinas was liberated from prison after about a year. In 1245 the Dominicans sent him to Paris where he met his mentor, the great Dominican scientist, philosopher, and alchemist, Albert the Great, whom he followed to Cologne in 1248. Ordained there, he returned to Paris in 1252 for graduate studies, first as a biblical bachelor (1252–1254) and next as a bachelor of the *Sentences* and lecturer on Scripture (1254–1256). In 1256 he was promoted to master of theology by a special papal dispensation because he was four years underage. After teaching theology in Paris from 1257 to 1259, he set out for Italy when he was called to the papal court at Anagni, Orvieto, Rome, and Viterbo. In 1269 he returned to teach in Paris, where he stayed until 1272, when he returned to Naples as master of theology at the university and the Dominican House of Studies. The following year, while celebrating the Eucharist in the chapel of St. Nicholas on December 6, he had an experience that rendered him mute. His closest relatives and associates thought he had gone crazy. The only words he spoke were as follows: "such things have been revealed to me that all that I have written seems to me as so much straw." He wrote not a word after this event, and he fell silent. He died on March 7, 1274, in a Cistercian monastery of Fossanuova, where he was taken when he fell ill on the road. He was forty-nine years old and on the way to the Church Council of Lyons called by Pope Gregory IX.

On March 7, 1277, Stephen Tempier, Bishop of Paris, condemned 219 statements, including many of Thomas's. The same year Robert Kilwardby, O.P., archbishop of Canterbury, condemned the philosophic positions of Thomas. In 1278 the General Chapter of the Dominicans upheld Thomas's teaching, while in 1282 the General Chapter of the Franciscans prohibited the reading of his *Summa theologiae* in their schools. In 1284 a later archbishop of Canterbury, John Peckham, again condemned Thomas's ideas. In 1323 Pope John XXII canonized Thomas Aquinas, and in 1324 the archbishop of Paris, Stephen Bourret, revoked the condemnation of Aquinas by the bishop of Paris in 1277. The man was at least as controversial in his death as he had been in his life.

A bizarre story ensues that reinforces the controversy that was Aquinas throughout his life. It seems that the Cistercian monks where he died exhumed his corpse and cut off the head so that, if the Dominicans came to claim the body, they would have a hardy relic of their own. Later they also boiled the flesh off the corpse so that they could keep the bones in a small container. Eventually the Dominicans retrieved all that was left of the body for internment in Toulouse, France, where it lies today and where Dominic had founded his order years earlier.[35]

There is much discussion about what transpired in Aquinas's final year, whether his going mute was a mystical experience, or whether it was a mental "breakdown" (James Weisheipl's word) brought on by his intense work schedule and vociferous intellectual battles against right-wing Christians who hated his embrace of the "pagan" scientist Aristotle as well as against atheistic Aristotelians of the camp of Siger of Brabant. I reproduce at the end of our "Second Conversation" a portion of a work, ascribed by some scholars to Aquinas, of a theologian undergoing a kind of schizophrenic episode resulting from, as Louise von Franz puts it, a rupture from his anima. All these theories may in fact be quite compatible with one another. The volume of his output was not only extraordinary in its quantity but heroic in its quality for many years. The battles in which he was ensnared would not let up. On at least one occasion the king of France had to call out his troops to surround the convent Aquinas occupied in Paris because the crowds were so anxious for his blood. Perhaps one episode that most punished the anima side of his soul was the abandonment he must have felt when his lifelong companion in theology, the Franciscan Bonaventure, drew back from Aquinas when he explored Aristotle in his final years and retreated to a safer, Augustinian worldview. (Bonaventure also accepted a political office, that of master general of the Franciscans, whereas Aquinas is said to have rejected an offer to become a cardinal, for example.) I suspect that some of the strong things that Aquinas says about the need to love truth more than friends, indeed to love truth as a friend, may have stemmed from that traumatic episode in his life (see "Third Conversation"). When we reflect on the tragic story that Aquinas's life became—not unlike the tragedy of Francis of Assisi, who had his order taken from him before he died, or Jesus' execution—one of Aquinas's own astute observations might provide some insight. He writes:

> It is related of Blessed John the Evangelist in the *Conferences of the Fathers* that when some people were scandalized on finding

him playing together with his disciples, he is said to have told
one of them who carried a bow to shoot an arrow. And when
the latter had done this several times, he asked him whether
he could do it indefinitely, and the man answered that if he
continued doing it, the bow would break. Whence the
Brother John drew the inference that in like manner a person's
mind would break if its tension were never relaxed.[36]

I think the evidence of Aquinas's exertion and burnout is
overwhelming. His bow simply broke.

I sketched above the basic elements of his life journey. Let us
now consider his writings, which were the bow that he wielded
in his battles to bring a cosmic spirituality to Western theology.
It is estimated by Professor Weisheipl that a complete edition of
Aquinas's works would fill forty to fifty volumes. Current edi-
tions we have fill twenty-five volumes of encyclopedic-sized
pages averaging 650 pages apiece. Among these volumes—all
handwritten, often in nearly unintelligible shorthand, or dictated to secretaries, who of course wrote them by hand or took
them down as notes during his lectures—are the following major works:

Commentary on the Book of the Sentences (by Peter Lombard)

Summa contra Gentiles

Summa theologiae

Debated questions: special topics, including *On Evil; On the
Power of God; On Spiritual Creatures; On the Soul; On Truth;
On the Union of the Incarnate Word; On the Virtues*

Commentaries on Scripture, including the Psalms; Isaiah; Jeremiah; Lamentations; Job; the Gospel of Matthew; the Gospel of John; Paul's Epistles; Letter to the Hebrews; and
Catanea aurea, which is a collection of patristic commentaries on the four Gospels.

Commentaries on Aristotle, including *On Generation and Corruption; On the Heavens and Earth; On Interpretation; On
Memory and Recall; On the Metaphysics; On Meteorology; On
the Nicomachean Ethics; On the Physics; On the Politics; On the
Posterior Analytics; On Sensation; On the Soul.*

Other commentaries, including *On Boethius's treatise "How Substances, Insofar as They Are, Are Good"; On Boethius's "On the Trinity"; on Dionysius's "On the Divine Names"; On Proclus's "The Causes."*

Treatises on special topics, including *On Being and Essence; On the Combining of the Elements; On the Commendation and Division of Sacred Scripture; A Compendium of Theology (Treatise of Faith, Hope and Charity); On Fallacies; On Kingship, to the King of Cyprus; On Modal Propositions; On the Principles of Nature; On Separate Substances.*

General debates, including *On the Admission of Boys into Religion; On the Meanings of Holy Scripture; On the Divine Attributes; On the Manual Work of Religious; On the Immortality of the Soul; Whether the Conjoined Soul Knows Itself Through Its Essence.*

Polemical writings, including *Against Those Attacking the Worship of God and Religion (Apologia for Religious Orders); On a Common Intellect (Against Averroists); Against the Destructive Doctrine of Those Who Would Deter Boys from Entering Religious Life (Apologia for Religious Orders); On the Eternity of the World; On the Perfection of Religious Life.*

Five "opinions rendered" and numerous letters, ranging from a discussion on usury to "How to Study" to "Astrology" to "The Movement of the Heart."

Liturgical pieces, including *On the Angelic Salutation; On the Apostles' Creed; On the Lord's Prayer; Office of the Feast of Corpus Christi;* prayers, such as "Adoro te" and other poems; also some sermons.

It is almost exhausting to list these works, much less read them! It is little wonder that Professor Weisheipl reports that Aquinas always had four secretaries with him to help with his work. What a life's work to have composed them all in a twenty-one-year period (1252–1273) and with the attention to quality and depth that for the most part characterizes them. And of course, this was before photocopiers, computers, typewriters. It is important to remember that his great *Summa theologiae* was not finished when he went mute and died. It is a great unfinished symphony, and I suspect there is a deeper meaning to this: it stands unfinished and therefore open-ended.

Does it seem strange, on reading this list of accomplishments and gifts from this great artist of ideas, that he burned out or broke down or was "completely out of his senses" (as his sister said of him), and fell exhausted before he was fifty? One thing he is reported to have said after laying down his pen was the following: "The only thing I want now is that as God has put an end to my writing, he may quickly end my life also." Three days following this statement he set out for his final journey. To me the statement reveals how thoroughly he had identified his writing with his being. He was an artist. His vocation was to write and to think; when he could not do so, he was finished living. To end one was to end the other. More of his love of his creative vocation emerges in our "Third Conversation" when he speaks of the power of teaching, writing, and sharing the "fruits of one's contemplation with others."

His life was not only controversial; it was ironic—here was the greatest thinker and most prodigious writer in Christendom struck mute. His life in its entirety is a kind of parable filled with paradox. Part of that paradox indeed has been the use to which his life and work has sometimes been put by rigid enforcers of orthodoxy who ignore his teachings on conscience and justice (see the "Fourth Conversation") as facilely as they do his commitment to Scripture and to creativity. This misuse to which Aquinas has been put ignores entirely the Zenlike quality of his call for emptying the mind of all things and undergoing the apophatic God of darkness about whom we can know nothing except that we know nothing (see the "Second Conversation").

Sources of Aquinas's Spirituality

Another result of Aquinas having become an "ism" has been the "freezing" of his thought into dogmatic statements and proof-texts. It is hard to imagine anything further from his own spirit, which is so deeply ecumenical.[37] Aquinas sought truth like a wild animal seeks food, and he sought it wherever he could get it. The story is told that when he was first shown the rising new Cathedral of Notre Dame being constructed on the *Ile de la Cité* in Paris, his response was: "I would give it all for just one of

Gregory's commentaries." His intellectual appetite was even more insatiable than his culinary one. He himself declared that "authority is the weakest form of proof"[38] — yet he has suffered since his death by being reduced to a provider of proof-texts and a bastion of authority.

What the West has forgotten about scholasticism is that it was, in its healthy days, a radical intellectual movement that came to Europe from Islam and that was essentially *a methodology of asking questions*. This is why it appealed to the radical new movements of the renaissance of the twelfth and early thirteenth century: it assisted the overthrow of the established intellectual methodology of simply citing authorities, usually fathers of the church. The disdain in which the new thinkers were held by those who fancied themselves guardians of the status quo and the "eternal tradition" is evident in the following comment by Bishop Stephen of Tournai (1192–1203) in a letter complaining to the pope:

> Scriptural studies have lapsed into a state of confusion in our time, for students applaud nothing but novelties and the masters are more intent on glory than doctrine; everywhere they draw up new and modern little summaries and supporting commentaries on theology, and with these they lull, hold, and deceive their listeners, as if the works of the sacred fathers did not still suffice.[39]

In response, the new thinkers fought back. Rupert of Deutz wrote:

> Necessity compels me to say that the writings of St. Augustine are not part of the canon, that they are not to be trusted in all matters as are the canonical books. . . . Moreover they [his intellectual enemies] have begun to denounce me as a heretic for saying that St. Augustine was not canonical.[40]

Richard of Saint-Victor accused the old guard of "inertia." They "dawdle about lazily and deride, ridicule, and mock the industriousness shown by others in the quest and discovery of truth. But he who dwells in heaven shall ridicule them; the Lord shall mock them."[41] Abelard of Bath also fought the establishment's complacency. He writes:

> This generation has an innate vice, namely, that it can accept
> nothing which has been discovered by contemporaries; as a
> consequence, when I wish to publish something I myself have
> discovered, I ascribe it to someone else, saying: "A certain
> man, not I, has said . . ."[42]

What one senses in the polemic and the passion of these statements is indeed a clash of cultures and a paradigm shift. Thomas
Kuhn observes that one of the signs of a paradigm shift is the
depth of resistance the new paradigm encounters, and there is
no doubt that the old monastic theology, supportive as it was
of feudal privileges in which it was heavily favored, and relying
as it did on argument by authority, was being asked to step aside
for a new paradigm. That paradigm was represented by a movement to cities, a rediscovery of nature, and the founding of universities that studied among other things the new science and
cosmology and that took away from the land-based monastic
schools their monopoly on education and indeed their very
methods of learning. Scholasticism was part of the new paradigm, for it celebrated questioning and reasoning over the citing
of authorities.

There can be no question as to which side of this paradigm
shift Aquinas was on. He knew the old ways, for he had come
of age in a monastic community; but he opted for the new and
paid a personal price for that decision that no doubt hardened
him in his resolve. Aquinas opts for questions and reason over
proof by authority when he writes:

> There are some who think that nothing is convincing enough
> unless a poet or some authority is cited. This is also a result
> either of custom or of poor judgment, because they cannot
> decide for themselves whether the conclusion of an argument
> is certain; and therefore having no faith in their own judg-
> ment, as it were, they require the judgment of some recog-
> nized authority.[43]

One can sense in this comment a kind of disdain for those
who refuse to use the intellect God has given them. For Aquinas
there was not "Christian truth" any more than there was such
a thing as "Christian grace" or "Christian ecstasy." (*"Amor facit
ecstasim,"* he writes—"love of anything at all makes ecstasy."[44])
Truth was truth and grace was grace and ecstasy was ecstasy and

no human group had a monopoly on any of it. He says: "Whatever truth is known by anyone is due to a participation in that light that shines in the darkness; for every truth, no matter by whom it is spoken, comes from the Holy Spirit."[45] He sought truth from Jewish and Muslim philosophers and pagan scientists, from Christian theologians of the past and from Roman philosophers. (Chenu says that Aquinas was influenced as much by the Muslim philosophers as by Dionysius.[46]) But he did not encounter diversity of ideas merely as a kind of intellectual cafeteria—rather he argued with each, honing what he agreed with and what he disagreed with, always offering the reasons for his opinions. He was subtle for the most part in his disagreements with Augustine or with Dionysius, for example, but his disagreements were massive in size, for he wanted faith to move in great new directions.

How telling it is, for example, that Aquinas wrote whole commentaries on ten of Aristotle's works—but not one on Plato, who was Augustine's mentor. He is explicit about his preference for Aristotle over Plato; it has to do with the former's trust of matter and his cosmology and what Pieper calls the "decisive turn to concreteness, to the empirical reality of the world . . . to the senses. . . . The body, the senses, and what the senses grasp—is all to be taken seriously in a manner hitherto unknown."[47] Aquinas found Aristotle far more incarnational than Plato and therefore worthy of studying further and incorporating into Christian theology. He loved what we would today call the "scientific" dimension of Aristotle, who explored nature to find truth. For Aquinas the truth of nature—and the need to enfold the greatest scientist of his day, Aristotle, into theology—was absolutely essential to faith. He says: "They hold a plainly false opinion who say that in regard to the truth of religion it does not matter what a person thinks about the creation as long as he or she has the correct opinion concerning God. An error concerning the creation ends as false thinking about God."[48] In a revealing passage contrasting Plato and Aristotle, Aquinas writes that the latter formed a middle ground between the "physical philosophers," who "felt no hankering for universal substances and kept to facts," and Platonic philosophers, who sought "the pure and essential soul, the cause and idea of all that is in particular souls." Says Aquinas: "Aristotle sought to keep the balance between the Platonist and the physical philosophers, between the general nature of soul and the specific characteristics of each type."[49] Aquinas not only admired Aristotle's "balance"; he sought balance himself. In one sentence Aquinas reveals why he preferred the controversial Aristotle over the established Plato. "Aristotle's doctrine, rather than Plato's, is corroborated by experience."[50]

I believe it is equally clear why Aquinas owes more in his spirituality to Dionysius than to Augustine. (He cites the former over seventeen hundred times, in addition to having written a major commentary on his work—something he never did with any of Augustine's works.) Dionysius is more of a creation mystic than Augustine; his eastern spiritual sensibilities are more about *theosis,* the divinizing of the universe, than about guilt and redemption. As Chenu points out, "the Augustinian bias led to considering the sacraments as so many remedies for a fallen world," whereas with Dionysius "symbolic action is a normal part of the dynamism of a cosmos reaching upward toward God."[51] A sacralization of all of nature was as important for Dionysius as for Aquinas. Dionysius had a creation-centered approach to spirituality and a cosmic one that Augustine lacked. Chenu observes that Augustine internalized the image of God or *mens* (mind), rendering it overly psychologized. In contrast, both Aquinas and Dionysius speak of the image of God or *mens* of the human in the context of creativity and cosmology.[52] In addition, Aquinas sees in Dionysius a substantive observer of the spiritual process when he says: "It is evident that Dionysius describes the movement of contemplation with much greater fullness and depth [than does Richard of Saint Victor]."[53] The cosmic dimension—totally lacking in Augustine's introspective psychology—is rich in Dionysius. So eager was Aquinas to present a cosmology that at first he felt Dionysius's mysticism coincided with Aristotle's science. When later he realized their vast differences, he sided with Aristotle. Though excited by Dionysius early in his career (his mentor Albert the Great taught him Dionysius's work), he always kept his critical edge about him, writing of Dionysius's "obscure style" that is "uncommon among the moderns." As Chenu puts it, Aquinas "internally resisted" the "style, way of thinking and mentality of Pseudo-Denys."[54] It was cosmology that fully attracted

Aquinas, as Chenu comments. "Humanity is encountered in the *Summa,* not primarily as the mystical body of Christ, but as part of a cosmology."[55] And he sought it wherever he could, whether in pagan scientists or in Eastern theologians.

I think it can be said that Aquinas's very early training as a Benedictine also influenced him considerably. The monastic tradition did not indulge in spirituality as a series of techniques so much as a way of life. I think Aquinas kept this sense about him his whole life long. The Benedictine tradition in its purity is also very creation-centered, and while its worldly success during the late Middle Ages robbed it of its spiritual roots, nevertheless its basic spirituality must have impressed Aquinas deeply. This is particularly evident in his lifelong love of wisdom and wisdom literature and the Psalms, which of course the monks chanted daily. Indeed, Aquinas introduces his commentary on the Psalms by noting that "this book deals with the general matter of all theology. . . . It contains all Scripture."[56]

From the monks Aquinas no doubt also learned the value of meditation or what we might call "right-brain" activity. Aquinas rejects Augustine's distinction in dividing the mind dualistically between a *"ratio* superior" that attains wisdom and eternal things and a *"ratio* inferior" that deals with science and temporal things and includes memory, imagination, and instinct. For Aquinas the two dimensions of the mind are "one and the same power of reason" with different tasks. Augustine had taught that the Trinity works in the *"ratio* superior" only. Not so for Aquinas. "In no way are they two different powers of the soul . . . one is the medium for knowing the other." [57] As Chenu puts it, Aquinas had "nothing but disdain" for any dualistic theory of *"ratio* inferior" separate from *"ratio* superior." "There is no specific faculty for things divine. . . . No science of the human is totally true which does not find its object among the material realities in which the human's body is immersed, both in its being and in its operations."[58] We cannot escape matter, nor should we seek to do so.

A commitment to matter is a commitment to history, and Aquinas's commitment to history was not just in theory but in practice. He was so controversial a figure—and the controversies that embroiled him led to his early death—precisely because he lived what he fought for. He refused to try to escape history and paid a dear price for attempting to offer Christianity a paradigm shift—an offer it has for the most part refused to take.

Scripture was key to Aquinas's spirituality as well as his theology. "It is a heavenly way of life to spend one's days in the study of sacred Scripture" he writes.[59] And he speaks of its importance to preachers in particular: "Study among religious should be commended and particularly study of the Scriptures, especially in the case of people who are appointed to be preachers."[60] Chenu picks up on this commitment to biblical spirituality on Aquinas's part when he writes: "The very pith of his work was scriptural, and his theology had at its roots the Gospel movement of his day, just as it did the renaissance movement of which it was one of the effects."[61] In this one sentence Chenu underscores the dialectic of mysticism/prophecy that was key to Aquinas's spirituality, as it is to all creation-centered spirituality: the prophet is the mystic in action.[62] To say that his work was an effect of the renaissance of his day is to give an ultimate compliment to Aquinas, who was consciously and deliberately a part of the poverty movement such as Peter Waldo or Francis of Assisi represented, because Christ was himself poor. Josef Pieper recognizes the role of Scripture in Aquinas's work and spirituality when he points out that his *Summa theologiae* contains three extensive tracts on biblical theology—a fact that was an innovation at the time and a

> far cry from the "systematic" theology of the commentaries
> on the *Sentences*. In this, Thomas was showing the influence of
> the voluntary poverty movement. Thomas drew upon Biblical
> example to justify the incursions of the mendicant orders into
> the fields of preaching and pastoral care: "There are to be
> found [in the parish clergy] only very few who know Holy
> Scripture—although the proclaimer of the Word of God must
> be conversant with Holy Scripture."[63]

At the very time that Aquinas was writing his commentary on Aristotle's *Physics,* his Dominican brothers with whom he lived at St. Jacques in Paris were compiling the first concordance of the Bible, and a quest for the original texts of the Scriptures was undertaken with the help of a converted Jew who collated the Hebrew text. Chenu says: "In XIIIth century theological teaching the Bible was the basic book. . . . Here, then, is the

fact: Saint Thomas, master in theology, took the text itself of
the Old and the New Testament as the subject matter of his
official course."[64] If Thomists had been true to the spirit of their
master they would not have misunderstood Luther so fully in
his efforts to return theology to a biblical basis. Chenu observes
that Thomists in the sixteenth century

> lost the eminent spiritual equilibrium of their master which
> would have enabled them to understand, assess and assimilate
> the rational values of this second Renaissance. They should
> have been well supplied with balanced solutions because the
> work of St. Thomas was done during a very rationalistic ren-
> aissance in the thirteenth century (the Aristotelian movement)
> and Thomas succeeded in attaining a coherence of faith and
> reason within the realm of faith itself. But their theology had
> lost the spirit of daring as well as its original freshness and had
> forgotten the need of continual discovery.[65]

Thomism's failure was a failure in nerve, a failure in courage,
a failure in trust (which is the biblical meaning of "faith"). It was
ultimately a failure in spirituality—praxis as much as theory.
Chenu cites approvingly the analysis of Professor Gilson.

> The Thomistic school of the Renaissance can be said to have
> failed completely in so far as it opposed the Renaissance in-
> stead of assimilating it and taking its spiritual direction from it
> as St. Thomas had done with the philosophical movement of
> the thirteenth century. Not only did Thomism have the re-
> sources for doing that, but it was its duty to do it . . . and
> one may well ask why such a man as Cajetan failed in this
> regard. It may be that the original, creative work of Thomas
> had given way to the unoriginal work of the commentator.[66]

All this has immense relevance for today: Will those who
claim a lineage to Thomas Aquinas miss the great renaissance of
the West that is occurring today, with the excitement of a new
creation story emerging from science, as they did the sixteenth-
century renaissance? Or is there still some life left in Western
Christianity with which to respond to a cosmology when one
hears it?

Leaving Rationalism Behind: Thomas Aquinas in a Postmodern Era

For this authentic response to a renaissance to occur in Western religion there must be, especially at this end of the rationalistic era of the modern period, an awakening to the mystical. Our hearts need to be expanded. Theology need not be an obstacle to this enterprise, provided it can recover its mystical, heart dimension. Benedictine monk Bede Griffiths comments on this fact from his ashram in India.

> St. Thomas Aquinas himself wrote this terribly logical, rational *Summa theologica,* and at the end of his life he said, "Everything I've written seems to me like empty straw compared to what I've seen." Then his followers take up the system, repeat the whole rationalization and conception, and lose this understanding. That's why you have to go behind the theological terms to the source of mystical experience that they're supposed to be serving.[67]

There has been immense confusion over the role reason or *ratio* plays in our understanding of Aquinas. One must remember that the rediscovery of the scientific method of Aristotle in the Middle Ages was a breath of fresh air after centuries of allegorisms and a heavy dose of superstition—a time in which one might say the right brain ran riot. Liberation movements of Aquinas's time called for being rational— for using one's God-given reason, for exercising one's "left brain" by way of definitions, distinctions, and syllogistic reasoning. Nevertheless, while Aquinas took in this mentality, which was a gift from the scholastic movement of his day, he by no means succumbed to it. That is to say, he was not a rationalist. On the contrary, he was a mystic—just as Bede Griffiths attests to. This is where Aquinas's amazing balance shows itself: he exercised to the full, it seems, both hemispheres of his brain. Creation spirituality is never anti-intellectual (Hildegard of Bingen said in the twelfth century that "all science comes from God"). Our left brain is as much a gift from God as our right brain. But we are always in danger of living one-sided lives and yielding either to the one or the other. Chenu comments that it is a "false modern idea that there is opposition between mysticism and scholasticism."[68]

Part of Aquinas's spiritual greatness was his ability to be equally true to both the right and the left brain. But his interpreters through the centuries have rarely been as balanced.

One difficulty we have today in seeing the mystical side of Aquinas is that the modern era has rendered us all so antimystical. As Jaraslov Pelikan has put it, "the Enlightenment deposed the Cosmic Christ and made the quest for the historical Jesus necessary."[69] The Cosmic Christ, of course, represents a primary archetype of the mystical tradition in the West. Aquinas knew it well.[70] The modern era has been a rationalistic one, and it has tainted our understanding of reason itself, divorcing it from wonder, awe, and therefore mysticism. What we mean by reason today is not what Aquinas meant, as Josef Pieper attests to: "The emphatic and ever recurrent stress on reason and the order of reason in the works of Aquinas is obviously not to be understood in the sense which the Enlightenment has given to these terms."[71]

What then is Aquinas's understanding of *ratio* or reason? Pieper says that *ratio* signifies "in its widest sense—man's power to grasp reality."[72] My conversations with Aquinas reveal something of the depth as well as the breadth of this understanding of reason as our "power to grasp reality," for we see it equated at times with creativity and imagination, as well as love. Reason, says Aquinas, is that "by which one is free in one's actions."[73] Indeed, if painted into a corner, Aquinas insists on love over knowledge when he says: "Loving draws us more to things than knowledge does."[74] Yet he continually pursues the knowledge question, because love and knowledge are so intimately related: we can love only what we know. Ultimately, rather than just know about God, we are called to love God. "It is better to love God than to know about God, for the divine goodness is most perfectly in God, which is how it is desired by the will, than it is as shared in us or conceived by the mind."[75] Aquinas also resists abstractionism when he states that "reason, we must remember, is both speculative and practical."[76] Does the following observation of Aquinas sound like a rationalist at work? "In the midst of a person's body lies the heart, to which is attributed a certain wisdom and understanding; hence, although the intellect has no bodily organ, yet because the heart is our chief organ, it is the custom to take it for the intellect."[77]

Or this statement: "The objects of the heart are truth and justice."[78]

The format of this book, because it leaves behind the rationalistic bias of the modern era in the questions and fourfold mystical/prophetic path that it follows, might actually be understood as a journey of the heart. We can see Thomas's mysticism coming alive in the Four Paths:

1. The heart of exaltation, awe, wonder, and delight. (Via Positiva)

2. The heart of silence, letting go, suffering, sorrow, grieving, and "roaring" (his word). (Via Negativa)

3. The heart of passion for creativity, cocreating, birthing life and power (virtue) in all its forms: the art of empowerment. (Via Creativa)

4. The heart that is compassion: moral outrage at injustice that leads to the passionate work of justice making and healing and the heart-work that celebration entails and demands. (Via Transformativa)

Aquinas does not let off the hook easily those who ignore the search for truth as a matter of both head-work *and* heart-work. He insists that to fail to know what we should or to refuse to know what we should is a sin. "Error is imputed to the reason as a sin when it is in ignorance or error about what it is able and ought to know."[79] Fundamentalist or literal thinking or nonthinking is sinful, as Aquinas sees it. "Ignorance denotes a privation of knowledge, that is, a lack of knowledge of those things that one has a natural aptitude to know. Some of these we are under an obligation to know, those namely without whose knowledge we are unable to accomplish a due act rightly. . . . Wherefore, through negligence, ignorance of what one is bound to know is a sin."[80] It strikes me that, for example, cosmology is something we need to know if we are to act rightly today. And knowledge of the ecological. And of our own capacity for mysticism that gives us hope and strength and moves us beyond the pessimism and despair that anthropocentrism breeds. Indeed, anthropocentrism, using Aquinas's criteria, is a sin, a deviation from what we can and ought to know.

Aquinas realizes that often our refusal to learn comes from a hard heart—one more instance in which he sees the intimate relationship between heart and head. "Spiritual blindness and hardness of heart imply the movement of the human mind in cleaving to evil and turning away from the divine light. . . . Spiritual blindness corresponds to sight (and discovery), and heaviness of the heart to hearing (and teaching), and hardness of heart to the affections."[81] Thus the purity of our minds is affected by our affections, our teaching, and our willingness to discover. Envy also can interfere with our responsibility to learn, as Aquinas astutely observed. "Envious persons hinder the progress of souls 'who say to the seers, See no visions' (Isa. 30:10). They ask questions not to learn but to obstruct."[82] (Indeed, Aquinas talks of fear as a "sin" in "Third Conversation.") There are lessons here for all who are unwilling to let go, unwilling to trust the creative spirit, which, as scripture says, "makes all things new."

Gifts of Aquinas to the Spiritual Needs of Our Time

I would like to list briefly and succinctly some of the contributions that Aquinas makes to our search for an authentic spiritual vision, the emerging renaissance in our time. The reader of this book will no doubt be inspired to find many more. The list I present here may assist the reader in her or his appreciation of the conversations that follow.

1. I believe that Aquinas understood more than any other theologian of the past one thousand years the importance of cosmology for faith, life, and practice. Science, mysticism, and art — the three elements of a living cosmology—all find ample and deep expression in Aquinas's spirituality. For him, as for Job, our lives need to be put in the context of the whole of creation, for "Divinity is better represented by the whole universe than by any single thing" (see "First Conversation").[83] Henry Adams understood the prophetic impact of Aquinas's cosmology on our own civilization when he wrote:

An economic civilization troubles itself about the universe
much as a hive of honey-bees troubles about the ocean, only
as a region to be avoided. The hive of St. Thomas sheltered

God and man, mind and matter, the universe and the atom,
the one and the multiple, within the walls of an harmonious
home.[84]

2. All being is holy. Because Aquinas helps us to find the
infinite in the finite, he helps us to rediscover the true meaning
and experience of spirit itself, which he understands as our capacity to be open to all of being, our capacity for the infinite.
The implications of this are very great in our time, for example
as concerning our culture's problems with addiction. Is all addiction a kind of quest for the infinite? But a quest that the objects of our addiction cannot satisfy? Aquinas teaches how we
can indeed experience the infinite in the finite, in creation itself.
For him all being is holy. It is sacramental, a revelation of the
divine. Being, for Aquinas, is not a noun, not a static substance,
but a dialectical dance of act/potency or matter/form or poten-
tial/fruitfulness. Everything is about to blossom into being.
Birth, creativity, is everywhere.

3. Ecumenism: as I indicated above, Aquinas was anything
but a narrow thinker; he was an eager and hungry searcher after
truth who insisted it could be found anywhere and everywhere.
He writes:

> Every truth without exception—and whoever may utter it—is
> from the Holy Spirit.[85]
> The old pagan virtues were from God.[86]
> Revelation has been made to many pagans.[87]

His commitment to Aristotle was disturbing to narrow-
minded Christians not only because Aristotle was a scientist but
also because he was a "pagan."

4. Wonder, the Via Positiva, is the starting point of all
knowledge for Aquinas. How different this is from the modern
era, when Descartes, for example, posited *doubt* as the starting
point for learning. How anthropocentric and filled with self it
is to begin learning with doubt! In contrast, how childlike and
cosmic is wonder. Underlying Aquinas's commitment to wonder is a reverence for all things. He says: "The cause of that at
which we wonder is hidden from us" and "no philosopher has
ever been able to grasp the being of a single fly." The world is
too rich to "grasp," but it is ours to wonder at forever. There
is great *puer power*[88] in Aquinas's love of wonder that a tired

civilization with its tired educational systems derived from a cynical negative *senex* has not felt for a long, long time.

5. Blessing—which is the theological word for goodness—is at the heart of existence and at the heart of all things for Aquinas. Every being in its essence is good and participates in the divine goodness. All desire is a yearning for the good, a yearning for blessing. Aquinas's spirituality is clearly one of original blessing. It is interesting in fact that he does not treat the concept of original sin in his *Summa theologiae* until Part II, and then only in questions 82 and 83. Preceding this treatment of original sin are his treatises on God, on the Creation, on the Work of the Six Days, on humanity, and on the divine government (questions 1–119 of Part I).

6. Aquinas represents a giant step forward in the West's rediscovery of an ecological consciousness. For Aquinas, every creature shares in what he calls the "dignity of causality." He respects the "soul" in both animals and plants. He totally deanthropocentrizes salvation when he says: "The meaning of salvation consists first and principally in this, that something is preserved in the good."[89] I cannot imagine a more basic principle to an ecological ethic than this requirement: to preserve things in their good, in their blessinghood. This and his other teachings about cosmology and the goodness of things and the interdependence of all things establishes him as an important ecological thinker. In his teaching that all creatures share in bringing about the divine purpose, he acknowledges what scientist Erich Jantsch calls the divine "mind" that is intrinsic to the entire evolutionary process.

7. Aquinas celebrates the greatness and grandeur of each and every human being, reminding us we are *capax universi* (capable of the universe) and that we are infinite in our capacities to know, to love, and to create. In this insight lies the resolution to much addiction, including the enticements of greed, which is, in Aquinas's brilliant analysis, a sin of the spirit—that is, a quest for the infinite—rather than a sin of materialism as such.

8. He celebrates silence and letting go in a startlingly Zenlike manner. He talks about emptying the mind and how it is that we know what God is not but not what God is (see "Second Conversation"). He celebrates both the Cataphatic God of light and creation and the apophatic God of silence and mindlessness.

Not only is the human mind radically receptive, it is an abyss of emptiness. "All I have written is straw."

9. Aquinas also analyzes—in tremendous depth—humanity's weaknesses; especially relevant for today are his brilliant analysis of fear, of despair, of pusillanimity (puny-souledness), of acedia, which is the burnout and spiritual sadness that so depresses us that we "refuse to begin new things." Rightly does he call fear—so rampant in fundamentalisms around the world today—a "sin," and sound is his teaching that despair is the "most dangerous of all sins," for one in despair "flounders in wickedness." And he warns that the greatest of all evils is a teacher who teaches despair.

10. His psychology is so rich because it is not anthropocentric, nor is it deadeningly introspective. It is, like that of Hildegard of Bingen, a psychology of microcosm/macrocosm. Yet his understanding of human motivation and feelings and powers is brilliant. Indeed, of all his writings, I feel that his genius is most revealed in his writings on human psychology.

11. Aquinas celebrates the *deification* of our species and elaborates at length on what this means. Thus, by developing a theology both of the blessing of creation and of our deification or sanctification, he corrects the unbalance that has crept into Western theology around the classical "three articles" of faith: Creation, Redemption, and Sanctification (or deification). Western theology has tended to subsume the first and third articles under the second or even to ignore the first and third altogether. Aquinas would have none of this neglect of articles One and Three.

12. His morality is based not on laws and commandments but on the Via Creativa, that is, on birthing our biggest and best selves by way of virtue (which in his language also means "power"). His morality is clearly an ethics of empowerment. An example would be his wonderful treatises on the virtue of magnanimity, which is the antidote to pusillanimity, which derives from fear and despair. Key to the moral act in Aquinas's opinion is *the act of choice*. We do choose and we must choose, and the ultimate act of empowerment lies in the choices we make.

13. Aquinas's spirituality is hopeful. He has solutions to despair—falling in love with creation, *"amor facit ecstasim,"*

("ordinary love produces ecstasy") is one of them. "Joy expands
the heart" he observes. His spirituality contains eschatological
power. It speaks to the future and not just to a tired past. "Joy,"
Aquinas declares, "is humanity's noblest act." Wouldn't it be
something if our educational, religious, political, and economic
systems were reformulated around this one idea: that our species
existed to bring out the "noblest" of our acts from one another?

14. He celebrates the senses and the passions, seeing the latter
as the "seat of the virtues." For him, anger has its rightful place,
for example, and sensuality is not a problem but a blessing.
Pleasure is not a problem for him; indeed, it lies at the heart of
our healthy motivation. "Pleasure is the perfection of activity."[90] The universe has come about because of God's pleasure.
"Sheer joy is God's and from this creation happens." "God is
always rejoicing." Consciousness comes about through joy, for
"God is most joyful and is therefore supremely conscious." Indeed, one of the reasons why Aquinas preferred Aristotle over
Plato was that the former was less suspicious of pleasure. Aristotle refutes Plato's arguments against pleasure.[91] For Aquinas, it is sinful to "choose to avoid pleasure," though of course
it is necessary to distinguish authentic from inauthentic pleasures.

15. He insists that matter and spirit are not antagonists. For
Aquinas, body and soul are truly companions in the human.
This move away from dualism was at the heart of the three
formal condemnations of his thought. It represented a radical
paradigm shift from Augustine's and neo-Platonist thinking, in
which the "soul makes war with the body" and "spirit is whatever is not matter" (Augustine).[92] Aquinas insists on the "consubstantiality" of soul and body that together constitute a
"wonderful communion."[93] He says: "The soul united with the
body is more like God than the soul separated from the body
because the soul in the body possesses its nature in more complete fashion."[94]

For Aquinas sexuality is good. He dismisses the Augustinian
idea that sexual love always contains sin because the abundance
of pleasure overwhelms reason. Several fathers of the church
had taught that reproduction of the human race in the Garden
of Eden must have taken place in some nonsexual manner.
Aquinas replies: "This cannot be said reasonably; for what

belongs to the nature of human beings is neither taken from them nor given to them by reason of sin."[95] With Aquinas, sensuality is "a very great blessing" (see "First Conversation") and unsensuality is a moral deficiency.

We have been told that Aquinas's commentary on the Song of Songs has been lost to us. This is very odd, both because we possess all the rest of his work and because he loved this book so dearly, citing it untold times in the works we do possess. Sometimes I wonder if his commentary on the Song of Songs was deliberately confiscated by persons who might have found his less allegorical and more literal or historical exegesis too hot to handle in his day.

16. Aquinas insists on justice, and he had a lifelong commitment to justice and the justice movements of his day. It is telling that in his long treatise on virtues, which in many ways represents the Via Creativa in his thought, the largest section by far is that on justice. In his commentary on Aristotle's *Ethics,* one entire book is dedicated to his treatise on justice, and in his *Summa theologiae* justice is treated at far greater length than any other virtue. On numerous occasions Aquinas equates redemption (*redemptio*) with liberation (*liberatio*). He also defines justice as preservation of creation, and Christ, he says, "is justice itself."

17. Aquinas showed great fidelity to his prophetic vocation. His life story, as we have seen, parallels that of many prophets, not only in his condemnation but also in the enforced isolation and solitude that was the result of his being ahead of his time. I believe his very rich teaching on prophecy (see "Fourth Conversation") is at times deeply personal, for he lived what he taught. If a prophet is one who "interferes," as Rabbi Heschel puts it, then Aquinas, who interfered with a centuries-old religious paradigm by preferring Aristotle's cosmology to Augustine's introspective conscience, was indeed a prophet who paid the price.

18. We must also praise him for his courage and his rich teachings on courage and magnanimity. How magnificently he lived out his own teaching on the magnanimous person in his daring effort to bring together radical, prophetic politics with the deepest study of nature. He demonstrated courage as a young man in joining the upstart Dominican order, leaving his

family's wishes aside, to set out to new lands, to appropriate Aristotle, to debate his opponents publicly, to stay true to the course. When he writes that it takes more courage to sustain a battle than to get it over quickly, I suspect he is speaking from personal experience. For his whole life was—especially in the last years—a great battle. Yet he never lost his own equilibrium in the fray. He was as true to his mysticism as to his prophecy. Both took a very big heart—which is, after all, the etymological meaning of the word "courage."

19. Aquinas provides a wealth of images for God and the Godhead and for Jesus Christ, whose person and life he sees in a multitude of ways. He develops a Cosmic Christ theology as well as a rich theology of Jesus as prophet and indeed of the entire prophetic vocation—a vocation he closely allies to the right use of imagination or artistic consciousness. He remains true to the dynamic sense of Trinitarian consciousness as distinct from rigid monotheism, and he offers many images of God that are deeply feminist, for example, that God is "the Source behind the Source" and that Christ is a "mother" (see "Third Conversation"). An often-repeated image of God in Aquinas is that "God is an Artist and the universe is God's work of art."

20. For Aquinas, art and creativity are essential components of human consciousness and of the spiritual path. Indeed, he develops an entire spirituality of work based on the image of God in us as expressed in our creativity. "In God there is perfect fecundity" he declares. (See Conversation Three below.) The mind is productive of artifacts, and evil results from our failure to act and from hiding our light under a bushel. He revisions power as the *empowerment* that creativity brings, including the creativity to develop our own powers or virtue and make this the basis of our living in the world, that is, of our morality.

21. Lastly, I think it can be safely said that the essence of Aquinas's work is not only his lifelong search for truth but his eager search for wisdom. Wisdom called Aquinas all his life. And he responded. For example, his inaugural address to the University of Paris as well as the prologues to his first major work, the *Commentary on the Sentences,* which he wrote when he was twenty-eight years old, are based on wisdom texts from Psalm 103, from the Book of Ecclesiastes (1:7), and from the Book of Ecclesiasticus (24:40), respectively. Aquinas taught that

the "wisdom of God is manifest in creatures" and called Jesus "incarnate wisdom," insisting that wisdom rules the cosmos. He wrote that there are four tasks to Wisdom and connected these to the mystery of the Incarnation in his Prologue to the First Book of the *Sentences:* first, to reveal the mysteries of God; second, to produce creation "like an artist births art"; third, to restore creation; and fourth, to perfect creation. Notice that this theology of Incarnation never even mentions the word "redemption"—he uses the word "restoration"—and even this is only the *third* task of wisdom.[96]

Wisdom, he felt, was given us "on loan"; it is not something we possess. Wisdom is "of the heart." It is "manifest in creatures." It is woman; it is riches; it comes from the prophets and accompanies justice; it is hidden and mysterious, but we participate in the wisdom of God because, like Christ, who is "incarnate wisdom who produces prophets," we are sons and daughters of God. Aquinas's rich development of a wisdom theology and of Christ as wisdom—a theme feminist theologians are rediscovering in our time—demonstrates how impoverished our theologies have been rendered by fall/redemption agendas in the West.

The medieval renaissance was so much like our own times, involving the breakup of a dominant worldview and economic/political system; the emergence of Earth consciousness and the goddess; a new cosmology emerging from a new scientific view of nature; a birth of social justice movements out of base communities and the history of the oppressed; and therefore new vitality at the level of mystical and prophetic consciousness. All this, along with the reasons I have just cited, suggests that Aquinas's accomplishments are nourishment for our own struggle to become spiritually awake and prophetically involved.

The "Clay Feet" of Thomas Aquinas

Having praised Aquinas for some of his lasting accomplishments, I believe it is equally important to meditate on his "clay feet," or his shortcomings. We should always do this with our saints, for several reasons: first, because no human is perfect (and only a neurotic one would want to be). If hagiography paints saints as perfect, then it does the rest of us a serious disservice, for we cannot identify with perfection. Most of us have access to the saints by way of their weaknesses, not their so-called "perfections." We find it easier to identify with them and their journeys if we know something of their "clay feet."

In addition, there is genuine false consciousness if we are led to believe that any saint is "perfect." Then when the truth becomes known to us we dismiss the hero from his or her pedestal. If the truth stays hidden we do a worse thing—we project the greatness of our souls and the uniqueness of them onto the saints instead of living out our own spiritual journey. We create hero relationships—which are invariably love-hate relationships—rather than filial relationships.

All saints have clay feet. Gandhi was cruel to his wife; Martin Luther King, Jr., apparently cheated on his doctoral thesis and was not altogether faithful in his marriage; Dorothy Day was a clericalist in her ecclesiology and somewhat of a sexist in her attitudes toward women. Saints' clay feet do not make them less saintly. Aquinas speaks to this in our "Fourth Conversation" when he points out that prophets aren't prophets twenty-four hours a day. Prophecy, he writes, "is not something abiding in the prophet, but a kind of transient impression."[97] If prophets were always right we would not need one another! We would not need the church, the community of mystic/prophets who can support and challenge one another, and who can celebrate together the whole of life, its joys and its struggles. As Aquinas points out, revelation via the prophets is given "not all to every one, but one to one, and some to another."[98]

Thomas Aquinas, while he bears the heavy and even archetypal burden of having been declared a saint by the Roman Catholic Church, nevertheless also had clay feet. In particular, I see the following four weaknesses in Thomas Aquinas.

First, regarding women, Aquinas is at best ambivalent and at worst sexist. Sometimes he has favorable things to say about women, as for example when he celebrates marriage as a "perfect friendship" and a unique vocation, saying: "Perfect friendship, such as exists between a man and his wedded wife, for whom a man leaves even his father and mother (Gen. 2), cannot be for many."[99] He calls for a relationship of mutuality between husband and wife when he says: "Man and wife ought to live together in such a way that each fulfills what is just to the other. This will be different for different persons."[100] Virtue lies at the heart of man–woman relationships in marriage: "There is a virtue proper to both husband and wife that renders their friendship delightful to each other. Clearly, then, friendship of this kind can be based on virtue, utility, and pleasure."[101] Indeed, it is this dimension of friendship that provides Aquinas with his firmest argument for marital fidelity. He writes:

> Superabundant love is not designed by nature for many but for one only. This is evident in sexual love, according to which one man cannot at the same time love many women in an excessive manner. Therefore, the perfect friendship of the virtuous cannot extend to many persons.[102]

Speaking of "superabundant love" between man and woman reveals, among other things, Aquinas's celebration of marriage as a sacrament—a theological accomplishment that was less than one century old in the church of his day. He develops a theology of marriage as friendship when he says: "The greater the friendship, the more permanent it should be. The greatest friendship is that between man and wife."[103] Commitment makes public this greatest of friendships. "The form of marriage lies in an inseparable union of minds by which either is unalterably plighted to serve the other loyally."[104] His argument against polygamy is as follows: "Friendship spells equality. Experience shows that women are treated like servants when polygamy is the rule."[105] He states that humans are "inclined by nature more to conjugal than political society," for humans are "by nature more a conjugal than a political animal."[106] He considers "conjugal friendship" to be unique to the human species.

> Aristotle concludes . . . that pairing of male and female among other animals exists exclusively for generation of offspring. But union of male and female among humans occurs not only for the procreation of children but also for the functions needed in human living. . . . Mutual needs are provided for when each (man and woman) contributes his or her own services for the common good.[107]

His basic argument against sex outside of marriage is the risk at which it puts the children who might be born of such a union.

In the human species offspring requires not only nourishment
of the body, as in the case of other animals, but also education
for the soul. For other animals naturally possess their own
kinds of prudence whereby they are enabled to take care of
themselves. But a human being lives by reason, which one
must develop by lengthy, temporal experience so that one
may achieve prudence. Hence, children must be instructed by
parents who are already experienced people.[108]

Children are a blessing to their parents, for "children are a
common good of both husband and wife, whose union exists
for the sake of the children."[109]

Aquinas commends the women in the Gospels for their
steadfastness toward Jesus—a steadfastness that put Jesus' male
friends to shame.

Due to the fact that both women were standing near the cross
and his disciples had fled, leaving him behind, John commends the devoted constancy of the women. Job 19:20 says:
"My flesh having been eaten away, my bone clings to my
skin." In other words, it is as if the disciples, being signified
through the flesh, had withdrawn and the women, signified
through the skin, had hung on.[110]

He also celebrates women as prophets or prophetesses. For
example, he admires Mary Magdalene for her courage and
"boldness" and calls her a "prophet" and the "Apostle of the
apostles" who was the first to announce the good news of resurrection. "The announcement of the Lord's resurrection to the
disciples was entrusted to her; just as woman first announced
the words of death to man, so also woman first announced the
words of life."[111]

There is another side to Aquinas's teaching about women,
however. Having in one place celebrated Mary Magdalene as
the first preacher of the good news and the "Apostle of the apostles," in another he says that women should not be preachers in
the church.[112] Having in one place praised marital love as the
greatest of friendships and a relationship of equals as we saw
above, in another place he talks about husband-wife relationships as a friendship of "inequality"[113] and says that "the husband being more worthy is placed over the wife; however, the
husband does not direct the affairs belonging to the wife."[114]

Having taught in one place that marriage is ideally a relationship of justice among equals, he later writes of the natural inferiority of women.

> It is clear that the generation of a female is apart from the intention of a particular nature, that is, of the power that is in this semen, which, as much as possible, tends to a perfect result of conception; but it is in accord with the intention of the universal nature, that is, of the power of the universal agent for the generation of inferior beings, that a female is generated; for without a female the generation of a number of animals could not be accomplished.[115]

Having taught that women are inferior beings, he also teaches that their bodies are part of the cause of their inferiority and that their emotions rule over their reason.

> Aristotle offers the example of women in whom, for the most part, reason flourishes very little because of the imperfect nature of their body. Because of this they do not govern their emotions in the majority of cases by reason but rather are governed by their emotions. Hence wise and brave women are rarely found, and so women cannot be called continent and incontinent without qualification. The same argument seems valid for those who are ill, that is, have a diseased temperament because of bad habits, which oppresses the judgment of reason after the manner of a perverse nature.[116]

In his treatise "On the Production of Woman" in the *Summa theologiae,* Aquinas says that

> as regards the individual nature, woman is defective and misbegotten, for the active force in the male seed tends to the production of a perfect likeness in the masculine sex; while the production of woman comes from defect in the active force or from some material indisposition, or even from some external influence, such as that of the south wind, which is moist, as the Philosopher observes.[117]

He does concede, however, that "as regards human nature in general, woman is not misbegotten, but is included in nature's intention as directed to the work of generation."[118]

This is very unsavory stuff, repugnant to contemporary women and men alike. It is almost bizarre, this search for straws, as when he cites Aristotle about the influence of the south, moist wind. But what is clear in all of it is his ambiguity. Aquinas contradicts himself time and again on the subjects of women and of male-female relationships.

There is an obvious attraction in the sexual theory he expounds to men who want their privileges legitimized. Here too Aquinas's clay feet are revealed. "Woman is naturally subject to man, because in man the discretion of reason predominates."[119] And again, "man is the head of the woman."[120] He does give a hint of a caution to male egoism, however, when he reminds men that the infinite divine power made man "from the slime of the earth, and a woman from a man."[121] And he reminds men too that women "are not called the daughter of Adam" but are made "by the divine power alone."[122] And, breaking with Augustine, he insists that men and women are both made in the image and likeness of God. "The image of God is common to both sexes, since it is according to the mind, in which there is no distinction of sexes."[123]

In addition to his overreliance on Aristotle, another reason can be put forward for Aquinas's ambivalence—even schizophrenia—toward women. That is that he knew so few. Women taught in the University of Paris in its early days and otherwise played some prominent roles there (Heloise was recognized as the most outstanding student in the university in her day—and her brilliant correspondence later in life corroborates her intellectual genius and her spiritual depth). Yet by Aquinas's day women were no longer visible in the university. It is doubtful that he had any women students, and certainly he had no women teachers. He lived in an all-male and celibate community from the age of five to his death. The only women I find mention of in his life are his mother, his sisters, and a prostitute.

His mother, according to Professor James Weisheipl, was the instigator of Thomas's kidnapping by his brothers, five months after his father died. Aquinas's mother had great ambitions for him, ambitions that depended on his entering the monastic/feudal establishment of her day. She was not a willing participant in the new culture that attracted Thomas. According to Weisheipl, "Donna Theodora and her husband, Landulf, had made careful plans for the future of the family, and Thomas was to play an important part in its security."[124] Entering the new and antiestablishment Dominican Order was not part of her plans for her son.

A second woman in his life was the prostitute or "very beautiful girl seductively attired" whom Aquinas's brothers put into his cell during his captivity to seduce him. As Weisheipl points out, "there is every reason to think that the prostitute episode is historical fact,"[125] and while Aquinas resisted the allurement, one can only speculate about how this violent episode might have colored his understanding of women for the rest of his life. There is considerable evidence that Aquinas remained a virgin all his life, and a deeper understanding of women would not ordinarily be the result of such a life-style.

A third experience of women in Aquinas's life was that of his five sisters. Among these was the Countess Theodora of San Severino, who commented in his last days that her brother was "completely out of his senses" (*stupefactus*).[126] Another sister, who is unnamed for us, died as a young child in a severe lightning storm that made Thomas afraid of thunderstorms his whole life. Marotta became a Benedictine and was the abbess of Santa Maria de Capua. She died about 1259. Maria married Guglielmo of San Severino and died in 1286. Their daughter, Catherine, was active at the canonization process of her uncle. Aquinas's younger sister Theodora was married to Count Roger of San Severino and died about 1310. We know nothing about his fifth sister, except for her name, Adelasia. One must ask how close Aquinas was to his sisters when he left home at five years of age.

In understanding Aquinas's often dismal record on women, Marie-Louise von Franz has something notable to say about the author of *Aurora consurgens,* whom she believed (and Dominican Victor White concurred) was Thomas Aquinas. (Portions of that text are reproduced at the end of our "Second Conversation.") She writes:

> We must conclude that this author had no relationship with the feminine principle before. It is quite obvious from the text that he is a clerical man, and I would imagine he had a negative mother complex and for that, or some other reason, had no relationship to the feminine principle, which means neither to his own feminine side nor to women.[127]

It is because of Aquinas's clay feet regarding women that in my "Family Tree" of creation spirituality thinkers I give Aquinas not four stars but only three and one-half.[128] This is sad because in so many ways he was an ally, not an enemy, of feminist consciousness. That he is not consistent when teaching about women is perhaps evidence of his own doubts as he took upon his conscience the cross of centuries of Christian dualism and tried to dismantle it.

The second of Aquinas's "clay feet" is his teaching on sexuality. While we saw above how he celebrates sexuality as a blessing, still his biological grasp of the subject is a woefully inadequate base on which to construct an ethics of sexuality. Twentieth-century persons can readily forget that it was not until the mid-nineteenth century that it was learned that women produce the egg that together with the sperm makes the child. The human race's ignorance of the facts of sexuality has at times been a source of immense violence to women. Thomas Aquinas learned his sexual biology from Aristotle, who taught that the father provided the form, the mother the matter. The male provided the seed; the female the soil. "The father disposes the son's principal part, the form; and the mother disposes the matter."[129] Citing Aristotle's book *On the Generation of Animals,* Aquinas says that "in perfect animals, generated by coition, the active force is in the semen of the male; but the fetal matter is provided by the female."[130] He reiterates this theory of sexuality. "Among perfect animals the active power of generation belongs to the male sex, and the passive power to the female."[131] To his credit, Aquinas is consistent in this bizarre sexual biology when he declares that a man who emits semen other than for the purpose of generation of children takes "next place" to a sin of homicide.[132] He is being consistent because if the male provides all the active principle or form of his offspring, then all semen is sacrosanct. It is to Aquinas's credit also that he teaches the sacredness of the male seed, which he understood as the basis of human life. This position is a far cry from some other medievals who wrote about semen as "fetid" and "foul" and "stinking."[133]

What is most important to remember is that Aquinas's ethics is based on false biology. Were Aquinas living today, he would surely be the last one to subscribe to his own ethics, because he would not take Aristotle's sexual theories as a starting point. Given Aquinas's commitment to science—a commitment that got him into so much trouble theologically—we know that he would not and could not justify his sexism in today's context. If, as he says, a mistake about nature can result in a mistake about God, how much more true is it that a mistake about nature can result in a mistaken morality. Clearly his morality depends on his understanding of what is or is not natural. He says, for example, that "natural love is a kind of natural inclination engrafted in a nature by God. But nothing natural is perverse, therefore it is impossible for any natural inclination or love to be perverse."[134] The idea that his church could or would want to continue to teach his sexual ethics based on a bizarre biology is beyond imagination.[135]

Third, we must also raise questions about Aquinas's attitude toward his own body and toward animals. A man of considerable appetite, his girth might suggest that in praxis he was less in touch with his body than in theory when he writes about the body as equal to the soul. In addition, he sometimes has flights from his body that seem less than incarnational, as when he writes: "The life of the gods (that is, the intellectual substances) is completely happy because they have only intellectual life."[136] Is he announcing his own breakdown here when he praises the intellectual life over bodily life? While he pronounces that sexual activity drains one's intellectual life, on what basis did he arrive at this conclusion, since he himself was a virgin? Who is to say that erotic love cannot feed intellectual and creative work and a deep spirituality?

As for animals, we have seen how Aquinas celebrates the soul in animals. He admires their "wonderful sagacity," calling them "keen and clever."[137] And he honors the fact that all creatures share in the "dignity of causality." We have also seen how he dismisses a distinction between an "inferior" and a "superior" reason in humans. Nevertheless, he often seems to be putting down animals. Perhaps this is partly explainable by the fact that he was urging humans to use their intellects more, fighting as he was against the anti-intellectualism of much of the Dark Ages. But animals are not treated with as much reverence as one would wish in Aquinas's work. Human chauvinism does creep into his writings. For example, Aquinas is adamant about how the human resurrection will include the body—indeed the human will be at the "perfect age" of about thirty-three years. But he is deeply anthropocentric when he denies other creatures will be part of the resurrection.

A fourth issue is Aquinas's latent anti-Semitism. I say "latent" because he is a deeply biblical thinker whose pastoral theology is found most of all in his numerous biblical commentaries, which are dependent on a Jewish worldview. To cite just one example in this regard, he says that "the ancients erred in supposing the just God to be the God of the Old Testament and another God to be good, namely, the God of the New Testament."[138] Aquinas is in many ways a deep ecumenist, as we have seen. He in no way devalues the wisdom or ways of the Jewish and biblical tradition—in fact, his commitment to a nondualistic philosophy is a movement away from Hellenism to a more Jewish and biblical spirituality. However, while it does not play a prominent part in his overall philosophy, Aquinas does regrettably express anti-Semitism at times. In fact, in a sermon given in Naples the last year of his life in response to the question whether "the Jews, since they did not kill the Godhead, sinned no more than if they had killed any other man," Aquinas said: "I reply that a man who bespatters a king's robe is as guilty as though he had bespattered the king himself. Hence the Jews, though they could not slay God, yet for slaying the human nature wherewith Christ was clothed, were punished as though they had slain the Godhead."[139] This identifying of the killing of Jesus with the whole of the Jewish people is unacceptable, and, as it was offered in a public sermon and at the supposedly mature apex of his life, makes it all the more reprehensible.

The Unfinished Work of Thomas Aquinas

It seems to me that each of these "clay feet" of Aquinas only demonstrates how unfinished was his effort to move Western religion into a less dualistic mode, and how unfinished it remains to this day. For example, what I think is most important in evaluating Aquinas in reference to feminism is the following. While he was confused about the role of women in culture and his knowledge of the biology of sex was as abysmal as that of most people in the West for the past twenty-five hundred years, still his overall philosophy can justifiably be understood as feminist. The issues that preoccupied him—cosmology, wisdom, relationship, creation, spirit in matter and not opposed to matter, science, creativity, justice, truth found among the pagans, passion as the seat of all virtue, sensuality, nature, compassion, Christ as Wisdom, alternative images of God, conscience—these are all issues that concern feminist thinkers. His condemnation so soon after his death for espousing the consubstantiality of body and soul is proof that his own contemporaries and guardians of the status quo understood how radical his non-dualistic positions were.[140] Some of his most cherished principles—those, in fact, that resulted in his condemnation—are feminist. That he did not know women is a great tragedy. And history cannot dismiss the weight he lent to their ongoing oppression.

In spite of his ambivalence toward women and the body and in spite of his sexism, many women can find in Aquinas an ally and not an enemy at the deepest levels of their spiritual struggle. What happens, for example, when women apply his teaching on magnanimity and fortitude to themselves? What esteem results from the affirmation of women's being and creativity and empowerment? What happens when women are affirmed in their quest for a living cosmology? The thirteenth-century mystic and activist, Mechtild of Magdeburg, whom no one could accuse of being an uncritical woman since she was an active member of the Beguine community, the feminist movement of the Middle Ages, was a great devotee of Thomas Aquinas. She saw in his work the groundwork for a liberation of women, and with good reason. For while his experience of women was deeply limited and his understanding of biology was irredeemably flawed, still his basic philosophical effort was feminist.

Aquinas tried to move Western civilization away from the dualisms of Hellenistic and neo-Platonic thought. He paid a price for his prophecy, both politically and personally. Politically it is a fact that, pious accolades notwithstanding, the church never chose to embrace the route of nondualism that Aquinas forged for it seven centuries ago. As Chenu puts it: "Christianity was scarcely ever able to effectively oppose the attractions of the dual spiritualism of Augustine and Descartes."[141] Again, Chenu comments:

In the finest hour of the University of Paris, in the emancipated world of the Communes, Thomas Aquinas roused the anger and disdain of intellectuals and religious people *by proclaiming the importance of matter in the metaphysics of the universe, in the constitution of man and in the evolution of society.* And the subtle analysis he used to vindicate the interiority of consciousness and the freedom of spirit, despite the limitations of matter, did nothing to allay suspicion. . . . The delayed approval of his theology was destined to make it official rather than practically effective.[142]

Historically and politically speaking, Aquinas failed. Personally, Aquinas underwent the pain that a postpatriarchal mindset demands of people, for, if Marie-Louise von Franz is correct in understanding his breakdown as a rupture with his own anima or feminine side, then *Aquinas himself died as a result of the excessively patriarchal milieu in which he worked and struggled.* While he did not support women well during his lifetime, he stands with them in his death. His record on women is not at all consistent with his lifelong and ardent struggle against dualism. That he suffered a breakdown over the loss of the feminine in a mystical insight while celebrating the Eucharist only heightens the irony of the event, while it deepens the lesson passed on to us by his teachings and by the parable of his life and death. The tragic ending in Aquinas's life reminds us of the difficulty involved in making a paradigm shift that touches the psychic and bodily as well as the intellectual and political levels of our being.

It also deepens the challenge to us today who dare not fail another time in this great undertaking to move away from dualism to a more reverent relationship to the whole of creation. As we embark on the third millennium of Christianity with the survival of our fragile planet in human hands, the Earth awaits our choices. Aquinas himself taught that choice lies at the heart of the moral acts of humans. I hope that this book, and that portion of wisdom that Aquinas names for us within it, might contribute to the renaissance our times demand of us. In this way the planet might once again partake in the "sheer joy" that imagined it into being in the first place. For, as Aquinas would put it, the "success in knowing the sheer joy of God should not be restricted to the few or to the old."

1. "Letter to Fr. Victor White, O.P." (December 31, 1949), in Gerhard Adler and Aniela Jaffes, eds., *C. G. Jung Letters* (Princeton, NJ: Princeton Univ. Press, 1973), I: 540.
2. CG I, ch. 4 n. 4. Gilby translation.
3. DV II, q. 14, a. 11.
4. For instance, see Thomas Gilby, *St. Thomas Aquinas: Philosophical Texts* (Durham, NC: Labyrinth Press, 1982); Gilby, *St. Thomas Aquinas: Theological Texts* (Durham, NC: Labyrinth Press, 1982); Mary T. Clark, ed., *An Aquinas Reader* (Garden City, NY: Doubleday, 1972); and Vernon J. Bourke, *The Pocket Aquinas* (New York: Pocket Books, 1960).
5. The old philosophical categories reflect the sexism of that enterprise. Please read an invisible "sic" each time the term "man" appears.
6. Perhaps we find scholasticism so cumbersome because today we have our own scientific methodologies that have supplanted it. Carl Jung gives scholasticism credit for today's scientific method when he says: "The scholastic spirit . . . is the mother of our modern scientific method. . . . The great achievement of scholasticism was that it laid the foundations of a solidly built intellectual function, the sine qua non of modern science and technology" (*Symbols of Transformation* [Princeton, NJ: Princeton Univ. Press, 1956], 20).
7. M. D. Chenu, *Toward Understanding Saint Thomas* (Chicago: Univ. of Chicago Press, 1963), 243.
8. Ibid., 233–34.
9. For this book I have translated the following volumes of Aquinas's work never before translated into English: the *Commentary on Dionysius;* his commentaries on Job, Isaiah, Jeremiah, Lamentations, the Psalms (he commented on only the first fifty-four), Matthew's Gospel, John's Gospel (one-half of this had previously been translated). I confess that I only discovered an English translation of the commentary on Job after this book was entirely completed. It is mentioned in the bibliography. Scholars distinguish between a *reportatio* and an *ordinatio.* The former is a live lecture taken down by a student or scribe; the latter is a finished product written or dictated by the author. Among the former are Thomas's lectures on Paul's letter to the Corinthians, chapter 11 to the end of

Hebrews, the lecture on Matthew. We can presume his other Biblical works are from his own hand. His commentary on John's Gospel was corrected by him. (See James A. Weisheipl, *Friar Thomas D'Aquino* [Garden City, NY: Doubleday, 1974], 117.)

10. Weisheipl, p. 117.
11. See the Appendix for a sample of Aquinas's critical passion for scientific cosmology.
12. Weisheipl, *Friar Thomas D'Aquino*, 322–23. Also see Marie-Louise von Franz, *Alchemy: An Introduction to the Symbolism and the Psychology* (Toronto: Inner City Books, 1980), 216.
13. From notes I took during Louis Cognet's class in the history of Western spirituality, spring 1969.
14. Abraham Heschel, "On Prayer," *Conservative Judaism* 25 (Fall 1970): 8.
15. See my *Creation Spirituality: Liberating Gifts for the Peoples of the Earth* (San Francisco: HarperCollins, 1991), 17–26.
16. While Simon Tugwell in *Albert & Thomas: Selected Writings* (New York: Paulist Press, 1988) is to be commended for translating some of Aquinas's rich wisdom texts (though many of these were already in Gilby), nevertheless his narrow definition of spirituality generated by a complete lack of awareness of the Via Transformativa provides a perfect example of what happens without a hermeneutic. While offering us far too many selections built around a search for Aquinas's literal definitions of prayer, he gives us none of Aquinas's thoughts on creativity and the prophetic vocation. A brief section on prophecy belies the author's charismatic ideology. Contrast this with Aquinas's rich development of the prophetic vocation and its relation to the struggle for justice as found in Conversation Four below. One gets the impression that Tugwell does not consider the struggle for justice a constitutive element of the Gospel or part of Aquinas's spiritual agenda. Yet it surely was.

    Another example of the lack of a spiritual hermeneutic can be found in Walter H. Principe, *Thomas Aquinas' Spirituality* (Toronto: Pontifical Institute of Mediaeval Studies, 1984). In this lecture the author wisely calls for more attention to the scriptural commentaries of Aquinas, yet he offers no understanding of the Via Negativa in Aquinas, nor of the Via Transformativa (neither the justice element so important to Aquinas nor the role of the prophet is treated; instead, the phrase "serve others in charity" is employed). Nor is there mention of cosmology or even of Aquinas's *Commentary on Dionysius,* which was so seminal a work in his early mysticism.

17. In Ethics I, L. 1, p. 6.
18. In Pss, Preamble, 148.
19. For these same Four Paths and how they are present in Meister Eckhart's work, see my "Meister Eckhart on the Fourfold Path of

a Creation-Centered Spiritual Journey," in Matthew Fox, ed., *Western Spirituality: Historical Roots, Ecumenical Routes* (Santa Fe, NM: Bear & Co., 1980), 215–48.

20. See David Griffith, *Sacred Interconnections: Postmodern Spirituality, Political Economy, and Art* (Albany, NY: State Univ. of New York Press, 1990), Introduction; also Georges DeSchrijver in *Lectures at Katholieke Universiteit Leuven,* Belgium, Fall 1990.

21. See "Your Mother is Dying" in my *The Coming of the Cosmic Christ* (San Francisco: Harper & Row, 1989), 11–33.

22. See Henry Adams, *Mont-Saint-Michel & Chartres* (Garden City, NY: Doubleday, 1959); and William Anderson, *Green Man: The Archetype of Oneness with the Earth* (San Francisco: Harper, 1990).

23. M. D. Chenu, *Nature, Man and Society in the Twelfth Century* (Chicago: Univ. of Chicago Press, 1968), 3.

24. Consider for example the contrast between St. Peter's sixteenth-century Basilica in Rome, where not a single blade of grass lives and whose interior is cold marble with gigantic statues of exaggerated human forms—mostly male—with the twelfth-century temples of France, where the cosmos, nature, and its processes are all celebrated.

25. Josef Pieper, *Guide to Thomas Aquinas* (New York: Pantheon Books, 1962), 30–31.

26. Josef Pieper, *The Silence of Thomas Aquinas* (Chicago: Regnery, 1957), 85.

27. See my *Breakthrough: Meister Eckhart's Creation Spirituality in New Translation* (Garden City, NY: Doubleday, 1980); *Meditations with Meister Eckhart* (Santa Fe, NM: Bear & Co., 1983); *Illuminations of Hildegard of Bingen* (Santa Fe, NM: Bear & Co., 1985); *Hildegard of Bingen's Book of Divine Works with Letters and Songs* (Santa Fe, NM: Bear & Co., 1987); "Creation Spirituality from Hildegard of Bingen to Julian of Norwich: 300 Years of an Ecological Spirituality in the West," in Philip N. Joranson and Ken Butigan, eds., *Cry of the Environment* (Santa Fe, NM: Bear & Co., 1984), 85–106; and "The Cosmic Christ and the Creation Mystics—The Medieval West," in *Coming of the Cosmic Christ,* 109–26.

28. ST, Prologue.

29. Ibid.

30. Chenu, *Faith and Theology* (New York: Macmillan, 1968), 33.

31. In Meta XI, L. 1, p. 119.

32. See Jean Delumeau, *Sin and Fear: The Emergence of a Western Guilt Culture 13th—18th Centuries* (New York: St. Martin's Press, 1990), 70, 145.

33. See my *Original Blessing* (Santa Fe, NM: Bear & Co., 1983), 309, 316. Having criticized the "ism" of Thomism I do wish to acknowledge my debt to those deep students of Aquinas who have gifted us with some of Aquinas's spiritual genius. In particular I wish to honor my mentor, Père Marie Dominic Chenu;

Josef Pieper (see *Leisure the Basis of Culture* [New York: Mentor Books, 1952]; *Fortitude and Temperance* [New York: Pantheon Books, 1954]; *In Tune with the World: A Theory of Festivity* [Chicago: Franciscan Herald Press, 1965]); Athanasius Weisheipl, with whom I studied for three years; Etienne Gilson; and even G. K. Chesterton, whose book on Aquinas, totally lacking Aquinas's spirit of ecumenism, nevertheless captures much of the heart of Aquinas as a "revolutionary" (see *Saint Thomas Aquinas: The Dumb Ox* [Garden City, NY: Doubleday, 1956]). Mention should also be made of Jacques Maritain, and of Rudolf Steiner and John D. Caputo, who have wrestled with Aquinas's mysticism in this century (see Rudolf Steiner, *The Redemption of Thinking* [Spring Valley, NY: Anthroposophic Press, 1956]; John D. Caputo, *Heidegger and Aquinas* [New York: Fordham Univ. Press, 1982]). Also part of the shoulders on which I stand is the work of the English Dominican Thomas Gilby.

34. One wonders how much the trauma of the latter enticements wounded his attitude toward women and sexuality in his later thinking, a subject I shall explore later in this introduction.
35. Weisheipl, *Friar Thomas D'Aquino,* 330–31.
36. ST II-II, q. 168, a. 2.
37. I am using this term in the technical way in which I first define it in my *Coming of the Cosmic Christ,* 228–44, namely, as world religions coming together around their cosmic wisdom or mystical traditions.
38. ST I, q. 1, a. 8, ad 2.
39. In Chenu, *Nature, Man and Society in the Twelfth Century,* 311.
40. Ibid., 315.
41. Ibid., 310.
42. Ibid., 312.
43. In Meta II, L. 5, 135–36.
44. DDN, n. 430, p.142.
45. In Jn 1.4b, n. 103, p. 61.
46. Chenu, *Nature, Man and Society,* 24.
47. Pieper, *Guide to Thomas Aquinas,* 44ff.
48. CG II, ch. 3 n. 6.
49. In DA I, L. 1, p. 3.
50. ST I, q. 88, a. 1.
51. Chenu, *Nature, Man and Society,* 135.
52. Chenu, *Toward Understanding Saint Thomas,* 51.
53. ST II-II, q. 180, a. 6, ad 3.
54. Chenu, *Toward Understanding Saint Thomas,* 228.
55. Ibid., 314.
56. In Pss, Preamble, 148.
57. ST I, q. 79, a. 9.
58. Chenu, *Faith and Theology,* 133.
59. CI, ch. 11.

60. Ibid.
61. Chenu, *Toward Understanding Saint Thomas,* 68.
62. This phrase is from the American philosopher William Hocking. I have dealt with this dialectic at considerable length, for example, in my *On Becoming a Musical, Mystical Bear: Spirituality American Style* (Paramus, NJ: Paulist Press, 1976) and *A Spirituality Named Compassion* (San Francisco: Harper & Row, 1979).
63. Pieper, *Guide to Thomas Aquinas,* 29ff. Thomas's statement is from CI, ch. 3 n. 121.
64. Chenu, *Toward Understanding Saint Thomas,* 233ff.
65. Chenu, *Faith and Theology,* 33.
66. Cited in ibid., note 10. The original is in E. Gilson, "La tradition francaise et la chrétienté," in *Vigile,* IV, 1931, Book I, 74 n. 1.
67. Cited in Renee Weber, *Dialogues with Scientists and Sages: The Search for Unity* (London: Routledge, Kegan Paul, 1986), 169.
68. Chenu, *Toward Understanding Saint Thomas,* 63.
69. Jaroslav Pelikan, *Jesus Through the Centuries* (New Haven, CT: Yale Univ. Press, 1985), 63.
70. See my *The Coming of the Cosmic Christ,* 114–16. See also Aquinas's treatise on glory as found in his treatment of the Transfiguration in ST III, q. 45.
71. Pieper, *Fortitude and Temperance,* 58. Pieper comments: "We must avoid the temptation of transferring our justifiably contemptuous lack of confidence in the dictatorial 'reason' of the idealist philosophers of the nineteenth century to the ratio of scholasticism always closely related to reality" (22).
72. Ibid., 57.
73. In Ethics X, L. 9, p. 904.
74. ST I-II, q. 22, a. 2.
75. DV, q. 22, a. 11.
76. In Ethics I, L. 5, p. 29.
77. In Jn 1.26, n. 246.
78. In Pss 36, p. 281.
79. ST I-II, q. 74, a. 5.
80. Ibid., q. 76, a. 2.
81. Ibid., q. 79, a. 3.
82. In Jn 1.25, n. 243.
83. Thomas Gilby observes that the "*Summa theologica* follows the order of the first chapter of Genesis. The treatise on man [sic], rather an anthropology than a psychology, comes as a climax to the questions on the different days of creation and should be set against that zoological background" (Gilby, *Philosophical Texts,* 193 n. 1).
84. Cited in R. P. Blackmur, *Henry Adams* (New York: Harcourt, Brace, Jovanovich, 1980), 178–79ff.
85. ST I-II, q. 109, a. 1, ad 1.
86. DP, q. 6, a. 5, ad 5.

87. ST II-II, q. 2, a. 7, ad 3.
88. For a discussion of this term and its opposite, the sin of adultism, see *Coming of the Cosmic Christ,* 180–98.
89. DDN, n. 792, p. 296.
90. In Ethics X, L. 6, p. 886.
91. See ibid., L. 2 and 3, pp. 867, 871ff.
92. St. Augustine, *De Genesi ad Litterum,* Book XII, 7.16.
93. CG II, ch. 68 n. 6.
94. DP, q. 5, a. 10, ad 5.
95. ST I, q. 98, a. 2.
96. In I Sent, Prologue. See also his connection of Christ, wisdom, and "glory" in In Heb, Prologue and ch. 1, pp. 666–71.
97. DV II, q. 12, a. 13, ad 3.
98. ST II-II, q. 171, a. 4, ad 1.
99. In Is 4, p. 446.
100. In Ethics VIII, L. 12, p. 769.
101. Ibid, 768.
102. Ibid., L. 6, p. 731.
103. CG III, ch. 123 n. 6.
104. ST III, q. 29, a. 2.
105. CG III, ch. 124 n. 4.
106. In Ethics VIII, L. 12, p. 768.
107. Ibid.
108. CG III, ch. 122 n. 8.
109. In Ethics VIII, L. 12, p. 768.
110. In Jn 19.26, n. 2438.
111. In Jn. 20.17, n. 2519.
112. ST II-II, q. 177, a. 2.
113. In Ethics VIII, L. 7, p. 736.
114. Ibid., L. 11, p. 759.
115. CG III, ch. 94 n. 11.
116. In Ethics VII, L. 5, p. 642.
117. ST I, q. 92, a. 1, ad 1.
118. Ibid.
119. Ibid., ad. 2.
120. Ibid., a. 2.
121. Ibid., ad 2.
122. Ibid., ad 3.
123. Ibid., q. 93, a. 6, ad 2.
124. Weisheipl, *Friar Thomas D'Aquino,* 29.
125. Ibid., 31.
126. Ibid., 322.
127. Von Franz, *Alchemy,* 216.
128. See my *Original Blessing,* appendix A, p. 309.
129. In Ethics VIII, L. 12, p. 766.
130. ST I, q. 118, a. 2, ad 4.
131. Ibid., q. 92, a. 1.

132. CG III, ch. 122 n. 9.
133. Thus the future Pope Innocent III wrote: "Man is formed of dust, mud, ashes, and what is even viler, foul sperm." See Delumeau, *Sin and Fear*, 16, 44, passim.
134. QQ 1, q. 4, a. 3.
135. A critical evaluation of Aquinas's views of sexuality and especially on the topic of homosexuality can be found in John Boswell, *Christianity, Social Tolerance, and Homosexuality* (Chicago: Univ. of Chicago Press, 1980), 318–32.
136. In Ethics X, L. 12, p. 920.
137. ST I-II, q. 13, a. 2, ad 3.
138. In Jn 17.25, n. 2264.
139. AC, 37–38.
140. Rosemary Radford Ruether sheds light on the essence of a post-patriarchal age when she names the essential struggle of feminism as a struggle against dualism. See Rosemary Ruether, "Women's Liberation in Historical and Theological Perspective," in Sarah Bentley Doely, ed., *Women's Liberation and the Church* (New York: Association Press, 1970), 26–36.
141. Chenu, *Faith and Theology*, 225.
142. Ibid., 113.

First Conversation:

ON THE VIA POSITIVA

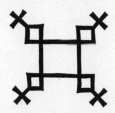

Sacred writings are bound in two volumes—that of creation and that of the Holy Scriptures.

(CG II, ch. 4 n. 5)

FOX: Brother Thomas, I am drawn to your work, first of all, because of what G. K. Chesterton was inferring when he called you "Thomas of the Creator who reminded people of the creed of creation when many of them were still in the mood of mere destruction." Humanity's anthropocentrism and religion's preoccupation with sin and redemption, together with the ecological devastation of the industrial revolution, have rendered creation deeply vulnerable in our time. How do you understand creation and what role does creation play in your spirituality?

AQUINAS: Creation is the emanation of the whole of being from the universal cause.[1] It is the primordial action that presupposes no other action and is presupposed in all others. In this sense creation is an action unique to God, who alone is the universal cause of being.[2] Creation means divine action invested with a certain logical relationship. . . . In its passive sense it signifies a real relation, which is a created entity; though to speak more precisely, . . . this relationship is not a thing, but a reality inhering in a thing.[3]

FOX: It is telling to me how much emphasis you put on relation when you speak of creation. It makes me think of the prayer of the Lakota people: "All our relations."

AQUINAS: Creation is original freshness related to God.[4]

FOX: Many people say that a theologian's work is exclusively with the Bible, yet you seem eager to exegete creation as much as the Bible and to follow scientists who do so as well.

AQUINAS: Theologians seek an answer to the following question: How do the relationships within creatures open out to Divinity?[5] Sacred writings are bound in two volumes—that of creation and that of the Holy Scriptures.[6]

---

1. ST I, q. 45, a. 1.   2. CG II, ch. 21 n. 2.   3. DP, q. 3, a. 3 ad 2.
4. DP, q. 3, a. 3. (Gilby's translation for *"relatio quaedam ad Deum cum novitate essendi."*)   5. CG II, ch. 4 n. 5.   6. Sermo, 6.5, p. 129.

FOX: Are you saying that creatures are a Bible, a kind of revelation, as if they were sacred words of God?

AQUINAS: Visible creatures are like a book in which we read the knowledge of God.[7] One has every right to call God's creatures God's "words," for they express the divine mind just as effects manifest their cause. "The works of the Lord are the words of the Lord" (Eccles. 42:15).[8]

FOX: Creation, then, is a kind of revelation of the divine.

AQUINAS: God is manifested in two ways to humans. First, by an infusion of interior light through which a person knows: "Send out your light and your truth" (Ps. 42). Second, by placing before us the exterior signs of the divine wisdom, namely, sensible creatures. "God diffuses it, namely wisdom, over all of God's works" (Eccles. 1).[9]

FOX: Thus creatures reveal God to us?

AQUINAS: In this life we know God insofar as we know the invisible things of God through creatures, as it says in Romans, chapter 1. And thus every creature is for us like a certain mirror. Because from the order, goodness, and magnitude that are caused by God in things, we come to a knowledge of the divine wisdom and goodness and eminence. And this knowledge we call a vision in a mirror.[10]

FOX: If creation is a "word" of God like the Scriptures are, it presupposes a listener.

AQUINAS: The doctrine of wisdom that is God's voice is not ordered only toward the teaching of people who hear it but also toward the perfection of natural works that come from the teaching of divine wisdom.[11]

FOX: You cited the Scriptures that used the word "Lord," as they often do. But for us today the word "Lord" conjures up feudal political systems. What do you understand this word "Lord" to mean?

AQUINAS: The word "Lord" means the maker of all creation. As in Judith 16: "All your creation serves you."[12]

FOX: The term "Lord" is really a cosmic title, that of the governor of the universe. No wonder it gets politically oppressive

---

7. In Rom, ch. 1, p. 21.   8. DV, q. 4, a.1.   9. In Rom, ch. 1, p. 21.
10. In I Cor, ch. 13, p. 263.   11. In Job, ch. 37, p. 123.   12. In Pss 17, p. 203.

when it is taken out of its cosmological context and put into an anthropocentric one.

AQUINAS: The word "God" signifies the governor and provider of all things. To believe there is a God is to believe in one whose government and providence extend to all things.[13]

FOX: What further is implied when you use the term "creation"?

AQUINAS: Creation imports a relation of the creature to the Creator, with a certain newness or beginning.[14]

FOX: I am struck by the emphasis you put on "newness or beginning." Is this why you used the term "original freshness" in your definition of creation?

AQUINAS: When Moses uses the words, "in the beginning God created heaven and earth," he is referring to the newness of the world. The newness of the world is known only by revelation; therefore, it cannot be proven.[15]

FOX: One gets the impression that the "newness" or "original freshness" of creation never ceases. Apparently creation is still going on.

AQUINAS: If things have eternally emanated from God, we cannot give a time or instance at which they first flowed forth from God. So either they never were produced by God, or their being is always flowing forth from God as long as they exist.[16]

FOX: You obviously opt for the latter option.

AQUINAS: This is what it means to say that God preserves things in being by the divine operation.[17] The preservation of things by God is a continuation of that action whereby God gives existence. This action is without either motion or time, just as the preservation of light in the air is by the continual influence of the sun.[18]

FOX: If creation is continuous, then our experience of the Creator is meant to happen here and now.

AQUINAS: Nothing exists of time except now. Hence time cannot be made except according to some now; not because in the first now is time, but because from it time begins.[19]

---

13. AC, p. 8.   14. ST I, q. 45, a. 3, ad 3.   15. Ibid, q. 46, a. 2.   16. CG III, ch. 65 n. 8.   17. Ibid.   18. ST I, q. 104, a. 1.   19. Ibid., q. 46, a. 3, ad 3.

FOX: This sounds like what the mystics refer to as an "eternal now" experience.

AQUINAS: The apprehension of time is caused by the perception of the changing instant, the apprehension of eternity by that of the enduring instant.[20] The "now" of time is not time, the "now" of eternity is really the same as eternity.[21]

FOX: Does creation elicit for you an "eternal now" experience?

AQUINAS: Things are said to be created in the beginning of time not as if the beginning of time were a measure of creation, but because together with time heaven and earth were created.[22]

FOX: This sounds like physicist Stephen Hawking writing in his book, *A Brief History of Time.* When you speak of creation as a relationship with Divinity that is intrinsic to all things and ever fresh, I feel a sense of dynamism and flow.

AQUINAS: When we say "in him was life" (John 1:32), we mean that God could not only produce all things but that God also has an unfailing flow and a causality for producing things continually without undergoing any change. God is a living fountain that is not diminished in spite of its continuous outflow. Collected water, on the other hand, water that is not living or running water, is diminished when it flows out. It gets used up and becomes stagnant.[23]

FOX: God, you say, has "an unfailing flow." Your God sounds wet.

AQUINAS: I understand the Word to be the source from which realities stream, flowing into the very being things have within themselves.[24] You see, love works in a circle: the beloved moves the lover by stamping a likeness and the lover then goes out to hold the beloved in reality. The one who was first and the beginning now becomes the end of the movement.[25]

FOX: The circle imagery seems important to you.

AQUINAS: There is manifested a kind of circle in existing things, for they have the same beginning and the same end.[26]

FOX: I certainly prefer this circle imagery to that of "climbing Jacob's ladder," which has for so long dominated the patriarchal

---

20. Ibid., q. 10, a. 2, ad 1.   21. In I Sent 19.2.2.   22. ST I, q. 46, a. 3, ad 1.   23. In Jn 1.4a, n. 94.   24. ST I, q. 58, a. 6.   25. Ibid. I-II, q. 158, a. 1.   26. DDN, n. 605, p. 224.

spiritual consciousness in the West. After all, we live in a curved universe.

AQUINAS: A certain circulation appears in love because it is from good and toward good and that circling agrees with the divine eternity of love, since circular motion alone can be perpetual. Thus Dionysius says that love is "like a kind of eternal circle," insofar as it is because of the good as an object, and from the good as from a cause, and persevering in the good, and striving for the purpose of achieving the good. Thus the good circles by a certain unwavering convolution.[27]

FOX: I notice that your great work, the *Summa theologiae,* is structured in a kind of circular fashion, that is from *exitus* (creation flowing from God) to *reditus* (creation returning to God).

AQUINAS: In the process of reason there is a kind of convolution like a circle, for reason, beginning from one, proceeds through many and back to the one.[28]

FOX: So you are saying that both love and knowing are circular in nature?

AQUINAS: The truth of existing things consists fundamentally in the apprehension of the essence of things, an essence that rational souls cannot apprehend immediately by themselves. Instead, they scatter themselves throughout the properties and effects that surround the essence of the thing, so that from these they come upon the proper truth. Thus their investigation takes place in a kind of circle, for from the properties and effects they discover causes and from the causes they make judgments about the effects.[29]

FOX: Do you envision Divinity as circular?

AQUINAS: In circular motion consider three things: first, that whatever is the assigned point in the circle is both the beginning and the end. Second, it is possible to consider a concave and a convex in the circular line itself, and the line contains something on the concave side while it can be contained by others on the convex side. Third, what is moved in a circular motion returns by its circular motion to the first point from which it began to be moved.

---

27. Ibid., n. 450, p.148.   28. Ibid., n. 713, p. 267.   29. Ibid.

In this way therefore God is said to be moved like a circle: insofar as the Godhead contains in itself all Identity, all midpoints, and all extremes, in this way God touches the first property mentioned above; and insofar as God contains the surrounding points because God pertains to the measure of the concave and the surrounded points and because God pertains to the measure of the convex, it touches the second property; and insofar as it contains the turning toward God as toward a goal of those who have proceeded from God, as from a beginning, it touches the third property.[30]

FOX: When I hear you speak, I am reminded of the definition of mysticism as a "return to our origins."

AQUINAS: The vision of the divine essence fills the soul with all good things because it unites it to the source of all goodness.[31] In the emergence of creatures from their first Source is revealed a kind of circular motion in which all things return, as to their end, back to the very place from which they had their origin in the beginning.[32]

FOX: It is a good thing, you are saying, for people to return to their source?

AQUINAS: It is desirable for each thing to be united to its source since it is in this that the perfection of each thing consists.[33]

FOX: Why is this so?

AQUINAS: An effect is most perfect when it returns to its source; thus, the circle is the most perfect of all figures, and circular motion the most perfect of all motions, because in their case a return is made to the starting point. It is therefore necessary that creatures return to their principle in order that the universe of creatures may attain its ultimate perfection. Now, each and every creature returns to its source so far as it bears a likeness to its source, according to its being and its nature, wherein it enjoys a certain perfection.[34]

FOX: God then is a Source?

AQUINAS: The Source who has no Source.[35]

FOX: Your use of the word "original" with creation strikes me as a mystical way of understanding creation.

---

30. Ibid., n. 842, pp. 317–18.   31. ST I-II, q. 5, a. 4.   32. In I Sent 14.2.2.   33. In Meta I, L. 1, p. 7.   34. CG II, ch. 46 n. 2.   35. In V Sent 4.15.4.

AQUINAS: Each thing is perfected when it returns to its beginning. Tobias (12:20) says: "It is time for me to return to the One who sent me." Ecclesiastes 1:7: "Rivers return to the place from whence they came." Indeed, in accordance with his humanity, Jesus was going to God with whom he was from eternity in accordance with his divinity [as he says in John's gospel].[36]

FOX: So Christ was one with his beginning or source?

AQUINAS: The divine Word is of necessity perfectly one with the Source from which it proceeds, without any kind of diversity.[37]

FOX: So Divinity is indeed our source and beginning?

AQUINAS: Divine wisdom is the beginning from which the entire emanation of knowledge begins and the cause pouring itself forth and the maker of substance insofar as it makes wisdom come to be in each creature and perfection insofar as it leads knowledge to its completion. It is also a defense for it perseveres to the end, since in this all knowledge finds its end, namely, in the fact that God is known. Therefore divine wisdom is both the beginning and the cause of wisdom itself, which has been received in common in accordance with itself; and of every mind, that is, of intellect, with regard to the angels; and of every reason, with regard to human beings; and of all sense, with regard to animals.[38]

FOX: Your image strikes me as being a dynamic, multidimensional spiral motion rather than simply a circular one. Your imaging of the relationship between God and creature as being that of Lover to beloved moves me to ask you further about Divinity. Who is God? How might we image God with power and with intimacy?

AQUINAS: God is an artist and the universe is God's work of art.[39] All natural things are produced by divine art and can rightly be called God's works of art.[40] Divine art is not exhausted in the making of creatures. Diversity reigns because artists have the right to change their style and make things differently as time goes on.[41]

---

36. In Jn 16.5, n. 2083.   37. ST I, q. 27, a. 1, ad 2.   38. DDN, n. 716, p. 267.   39. ST I, q. 45, a. 6.   40. ST I, q. 91, a. 3.   41. DP, q. 6, a. 1, ad 12.

FOX: Speaking of God as artist is a powerful metaphor for me. One thing it implies is that God is not neutral but quite passionate about God's work.

AQUINAS: All artists love what they give birth to—parents love their children; poets love their poems; craftspeople love their handiwork. How then could God hate a single thing since God is the artist of everything?[42]

FOX: Now I understand more fully your emphasis on creatures as "words" of God that express the divine Artist just as all works of art tell us about the artist.

AQUINAS: The Godhead goes forth when a creature proceeds from God. Because of this procession there is a multitude of things and a distinction of creatures from God.[43] At the origin of everything lies God's simple will and pleasure.[44]

FOX: I sense that you have a well-developed appreciation of the divinity inherent in all creatures. Can you elaborate on this?

AQUINAS: Every creature participates in some way in the likeness of the divine essence.[45] All creatures are images of God, who is the first agent.[46] An image of the Trinity pulsates in all conscious and loving creatures to the extent that they too conceive words and expand in love.[47]

FOX: As God does?

AQUINAS: Every effect demonstrates some trace of its cause—smoke with fire, for example; or a footprint that tells us that someone has passed but not who. In all creatures there is a footprint of the Trinity.[48]

FOX: Elaborate more on your understanding of the creature as "image of God."

AQUINAS: The Word of God is a spotless mirror that reflects all being.[49] Not only are individual creatures images of God but so too is the whole cosmos. God has produced a work in which the divine likeness is clearly reflected—I mean by this, the world itself.[50] God's love is not about a private conversation; it goes out universally to all the divine works.[51]

FOX: You hold creatures and the world in such divine esteem. Don't you ever get accused of pantheism?

---

42. CG I, ch. 96 n. 5.   43. DDN, n. 153, p. 48.   44. DV, q. 6, a. 2.
45. ST I, q. 15, a. 2.   46. CG III, ch. 19 n. 4.   47. ST I, q. 45, a. 7.
48. Ibid.   49. In Eph 3.10, p. 470.   50. In Jn 1.10, n. 136.   51. CT II, 5.

AQUINAS: On the contrary, to hold creatures cheap is to slight divine power.[52] Creatures resemble God, yet God does not resemble creatures.[53] All creatures exist in God and are God's life, so great is the divine understanding and cherishing of all that God has made.[54]

FOX: To say "creatures exist in God" sounds like panentheism.

AQUINAS: The Scriptures say, "of God, and by God, and in God are all things" (Rom. 11:36).[55] God embraces in the divine self all creatures.[56] God holds all things in Godself and not successively according to time nor divided into parts, but together.[57] Indeed, the Godhead contains all things.[58] God contains every place.[59] God does not rest in some thing but all things rest in God.[60] All things are in God[61] since in the Godhead God has all being, all substance, and all existence; and again as around the Godhead insofar as they are derived from God.[62] Christ says, "Remain in me" by receiving grace; "and I remain in you," by helping you.[63]

FOX: You certainly are familiar with the idea of panentheism! What does it mean to say creatures are "in God"?

AQUINAS: A creature is said to be in God in two ways. First as in its governing cause and preserver of its being: and in this sense the creature is understood as already existing apart from the Creator, so that we may say that the creature derives its being from the Creator. For the creature is not understood to be preserved in being except as already having being in its proper nature, in respect of which being the creature is distinguished from God. Wherefore in this sense the creature as existing in God is not the creative essence. Second, the creature is said to be in God inasmuch as it exists virtually in its effective cause or as the thing known in the knower.[64]

FOX: The Book of Acts says that God is the one "in whom we live, move, and have our being." Would you comment on that?

AQUINAS: Creatures are said to be in God in a twofold sense. In one way, so far as they are held together and preserved by the divine power—even as we say that things that are in our power

---

52. CG III, ch. 69 n. 15. 53. ST I, q. 4, a. 3, ad 4. 54. Ibid., q. 8, a. 4. 55. Ibid., q. 44, a. 1. 56. CG II, ch. 46 n. 7. 57. DDN, n. 959, p. 359. 58. Ibid, n. 948, p. 356. 59. Ibid, n. 806, p.301. 60. In Is 66, p. 574. 61. DDN, n. 619, p. 233. 62. Ibid., n. 629, p. 234. Cf. nn. 661, 811. 63. In Jn 15.3, n. 1988. 64. DP, q. 3, a. 16.

are in us. And creatures are thus said to be in God, even as they exist in their own natures. In this sense we must understand the words of the Apostle when he says, "in God we live, move, and have being," since our being, living, and moving are themselves caused by God. In another sense things are said to be in God, as in the one who knows them, in which sense they are in God through their proper ideas, which in God are not distinct from the divine essence.[65]

FOX: Could you explain that phrase, "not distinct from the divine essence"?

AQUINAS: All things are life in God. Since all things that have been made by God are in God as things understood, it follows that all things in God are the divine life itself.[66]

FOX: You do not seem shy about talking about the divinity of creatures when you speak of our being "in God."

AQUINAS: All that exists in God is God.[67] All that exists in God is one with the divine nature.[68]

FOX: What do you mean by the phrase, "the divine life itself"?

AQUINAS: "Divine life" is supereminently living and the active and preserving cause of life per se, that is, of common life. Consequently, all particular life and all vital motion and every beginning of each life proceeds from divine life, which is above all other life.[69]

FOX: You seem to have great reverence for the mystery of life.

AQUINAS: From divine life, even human souls are able to live incorruptibly, and from divine life come those animals that live a life with sensation and all the plants that hold life according to the last resonance, that is, according to the final and most extreme participation in life, since life does not proceed beyond plants. Even when life is destroyed it participates in creation. . . . Insofar as the things that, through the weakness of their nature, are lacking in a participation of life yet are turned toward life again, they become animals or living things of some kind or other, as is clear in plants and animals generated from putrefaction. On account of this there is said in the Scriptures: "Send

---

65. ST I, q. 18, a. 4, ad 1.   66. Ibid., a. 4.   67. Ibid., q. 27, a. 3, ad 2.
68. Ibid., a. 4, ad 1.   69. DDN, n. 680, p. 255.

forth your Spirit and they will be created and you will renew the face of the earth" (Ps. 104).[70]

FOX: Speak more about God and life.

AQUINAS: God is the cause of all life. Whether one calls it intellectual life as in the case of angels or rational life as in the case of human beings or sensible life as in the case of plants or whatever kind of life—even if there were other modes of living. And not only all life, but even every beginning of life and all substance having life is from divine life.[71]

FOX: What are some characteristics of divine life as you understand it?

AQUINAS: Divine life is praised above all life because of its fecundity, by which it produces all lives. It is most generous because it is not narrowed toward one kind of life but has a comprehensive fullness of all life.[72]

FOX: You say God is most generous. Please elaborate on that statement, as I believe that we human beings can use all the models of generosity we can find.

AQUINAS: God does not will to give to someone the divine goodness so that thereby something may accrue to the divine benefit, but because for God to make such a gift befits the Godhead as the fount of goodness. But to give something not for the sake of some benefit expected from the giving, but because of the goodness and befittingness of the giving, is an act of generosity. . . . God, therefore, is supremely generous . . . and alone can truly be called generous, for all agents other than God acquire some good from their actions, which is the intended end.[73]

FOX: And among God's gifts freely given is life itself?

AQUINAS: Divine life is per se alive since it is not vivifying some other things in God. It is supereminently alive . . . and ineffable.[74]

FOX: Is this divine life of which you speak the same as the term we hear used frequently, "eternal life"?

AQUINAS: John's epistle (1 John 5) says, "This is the true God and eternal life." This means that God is the One from whom

---

70. Ibid., n. 681, p. 255. 71. Ibid., n. 692, p. 259. 72. Ibid., n. 693, p. 259. 73. CG I, ch. 93 n. 7. 74. DDN, n. 694, p. 259.

there is life itself per se, that is, common life itself and all particular life and divine life is spread abroad from itself. For the capacity for living is distributed to all things that participate in life in whatever way according to the capacity of each thing. It is as if John said that God is called eternal life insofar as God is the cause of common and particular life and of all living things. [75]

FOX: It is amazing to me that you never once spoke of "life after death" in describing what we mean by "eternal life"! You seem to understand eternal life as beginning in this lifetime. Your theology has a well-developed sense of realized eschatology. Let us now turn to that other aspect of panentheism, that of God being in creatures and in creation.

AQUINAS: God must be everywhere and in all things. [76] Since God is the universal cause of the whole of being . . . it must be that wherever being is found, the divine presence is also there. [77] It belongs to the infinite to be present everywhere, and in all things. God is in all things; not, indeed, as part of their essence, nor as an accident; but as an agent is present to that upon which it works. [78]

FOX: You say God is in all things. But is there a special kind of dwelling of God in human beings as well?

AQUINAS: God dwells in the saints in three ways: by faith: "That Christ may dwell in your hearts by faith" (Eph. 3:17); by love: "He or she that dwells in love, dwells in God and God in him or her" (1 John 4:16); and by the fulfillment of God's commandments: "If anyone love me, they will keep my word and my Creator will love them, and we will come to them, and make our abode with them" (John 14:23). [79]

FOX: You make God's presence in us sound very intimate and sacred indeed.

AQUINAS: We need to bear in mind that God is near us, indeed, within us — since God is said to be in the heavens, that is, in the saints, who are called "the heavens": "The heavens declare the glory of God" (Ps. 18:2) and "You, O Lord, are among us" (Jer. 14:9). [80]

---

75. Ibid., n. 675, p. 254.   76. CG III, ch. 68 n. 1.   77. Ibid., n. 4.
78. ST I, q. 8, a. 1.   79. AC, p. 113.   80. Ibid., p. 115.

FOX: You connect psyche and cosmos here when you talk of us humans as the heavens declaring God's glory. What follows practically from our practicing panentheism more deeply?

AQUINAS: Confidence comes from God's nearness: "The Lord is near to all that call upon God" (Ps. 145:18). Hence it is said: "But you when you pray enter into your chamber" (Matt. 6:6), that is, into your heart.[81]

FOX: So our hearts grow and become fuller when trust increases. In your opinion, just what is the primary work of God vis-à-vis creation?

AQUINAS: Since God is very being by the divine essence, created being must be God's proper effect, as to ignite is the proper effect of fire. Now God causes this effect in things not only when they first begin to be, but as long as they are preserved in being; as light is caused in the air by the sun as long as the air remains illuminated. Therefore, as long as a thing has being, God must be present to it, according to its mode of being. But being is innermost in each thing and most fundamentally inherent in all things, since it is formal in respect to everything found in a thing. Hence it must be that God is in all things, and most intimately so.[82]

FOX: But what about the idea that God is "above all things," which we find even in Scripture, for example, Psalm 103: "The Lord is high above all nations"?

AQUINAS: God is above all things by the excellence of the divine nature; but God is in all things as the cause of the being of all things.[83] In a certain sense, one can say that God is more closely united to each thing than the thing is to itself.[84]

FOX: But if God is in all things, doesn't it follow that God is contained by all things?

AQUINAS: Although corporeal things are said to be in another as in that which contains them, nevertheless spiritual beings contain those things in which they are: for example, the soul contains the body. Hence also God is in things as containing them. Still, by a certain similitude to corporeal things, it is said

---

81. Ibid., p. 116.   82. ST I, q. 8, a. 1.   83. Ibid., ad 1.   84. Ibid., a. 17.

that all things are in God inasmuch as they are contained by God.[85]

FOX: How wonderful to hear you say that the soul contains the body rather than the tired notion that the body holds the soul! What about the notion that God is "in heaven" as we pray in the "Our Father" prayer?

AQUINAS: "In heaven" does not mean God is content to stay in the heavens but that God comprehends the universe in one sweep of power. "None but I span the vault of heaven" (Eccles. 24:8).[86]

FOX: What about evil persons or demons? Can we say God is in them too?

AQUINAS: In the demons there exists their nature, which is from God, and also the deformity of sin, which is not from God. Therefore God is in the demons only inasmuch as they are beings.[87]

FOX: Do you believe God is everywhere?

AQUINAS: God must be everywhere and in all things.[88] Scriptures say: "I fill heaven and earth" (Jer. 23:24). In some way God is in every place; and this is to be everywhere. First, as God is in all things as giving them being, power, and operation. God fills every place—not indeed like a body, for a body is said to fill place inasmuch as it excludes the simultaneous presence of another body. However, when God is in a place, others are not thereby excluded from it. Indeed, by the very fact that God gives being to the things that fill every place, Godself fills every place.[89] Just as the soul is whole in every part of the body, so is God whole in all things and in each one.[90]

FOX: Is this capacity to be everywhere unique to Divinity, would you say?

AQUINAS: To be everywhere primarily and absolutely is proper to God. To be everywhere primarily is said of that which in its whole self is everywhere. To be everywhere belongs to God and is proper to God because whatever number of places are supposed to exist, God must be in all of them, not just a part of God but God's whole self.[91]

---

85. Ibid., a. 1, ad 2.   86. CT II, 6.   87. ST I, q. 8, a. 1, ad 4.   88. CG III, ch. 68 n. 1.   89. ST I, q. 8, a. 2.   90. Ibid., ad 3.   91. Ibid., a. 4.

FOX: In some respects, what you are saying simply seems an elaboration of the divine name of "Emmanuel" or "God-with-us."

AQUINAS: Since God is everywhere, God is with all who are anywhere. [92]

FOX: But we speak of the universe itself being everywhere as well.

AQUINAS: The whole body of the universe is everywhere, but not primarily. For it is not wholly in each place, but according to its parts. Nor is it everywhere absolutely, for if other places existed besides this universe, it would not be in them. [93]

FOX: Please elaborate more on the presence of God in things.

AQUINAS: God is in all things that God created, and in another way God is in things as the object of operation is in the operator. God is in all things by the divine power, inasmuch as all things are subject to divine power; God is in all things by the divine presence, inasmuch as all things are bare and open to God's eyes; and God is in all things by the divine essence, inasmuch as God is present to all as the cause of their being. [94] God, through the divine essence, through which God creates all things, is in all things. [95]

FOX: But we confuse ourselves if we say that God belongs to the essence of things.

AQUINAS: God is in all things by essence—not by the essence of the things themselves, as if God were of their essence, but by God's own essence, because the divine substance is present to all things as the cause of their being. [96]

FOX: This seems to be one of the differences between pantheism and panentheism. Have you ever been accused of pantheism?

AQUINAS: God forms no part of the essence of created things. It is the existence that permeates things that cannot be understood except as derived from the divine existence. [97]

FOX: I am troubled when you say God acts in all things, because it seems to belittle the autonomy of creatures.

---

92. In Jn 17.24, n. 2258.   93. ST I, q. 8, a. 4, ad 3.   94. Ibid., a. 3.
95. In Jn 1.10, n. 134.   96. ST I, q. 8, a. 3, ad 1.   97. DP, q. 3, a. 5,
ad 1.

AQUINAS: Some have understood God to work in every agent in such a way that no created power has any effect in things, but that God alone is the immediate cause of everything that comes about. For example, that it is not fire that gives heat, but God in the fire, and so forth. But this is impossible.[98]

FOX: Why is it impossible?

AQUINAS: First, because the order of cause and effect would be taken away from created things, and this would imply lack of power in the Creator: for it is due to the power of the cause that it bestows active power on its effect. Second, because the active powers that are seen to exist in things would be bestowed on things to no purpose, if these brought about nothing through them. Indeed, all things created would seem in a way to be purposeless, if they lacked an operation proper to them, since the purpose of everything is its operation. We must therefore understand that God works in things in such a manner that things have their proper operation.[99]

FOX: Your passion about respecting the autonomy of secondary causes always comes through to me. Why are you so passionate about this issue?

AQUINAS: If we minimize secondary causes it derogates from the order of the universe, which is made up of the order and connection of causes. For the first cause, by the preeminence of its goodness, gives other beings not only their existence but also their existence as causes.[100] There is no contradiction between secondary causes and providence; secondary causes in fact bring about the accomplishment of providence.[101]

FOX: I see why your passion is so strong—it is a cosmic passion for you! A law of the universe is at stake. It seems to follow from this discussion on creation and Divinity that study and meditation on creation is important to our spiritual growth. After all, you said that creation as well as Scripture constitutes the holy book of God. I have known many theologians who have spent decades studying biblical languages and the works of classical theologians (including your own) but almost entirely ignore science and meditation on nature. Am I understanding you properly when I criticize education and theological education in particular for ignoring creation?

---

98. ST I, q. 105, a. 5.   99. Ibid.   100. Ibid. II, q. 11, a. 1.   101. CG III, ch. 96 n. 8.

AQUINAS: Errors made about creation will result in errors about God as well.[102] The opinion is false of those who assert that it makes no difference to the truth of the faith what anyone holds about creatures, so long as one thinks rightly about God. For error about creatures spills over into false opinion about God, and takes people's minds away from God, to whom faith seeks to lead them.[103] For this reason Scripture threatens punishment to those who err about creatures: (Ps. 28:5) "Because they have not understood the works of the Lord and the work of God's hands, you will destroy them, and not build them up."[104] There can be no question that to study creatures is to build up one's Christian faith.[105]

Suppose a person entering a house were to feel heat on the porch, and on going further, were to feel the heat increasing, the more they penetrated within. Doubtless, such a person would believe there was a fire in the house, even though they did not see the fire that must be causing all this heat. A similar thing will happen to anyone who considers this world in detail: one will observe that all things are arranged according to their degrees of beauty and excellence, and that the nearer they are to God, the more beautiful and the better they are.[106]

FOX: You say it is a sin to misread nature. Can you give an example of how our ignorance of creation can be sinful?

AQUINAS: Those things that are knowable to individual persons, that is, to this or to that particular man or woman, and are first in the process of knowing, are often only slightly knowable by nature. This often happens because they have little or nothing of being; for a thing is knowable to the extent that it has being. For example, it is evident that accidents, motions, and privations have little or nothing of being, yet they are more apparent to us than the substances of things; for they are closer to the senses, since of themselves they fall under sensory perception as proper or common objects of sense. But substantial forms do so only accidentally.[107]

FOX: Your explanation helps elucidate for me how it is that titillation, to which our contemporary mass media frequently appeals, often overpowers the human mind. To find the substance of things takes some work. Can you recommend places

---

102. CG II, ch. 2 n. 3.   103. Ibid., ch. 3 n. 6.   104. Ibid., n. 7.
105. Ibid., ch. 2 n. 6.   106. AC, pp. 13–14.   107. In Meta VII, L. 2, pp. 502–503.

to go to understand the substance, rather than the superficialities or "accidents" of things?

AQUINAS: Matter itself cannot be adequately known except through motion. Its investigation is the physicist's job; the philosopher should accept the physicist's findings.[108]

FOX: So science is an avenue to marveling at creation?

AQUINAS: Science ensures right judgment about creatures.[109]

FOX: You seem so wonder-filled about the diversity of creation, and you refer to this amazing diversity so often. I suppose the diversity follows from calling God a fruitful and creative artist: no two creatures are exactly the same.

AQUINAS: There is nothing redundant in what God has made.[110] This is what the philosopher and the poet share in common: both are concerned with the marvelous.[111] Amazement (admiratio) is the beginning of philosophy.[112]

FOX: Unfortunately, modern philosophers begin the act of philosophy not with wonder but with doubt. I get the impression you think wonder is good for all of us.

AQUINAS: Wonder was the motive that led people to philosophy.[113] Philosophy is to the cure of the soul what medicine is to the cure of the body.[114] Wonder is a kind of desire in knowing. It is the cause of delight because it carries with it the hope of discovery.[115] We wonder or admire when we see an effect and do not know the cause. A cause is doubly admirable either because it is totally unknown, or because the effect does not produce a perfectly clear cause. God produces an effect (see Rom. 1) but not one showing its cause perfectly. Therefore it remains wonderful.[116]

FOX: Give an example of an effect of God that leads us to wonder.

AQUINAS: The abundance of rain appears wonderful if the origin of the rain is considered, namely, that so much water is breaking out from the clouds, which do not have any solidity. Regarding this, Job speaks of "those waters which flow from

---

108. Ibid., 499.   109. ST II-II, q. 4, a. 4.   110. Ibid. III, q. 62, a. 2.
111. In Meta I, L. 3, p. 24.   112. ST I-II, q. 41, a. 4, ad 5.   113. In
Meta I, L. 3, p. 24.   114. In Ethics II, L. 4, p. 131.   115. ST I-II, q. 32,
a. 8.   116. In Pss 8, p. 167.

the clouds." But they do not flow in such a way that by an action such great rain comes from the clouds, but because the vapors of the clouds themselves are gradually condensed into rain. And there is also in rain another wonderful thing, that it is poured forth over a large area of the earth. For this reason Job adds, "which comes upon all things from above," namely, the places in the region in which it rains, so that no part of the land remains unflooded. . . . But from the clouds a flashing light proceeds because of the collision of wind, and so he adds, "and to flash with God's light from above." But clouds sometimes cover the sky even to the horizon of some region, within which the limits of the sea seem to be enclosed. And therefore Job says, "God covers the roots of the sea with a canopy of clouds."[117]

FOX: It sounds as if both you and Job had been moved to wonder by observing the forces of nature.

AQUINAS: Job enumerates the effects of divine power in natural things and begins with the most extreme, namely, the sky and the earth, in each of which something appears based on divine power, which surpasses human powers. . . . For nothing seems to be supporting the sky except divine power. . . . The earth, which is as it were the foundation of the sky, does not appear to be strengthened by something that can support it, but is supported by the power of God alone. And so Job says, "God suspends the earth above nothing." . . . The air seems wonderful because water is suspended in air, raised as a vapor, and does not fall wholly at once but drop by drop, as happens when it rains. And so he says, "God who encloses the waters in the clouds," that is, causes by the divine power, "so they do not fall," namely, the waters of the rain "flow equally downward," but by drops, as is right in conjunction with the temperature of the earth. As if by divine power, that which remained in the clouds has been bound up so that it would not fall from the beginning. For it happens by divine power that the vapors do not condense all together, so that, turned into water, they would rightly fall together, as rain falling from the clouds above with certain remnants of the vapors, from which little clouds are generated, remain, by means of which the sky is covered for us.[118]

---

117. In Job, ch. 36, p. 122.   118. Ibid., ch. 26, p. 93.

FOX: When I hear you speaking with such intensity about the wonder of rain and air and clouds and lightning, I also hear you saying God is wonderful.

AQUINAS: The Scriptures say "How wonderful is your name!" and "Why do you ask my name, which is wonderful?" (Gen. 32). Likewise of Christ incarnate, (Isa. 9): "His name will be called 'Wonderful.'" But does this apply to Judaea alone, as the Jews might say? or to Africa, as the Donatists say? No. It applies to the whole earth. "From the rising of the sun to its setting, great is my name among the nations." The reason for admiration is given when the psalmist says, "your glory has been raised up," because your majesty appears in the skies.[119]

FOX: Modern philosophy begins with doubt, not wonder. There has been more of this wonder, I think, in scientists pursuing the wonders of nature. What is wonder?

AQUINAS: Wonder is a kind of fear that results from an awareness of something that is too great for our capacity. It is an act that follows from the contemplation of some great truth. And, as I have said, contemplation culminates in our feelings.[120]

FOX: Then wonder seems the same as awe. How does this wonder of yours—so evident in all your work and in the very passion that sustained that work—apply to meditating on creation itself?

AQUINAS: The lover is not content with superficial knowledge of the beloved, but strives for intimate discovery and even entering into the beloved.[121] The more one knows the causes for love, the more reasonable it is that one love more.[122] One meditates on creation in order to view and marvel at divine wisdom.[123]

FOX: For you it seems that philosophy and wisdom go together.

AQUINAS: While this science [of philosophy] was first designated by the name wisdom, it was changed to the name philosophy, since they mean the same thing. . . . Pythagoras, when asked what he professed himself to be, refused to call himself a wise man as his professors had done, because he thought

---

119. In Pss 8, p. 167.   120. ST II-II, q. 180, a. 3, ad 3.   121. Ibid. I-II, q. 28, a. 2.   122. In Ethics VIII, L. 12, p. 765. · 123. CG II, ch. 2 n. 2.

this was presumptuous, but called himself a philosopher, that is, a lover of wisdom. And from that time the name "wise one" was changed to "philosopher," and "wisdom" to "philosophy."[124]

FOX: I hear you saying that meditation on creation leads us to God.

AQUINAS: To know God in some fashion is natural for the human intelligence no matter what state it is in. But in the beginning—that is, in this life—it is natural for it to know God through sensible creatures.[125] Each creature is made as a witness to God insofar as each creature is a witness to God's power and omnipotence; and its beauty is a witness to the divine wisdom.[126]

FOX: How does meditation on creation lead us to wonder at God's power?

AQUINAS: No one is so foolish as not to believe that the things of the physical world are subject to someone's government, providence, and disposition, seeing that they are regulated according to a certain order and time. For we see the sun, the moon, the stars, and other parts of the physical world all holding a certain course, which would not happen if they were the sport of chance.[127]

FOX: I sense in your thought the potential for retrieving in the West the true meaning of philosophy and the joy that comes with love of wisdom.

AQUINAS: Every human naturally has a desire for knowledge. As a result everyone enjoys knowing truth.[128]

FOX: Please elaborate on the enjoyable aspect of wisdom.

AQUINAS: Two features of play make it appropriate to compare the contemplation of wisdom to playing. First, we enjoy playing, and there is the greatest enjoyment of all to be had in the contemplation of wisdom, as Wisdom says in Ecclesiasticus (24:27): "My spirit is sweeter than honey." Second, playing has no purpose beyond itself. What we do in play is done for its own sake. The same applies to the enjoyment of wisdom. . . . The contemplation of wisdom contains within itself the cause of its

---

124. In Meta I, L. 3, p. 24.   125. ST II, q. 13, a. 1, ad 1.   126. In Jn 1.7, n. 116.   127. AC, p. 8.   128. ST II-II, q. 180, a. 7.

own enjoyment, and so it is not anxious about waiting for something that we lack. . . . It is for this reason that divine Wisdom compares her enjoyment to playing in Proverbs 8:30: "I delighted God day after day, ever at play in God's presence."[129]

FOX: Are you defining contemplation as play?

AQUINAS: Contemplation concerns ends that serve no ulterior purpose. Play, too, is concerned with ends when you play "for the fun of it." Sometimes it concerns means toward ends, when you take exercise in order to keep fit.[130]

FOX: But I hear you saying that contemplation is not possible without the discipline of meditation.

AQUINAS: The psalmist says: "I meditate on all your works, I muse on the work of your hands" (Ps. 143:5). Meditation is indispensable for well-instructed faith.[131]

FOX: Will you define meditation for us?

AQUINAS: Cogitation would seem to regard the consideration of the many things from which a person intends to gather one simple truth. Meditation would seem to be the process of reason from certain principles that lead to the contemplation of some truth. (Consideration has the same meaning.) But contemplation regards the simple act of gazing on truth.[132] One reaches the knowledge of truth by applying oneself by one's personal study, and this requires meditation.[133]

FOX: I hear you saying that study can be a kind of yoga or spiritual discipline. And so meditation and study of nature lead one to God?

AQUINAS: A work of art represents the mind of the maker. God's wisdom has produced all things real; from them we can catch a glimpse of the divine likeness, "poured forth on all creation" (Eccles. 1:10).[134] Also, from God's creatures we all are led to wonder at the divine power and in this way to hold God in reverence. The maker is nobler than the things that are made. . . . From wonder comes awe and reverence.[135] In addition, creatures have the capacity to warm our hearts to love the goodness of God. Since all perfections showered throughout the world in separate drops flow together, whole and complete,

---

129. CBH, Prologue.   130. CG III, ch. 2 n. 9.   131. Ibid. II, ch. 2 n. 1.
132. ST II-II, q. 180, a. 3, ad 1.   133. Ibid., ad 4.   134. CG II, ch. 2 n.
2.   135. Ibid., n. 3.

in the font of goodness, when we are drawn to the sweetness, beauty, and goodness of creatures, how boldly we ought to be borne away to the One in whom all these little streams commingle and course![136] In addition, when we meditate on creatures we grow like God, who sees everything by self-knowledge. As it is said: "But we all beholding the glory of the Lord with open face, are transformed into the same image" (2 Cor. 3:18).[137]

FOX: Thus creatures lead us to God?

AQUINAS: All creatures confess that they are made by God. Human beings ask questions of creatures when they consider them diligently. Those questioned respond when people perceive that the ordering that is found in the disposition of parts and order of action can in no way exist unless directed by some fuller wisdom.[138] Just as someone looking at a book knows the wisdom of the writer, so when we see creatures, we know the wisdom of God.[139] All natural things were produced by the divine art, and so may be called "God's works of art."[140]

FOX: The word "wisdom" arises so often when you talk about meditating on creation.

AQUINAS: God produces all things according to the divine wisdom.[141] God is both the origin of wisdom and the place of understanding. Wisdom is drawn from God, the first origin, into all creatures that are made through God's wisdom, just as art is drawn from the mind of artists into their work. Thus it is written in Ecclesiastes, "God has poured wisdom upon all God's works" (Ecclesiastes 1:10).[142] God is the origin of wisdom. . . . God does not acquire wisdom from creatures as we do, but rather produces creatures from divine wisdom.[143]

FOX: Let us go more deeply into our meditation and marveling at creation. Tell us more of the divine energy and image that you find pulsating in creatures.

AQUINAS: To exist is the most perfect thing of all, for compared to existence, everything else is potential. Unless it exists, nothing reaches actuality.[144] Existence is the actuality of all acts and the perfection of all perfections.[145] When it comes to living

---

136. Ibid., n. 4.   137. Ibid., n. 5.   138. In Job, ch. 12, p. 52.   139. In Pss 44, p. 31.   140. ST I, q. 91, a. 3.   141. CG II, ch. 24 n. 2.   142. In Job, ch. 28, p. 98.   143. Ibid., 99.   144. ST I, q. 4, a. 1, ad 3.   145. DP, q. 7, a. 2, ad 9.

things, their real aliveness is their very being.[146] Existence is all-pervading. When a person comes to be, the first appearance is that of existence; then of life; then of humanity. One must be an animal before one is a human being, one might say. And, at the end of life, one first loses the use of reason while life and breath remain. Then one loses these too and only existents are left.[147] Existence is innermost in each and deepest in everything that exists.[148] Consider creatures. They make it clear that they naturally desire to be. Those that are subject to death naturally resist deadly influences, tending toward where they are secure.[149]

FOX: So existence is both holy and all-pervading.

AQUINAS: Being is the most common first effect and more intimate than all other effects.[150]

FOX: You advocate the consideration of creatures. Meditate with me on some creatures.

AQUINAS: The whole earth is full of God's glory, since even to the farthest creatures, which are known throughout the earth, God manifests the spreading of Divinity's goodness.[151]

FOX: I sense that this word "glory"—which is so basic a word in the Cosmic Christ tradition—also plays a very important role in your theology of creation.

AQUINAS: Glory belongs preeminently to God alone. Isaiah (42:8) says: "I will not give my glory to another." And 1 Timothy (1:17) says: "Honor and glory to the immortal, invisible king of the world who is God alone." The knowledge therefore of divine goodness that is lofty and preeminent is spoken of as glory that is brilliant with praise and knowledge of the divine goodness.[152]

FOX: So "glory" and "goodness" are related for you, and both suggest the presence of the Divine, even in creation itself.

AQUINAS: Scripture, when it wishes to manifest the power of God, leads us back to the consideration of the skies. Thus Isaiah (40) writes: "Lift up your eyes on high, and see who created these things." Therefore the psalmist says, "I will look in your skies at the work of your fingers."[153] If we regard the corporeal

---

146. CG I, ch. 98 n. 2.   147. DCC, lect. 1.   148. ST I, q. 8, a. 3.
149. CG III, ch. 19 n. 3.   150. DP, q. 3, a. 7.   151. In Is 6, p. 457.
152. In Heb 1, p. 671.   153. In Pss 8, p. 168.

skies, they proclaim to us the glory of God, since in them there is a wonderful and regular order, which is a certain overflowing of the Divine in the strength of its glory. As Scripture says (Eccles. 43), "The appearance of the sky, the glory of the stars, the Lord on high illuminating the world." Therefore those material skies are understood to reveal God's glory to us, not like material living things, as Rabbi Moses says, but in their beauty, by which their maker is revealed much more. And the firmament shows us how magnificent God is. The firmament is called the sky, as in Gen 1: "God has called the firmament the sky." Thus in the division of the skies divine wisdom appears.[154]

FOX: What about a meditation on some living creatures?

AQUINAS: Jesus teaches us to avoid anxiety by considering the birds of the sky, since there is wisdom from them. Also in Job we read, "Ask the cattle and they will teach you" (Job 12:7).[155]

Job also recalls the strength of the horse when he says, "will you furnish a horse with strength?" He means not only strength of body, for a horse is powerful for carrying a burden; but also strength of mind, for a horse goes through dangers boldly. But he recalls another characteristic of the horse that is called forth by exterior appearance toward an object of desire: for it is said concerning horses that they are excited toward coitus by the beauty of the mane, and when the mane is cut off the desire is extinguished. Job implies this when he says "you have clothed its neck with whinnying," for horses are accustomed to whinny on account of desire. . . . But the horse has another quality, the fact that it leaps quickly, contrary to the accustomed habit of many quadrupeds. Thus he adds, "will you revive it anymore?" namely, by raising it on high. Another property of the horse is its boldness in war: he describes this more expansively, since it is noble and noteworthy. Its boldness is first manifested when it perceives war by smelling those who are approaching. Thus he writes: "its majestic snorting is terrible," that is, war, which is a terror for others, perceived by the horse through the nose, is a glory to him, that is, a kind of magnitude of soul. And this sign immediately appears when he writes, "his hoof digs the earth," as if the horse were preparing itself for fighting. But

---

154. In Pss 18, p. 207.   155. In Mt 6, p. 74.

from that which the horse perceives of war, he takes joy within. Thus Job adds: "He exults." Namely, the chance of fighting having been perceived, and he shows this through its effect when he adds: "he goes boldly in meeting armed forces." Nor is the horse cast down by terror when it is in battle. Thus he adds, "he mocks fear." And, what is more, he is not even affected by the pain of wounds, whence he adds, "nor does it yield to the sword." Most animals are terrified even by the sound of shrieking; but this does not affect the horse. Thus he adds, "the quiver will rattle over it," namely, full with arrows, when it is shaken in the movement of the soldier sitting on the horse. Likewise, some sound from the soldier's spear and his shield also come forth, and so he adds, "the flashing spear will shake," that is, while the spear flashes, it also emits a sound, and the shield as well, colliding with the weapons when it is moved, also makes noise. And so he adds, "excited," namely, within through boldness; "and snorting," namely, with whinnying, which he calls snorting. This is also characteristic of lions and demonstrates the boldness of the horse. And not only does he show an interior excitement of mind by the sounds he makes, but also by his exterior acts. So he adds, "he swallows the earth," that is, he seems to suck it in by digging it with his hooves. Not only is the horse not dazed by the sound of the quiver, spear, and shield, he is not even affected by the sound of the trumpet that they use in war. And so he adds, "when he has heard the trumpet, he says 'Ah!'" He actually emits a sound of exultation, for "Ah!" is the interjection of exultation. The horse also "smells war from afar," that is, when the enemy is still far away, he perceives war to be near at hand by the smell. He also seems to sense the preparation of war, namely, when leaders animate their soldiers with exhortations. And with regard to this he adds: "The shouting of the leaders," namely, the horse perceives this "and the shouting," that is, the confused clamor and clashing "of the army," namely, preparing itself for war.[156]

FOX: I am a bit surprised that you have observed horses so carefully, since as a Dominican friar you were forbidden to ride them.

---

156. In Job, ch. 39, p. 134.

AQUINAS: The consideration of creatures ought to be for the praise of God.[157]

FOX: Would you like to meditate with us on another earthly creature?

AQUINAS: In Isaiah (ch. 40) we take note of the statement, "they will mount up on wings like an eagle." The saints are compared to eagles first because of the height of their flying. "Will the eagle be lifted up to your bidding and build its nest up on the crags?" Here lies the prominence of contemplation.[158]

FOX: Yes—the archetype of soaring like a bird is indeed a well-known symbol for our mysticism and indeed for the divine child inside us (I think of the *puer*, Icarus).

AQUINAS: Isaiah says just before this in chapter 33: "They will see the king in his beauty." The second reason for invoking the eagle is the subtlety of its sense of smell. Luke 16: "Where there is a body, there also will eagles gather together." There is implied here the commotion of selection. Consider Songs of Songs 1: "Your anointing oils are fragrant." A third application is the sublimity of place. Proverbs 3 says: "There are three things most difficult for me and the fourth I am deeply ignorant of. The way of the eagle in the sky." Here there is a hint of an eagerness for celestial conversation, as in Philippians 3: "But our conversation is in the heavens." A fourth meaning is because of the speed of motion. (Lam. 4): "Our persecutors have been faster than the eagles of the sky." This implies a promptness to good work, as in Proverbs (22): "Have you seen one who is stifled in their work?" Fifth is the theme of renewal. Psalm 103 says: "Your youth shall be renewed like that of an eagle." In this there is an eagerness for correction and initiative. Consider 2 Corinthians 4: "Our outer nature is wasting away, our inner nature is being renewed day by day." Sixth is on account of the beauty of its limbs. Ezekiel (17) says: "An eagle came to Lebanon, great with huge wings and long pinions, full of a variety of plumage." This refers to the beauty of the virtues, as in Song of Songs 4: "You are wholly beautiful, my love, and there is no blemish in you." Also, the eagle cares for its children. "Like an eagle challenging her chicks to fly, and continuously flying

---

157. In Mt 6, p. 74.   158. In Is 40, p. 529.

above them" (Deut. 32). This applies to God's care of the saints: "Who is weak and I am not weak? Who is scandalized and I do not burn?" (1 Cor. 11).[159]

FOX: What lies at the heart of wisdom for you?

AQUINAS: When the psalmist says, "Taste and see the Lord is good," he first urges one to experience and he then posits the effect of experience. So he says, "taste and see," etc. Experience of a thing is taken in through the sense, but in one way with a thing at hand, in another of a distant thing. A distant thing is experienced through sight, smell, or hearing. A thing at hand, through taste of an interior sort. But God is not far from us, nor outside of us, but in us. Jeremiah 14: "Lord, you are in the midst of us." And so experience of divine goodness is called taste. But the effect of experience is put forth in two ways. One is certitude of the intellect, the other is confidence of feeling. With regard to the first he says "taste and see." For in corporeal things there is sight first, and then taste; but in spiritual things there is taste first but afterward there is sight, since no one knows who does not taste.[160]

FOX: So experience lies at the core of wisdom for you.

AQUINAS: Whoever desires something good seeks to have it as it really exists in nature—not as it exists merely in one's mind or one's consciousness.[161] The excellence of God's grandeur can come to the attention of humanity through the experience of divine power and wisdom in human events. Thus Job first shows how human beings come to the knowledge of things through experience by saying "Does not the ear try words," that is, when the ear hears words; "and the palate taste foods" and makes a judgment about the food. Since experience is from the senses, Job shows the power of experience through the judgment of the senses, especially through hearing and taste. For hearing is the most easily disciplined of the senses and is thus very valuable for contemplative knowledge. Taste, however, is perceptive about food, which is necessary for a person's life. Thus, through the judgment of taste, Job signifies the experience that we have of the things pertaining to the active life. Consequently, from the judgment of these two senses Job shows the

---

159. Ibid.   160. In Pss 33, p. 266.   161. DV, q. 22, a. 3, ad 4.

power of experience both in speculative and in practical things. Thus he says, "wisdom is with the aged," because the aged have heard much, "and in length of days prudence," which pertains to action. Because over a long period of time people taste and sample many things both useful and harmful.[162]

FOX: With this emphasis on taste and experience you seem to take seriously the etymological meaning of "wisdom," since in both Hebrew and Latin the word derives from the word meaning "to taste." Your marveling at the mystery of existence or "isness" seems to include Divinity in the heart of everything that is.

AQUINAS: God is in all things in the most intimate way. Insofar as a thing has existence, it is like God.[163] Just as flaming up comes with fire, so the existence of any creature comes with the divine presence.[164] The first fruit of God's activity in things is existence itself. All other fruits presuppose this one, namely, existence.[165]

FOX: You seem so confident about the absolute holiness and divinity of existence itself. Where do you derive this confidence about the graced mystery of existence?

AQUINAS: God is pure existence. The existence of all other things partakes of God's.[166] God is essential existence and all other things are beings by participation.[167] The essence of God is God's existence. Moses was taught this sublime truth when he asked: "If the children of Israel say to me, What is God's name? What shall I answer them? The Lord replied: "I am who am; so shalt thou say to the children of Israel: The One who is has sent me to you" (Exod. 3:13–14).[168]

FOX: Do you feel that the mystery of existence best names the mystery of God?

AQUINAS: The name "The One Who Is" determines no particular mode of being. Rather, it is indeterminate to all. Therefore it denominates the infinite ocean of being.[169] Divine names should be imposed from some perfections flowing from God to creatures. Among these the first is existence, from which comes this name, "The One Who Is."[170] It is precisely insofar as things are like God that they have being.[171]

---

162. In Job, ch. 12, p. 52.   163. ST I, q. 8, a. 1.   164. Ibid.   165. CT I, 68.   166. Ibid.   167. ST I, q. 4, a. 3, ad 3.   168. CG I, ch. 22 n. 10. 169. ST I, q. 113, a. 11.   170. Ibid, a. 11, ad 3.   171. CG III, ch. 19 n. 3.

FOX: How might we image this mystery of existence?

AQUINAS: The being of things is itself their light[172] and the measure of the being of a thing is the measure of its light.[173]

FOX: I am struck by your light imagery. Today's science has demonstrated that photons or light waves exist in all atoms and all beings in the universe. Also, your light imagery is about radiance and suggests the Cosmic Christ experience, which we will discuss later.

AQUINAS: Every creature is related to God like the air is related to the sun that lights its up.[174]

FOX: If what you are marveling at in the godlikeness of creation was true in your day, how much more amazing it is in ours, when we are beginning to learn more of the vastness and riches of the cosmos all around us. For example, we have learned that our universe is home to a trillion galaxies, each with billions of stars and countless atoms, and that it took eighteen billion years to expand to its present state, and that every atom contains photons or light waves. Do you detect purpose in this mystery of existence shared by so vast a universe?

AQUINAS: God created all things that they may be—not that they may sink back into nothingness. (See Wis. 1:14.)[175] Each and every single creature tends toward this—that it may participate in the Creator and be assimilated to the Creator insofar as it is able.[176] God gifts every single thing with its original being and sustains it as long as it lasts. God bestows on them their active powers and the divine activity runs through all of theirs.[177] All the natural course of things represents a certain movement of the creature toward the perception of God, according to Psalm 148: "Fire, hail, snow, ice, the blowing of the gale—these fulfill God's word."[178]

FOX: You speak of "all things." Can we move from a discussion of the microcosm, that of individual creatures, to a reflection on the macrocosm, the whole?

AQUINAS: Nature in its most usual sense includes the relationship of the whole cosmos to God.[179]

---

172. DCC, lect. 6.   173. In Tim 6.16, p. 618.   174. ST I, q. 104, a. 1.
175. QQ 4, q. 3, a. 4.   176. ST I, q. 103, a. 2.   177. Ibid., q. 105, a. 5.
178. In Job, ch. 39, p. 134.   179. DP, q. 6, a. 1, ad 1.

FOX: I find your sense of cosmology a very important corrective to today's thinking, which suffers from an excessive anthropocentrism.

AQUINAS: It is false to say that humanity is the most excellent being in the world.[180] When human beings are ignorant of nature and their place in the cosmos they may imagine that they are subject to forces that in fact they are beyond.[181]

FOX: Our ignorance of the universe subjects us to fear and paranoia, you say. If humanity is not the best thing in the universe, what is?

AQUINAS: The entire universe is one dominion and realm, governed by one ruler, who is the first mover, the first truth, the first good—God, blessed for ever and ever.[182] Now God and nature and every other cause work for the optimum total effect and for the completion of each and every part, not in isolation but in relation to the entire system.[183]

FOX: Your emphasis on the whole universe is a refreshing one in a world gone mad with anthropocentrism and psychologizing.

AQUINAS: God knows the whole body of creatures (*universitatem creaturum*).[184]

FOX: It is amazing to sense your passion for the root meaning of "university"—namely, a place where we learn to see the world as a whole, like God does. Our educational systems have totally lost this sense of the whole. We live in worlds of parts and pieces.

AQUINAS: A part is not perfect except in the whole, whence naturally the part loves the whole and the part is willingly exposed for the safety of the whole.[185]

FOX: You seem to be celebrating a very contemporary "law" of the universe—that of interdependence as opposed to isolation or competition.

AQUINAS: The very order of things created by God shows the unity of the world. For this world is called one by the unity of

---

180. In Ethics VI, L. 6, p. 569.   181. CG II, ch. 3 n. 5.   182. In Meta XII, L. 12, p. 925.   183. ST I, q. 48, a. 2, ad 3.   184. In Job, ch. 28, pp. 98–99.   185. DDN, n. 406, p. 135.

order, whereby some things are ordered to others. But whatever things come from God have relation of order to each other as well as to God.[186]

FOX: And so relationship permeates the universe?

AQUINAS: Aristotle says that all things in the universe are ordered together in some way, but not all are ordered alike, for example, sea animals, birds, and plants. Yet even though they are not ordered in the same way, they are still not disposed in such a way that one of them has no connection with another. For plants exist for the sake of animals, and animals for the sake of human beings. That all things are related to each other is evident from the fact that all are interconnected together to one end.[187]

FOX: I hear you praising interconnectivity!

AQUINAS: Indeed, the perfection of any one thing considered in isolation is an imperfection, for one thing is merely one part of the entire integrity of the universe arising from the assembling together of many singular perfections.[188]

FOX: So human beings too are interconnected with all things.

AQUINAS: Human nature is of an excellent making—it communicates with all the creatures. We have being in common with the stones; life in common with the trees; sense knowledge in common with animals; intelligence in common with the angels.[189] Human beings occupy a middle place between God and the brute animals, and they communicate with each of these extremes. With God according to intellectuality; with brute animals according to sensuality.[190]

FOX: You say that our interconnectivity is toward "one end."

AQUINAS: All things issuing from God are ordered to one another and to God, and this is the reason why all belong to one world.[191] Things relate to God too in the fashion of an interpenetration (*impermixtio*).[192]

FOX: And they relate to one another as well?

AQUINAS: One indissoluble connection consists in all things.[193] All are joined together in a common bond of friendship with all

---

186. ST I, q. 47, a. 3.   187. In Meta XII, L. 12, p. 920.   188. DV, q. 2, a. 2.   189. In Rom, ch. 1, p. 16.   190. Ibid., 18.   191. ST I, q. 48, a. 3. 192. DCC, lect. 20.   193. DDN, n. 910, p. 337.

nature (*connaturalem amicitiam*).[194] In no way is it possible for something to exist by itself or for something to be among beings as an accident or partially, for then it would have altogether fallen out of the unity [of the whole].[195]

FOX: You say all things share friendship?

AQUINAS: Nothing among creatures is so weak that it does not share in some divine gift, from which sharing it takes a part so that it has a friendship of shared nature with the other creatures.[196] If all things are united with all things, they not only come together in the one shape of the whole, but they also come together in this fact: that all things are united according to one form, devised by the One who is the Author of all things. For this very unity of all things proceeds from the unity of the divine mind, as the shape of a house that is in the materials comes from the shape of the house that is in the mind of the architect.[197]

FOX: Does this friendship among all things also include a friendship with the Creator?

AQUINAS: There exists a natural friendship with God according to which anything whatsoever, insofar as it exists, seeks God and desires God as the first cause and the highest good and as its own end.[198]

FOX: When you celebrate the interconnectivity of all things, you seem to be celebrating the true meaning of cosmos, the whole *order* of the universe, since *kosmos* in Greek means *order*.

AQUINAS: There is a certain single and indissoluble combination of all things, namely, to the extent that all things come together in a single order of the universe. This [unity] remains indissoluble insofar as there is caused by God a kind of harmony in the universe that is a proportioned concord. Dionysius describes this when he says that a "perfect consonance is harmonized." For harmony is nothing other than a concordant consonance.[199]

FOX: What follows from this harmony?

AQUINAS: This harmonious combination or concordant consonance possesses order and strength. Confusion destroys order. As for strength, there is an indissoluble strength in the

---

194. Ibid.   195. Ibid., n. 921, p. 342.   196. Ibid., n. 910, p. 337.   197. Ibid., n. 979, p. 364.   198. In I Cor, ch. 13, p. 263.   199. DDN, n. 908, p. 336.

connection of things, not from the multitude of the things assembled but by virtue of the one cause containing and assembling them into one.[200]

FOX: And this is God?

AQUINAS: God contains all things and hugs them in an embrace
insofar as all things are under the divine providence. . . . The
Godhead is both a place and foundation and chain connecting all
things.[201]

FOX: Your images, including that of God "hugging" all
things, makes the cosmos sound like a place in which creatures
should feel very much at home.

AQUINAS: It would not be good for different families who
shared nothing in common to live in a single home. Hence it
follows that the whole universe is like one principality and one
kingdom, and must therefore be governed by one ruler. Aristotle's conclusion is that there is one ruler of the whole universe,
the first mover, and one first intelligible object, and one first
good, whom . . . Aristotle called God, who is blessed for ever
and ever. Amen.[202]

FOX: It sounds like interconnectivity and the relation among
things is itself a source of wonder for you.

AQUINAS: We are able to contemplate the marvelous connection of things. For it is always found that the lowest in the
higher genus touches the highest of the lower species. Some of
the lowest members of the animal kingdom, for instance, enjoy
a form of life scarcely superior to that of plants; mussels, which
are motionless, have only the sense of touch and are fixed to the
earth like plants.[203]

FOX: Give another example of interconnectivity in nature.

AQUINAS: Our palpable sun—the one light existing—uniformly
pours out to all things and renews all palpable things, especially
in regard to their substances and their qualities, by generating
things anew when certain things have been corrupted. This
happens with plants and vines stricken by frost. The sun also
nourishes all living things; it guards or preserves all things

---

200. Ibid.   201. Ibid., n. 851, p. 320.   202. In Meta XII, L. 12, p. 925.
203. CG II, ch. 68 n. 6.

universally, both living and nonliving; it perfects them by leading them toward life and the requisite perfection. It discerns or distinguishes among the diversity of sense objects. It unites by composing one out of many; and it makes the plants dried up in the winter through cold to flourish again; it even makes them germinate when they are closed up under roofs. Both plants and animals are generated by its power. It alters the things that are altered in the nature of things, and it arranges or makes each thing exist firmly and grow strong in its own place and even in its foundations. From the plants the sun causes the production of fruit and seeds and other plants. It moves the nourishment upward from the root of the plants to their tops; and it vivifies all the things that are alive and even every one of the natural bodies according to its own property, which shares in the power of one and the same sun.[204]

FOX: And the human being—what role does it play in this interpenetrating and interdependent universe?

AQUINAS: God wills that human beings exist for the sake of the perfection of the universe.[205]

FOX: "Perfection of the universe"? What do you mean by "perfect"?

AQUINAS: To fulfill one's proper function.[206] The terms "perfect" and "whole" have the same or nearly the same meaning. . . . For example, one is said to be perfect when no part of one is missing.[207]

FOX: You say that perfection has to do with fulfilling one's proper function.

AQUINAS: The reason why a thing is said to be perfect in the line of its particular ability is that an ability is a perfection of a thing. One is said to be a perfect physician or a perfect flute player when one lacks nothing pertaining to the particular ability by reason of which one is said to be a good physician or a good flute player.[208]

FOX: You are saying that the human being exists to fulfill the overall function of the universe and to make its unique contribution to the destiny of the universe. Humanity too, then, is utterly interdependent with all the rest of creation.

---

204. DDN, n. 662, p. 246.   205. In Eph 1.6a, p. 457.   206. CG II, ch. 89 n. 18.   207. In Meta V, L. 18, p. 391.   208. Ibid.

AQUINAS: The human body is something supreme in the genus of bodies and is harmoniously tempered. It is in contact with the lowest of the higher genus, namely, the human soul, which holds the lowest rank in the genus of intellectual substances, as can be seen from its mode of understanding. Thus one can say that the intellectual soul is on the horizon and on the confines of things corporeal and incorporeal.[209]

FOX: Our souls are "on the horizon," you say, between the material and the spiritual.

AQUINAS: Soul is that in us through which we have communion with animals, spirit is that through which we have relationship with spiritual substances. Yet it is one and the same substance that makes the body alive and that, by its power called the mind, is able to understand.[210]

FOX: You say our souls are "on the horizon." What are the limits to this horizon that we can stretch for?

AQUINAS: Aristotle says that the human soul is potentially everything, and it is what it is by becoming all things. So it is possible for the perfection of the whole world to exist in one thing. Such is the fullness the soul may achieve. According to philosophers, the entire system of the cosmos, complete with all its causes, may be delineated in the soul. This, they maintain, is the last end of human beings. We, however, set it in the vision of God, for, as Gregory remarks, for those who see God, who sees everything, what is there they do not see?[211]

FOX: You have so often brought up the topic of goodness in this conversation on creation. Just how good is creation in your estimation? Isn't it true that much of the despair of our times derives from our loss in a belief that life is good? Or even that goodness is possible? A religion that centers itself around human sin and evil contributes, it seems, to the despair of a pessimistic culture and thereby forfeits its opportunity to redeem it from its most destructive tendencies.

AQUINAS: Despair consists in one's ceasing to hope for a share of God's goodness. Despair is against God insofar as we lose hope that we can partake of God's goodness.[212]

---

209. CG II, ch. 68 n. 6.   210. In Heb, ch. 4, p. 705.   211. DV, q. 2, a. 2.   212. ST II-II, q. 20, a. 3.

FOX: I hear you saying that despair comes from the loss of belief in one's own goodness and a loss of awareness of how that goodness of ours relates to the divine goodness.

AQUINAS: Despair consists principally in a flight from God, who is the immutable good.[213]

FOX: That despair comes from an unbelief in goodness is a powerful insight for our depressed and pessimistic—even cynical—times. All the more reason to pursue this issue of the goodness—or as theologians say, the blessing that creation is in depth.

AQUINAS: To bless is nothing else than to speak the good. In one way we bless God, and in another God blesses us. We bless God by recognizing the divine goodness. As Scripture says, "Bless the God of heaven" (Tob. 12). and "Bless and exalt the Lord as much as you can" (Eccles. 43). But God blesses us by causing goodness in us.[214]

FOX: How does God bless us creatures?

AQUINAS: God's accepting or loving someone (for they are the same thing) is nothing else but God's willing a person some good. Now God wills the good of nature for all creatures. On this account God is said to love all things: "For you love all things that are . . . " (Wis. 11:25), and to approve all: "And God saw all the things that were made, and they were very good" (Gen. 1:31).[215]

FOX: Elaborate on the blessing or goodness that creatures are.

AQUINAS: Every being as being is good.[216] For all things, to be and to be good are the same.[217] Good and being are interchangeable.[218]

FOX: Why do you say that?

AQUINAS: Two things are essential to an end: it must be sought or desired by things that have not yet attained the end, and it must be loved by the things that share the end, and be, as it were, enjoyable to them. For it is essentially the same to tend to an end and in some sense to repose in that end. . . . Existence itself, therefore, has the essential note of goodness. . . . It is necessary that every thing be good by the very fact of its having

---

213. Ibid., a. 1, ad 1.   214. In Pss 40, p. 308.   215. DV, q. 27, a. 1.
216. ST I, q. 5, a. 3.   217. CBH, 3.   218. DV, q. 21, a. 2.

existence, even though in many beings many other aspects of goodness are added over and above the act of existence by which they subsist.[219]

FOX: So all creation is good, all creation is a blessing.

AQUINAS: All nature is good.[220] Every existing thing, whatsoever the mode of its existence, is a good thing to the extent that it is a being.[221] Moreover, every act of being, whatever its type may be, comes from God . . . who is the perfect good. Now, since evil could not be the product of a good thing, it is impossible for any being, as a being, to be evil.[222] "Every creature of God is good" (1 Tim. 4:4).[223]

FOX: And, you are saying, the blessing or goodness of things goes beyond just our sacred existence?

AQUINAS: God is Author of effects such that they can in no way be contrary to the human will, since to be, to live, to understand, which are effects of God, are desirable and lovable to all.[224]

FOX: These are certainly the basics of life, aren't they? To be, to live, to understand. And they are blessings we can so easily take for granted.

AQUINAS: Dionysius says that if one considers carefully, it is not possible to find something that does not have [some] being and perfection and health.[225]

FOX: Why do you ground creation so thoroughly in blessing or goodness?

AQUINAS: Just as human beings are distributors of human goods, such as money and honor, so too God is the distributor of all the goods of the universe.[226] All things are good because they flow from the fount of goodness. We can praise God through all things![227]

FOX: You certainly seem to do so!

AQUINAS: Nature is related to blessedness as first is related to second. Blessedness is grounded on nature.[228] There is nothing that does not share in goodness and beauty. Each thing is good

219. Ibid.   220. DSS, 18.   221. CG III, ch. 7 n. 8.   222. Ibid., n. 9.
223. Ibid., n. 10.   224. ST II-II, q. 34, a. 1.   225. DDN, n. 987, p. 368.
226. CG I, ch. 93 n. 12.   227. CBH, 5.   228. ST I, q. 63, a. 7.

and beautiful by its proper form.[229] Everything images the divine goodness in its way.[230] By the first essential existent and good, each and every other thing exists and is good. It partakes of God and is made like God, though deficiently so. The likeness to divine goodness is intrinsic to each. Thus there is one goodness throughout the world, yet also so many goodnesses.[231]

FOX: If things are so good, why are there so many things in the universe?

AQUINAS: Distinction and variety in the world is intended by God, who brings things into existence in order to communicate and manifest the divine goodness. One solitary creature would not be adequate. Therefore God makes creatures many and diverse, so that what is lacking in one may be supplied by another.[232]

FOX: You are naming one more instance of interdependence here.

AQUINAS: Goodness in God is single and consistent, while in creatures it is scattered and uneven. Divinity is better represented by the whole universe than by any single thing.[233]

FOX: So there are limits to creatures' goodness?

AQUINAS: The participated good that is in an angel, and in the whole universe, is a finite and restricted good.[234]

FOX: You really part ways here with many neo-Platonic mystics who see the physical world as mere "shadow" and regret the multitude of physical creatures in the world, pining as they do for a God who is exclusively "One."

AQUINAS: God deliberately brings about multitude and distinction in order that the divine goodness may be brought forth and shared in many measures. There is beauty in the very diversity.[235]

FOX: Some theologians teach that the imperfections in things are all due to sin.

AQUINAS: The contrast and uniqueness of creatures does not happen by chance nor from flawed materials nor from interference with the divine plan, nor from punishment for human

---

229. DDN, n. 355, p. 115.   230. CG III, ch. 20 n. 2.   231. ST I, q. 6, a. 4.   232. Ibid., q. 48, a. 1.   233. Ibid.   234. Ibid., I-II, q. 2, a. 8, ad 3.   235. CT I, 102.

sin, but from God's own purpose.[236] For example, the nature of animals was not changed by humankind's sinning, as if those whose nature it now is to devour the flesh of others, such as the lion or the falcon, would previously have lived on herbs.[237]

FOX: You speak of "the divine purpose." How would you name that divine purpose?

AQUINAS: God wills to impart divine perfections to creatures, as much as each can endure.[238] The final end of all things is the divine goodness, toward which as toward a goal all journeys and particular ends toward which things are naturally inclined are ordered. In this way the very natural inclinations of things toward their natural ends—which we call natural laws—are a kind of "sweet offspring," that is, an effect that is in harmony with the natural appetite. I call it effect or "the offspring of love" by which divine goodness is loved. This love indeed is divine and holds all things; it is also indissoluble. . . . The divine love that is bestowed on all things and through which all things are held by God cannot be dissolved, since all things of necessity love God, at least in God's effects.[239]

FOX: You make it seem as if the "laws of God" that operate in nature are a very pleasurable thing.

AQUINAS: The law of God is the fixed natural inclination for each creature for doing what is agreeable to itself according to its own nature. For this reason it says in Wisdom (8), concerning divine Wisdom, that "it disposes all things pleasantly."[240]

FOX: You said above that God wills to impart as much divine perfection to things "as each can endure." Are you saying that the whole of creation endures, if you will, more of God's goodness or blessing than the parts?

AQUINAS: In the Book of Genesis it says: "God saw all the things that God had made, and they were very good," each one of them having been previously said to be good. For each thing in its nature is good, but all things together are very good, by reason of the order of the universe, which is the ultimate and noblest perfection in things.[241]

---

236. CG II, ch. 45 n. 9.   237. ST I, q. 96, a. 1, ad 2.   238. Ibid.   239. DDN, n. 858, pp. 321–22.   240. Ibid., n. 857, p. 321.   241. CG II, ch. 45 n.10.

FOX: It would seem to follow, in your consummate praise of the goodness in things, that one's own self is also a good to be enjoyed and praised.

AQUINAS: Self-love is the form and root of all friendship.[242] Well-ordered self-love is right and natural[243]—so much so that the person who hates himself or herself sins against nature.[244] To know and to appreciate your own worth is no sin.[245]

FOX: What would you say follows from this healthy self-love?

AQUINAS: It is natural for human beings to love their neighbor and the truth.[246]

FOX: Would you elaborate more on your understanding of God's goodness, which you describe as "the fount of all goodness"?

AQUINAS: Goodness is the self of God, since God is the being of goodness.[247] God's goodness is consummate and lacking nothing of perfection found anywhere.[248] God is sheer goodness.[249]

FOX: Then how does God's goodness relate to creatures?

AQUINAS: Whatever we call good is good by the divine goodness.[250]

FOX: One would think that creation would be utterly unnecessary if God were so supremely good.

AQUINAS: Nothing but the divine goodness moves God to produce things.[251] God produced creatures not because God needed them, nor because of any other extrinsic reason, but on account of God's own goodness. So Moses, when he says, "God saw the light that it was good," shows the proof of the divine love. The same is also found in the other works of creation.[252]

FOX: God's blessing or God's goodness seems difficult to fathom.

AQUINAS: God is so good that it would be out of character for Divinity to keep its knowledge of itself to itself and never to give itself intimately, for goodness of itself is generous.[253] God

---

242. ST II-II, q. 25, a. 4.   243. Ibid. I-II, q. 77, a. 4, ad 1.   244. In Eph 5.28b, p. 496.   245. ST II-II, q. 132, a. 1.   246. Ibid. I-II, q. 100, a. 5, ad 5.   247. In Pss 24, p. 231.   248. In Meta V, L. 18, p. 392.   249. CBH, 5.   250. ST I, q. 6, a. 4.   251. CG II, ch. 46 n. 6.   252. ST I, q. 32, a. 1, ad 3.   253. DDN, n. 36, p. 10.

is supremely good and therefore supremely generous. Sheer joy is God's and this demands companionship.[254]

FOX: Are you talking about unconditional love?

AQUINAS: No antecedent merit prompts God's love. It is gratuitous.[255] The corporeal and visible creatures were made because it is good for them to be; this is in keeping with God's goodness, and not because of any merits or sins of rational creatures.[256] God's love for things is better than ours. For our will is not the cause of goodness, rather it responds to goodness. But God's love impregnates all the goodness things have.[257] The Holy Spirit is the love whereby God loves creatures and imparts to them the divine goodness.[258] God has so communicated God's goodness to creatures that one thing can shed on another what it has received.[259]

FOX: You seem to be speaking of our holy origins once again.

AQUINAS: Creatures are the streams; God is the main river.[260] Many rivers rise from one source, and water from a spring spills into numerous streams. . . . So too, the flowing out and the sharing of particular goods from the divine goodness happens. Yet in this case there is no loss of the original goodness involved in the sharing, for the divine goodness remains undivided in its essence, undepleted and simple.[261]

FOX: Your phrase "original goodness" and your previous phrase "original freshness" both sound like "original blessing" to me! I find your explanation of divine goodness deeply attractive.

AQUINAS: Goodness attracts. The divine goodness attracts creatures beyond themselves at the same time that the principal good existing in things themselves is the perfection of the universe itself.[262] Whatever God communicates to a creature, God communicates from the divine goodness.[263]

FOX: Now I see why, if creatures are so imbued with blessing or divine goodness, meditation on them would be an important spiritual discipline in our lives.

---

254. In I Sent 2.1.4.   255. DV, q. 6, a. 2.   256. CG II, ch. 44 n. 14.
257. ST I, q. 20, a. 2.   258. In I Sent 14.1.1.   259. CG III, ch. 69 n. 16.
260. Ibid. II, ch. 2 n. 4.   261. DDN, nn. 214–15, p. 68.   262. ST I, q. 22, a. 3.   263. DDN, n. 213, p. 68.

AQUINAS: By dwelling on creatures the mind is inflamed to love the divine goodness.[264] We love God and know God in the mirror of God's creatures.[265]

FOX: You are saying that creatures mirror God?

AQUINAS: To see a thing in a mirror is to see a cause in its effect wherein its likeness is reflected.[266]

FOX: How do you recommend our meditating on creatures to experience God there?

AQUINAS: When anyone knows an effect, and knows that it has a cause, there naturally remains in that person the desire to know about that cause, what it is. This desire is one of wonder. It causes inquiry . . . from wonder a person proceeds to inquire. And this inquiry does not cease until she arrives at a knowledge of the essence of the cause.[267]

FOX: Wonder or amazement, then, are the beginning of our God experience?

AQUINAS: Amazement is the beginning of philosophical research. One who is amazed shrinks at present from forming a judgment of that which amazes them, fearing to fall short of the truth, but inquires afterward.[268]

FOX: You are speaking of the nonaction that awe is about and the receptivity that precedes judgment making?

AQUINAS: Two things pertain to the contemplative life. First, that someone uses what is well known for inquiring into other things, and second, that one learns unknown things. The second is learned not only through Scripture and creatures, but also interiorly.[269]

FOX: It is telling to me that you link together Scripture and creation as sources of divine knowledge and interior contemplation.

AQUINAS: Indeed, divine wisdom first appears in the creation of things. Because our intellects are weak, what we know of God we have to learn from creatures around us. Consequently, to know how God is said to be provident, we have to see how creatures are provident.[270]

---

264. CG II, ch. 2 n. 4.   265. ST II-II, q. 171, a. 2, ad 3.   266. Ibid., q. 180, a. 3, ad 2.   267. Ibid. I-II, q. 3, a. 8.   268. Ibid., q. 41, a. 4, ad 5. 269. In Pss 24, p. 230.   270. In Job, ch. 35, p. 119.

FOX: When you speak this way about revelation via creation, I hear you talking of the works of God as the word of God.

AQUINAS: All the knowing and speech of human beings comes from God through God's works, which, however, neither Job nor any other human can understand perfectly.[271] When Job says, "all people see God," he means through the divine works. For no one is so deficient in wisdom that they fail to perceive some of the divine works.[272] God communicates something to human beings in two ways. One way is through the infusion of light internally, through which the people understand. (Ps. 43:3: "Send forth your light and your truth.") The other way is by showing divine wisdom through external signs, that is, through creatures perceived by the senses. (Ecclesiastes 1:10: "God has poured her [that is, wisdom] over all the divine works.") Thus the Godhead has made itself known to human beings either interiorly through the infusion of light or exteriorly through visible creatures, in which, as if in a book, the knowledge of God is read.[273]

FOX: You are telling us to read the book of nature as one would read the Sacred Scriptures—as a source of wisdom and revelation.

AQUINAS: Just as art is manifested through the work of the artist, so God's wisdom is manifested through creatures. (Wis. 13: "For, from the greatness and beauty of created things, their original author by analogy is seen.")[274]

FOX: You have used the term "beauty" frequently in our conversation. In what way is "beauty" an important dimension of a spiritual relationship to creation?

AQUINAS: The highest beauty is in the Godhead, since beauty consists in comeliness: but God is beauty itself, beautifying all things. The Creator of beauty has set up all the beauty of things.[275] Divinity is manifest through the names of Wise and Beautiful. Dionysius says that theologians praise God as "wise and beautiful," since all beings . . . "are full of every divine harmony," that is, they exist with perfect consonance or order from God and are full "with a holy beauty." When he says, "harmony," he is alluding to wisdom, a characteristic of which

---

271. ST I, q. 5, a. 1.   272. In Job, ch. 36, p. 122.   273. In Rom, ch. 1, p. 16.   274. Ibid.   275. In Pss 26, p. 238.

is to order and measure things. When there is something lacking in harmony or beauty, corruption occurs in things, an excess of their proper nature takes over. This happens with disease in bodies and with sin in the soul.[276]

FOX: You are saying, then, that beauty and wisdom go together?

AQUINAS: Dionysius teaches that the supersubstantial "Good" that is God "is praised by the holy theologians" in Sacred Scripture "as the beautiful." Cant. 1: "Behold, you are beautiful, my love."[277]

FOX: Thus, beauty and goodness go together. You have said that every being is good. Is every being also beautiful? What about beauty in God and in creatures?

AQUINAS: Beauty and goodness in a thing are identical fundamentally . . . and consequently goodness is praised as beauty. But they differ logically, for goodness properly relates to the appetite, while beauty relates to the cognitive faculty: for beautiful things are those that please when seen. Thus beauty consists in due proportion—for the senses delight in due proportion, as in what is after their own kind, because even sense is a sort of reason, just as is every cognitive faculty.[278]

The beautiful and beauty are attributed in different ways to God and to creatures.[279] In God, as Dionysius says, "the beautiful and beauty must not be divided," as if the beautiful were one thing in God and beauty another.[280]

FOX: And for creatures?

AQUINAS: Dionysius says that "in existing things" the beautiful and beauty are distinguished as the sharer and the shared, so that "the beautiful" is said to be "that which participates in beauty"; but beauty is a sharer in the first Cause, which makes all things "beautiful." For the beauty of a creature is nothing other than a likeness of the divine beauty sharing in things.[281]

FOX: Speak more to me about beauty and God. Rarely have rational theologians of the past three hundred years admitted that beauty was a theological category of note.

---

276. DDN, n. 59, p. 19. 277. Ibid., n. 334, p. 113. 278. ST I, q. 5, a. 4, ad 1. 279. DDN, n. 335, p. 113. 280. Ibid., n. 336. 281. Ibid., n. 337.

AQUINAS: God, who is supersubstantial beauty, is called beauty because God bestows beauty on all created beings. Beauty of the spirit is one thing and that of the body is another, and that of one body is different from that of another.[282]

FOX: How would you define beauty?

AQUINAS: The measure of beauty consists in there being a cause of harmony and brightness in each thing: for in this way we call anyone beautiful on account of a handsome proportion of size and arrangement and because they have a bright and shining complexion. Whence proportionately, it must be accepted in the case of other things, that each one is called beautiful to the extent that it possesses a brightness of its own kind either spiritual or corporeal and has been established in terms of a required proportion.[283]

FOX: Is God a cause of this "brightness" or radiance that is found in things?

AQUINAS: God puts into creatures, along with a kind of "sheen," a reflection of God's own luminous "ray," which is the fountain of all light.[284]

FOX: This sounds similar to the contemporary scientific theory that photons, as light waves, are indeed present in every atom and in every being.

AQUINAS: Shining reflections of the divine radiance must be understood as the sharing of God's likeness and constitute those "beautifying" reflections that make beauty in things.[285]

FOX: At times you define beauty as "harmony" as well.

AQUINAS: God is the cause of the harmony in things, of which there is a twofold kind. The first is according to the ordering of the creatures toward God, and Dionysius alludes to this when he says that God is the cause of harmony "like one calling all things toward itself." God does this insofar as God turns all things toward the Godself as an end. "Beauty" in Greek is called *kalos* because it is derived from the word for "calling." The second harmony is in things according to the ordering of those things among one another.[286]

---

282. Ibid., n. 339.   283. Ibid.   284. Ibid., n. 340.   285. Ibid.   286. Ibid.

FOX: Thus you recognize the interdependence of things as a kind of harmony and beauty?

AQUINAS: God assembles all things in all things, toward the same end. This can be understood, in accordance with the opinion of the Platonists, that higher orders of things are in the lower orders by participation; the lower things in truth are in the higher through a certain kind of excellence, and thus all things are in all things. And from this fact, namely, that all things are found in all things by a certain kind of ordering, it follows that all things are ordered to the same end.[287] God is the most beautiful and the superbeautiful.[288]

FOX: Why do you say that?

AQUINAS: Suppose we say that fire exceeds in heat by an excess in kind, we call this "most hot." But the sun exceeds not from kind and so it is not called most hot but superhot, since the heat is not in it in the same way but in a more surpassing way.[289]

FOX: How else is God's beauty different from that of creatures?

AQUINAS: There are certain things that have a variable beauty, as appears from corruptible things, and this defect is excluded from God, because, as Dionysius says, God is "always" beautiful. The generation and corruption of beauty are not in God, nor is there increase or diminution, as appears in corporeal things. Also, God is not in some part beautiful and in another ugly, as happens in particular things; nor is God beautiful at some time and not at another; nor again is God beautiful with regard to one thing but not with regard to another, as happens in all the things that have been determined with regard to one determined use or end; nor is God beautiful in some place and not in another place. God is beautiful both in every way and simply.[290]

FOX: You are saying that God's beauty does not waver.

AQUINAS: What is in harmony with anything according to itself and primarily, is in harmony both with everything and always and everywhere. Again, the divine is beautiful in itself, not with respect to some determination, and therefore it cannot be said that God is beautiful to one thing and not beautiful to another, nor beautiful to certain ones and not beautiful to certain

287. Ibid. 288. Ibid., n. 343, p. 114. 289. Ibid. 290. Ibid., n. 345.

others. God is "always" and uniformly beautiful. Because of this the first defect of beauty, which is variability, is excluded from God.[291]

FOX: How does God cause beauty?

AQUINAS: God is a fountain of total beauty.[292] The beautiful is said to be from God as a cause.[293] From this beautiful One beauty comes to be in all beings, for brightness comes from a consideration of beauty, as has been said. But all beauty, through which a thing is able to be, is a kind of participation of the divine brightness. Likewise it has even been said that harmony comes from the measure of beauty, whence all the things that pertain to harmony in whatsoever a way proceed from the divine beauty. And it follows that on account of the beautiful, which is divine, the concord of all rational creatures derives; and friendship also with regard to emotional concord; and association with regard to external acts; and universally all creatures, whatsoever union they may possess, possess it from the power of beauty.[294]

FOX: Are there additional ways in which beauty is a cause of things?

AQUINAS: First, the beautiful indeed is the foundation of all like an efficient cause giving being. Like a cause moving and a cause containing, it preserves all things. For these three things seem to pertain to the nature of an efficient cause: that it give being, that it move, and that it preserve. . . . It is characteristic of a perfect agent that it act through love of that which it possesses, and on account of this Dionysius adds that the beautiful, which is God, is an efficient, moving, and containing cause, "by the love of its own beauty." For since it possesses its own beauty, it wishes to multiply it as much as possible, namely, through communication with its own likeness.[295]

FOX: What about beauty as a final cause?

AQUINAS: The beautiful, which is God, is the end of all like the final cause of all things. For all things have been made in order that they imitate the divine beauty in whatever way possible.[296] The divine beauty is the cause of all states of rest and of motion,

---

291. Ibid., n. 346.   292. Ibid., n. 347.   293. Ibid., n. 348.   294. Ibid., n. 349.   295. Ibid., n. 352, p. 115.   296. Ibid., n. 353.

whether of minds, spirits, or bodies. Motion and rest are reduced to the causality of the beautiful.[297] Beauty is also an exemplary cause insofar as no one goes to the trouble of making a likeness or representation unless for the sake of the beautiful.[298]

FOX: But don't we say that the good is the final cause of all things, the reason why we choose to do something?

AQUINAS: The good and the beautiful are the same, since all things desire the beautiful and the good as a cause in every way. There is nothing that does not participate in the beautiful and the good, since each thing is beautiful and good according to its own form.[299]

FOX: But surely the good is not altogether synonymous with the beautiful?

AQUINAS: Although the beautiful and the good are the same in subject, since brightness and harmony are equally contained under the nature of the good, nonetheless they differ in reason: for the beautiful offers something beyond the good, namely, a due course toward the power of knowing that the beautiful is of the good.[300] What beauty adds to goodness is a relation to the cognitive faculty. Thus "good" means that which simply pleases the appetite, while the "beautiful" is something pleasant to apprehend. The senses most drawn to the beautiful are the most cognitive ones, such as sight and hearing, insofar as they serve reason; for we speak of beautiful sights and beautiful sounds. But in reference to the other objects of the other senses, we do not use the expression "beautiful," for we do not speak of beautiful tastes or beautiful odors.[301]

FOX: Is there anything else that distinguishes the beautiful from the good?

AQUINAS: In addition to holding both beautiful things and good things in reverence, it is necessary for good things to be conspicuous, because to be conspicuous pertains to the nature of beauty.[302]

FOX: You have discoursed on God as beauty and the divine beauty in things. Can our contemplation of all this beauty move

---

297. Ibid., n. 367, p. 116.   298. Ibid., n. 354, p. 115.   299. Ibid., n. 355.   300. Ibid., n. 356.   301. ST I-II q. 27, a. 1, ad 3.   302. DDN, n. 947, p. 355.

us to love? What is the relationship between beauty, blessing, and love?

AQUINAS: Nothing is loved except to the extent that it possesses a measure of the beautiful and the good. God, who is beautiful and good, is the proper object of love.[303]

FOX: What does love do in the lover?

AQUINAS: Dionysius shows what love does in the lover. Since love is the common root of appetite, it is necessary that every operation of appetite be caused from love. It follows that every action of each thing is caused from love. This is what he teaches when he says that "all things act and wish whatever they do and wish" from a desire of the beautiful and the good.[304]

FOX: You seem to find much love in the universe, then, if, as you say, all things act out of love.

AQUINAS: The habitual or conditioned appetite for something as for its own good is called love.[305]

FOX: Where does all this love come from?

AQUINAS: God, who is the cause of all, on account of an excess of the goodness that is God's own, loves all things. And from love God makes all things, giving them being. And God perfects all things by filling them individually with their own perfections. And God contains all things by preserving them in being. And God converts all things, that is, God orders them toward the Godself as toward an end. . . . Love, by which God loves, is the actual existence of goodness in the things themselves, and on account of this one says that everything is good, since it preexists causally in the good. . . . For out of the love of God's own goodness it happened that God wished to pour forth and share the divine goodness with others, as far as was possible, namely, through the mode of likeness, with the result that the divine goodness not only remained in God but also flowed out to other things.[306]

FOX: Your language is very luxurious; you speak of Divinity "pouring forth" and "flowing out" to all things.

AQUINAS: God gives "lavishly to all," as is said in James 1. The divine offering is overflowing—it can never diminish because of

---

303. Ibid., n. 425, p. 137.   304. Ibid., n. 408, p. 135.   305. Ibid., n. 401, p. 143.   306. Ibid., n. 409, p. 135.

the abundance of its effusion. According to this offering the divine makes all things perfect insofar as it "fills them up" with the likeness of the divine perfection.[307]

FOX: Your descriptions of God's love for the beloved, namely, for creation, are beginning to sound quite erotic.

AQUINAS: A love that produces ecstasy puts lovers outside of themselves.[308]

FOX: Are you saying that God undergoes ecstasy at creation?

AQUINAS: The Godhead, who is the cause of all things, through its beautiful and good love by which it loves all things, according to the abundance of the divine goodness by which it loves things, becomes outside of itself. This happens insofar as the divine provides all beings through its goodness and love and delight, and in a certain way is drawn out and in a certain way is displaced from its own excellence insofar as it exists above all things and is separated from all things, toward this thing that is in all things, through the effect of its goodness, in accord with a certain kind of ecstasy.[309]

FOX: How does God's ecstasy affect ours?

AQUINAS: Divine love can be understood in two ways: in one way, the love by which God is loved, and thus we can explain this statement, that "divine love produces ecstasy," that is, it puts lovers outside of themselves. . . . In another way, the divine love that is derived from God can be understood as directed not only toward God but even toward other things, namely, equal or inferior ones, and thus must be understood the phrase "not allowing the lovers to be directed toward themselves" only, but toward the beloved ones, that is, toward those who are loved. For love brings it about that lovers are directed not only toward themselves, but also toward others.[310]

FOX: Can you offer an example of such love?

AQUINAS: In the Song of Songs (chapter 5) we read: "My beloved, you are drunk with love." Those who are drunk are not inside of themselves but outside of themselves. Those who are filled with spiritual gifts, all their intention is carried toward God. . . . It seems pleasurable, since it makes pleasure and

---

307. Ibid., n. 968, p. 360.　308. Ibid., n. 430, p. 142.　309. Ibid., n. 437, p. 143.　310. Ibid., n. 433, p. 143.

sweetness in the soul, as the book of Wisdom says: "O how good and sweet, Lord, is your spirit in us!" (12). And the good drink in this drink: 1 Corinthians 10: "They drank the same spiritual drink." There is a rushing of your pleasure, namely, of God, who is called a gushing stream in Proverbs 18: "Flowing torrent, fountain of wisdom." For God's will is so effective that God cannot be resisted, as a gushing stream cannot be. Romans 9: "Who can resist God's will?" But the matter of restoration is such that they are joined together in a fountain. And just as those who hold their mouth to a fountain of wine are drunk, so those who hold their mouth, that is their desire, at the fountain of life and sweetness are drunk. And so they are drunk, since "with you there is a fountain of life." If this refers to the Creator, then the sense is, "with you is the fountain of life, that is, your word enlivening all things."[311]

FOX: This language of drunkenness is quite inebriating to me.

AQUINAS: Spiritual restoration consists in two things: namely, in the gifts of God, and in God's sweetness. With regard to the first, the psalmist says, "they will be drunk with the abundance of your house." . . . Psalm 65 says: "we will be satisfied with the goodness of your house." But what is more, they will be drunk, meaning their desires will be filled beyond all measurement of merit. For intoxication is a kind of excess, as the Song of Songs says, "my beloved, you are drunk with love" (5).[312]

FOX: Can you offer another example of ecstasy in love?

AQUINAS: In Galatians, Paul writes: "I am alive, now not I, but Christ lives in me" (Gal. 2). This means that since departing from himself he had cast himself forth wholly into God, not seeking that which is his own, but that which is God's, like a true lover or one experiencing ecstasy, living for God and not living a life of his own, but the life of Christ as a "beloved," which life was especially desirable for him.[313] Ecstasy makes Paul live not his own life but that of God.[314]

FOX: Paul was an exceptional man who underwent some extraordinary experiences. You have spoken of "amor"—ordinary love—causing ecstasy. Is the ecstasy of creation not available to us all?

---

311. In Pss 35, p. 278.   312. Ibid.   313. DDN, n. 436, p. 143.   314. In Pss 30, p. 250.

AQUINAS: Every love causes ecstasy. To suffer ecstasy means to be placed outside oneself. This happens both to the apprehensive power and to the appetitive power. As to the apprehensive power, persons are said to be placed outside themselves when they are placed outside the knowledge proper to them. This may be due to their being raised to a higher knowledge; thus, persons are said to suffer ecstasy inasmuch as they are placed outside the connatural apprehension of their sense and reason, when they are raised up so as to comprehend things that surpass sense and reason. Or, it may be due to one's being cast down into a state of debasement; thus one may be said to suffer ecstasy when one is overcome by violent passion or madness.

As to the appetitive power, one is said to suffer ecstasy when that power is born toward something else, so that it goes forth out from itself, as it were.

The first of these ecstasies is caused by love dispositively, insofar, namely, as love makes the lover dwell on the beloved and to dwell intently on one thing draws the mind from other things. The second ecstasy is caused by love directly: by love of friendship, simply; and by love of desire, not simply but in a restricted sense. For in love of desire lovers are carried out of themselves in a certain sense, insofar, namely, as not being satisfied with enjoying the good that they have, they seek to enjoy something outside themselves. But since they seek to have this extrinsic good for themselves, they do not go out from themselves simply, and this movement remains finally within them. On the other hand, in the love of friendship, one's affection goes out from itself simply because one wishes and does good to one's friend, by caring and providing for them, for their sake.[315]

FOX: Does this mean the lover loves the beloved more than him- or herself?

AQUINAS: Lovers go out from themselves insofar as they will the good of a friend and work for it. Yet they do not will the good of their friend more than their own good: and so it does not follow that they love another more than themselves.[316]

FOX: Ecstasy, then, is available to us all?

AQUINAS: In the Scriptures, transport of mind, ecstasy, and rapture are all used in the same sense and indicate some raising

---

315. ST I-II, q. 28, a. 3.   316. Ibid., ad 3.

up of the mind beyond objects of sense outside of us toward which we naturally turn our attention to things that are beyond human beings. . . . At times, this transport from things outside is taken to refer to attention only, as when one makes use of the external senses and things about one, but one's whole attention is engaged in contemplating and loving things divine. Such is the state of anyone who contemplates and loves things divine in transport of the mind, whether ecstasy or rapture. For this reason Dionysius says: "Divine love brings about ecstasy."[317]

FOX: Is love the cause of all that we do?

AQUINAS: Love is cause of all that the lover does. As Dionysius says, "all things, whatever they do, they do for the love of good" (De divinis nominibus, ch. 4). Every agent acts for an end. Now the end is the good desired and loved by each one. Wherefore, it is evident that every agent, whatever it be, does every action from love of some kind.[318]

FOX: Does this apply only to human beings loving or to all creatures loving?

AQUINAS: Here we are speaking of love in a general sense, inasmuch as it includes intellectual, rational, animal, and natural love: for it is in this sense that Dionysius speaks of love in chapter 4 of De divinis nominibus.[319]

FOX: What else does love do?

AQUINAS: Love, when it is perfect, first assembles all its powers into one place, and moves them toward the beloved.[320]

FOX: Is love a passion that wounds us?

AQUINAS: Dionysius says that "everything loves itself with a love that holds it together," that is, that preserves it. Therefore love is not a wounding passion, but rather one that preserves and protects. . . . Love of a suitable good perfects and betters the lover; but love of a good that is unsuitable to the lover wounds and worsens the lover.[321]

FOX: Yet there is pain when we love, is there not?

AQUINAS: Four proximate effects may be ascribed to love: namely, melting, enjoyment, languor, and fervor. The first is

---

317. DV, q. 13, a. 2, ad 9.   318. Ibid., a. 6.   319. Ibid., ad 2.   320. In Pss 26, p. 237.   321. ST I-II, q. 28, a. 5.

melting, which is opposed to freezing. For things that are frozen are closely bound together, so as to be hard to pierce. But it belongs to love that the appetite is fitted to receive the good that is loved inasmuch as the object loved is in the lover. Consequently, the freezing or hardening of the heart is a disposition incompatible with love, while melting denotes a softening of the heart, whereby the heart shows itself to be ready for the entrance of the beloved. If, then, the beloved is present and possessed, pleasure or enjoyment ensues.

But if the beloved is absent, two passions arise: namely, sadness at its absence, which is denoted by languor; and an intense desire to possess the beloved, which is signified by fervor.[322]

FOX: Is union an effect of love?

AQUINAS: Every love is a unitive force. The union of lover and beloved is of two kinds. The first is real union and occurs when the beloved is present with the lover. The second is union of affection. The first of these unions is caused effectively by love because love moves one to desire and seek the presence of the beloved as something suitable and belonging to the one. The second union is caused formally by love because love itself is this union or bond. Desire implies the real absence of the beloved; but love remains whether the beloved be absent or present.[323]

FOX: Does mutual indwelling occur because of love?

AQUINAS: Every love makes the beloved to be in the lover, and the lover in the beloved. This effect of mutual indwelling may be understood as referring both to the apprehensive and to the appetitive power. As for the apprehensive power, the beloved is said to be in the lover because the beloved abides in the apprehension of the lover; while the lover is said to be in the beloved because the lover is not satisfied with a superficial apprehension of the beloved, but strives to gain an intimate knowledge of everything pertaining to the beloved, so as to penetrate into the very soul.[324]

As for the appetitive power, the object loved is said to be in the lover because it is in one's affections by a kind of pleasure, causing one either to take pleasure in it, or in its good, when present; or in the absence of the object loved by one's longing, to tend

322. Ibid. 323. Ibid., a. 1. 324. Ibid., a. 1, ad 1.

toward it with the love of desire or toward the good that one wills to the beloved with the love of friendship. This does not happen from any extrinsic cause but because the pleasure in the beloved is rooted in the lover's heart. For this reason we speak of love as being intimate and of the "bowels" of charity. Further, the love of desire is not satisfied with any external or superficial possession or enjoyment of the beloved but seeks to possess the beloved perfectly, by penetrating into his or her heart, as it were.

In the love of friendship the lover is in the beloved to the extent that one reckons what is good or evil to one's friend as being the same for oneself, and one's friend's will as one's own, so that it seems as though one felt the good or suffered the evil in the person of one's friend.

In still a third way, mutual indwelling in the love of friendship can be understood in regard to reciprocal love: inasmuch as friends return love for love, and both desire and do good things for one another.[325]

FOX: It has been suggested today that we lack a zest for living. I suppose this comes from our lack of being in love with being and creation or its Maker.

AQUINAS: Zeal arises from the intensity of love. For it is evident that the more intensely a power tends to anything, the more vigorously it withstands opposition or resistance. One is said to be zealous on God's behalf when one endeavors to the best of one's means to repel whatever is contrary to the honor or the will of God. In the words of John (2:17): "The zeal of your house has eaten me up." A gloss on these words says that one is eaten up with a good zeal when one strives to remedy whatever evil one perceives, and if one cannot, bears with it and laments it.[326]

FOX: It would seem that if we human beings loved the earth passionately enough we would indeed defend it—against ourselves. Where does zeal come from?

AQUINAS: Love and also zeal are caused in us from beauty and goodness, for a thing is not beautiful because we love it, but we

---

325. Ibid., a. 2.   326. Ibid., a. 4.

love it because it is beautiful and good. . . . God is called zealous because through God things become objects of zeal, that is, intensely lovable.[327]

FOX: As I listen to you I am beginning to feel that the joy we take in creation—or the lack of it—is a political issue. Talk to me more about the value of joy and pleasure in our lives.

AQUINAS: Enjoyment belongs to the best human activity.[328] Indeed, the perfect activity of a conscious being is invariably pleasurable activity.[329] No one can live without delight and pleasure.[330] Delight is connatural to human nature! For this reason morality must consider pleasure when it studies human acts.[331] Delight drives out sadness.[332] All wonderful things are delectable as well![333] Those who avoid all pleasure can in no way be said to be leading a reasonable life. One who abhors pleasures because they are pleasurable is rightly called an ungrateful boor.[334] If something is contrary to the natural order it is vicious. Now nature provides pleasure in vitally necessary activities, and the natural order requires that a person ought to enjoy what is required for the well-being of the individual and the species. A person who chooses to avoid pleasure and thereby to omit doing what is a natural necessity would commit a sin of resisting the design of nature. That would be a vice of lack of feeling.[335]

FOX: Your spirituality seems to be a far cry from that dominant kind we have heard of for centuries that decries pleasure and promotes purgation. It seems to have little in common with the classic phrase heard in the Catholic confessional, "did you take pleasure in it?"

AQUINAS: We only possess a gift when we enjoy it freely.[336]

FOX: What is gift?

AQUINAS: The name Gift involves the idea of belonging to the Giver through its origin.[337]

FOX: Creation as gift, then, implies a relationship to the Creator or gift giver. I suppose this also gives us permission to enjoy creation deeply, since the gift giver desires the enjoyment of the gift receiver.

---

327. DDN, n. 439, p. 143.   328. In I Sent 1.1.1.   329. In Ethics X, L. 6, p. 886.   330. ST II-II, q. 35, a. 4, ad 2.   331. In Ethics X, L. 1, p. 861.   332. In Pss 26, p. 238.   333. ST I-II, q. 32, a. 8.   334. Ibid. II-II, q. 142, a. 1, ad 2.   335. Ibid., a. 1.   336. Ibid. I, q. 43, a. 3.   337. Ibid., q. 38, a. 2, ad 2.

AQUINAS: Since the very fact of taking pleasure in the good one loves is a kind of good, it follows that pleasure causes love.[338] Delight of mind does not interfere with the use of reason. The opposite is the case—for we are more intent on what we more enjoy.[339] Delight that is attendant upon the operation of the intellect does not hinder it—in fact, it perfects it, for what we do with delight we do with greater care and perseverance.[340]

FOX: What is delight?

AQUINAS: Delight or enjoyment implies repose of the lover in the beloved object.[341] Delight is the resting of appetite in what is good.[342]

FOX: It would seem, from all that we have discussed up to now, that creation exists to delight us as well as God.

AQUINAS: It is very delightful to know the knowledge of all things that are in the world, . . . willed and arranged by God.[343]

FOX: Are delight and joy the same thing?

AQUINAS: We do not speak of joy except when delight follows reason. And so we do not ascribe joy to irrational animals, but only delight. Delight extends to more things than does joy.[344] The effect of hope is spiritual joy. Romans 12: "Rejoicing in hope." Exultation is joy leaping out through exterior things. Indeed, joy means an interior dilation of the heart. Therefore exultation signifies a fullness of joy. A person inflamed by the love of God in the beginning takes more joy and later moderate joy.[345] Joy expands the heart, while sorrow contracts it.[346] Delight is beyond time.[347] In fact, the desire for joy is inherently stronger than the fear of sadness.[348] The only person who truly has joy is one who lives in love.[349] Pleasure lies in being more than in becoming[350]—it comes as a kind of quiet after obtaining one's goal. Looking forward to pleasure can actually cause desire and love. In this sense pleasure is the enjoyment of a good and is final.[351] Enjoyment implies an absolute repose in the end.[352]

FOX: I hear you celebrating the fact that pleasure attracts us and draws us—even pulls us, if you will. And thus, as you say, it is

---

338. Ibid. II-II, q. 34, a. 6, ad 1.   339. Ibid. I-II, q. 33, a. 3.   340. Ibid., q. 4, a. 1, ad 3.   341. Ibid., a. 3.   342. Ibid., q. 34, a. 2.   343. In Pss 26, p. 238.   344. ST I-II, q. 31, a. 3.   345. In Pss 30, p. 251.   346. ST I-II, q. 37, a. 2.   347. Ibid., q. 31, a. 2.   348. Ibid., q. 35, a. 6.   349. DC, 35.   350. ST I-II, q. 31, a. 1.   351. Ibid., q. 25, a. 2.   352. Ibid., q. 12, a. 5, ad 2.

final or a final cause. Creatures can lead us to repose with God, it seems.

AQUINAS: In the making of the very least creature there is manifested the infinite power, wisdom, and goodness of God, because every single creature leads to the knowledge of the first and highest One, which is infinite in every perfection. Nor is it necessary that the infinite power or the infinite goodness be manifested through an infinite mode of communication. But this suffices to display the infinite goodness: that it is bestowed on each creature according to its unique capacity.[353]

FOX: What a challenge you put to us! To find the infinite in the smallest, finite thing! It seems that you are also saying that the goodness of creatures is so deep and real—so spiritual and divine, in fact—that creatures are no obstacle to our spiritual growth.

AQUINAS: In themselves creatures are no obstacle to eternal happiness. We make them so by abusing them and by committing ourselves to them as if they were our ultimate goal.[354] Creatures of themselves do not withdraw us from God, but lead us to God. For "the invisible things of God are clearly seen, being understood by the things that are made" (Rom. 1:20). If, then, they withdraw people from God, it is the fault of those who use them foolishly. Thus it is said, "creatures are turned into a snare for the feet of the unwise" (Wis. 14:11).[355]

FOX: Then spirituality is not about keeping the lid on? It is not, after all, a partner to repression?

AQUINAS: Faith does not quench desire. It inflames it.[356] Precisely what makes the contemplative life better than a purely activist one is that it ensures greater delight. The contemplative life is a kind of holiday. In the Martha-Mary story from the Gospels, Martha was fretting while Mary was busy enjoying herself. For this reason Mary was said to have chosen the "better part."[357] When discussing delight, however, it should be noted that the attraction of delight is not based on itself. What matters is the object that gives delight. The fact is that delight has its goodness and attraction from elsewhere. Delight accompanies the ultimate end but is not the ultimate end itself.[358]

---

353. In III Sent 1.3, ad 3. 354. In I Sent 1.3, ad 2. 355. ST I, q. 65, a. 1, ad 3. 356. CG III, ch. 40 n. 5. 357. ST II-II, q. 182, a. 1. 358. CG III, ch. 26 n. 13.

FOX: Thus there is a difference between our desires and our choices?

AQUINAS: It is true that not every delight may have moral goodness to it. This happens because what is delightful is decided by desire and this may not match the reason. For what is worthy and what is useful is for the reason to decide.[359] Creaturely goods do not stir us to spiritual joy unless we take them in relation to the divine good. It is from divine good that spiritual peace and accompanying joy arise—the fruits of the Spirit corresponding to the gift of wisdom.[360]

FOX: We will want to deal more with the topic of the fruits of the Spirit later when we deal with the Via Transformativa. For now, I want to ask you to please elaborate on the relationship between contemplation and delight.

AQUINAS: Through loving God we are aflame to gaze on the divine beauty. And since everyone delights when they obtain what they love, it follows that the contemplative life terminates in delight.[361]

FOX: For you delight and beauty accompany the experience of "tasting" wisdom.

AQUINAS: Both the light that makes beauty seen and the establishing of due proportion among things belong to reason. Hence, since the contemplative life consists in an act of the reason, there is beauty in it by its very nature and essence. For this reason it is written about the contemplation of wisdom that "I became a lover of her beauty" (Wis. 8:2).[362]

FOX: Where do you ground your deep conviction that joy and delight are so central to the spiritual experience? I find your teaching to contradict centuries of teaching that told us to begin spiritual practices with purgation.

AQUINAS: God delights. God is always rejoicing and doing so with a single and simple delight. In fact, it is appropriate to say that love and joy are the only human emotions that we can attribute literally to God.[363] Love and joy exist properly in God. They constitute the basis of all attraction—love is the origin and joy is the end result.[364] God is happiness by the divine essence,

---

359. ST I-II, q. 34, a. 2, ad 1.   360. Ibid. II-II, q. 9, a. 4, ad 1.   361. Ibid., q. 180, a. 1.   362. Ibid., a. 2, ad 3.   363. CG I, ch. 91 n. 12. 364. Ibid., n. 17.

for God is happy not by acquisition or participation of something else, but by God's essence. On the other hand, human beings are happy, as Boethius says, by participation.[365]

FOX: Now I am beginning to realize the power of what you said earlier, when you declared that "God's love for things is better than ours." You seem to be saying that we are to be joyful and delightful from our very spiritual roots, for the simple reason that God is that way and we are about imitating God.

AQUINAS: One walks before God not with steps taken by the feet, but by the desires of the mind.[366] God is most joyful and is therefore supremely conscious.[367] It is unique to God that the divine joy is identical with the divine being.[368] The divine joy gathers up within itself and consummates all joys.[369] I maintain that whatever is joyful in any joy whatsoever preexists wholly and supremely in the divine joy. Regarding contemplative joy, God has the continuous and most certain contemplation of Divinity and all else; regarding active joy, God has the operation of the entire universe. Regarding earthly joys, which lie in pleasure, riches, power, dignity, or fame, God possesses joy in Godself and in all other things through the divine delight. In place of earthly riches, God possesses complete self-sufficiency that is desired in riches; in place of power God has omnipotence; in place of dignity God has sovereignty over all. And in place of fame, God has the wonder of creation.[370]

FOX: If creation is good enough for God it ought to be good enough for us! The wonder of creation moves God and so it ought to move us.

AQUINAS: God loves all things with a single and simple act that does not vary and does not cease.[371] God cannot hate anything—no hatred of anything can be ascribed to God. God wills things because of their likeness to divine goodness, and this assimilation constitutes the good that is in each and every thing.[372] God did not make things except on account of good, for which reason it says in Genesis 1: "God saw that it was good." Thus it is clear that a good thing is pleasing to God.[373] The Holy Spirit, who is the lover whereby the Father loves the Son, is also

---

365. ST I-II, q. 3, a. 1, ad 1.   366. De perf, ch. II.   367. In Meta III, L. 11, p. 192. Gilby's translation.   368. ST I-II, q. 3, a. 2, ad 1.   369. CG I, ch. 102 n. 8.   370. ST I, q. 26, a. 4.   371. Ibid., q. 20, a. 3.   372. CG I, ch. 96 n. 9.   373. In Job, ch. 35, p. 119.

the love whereby God loves creatures and imparts to them the divine goodness.[374]

FOX: It would seem to follow from what you are saying that God, so steeped in joy and delight, must also be a great source of joy and delight.

AQUINAS: God's lovableness is infinite.[375] God knows this, you might say, because God perfectly delights in the Godhead since it perfectly knows and totally loves itself in as much as it is knowable and lovable.[376] Furthermore, since the supreme good is desired in every good,[377] it follows that any likeness or promise of joy, however meager, has its perfect origin and fulfillment in God.[378]

FOX: God, then, is our enjoyment and our delight?

AQUINAS: Delight is not best just because it is delight, but because it is repose in the best.[379] The very sight of God causes delight. At the sight of God the mind can do nothing but delight.[380] Human salvation consists in the enjoyment of God, who gives bliss to human beings. How appropriate, then, that Jesus took delight in God, for the originator of a process should be its master.[381] Our ultimate and principal good is to enjoy God.[382] Eternal life consists in enjoying God.[383] Joy is a human being's noblest act, and this happens when we enjoy the sublime, not when we achieve moral perfections or particular arrangements.[384]

FOX: Do other creatures besides human beings take delight in God?

AQUINAS: All things desire God as their end whenever they desire any good whatsoever. Whatever attracts them—be it intellective, sensitive, or unconscious desire—all of it is attractive because of some likeness it has to God.[385]

FOX: A likeness to God?

AQUINAS: Every creature participates in some way in the likeness of the divine essence.[386] Every creature represents God and is like God insofar as it possesses some perfection.[387]

---

374. In I Sent 14.1.1.   375. In Jn 1.14b, n. 188.   376. In Eph 5.5, p. 490.   377. In II Sent 1.2.3.   378. ST I, q. 26, a. 4, ad 1.   379. Ibid. I-II, q. 34, a. 3, ad 3.   380. Ibid., q. 4, a. 1, ad 2.   381. CT I, 213.   382. ST II-II, q. 23, a. 7.   383. Ibid. I-II, q. 114, a. 4.   384. CG III, ch. 35 n. 3. 385. ST I, q. 44, a. 4, ad 3.   386. Ibid., q. 15, a. 2.   387. Ibid., q. 13, a. 2.

FOX: Things are attracted, you say, to God?

AQUINAS: All things love God.[388] Everything in its own way naturally loves God more than itself.[389] God is loved by everything with natural love.[390] All things are united according to friendship to each other and to God.[391]

FOX: How is this possible?

AQUINAS: God, through divine providence, orders all things to the divine goodness, as to an end. . . . In this way the likeness of the divine goodness, as much as possible, is impressed on things.[392] God wishes and does good things in regard to every creature, for the very being of the creature and all its perfection result from God's willing and doing. Thus the Scriptures say: "For you love all things that are, and hate none of the things which you have made" (Wis. 11:25).[393]

FOX: You are saying that all things are good and attractive because they have being?

AQUINAS: Everything was brought into being for the reason that it was good for it to be.[394] Goodness and being are really the same. . . . The essence of goodness consists in this, that it is in some way desirable. . . . Goodness presents the aspect of desirableness, which being does not present.[395]

FOX: But you talked about a "friendship" that all beings have with one another. Please elaborate on this point.

AQUINAS: It is common to every nature to have some inclination: and this is its natural appetite or love. This inclination is found to exist differently in different natures, but in each according to its mode.[396] Natural love is nothing else but the inclination implanted in nature by its Author.[397] It is clear that in things devoid of knowledge everything naturally seeks to procure what is good for itself. For example, fire seeks to mount upward.[398] Everything loves another that is one with it in species, with a natural affection, insofar as it loves its own species. This is clear even in things devoid of knowledge, for fire has a natural inclination to communicate its form to another thing, wherein consists this other thing's good. Just as it is naturally inclined to seek its own good, namely, to be borne upward.[399]

---

388. DDN, n. 445, p. 147. 389. ST I, q. 60, a. 5, ad 1. 390. Ibid., ad 4. 391. DDN, n. 910, p. 337. 392. CG III, ch. 97 n. 2. 393. Ibid., ch. 150 n. 2. 394. ST I, q. 65, a. 2. 395. Ibid., q. 5, a. 1. 396. Ibid., q. 60, a. 1. 397. Ibid., ad 3. 398. Ibid., a. 3. 399. Ibid., a. 4.

FOX: Thus every being is a blessing, that is, a source of goodness.

AQUINAS: None of God's works has been made in vain.[400]

FOX: Isn't there a tension between the delight God takes in creation and the creature's need to pursue its own delight?

AQUINAS: God wishes the universe with all its creatures for their own sake, although God also wishes it for God's own sake; these two things are not repugnant. For God wills that creatures exist on account of the divine goodness specifically in order that they may imitate and represent it in their own way; this they in fact do insofar as they have existence from the divine goodness and subsist in their own nature. . . . For thus God has instituted each and every single nature, in order that it may not lose its own uniqueness (*proprietatem*).[401]

FOX: Do all things tend to good?

AQUINAS: All things—not only those that have knowledge, but also those without it—tend to good. . . . All things are destined and directed by God to good, and this is done in such a way that in each one is a principle by which it tends of itself to good as if seeking good itself, as if reaching for it of its own accord. For this reason it is said in the Book of Wisdom (8:1) that divine wisdom "orders all things sweetly" because each one by its own motion tends to that for which it has been divinely destined.[402]

FOX: Every being, you say, has a "destiny."

AQUINAS: To desire or have appetite is nothing else but to strive for something (*ad aliquid petere*), stretching, as it were, toward something that is destined for oneself.[403]

FOX: Then every being desires blessing. Perhaps this is the meaning of prayer among humans: to stretch for blessing and thereby enter into the process of creation's ongoing goodness?

AQUINAS: Prayer is the expression of desire.[404]

FOX: What is the best thing in creatures?

AQUINAS: The principal good in things themselves is the perfection of the universe.[405]

---

400. Ibid., q. 67, a. 4, ad 2.   401. DP, q. 5, a. 4.   402. DV, q. 22, a. 1.
403. Ibid.   404. OF, p. 103.   405. ST I, q. 22, a. 4.

FOX: The perfection of the universe? You are saying that every being contains the perfection of the universe? How perfect is this universe?

AQUINAS: The universe, given the present creation, cannot be better than it is. This is because of the most beautiful order given to things by God, in which the good of the universe consists. For if any one thing were bettered, the proportion of order would be destroyed.[406]

FOX: Why do you say this?

AQUINAS: Nature always does what is best, not with regard to the part, but with regard to the whole. Otherwise it would make a person's body all eye or all heart—for it would be better for the part but not for the whole.[407]

FOX: You seem to be carrying the principle of interdependence to its logical—though a very radical—conclusion.

AQUINAS: If one string in a harp were stretched more than it should be, the melody of the harp would be destroyed. Yet God could make other things, or add something to the present creation. And then there would be another and a better universe.[408]

FOX: When you use the analogy of the musical instrument, I sense that you have even deeper feelings of wonder for the universe as a whole than you do for any particular creature—even though you have praised them for their godliness.

AQUINAS: God brought things into being in order that the divine goodness might be communicated to creatures and be represented by them. And because the divine goodness could not be adequately represented by one creature alone, God produced many and diverse creatures, that what was wanting in one in the representation of the divine goodness might be supplied by another. For goodness, which in God is simple and uniform, in creatures is manifold and divided. Thus the whole universe together participates in the divine goodness more perfectly, and represents it better, than any single creature whatever.[409]

FOX: But didn't you say that creation is the best it can be?

AQUINAS: God made the universe to be the best as a whole, according to the mode of a creature. God did not make each

---

406. Ibid., q. 25, a. 6, ad 3.   407. DP, q. 3, a. 6, ad 26.   408. ST I, q. 25, a. 6, ad 3.   409. Ibid., q. 47, a. 1.

single creature best, but one better than another. But we find it said of each creature, "God saw the light that it was good" (Gen. 1:4); and in like manner of each one of the others. But of all together it is said, "God saw all the things that God had made, and they were very good" (Gen. 1:31).[410]

FOX: The goodness of the cosmos—what does it do for us to know how "very good" the whole cosmos is?

AQUINAS: The psalmist sings: "You have given me, O Lord, a delight in your doings: and in the works of your hands I shall rejoice" (Ps. 40:3). And also, "they shall be drunk with the plenty of your house"—that is, the universe. "And you will make them drink of the torrent of your pleasure. For with you is the fount of life" (Ps. 36:8–9).[411]

FOX: So all we have said of the goodness and beauty and delight in creatures is multiplied in your opinion when we meditate on the macrocosm—the beauty of the whole. Drunkenness. We are here to get drunk on the universe.

AQUINAS: The mutual relationship of creatures makes up the good of the universe. But no part is perfect if separate from the whole.[412]

FOX: And what do we know about the relationship of the whole and its parts?

AQUINAS: The entire universe is constituted by all creatures, as a whole consists of its parts. In the parts of the universe every creature exists for its own proper act and perfection, and the less noble for the nobler . . . each and every creature exists for the perfection of the entire universe. Furthermore, the entire universe, with all its parts, is ordained toward God as its end inasmuch as it imitates, as it were, and shows forth the divine goodness, to the glory of God. . . . The divine goodness is the end of all corporeal things.[413]

FOX: How do you come to this conclusion?

AQUINAS: The fellowship of natural goods bestowed on us by God is the foundation of natural love in virtue of which every single creature loves God above all things and more than itself . . . at least by a natural love. Stones, for instance, and other

---

410. Ibid., a. 2, ad 1.   411. CG II, ch. 2 n. 4.   412. ST I, q. 61, a. 3.
413. Ibid., q. 65, a. 2.

things bereft of knowledge, love God in this way because each part naturally loves the common good of the whole more than its own particular good. This is evidenced by its operation, since the principal inclination of each part is toward common action conducive to the good of the whole.[414]

FOX: You say that all things love God. What does God love the most in all of creation?

AQUINAS: The ultimate end of the divine will is the divine goodness, and the nearest thing to that, among created things, is the good of the whole universe. . . . Thus, among created things, what God cares for most is the order of the universe.[415]

FOX: This certainly underscores the importance of a cosmology—for if we human beings want to know God it behooves us to know what God "cares for most" in all of creation.

AQUINAS: That which is the greatest good in created things is the order of the universe, for it is most perfect, as the Philosopher [Aristotle] says. With this, divine Scripture is also in agreement, for it is said in Genesis (1:31): "God saw all the things which had been made, and they were very good," while God simply said of the individual works, that "they were good."[416]

FOX: Your stress on the cosmological certainly forestalls any temptations by human beings to anthropocentrism. It also puts even more importance on scientific explorations into how we creatures arrived in the universe. Therefore, let us talk a little about evolution. Now we all know that the medieval world had not heard of evolution as we understand it today. Yet I detect in your work a clear belief in the ongoing creation of things.

AQUINAS: God's work whereby God brings things into being must not be taken as the work of a craftsman who makes a box and then leaves it. For God continues to give being.[417]

FOX: You have just destroyed the Newtonian and deistic God of the past three hundred years in the West.

AQUINAS: After being produced, the creatures are multiplied and preserved, and this work also belongs to the divine goodness. Indeed, the perfection of this goodness is made abundantly

---

414. Ibid. II-II, q. 26, a. 3.   415. CG III, ch. 64 n. 10.   416. Ibid., n. 9.
417. DP, q. 3, a. 14, ad 10.

clear by the fact that in it alone God finds the divine rest—and we may find ours in its fruition.[418]

FOX: And so the goodness of creating has by no means come to an end—it was not all accomplished in the past?

AQUINAS: God indeed "works until now" (John 5:17) by preserving and providing for the creatures God has made.[419]

FOX: What is this act of preserving things that you speak of?

AQUINAS: God does not preserve things in existence except by continually pouring out existence into them.[420]

FOX: Do you envision that God makes new things?

AQUINAS: It is impossible that God has made everything that God can make, for thus God would have made so many things that God could not make any more. If this were the case, God's power would be limited to the creatures actually in existence. Similarly, it is impossible to hold that whatever God can disclose has been disclosed to any creature.[421] Something can be added every day to the perfection of the universe, as to the number of individuals, but not as to the number of species.[422]

FOX: Of course the last statement of yours can be challenged by evolutionary science today.

AQUINAS: Species that are new, if any such appear, existed beforehand in various active powers; so that animals, and perhaps even new species of animals, are produced by putrefaction by the power that the stars and elements received at the beginning. Again, animals of new kinds arise occasionally from the connection of individuals belonging to different species, as the mule is the offspring of an ass and a mare; but even these existed previously in their causes.[423]

FOX: Now this statement rings closer to today's science when you emphasize the link between the ages, namely, that the powers produced by elements at the beginning are still in effect. This would surely apply to theories about the original fireball birthing galaxies and the sun, and so on. How would you characterize this coming to be of things?

AQUINAS: Natural processes develop from simple to compound things, so much so that the highly developed organism

---

418. ST I, q. 73, a. 3, ad 2.   419. Ibid., a. 2, ad 1.   420. Ibid., q. 104, a. 3.   421. Ibid. II, q. 20, a. 5, ad 4.   422. Ibid. I, q. 118, a. 3, ad 2. 423. Ibid., q. 73, a. 1, ad 3.

is the completion, integration, and purpose of the elements. Such indeed is the case with any whole in comparison with its parts.[424]

FOX: You are being very non-Platonic when you celebrate the diversity of creation as you do.

AQUINAS: [Since] the good of the species is greater than the good of the individual, . . . a multiplicity of species adds more to the goodness of the universe than a multiplicity of individuals in one species. It therefore pertains to the perfection of the universe that there be not only many individuals, but also diverse species of things, and, consequently, diverse grades in things.[425]

FOX: I think you would be pleasantly astounded to learn what we are now learning about this "multiplication of species" that in your words contributes to the goodness and perfection of the universe. Again, it is striking how you part ways with the neo-Platonists, who associated diversity with the Fall and with sin in the universe. In addition to celebrating diversity in creation, you also comment on how creation did not take place all at once.

AQUINAS: All things were not distinguished or adorned together, not from a want of power on God's part, as requiring time in which to work, but that due order might be observed in the instituting of the world. Hence it was fitting that different days should be assigned to the different states of the world, as each succeeding work added to the world a fresh state of perfection.[426]

FOX: This is one of the finest endorsements of evolution I have ever heard from a theologian—celebrating the "due order" needed in the unfolding of the world and the "fresh state of perfection" that each "state of the world" offered.

AQUINAS: Divine art is not exhausted in the production of creatures, and therefore can operate otherwise than according to the customary course of nature. But it does not follow that by acting against the general run of things divine art contravenes its own principle, for artists are well able to devise a work of art in a style different from their first production.[427]

---

424. In I Pol, lect. 1, p. 366. 425. CG II, ch. 45 n. 6. 426. ST I, q. 74, a. 2, ad 4. 427. DP, q. 6, a. 1, ad 12.

FOX: Unlike today's fundamentalists, you don't seem threatened by the idea that God might create in time.

AQUINAS: Certain persons totally denied the existence of providence, as Democritus and the Epicureans, maintaining that the world was made by chance. Others taught that only incorruptible things were subject to providence and corruptible things not in their individual selves, but only according to their species. . . . We must say, however, that all things are subject to divine providence, not only in general, but even in their own individual selves.[428]

FOX: Thus for you the fundamentalist position is one of denying the providence of God.

AQUINAS: Two things belong to providence, namely, the type of the order of things foreordained toward an end and the execution of this order, which is called government. As regards the first of these, God has immediate providence over everything, even the smallest; and whatsoever causes God assigns to certain effects, God gives them the power to produce those effects. . . . As for the second, there are certain intermediaries of God's providence; for God governs things inferior by superior, not on account of any defect in the divine power, but by reason of the abundance of the divine goodness, so that the dignity of causality is imparted, even to creatures.[429]

FOX: I love this phrase of yours, "the dignity of causality" that "is imparted" to all creatures. What a wonderful way to name our sharing in the divine act of cocreation and evolution. Indeed, it seems to me that what most distinguishes your thinking from today's evolutionary science is the length of the days of creation or the naming of the varied states or stages of the world's unfolding. For I sense a certain evolutionary character to your thinking about creation, though of course it lacks the awareness of the immense history in which creation has unfolded.

AQUINAS: The first day of the "work of adornment" is the fourth day of creation, and on that day lights are produced to adorn the heavens by their movements. On the second day of the "work of adornment" (which is the fifth day of creation)

---

428. ST I, q. 22, a. 2.   429. Ibid., a. 3.

birds and fishes are called into being to make beautiful the intermediate element, for they move in air and water, which are taken as one [in the Genesis creation story]. While on the third day of adornment (which is the sixth day of creation), animals are brought forth to move upon the earth and adorn it.[430]

FOX: What about the plants?

AQUINAS: The earth owes its comeliness to the plants that clothe it, as it were, with a garment.[431] Jesus says that "neither Solomon in all his glory was adorned like one of these" [flowers]. Although art imitates nature, it does not however attain to it. For art has never made colors so pure as are made in nature in flowers.[432]

FOX: You seem smitten with plants.

AQUINAS: Plants are higher than inanimate bodies, for in them there is an issuing from within, for the sap is converted into seed, and this when planted in soil grows into a plant. Here the first degree of life may be discerned, for living things are those that set themselves into activity, whereas things that are in motion only inasmuch as they are acted on from outside are lifeless. This is the index of life in plants, that within them is a principle of motion. Nevertheless, their life is imperfect, for though the emanation is from within at the beginning, that which comes forth gradually becomes wholly extraneous in the end; the blossoms change into fruit distinct from the boughs on which they grow, and presently these, when ripe, fall to the ground and in due course become other plants. Scrutiny shows that the principle of this process is extrinsic to the plant.[433]

FOX: Do you believe that plants were produced "all at once," as it seems to say in the Scriptures?

AQUINAS: In the first days God created all things in their origin or causes. . . . Afterward, by governing the creatures, in the work of propagation, "God works until now." Now the production of plants from out of the earth is a work of propagation, and therefore they were to be produced in act on the third day, but in their causes only.[434]

---

430. Ibid., q. 70, a. 1.   431. Ibid., q. 69, a. 2.   432. In Mt 6, p. 74.
433. CG IV, ch. 11 n. 3.   434. ST I, q. 69, a. 2.

FOX: I think today's scientists would simply say that all of the emergence of the universe has been, in your words, "a work of propagation," and therefore the world as we know it was produced "in its causes only."

AQUINAS: Some people say that the first constitution of a species belongs to the work of the six days [of creation], but the reproduction among them of like from like belongs to the government of the universe. Scripture indicates this in the words, "before it sprung up in the earth," and "before it grew," that is, before like was produced from like. This same thing now happens in the natural course of things by the production of seed. Wherefore Scripture says pointedly (Gen. 1:11): "Let the earth bring forth the green herb, and such as may yield seed." This indicates the production of perfection of perfect species, from which the seed of others should arise. Nor does the question of where the seminal power may reside—whether in root, stem, or fruit—affect the argument.[435]

FOX: Even for you then, from your limited evolutionary perspective of the Middle Ages, creation was by no means finished in six days?

AQUINAS: In the first six days creatures were produced in their first causes, but after being produced, they are multiplied and preserved, and this work also belongs to the divine goodness. And the perfection of this goodness is made most clear by the knowledge that in it alone God finds God's own rest, and we may find ours in its fruition.[436]

FOX: You have celebrated the creation of plants, but what about minerals? Why aren't they important enough to be mentioned in the Genesis creation story?

AQUINAS: Moses put before the people such things only as were manifest to their senses, as we have said. But minerals are generated in hidden ways within the bowels of the earth. Moreover, they seem hardly specifically distinct from earth, and would seem to be a species thereof. For this reason, then, he makes no mention of them.[437]

FOX: Today's science, knowing so much more about the immense age of the universe, has indeed arrived at some awareness

---

435. Ibid.   436. Ibid., q. 73, a. 3, ad 2.   437. Ibid., q. 69, a. 2, ad 3.

of the "hidden ways" by which minerals too evolve and come to be—the "seminal power," in your words, that makes minerals and earth itself come to be. But don't you write elsewhere not about Moses' understanding of minerals, but about Job's?

AQUINAS: Job also speaks according to the thinking of common folk, for this is the custom in sacred Scripture.[438] Job first treats of those metals that people consider valuable. We should note that metals are generated from humid vapors that are released from the earth by the power of the sun and the other stars and retained in the earth. Hence metals are malleable and can be liquefied, whereas, on the contrary, rocks and other such things that are nonmalleable and cannot be liquefied are generated from dry exhalations retained beneath the earth. The types of metals are distinguished by the greater or lesser purity of the vapor released and by the degree of heat expended. Thus gold is the purest, then silver, then copper, the least pure being iron. These metals have different origins according to their greater or lesser purity. Because gold is the purest, it is found usually in the sand of rivers due to the greater amount of evaporation and the heat of the sand. Silver is usually found in certain veins in the earth or in rocks. Copper is found mixed with rock, and iron is found in earth, which is in the process of producing rock. Therefore Job, listing the various locations where the metals are found, says "silver has its origin in a mine," that is, it is found in certain places from which those vapors are released that are apt for generating silver. Thus, when these vapors are mixed with earth or rock, veins of silver are produced in those places. In regard to gold he adds, "and for gold there is a place in which it is formed," because from many grains of sand a certain number of grains of gold are collected that are then pressed together into one nugget. This takes place only in certain places where there occur the proper proportions of active power and matter. Then for iron he says "and iron is taken from the ground," because it is found in the earth, as it were, unformed. Of copper, he says "and copper is smelted from ore." This means that the rock has a vapor within it, and, under the influence of an extremely hot fire, the copper is drawn out of the rock.[439]

---

438. In Job, ch. 26, p. 93.   439. Ibid, ch. 28, p. 96.

FOX: Thank you for that surprising discourse on metallurgy with its intimations of alchemy. Let us get back now to the creation story in Genesis. What about the last day of creation?

AQUINAS: For the Israelites the seventh day was so called on account of the work of creation—until now nothing more worthy has gone forth. For us [Christians] it is the first day—or the eighth—on account of the mystery of the resurrection, when established nature was repaired for the better.[440] The seventh day represents the consummation of nature. In Christ's Incarnation was the consummation of grace and at the end of the world will be the consummation of glory.[441]

FOX: Yet you insist on studying science, and certainly your favorite scientist, Aristotle, did not know the Genesis creation story. I see you yourself relating the creation story to some physical theories of your day, as for example when you answer the question "Whether light is a physical body?"[442] and "Whether light is a quality?"[443] I experience you actually digging for the works of scientists who can explain the firmament or sky or air for you. Astronomy enters into your worldview and your theology, and you even contrast Aristotle to Ptolemy and to Moses in Genesis.

AQUINAS: The Scriptures were immediately addressed to uncultured persons.[444] Moses describes what is obvious to sense, out of condescension to popular ignorance.[445]

FOX: You even employ astrology at times.

AQUINAS: Although celestial bodies cannot be directly the causes of our understanding, they may do something indirectly to affect it. The operation of understanding cannot be accomplished in us without the operation of corporeal powers: that is, the imagination, the power of memory, and the cogitative power. . . . Now, the condition of the human body does come under the influence of celestial motions. In fact, Augustine says, in the *City of God,* Book V, that "it is not utterly absurd to say that certain influences of the stars are able to produce differences in bodies only." And Damascene says, in Book II, that "different planets establish in us diverse temperaments, habits and dispositions." So the celestial bodies work indirectly on the

440. In Is 56, p. 558.   441. ST I, q. 73, a. 1, ad 1.   442. Ibid., q. 67, a. 2.   443. Ibid., a. 3; cf. q. 66, aa. 2, 3.   444. Ibid., q. 91, a. 1, ad 4. 445. Ibid., q. 70, a. 1, ad 3. See q. 70, aa. 1, 2; q. 67, a. 4; q. 68, a. 3.

good condition of understanding. Thus, just as physicians may judge the goodness of an intellect from the condition of the body, as from a proximate disposition, so also may an astronomer judge from the celestial motions, as from the remote cause of such dispositions. In this way, then, it is possible that there is some truth in what Ptolemy says in his Centiloquium: "When, at the time of a person's birth, Mercury is in conjunction with Saturn and is itself in a strong condition, it gives inwardly to things the goodness of understanding."[446]

FOX: You do not seem to be frightened by astrology.

AQUINAS: By faith in God one may be guided to one's final goal. Still, one may imagine that one is subject to certain forces when in point of fact the individual is above them. This happens because one is ignorant of nature and of one's place in the cosmos. We are warned by Jeremiah: "Be not afraid of the signs of heaven which the heathen fear" (Jer. 10:2).[447]

FOX: Why do you think creation stories are so important to us?

AQUINAS: Since the end of a thing corresponds to its beginning, it is not possible to be ignorant of the end of things if we know their beginning.[448]

FOX: I hear you saying that we derive our basic morality from our shared origin stories. We shall, of course, be dealing more with the "end of things" as we progress to discussing the Via Negativa, Via Creativa, and Via Transformativa in our conversations. It is striking to me—and it reveals the depth of your commitment to cosmology—that in your very brilliantly structured work, the *Summa theologiae,* you put your discussion of creation in so prominent a place as you do.

AQUINAS: Of the works proper to the Godhead, the first is the order of nature. It is for this reason that the article about creation is proposed to us.[449]

FOX: But isn't your *Summa* a discourse on faith?

AQUINAS: Faith is about those things we will enjoy in eternal life, namely, the secret of the Godhead. To see this is to possess happiness. Faith also concerns the mystery of Christ's Incarnation, "by whom we have access to the glory of the sons of

---

446. CG III, ch. 84 n. 14.   447. Ibid. II, ch. 3 n. 5.   448. ST I, q. 103, a. 2.   449. Ibid. II-II, q. 1, a. 8.

God," according to Romans (5:2). . . . Some matters of faith concern the majesty of the Godhead, while others pertain to the mystery of Christ's human nature.[450]

FOX: Thus for you, creation pertains to the very "mystery of the Godhead." It is not just about "objects out there" but about its sacred, indeed divine, origins. Let us continue, then, our discussion about creation. We have been talking about created things—horses and sky, plants and minerals. Now it is time to talk of our own species. What about the human person? How do you see humanity?

AQUINAS: In God's hand is the life of every living thing, and not only of the animals, but also the breath of all humanity.[451] God has a special care for human beings. Not only does God care for humans, but God has familiarity with them. This is what the psalmist says, "since you visit him." The rational nature alone is able to grasp God, by knowing and loving. Therefore, to the extent that God is made present to us through loving and knowing, God visits us. Job 10: "Your visitation has preserved us." Therefore the great compassion of God is in the comparison of humanity with God.[452]

FOX: How can humanity be compared to God?

AQUINAS: To be crowned is to reign. God made human beings like royal persons of lesser creatures, and human beings are "with glory," namely, with the clarity of the divine image. And this is a kind of crown for humanity: 1 Corinthians 11: "The human being is the image and glory of God."[453]

FOX: You are celebrating the theme of our royal personhood.

AQUINAS: Christ was anointed with the oil of the Holy Spirit (Ps. 45: "God has anointed you, etc." applying to the king and the priest). And this anointing is even drawn down to us, as we read in Psalm 133: "like an ointment of the head which goes down to the beard, the beard of Aaron." And in John 1: "We have all received of his fullness." First therefore we are anointed with a priestly ointment in the form of a future kingdom: for we will be kings and queens and free. And since before this happens we suffer as regards our enemies, afterward we are doubly

---

450. Ibid.   451. In Job 12, pp. 52–53.   452. In Pss 8, p. 168.   453. Ibid., 169.

anointed with actual glory: namely, the stole of the glory of the soul and body. But Christ was first anointed with the ointment of grace, later of glory.[454]

FOX: What else is implied in the tradition that every human being is a "royal person"?

AQUINAS: That person is honored who is subject to no other. The human being is subjected to no creature with a corporeal nature, just as the soul, neither in its going in nor in its going forth, perishes with the body. The psalmist posits the compassion of God to humanity through a comparison with the things that are beneath the human, since human beings wished to have lordship over those inferior things. In doing this he does three things: first, he proposes lordship. Second, a means of ruling. Third, a number of subjects. Therefore he says, due to the fact that human beings are royal persons, you gave them lordship "over the works of your hands" (Gen. 1). "In order that they may preside over the fish of the sea, and the birds of the sky, and the beasts of all the earth, and the reptile which moves over the earth." Humanity has this through reason, since it surpasses all animals. And therefore as soon as he has said, "with glory and honor," he adds, "you have established"—that is, you have given lordship. But note that he says that humanity has authority over the works of God's hands, not God's fingers. Since they are not subtle like the skies, which are the works of God's fingers. Human beings are not able to subject these things to themselves.

Second, he shows the means of ruling. He says, "you have subjected all things" so that he commands and rules with a nod. This is signified in Genesis 2, when God has led all the animals to Adam. And this subjection was completed before sin, though in the punishment of sin some now resist. Third, when he says "sheep and cattle, etc." he numbers the subjects. He posits living things so that even plants may be understood. But among living animals, certain ones are subjugated in accordance with their whole genus, namely, animals tame and domesticated according to their nature, such as sheep and cattle . . . There are others that are not subjugated according to their own genus. Of these certain ones can walk, and regarding this he says, "also

---

454. In Pss 26, p. 236.

above the beasts of the field, etc." referring to boars, deer, and the like. Certain flying creatures, namely, birds; and certain swimming creatures like fish.[455]

FOX: I believe that you speak of our responsibility to creation as being intrinsic to our dignity in it. That one who "presides," that is, the royal person, is one who does justice. No doubt we will be discussing this more when we discuss the Via Transformativa.

AQUINAS: The creature becomes like God by moving others to be good. For there are two effects of government, the preservation of things in their goodness, and the moving of things to good.[456]

FOX: Speak to me more about the dignity of our species.

AQUINAS: "Person" signifies what is most perfect in all of nature—that is, a subsistent individual of a rational nature.[457] Indeed, some people define "person" as "hypostasis distinct by reason of dignity." Because subsistence in a rational nature is of so lofty a dignity, therefore every individual with a rational nature is called a person.[458]

FOX: Some believers would have trouble with your celebration of the personhood of the human, because they would say that "person" is not a biblical category. What do you say to that?

AQUINAS: If we could speak of God only in the very terms themselves that Scripture uses, it would follow that no one could speak about God in any but the original language of the Hebrew Bible or the New Testament! The urgency of confuting heretics made it necessary to find new words to express the ancient faith about God. Nor is such a kind of novelty to be shunned; since it is by no means profane, for it does not lead us astray from the meaning of Scripture.[459]

FOX: Thank you for that response to a common fundamentalist problem. Certainly the dignity of the human is, as you say, the "meaning" of the rather elaborate exegesis you offered regarding Psalms 8 and 26. You celebrate the unique gift of reason and rationality in the human. Tell me what makes you wonder so much at this gift.

---

455. In Pss 8, p. 169.   456. ST I, q. 103, a. 4.   457. Ibid., q. 29, a. 3.
458. Ibid., ad 2.   459. Ibid., a. 3, ad 1.

AQUINAS: The intellectual soul as comprehending universals has a power extending to the infinite.[460] Since our intellect is infinite in power, so it knows the infinite. For its power is indeed infinite inasmuch as it is not terminated by corporeal matter. Moreover, it can know the universal, which is abstracted from individual matter, and which consequently is not limited to one individual, but, considered in itself, extends to an infinite number of individuals.[461]

FOX: The infinite, you say? Our minds are infinite — what does that mean?

AQUINAS: Aristotle said that the soul is in a certain sense "all things," because it is in potentiality to all things through the objects of sense, that is, to all sensible things; and it exists in potentiality to all things intelligible through the intellect.[462]

FOX: We are "all things"?

AQUINAS: The human being is called "a little world" because all creatures of the world are in a way found in the human being.[463] Intellectual natures have a closer relationship to a whole than do other natures; indeed, each intellectual substance is, in a way, all things. For it may comprehend the entirety of being through its intellect; on the other hand, every other substance has only a particular share in being.[464]

FOX: Although we are a microcosm, the macrocosm dwells in us. Is this part of the notion of our "infinity" of which you speak?

AQUINAS: Our intellect never understands so many things, that it could not understand more.[465] It follows that our psyches cannot be limited by nature to certain fixed natural notions, or even to certain fixed means whether of defense or of clothing, as is the case with other animals, the souls of which are endowed with knowledge and power in regard to fixed and particular things.[466]

FOX: But we are bodily. How can a finite creature be infinite?

AQUINAS: Union with the body does not rob the intellect of its infinite power.[467]

---

460. Ibid., q. 76, a. 5, ad 4.   461. Ibid., q. 86, a. 2, ad 4.   462. Ibid., q. 84, a. 2, ad 2.   463. Ibid., q. 91, a. 1.   464. CG III, ch. 112 n. 5.   465. ST I, q. 86, a. 2.   466. Ibid.   467. CG II, ch. 69 n. 12.

FOX: When I listen to you I feel that you are reminding us that human nature is very great.

AQUINAS: Reason in the human being is much like God in the world.[468] There is nothing that the human mind cannot understand potentially. It is capable of knowing all things.[469] The greatness of the human person consists in this: that it is capable of the universe (*capax universi*).[470] Other beings take only a limited part in being. But the spiritual being is capable of grasping the whole of being.[471] We are also capable of embracing the whole of being.[472]

FOX: It seems that by the word *ratio* or reason you are really celebrating our creativity, which you name as "infinite" in its capacity.

AQUINAS: Instead of the knowledge and power in regard to fixed and particular things, human beings have by nature their reason and their hands. . . . The hand is called by Aristotle the "organ of organs," since by these means human beings can make for themselves instruments of an infinite variety and for any number of purposes.[473]

FOX: No doubt we will want to pursue this topic more fully when we discuss the Via Creativa. Why is it, would you say, that the "rational"—or maybe we would say today the most creative—of species is so noble?

AQUINAS: Knowledge and will require that the thing known should be in the one who knows, and the thing willed in the one who wills. Hence, by knowledge and will things are more truly in God than God is in things.[474]

FOX: But didn't we establish previously that God is in all things?

AQUINAS: God is said to be in a thing in two ways: in one way as an efficient cause—and in this way God is in all things created by the Godhead. But in another way God is in things as the object of operation is in the operator: this is proper to the operations of the soul to the extent that the thing known is in the one who knows and the thing desired is in the one desiring. In this second manner, God is in the rational creature in a special

---

468. DRP I, 12.   469. DV, q. I, a. 2, ad 4.   470. Ibid., q. 2, a. 2.
471. CG III, ch. 112 n. 5.   472. Ibid. II, ch. 98 n. 10.   473. ST I, q. 91, a. 3, ad 2.   474. Ibid., q. 8, a. 3, ad 3.

way, for that creature knows and loves God actually or habit-ually.[475] While there is some kind of likeness to God in all crea-tures, in the rational creature alone do we find a likeness of image. Whereas in other creatures we find a likeness by way of a trace. Now the intellect or mind is that whereby the rational creature excels other creatures.[476]

FOX: How is that so?

AQUINAS: One must know that the human being is composed of a rational nature and a sensitive one. According to the rational nature the human being has a likeness with God and the angels. Genesis 1 says "Let us make humankind in our image and like-ness," and Psalm 8 says "You have made them a little less than the angels." According to their sensitive nature, human beings have a commonality with the animals.[477]

FOX: How are we human beings like the angels?

AQUINAS: Human beings have an intellect somehow equal to the angels because of the property and capability of souls. For the inquiry that reason makes is completed in the simple un-derstanding of the truth, just as it begins with the simple under-standing of the truth that is known in the first principles.[478]

FOX: And so our intellects render our species to be so dignified?

AQUINAS: The perfection and dignity of the intellect consists in this, that the image of the thing that is understood is in the in-tellect itself, since in this way it actually understands, and from this its whole dignity is seen.[479]

FOX: Why is there so much dignity in knowing?

AQUINAS: There is a mode of perfection in creatures by which an excellence proper to one thing may show itself in another. This is the glory of a thing that can know, to the extent that it knows. For a thing is known inasmuch as it has come home to the knower.[480]

FOX: I hear you saying that we, by our infinite capacity to know, actually become in a way the beauty and goodness, the awe and wonder, that we take in—and there lies our "glory," as you call it. Surely our capacity to love is a sign of our dignity as well, though it depends on what we know, for we can love only what we know.

---

475. Ibid., a. 3.   476. Ibid., q. 93, a. 6.   477. In Pss 48, p. 337.   478. DDN, n. 713, p. 267.   479. DV, q. 22, a. 11.   480. Ibid., q. 2, a. 2.

AQUINAS: The nobility of the will and of its act consists in this, that the soul is directed to some noble thing in the very existence that that thing has in itself. Now, it is more perfect, simply and absolutely speaking, to have within oneself the nobility of another thing than to be related to a noble thing outside oneself. Hence, if the will and the intellect are considered absolutely, and not with reference to this or that particular thing, they have this order, that the intellect is simply more excellent than the will.[481]

FOX: But what about when we consider intellect and will in a less than absolute fashion?

AQUINAS: When you compare the intellect to the will as regards material and sense objects, the intellect is simply nobler than the will. For example, to know a stone intellectually is nobler than to will it, because the form of the stone is in the intellect, inasmuch as it is known by the intellect, in a nobler way than it is in itself, as desired by the will. But in reference to divine things, which are superior to the soul, to will is more excellent than to understand, as to will God or to love the Godhead is more excellent than to know God.[482]

FOX: You have compared the human being's likeness to God and to the angels. What follows from this comparison?

AQUINAS: The psalmist posits the honor of human nature in this respect, that it has a likeness to the angels. According to the Philosopher [Aristotle], honor is more excellent than praise, for praise is directed toward other things, but honor is through itself and in itself.[483]

FOX: Human nature, then, is honorable in itself.

AQUINAS: Light was given to the earth for the service of the human being, who, by reason of the human soul, is nobler than the heavenly bodies themselves.[484] There are two privileges of the rational creature. One, that the rational creature sees the light of God, and since other animals do not see in the light of God, the psalmist (Ps. 37) says, "in your light." This is not understood as the light created by God, for that which is spoken of in Genesis 1 is understood in this way: "Let there be light." But "in your light" means the light by which you shine, which is a likeness of your substance. That light animals do not share.

---

481. Ibid., q. 22, a. 11.   482. Ibid.   483. In Pss 48, p. 337.   484. ST I, q. 70, a. 2, ad 4.

But the rational creature first shares it in its natural thinking: for reason is nothing other than the light of divine brightness reflected in the soul. It is because of this brightness that the soul is close to the image of God, as the psalmist says: "Lord, the light of your face has shown upon us" (Ps. 4).[485]

FOX: You spoke of two privileges accorded the human being. What is the second?

AQUINAS: "In your light," that is, Christ. The other privilege is in this, that the rational creature alone sees this light, whence the psalmist says, "we will see the light." His light is either created truth, that is, Christ as a human being, or uncreated truth, by which we know some true things. For spiritual light is truth, since just as something is known through light inasmuch as it is clear, so it is known inasmuch as it is true. Animals know some truths well, for example, that this is sweet; but they do not know the proposition "this is true," since this consists in the matching of the intellect with the thing, which animals are unable to do. Therefore, animals do not have created light. Neither do they have uncreated light.[486]

FOX: In what way is the human being an "image of God"?

AQUINAS: The image of God is in the human being first inasmuch as the human being possesses a natural aptitude for understanding and loving God; and this aptitude consists in the very nature of the mind, which is common to all people.[487] The human being's likeness [to God] is indicative of a certain imperfect image rather than one of any consubstantiality. Indeed, Scripture implies this in saying that the human being was made "to the image" of God. Thus the "breathing" of which Genesis speaks signifies the pouring forth of life from God into the human being according to a certain likeness, and not according to unity of substance. . . . God is said to have breathed the spirit into the human being's face, because God gave the human the spirit of life, but not by detaching it from God's own substance.[488]

FOX: How do you define "spirit"?

AQUINAS: The name "spirit" expresses a kind of "elan" or vital impulse, as when we say that "love moves us" or "love urges

---

485. In Pss 36, p. 279.   486. Ibid.   487. ST I, q. 93, a. 4.   488. CG II, ch. 85 n. 15.

us" to do something.[489] Now it is a property of love to move and impel the will of the lover toward the object loved.[490] There is something that relates to the totality of existing things. The soul is such a being that, as is said in [Aristotles's] *The Soul,* "in some way is all things."[491]

FOX: Thus "spirit" for you is about vitality, being fully alive, being in touch with life at its source and with all of being?

AQUINAS: When we say "God is Spirit" we say God is a life giver, because our entire life is from God, as its creative source.[492]

FOX: Do all humans partake of the image of God?

AQUINAS: The image of God in its principal meaning, namely, the intellectual nature, is found both in man and in woman. That is why after the words, "in the image of God God created him," there is added, "male and female God created them" (Gen. 1:27).[493] The image of God always abides in the soul, whether this image be obsolete and clouded over as to amount to almost nothing; or whether in those who have not yet reached the age of reason; or whether it be obscured and disfigured, as is the case with sinners; or whether it be clear and beautiful, as is the case with the just.[494]

FOX: Fundamentalists today lack a sense of the Trinity, and if they concede an image of God in the human being at all they think only of Christ. What do you say to this?

AQUINAS: When it is written, "The Creator made him to the image of God," the sense is not that the Father made the human being in the image of the Son only, Who is God, as some explained it, but that the divine Trinity made the human being in Its image, that is, of the whole Trinity.[495]

FOX: Where do you find this image of God in the human being?

AQUINAS: First and chiefly, the image of the Trinity is to be found in the acts of the soul, that is, inasmuch as from the knowledge that we possess, by actual thought we form an internal word and from this we break forth into love.[496]

FOX: You are celebrating our creativity as the essence of the divine image in us. This "internal word" that "breaks forth into

---

489. ST I, q. 27, a. 4.   490. Ibid., q. 36, a. 1.   491. DV, q. 1, a. 1.
492. In Jn 4.24, n. 615.   493. ST I, q. 93, a. 4, ad 1.   494. Ibid., a. 8, ad 3.   495. Ibid., a. 5, ad 4.   496. Ibid., a. 7.

love" sounds like as good a definition as any I have heard for the creative process. We will no doubt be discussing this more in the Via Creativa conversation we will have. Perhaps this is one way of celebrating the Trinitarian presence in the soul, because every creative act is a Trinitarian one; that is, it is a coming together of two things to give birth to a third.

AQUINAS: We refer the divine image in the human being to the verbal concept born of the knowledge of God, and to the love derived from this.[497]

FOX: When we call the human being an "image of God" are we saying that God is more fully seen in the human being than in other creatures?

AQUINAS: The higher a creature is, and the more like it is to God, the more clearly is God seen in it. For instance, one is seen more clearly through a mirror in which one's image is the more clearly expressed. Thus God is seen in a much more perfect manner through God's intelligible effects than through those that are sensible or corporeal only.[498]

FOX: This smacks of human chauvinism, but I suppose what you are saying might mean that because of the complexity of the human and our added gifts there is even more of God—potentially speaking—in us than in some other creatures.

AQUINAS: The image of God is not found even in the rational creature except in the mind (*secundum mentem*) [or intellect or imagination].[499] The mind [or imagination] of a human being is like the lamp of God lit with divine light.[500] In the other parts of a person that the rational creature may happen to possess, we find the likeness of a trace, just as we do in other creatures. An image represents something by likeness in species, while a trace represents something by way of an effect. This effect represents the cause in such a way that it does not attain to the likeness of species. Thus imprints that are left by the movements of animals are called "traces," and ashes are a trace of a fire and desolation of the land is a trace of a hostile army.[501]

FOX: How then do human beings differ from other creatures as to our being "like God"?

---

497. Ibid., a. 8.　498. Ibid., q. 94, a. 1.　499. Ibid., q. 93, a. 6.　500. In Pss 17, p. 202.　501. ST I, q. 93, a. 6.

AQUINAS: An image adds something to likeness—namely, that it is copied from something else. For an image is so called because it is produced as an imitation of something else. There is in the human being a likeness to God—not indeed a perfect likeness, but imperfect.[502] When it comes to the likeness of the divine nature, rational creatures seem to attain, after a fashion, to the representation of the species, inasmuch as they imitate God not only in being and life but also in intelligence. In contrast, other creatures do not understand, although we observe in them a certain trace of the Intellect that created them, if we consider their disposition.[503]

FOX: I like your phrase "to imitate God." How else do we imitate God?

AQUINAS: In rational creatures wherein we find a procession of the word in the intellect, and a procession of the love in the will, there exists an image of the uncreated Trinity, by a certain representation of the species. In other creatures, however, we do not find the principle of the word, and the word and love; but we do see in them a certain trace of the existence of these in the Cause that produced them.[504]

FOX: I am not totally at ease with all of your wondering at the marvel of the human being—especially when it seems to diminish other creatures. I feel you presume to know more about other creatures than you (and we today) in fact do know. Perhaps, however, that is why you use the term "brute animal" so often when you are speaking of animals. Perhaps you are signifying those animals that appear to be less bearers of the spirit than others. At the same time, I concede that you are not so anthropocentric in the long run, since you said above that the greatest love of God is for the universe and creation as a whole and for the order intrinsic to this whole. All of this contributes to putting human beings in their place, so to speak. I suspect that a lot of your emphasis on the "reason" side of humanity (though we have pretty much established that that would be called "creative side" in today's parlance) may be due to the cultural period in which you lived. The emergence of human consciousness from the feudal era into the light of day, signified

---

502. Ibid., a. 1.   503. Ibid., a. 6.   504. Ibid.

by the invention of universities in your time and by Gothic Cathedrals and translations from Arabic of Greek masters like Aristotle, for the first time created a cultural imperative to wake people up to their divine and intellectual potential—and I believe that you, being a good member of the Order of Preachers, were trying to do that in your work. To do so you had to challenge a very low self-image that people had ingested during the feudal era, particularly as regards the capacity for learning. The monks were almost the only ones who could be schooled in that era. But your times were all new, and the young and freed serfs were eager to exercise their minds. For this reason—to urge the youth on to discover the more "rational" side of their nature—I suspect you emphasized the mind the way you did.

AQUINAS: On reaching the use of reason, the first thing that occurs to a person to think about is to deliberate about oneself.[505] The reasoning mind is the predominant part of the human being, while the sensitive and corporeal nature takes the second place. The Apostle [Paul] calls the former the inward person, and the latter the outward person (2 Cor. 4:16). Now good persons look upon their rational nature or the inward person as being the chief good in them, wherefore in this way they think themselves to be what they are. In contrast, the wicked reckon their sensitive and corporeal nature, or the outward person, to hold first place.[506]

FOX: One way to foster deliberation on oneself seems to be to contrast the human with the animal.

AQUINAS: Scripture teaches that land animals, from the higher perfection of their life, are, as it were, living souls with bodies subject to them. But the life of the human being, as being the most perfect grade, is not said to be produced, like the life of other animals, by earth and water, but immediately by God.[507]

FOX: What are the consequences for human behavior?

AQUINAS: Brute animals are motivated by passion. This is clear from the fact that as soon as a dog is angered, it barks, and as soon as a horse is aroused, it whinnies. But it is not credited to them, since they lack reason. But if a human being pursues passion as soon as one is aroused, and if one strikes out the moment

---

505. Ibid. I-II, q. 89, a. 6.   506. Ibid. II-II, q. 25, a. 7.   507. Ibid. I, q. 72, a. 1, ad 1.

one is angered, one is compared to a brute beast in one's behavior. As the psalmist says (Ps. 32): "Don't become like a horse
or mule." Thus, the Philosopher says that a bad man is worse
than a bad beast. Since, when the human being has an intellect
accompanied by ill-will, then they invent diverse evils.[508]

FOX: You seem to be saying that human beings are capable of
worse evil than other species and possibly of greater good. We
will be dealing with human evil shortly, and the emphasis you
have given the matter of our intellect and creativity vis-à-vis our
capacity for evil is something we will bring up in our discussions on the Via Creativa. But now it seems like an appropriate
time to discuss that side of human nature that we share with the
animals. This seems like an especially important topic to you,
since it was your apparently radical views on the "consubstantiality of soul and body" that got you into so much difficulty in
your day.

AQUINAS: The soul is in the body as containing it, not as contained by it.[509] The soul contains the body and is like its foundation. Part of the soul is part of the body. Thus, when the
foundation is stricken the wall is stricken, and when the powers
of the soul are stricken the limbs are stricken. Thus when an
animal gets angry it trembles. In human beings there are four
things: namely, reason, sensitive powers, nature, matter and
body. And in the world there are God, angels, animals, plants,
and elements.[510]

FOX: I am struck when I hear you picture the body as being in
the soul, for this certainly opens the human being up to vast
possibilities of spirit and experience beyond the confines of the
space our bodies occupy. It also renders the soul less antago-
nistic toward the body, as opposed to the body being some kind
of cage imprisoning the soul. How do you envision the relationship of soul and body in the human being?

AQUINAS: A particular human being is composed of this soul,
of this flesh, and of these bones. So it belongs to the notion of
humanity to be composed of soul, flesh, and bones.[511]

FOX: Then it is not part of your spirituality to overly spiritu-
alize the human being and to see spirit exclusively in the soul or
apart from matter?

---

508. In Pss 48, p. 337.   509. ST I, q. 52, a. 1.   510. In Pss 17, p. 196.
511. ST I, q. 75, a. 4.

AQUINAS: Sensation is not an operation of the soul only. Therefore human beings are not soul only, but something composed of soul and body. Plato, by supposing that sensation was proper to the soul, could maintain the human being was a soul making use of the body.[512]

FOX: Where is the soul in relation to the body?

AQUINAS: The whole human soul is in the whole body and also in every part of the body, just as God is present to the entire universe.[513]

FOX: Sort of as in panentheism, the soul is in the body and the body is in the soul. In addition you seem to be saying that the soul does not have to be cut off from matter and body to be spiritual?

AQUINAS: The soul is more like God when united to the body than when separated from it.[514]

FOX: Why?

AQUINAS: Because its nature is then more perfect. For a thing is like God insofar as it is perfect.[515]

FOX: But why is the soul more perfect or complete when united with the body than when separate from it?

AQUINAS: No part has the perfection of a nature when separated from the whole. And therefore the soul, since it is a part of a human nature, does not have the perfection of its own nature, save in union with the body. . . . And hence the soul, although it can exist and can understand separated from the body, nevertheless does not have the perfection of its own nature when it is separated from the body.[516] Spirit fits in with spirit rather than with body by a congruity of nature. But by a congruity of relationship that is required between form and matter, spirit fits in with body more than spirit does with spirit since two spirits are two acts, whereas the body is related to the soul as potency is to act.[517]

FOX: Do you believe this about the resurrection of the body as well?

AQUINAS: Elements that are by nature destined for union naturally desire to be united to each other; for any being seeks what

---

512. Ibid. 513. Ibid., q. 93, a. 3. 514. ST II, q. 5, a. 10, ad 5. 515. Ibid. 516. SC, a. 2, ad 5. 517. Ibid., ad 10.

is suited to it by nature. Since, therefore, the natural condition of the human soul is to be united to the body, it has a natural desire for union with the body. Hence the will cannot be perfectly at rest until the soul is again joined to the body. When this takes place, the human being rises from the dead. . . . In order that the human soul may be brought to complete wholeness with regard to its end, it must be complete in its nature. This is impossible unless the soul is united to the body. For by nature the soul is a part of the person as its form. But no part is whole in its nature unless it exists in its whole. Therefore the human being's final happiness requires the soul to be again united to the body.[518]

FOX: And for you the resurrection of the body is very much a resurrection of the bodies we now possess?

AQUINAS: At the resurrection the soul will not resume a celestial or ethereal body, or the body of some animal, as certain people fancifully prattle. No, it will resume a human body made up of flesh and bones, and equipped with the same organs it now possesses.[519] The human beings that rise again are the identical human beings who lived before, though their vital processes are performed in a different way. . . . Human beings do not assume a heavenly or ghostly kind of body. Their bodies remain truly human, though they are invested with an immortality coming from a divine strength that enables the soul so to dominate the body that corruption cannot enter.[520] Entirely possessed by soul, the body will then be fine and spirited. Then also it will be endowed with the noble lightsomeness of beauty . . . it will be lissome and agile, entirely responsive to the soul, like an instrument in the hands of a skilled player.[521]

FOX: Let us return to our present life. When you praise the body for its beauty, you are insisting on its contribution to the "perfection" of the human being.

AQUINAS: Natural love is not only in the powers of the vegetative soul, but in all the soul's powers, and also in all the parts of the body, and universally in all things, as Dionysius says: "Beauty and goodness are beloved by all things." For each sin-

---

518. CT I, 151.   519. Ibid., 153.   520. Ibid., 155.   521. Ibid., 168.

gle thing has a connaturalness with that which is naturally suitable to it.[522]

FOX: And this beauty of the body blesses God and pleases God?

AQUINAS: Just as men and women are decorated by a handsome garment, so all the beauty of the holy angels and of human beings streams back to the embellishment of God, insofar as from this the good of God is commended in the manner that Isaiah speaks of (49): "You have clothed yourself in all these things as with a garment." One should meditate on how this pertains to the compassion of God, to make all the saints beautiful, but God uses this beauty for the divine glory.[523]

FOX: What ought our attitude toward the body be?

AQUINAS: We ought to cherish the body. Our body's substance is not from an evil principle, as the Manicheans imagine, but from God. And therefore we ought to cherish the body by the friendship of love, by which we love God.[524] Vice does not come to the soul from the body, but to the body from the soul.[525] In fact, it is a law of nature that we should care for our body.[526]

FOX: Why is it a law of nature to care for our bodies?

AQUINAS: It is a sin not to eat when necessity demands.[527] When we nourish our own flesh we are loving it, just as we love anything whose powers we sustain.[528] Furthermore, the mind itself cannot play freely if the senses are not fit and vigorous.[529] Perfection of the body is necessary, lest the body hinder the mind from its full potential.[530]

FOX: From all the pictures I've seen of you, I have the impression you practiced what you are currently preaching and that you truly loved to eat! All this sounds like you are praising our sensuality.

AQUINAS: Sensuality is the name given the sensitive appetite.[531] The sensitive appetite, which we call our sensuality, is one of the perfections of animal nature that is included in human nature. Of course, it is called to follow the path that reason lays out.[532]

---

522. ST I-II, q. 26, a. 1, ad 3.   523. In Job, ch. 40, p. 136.   524. ST II-II, q. 25, a. 5.   525. CG III, ch. 127 n. 4.   526. In Thess, 4.1, p. 566. 527. In Eph 4.28, p. 486.   528. Ibid. 5.29, p. 496.   529. In 2 Cor, ch. 12, p. 367.   530. ST I-II, q. 4, a. 6, ad 2.   531. Ibid. I, q. 81, a. 1. 532. Ibid. III, q. 18, a. 2.

When Scriptures celebrate this fact, that "the flesh rejoices in the living God" (Ps. 84:2), the rejoicing is not by carnal activity reaching up to God but by the overflowing of the heart, as when feeling follows willing.[533]

FOX: Isn't the source of one of your bitter arguments with the Augustinians and even with Bonaventure the fact that you insisted that the seat of virtue lies not in the will but in the passions?

AQUINAS: I understand the sensitive appetite and passions to be the subject and seat of the virtues.[534]

FOX: You seem so free from the body-soul dualism that so much of Western spirituality has presumed or espoused, consciously or unconsciously.

AQUINAS: We ought to celebrate the "wonderful communion" (*communio admirabilis*) of body and soul. God fashioned the human body in the disposition that is best suited for a rational soul and its activities, for the proximate purpose of the human body is the human soul. Take a person who makes a saw in order to cut with: Does he choose glass, though a beautiful material in itself? Would this not defeat the purpose of what a saw is for? The person chooses metal because that best suits the purpose.[535]

FOX: People should not regret being embodied, then?

AQUINAS: The soul, as part of human nature, has its natural perfection only as united to the body. Therefore it would have been unfitting for the soul to be created without the body.[536] Sensation is not an activity of pure soul. Though sensation is not unique to human beings, it is truly human. Therefore, a person is not just soul, but a compound of body and soul.[537]

FOX: Furthermore, God, who made the elements of the universe, also made the body, and surely God does not regret the body.

AQUINAS: The power of the divine Creator was manifested in the human body when its matter was produced by creation. And it was fitting that the human body should be made up of the four elements—in order that human beings might have

---

533. Ibid., q. 21, a. 2, ad 1.   534. Ibid. I-II, q. 56, a. 5, ad 1.   535. Ibid. I, q. 91, a. 3.   536. Ibid., q. 90, a. 4.   537. Ibid., q. 85, a. 4.

something in common with lesser bodies—since it is something existing between spiritual and corporeal substances.[538]

FOX: How striking that you celebrate the fact that the elements of the universe as science understood them in your day make up the human body! In naming the relationship of body to universe you lay out a microcosmic/macrocosmic psychology that reveals a deep sense of the cosmological setting for our human existence. Today we celebrate how the elements of our bodies were birthed by a supernova explosion in the universe five and a half billion years ago. The facts are different from the science of your day, but the dimension of wonder is not only similar, it is increased. I notice too that when you speak of the body-soul relationship, you seem to avoid that ultimate error in dualism, that of pitting soul against body and of relegating the spirit exclusively to soul. I suppose, given your definition of spirit as "elan," which we heard earlier, that you are saying that body too has spirit to it. This strikes me as very modern—much like Einstein's thesis on the convertibility of matter and energy.

AQUINAS: Human souls and pure spirits are different kinds of things.[539] It is contrary to the nature of the soul to be without the body.[540]

FOX: You certainly state your case against dualism strongly.

AQUINAS: To be united to body is not to the detriment of soul but to its enrichment.[541] There follows from this the substantial benefit of completing human nature and a more modest advantage of achieving knowledge that can only be acquired through the senses.[542] Sensitive activity is always that of soul and body in unison.[543] The natural body is a certain fullness of the soul. The soul is unable to exercise its activities fully if the body parts are less than integral.[544]

FOX: I don't get the impression that your nondualistic approach to body-soul relationships has held sway in Western thought.

AQUINAS: Plato taught that a human being was not a thing composed of soul and body, but that it was a soul using the body. But this is impossible, since animals and people are natural and sensitive beings. This could not be the case if bodies and bodily organs were not integral to their essence, that is, if they

---

538. Ibid., q. 91, a. 1, ad 1.   539. Ibid., q. 85, a. 7.   540. CG IV, ch. 79 n. 10.   541. DA 2, ad 14.   542. Ibid. 1, ad 7.   543. ST I, q. 75, a. 3. 544. In Eph 1.23, p. 456.

were wholly souls.[545] Furthermore, soul and body share common actions like sensing and feeling, which are functions of soul and body acting in unison and out of one single being simultaneously.[546] Origen said that souls were united to bodies by divine decree, but as a punishment. For Origen thought that souls had sinned before bodies existed, and that according to the gravity of their sin, souls were imprisoned in bodies of higher or lower character, as in so many prisons. This doctrine, however, is untenable, for being contrary to a good of nature, punishment is said to be an evil. If, then, the union of soul and body is something penal in character, it is not a good of nature. But this is impossible, for that union is intended by nature, since natural generation terminates in it. And again, on Origen's theory, it would follow that a person's being would not be a good according to nature, yet it is said, after human beings were created: "God saw all the things that God had made, and they were very good."[547]

FOX: And so our nature is "very good." What about our sexuality? There are those theologians, such as Gregory of Nyssa, who say that in the Garden of Eden generation of our species would not happen by lovemaking but in the manner that angels generate. What do you say to this?

AQUINAS: In the state of innocence there would have been generation of offspring for the multiplication of the human race. Otherwise, human sin would have been very much necessary, in order to bring about such a very great blessing.[548] Gregory of Nyssa's position is unreasonable. For what is natural to human beings was neither acquired nor forfeited by sin. Now it is clear that generation by sexual intercourse is natural to human beings by reason of their animal life, which they possessed even before sin, just as it is natural to other perfect animals. The bodily parts we possess make this clear. We cannot agree that these bodily parts would not have had a natural use, as other of our bodily parts had, before sin.[549] God made man and woman before sin (Gen. 1, 2). But nothing is void in God's works. Therefore, even if human beings had not sinned, there would have been sexual intercourse to which the distinction of sex is ordained.[550]

---

545. CG II, ch. 57 n. 5.   546. Ibid., n. 6.   547. Ibid., ch. 83 n. 22.
548. ST I, q. 98, a. 1.   549. Ibid., a. 2.   550. Ibid.

FOX: You called our sexuality "a very great blessing." So for you our sexuality is good and one of the blessings of our lives?

AQUINAS: The blessing of generating offspring is repeated in the case of the human being (in Genesis) . . . to prevent anyone from saying that there was any sin whatever in the act of begetting children. When it came to plants, since they experience neither desire of propagation nor sensation in generating, they are deemed unworthy of a formal blessing.[551]

FOX: Can sexual union be evil in itself?

AQUINAS: Natural inclinations are present in things from God, who moves all things. So it is impossible for the natural inclination of a species to be toward what is evil in itself. But there is in all perfect animals a natural inclination toward carnal union. Therefore, it is impossible for carnal union to be evil in itself.[552]

FOX: But what about the objection that continence is praiseworthy because sexual intercourse is so vehemently delightful that a good person should refrain from such pleasures?

AQUINAS: Natural love is nothing else than the inclination implanted in nature by its Author. To say that a natural inclination is not well regulated is to derogate from the Author of nature.[553] Animals are without reason, and human beings become like them in a certain manner in the act of sexual intercourse, because human beings cannot moderate desire. In the state of innocence nothing of this kind would have happened that was not regulated by reason—not because delight of sense was less, as some people say, but because the force of desire would not have so inordinately thrown itself into such pleasure, being moderated by reason, whose place it is not to lessen sensual pleasure, but to prevent the force of desire from cleaving to it immoderately. In fact, in that state the sensible delight would have been greater than it is now in proportion to the greater purity of nature and the greater sensibility of the body.[554]

FOX: Your point that reason does not diminish pleasure but regulates our attachment to it is an important one. What is the "immoderate" pleasure you speak of? When is pleasure immoderate?

---

551. Ibid., q. 72, a. 1, ad 4.   552. CG III, ch. 126 n. 3.   553. ST I, q. 60, a. 1, ad 3.   554. CG III, ch. 126 n. 3.

AQUINAS: By "immoderate" I mean going beyond the bounds of reason, as a sober person does not take less pleasure in food taken in moderation than the glutton, but his desire lingers less in such pleasures. Intensity of pleasure is not excluded from the state of innocence, but ardor of desire and restlessness of the mind is. Therefore continence would not have been praiseworthy in the state of innocence, whereas it is praiseworthy in our present condition—not because it removes fecundity, but because it excludes inordinate desire.[555]

FOX: This is interesting, and there is room for further dialogue with you on the topic of sexuality. However, I'm grateful that humanity's thinking on gender and sexuality have evolved so that we also could teach you some things. For example, that the "active principle" is not always male and the "passive principle" female, as you say it is.[556] Or that women are not inferior to men. Dualisms seem to die hard in the Western consciousness, and, as we have seen, you battled hard to lay so many of them to rest. Yet you also succumb at times.

Speaking of dualisms, and also about the human condition, what about the belief that God became a human being, thus overcoming the dualism between God and humanity? And that God took on a human body, thus contributing to the celebration of matter and the accomplishments of the universe in birthing our bodies? How does this discussion on creation relate to your understanding of the Incarnation of God in Jesus Christ?

AQUINAS: Paradoxes meet through divine and human nature in Christ's single person.[557]

FOX: I hear you celebrating Christ as the Ultimate Paradox—that of human and divine commingling. There lies the end of dualism and the beginning of healing by way of converting our either/ors into both/ands. You are truly a dialectical thinker!

AQUINAS: The Incarnation is indeed a unique union—one that surpasses every communion known to the human race.[558] Now the motive for the Son's taking to himself our flesh was the exceedingly great love of God.[559] The Son of God became human in order that human beings might become gods and become the children of God.[560]

---

555. Ibid.   556. ST I, q. 98, a. 2.   557. DVI 3, ad 13.   558. Ibid., 1.
559. ST III, q. 32, a. 1.   560. CT I, 214.

FOX: You say that the purpose of the Incarnation was our becoming godlike.

AQUINAS: The Incarnation holds up to humanity an ideal of that blessed union whereby the created intellect is joined, in an act of understanding, to the uncreated Spirit. It is no longer incredible that a creature's intellect should be capable of union with God by beholding the divine essence, since the time when God became united to humanity by taking a human nature to the very self of God.[561]

FOX: Do you believe that humanity's union with God was accomplished so that, as you say, it is no longer incredible?

AQUINAS: The Incarnation accomplished the following: that God became human and that human beings became God and sharers in the divine nature. (See 2 Pet. 1:4.)[562] The only-begotten Son of God intended to make us "partakers of his divine nature" (2 Pet. 1:4). For this reason the Godhead did take our nature on itself and became human in order to make humans gods.[563]

FOX: What does it mean to become God's children and take on God's nature?

AQUINAS: We are meant to become more and more like God.[564] We are called God's children by taking on the likeness of this natural and only-begotten Son, who is himself begotten wisdom.[565] Christ as the Word is expressive of God the Father and both expressive and creative of the universe itself.[566]

FOX: It sounds like you are celebrating Christ as cosmic wisdom or the Cosmic Christ.

AQUINAS: All nature obeyed Christ and heeded his slightest command as something established by him, because "all things were made through him" (John 1).[567] When we read in John's Gospel that "he came unto his own," this means he came to the world, since the whole universe is his own.[568] "Unto his own" does not mean he came to the Jews but into the world created by him. "The earth is the Lord's" (Ps. 24:1). . . . God came where God already was![569]

FOX: And God comes to us personally?

561. Ibid., 201. 562. In Eph 3.20, p. 475. 563. BCC. 564. DT ii, 1 ad 7. 565. ST II-II, q. 45, a. 6. 566. Ibid. I, q. 34, a. 3. 567. In Jn 1.14b, n. 186. 568. In Jn, Preamble, n. 3. 569. In Jn 1.11, n. 143.

AQUINAS: The Word of God, that is, Christ who is God's Word, dwells in us, or to quote the Apostle: "That Christ may dwell in your hearts by faith" (Eph. 3:17). And, "You have not God's word abiding in you" (John 5:38).[570]

FOX: Your language about our becoming gods and like God may be unsettling to many Western believers. I suppose our "becoming like God" has gradations to it.

AQUINAS: It is possible for a thing to become more or less like God.[571]

FOX: How do we go about growing into the image of the Cosmic Christ in us?

AQUINAS: Grace renders us like God and a partaker of the divine nature.[572]

FOX: What is grace?

AQUINAS: Grace is nothing else than a beginning of glory in us.[573] Grace is a habit, a settled quality infused into the soul, whereby the Holy Spirit is said to dwell in human beings.[574] Grace is called the "seed" of God (1 John 3:9).[575] Grace is a radiance of the soul, a real quality such as beauty is to a body.[576] Grace dwells in the substance of our souls, rendering them like God and partakers of the divine nature.[577] It is necessary that we understand divine things according to the unity of grace, that is, by not drawing divine things toward our agendas but rather setting all of ourselves outside of ourselves in God so that through this unity we will be totally deified.[578]

FOX: It is interesting to me that when you speak of "grace" you pit it not against nature but against sin. Creation itself is graceful, after all.

AQUINAS: Grace does not destroy nature but completes it.[579]

FOX: Where does the word "grace" come from?

AQUINAS: Since what is given anyone, without any preceding merit on their part, is said to be given to them gratis, and because the divine help that is offered to people precedes all human merit, it follows that this help is accorded gratis to human beings, and as a result it quite fittingly took the name grace.

---

570. AC, pp. 25–26.   571. CG III, ch. 58 n. 3.   572. DV, q. 27, a. 6.
573. ST II-II, q. 24, a. 3, ad 2.   574. In I Sent 17.1.1.   575. ST I, q. 62, a. 3.   576. Ibid. I-II, q. 110, a. 2.   577. DV, q. 27, a. 6.   578. DDN, n. 705, p. 262.   579. ST I, q. 1, a. 8, ad 2.

Hence, the Apostle says, in Romans (11:6): "And if by grace, it is not now by works: otherwise grace is no more grace."[580] But there is another reason why the aforesaid help of God has taken the name grace. In fact, one is said to be in the "good graces" of another when one is well liked by the other. Consequently, one who is loved by another is said to enjoy their grace.[581]

FOX: Your mention of the Christ who is wisdom incarnate and creative of the universe suggests that Christ has much to teach us about creation and divine grace.

AQUINAS: Through the Incarnation we are led to enjoy goodness perfectly.[582]

FOX: Can you elaborate on this, please? It certainly sounds as if Christ came to teach us the path of the Via Positiva and a blessing consciousness.

AQUINAS: Take note of Isaiah's statement "all you who are thirsty, come to the waters," because divine teaching is first called "water." Why? Because it makes the sick well, as in Ecclesiasticus (15): "She will give him the water of wisdom to drink." Also, because it cleans the unclean, as in Ezekiel (36): "I will pour out clean water over you, and you will be cleansed of all your impurity." Third, because God satisfies those who thirst, as John says (4): "If anyone drinks from the water which I will give him, he will never be thirsty."

But divine teaching is also called "wine." The first reason for this is that it pierces by making things clear, as it says above in Isaiah chapter 1, "your wine has been mixed with water." Second, because it inflames by exhorting, as in Psalm 104: "The word of the Lord inflamed him." Third, because it intoxicates by consoling, as in Isaiah below, "you are becoming drunk with the richness of your consolation." Divine teaching is also called "milk" because of its beauty, as in Genesis, near the end, "Nephtali is a doe giving forth words of beauty." Also, because of its sweetness, as in the Song of Songs (2): "Let your voice sound in my ears, for your voice is sweet." Third, because of the ease of understanding, as 1 Peter 2: "Desire milk as if in the manner of newborn babes."[583]

FOX: With your talk of "intoxication" and "beauty" and

---

580. CG III, ch. 150 n. 1.   581. Ibid., n. 2.   582. In Eph 1.9, p. 448.
583. In Is, ch. 55, p. 557.

"wine" and "milk" and "waters of wisdom," you appear to find the teachings of Christ to be ecstasy-producing, a kind of wonder in themselves.

AQUINAS: The goodness of God cannot be expressed, and if it is expressed, still it is expressed imperfectly. And so Jeremiah says (1): "Ah, ah, ah, I don't know how to speak."[584]

FOX: And so Jesus, among other things, helps to articulate the ineffable goodness of God?

AQUINAS: Before Christ's coming no philosopher by his entire sustained effort could have known as much about God and the truths necessary for salvation as can a humble old woman now that Christ has come. . . . Our knowledge is so meager that no scientist can ever completely expose the nature of a fly—we read of one researcher who spent thirty years in solitude in order to learn all about bees.[585]

FOX: How are knowledge by science and knowledge by faith different?

AQUINAS: Science shines only on the mind, showing that God is the cause of everything, that God is one and wise, and so forth. Faith enlightens the mind and also warms the affections, tells us not merely that God is first cause, but also that God is savior, redeemer, lover, made flesh for us.[586]

FOX: And so faith touches the heart. You seem to have put your finger on a limit that science has—that it can fall short of heart-knowledge and therefore compassion.

AQUINAS: When Paul says (1 Cor. 8:1) "knowledge puffs up," the text applies when science is without love.[587]

FOX: What else did Jesus teach us?

AQUINAS: To assume flesh was a sign of incomprehensible compassion on God's part.[588] God has produced a work in which the likeness of God is clearly reflected—that is, the world itself.[589] Christ assumed flesh and came into the world to enlighten all people with grace and truth.[590] The purpose of John's Gospel [is] to lead us specifically to a knowledge of the Creator's very self.[591] Christ is God's wisdom,[592] and the necessity for the

---

584. In Pss 46, p. 330. 585. AC, p. 6. 586. In 2 Cor, ch. 2, p. 310.
587. CI, ch. 11, p. 54. 588. In Jn 1.14a, n. 169. 589. In Jn 1.10, n.
136. 590. In Jn 1.5, n. 104. 591. In Jn 1.3, n. 78. 592. Ibid., n. 76.

Word's coming is seen to be the lack of divine knowledge in the world.[593]

FOX: Will you elaborate more on the idea of Christ as the Word of God?

AQUINAS: Nothing was made outside of the Word, because it encompasses all things, preserving them.[594] The Word is per se life, always perfect life.[595] The spiritual power of the whole world belongs to Christ.[596] Because God by one act understands the Godhead and all things, God's one only Word is expressive not only of the Father, but of all creatures. . . . The Word of God is both expressive and productive of creatures; and therefore it is said (Ps. 33:9): "God spoke, and they were made," because in the Word is implied the operative idea of what God makes.[597]

FOX: Just as every creature is a word of God, so too every creature is a Cosmic Christ or an expression of the Word of God?

AQUINAS: "Word" implies not only the notion of origin and imitation, but also that of manifestation. Consequently, the Word is, in a fashion, the word of creatures, because creatures are manifested by means of the Word.[598] As we say that a tree flowers by its flower, so do we say that the Father, by the Word or the Son, speaks Godself and God's creatures. And that the Father and the Son love each other and us, by the Holy Spirit, or by Love proceeding.[599] Furthermore, the Father speaks the Godhead and every creature by God's begotten Word inasmuch as the Word "begotten" adequately represents the Father and every creature. Thus also God loves the Godhead and every creature by the Holy Spirit inasmuch as the Holy Spirit proceeds as the love of the primal goodness whereby the Creator loves the Godhead and every creature.[600] Indeed, all the movements of nature are from the Word of God itself.[601]

FOX: Can you elaborate more on Jesus as the Word of God and as the Cosmic Christ?

AQUINAS: God conceived the Word in eternity, and according to that all things have been made. In other words, God engendered the Word in such a way that it became all things.[602] Paul says, "In him everything in heaven and on earth was created"

---

593. In Jn 1.9, n. 124.   594. In Jn 1.3, n. 86.   595. Ibid., n. 93.   596. In Pss 21, p. 224.   597. ST I, q. 34, a. 3.   598. DV, q. 4, a. 4, ad 6. 599. ST I, q. 37, a. 2.   600. Ibid., ad 3.   601. In Jn 15.5, n. 1993. 602. In Pss 32, p. 262.

(Col. 1:16). In regard to this statement we should note that the Platonists have a theory of ideas according to which things come into being inasmuch as they correspond to an idea, a human being for example. In the place of all these ideas we have one thing, that is, the Son, the Word of God. For an artist makes an artifact by making it correspond to a form that he himself has conceived, as if mixing the form into some external matter. Thus we might say that the builder makes a house through the form he has conceived within himself. So God is said to make all things in the divine wisdom, because the wisdom of God is related to created things as the art of the builder is related to the completed house. This form, this wisdom, is the Word, and therefore everything is founded in the Word as in an exemplar. Genesis 1 says: "God spoke, and they were made," because in God's eternal Word, Divinity made all things.[603]

FOX: Speak more about who Jesus was.

AQUINAS: The Son of God has been made in reference to us, that is, a man like us in nature. His flesh was "taken up"—not brought down from heaven as Valentinus has it; and "totally"— that is, not removed by spirit or intellect as Arius and Apollinarius have it; "and truly"—not like a phantasm as the Manicheans have it. As for this humanity that is his, he was conceived, he was born, he ate, drank, slept, was crucified, and the like. He was not made a human being to lose his Divinity, but stepping forth as a human being, he had the divine ability, which was shared by himself and the Father and the Holy Spirit.[604] In its first coming the Godhead came hidden in the weakness of humanity, as Ezekiel says, "I will cover the sun with a cloud" (Ezek. 32). And as Isaiah says, "Truly you are a hidden God" (Isa. 45). Likewise, in its first coming the Godhead showed gentleness (Isa. 53): "Like a lamb he was led to the shearer." Thus he said nothing before the leaders and priests, nor before Pilate.[605]

FOX: In other words, Christ became a creature—a full-fledged participant in creation—just like all the other beings of creation we have been considering in our discussion of the Via Positiva?

---

603. In Col, ch. 1.16, p. 535.   604. DDN, n. 168, p. 53.   605. In Pss 49, p. 340.

AQUINAS: The Son assumed the visible creature, wherein he appeared, into the unity of his person, so that whatever can be said of that creature can be said of the Son of God.[606]

FOX: What else did Jesus do?

AQUINAS: Christ has done marvels, such as the nativity, the passion, the resurrection, and the ascension. Ecclesiasticus 42 says: "God has made the saints tell all the divine wonders, has God not? And Isaiah says: "Announce this to all the earth." And Psalm 92 says: "Tell it among all the nations, tell God's wonders to all peoples." Or, "the skies proclaim God's wonders," since the skies have sent a new star, one that rises to make known the Savior (Matt. 2). "We have seen his star in the east."[607]

FOX: And so the wonders of the universe multiplied as a result of Jesus. What else has the Incarnation accomplished?

AQUINAS: About the peace made through the Incarnation of Christ, nothing sufficient can be said. . . . Peace is spread across the world through Christ, and following this peace now we are freed from sin by the teaching and example of Christ and the interior inspiration of the Holy Spirit. We have learned not to make war either by sinning against ourselves or by opposing the holy angels. Rather, through this peace, in accordance with our virtue, we do the works that are of God, along with the holy angels. And this according to the providence and grace of Jesus, who does "all things in all things" and who makes that "ineffable peace" that is preordained from eternity. Through this peace we are reconciled with Christ himself in the Holy Spirit, who is the Spirit of delight and peace. Through Christ himself and in Christ himself we are likewise reconciled with God the Father.[608]

FOX: You say Christ is teacher. What are some of the things he teaches us?

AQUINAS: Christ is the way directing us to God.[609] The mystery of the Incarnation is fulfilled in the fact that God united the Godhead to the creature in a new way, or it might be better to say, God united the creature to the Godhead in a new way.[610]

FOX: It sounds like you are saying that creation itself and its relationship to the Creator is what the Incarnation is all about.

---

606. ST I, q. 43, a. 7, ad 1.   607. In Pss 18, p. 207.   608. DDN, n. 923, p. 343.   609. ST I, q. 2, Prologue.   610. Ibid. III, q. 1, a. 1, ad 1.

AQUINAS: The mystery of the divine Incarnation is what John says it is: "God has so loved the world that God sent the only begotten son and all who believe in him will not perish but will have eternal life" (John 3:16).[611]

FOX: What else does Christ teach us?

AQUINAS: He teaches the dignity of human nature . . . and the full participation in Divinity, which is truly humanity's happiness and the goal of human life.[612]

FOX: A "full participation in Divinity"? Please explain.

AQUINAS: Heaven had been closed to humankind through sin (Gen. 3:24). But it was opened through Christ. Consequently, when Matthew's gospel says "Behold a voice speaking from heaven, 'This is my son,'" notice that baptism not only makes one spiritual but makes one the child of God (John 1:12): "He gave them the power to become children of God."[613] Christ is the author of sanctification.[614]

FOX: What you are naming is so important, for it takes us beyond the traditional "second article of faith," redemption and Christ's role in that, to the "third article of faith," that of our sanctification. When you refer to sanctification, you seem to be returning to a theme you touched on earlier, that of deification, or our becoming children of God who are like God.

AQUINAS: The mystery of Christ's human nature is the mystery of godliness (1 Tim. 3:16).[615] The saints have their name from divine adoption. 1 John 3: "See what sort of charity God the Father has given us, so that we are called the children of God and that is what we are."[616] Divine virtue gives deification itself, that is, participation in the Godhead, which is through grace.[617]

FOX: What does it mean to say we are deified?

AQUINAS: A rational creature is said to be deified through the fact that, in its own way, it is united to God. Thus, the Godhead itself principally belongs to God, but secondarily and individually it belongs to those who are deified.[618] God deifies all who are turned toward the Godhead. "God deifies," I say, that is, God makes them gods through sharing the divine likeness, but not through their proper nature.[619]

---

611. Ibid., a. 2.   612. Ibid.   613. In Mt 3, p. 36.   614. ST I, q. 43, a. 7, ad 4.   615. Ibid. II-II, q. 1, a. 8.   616. In Is 56, p. 558.   617. DDN, n. 761, p. 286.   618. Ibid., n. 50, p. 17.   619. Ibid., n. 953, p. 356.

FOX: To be deified is to share in the selfhood of God?

AQUINAS: Human beings are called "gods" by participation.[620] The Godhead per se is a certain gift of God through which one becomes a sharer of Divinity. In like manner we also speak of "beauty per se," which is an effusion of beauty through which both the universal and particular beauty in things is caused and through which some things come to be beautiful.[621] God gives Godself for the deification of the converted, that is, in order that God may make like the Godhead those whom God converts to itself.[622] As long as human beings live innocently, they are gods, but when they sin they fall into the human condition. The psalmist says (82:6–7.): "I said to you, 'You are gods' . . . but you will die like human beings.'"[623]

FOX: It seems that the divine beauty we assimilate is not all of God's beauty.

AQUINAS: It is not possible that the entire beauty of God be received in any created mirror. But in certain created mirrors, on account of their purity and clarity, the entire beauty is received perfectly according to the capacity a creature possesses through its likeness to God. A creature's godlike form or godly beauty is always partial and not entire.[624]

FOX: By using the analogy of the mirror again, you are recalling the theme of our being images of God. Clearly, then, Christ's act of restoration is one of restoring us as images of God and mirrors of God.

AQUINAS: The image of the beholder is represented in a mirror, and in a mirror there is required a certain ability for receiving the image of another thing.[625]

FOX: For all your celebration of the divinity of human beings, you still qualify our divinity as somewhat different from God's?

AQUINAS: God's likeness in human beings can be compared to the likeness of a statue, say of Hercules, in marble. There is a likeness of form [between the statue and Hercules], but a disparity of nature.[626] We resemble God but God does not resem-

---

620. ST I-II, q. 3, a. 1, ad 1.   621. DDN, n. 938, p. 347.   622. Ibid., n. 824, p. 308.   623. In Mt 6.15. Version in Simon Tugwell, *Albert & Thomas: Selected Writings* (New York: Paulist Press, 1988), 474.   624. DDN, n. 525, p. 188.   625. Ibid., n. 524, p. 188.   626. CG IV, ch. 26 n. 7.

ble us, just as a painting is the expression of a painter but the painter is not the expression of her painting.[627]

FOX: To talk of our being "children of God" is to talk of God as parent.

AQUINAS: God is called the Father first of all from creation. Matthew 11: "I confess to you, Father, Lord of heaven and earth."[628] Deuteronomy says (32): "That one is your father who established you and made you and created you."[629]

FOX: Then Jesus teaching us to call God "Father" or "Abba" is his teaching us to pray to God as Creator, first of all.

AQUINAS: Second, God is called the Father by adoption, as in Romans 8: "You have accepted the spirit of the adoption of the children of God, to whom we cry, 'Abba, Father!'" Third, by instruction, as in Isaiah 38: "The father will make your truth known to the sons." Fourth, by correction, as in Proverbs 3: "For the Lord reproves the one he loves, even as a child in whom God takes pleasure."[630]

FOX: What else is implied in the word "father"?

AQUINAS: "Father" is relative to "child," and "child" implies freedom.[631]

FOX: A child inherits a father's world.

AQUINAS: The inheritance of the celestial fatherland is outstanding with the brightness of the divine vision. Consider Wisdom 6: "Radiant is that wisdom which is unfading and is easily seen by those who love it." It is also outstanding from the sweetness of divine love, as in Psalm 23: "How wonderfully my cup is overflowing." And from the familiarity of divine consolation, as in Wisdom 8: "The wonder in the sharing of her words." From the magnificence of God's working, as in Ecclesiasticus 43: "Thence strange and marvelous works." And from the greatness of God's exultation, as in Zechariah 8: "The house of Judah and the home of Israel will be a blessing." And from the consolation of companionship, as in Ezekiel 31: "no tree in the garden of God could rival its beauty."[632]

FOX: Thus you are saying that the wisdom that Christ, who is wisdom, teaches us is sweet, consoling, magnificent, exultant, and friendly.

---

627. ST I, q. 4, a. 3, ad 4.   628. In Jer 3, p. 587.   629. In Is, ch. 63, p. 571.   630. In Jer 3, p. 587.   631. In Mt 6, p. 70.   632. Ibid.

AQUINAS: From God comes all wisdom—and all order and all harmony, which is attendant to order.[633] Christ is the begotten Wisdom of the Father, as is indicated in 1 Corinthians 1:24: "Christ the power of God and the wisdom of God." . . . Since the Word of God is perfect and is one with God, Christ must be the perfect conception of the wisdom of God the Father.[634]

FOX: This recovery of Christ as wisdom is a very important movement in contemporary Scripture and cosmology. I am pleased you have it so richly in your theology. How would you characterize the kind of teaching Jesus did?

AQUINAS: Matthew's gospel (chapter 7) says that Jesus was admired because "he was teaching with power." Thus there was fulfilled in him what is said in Ecclesiastes 8:4: "His word is full of power." To "teach with power" means he had the power to penetrate the heart.[635]

FOX: How would you summarize the work of Christ in Jesus?

AQUINAS: The excellent work of Christ is threefold. One task he accomplished is that he extended himself to all of creation, that is, to the work of creation. John 1:3 says: "All things were made through him." In addition, in the work of enlightenment he extended himself to the rational creature in a unique way, for it is through Christ that they are enlightened, as John 1:9 says: "He was the true light which enlightens everyone who comes into this world." Third, was the work of justification, which pertains only to the holy ones who are vivified and made just through Christ by a life-giving grace. As John 1:4 puts it, "and that life was the light of humanity."[636]

FOX: I am struck by how for you redemption or justification is mentioned as only the third accomplishment of Christ following on creation and enlightenment. How far a fall/redemption Christianity has wandered from this awareness! And from an awareness of the Cosmic Christ.

AQUINAS: When Scripture says (John 1:26): "There is one standing in your midst," this means that Christ is in the midst of all things because he, as word, has filled all from the beginning of creation. "I fill heaven and earth" (Jer. 23:24).[637]

---

633. DDN, n. 650, p. 238.   634. CT I, 216.   635. In Mt 7, p. 81.
636. In Heb, Prologue, p. 666.   637. In Jn 1.26, n. 246.

FOX: Is there more that the Incarnation accomplished?

AQUINAS: The Incarnation puts the finishing touch to the whole vast work envisaged by God. For humanity, which was the last to be created, returns by a sort of circulatory movement to its first beginning, being united by the work of the Incarnation to the very origin of all things.[638]

FOX: And so Christ returns us to our Source and Origin.

It is time to turn to a question only lightly touched on up to now: that of evil. Some people will say, on listening to your exposition up to now of the blessing that creation is in the Via Positiva, that you are hopelessly optimistic. What role does evil play in your cosmology?

AQUINAS: No existing thing is corrupted through evil so as to be called evil as to its very substance or nature. For example, in an evil person, the substance and the nature of the person remain. We call something evil on account of this, that the measure that is the proportion of harmony and like dimension that is according to its nature is weakened through some defect of order. It is not totally destroyed, however, but remains to some small extent. That weakness, however, by which such a proportion is weakened, is not total, since if it were total it would destroy the subject itself.[639]

FOX: You are saying that the subject of evil remains good.

AQUINAS: The subject is not evil by nature, but a good with a defect. For that which is altogether devoid of good cannot be found among beings. Nothing is evil according to its nature.[640] There is no first principle of evil as there is of good. First, because the original principle of things is essentially good. Nothing can be essentially bad. Every being as being is good; evil does not exist except in a good subject.[641]

FOX: You are saying that nature is never of itself evil—and cannot be because it is blessing at its core?

AQUINAS: Nature by itself is not evil, but this is the evil of nature: not to be able to pursue the things that pertain to the perfection or completion of one's proper nature.[642]

---

638. CT I, 201.   639. DDN, n. 530, p. 193.   640. Ibid.   641. ST I, q. 49, a. 3.   642. DDN, n. 552, p. 206.

FOX: But doesn't the deer experience an evil on being eaten by a lion?

AQUINAS: If you take away from animals of this kind their fury and lust and other such passions, which some people call "evil"—and nonetheless they are not simply evils of their nature—if, I say, those things are taken away, their nature is straightaway destroyed. For when a lion has lost its animosity and pride it will be a lion no longer. And likewise a dog, when it has lost its fury and when it has been rendered gentle toward all, will no longer be a dog. This is clear in the utility that the dog performs in human affairs, in which the duty of the dog is to guard the home or other things of this kind. He does this by yielding to the familiar and by resisting the stranger.[643]

FOX: It seems that by putting evil within a larger context of cosmology you make it more palatable, if you will. Somehow what appears evil in a particular instance in fact serves a larger purpose.

AQUINAS: Each thing that is generative of beings contributes to the perfection of all. Therefore, it follows that evil is contributing to the completion of each thing, that is, of all, and that it gives bountifully to the whole, that is, to the all, which is not imperfect. It does this through itself, which is not inharmonious, since that which evil contributes accidentally toward the beauty and perfection of all is not inharmonious, insofar as good things follow accidentally from evils, as Augustine says in *The Enchiridion.*[644]

FOX: I am struck by how your cosmology provides a different setting for our grasp of evil. Our culture became mired in pessimism at the very time that we lost a cosmology.

AQUINAS: Every evil that God does or permits to be done is directed to some good—yet not always to the good of those toward whom the evil is done. Sometimes it is to the good of others, or of the whole universe: thus God directs the sin of tyrants to the good of the martyrs, and the punishment of the lost to the glory of divine justice.[645]

FOX: Why does evil happen?

---

643. Ibid., n. 546, p. 201.   644. Ibid., n. 490, p. 170.   645. ST I-II, q. 79, a. 4, ad 1.

AQUINAS: The things that come to be from irrational causes come to be either for the benefit of humanity or for the perfection of the universe, as is held in 3 Kings 13, when a certain prophet was killed by a lion, and this on account of his own fault. A mouse is killed by a cat for the preservation of the universe. For this is the order of the universe, that one animal lives from another.[646]

FOX: Try telling the mouse that!

AQUINAS: Since God provides universally for all being, it belongs to Divine providence to permit certain defects in particular effects in order that the total good of the universe may not be hindered. For if all evil were prevented, much good would be absent from the universe. A lion would cease to live, if there were no slaying of animals. And there would be no patience of martyrs if there were no tyrannical persecution.[647]

FOX: And there would be no cat if there were no mice to eat? It seems that a cosmology provides a context for our entire discussion of "evil" and teaches us how truly relative so much evil is.

AQUINAS: It is because we do not know God's reasons that we think many things happen without order or plan. We are like people who enter a carpenter shop and think that there is a useless multiplication of tools because they do not know how each one is used. But one who knows the trade will see that this number of tools exists for a very good reason.[648]

FOX: How can a good providence allow evil to happen?

AQUINAS: If complete equality were present in things, there would be but one created good, which clearly disparages the perfection of the creature. Now, it is a higher grade of goodness for a thing to be good because it cannot fall from goodness; lower than that is the thing that can fall from goodness. So the perfection of the universe requires both grades of goodness. But it pertains to the providence of the governor to preserve perfection in the things governed, and not to decrease it. Therefore, it does not pertain to divine goodness entirely to exclude from things the power of falling from the good. But evil is the consequence of this power, because what is able to fall does fall at

---

646. In Mt 10, p. 104.   647. ST I, q. 22, a. 2.   648. Ibid. I, q. 5, a. 5, ad 6.

times. And this defection of the good is evil. Therefore, it does not pertain to divine providence to prohibit evil entirely from things. [649]

FOX: Then what is the concern of providence when it comes to evil?

AQUINAS: It is the concern of divine providence not to safeguard all beings from evil, but to see to it that the evil that arises is ordained to some good. [650]

FOX: What about earthquakes, for example?

AQUINAS: God is said to make or create evils, insofar as God creates things that in themselves are good, yet are injurious to others; the wolf, though in its own kind a good of nature, is nevertheless evil to the sheep. [651]

FOX: But what about the evil that strikes us personally, for example, snakes that bite us or the sun that burns us?

AQUINAS: To those who judge things not by the nature thereof, but by the good they themselves can derive therefrom, everything that is harmful to themselves seems simply evil. For they do not reflect on the fact that what is in some way injurious to one person is beneficial to another, and that even to themselves the same things may be evil in some respects, but good in others. [652]

FOX: You appear to be discoursing on the relativity of evil and how important it is that we judge evil in its context—including the cosmological context, of which, in fact, we know very little. In short, I hear you calling for a kind of humility when it comes to making judgments about good and evil.

AQUINAS: The judgment on the goodness of anything does not depend upon its order to any particular thing, but rather upon what it is in itself, and on its order to the whole universe, wherein every part has its own perfectly ordered place. [653]

FOX: "What it is in itself"—this requires a lot of study. What are things in themselves? I suppose our entire discussion up to now has been about that topic, namely, that things are essentially blessings, and wonders and traces of God's wisdom and words of God. I am beginning to see why evil does not preoccupy you.

---

649. CG III, ch. 153 n. 3.   650. CT I, 142.   651. CG II, ch. 41 n. 13.
652. ST I, q. 65, a. 1, ad 2.   653. Ibid., q. 49, a. 3.

AQUINAS: Nothing can be essentially bad. For it was shown above that every being, as such, is good. Evil can exist only in good as in its subject.[654]

FOX: How much power does evil have?

AQUINAS: Although evil always lessens good, yet it never wholly consumes it. Thus, while good always remains, nothing can be wholly and totally bad. Every evil is caused by good.[655]

FOX: This sounds like the thinking of psychologist Alice Miller, who has worked for over twenty years with the worst criminals of Germany but who concludes that all human beings are born blessings and that it is the wounds inflicted on them, usually as children—"the killing of their souls," as she puts it—that turns them into killers.

AQUINAS: Evil does not wholly destroy good—no matter how much evil be multiplied, it can never destroy the good wholly.[656] In fact, there must always continue to be a subject for evil, if evil is to endure. Of course, the subject of evil is the good, and so the good will always endure.[657]

FOX: What about human evil or sin?

AQUINAS: Sin is nothing else than a deviation from that rectitude that an act ought to have, whether we speak of sin in nature, art, or morals.[658] Because good in itself is the object of the will, evil, which is the privation of good, is found in a special way in rational creatures that have a will.[659] Moral evil is present in a natural good.[660]

FOX: We will no doubt be pursuing that issue in greater depth in the Via Creativa when we discuss the choices that people make as a result of their creativity. What is lost when we sin?

AQUINAS: There is in sin a loss of the light of reason and consequently of the wisdom of God in the human being, since that light is a certain participation in divine wisdom. As Baruch 3:28 says: "Because they did not have wisdom, therefore they perished." . . . There is also due to sin a disfiguring of the likeness to God in the human being.[661]

FOX: Some people say that to celebrate our divinization or to seek it or even to theologize about it is sinful.

---

654. Ibid.   655. Ibid.   656. CG III, ch. 12 n. 1.   657. Ibid., n. 2.
658. ST I, q. 63, a. 1.   659. Ibid., q. 48, a. 5.   660. CG III, ch. 11 n. 7.
661. In Heb, ch. 1, p. 673.

AQUINAS: To desire to be as God according to likeness can come about in two ways. In one way, as to that likeness whereby everything is made to be like God. And so, if anyone desires to be godlike, he or she commits no sin, provided that they desire such likeness in due order, that is to say, that they may obtain it from God. But someone would sin if they were to desire to be like God even in the right way, on their own, and not from God's power. Or if one were to desire to create heaven and earth.[662]

FOX: Some people say that evil in life is a punishment for our sins.

AQUINAS: Even before the earth was accursed, thorns and thistles had been produced, either virtually or actually. But they were not produced in punishment of human beings, as if the earth, which human beings tilled to gain their food, produced unfruitful and noxious plants.[663]

FOX: Perhaps we've covered this topic already, but it seems necessary to bring it up in the context in which we are currently speaking. Some people say that matter is evil.

AQUINAS: Among many of the ancients it was commonly said that matter in and of itself is evil, because they did not distinguish between privation and matter. For privation is nonbeing and in that sense evil. Whence, like Plato, they said that matter was nonbeing and thus matter was in and of itself evil. But Aristotle in 1 *Physics* says that matter is neither nonbeing nor evil, save accidentally. In other words, by reason of a privation that happens to it. This is also what Dionysius says here, that "in matter evil is not, insofar as it is matter."[664]

FOX: Now I realize why you preferred Aristotle so much over Plato and also why you jeopardized your standing as a Christian theologian to set so much of your theology on the cosmology of this "pagan" or "heathen" scientist. It also follows from what you are saying that the body is not a curse or a cause of evil, is it?

AQUINAS: Some say that visible bodies are joined to spiritual creatures because of sin—a notion seemingly akin to the error of

---

662. ST I, q. 63, a. 3.   663. Ibid., q. 69, a. 2, ad 2.   664. DDN, n. 559, p. 207.

the Manicheans, who asserted that these visible things originated from an evil principle. This opinion is clearly contradicted by the authority of Sacred Scripture, for in regard to the production of visible creatures, Moses says: "God saw that it was good."[665] The cause of malice of spirit is not the body. In actual sin, it is manifest that malice of spirit comes from free will, which is used in an evil way in corporeal beings.[666] The evil in spirits does not come from matter, but from the inordinate motion of free will, which is sin itself.[667]

FOX: After all, matter is good as all creation is good, is it not?

AQUINAS: If in truth matter exists, since all things that exist come from the good, it follows that matter comes from the good. But that which comes from the good is not in and of itself evil. Therefore matter is not in and of itself evil.[668]

FOX: But doesn't matter lead us to sin and evil? For example, doesn't matter fuel the greed that urges us to live luxurious lifestyles or the lust for the beautiful body of someone other than our committed partner?

AQUINAS: Corporeal matter in some way attracts and diverts things joined with the soul. But it does so . . . because the matter in and of itself is good. For something can be an occasion of some evil that nonetheless is good in and of itself.[669] We do not do evil except from a desire for some good. For no one does the things that they do with regard to evil intentionally. Just as anyone who commits adultery is not enticed by the disorder that renders adultery evil, but by delight, which is something good. Therefore, the end of evil is good. And it follows that good is also the foundation of evil.[670] Indeed, evil is caused only by the good.[671]

FOX: You say "the end of evil is good." How can this be?

AQUINAS: Evil by itself is able to corrupt, but it is also able to generate—but only accidentally or on account of the good. Accidentally speaking, evil can be an efficient cause of good things.[672] Every evil is based on some good.[673]

FOX: But doesn't evil cause injury and harm?

---

665. CG II, ch. 44 nn. 13, 14.   666. DDN, n. 555, p. 207.   667. Ibid., n. 566, p. 208.   668. Ibid., n. 561, p. 207.   669. Ibid., n. 567, p. 208. 670. Ibid., n. 581, p. 214.   671. CG III, ch. 10 n. 1.   672. DDN, n. 492, p. 175.   673. CG III, ch. 11 n. 1.

AQUINAS: Something is called evil due to the fact that it causes injury. But this is only so because it injures the good, for to injure the evil is a good thing, since the corruption of evil is good.[674]

FOX: You keep returning to the absolute primacy of blessing and goodness in the universe and in things.

AQUINAS: Every being, as being, is good.[675] No being can be spoken of as evil, formally as being, but only insofar as it lacks being. Thus one is said to be evil because one lacks some virtue. And an eye is said to be evil because it lacks the power to see well.[676] All movement in the act of limping comes from the power to walk, while the defect is owing to a misshapen leg.[677]

FOX: It almost sounds as if, in your view of things, evil were not intended.

AQUINAS: Evil occurs in things apart from the intention of the agents.[678] For evil is different from the good that every agent intends. Therefore, evil is a result apart from intention.[679]

FOX: Can you give an example of what you mean?

AQUINAS: A defect in an effect and in an action results from some defect in the principles of the action. For instance, the birth of a monstrosity results from some corruption of the semen, and lameness results from a bending of the leg bone. Now, an agent acts in keeping with the active power that it has, not in accord with the defect of power to which it is subject. According as it acts, so does it intend the end. So, that which results as an effect of the defect of power will be apart from the intention of the agent. Now, this is evil. Hence, evil occurs apart from intention.[680]

FOX: Do you have another example?

AQUINAS: When the power of an organ of digestion is weak, imperfect digestive functioning and undigested humor result; these are evils of nature. Now, it is accidental to the agent, as agent, for it to suffer a defect in its power; for it is not an agent by virtue of the fact that its power is deficient, but because it possesses some power. If it were completely lacking in power, it would not act at all. Thus, evil is caused accidentally on the

---

674. Ibid., n. 4. 675. ST I, q. 5, a. 3. 676. Ibid., ad 2. 677. Ibid., q. 1, a. 6, ad 5. 678. CG III, ch. 4 n. 1. 679. Ibid., n. 2. 680. Ibid., n. 3.

part of the agent insofar as the agent is defective in its power. This is why we say that "evil has no efficient, but only a deficient cause."[681]

FOX: It seems appropriate to bring up the topic of original sin. What strikes me is that you first take up the topic in your *Summa theologiae* only in Part I-II, at question 81. In other words, halfway through your major opus. A great deal of discussion about the blessing of nature and God precedes that topic for you. How do you see original sin?

AQUINAS: Original sin is a disordered disposition arising from the loss of harmony essential to original justice, as illness in the body is a disordered disposition of the body caused by loss of balance essential to health. Thus original sin is spoken of as the "languor of nature."[682]

FOX: If original sin is a kind of illness in the soul, what parts of the soul are most infected by it?

AQUINAS: Original sin is related primarily to the will.[683]

FOX: How do you believe humanity received this loss of balance and harmony?

AQUINAS: Original sin is contracted not from the mother, but from the father, so that if Eve and not Adam had sinned, their children would not contract original sin. Whereas if Adam and not Eve had sinned, they would contract it.[684]

FOX: This idea of yours, obviously based on sexual misinformation, is ironic in what it says to the feminist movement. It would seem to encourage women to be angry with men, since it is through men that we all contract original sin.

We are coming to the end of our discussion on the Via Positiva. We have covered much theological ground, we might say, and it seems a bit incongruous to end on the note of evil and sin, since your message seems to be essentially to combat evil with good and to begin spirituality—as you begin your *Summa*— with the goodness and blessing of things.

AQUINAS: It is the mark of a happy disposition to see good rather than evil.[685]

---

681. Ibid., ch. 10 n. 7.　682. ST I-II, q. 82, a. 1.　683. Ibid., a. 3.
684. Ibid., q. 81, a. 5.　685. Ibid. II-II, q. 106, a. 3, ad 2.

FOX: "A happy disposition." Maybe this is why we begin our spiritual journeys with blessing, because blessing empowers us. It empowers us to love, healthy self-love, and to do loving action, thus returning blessing for blessing, and to return to our origins in blessing.

AQUINAS: It belongs to the wise to share their pleasures with those among whom they dwell, not lustful pleasures, which virtue shuns, but honest pleasures, as the psalmist says (133:1): "Behold how good and how pleasant it is for brethren to dwell together in unity."[686]

FOX: You speak of "lustful pleasures." What is lust?

AQUINAS: Lust in its most general sense is the unbridled desire for one's own pleasure.[687]

FOX: In other words, when pleasure it utterly selfish it is out of bounds. Just how much happiness can persons expect in this life? When you look at our culture, happiness seems rather rare a good deal of the time.

AQUINAS: A certain participation in happiness can be had in this life; but perfect and true happiness cannot be had in this life.[688] Joy is full when there remains nothing to be desired. But as long as we are in this world, the movement of desire does not cease in us, because it still remains possible for us to approach nearer to God by grace.[689]

FOX: Is anybody in the universe truly happy?

AQUINAS: Beatitude belongs to God in a very special manner.[690] Of God alone is it true that one's being is one's happiness.[691] The blessed are called blessed (*beati*) by reason of their assimilation to God's happiness.[692]

FOX: We seem to have returned to the subject of blessing once again. Where do we human beings come by happiness?

AQUINAS: Human happiness does not consist in believing things about God.[693]

FOX: What does human happiness consist in, then?

AQUINAS: By enjoying God, people are made happy.[694] Since no creature is capable of the joy truly belonging to God, it

---

686. Ibid., q. 114, a. 1, ad 3.   687. Viii De malo 1, ad 1.   688. ST I-II, q. 5, a. 3.   689. Ibid. II-II, q. 28, a. 3.   690. Ibid. I, q. 26, a. 1.
691. Ibid. I-II, q. 3, a. 2.   692. Ibid., ad 2.   693. CG III, ch. 40 n. 6.
694. ST I-II, q. 5, a. 2.

follows that this perfectly full joy is not something that enters into human beings; but rather, humanity enters into it, as Matthew puts it in his gospel (25:21): "Enter into the joy of your Lord."[695]

FOX: Again, you are sounding very panentheistic: you say we enter into joy. What causes this joy?

AQUINAS: Spiritual joy, which is about God, is caused by charity.[696]

FOX: And what do you mean by "charity" in this statement?

AQUINAS: Charity is love of God, whose good is unchangeable, since God is the divine goodness, and from the very fact that God is love, God is in those who love God by God's most excellent effect. According to 1 John (4:16), "Those who abide in love abide in God and God in them."[697]

FOX: And some persons enjoy God more than others?

AQUINAS: As to the attainment or enjoyment of this Good, one person can be happier than another; for the more anyone enjoys this Good, the happier they are. Now, the fact that one person enjoys God more than another results from that person being better disposed or ordered to the enjoyment of God. Thus, in this sense one person can be happier than another.[698]

FOX: But authentic happiness is always communal in some way, is it not?

AQUINAS: As regards the participation of happiness, our neighbor's soul is more closely associated with our own soul than even our body is.[699]

FOX: We are talking about pleasure and enjoyment again. No wonder the first path in creation spirituality is the path of the Via Positiva.

AQUINAS: The root of all virtue is the very desire for joy and happiness.[700]

FOX: Then joy builds up strength?

AQUINAS: Pleasure itself is a stronger motive of attraction than sorrow, for the lack of pleasure is a motive of withdrawal, since lack of pleasure is a pure privation.[701] There is no question in my mind that love is absolutely stronger than hate.[702]

---

695. Ibid. II-II, q. 28, a. 3.   696. Ibid., a. 1.   697. Ibid.   698. Ibid., a. 3.   699. Ibid., q. 26, a. 5, ad 2.   700. Viii De malo 1, ad 1.   701. ST II-II, q. 138, a. 1.   702. Ibid. I-II, q. 29, a. 3.

FOX: When I meditate on the themes we have discussed under the heading of the Via Positiva, and when I swim in the marvels that you have helped name for us—creation as "original freshness flowing from God" and "original goodness"; the holiness of "isness" or existence itself; the wonder of the universe in its parts and in its entirety; God as beauty and all things as participants in that beauty; the wisdom of things; the blessing of body and bodiliness; the greatness of the human soul and intellect and creativity with its capacity for the infinite; the goodness inherent in all being, including oneself; the response of delight and joy and pleasure in the gift of creation; the interconnectivity of all things; the activity of God cocreating with secondary causes; the Incarnation of Jesus Christ to underscore blessing and all this cosmic connecting, including the connecting between the human and the divine; the dependence of evil on good—all these meditations lead me to say simply, "Thank-You," to the Creator.

AQUINAS: Of all the divine gifts to be commemorated, the first and foremost was that of the Creation, which was called to mind by the sanctification of the Sabbath. This is why the reason for this precept is given in Exodus 20:11: "In six days the Lord made heaven and earth," etc.[703] The sanctification of the Sabbath [is] in memory of the creation of all things.[704]

FOX: Isn't this what ritual and worship are meant to be about—the great "Thank-You"? (*Eucharistein* in Greek, after all, means "thank-you.")

AQUINAS: Worship does not exist for God's sake but for ours. God has no need of human worship. It is we who need to demonstrate our gratitude for what we have received.[705]

FOX: And that which we first of all give thanks for is existence itself and creation itself?

AQUINAS: Worship under the Old Law was instituted in celebration of some divine gift, either in memory of past gifts or in sign of some gift to come. All the sacrifices were offered up for the same purpose. Now, of all the divine gifts to be commemorated, the chief was that of the Creation. . . . And of all the future blessings, the chief and final was the repose of the mind

---

703. Ibid., q. 100, a. 5, ad 2.   704. Ibid., a. 5.   705. In III Sent 9.1.3, sol. iii.

in God, either, in the present life, by grace, or, in the future life, by glory. This repose was also foreshadowed in the Sabbath-day celebration. Scripture says: "Call the Sabbath delightful and the holy of the Lord glorious" (Isa. 58:13). This is because these blessings are the first and foremost ones to be remembered by people, especially the faithful.[706]

FOX: I am struck that you say the primary reasons for worship are to give thanks for blessings past and future, beginning with the blessing of creation. One more reason for beginning our spiritual journeys with the Via Positiva! And for beginning our worship that way also, instead of with an anthropocentric reflection on sin and guilt.

AQUINAS: When we give thanks to God we bless God for God's very self—that is, we recognize God as good and as the giver of all good things. As Scripture says (Tob. 12:20): "Bless the God of heaven and tell all the wonders of God." And Daniel (3:57): "Bless all the works of the Lord to the Lord, praise and exalt God above all things for ever."[707]

FOX: And so you link our "Thank-You" to a theology of blessing, and you say that we can actually bless God?

AQUINAS: We bless God and God blesses us, but differently one from the other. For God to speak (and therefore to bless) is to make something, as Psalm 148:5 puts it: "God spoke, and things were made." Thus the blessing of God infuses things; it has the nature of causality. . . . But for us to speak (and therefore bless) is not causal, but it is to recognize or express. Thus our blessing is the same as to recognize the good.[708]

FOX: This is an important point you are making, for in our time of cynicism and despair brought on by our anthropocentric civilization, we have to dig hard for a consciousness of blessing. You emphasize worship as an act of gratitude for the blessing of creation. What about the salvific events that worship is also meant to commemorate?

AQUINAS: Other solemnities were celebrated [among the Jewish people] on account of certain particular blessings temporal and transitory, such as the celebration of the Passover in memory of the past grace of the liberation from Egypt, and as a sign

---

706. ST I-II, q. 100, a. 5, ad 2.   707. In II Cor, ch. 1, p. 301.   708. Ibid.

of the future Passion of Christ, which, though temporal and transitory, brought us to the repose of the spiritual Sabbath.[709]

FOX: That is an interesting reference to the Christ-event—that it brings us to "the repose of the spiritual Sabbath." You said that "we need to demonstrate our gratitude for what we have received." How do we do that?

AQUINAS: Gratitude depends chiefly on the heart.[710] The debt of gratitude flows from the debt of love.[711]

FOX: If gratitude comes chiefly from the heart, then our task is to enlarge the heart and stretch it.

AQUINAS: Isaiah says (ch. 54): "Spread out your tent," meaning that the heart must first be spread out on account of the greatness of the guest. Jeremiah says (23): "Do I not fill heaven and earth?—it is Yahweh who speaks." Also, we spread out the heart on account of the number of gifts, as Isaiah says (60): "You will see, and you will grow radiant, and your heart will be throbbing and full."[712]

FOX: I am amazed to read in your writings that the symbolic organ for the intellect is the heart![713] You don't sound like a rationalist to me. This expansion of the heart seems to come with an expansion of mind as well. Awe penetrates a frozen heart.

AQUINAS: The freezing or hardening of the heart is a disposition incompatible with love: while melting denotes a softening of the heart, whereby the heart shows itself to be ready for the entrance of the beloved.[714] Faith is in the heart.[715] The Holy Spirit dissolves the hardness of hearts. Luke says in his gospel (12): "I have come to set fire upon the earth."[716]

FOX: Thus our increased love and awe at creation opens our hearts to the Creator?

AQUINAS: Knowledge of the Creator through creatures is "evening knowledge."[717] Not any knowledge of things in their own nature can be called "evening knowledge," but only that which is referred to the praise of the Creator.[718]

FOX: Can we fail to praise the Creator?

---

709. ST I-II, q. 100, a. 5, ad 2.   710. Ibid. II-II, q. 106, a. 3, ad 2.
711. Ibid., q. 107, a. 1, ad 3.   712. In Is, ch. 54, p. 555.   713. In Jn 1.26, n. 246.   714. ST I-II, q. 28, a. 5.   715. In Pss 44, p. 326.   716. In Pss 45, p. 329.   717. ST I, q. 8, a. 16, ad 9.   718. Ibid., a. 17.

AQUINAS: There is no praise on the lips of sinners.[719]

FOX: So the ultimate sin against the Via Positiva is to fail to praise, to fail at gratitude—even to take for granted.

AQUINAS: The supreme degree of ingratitude is when a person fails to recognize the reception of a favor, whether by forgetting it or in any other way. . . . It pertains to this degree of ingratitude to esteem kindness as though it were unkindness.[720]

FOX: I think we do indeed esteem the kindness and blessing of creation as unkindness and even curse when we fail to be thankful for it. An original blessing theology certainly urges us to gratitude. Since this is expressed in praise, as you say, the obvious question remains: How are we encouraged to praise?

AQUINAS: The psalmist says, "I will sing to the Lord," that is, I will praise God. And, "you who fear the Lord, praise God" (Ps. 22). For praise of God is very strong in assailing the devil, as Matthew says (17): "This kind of demon is not cast out except by prayer and fasting." And Habakkuk says (3): "I will rejoice in the Lord." And we do this because kindness has been shown to us. There are certain temporal goods that the Lord has given, as in Matthew 15: "He has given them his goods, and to one he has given five talents, etc." Likewise, we have been given spiritual goods, which are good graces and virtues, as in 1 Corinthians (12): "The varieties of the graces. . . . "[721] God, who is "per se goodness," first brings goodness forth and distributes to created things this gift that is per se being. This God is praised.[722]

FOX: Where does praise come from?

AQUINAS: The praise of God ought to come from joyfulness of heart (*jucunditate cordis*).[723] For the principle of praise is an interior joy.[724] Prayer itself proceeds from trust.[725] What I have in my heart, I confess with my mouth.[726]

FOX: Even though praise is good for us, a kind of self-love, nevertheless it is voluntary, isn't it? We can choose not to praise, which would constitute a kind of sin of omission.

AQUINAS: Both angels and human beings naturally seek their own good and perfection. This is to love self. Hence angel and

---

719. In Is, ch. 6, p. 457.   720. ST II-II, q. 107, a. 2.   721. In Pss 12, p. 183.   722. DDN, n. 641, p. 236.   723. In Pss 38, p. 297.   724. In Pss 33, p. 265.   725. In Pss 38, p. 297.   726. In Pss 50, p. 349.

human being naturally love self, insofar as by natural appetite each desires what is good for the self. On the other hand, each loves self with the love of choice, insofar as from choice one wishes for something that will benefit oneself.[727]

FOX: Our heart-work culminates in praise, then?

AQUINAS: Only God can know the thoughts of hearts and affections of wills, because the rational creature is subject to God alone, and only God can work in it.[728] The "One who searches hearts" is God, and this is unique to God. "God who searches hearts and reins" (Ps. 7:10). God is said to search hearts, not in the sense that God discovers the secrets of our hearts by investigating them, but because God knows clearly all that is hidden in our hearts.[729]

FOX: How do we praise God?

AQUINAS: Love of God presupposes knowledge of God. And because this knowledge does not rest in creatures, but, through them, tends to something else—love begins there and then goes on to other things by a circular movement, so to speak: for knowledge begins from creatures and tends toward God. Love, on the other hand, begins with God as the last end and passes on to creatures.[730]

FOX: Who is this God we praise who alone knows our heart-thoughts and alone works in our hearts?

AQUINAS: The Godhead is before all days and before all times.[731] God is called ancient or elder because of God's antiquity, namely, that the Godhead always existed "from the beginning" of eternity. But God is called "new" or "younger" because God is ancient "without old age," that is, without any deficiency or even change.[732]

FOX: Then God is beginning and end, elder but ever young?

AQUINAS: Since old age and antiquity seem to pertain to a beginning on account of their priority in youth and toward an end on account of their posteriority, and through the fact that both are attributed to God, we are taught that God proceeds through all things from the beginning to the end.[733] God is said to be

---

727. ST I, q. 60, a. 3.   728. Ibid., q. 57, a. 4.   729. In Rom, ch. 8, p. 85.   730. ST II-II, q. 27, a. 4, ad 2.   731. DDN, n. 860, p. 324.   732. Ibid., n. 864, p. 324.   733. Ibid.

before all ages because God is the lifetime of lifetimes, that is, the measure of all measurings.[734]

FOX: How else is God praised?

AQUINAS: Although God is above all wisdom, God is praised in Scripture both as mind and as reason and as knower.[735]

FOX: How is God known as "reason"?

AQUINAS: God is praised in Sacred Scripture as "reason" because God is called the Word there according to the passage in John 1: "And God was the Word." For *Logos* in Greek, as Augustine says, signifies both reason and word.[736]

FOX: How else do we praise God?

AQUINAS: Even the very ones who were experienced concerning Divinity, such as the apostles and prophets, praise God as the Cause of all things from the many things caused. They praise God as good (Luke 18); as beautiful (Song of Songs 1); as wise (Job 9); as beloved (Song of Songs 5); as God of gods (Ps. 50): as holy of holies (Dan. 9); as eternal (Bar. 4): as manifest (Job 14); as the cause of the ages (Eccles. 24); as the bestower of life (Acts 17); as wisdom (1 Cor. 1): as mind or intellect (Isa. 29.); as reason (Isa. 63: "I who speak justice"); as the knower (2 Tim. 2); as the one possessing in advance all the treasures of universal knowledge (Col. 2); as virtue (1 Cor. 1); as the powerful (Ps. 89); as King of kings (Apoc. 19); as the Ancient of days (Dan. 7); as without age and unchanging (James 1); as salvation (Matt. 1); as justice, or as one justifying, as it were, deliverance or redemption according to another translation (1 Cor. 1); as magnitude exceeding all things (Job 23); as in the light breeze (3 Kings 19). And they say that God is even in minds or hearts (Eph. 3); in spirits (Wis. 7); and in bodies (1 Cor. 6); in heaven and on earth (Jer. 23); and at the same time in the same place, that is, with regard to the same material, they say that the same one is worldly, that is, in the world (John. 1); involved in the world (Eccles. 24); above the world (Isa. 66); and supercelestial, or above the heavens (Ps. 113: "The Lord on high above all the nations whose glory is above all the skies"); supersubstantial (Matt. 6); the sun (Mal. 4); a constellation, that is, a star (Apoc. 22); fire (Deut. 4); water (John 4); air (Joel 2); and dew (Hos. 14);

---

734. Ibid., n. 630, p. 235.   735. Ibid., n. 719, p. 271.   736. Ibid., n. 735, p. 277.

cloud (Hos. 6); stone (Ps. 118); rock (1 Cor. 10); and all the other beings attributed to God as cause. And the Divine One is none of these beings insofar as God surpasses all things.[737]

FOX: We will surely be dealing with this last point in our next conversation, that on the Via Negativa. What so strikes me about this list of divine names that you offer for our praise, however, is two things: first, hearing so many names gives us permission, if you will, to trust our experience, hearts, minds, and imagination to birth a multitude of names and images for God. No one image suffices. How far this takes us from a fundamentalist need to pin God down to one name! Second, you are connecting God to the physics of your time and that of the Bible when you call God earth, air, fire, water—God as the elements of the universe, because God is cause of them and is present in them all, as we saw in our discussion of panentheism. As science learns more about the universe, we learn more names with which to praise God.

It would seem then, that if the gift of being created is the first and foremost of all divine gifts, and if worship is gratitude publicly and cosmically expressed, then a true renewal of worship would require a new immersion of humanity in the blessings of creation such as we have discussed in the Via Positiva. If we fail to do this we sin.

AQUINAS: The sin of acedia is opposed to the precept about hallowing the Sabbath day. For this precept, insofar as it is a moral precept, implicitly commands the mind to rest in God. And sorrow of the mind about the divine good is contrary to this.[738]

FOX: It would seem then that acedia, which is the opposite of the Via Positiva, is a serious evil in the human being.

AQUINAS: Mortal sin is so called because it destroys the spiritual life, which is the effect of charity, whereby God dwells in us. Wherefore any sin that by its very nature is contrary to charity is a mortal sin by reason of its genus. And such is acedia, because the proper effect of charity is joy in God, while acedia is sorrow about spiritual good inasmuch as it is a divine good.[739]

---

737. Ibid., n. 98, p. 30.   738. ST II-II, q. 35, a. 3, ad 1.   739. Ibid., a. 3.

FOX: Describe acedia in greater detail, please, for it seems to me that the spiritual depression of our culture, which is without joy and cosmology, is a serious problem.

AQUINAS: Acedia is sadness about an inward, eternal good.[740] According to John Damascene, it is an oppressive sorrow that so weighs upon one's mind that one wants to do nothing. Hence acedia implies a certain weariness of work. Others define it as a sluggishness of the mind, which neglects to begin good.[741]

FOX: It almost sounds like what we call "burnout" today. Are you saying acedia is a sin?

AQUINAS: Whatever is forbidden in Holy Scripture is a sin. Now such is acedia, for it is written (Eccles. 6:26): "Bow down thy shoulder, and bear her," that is, spiritual wisdom, "and be not grieved (*acedieris*) with her bands." Therefore acedia is a sin.[742]

FOX: But surely not all sorrow is a sin?

AQUINAS: Since spiritual good is a certain good, sorrow about spiritual good is evil in itself. And that sorrow that is about a real evil is also evil in its effect: it so oppresses people as to draw them away entirely from good deeds. Hence the Apostle (2 Cor. 27) did not wish those who repented to be "swallowed up with overmuch sorrow." [743]

FOX: You are not saying that all our sadness is blameworthy, are you?

AQUINAS: Sorrow in itself calls for neither praise nor blame. In fact, moderate sorrow for evil calls for praise. Yet sorrow over good or immoderate sorrow over evil does call for blame. It is in this sense that acedia is said to be a sin.[744]

FOX: Where does acedia come from? How do we fall into acedia?

AQUINAS: Acedia comes from a shrinking of the mind—not from any spiritual good but from that to which we should cleave as a duty, namely, to the goodness of God.[745]

FOX: A shrinking of the mind—how important it is, then, to teach awe and wonder and cosmology and thereby expand the mind to what you described earlier as our "infinite" capacities for expansion!

---

740. xi De malo 1, ad 4.   741. ST II-II, q. 35, a. 1.   742. Ibid.   743. Ibid.   744. Ibid., ad 1.   745. xi De malo 3, ad 4.

AQUINAS: The very neglect to consider the divine gifts arises from acedia.[746] Isaiah writes: "Raise your eyes on high." Here he is addressing those who despair, and first of all by mentioning the divine majesty [known] from the creation of things. "Who created?" he asks, meaning who created the things in the skies. The psalmist says (148): "God spoke, and things were made; God commanded, and they were created."[747]

FOX: So if we were to cease taking for granted the creation of which we are a part, we would learn to marvel and would banish acedia.

AQUINAS: The more we think about spiritual goods, the more pleasing they become to us, and immediately acedia dies away.[748] A person's mind is said to be magnified or expanded by pleasure.[749] Isaiah talks about "an army" of celestial wonders, such as the heavens, the stars and angels. Consider Psalm 147: "The One who numbers the multitude of the stars, and calls all things by their names."[750] You see, it is very delightful to know the knowledge of all things that are in the world.[751]

FOX: You are saying that recognizing creation as blessing heals us of the sin of acedia, but I have to honestly report that I believe that Christianity's emphasis on redemption by Christ has cut us off from experiencing creation as blessing.

AQUINAS: We can consider the goodness and effect of divine love from a fourfold perspective. First, because God made us to exist. Second, because God made us in God's own image and rendered us capable of divine joy. Third, because God repaired the brokenness of humanity due to sin. And fourth, because God gave the divine Son for our salvation.[752]

FOX: I appreciate the order in which you lay out the love of God for us. A kind of intellectual laziness and self-satisfaction seem to accompany all anthropocentrism, whether religious or secular. What a pity that we do not employ the minds God has given us by which to examine the wonders and blessings of life that we so easily take for granted.

AQUINAS: The light of reason is nothing other than a certain participation in the divine light.[753] God is light; and whoever

---

746. ST II-II, q. 20, a. 4, ad 3. 747. In Is, ch. 40, p. 529. 748. ST II-II, q. 35, a. 1, ad 4. 749. Ibid. I-II, q. 33, a. 1. 750. In Is, ch. 40, p. 529. 751. In Pss 26, p. 238. 752. In Eph 2.4, p. 458. 753. In Pss 30, p. 253.

approaches the light is illuminated, as Isaiah said: "Rise, through longing (*per affectum*), and be enlightened."[754]

FOX: Blessing as illumination.

AQUINAS: When a person is happy, all things seem clear to him or her; but when they are sad, all things seem dark to them. Therefore the psalmist says: "you light my lamp, O Lord," since you have given me prosperity and you give it continually. And he says, "lighten my darkness," meaning that if any adversity remains in me, drive and remove it from me. Consider Proverbs (20): "The lamp of the Lord is the human spirit."[755]

FOX: It would seem that if our culture were not able to restore the experience of illumination or blessing we would be inundated by sins of despair and acedia instead.

AQUINAS: Sins against hope are more dangerous than sins against faith or against love—for when hope dies we lose heart and we flounder in wickedness.[756] Despair is the path to unrestrained sin. There is nothing more dangerous than teaching that would cast people into the pit of despair.[757]

FOX: It would follow, then, that our sins of omission in our failing to teach people wonder, awe, and a living cosmology contribute to the "most dangerous of all sins"—that of despair. This is one more reason for our teaching the Via Positiva in our time, one that awakens that "original freshness" that you said early in our conversation is present in all creation.

AQUINAS: When a person is joyful, that person has greater hope. And, on the other hand, those who are sorrowful fall more easily into despair.[758] Isaiah says "my eyes have grown small," meaning the eyes are dilated through depression.[759]

FOX: And just how do we open up our eyes and make them fuller?

AQUINAS: Isaiah says: "Look up on high," because our eyes are first lifted up by the elation of the heart. As the psalmist puts it (131): "Lord, my heart has not been exalted, nor have my eyes been lifted up." A second way is through the curiosity of questioning. Job says (18): "When you think great things, your eyes

---

754. In Pss 33, p. 266.   755. In Pss 17, p. 202.   756. ST II-II, q. 20, a. 3.   757. CG IV, ch. 71, n. 6.   758. ST II-II, q. 20, a. 4, ad 2.   759. In Is, ch. 38, p. 525.

are astonished." And third, our eyes are opened by contemplation. As Isaiah says (40): "Lift up your eyes on high, and see the joy which is coming to you."[760]

FOX: Once again, you seem to have underscored the importance of our recovering a Via Positiva in our lives and civilization wherein we can exalt the heart, pursue our scientific questioning, and contemplate with joy. Brother Thomas, this is your last chance to say something about the Via Positiva. What do you want to say?

AQUINAS: Remember this: God's love for us is no greater in heaven than it is right here and now.[761]

---

760. Ibid.   761. QQ 5, q. 3, a. 6, ad 2.

Second Conversation:

ON THE VIA NEGATIVA

*God is beyond all that which we can
comprehend by the intellect.*

(DDN, n. 180, p. 57)

FOX: In our previous conversation we spoke about the Via Positiva, the experience of the God of light, the cataphatic God, who is the "freshness" of creation, as you put it. Now let us direct our attention to the Via Negativa, the apophatic God, the God of darkness, mystery, silence, and grief. Brother Thomas, we experience nothingness at times. Where does this experience come from? After all, we established in the Via Positiva discussion that things are good and beautiful and images of Divinity.

AQUINAS: Even though God is supremely good and supremely generous, God cannot supremely give the Godhead to creatures, for they cannot receive the entirety of the divine goodness.[1]

FOX: You are saying that creatures, for all their glory, also exhibit limits and weaknesses, and that this shows especially when it comes to Divinity's desire to give of itself?

AQUINAS: The reason why no created species can represent the divine essence is plain: for nothing finite can represent the infinite as it is; but every creature is finite.[2] To be incapable of receiving love's gift is a mark of great weakness. To be able to sustain it is a mark of great strength.[3]

FOX: I find your point that it takes great strength to receive and sustain love very important indeed. In our culture we tend to praise love that gives in preference to love that receives. But you also speak of our weakness in not receiving love's gift. Where does this weakness come from?

AQUINAS: Creatures are vanity insofar as they exist on the brink of nothingness. They are not vanity, however, insofar as they are made to God's likeness.[4]

---

1. In I Sent 2.1.4.   2. In Jn 1.18, n. 211.   3. DP, q. 9, a. 9.   4. DC, 1, ad 11.

FOX: You seem to be dancing a dialectical dance, a both/and process, wherein on the one hand you celebrate the splendor of creatures, and on the other hand you name their darkness.

AQUINAS: Created things are darkness insofar as they proceed from nothing, but insofar as they proceed from God, they participate in some likeness of God and thus lead to God's likeness.[5]

FOX: How is it that creatures—which you hailed in the Via Positiva as traces of God and godlike in their existence—proceed from nothing?

AQUINAS: Positively speaking, the leaning in creatures toward nothingness is merely their dependence on the causal principle of their being.[6]

FOX: And we have experiences of nothingness at times. Could you give some examples of this?

AQUINAS: John the Baptist spoke of "the strap of whose sandal I am not worthy to unfasten," which is the least service that can be done for another human being. It is clear from this that John had made great progress in the knowledge of God, so far that from the consideration of God's infinite greatness, he completely lowered himself and said that he himself was nothing. So did Abraham, when he recognized God, and said (Gen. 18:27), "I will speak to my Lord, although I am but dust and ashes." And so also did Job, saying, "Now I see you, and so I reprove myself, and do penance in dust and ashes" (Job 42:5). Isaiah also said, after he had seen the glory of God, "Before him all the nations are as if they are not" (Isa. 40:17).[7]

FOX: It seems that a kind of tendency toward nothingness is part of our makeup and that we are bound to experience this reality in the Via Negativa.

AQUINAS: Creatures do come forth from nothing and creatures would go back there if God permitted it.[8] A creature has this tendency to nonexistence of itself, since it is produced from nothing.[9]

FOX: And so our existence is bounded by nothingness—we are surrounded by nothingness?

---

5. DV, q. 18, a. 2, ad 5.   6. In II Sent 19.1.1, ad 7.   7. In Jn 1.27, n. 249.   8. DP, q. 5, a. 4, ad 10.   9. ST I, q. 104, a. 3, ad 1.

AQUINAS: Creatures are kept existing by God. . . . Every creature is preserved by God, for every creature's existence so depends upon God that it could not subsist for a moment but would cease to be anything if God by the divine action did not preserve it in existence.[10] If God for even a moment were to withhold the divine power from the things God established, all would return to nothing and cease to be.[11]

FOX: You make our existence, as glorious as it is, sound extremely precarious.

AQUINAS: Absolutely speaking, God could withdraw the divine sustaining action and things would cease to be. But relative to the divine wisdom and prevision, God would not have it so. "For death was not God's doing; God takes no pleasure in the extinction of the living. For God created all things that they might be" (Wis. 1:14)—not that they might fall into nothingness.[12]

FOX: And so our nothingness experiences are not something to be afraid of? You might say that we can trust the experience of nothingness because we can trust that existence endures?

AQUINAS: The nature of creatures demonstrates that none of them is reduced to nothingness—either because they are immaterial and so in them there is no potency to nonbeing, or because they are material, in which case they remain at least with respect to their matter, which is incorruptible, that is, it exists as the subject of generation and corruption. Likewise, to reduce something to nothingness does not pertain to the demonstration of God's graciousness: rather, the divine power and goodness are shown forth through things being conserved in being. Hence it must be said without any qualification that nothing at all is reduced to nothingness.[13]

FOX: It seems that no matter what we undergo in the Via Negativa, the Via Positiva remains firm. I hear you saying that our nothingness experiences are grounded in fact and are both real and salvific—that in undergoing them there is power to heal and be healed. Darkness is a teacher and a way of touching wisdom itself.

---

10. Ibid., a. 1.   11. In Jn 1.10, n. 135.   12. QQ 4, q. 3, a. 4.   13. ST I, q. 104, a. 4.

AQUINAS: We are taught not only by learning about things but by undergoing them. The secrets of Divinity can be reached only through a spiritual rebirth.[14]

FOX: A spiritual rebirth seems to imply some kind of dying as well. Birth is a kind of death and death a kind of birth. Also, a return to our origins seems to be part of a "rebirth" experience. Yet you have established that nothingness is part of our origins. You have spoken of the "secrets of divinity" and the "wonder" that is hidden from us.

AQUINAS: The cause at which we wonder is hidden from us.[15]

FOX: Please elaborate on this respect for mystery that I sense plays so important a role in your Via Negativa teaching.

AQUINAS: Take note of Isaiah's saying "hidden," because the great works of God are hidden first of all on account of their size. Matthew 19 says: "Not all grasp this word." And John 3 says: "If I spoke earthly things to you, and you do not believe, how will I speak of heavenly things to you, and you will believe?" Second, they are hidden on account of their dignity. Matthew 13 says: "It has been granted to us to know the mystery of the reign of God, but to others in parables." Third, they are hidden on account of the unsuitableness of others, as Matthew says (7): "Don't give what is holy to dogs."[16]

FOX: The mysteries of God remain just that—mysteries.

AQUINAS: Jeremiah says that "there was a sealed book." That book . . . has been sealed by the depths of the mysteries. First Corinthians 13 says: "For the spirit utters mysteries." An apostle is one so called who has brought forth the Sacred Scriptures: "It has been granted to you to know the mystery of the reign of God" (Matt. 13). It has also been sealed in the variety of its images, as also with the other books of the prophets. Proverbs 1 says: "Perceive the meaning of proverbs and obscure sayings, the sayings of the sages and their riddles." Hosea 12 says: "I have multiplied my visions, and through the prophets I will deal out death."[17]

FOX: The mystery of the reign of God is hidden.

AQUINAS: In truth, the way of the spirit is hidden. Thus Psalm 31:20 says: "How great the wealth of your sweetness, Lord,

---

14. In Jn 3.1, n. 431.   15. DP, q. 6, a. 2.   16. In Is 24, p. 500.   17. In Lam, Preamble, 668.

which you have hidden from those who fear you!" For since it is hidden, therefore also few find it. But some even find it and withdraw, and concerning these it was mentioned in Luke 9:62, "No one putting his hand to the plow and looking back is fit for the reign of God."[18]

FOX: And so the God we encounter remains radically mysterious.

AQUINAS: We are united to God as to One Unknown.[19]

FOX: Tell us more about this "unknown" God.

AQUINAS: It should be understood that there is something about God that is altogether unknown to persons in this life, namely, what God is. For this reason Paul found in Athens the altar inscribed to an "unknown God." This is so because human knowledge begins from those things that are connatural to it, that is, from creatures known from sense. Yet these are not proportionate to representing the divine essence.[20]

FOX: You have spoken of the "secrets of God," of the "hiddenness" of the God of wonder, and of God as one "unknown." What are some practical implications of encountering this apophatic God of darkness?

AQUINAS: God is worshiped in silence.[21] God is beyond all speech.[22]

FOX: Why is this?

AQUINAS: God alone knows the depths and riches of the Godhead, and divine wisdom alone can declare its secrets.[23]

FOX: You are saying that before the great mystery of Divinity we are necessarily rendered dumb or silent?

AQUINAS: There are various kinds of silences: that of dullness; that of security; that of patience; and that of a quiet heart.[24]

FOX: And when you speak of silence in the Via Negativa, I take it you are speaking of that of a quiet heart?

AQUINAS: The mind needs to be present to itself and to God before it is excited by ideas taken from the senses.[25]

---

18. In Mt 7, p. 78. 19. ST I, q. 12, a. 13, ad 1. 20. In Rom, ch. 1, p. 15. 21. DT ii.1 ad 6. 22. DDN, n. 77, p. 27. 23. In I Sent, Prologue. 24. In Jer 8, p. 600. 25. DV, q. 10, a. 2, ad 5.

FOX: I hear you—one of the greatest intellects of Western civilization, who spoke to us of the "infinity" of our intellects in our first conversation—here praising mindlessness and emptying of the mind. You certainly do practice the both/and dialectic that you preach! But why is it that silence is so valuable a path to God?

AQUINAS: The knowledge by which God is seen through creatures is not a knowledge of God's essence, but a knowledge that is dark and mirrored and from afar. We do not know what God is by all these acts of knowing, but what God is not. The perfect way in which God is known in this present life is by taking away all creatures and everything understood by us.[26]

FOX: Thus letting go is a deep avenue to the God experience. Indeed, you have called it the "perfect way" to God in this life.

AQUINAS: The mind's greatest achievement is to realize that God is far beyond anything we think.[27] This is the ultimate in human knowledge: to know that we do not know God.[28]

FOX: I hear you insisting on the preeminence of the mystery behind the mystery of God.

AQUINAS: God exceeds all speech. God is ineffable and nobody can sufficiently sound God's praises.[29] The chief way to consider the divine essence is the way of negation, for by its immensity the divine essence transcends every form attained by the human intellect. And so in apprehending it we do not know what it is. But by knowing what it is not we get some knowledge of it, and the more things we are able to deny of it, the nearer we come to knowing it.[30]

FOX: I sense that in the Via Positiva you were in pursuit of the God of life and existence and beauty and wisdom; but now you are in hot pursuit of "the divine essence," a phrase you repeat often. I am touched by your spiritual ambition in the good sense of the word, that is, that you want to encounter the essence of God.

AQUINAS: Since the perfection of a human being consists in one's union with God, it is required that one should in every

---

26. In Jn 1.18, n. 211.   27. DDN, n. 83, p. 28.   28. DP, q. 7, a. 5, ad 14.   29. In Dec I, p. 302.   30. CG I, ch. 14 n. 2.

possible way cling to and be led toward divine things. And that with everything that is in one.[31]

FOX: And one does not have to worry about being overly ambitious in one's search for God-experience?

AQUINAS: The more one occupies oneself with things that are of more worth than oneself, provided it be within the limits of one's measure, the more one will be benefited.[32]

FOX: It seems that in the Via Negativa we come up against what you call our "limits" in our knowledge of God.

AQUINAS: It is indeed not lawful, while we are in this world, so to scrutinize divine mysteries that it is our intention to grasp them completely. . . . Concerning divine things, we cannot know what they are, but what they are not.[33]

FOX: And you are pursuing in depth a knowledge of God's essence?

AQUINAS: Wisdom consists not only in knowing that God exists, but in attaining to a knowledge of what God is. But in this life we can know this only insofar as we know what God is not.[34]

FOX: And why is this?

AQUINAS: Since God infinitely transcends all creatures, no creature can be moved toward God in such a way as to be equal to God, whether in what it receives from the Godhead, or in what it knows of the Godhead.[35]

FOX: And the only way to know God's essence is the way of paradox, that is, of letting go of our mind's efforts to reach God.

AQUINAS: We not only gather information about divine things —we also submit ourselves to them. By that I mean that we do more than study things with our mind; we also fall in love with them and learn to cherish them.[36]

FOX: We did much falling in love and becoming awestruck and learning to cherish in the Via Positiva. But now you are speaking of another kind of cherishing, that of letting go and being in silence. I sense that the silence you are celebrating is a kind of *letting go* of images that allows *letting be* to happen. Letting go

---

31. DT ii, a. 1.   32. Ibid., ad 1.   33. Ibid., ad 4.   34. DV, q. 10, a. 12, ad 7.   35. DT ii, a. 1, ad 7.   36. DDN, n. 191, p. 59.

of our language for God allows the depths of Divinity to emerge. This would seem to lead to the emergence of even more wonder, since it allows a greater Divinity to break through.

AQUINAS: When God is worshiped in silence we come to appreciate how far God surpasses our comprehension.[37] God exceeds the comprehension of reason.[38] Demonstrative knowledge about God leaves so much unsaid.[39]

FOX: What a potent case you make for moving beyond the rational.

AQUINAS: The highest peaks of wisdom are beyond all human reasoning. "Hidden from the eyes of all the living" (Job 28:21); and again, "God makes the divine hiding place in darkness" (Ps. 18:11). These are the places where wisdom is said to dwell, and they are discovered by dedicated guides: "Your spirit searches all things, yes even the deep things of God" (1 Cor. 2:10).[40]

FOX: I hear you demonstrating one difference between knowledge and wisdom—wisdom includes mystery and response to an awe that carries us beyond knowledge and analysis or, as we would say today, beyond the work of the left hemisphere of the brain.

AQUINAS: A created mind may see God but cannot know all that God has done and can do: that would be to comprehend the divine power.[41] God is represented by no class, no definition, no genus, no difference.[42]

FOX: Why must our left-brain efforts to define God always fall short?

AQUINAS: Logical categories may frame the physical world, but not the first principles of reality. God's infinite simplicity rules out any attempt to classify God by genus and species; consequently, God is not the subject for scientific definition.[43]

FOX: And in the presence of the "infinite simplicity" of God we are to be and not to think, much less analyze. Are you saying that God really has no name?

AQUINAS: Divinity is incomprehensible. It can be neither embraced nor designated by a name.[44]

---

37. DT ii, 1, ad 6.   38. ST I, q. 1, a. 1.   39. CG III, ch. 39 n. 6.
40. IL.   41. ST I, q. 12, a. 8.   42. CG I, ch. 25 n. 10. Gilby translation.
43. DEE, 7.   44. In Eph 1.21, p. 454.

FOX: Why are you so confident that God is ineffable?

AQUINAS: The manifestation of the divine light is hidden from us on account of its excellence and simplicity.[45] No one is so wise whose knowing is not greatly surpassed by the excellence of divine brightness. Thus Job says: "Each one sees from afar," that is, the knowing of human beings is far from the perfect comprehension of divine essence. For it is not possible for human beings to know except through the divine works, yet these are infinitely distant from the excellence of the divine essence. In addition, human beings do not perfectly understand the divine works: Job concludes from this that God surpasses the knowledge of humanity through the divine excellence, as in Psalm 139: "Your knowledge is wonderful" and he adds, "behold the greatness of God transcending our knowledge." For the fact that God cannot be known by us does not happen because of a defect in God, as happens concerning motion and time, but because of the divine excellence.[46]

FOX: So the "divine excellence" is just too vast for creatures to grasp—it seems that you are giving us two reasons for our silence before the mystery of God.

AQUINAS: Creatures fail to represent their Creator adequately. Consequently, through them we cannot arrive at a perfect knowledge of God. Another reason for our imperfect knowledge is the weakness of our intellect, which cannot assimilate all the evidence of God that is to be found in creatures.[47]

FOX: I like that phrase of yours—that we "cannot assimilate all the evidence of God that is to be found in creatures" — for it celebrates the essential ineffability of our ecstatic experiences. It underscores the depths of the divine mystery we encounter in creation.

AQUINAS: The Apostle Paul says: "For the invisible things of God, from the creation of the world, are clearly seen, being understood by the things that are made; God's eternal power also and divinity" (Rom. 1:19). But this knowledge is imperfect, because not even creatures can be perfectly comprehended by human beings, and also because creatures are unable to represent God perfectly, since the excellence of the cause infinitely

---

45. DDN, n. 522, p. 188.   46. In Job, ch. 36, p. 122.   47. ST I, q. 5, a. 2, ad 11.

surpasses its effect. Therefore in Job 11:7 the question is put: "Might you comprehend the steps of God, and will you find out the Almighty perfectly?" and in Job 36:25, after affirming that "all human beings see God," the speaker adds, "every one beholds God from far off."[48]

FOX: Your point is well taken that even creatures elude our knowledge as to their essential mystery. Yet we do know some things about God, do we not?

AQUINAS: The essence of God, as has been said, we cannot see. (John 1:18): "No one has ever seen God," that is, as God is in the divine essence while living this mortal life. Consider 1 Timothy 1:17: "The king of ages, the immortal, the invisible." Paul speaks of the invisible things in the plural because the essence of God is not known to us as it is in itself; it is one, and this is how it will be known to us in heaven when the Lord will be one and God's name one, as Zechariah says. It is, however, made known to us through certain likenesses found in creatures that share in a diverse way in that which is one in God. In this way the human mind considers the unity of the divine essence under the aspects of goodness, wisdom, virtue, and other names of this kind, which do not as such exist in God. Paul calls these the "invisible things of God" because that one thing that in God corresponds to these names or aspects is not seen by us.[49]

FOX: The secrets of God and the invisible things of God represent the unknowability of God?

AQUINAS: God, by reason of the divine excellence, is unknown to us, according to Job (36:26): "If God comes to me, I shall not see God; if God departs, I shall not understand."[50]

FOX: And yet there is something of God that we do understand, is there not?

AQUINAS: The sight of God is twofold: one is perfect, whereby God's essence is seen; the other is imperfect, whereby though we see not what God is, yet we see what God is not; and whereby, the more perfectly we know God in this life, the more we understand that God surpasses all that the mind comprehends.[51]

---

48. CT II, 8.   49. In Rom, ch. 1, p. 16.   50. ST I-II, q. 112, a. 5.
51. Ibid. II-II, q. 8, a. 7.

FOX: Yet you declared in the discussion on the Via Positiva that we do know of, for example, the power of God and the beauty of God.

AQUINAS: From the knowledge of the objects of sense the whole power of God cannot be known; nor therefore can God's essence be seen. But because they are God's effects and depend on their cause, we can be led from them so far as to know of God whether God exists, and to know of God what must necessarily belong to God, as the first cause of all things, exceeding all things caused by God.[52]

FOX: Not even our imaginations—infinite as they are—can see God?

AQUINAS: The essence of God is not seen in a vision of the imagination; but the imagination receives some form representing God according to some mode of similitude; as in divine scripture divine things are metaphorically described by means of objects of sense.[53]

FOX: And why is this?

AQUINAS: Contemplation is natural to human beings by reason of their intellect but beyond the natural scope of the powers of one's imagination, which try to take an active part in the work of contemplation.[54] It is impossible for any created intellect to see the essence of God by its own natural power, [for] if the mode of anything's being exceeds the mode of the knower, it must follow that the knowledge of that object is beyond the nature of the knower.[55] It is impossible for any created intellect to comprehend God.[56]

FOX: Do angels also fail to comprehend Divinity?

AQUINAS: God is not unknown on account of obscurity, but on account of the abundance of brightness. For the vision of God is by its essence above the nature of any created intellect, not only human, but even angelic.[57] God's radiance is supersubstantial—that is, divine truth itself exceeds all boundaries and the ends of any knowledge.[58]

FOX: And yet we offer many images of God, as we did in the Via Positiva; and they all speak to our hearts and tell us something about God.

---

52. Ibid. I, q. 12, a. 12. 53. Ibid., a. 3, ad 3. 54. In Ethics VII, L. 14, p. 698. 55. ST I, q. 12, a. 4. 56. Ibid., a. 7. 57. DDN, n. 82, p. 27. 58. Ibid., n. 72, p. 21.

AQUINAS: Just as in the shadows of the north the shining gold is found, so too among the shadows of ignorance of this life some obscure reflection of divine knowing is found. Thus Job says: "the praise of God is full of fear," because if no divine light shone over us, in no way would we be able to praise God. Also, if divine truth shone upon us manifestly, as at noontime, we would praise God fearlessly; but since on earth something of divine light shines on us with a certain obscurity, we praise God with fear as a person does something out of fear that he knows he cannot do perfectly. And so Job adds: "We cannot find God truly," meaning of course that we arrive through our finding at knowing God as God is. This indeed happens through the divine excellence, and so Job adds "full of fear" because God's virtue surpasses all its effects infinitely. For this reason God cannot be found worthily from the divine effects.[59]

FOX: And so the Via Positiva discussion was not in vain—we really do experience God in creatures?

AQUINAS: In this life we cannot know God directly without first knowing something else.[60]

FOX: This explains why the Via Positiva and the study of creation is so important to our God-experience.

AQUINAS: We do not know God by seeing the divine essence, but we do know God from the order of the whole universe. For the universe of creatures is itself presented to us by God so that through it we may know God insofar as it possesses certain images and likenesses—albeit imperfect—of divine things. These images are compared to divine ones as primary models to their images.[61]

FOX: Then creatures are images that give us a mirror reflection of the divine?

AQUINAS: God can be seen in the divine substance in this life, but only as in a mirror. And this is what the Apostle professes concerning the knowledge of this life, for he says, "we see now through a glass darkly" (1 Cor. 13:12).[62]

FOX: But you celebrated in the Via Positiva the divine likeness the human mind possesses.

---

59. In Job, ch. 37, p. 125.   60. DV, q. 10, a. 11, ad 6.   61. DDN, n. 729, p. 274.   62. CG III, ch. 47 n. 8.

AQUINAS: Although this mirror, which is the human mind, reflects the likeness of God in a closer way than lower creatures do, the knowledge of God that can be taken in by the human mind does not go beyond the type of knowledge that is derived from sense objects, since even the soul itself knows what it is itself as a result of understanding the natures of sense objects, as we have said. Hence, throughout this life God can be known in no higher way than that whereby a cause is known through its effect.[63] God knows creatures through the divine nature; we on the other hand, know God through God's creatures.[64]

FOX: And so we both grasp God and fail to grasp God.

AQUINAS: Concerning God all things can be affirmed and denied. Yet the divine One is above all affirmation and denial, for God is beyond our entire intellect, which composes affirmations and denials.[65]

FOX: This phrase of yours, that God is beyond "affirmations and denials," explains why the "left brain," which affirms and denies, analyzes and judges, needs to be set aside in the Via Negativa if we are to experience God more fully. Of course, when you speak this way you are speaking of deep paradox along the path of the Via Negativa.

AQUINAS: There is no contrary to the object of contemplation, because contraries, as apprehended by the mind, are not contrary. Rather, one is the means of knowing the other.[66]

FOX: And paradox helps us to move beyond the ordinary processes of the mind?

AQUINAS: Through creatures God is both hidden from us and made manifest to us.[67]

FOX: So the relationship of the Via Positiva and the Via Negativa is somewhat paradoxical?

AQUINAS: It is necessary to understand God to be beyond all that which we can apprehend by the intellect.[68]

FOX: Now you are speaking of an "unknown" God.

AQUINAS: God is unknown to us by reason of our feeble intellect, which in its present state has a natural aptitude for material objects only. Therefore we cannot know God in our

---

63. Ibid., n. 9. 64. DDN, n. 729, p. 274. 65. Ibid., n. 143, p. 46.
66. ST I-II, q. 35, a. 5. 67. In Heb, ch. 1, p. 680. 68. DDN, n. 180, p. 57.

present life except through material effects.[69] We know through God's effects that God is, and that God is the cause of other beings, that God is supereminent over other things and set apart from all. And this is the ultimate and most perfect limit of our knowledge in this life, as Dionysius says in *Mystical Theology*. "We are united to God as the Unknown." Indeed, this is the situation, for, while we know of God what God *is not,* what God *is* remains quite unknown.[70]

FOX: I hear you speaking with paradox, since in the Via Positiva you celebrated the "infinity" of our intellects.

AQUINAS: The essential principles of things are unknown to us.[71]

FOX: If this is true regarding things in creation, how much more true it must be for divine things. For a so-called rationalist, you certainly bend over backward to insist on the essential mystery of our lives!

AQUINAS: The final limit to which contemplation can reach is the divine substance. Hence, the mind that sees the divine substance must be completely cut off from the bodily senses, either by death or by ecstasy. Thus, it is said by one who speaks for God, "No one shall see me and live" (Exod. 33:20).[72]

FOX: And so our experiences of the Divine in ecstasy teach us to let go before the holy presence of God.

AQUINAS: Ecstasy or rapture or transport of the mind take place . . . when one is also deprived of the use of one's senses and sensible things in order to see certain things supernaturally. Now, a thing is seen supernaturally when it is seen beyond sense, understanding, and imagination.[73]

FOX: And yet sometimes ecstasy seems to lead directly to imagination instead of away from it, so to speak.

AQUINAS: Augustine distinguishes two kinds of rapture. There is one in which the mind is carried out of the senses to a vision in the imagination. This is what happened to Peter and to John the Evangelist in the Apocalypse, as Augustine says. There is another in which the mind is at once transported out of the senses and out of the imagination to an intellectual vision. This

---

69. ST I, q. 86, a. 2, ad 1.   70. CG III, ch. 49 n. 9.   71. In DA I, L.1, p. 4.   72. CG III, ch. 47 n. 2.   73. DV, q. 13, a. 2, ad 9.

happens in two ways. In one, the intellect understands God through certain intelligible communications, and this is proper to angels. . . . In the other way, the understanding sees God through the divine essence. It was through this that Paul was enraptured.[74]

FOX: In either case, we do experience, by a process of letting go, something of the divine mystery.

AQUINAS: Chrysostom says that the heavenly secret is seen in its essence only through a medium. This is attained by some through divine illumination, such as the blessed in heaven or those who have been lifted up by rapture to this way of seeing. It is seen by those with a less perfect kind of vision in certain likenesses of God's goodness either through objects of sense or images or intelligible species [ideas]. This is the vision that the prophets have through the light of prophecy and that we have through faith, and also that the philosophers who knew God had through the light of reason, as Paul speaks about in Romans 1:20.[75]

FOX: Twice now you have mentioned ecstasy or rapture as a kind of "letting go" experience that allows God to enter.

AQUINAS: Our mind is compelled to represent by means of various forms that most simple being who is God and who is incomprehensible.[76] To see the essence of God there is required some similitude in the visual faculty, namely, the light of glory strengthening the intellect to see God.[77] Those to whom it is given to see God through the divine essence in this way are withdrawn completely from activity of the senses, so that the whole soul is concentrated on seeing the divine essence. Hence, they are said to be in a state of rapture, as if by virtue of a higher power they were separated from that which naturally belongs to them.[78]

FOX: Can you identify someone who had such an experience of ecstasy in this life?

AQUINAS: Moses is shown to have seen God through the divine essence in a rapture, as we are told of Paul in the second Epistle to the Corinthians (12:2), in order that the lawgiver of the Jews and the teacher of the Gentiles might be equal in this respect.[79]

---

74. Ibid.   75. In Is 6, p. 48.   76. DP, q. 1, a. 1, ad 13.   77. ST I, q. 12, a. 2.   78. DV, q. 10, a. 11.   79. Ibid., ad 1.

FOX: Once again I hear you calling for a dialectical understanding of the way we experience God, the dialectic of the Via Positiva and the Via Negativa.

AQUINAS: We ascend from creatures toward God both in the cleansing and excess of all things and in the cause of all things, because God is known *in all things* as in their effects. God is also known *outside all things* insofar as God is separate from all things and exceeds them all. Because of this also God is known through the knowledge we have, since whatever falls into our knowing, we receive as brought from God; and also God is known *through the ignorance we have,* namely, insofar as this is what it means to know God: that we know that we are ignorant concerning what God is.[80]

FOX: So God is both known and unknown, and the "ignorance" in letting go can in fact prove to be a holy knowing.

AQUINAS: We speak correctly concerning God when we say God is known and not known. For from all beings God is known and God is praised insofar as they have a symmetry with God, as those of whom God is the cause. However, there is another most perfect knowledge of God, namely, through separation, by which we know God through ignorance, through a certain unity with the divine things beyond the nature of the mind. This happens when our mind, receding from all other things, and afterward also letting itself go (*dimittens seipsam*), is united to the superresplendent rays of the Deity. Thus, insofar as it knows, God exists not only beyond all the things that are within it, but even beyond it and beyond all the things that can be comprehended by it. Knowing God in this way, in such a state of knowledge, one is illuminated by the very profundity of divine wisdom, which we cannot examine thoroughly. That we also understand God to be beyond not only all the things that are, but even all the things that we can apprehend, comes to us from the incomprehensible profundity of divine wisdom.[81]

FOX: You call this way of ignorance a "most perfect" way of knowing God. Why do you call it that?

AQUINAS: The "depth" of God is called the hidden and unknown essence of God, which is incomprehensible to existing

---

80. DDN, n. 731, p. 274.   81. Ibid., n. 732, p. 275.

beings.[82] The union of us with God—which is possible for us in this life—is brought to completion when we discover that we know that God is beyond the most excellent of creatures.[83]

FOX: And is not this experience of the depth that God is an experience of dark and unnameable mystery?

AQUINAS: Every name imposed by us onto God falls short of God.[84] To manifest his ignorance of this sublime knowledge, it is said of Moses that "he went to the dark cloud wherein God was" (Exod. 20:21).[85] We attribute to God that which is impalpable and invisible darkness insofar as God is inaccessible light, surpassing every light that can be seen by us either through sense or through intellect.[86]

FOX: But how about Christ? Is Christ not a word for God that is reliable?

AQUINAS: In the very wisdom of God, which is Christ, "all the treasures of wisdom and knowledge are hidden," as the Apostle says (Col. 2). "Treasures" refers to the eminence of divine knowledge, as far as it exceeds our intellect.[87]

FOX: So even Christ, who is called the "Word of God," remains in a sense hidden in the depths of the unknown and mysterious treasures of wisdom?

AQUINAS: Without doubt, nothing is more like the Word of God than the unvoiced word that is conceived in a person's heart. Now the word conceived in the heart is unknown to all except the one who conceives it; it is first known to others when the voice gives utterance to it. Thus the Word of God while yet in the bosom of the Father was known to the Father alone.[88]

FOX: Again, I hear you stressing the silence of the heart, and I particularly appreciate your example of the silence that precedes the creative act. After all, if we had words for what we give birth to, our birthings would not be new! But when you stress that we cannot give God a name, are you saying that God is nothing or nonbeing?

AQUINAS: God is said to be nonbeing (*non-existens*) not because God is lacking in being, but because God is beyond all beings.[89]

---

82. Ibid., n. 826, p. 308.   83. Ibid., n. 996, p. 370.   84. Ibid., n. 995, p. 369.   85. CG III, ch. 49 n. 9.   86. DDN, n. 721, p. 271.   87. Ibid., n. 708, p. 265.   88. AC, 29.   89. DDN, n. 463, p. 161.

God fills all things, because the Godhead is deficient in nothing due to its power.[90]

FOX: And we, to appreciate God's fullness, need to be emptied.

AQUINAS: Nothing receives what it already has, since as Aristotle remarks (*De anima* III, 4), the recipient must be devoid of the thing received.[91]

FOX: Clearly the Via Negativa is a path of *receptivity*. I find your teaching on this way to God to be deeply Zenlike. It is surprising to hear from you, so often depicted as the ultimate rationalist of the West, such Zenlike teachings of the "most perfect" path to God.

AQUINAS: Divine wisdom is excellently praised as "irrational," insofar as it exceeds reason; and as "mindless," insofar as it exceeds mind or intellect; and as "stupid," insofar as it exceeds the condition of the mind, namely, wisdom.[92]

FOX: These surprising phrases you use—"irrational, mindless, stupid"—seem to celebrate holy folly and other gifts of what we call today the right hemisphere of the brain.

AQUINAS: Divine truth is ineffable to us and exceeds all the reason we have.[93]

FOX: When you speak of the mind "letting itself go," you are clearly celebrating the *receptive* powers of the person that might otherwise be unused or underused. How is the Via Negativa a kind of exercise in receptivity?

AQUINAS: On God's side there is found a superabundant plenitude of goodness; from this abundant plenitude it follows that God does more; from the fact that God is the primordial cause, it follows that God's gifts are like a fountain, like a primordial fountain. Therefore, in accordance with God's superplenitude and magnificence and the divine fountainlike gifts, the gifts are shared by all according to the effusion of the gift. The gift is infinite on the part of the giver.[94]

FOX: If the gift is infinite, we surely do need emptying and strengthening—indeed, courage or a big heart—to absorb it.

AQUINAS: The gifts are altogether undiminished but always have the same superabundant plenitude and never are diminished, no matter how much they are shared. In fact, the more

---

90. Ibid., n. 437, p. 143.   91. CG II, ch. 73 n. 32.   92. DDN, n. 708, p. 265.   93. Ibid., n. 702, p. 262.   94. Ibid., n. 807, p. 301.

they are shared, so much the more do they spread forth from above, since by the amount that something receives from the divine gifts, to that extent is one made fit for receiving more. From the point of view of the flowing in, the inflowings of infinite virtue cannot be diminished.[95]

FOX: And so we need to prepare for this infinite flowing in of divine gifts by being emptied and made receptive?

AQUINAS: Whatever is received by a creature is as vanity in comparison with the being of God, since a creature cannot receive being in that perfection with which it is in God.[96] There is more power in God for making peace than there is in things for taking it up, and for this reason the emanation of peace from God is beyond the ability of things to receive it.[97]

FOX: Divinity, it seems, is just too big for us to grasp, too full of surprises.

AQUINAS: Job puts it this way: "Even if anyone shall have spoken" as if wishing to understand divine effects "they would be overwhelmed as if swallowed up" by the magnitude of the matter about which they speak. Proverbs says (25): "To conceal a matter, this is the glory of God, to sift it thoroughly, the glory of kings." Or it can be understood in another way so that the meaning is as follows: not only are human beings unable sufficiently and conveniently to explain divine effects, but even if God had told them to human beings, that is, by revealing them, human beings would be overwhelmed, as if unable to grasp so great a thing. Thus in John 16 it is said: "I have many things to say to you, which you cannot now bear" and in Deuteronomy 5 it is said: "What is all flesh, that it should hear the voice of the living God?" But lest someone think that the knowing of the divine truth might have been taken from humanity forever, for the purpose of excluding this notion, Job adds: "But now," that is, in the present time, "they do not see," namely, human beings, "the light," that is, the brightness of divine knowing.[98]

FOX: I hear you saying that when it comes to divine experience there are times when even our imaginations fall far short and need to be stilled and quieted.

---

95. Ibid. 96. DP I, q. 2, a. I, ad 11. 97. DDN, n. 912, p. 337.
98. In Job, ch. 37, p. 125.

AQUINAS: God is eminent above all and set apart from all—not only from things that exist, but also from things that can be conceived by the created mind.[99]

FOX: Since you praise the way of "mindlessness" and "ignorance" so profusely, I think it is an appropriate moment to ask a practical question: How does one learn to undergo this way of meditation?

AQUINAS: The first requirement, then, for the contemplation of wisdom is that we should take complete possession of our minds before anything else does, so that we can fill the whole house with the contemplation of wisdom. It is also necessary that we be fully present there, concentrating in such a way that our aim is not diverted to other matters. Thus Scripture says: "Return home quickly and gather yourself together there and play there and pursue your thoughts" (Eccles. 32:15–16). To "gather yourself together there" is to draw together your whole intention.[100]

FOX: So solitude is part of the experience of the Via Negativa?

AQUINAS: When we are engaged in outward activities we need many things to help us, but in the contemplation of wisdom we work all the more effectively the more we dwell alone with ourselves. So, in the words cited above, the wise person calls us back to ourselves: "Return home quickly," that is, be anxious to return from external things to your own mind, before anything else gets holds of it and any other anxiety distracts it. That is why it says in Wisdom 8:16: "I will enter my house and find rest with her," with wisdom, that is.[101]

FOX: And so the first step is letting go and "returning home." What is the next step in this kind of prayer?

AQUINAS: When our interior house is entirely emptied like this and we are fully present there in our intention, the text tells us what to do next: "And play there."[102]

FOX: Play, too, is a kind of letting go and another expression of the unself-consciousness that we can see is part of the Via Negativa.

AQUINAS: There are two features of play that make it appropriate to compare the contemplation of wisdom to playing.

---

99. CG III, ch. 49 n. 9.   100. CBH, Prologue.   101. Ibid.   102. Ibid.

First, we enjoy playing, and there is the greatest enjoyment of all to be had in the contemplation of wisdom. As Wisdom says in Ecclesiasticus 24:27, "My spirit is sweeter than honey."

Second, playing has no purpose beyond itself; what we do in play is done for its own sake. And the same applies to the pleasure of wisdom.[103]

FOX: Yes! Play is without a why. And so too is prayer at its deepest levels. No doubt we will play with the meanings of play further on in our discussions, but I think it is important here to return to this dimension of play that letting go is all about. What do we learn from this concentration and gathering up of ourselves that you are recommending so highly?

AQUINAS: We are to learn to be single-hearted. The more united and compact we are, the more like God we are.[104] Take note of what Isaiah says: "go back, collusions, to the heart."[105]

FOX: So we should begin with the heart? In other words, we should return to the heart?

AQUINAS: The heart is said to be in the midst of the person. Since God dwells in our hearts, God is said to be in the midst. There is a double effect to this: stability against evil and firmness with regard to good things. So the psalmist says, "Since God is in the midst of it," namely, of that city-state, "it will not be shaken," that is, it will be rendered firm and stable. Psalm 125 praises "those who are confident" and Matthew (16) promises that "the gates of hell will not prevail against it."[106]

FOX: And so we are to return to our hearts to pray the prayer of the Via Negativa?

AQUINAS: One ought to return to one's heart first as to the seat of a judge, in order to scrutinize oneself. Psalm 77 says: "I communed at night in my heart, and I trained myself and looked into my spirit." A second reason for returning to the heart is to go to the foundation of life, so that we may guard ourselves. Proverbs 4 says: "Preserve your heart with every defense, since life proceeds from it." A third reason is to approach the hearing of the divine word, so that we may attend diligently. Hosea 2 says: "I will lead her into solitude, and speak to her heart."

---

103. Ibid.   104. In I Tim, ch. 6, p. 616.   105. In Is 46, p. 542.   106. In Pss 45, p. 328.

Fourth, to approach the treasure of the divine eloquence, so that we may preserve it. The psalmist says (119): "I have hidden your eloquence in my heart, so that I may not offend you." Fifth, to enter the dining room of divine peace and refreshment. The opposite of this would be the kind of things spoken of in Psalm 28: "They spoke peace with their neighbor, but hid evil things in their heart."[107]

FOX: And so meditation in the way of the Via Negativa includes becoming emptied?

AQUINAS: In the soul there are two kinds of distraction that have to be removed prior to its coming to a kind of oneness: first, the distraction caused by the variety found in external things. This is the first element that Dionysius identifies in the soul's circular movement: its leaving behind external things in order to enter into itself. The second diversification that has to be removed is the one caused by discursive reasoning. We do this when all the soul's workings are reduced to a simple contemplation of intelligible truth. This amounts to the second thing Dionysius declared necessary, a uniform orbiting of the soul's intellectual powers, that is, the abandonment of discursive reasoning and a fixing of the soul's gaze in the contemplation of one unified truth. In this work of the soul there is no going astray, because there is no possibility of making mistakes about the understanding of first principles, which we know by simply seeing them. After these two steps, a third act of oneness occurs, which is like that of the angels. In it the soul ignores everything else and settles down to the sheer contemplation of God. Thus, in Dionysius's words, "having become one, in a way that is united with"—that is, conformed to—"the unified powers, the soul is led to the beautiful and the good."[108]

FOX: You seem to be advocating silence or the "abandonment of discursive reasoning" as a key way to open the heart up and to undergo the prayer of the Via Negativa.

AQUINAS: The contemplative life consists in a certain leisure and repose. "Be still and see that I am God" (Ps. 46:10).[109] Gregory, speaking of contemplation, says: "Those who are rapt in order to understand the things within close their eyes to visible things."[110]

---

107. In Is 46, p. 542.   108. ST II-II, q. 180, a. 6, ad 2.   109. Ibid., q. 182, a. 1.   110. DV, q. 13, a. 2, ad 9.

FOX: One of the etymological meanings of the word *mysteuein* or "mysticism" is "to shut one's senses." Why do you suppose silence is so useful a way to the knowledge of the unknown God?

AQUINAS: We are not now able to understand how great the love of God is for us, since the goods that God is going to give us, because they exceed our appetite and desire, cannot fall into our heart. Consider 1 Corinthians 2:9: "The eye does not see nor the ear hear, nor does it enter the hearts of humankind what God has prepared for those who love God."[111]

FOX: Does no one understand the vastness of this love that wants to "fall into our hearts"?

AQUINAS: The believing world, that is, the saints, understand through their experience how much God loves us.[112]

FOX: Let us return to experience. Speak more of how we undergo this silence that experiential prayer is about.

AQUINAS: Dionysius says that it is neither lawful nor possible for any human being, or indeed for any existing creature, to say by mouth or to think by heart divine peace as it is in itself or divine silence itself. Saint Justin calls this "the ineffability of God," because we are not able to utter God nor does God utter a word to us so that we are able to know perfectly the Godhead as it is.[113]

FOX: And so our silence is a silence before the silent mystery of God. Just a being still there?

AQUINAS: Dionysius teaches that we revere the unutterable aspects of the Godhead "with a chaste silence." For through this silence we reverence hidden things because we do not understand them, and through it we reverence ineffable things, because we are silent concerning them. And this silence indeed proceeds from the sanctity and chastity of the soul, not extending itself beyond its limits.[114]

FOX: No doubt one remains silent also to receive something into the heart.

AQUINAS: Jesus tells the story in Matthew's gospel about the seed that was sown on rocky ground. The rocks are an evil heart

---

111. In Jn 17.23, n. 2250.   112. Ibid.   113. DDN, n. 894, p. 334.
114. Ibid., n. 44, p. 16.

into which the word cannot penetrate, like rocky ground in which there is little earth. Thus some people do not present a penetrable heart.[115]

FOX: "A penetrable heart," you say. What is a penetrable heart?

AQUINAS: A heart is called penetrable when it places nothing ahead of the word, when it has the word as its radical principle. Thus Ezekiel says: "Remove from yourselves your heart of stone." And again, "he hears the word and immediately receives it with joy" (Ezek. 11:19). Therefore one takes delight in justice and is inclined toward good. . . . The seed (in Jesus' story in Matthew's gospel) takes delight but cannot be implanted because it has no roots, being sown among stones. The root is love. Consider Ephesians (3:17): "Rooted and grounded in love."[116]

FOX: And so silence roots us in love?

AQUINAS: Divine peace is the final cause of all things.[117] There is a triple union of peace: one is with oneself insofar as each thing by itself is some one thing; another union is with another to become truly one thing; and a third union occurs when things are united with the One source of the peace of all things, namely, God.[118]

FOX: And we can taste something of this peace through silence?

AQUINAS: Dionysius connects silence and peace, since a sign of troubled peace is noise and clamor. . . . Calm and immobility are joined to peace—as is silence as well—because the things that have peace, for this very reason, seem to have a kind of calm.[119]

FOX: When are we at peace with ourselves?

AQUINAS: Something is properly said to have peace in itself from the moment when its appetite becomes calm in the acquiring of its proper good. This indeed happens when there is nothing repugnant that impedes such a calm either internally or externally. In this way, therefore, something is said to have peace in itself and toward other things by a kind of union by which all repugnance is excluded.[120]

FOX: Elaborate, please, on this "calmness" you speak of.

---

115. In Mt 13, p. 128.   116. Ibid.   117. DDN, n. 886, p. 331.
118. Ibid., n. 888, p. 331.   119. Ibid., n. 895, p. 335.   120. Ibid., n. 880, p. 330.

AQUINAS: Becoming calm means calming our intellectual activities, lest anything be undergone beyond what is granted to us. After we have been united according to the godlikeness through the knowledge of divine things, as far as is possible for us, to this extent there remains something of the divine things hidden from us; to inquire about these matters it is necessary for us to calm our intellect.[121]

FOX: In the praxis you are describing as "calming the intellect," there seems to be an element of letting go of expectations and of waiting.

AQUINAS: The author of the Book of Lamentations brings up the condition of the one who waits, first as regards the elevation of contemplation. He speaks of being "solitary" so that one is not hindered, and he says that "he will be silent," meaning from the tumult of thoughts and of desires. For through this [letting go] "one has raised oneself above oneself" for the purpose of considering divine things. Consider Hosea (2): "I will lead her into solitude, and will speak to her heart." This is also indicated in the dejection of one who waits, since one stays in order to wait: "One will sit alone and will be silent" (when one is abject); and one will rise up (when one is exalted). This also occurs through humility of speech: "he will place his mouth in the dust" speaking of humility. As Isaiah says (29), "You will speak from deep in the earth."[122]

FOX: Solitude, silence, and prayer go together, then?

AQUINAS: Whatever our intellect apprehends is less than the essence of God and whatever our tongue speaks is less than the divine being. Neither is the divine essence able to be manifested perfectly by any created intellect so that it comprehends it.[123]

FOX: Can you offer us a model or example of someone who prays this kind of prayer of silence that you advocate so strongly?

AQUINAS: In Matthew's gospel the Sermon on the Mount begins by saying: "And opening his mouth, Jesus taught them." By saying the word "opening" the author is signifying that Jesus was silent for a long time before he taught.[124]

---

121. Ibid., n. 70, p. 21.   122. In Lam 3, p. 679.   123. DDN, n. 609, p. 232.   124. In Mt 5, p. 48.

FOX: So Jesus for you teaches us to pray in the manner of silence?

AQUINAS: It should be pointed out that Christ had three refuges as spoken of in Matthew's gospel: sometimes he fled to the mountains, as is said in Matthew 5:1 and also in John 8:1: "Jesus however proceeded to the Mount of Olives." Sometimes he took refuge in a boat (Luke 5): "When many crowds pressed upon him . . . boarding a boat, which was Simon's . . . sitting he taught." And his third refuge was into the desert (Mark 6:31): "Let us go into a desert place." And this suffices, for in the three instances persons can have a refuge in God.[125]

FOX: You find Jesus praying in mountains, on the lake in boats away from the people, and in the desert. You have cited Hosea frequently about the desert as a place of solitude. It is interesting that you recall Jesus choosing the same place for prayer.

AQUINAS: In Matthew's gospel (4:1) it says: "Then Jesus was led into the desert." This agrees with what precedes and what follows, since he had agreed that he would enter the desert after his baptism. This corresponds to the Israelite people who entered the desert after the crossing of the Red Sea, which crossing was a symbol of baptism. Through desert and solitude they came into the land of promise. So the baptized ought to seek a solitary and quiet life, leaving the world behind with both body and mind, as Hosea says (2:14): "I will lead her into solitude, and I will speak to her heart." Or as the psalmist puts it (Ps. 55:7): "How far I would take my flight, and make a new home in the desert!"[126]

FOX: And so Jesus knew well the prayer of silence?

AQUINAS: There is a difference between the speech of Christ and our speech. Our speech is for necessity alone, but Christ's speech is more for instruction. For no need of speaking inheres in the one who hears clearly together with the Father.[127]

FOX: Thus Christ relates to the Creator in silence. What else occurs when we undergo silence and solitude?

AQUINAS: Angels are announcers of divine silence. For it is clear that a conception of the heart or of the intellect that is

---

125. Ibid.   126. Ibid. 4, p. 37.   127. In Jn 17.1, n. 2179.

without voice is with silence. But it is through a perceptible voice that silence of the heart is proclaimed.[128]

FOX: And so in this fashion we learn to become "proclaimers of the silence of the heart" ourselves?

AQUINAS: Angels are always announcers of divine silence. But it is necessary after something is announced to someone that they understand the announcement. In addition, therefore, because we can understand by the intellect the things that are announced to us through the angels, they themselves by the brightness of their own light help our intellect to grasp the secrets of God.[129]

FOX: And so silence is essential, but it is not all there is.

AQUINAS: God is indeed respected by silence. But this does not mean that we may say nothing whatever about God, nor inquire about God, but that we should understand that we fall short of fully grasping God.[130]

FOX: Are there other dimensions to this prayer of silence that you wish to address?

AQUINAS: The author of the Book of Lamentations teaches the manner of praying according to the time of day: "Rise up from sleep, praise God through prayer in the night." In the night the time is more empty and it is a more quiet time, as he says, "in the beginning of the night watches." The watches of the night are distinguished according to the watchmen who guard the city, as is said in Song of Songs (3): "The watchmen of the city found me awake."[131]

FOX: So the night symbolizes the calm and gathering together of heart and mind that you have been speaking of?

AQUINAS: The time of night is the time of meditation on account of its quiet. Therefore in the quiet of the night a person meditates and devises many things from which he or she becomes a knowing person—that is why night is the time of knowledge. Therefore the psalmist (Ps. 19) says, "night declares its knowledge to the night," that is, of God. For in one night there is a different disposition of time than in another; and all of this happens because of the arrangement of the knowledge of God.[132]

---

128. DDN, n. 288, p. 90.   129. Ibid., 91.   130. DT, i, a. 2, ad 4.
131. In Lam 2, p. 677.   132. In Pss 18, p. 211.

FOX: Why else is night a particularly holy time?

AQUINAS: "At night" also means in calm and quiet when God visits us through consolation. Consider Matthew 25: "But at midnight there was a cry, 'The bridegroom is here! Go out and meet him.'"[133] God illuminates the shadows. These are the shadows concerning which in John 3 it is said that Nicodemus came to Jesus "at night."[134]

FOX: What other meanings are evoked by speaking of praying "at night"?

AQUINAS: Night holds the quiet of contemplation, in which there is first the desire of the excitement of love: "My soul has desired you in your decrees: In the middle of the night I rose up to praise you" (Ps. 119). And it signifies the silence of divine consolation as in the Book of Wisdom (18): "For when peaceful silence lay over all, and night had run the half of her swift course, from the royal throne there leapt your all-powerful Word."[135]

FOX: Of course we also dream at night, don't we?

AQUINAS: Job introduces the value of human instruction by which some are instructed toward the good by revelation. And he adds, "God who has given," namely, through revelation, divine "songs," the doctrines of human instruction, which were comprehended by the ancients many times in songs "in the night." This means literally in a nighttime dream, or in the calm of contemplation, or in the obscurity of a vision.[136]

FOX: Sometimes our visions are very obscure. Is this, too, symbolized by the darkness of the Via Negativa?

AQUINAS: Scriptures say that "the Lord answered Job out of the whirlwind." Understood as a metaphor, this response of God could have been an interior inspiration perceived by Job. Thus God would be said to speak from the whirlwind because of the disturbance that Job suffered and the obscurity, which is like a whirlwind. For in this life we cannot clearly perceive divine inspiration except with the cloudiness of sense symbols, as Dionysius says in the first chapter of *The Celestial Hierarchy*. The message from God would be the same as if God had made the divine voice heard in a material whirlwind.[137]

---

133. In Pss 16, p. 190.　134. In Jer 25, p. 636.　135. In Is 15, p. 484.
136. In Job, ch. 35, p. 119.　137. Ibid., ch. 38, p. 126.

FOX: Does "night" also signify pain and suffering?

AQUINAS: The psalmist (119) says: "I have shouted in my whole heart: hear me, Lord." And he summons a multitude of tears, "my eyes stream with tears." Jeremiah says (9): "Let our eyes rain tears, our eyelids run with weeping!" And the psalmist summons us to a continuation of grief when he says "throughout the day and the night," that is, in both prosperous times and adverse ones.[138]

FOX: Thus the night symbolizes pain and suffering, and no doubt these are also part of our Via Negativa experience.

AQUINAS: Job says: "At night my mouth is pierced with grief and this makes a burning sensation" (Job 50). It is harder to suffer lack of sleep at night than in the day, since during the day the mind of a person is lifted up by the association with others and the appearance of light. While night, on the other hand, is sleepless for someone who desires it to be finished quickly. Job says this when he says, "I hope for the light back after the shadows," meaning I hope that the light of day will return after the shadows of night.[139]

FOX: We associate grace with light or day and grief with darkness or night, it seems.

AQUINAS: In Jeremiah a time of grace is called "day" because of the appearance of light, as in Romans (13): "The night has passed, but the day is approaching: let us therefore cast off the works of the shadows, and put on the weapons of light." Security for the journey is also alluded to when we read in John (11): "If someone has walked during the day, he offends not, since he sees the light of this world; but if someone has walked in the night, he offends, since the light is not in him." Also, we apply this metaphor to the issue of vigilance and sobriety when we read in 1 Thessalonians (5): "For those who sleep, sleep at night; and those who are drunk, are drunk at night."[140] "At night" can also signify a defect of spiritual intelligence. Sometimes someone has the right heart, and temptation and forgetfulness overcome him—and this is at night. When this happens the Lord visits by helping against temptation and beats away forgetfulness and strengthens the person. As the psalmist prays, "when my virtue is deficient do not abandon me" (Ps. 50).[141]

---

138. In Lam 2, p. 677. 139. In Job, ch. 17, p. 70. 140. In Jer 23, p. 634. 141. In Pss 16, p. 190.

FOX: I sense that when you expound on grief and suffering in the Via Negativa you are beginning to name what we have come to know through John of the Cross as the "dark night of the soul."

AQUINAS: Any sadness and suffering of heart can be called a "darkness," just as any joy can be called a "light."[142] With regard to the state of adversity the psalmist (Ps. 42) speaks of "at night," meaning in the time of adversity, he gave "his song," that is, joy, which is the greatest consolation to one in tribulation, deriving from divine compassion. In another sentence he says "on the day he declared," meaning that divine compassion is declared and manifest in times of diversity. Ecclesiasticus 53 notes: "Apparent is the compassion of God in time of tribulation." and Psalm 51 says: "in your great tenderness," etc.[143]

FOX: Thus the Via Negativa is about paying attention to the pain of our hearts?

AQUINAS: One sign of great sadness is roaring. Thus the psalmist says, "I was roaring from the groaning of my heart" (Ps. 38). Roaring is said to be the sound that beasts make, such as the lion or the bear, on account of the vehemence of pain or hunger. Thus roaring is the vehemence of *wailing,* as in Job (3): "My roaring is like flooding water." Whence the phrase "I was roaring" means I was wailing most bitterly. But it sometimes happens that one wails externally, and not from a disturbance of the mind. But the psalmist does not wail thus, no, this roaring proceeds form the groaning of one's heart, as in Lamentations (1): "Many are the groans, and my heart is grieving." Consider Isaiah 59: "We will roar like all the bears."[144]

FOX: Wailing and roaring—and wailing and roaring like bears —these elements of touching the depths of darkness and pain need to be more fully taught and understood as prayer forms today.

AQUINAS: The compassion of the prophet is brought forth when the author of the Book of Lamentations speaks about external wailing: "My eye has been afflicted," weeping, "nor has it been silent" from tears, "quiet" from tribulations to the people (Lam. 3:17). Jeremiah says (9): "My eyes shed tears, since the

---

142. In Jn 1.5, n. 105.   143. In Pss 41, p. 312.   144. In Pss 37, p. 292.

voice of lamentation has been heard from Sion." And the end of wailing, "until he looked back," with the eye of compassion. Second, with regard to the sting of interior pain: "My eye," seeing the depredation of the earth, "has plundered my soul," despoiling it of its joy, or bewailing the whole pain of the heart it drags it externally.[145]

FOX: Imagery of the Via Negativa is certainly not lacking in the Scriptures, where there seems to be genuine permission to wail and lament.

AQUINAS: The author of the Book of Lamentations says, "my life slipped into the lake"—meaning of prison and captivity. This is similar to the psalmist who said (87): "They placed me in a lower lake, in shadows, and among the shades of death." The affliction of those in prison is also named: "They have flowed in," they have been multiplied, "the waters" of tribulation, "I have said," despairing and impatient. As Jonah says (2): "All your billows have passed over me."[146]

FOX: And do you believe that the heart is purified by this dark night of the soul?

AQUINAS: What happens through the poverty of the spirit, through grief, through gentleness, except that the heart is kept pure?[147] The heart is washed by the tears of compunction, as the psalmist says: "I wash my bed each night, I will drench my couch with my tears."[148]

FOX: The dark night of the soul can bring about almost a violent kind of pruning, wouldn't you say?

AQUINAS: A tree that does not produce good fruit will be cut down and thrown into the fire, as it is said in Matthew 3. But a fruitful tree is pruned so that it is purified, according to John 15: "Every branch of the vine which does not bear fruit he will cleanse so that it bears more fruit." So the impious are punished to destruction, but the just to perfection.[149]

FOX: And so all persons undergo pruning and purification in the trials of living?

AQUINAS: In a natural vine it happens that at times a branch with many shoots is less fruitful because of the moisture being

---

145. In Lam 3, p. 681. 146. Ibid. 147. In Mt 5, p. 53. 148. In Jer 4, p. 590. 149. In Job, ch. 19, p. 76.

divided among many branches. Therefore the vinedresser prunes it of its excess shoots. Thus it is with humans. For a person well disposed to God but with desire for many things will lose strength and be less able to act well. Thus God frequently cuts away these hindrances and purifies the person by sending trials and temptations by which one is made stronger so that one might bear more fruit. Therefore John's gospel says "God prunes," although one is already clean, because no one in this life is so pure that they cannot be more and more purified.[150]

FOX: I am struck by the context in which you put the pruning we all undergo—namely, that of being made stronger in order to bear more fruit. You place the Via Negativa in the context of the Via Creativa—or perhaps I should say that Jesus does this in John's gospel.

AQUINAS: In Matthew 25 it is said that the talent was taken away from the one who hid it and did not gain anything from it. In Luke 13 the Lord orders the sterile fig tree cut down. His efforts toward the good branches is that they be encouraged to bear more fruit. That is why he says: "Every one who bears fruit God will prune and they will bear more fruit."[151]

FOX: Can you give an example of this purification that comes about by pain and pruning?

AQUINAS: Rachel is said to lament because she was the mother of Benjamin. This is a figurative kind of speech (in Matthew 2:4) to express the magnitude of pain. In one way it can be referred to the captivity of the Israelites who, when they were led into captivity, are said to have lamented on the road near Bethlehem. And then Rachel is said to have lamented because she was buried there (Gen. 31). This use of speech is the same as saying that a place laments the evil things that happen in that place. So the prophet wishes to say that just as there was the greatest pain and grief when the tribe of Benjamin was destroyed, so it will again be greatest in the time of captivity. The Evangelist takes up the deed concerning the killing of the innocents and amplifies that grief in four ways: from the diffusion of the grief, from the multitude of the grief, from the subject of the grief, and from the inconsolability of it. And so he says, "a voice in Rama,"

---

150. In Jn 15.2, n. 1985.   151. In Jn 15.2, nn. 1984–85.

which is a certain city in the tribe of Benjamin . . . "has been heard on high," that is, in heaven with God. Thus Ecclesiasticus 35:21 says: "The prayer of the humble pierces the clouds, and he will not be consoled until he reaches the goal, nor will he desist until the Most High takes notice of him." And again, (35:15): "The tears of the widow descend down her cheeks, don't they, and she cries out against the man who caused them to fall." The grief of mothers is greater than that of sons. Likewise, the grief of mothers was continual, while that of boys was brief. For this reason Zechariah says (12:10): "They will wail over him as over an only child, and grieve over him, as is the custom to grieve over the death of the first-born." Likewise from the subject of the grief, since it is concerning the death of sons. Whence Rachel laments.[152]

FOX: So the Via Negativa is not just about experiencing the ineffable mystery of the unknown Godhead, but it is also about entering fully into the pain and grief of existence?

AQUINAS: Night holds terror. One such kind is that of an oppressing anticipation, as we read in Job (27): "At night a storm will carry him off." Another kind is that of present affliction, as in Proverbs toward the end, "Her lamp will not be extinguished at night." And a third kind of terror is that of eternal damnation, as in Wisdom (17): "Impious men . . . lay prisoners of the dark, in the fetters of the long night, confined under their own roofs, banished from eternal providence."[153]

FOX: We undergo much grief and suffering in this life, do we not?

AQUINAS: The author of the Book of Lamentations laments those who are wretched because of a defect of age. He mentions their death and the process of dying. First he demonstrates his compassion with an effusion of tears when he says, "my eyes are spent with weeping" as if they did not have the strength to weep any more. Jeremiah (9) says: "Who will give water to my head, and a fountain of tears to my eyes?" He also talks about the commotion going on in his innermost parts when he says, "they have been troubled," as if to say, as much as I grieve, there is such a pain of confusion inside, and it comes even to the

---

152. In Mt 2, p. 27.   153. In Is 15, p. 484.

innermost heart. Jeremiah says (31): "My stomach has been troubled." He also mentions the flowing of the bile, "my liver overflows onto the earth." He means, I grieve in such a way that my liver had overflowed or since my love, whose seat is in the liver, has been cast to the ground, the things that I was loving are prostrate. Hosea says (13): "I will tear the flesh around their hearts."[154]

FOX: Thus our passion in grief turns into compassion toward others' grief and suffering.

AQUINAS: The author of the Book of Lamentations explains the order of death so that it stirs up more compassion. First he speaks of the seeking of the dead ones by their mothers: "Where is wheat and wine?" as if it is lacking: give it to us to eat. In chapter 4 he says: "The little ones have sought bread, and there was no one to break it for them." He laments the necessity of seeking: "Since they were lacking," they died prematurely from hunger, "in the streets" as if with all watching, and no one able to offer a remedy.[155]

FOX: No doubt we will be dealing more with the relation between the Via Negativa and the Via Transformativa, the passion of sadness and the passion of compassion, when we discuss the Via Transformativa. It would seem that grief also relates to silence, since some grief is beyond words, wouldn't you say?

AQUINAS: Isaiah says: "This is why my loins are wracked with shuddering," that is, I grieve like one who suffers pain in the loins (Isa. 21). The psalmist speaks of "pains like those of one giving birth" and of collapsing under this burden (Ps. 48)—and with regard to the troubled countenance: "I have been troubled, and I have not spoken." And Psalm 55 says, "I have been troubled in my ordeal" and with regard to the feeling, "my heart has withered." This refers to the feeling of sadness.[156]

FOX: Sadness, then, is a part of the journey in the Via Negativa?

AQUINAS: There is a double sadness. There is a certain sadness leading to desperation, and this takes away desire and groaning since each of these happens in secret. So desire and groaning are known inwardly to God. And so the psalmist says, "Lord, before you are all my desires." Before you that which I desire is

---

154. In Lam 2, p. 676.   155. Ibid.   156. In Is 21, p. 493.

tested, and so I hope it to be granted to me through you. Proverbs says: "God's desire will be given to the just ones." And the psalmist says (10): "The Lord hears the desire of the poor." Desire is known to you who examine our hearts, as in 1 Kings 16: "God looks into the heart."[157]

FOX: Sadness is about touching the dark recesses of the heart.

AQUINAS: The psalmist says "My heart is troubled" (38). Here he shows his need for consolation, since there is nothing in his heart that is capable of being consoled. There are three things in the human, namely, the intellect, the will, and executive power: the intellect directs, the will orders, and the power executes. And these three are deficient in me [the psalmist is saying]. To say that "the heart is troubled" is to say that feeling is moved by sadness and disturbance. Consider Psalm 60: "You have made the earth tremble, torn it apart." The heart has been troubled because of the anxiety of the world. Likewise, the executive power that the psalmist had before sinning has abandoned him.[158]

FOX: Why are prayers of sadness so related to the heart and to a journey of the heart?

AQUINAS: The habitual or conditioned appetite for something as for its own good is called love. When love is absent there is caused dread and sadness concerning it and concerning the subsequent emotions that are derived from these.[159]

FOX: If we don't deal with this sadness, it can have an inordinate influence on the rest of our lives.

AQUINAS: Just as love arises from pleasure, so does hatred arise from sorrow. . . . Since envy is sorrow for our neighbor's good, it follows that our neighbor's good becomes hateful to us, so that "out of envy cometh hatred" (Gregory).[160]

FOX: Thus sorrow undealt with can lead to self-hatred and to hatred of others.

AQUINAS: Since envy of our neighbor is the mother of hatred of our neighbor, it becomes, in consequence, the cause of hatred toward God.[161]

---

157. In Pss 37, p. 292. 158. Ibid. 159. DDN, n. 401, p. 143. 160. ST II-II, q. 34, a. 6. 161. Ibid., ad 2.

FOX: Are there other examples you can offer of the dark night of the soul?

AQUINAS: The psalmist (Ps. 23) speaks of a person traveling through dangerous places, for whom security is essential. He says, "even if I walk in the shadow of death, I will not fear evil, since you are with me," as a leader and protector—and thus I will be secure. "The shadow of death" stands for a present tribulation, for a shadow is a presage of a body that will follow. Colossians 2 says: "Law, the shadow of future things, but the body of Christ." This tribulation is like a sign of death. "In the middle" means in the innermost part and fervency of tribulation, you will revivify me. But "the shadow of death" means the life of the present darkened by the darkness of sins, as Job says (3): "The darkness will seize him, etc." But the shadow of death can also mean that which does not bring evil when God is present, as Job speaks of (17): "Place me near you." And Isaiah (43): "When you pass through rivers, they will not swallow you up. Should you walk through fire, you will not be scorched."[162]

FOX: You have described the deep experience of fear as a part of entering the darkness. Are there other such journeys we ought to name?

AQUINAS: Job says that "I have empty months," that is, I have thought the months past have passed empty for me inasmuch as in them I did not gain final perfection. And he goes on, saying "the nights"—reckoned as a quiet time against affliction—"I numbered as laborious for me," that is, I considered them as if they were laborious inasmuch as in them I was delayed from pursuing the end.[163]

FOX: And so our experiences of ennui are also experiences of the Via Negativa and the dark night of the soul?

AQUINAS: Just how Job considered the months empty and nights laborious he explains when he says: "If I slept"—that is, when there was a time of sleeping at night, "I would ask, 'When will I rise?'" expecting the day, "and back again [to bed]," the day completed, "I will look for the evening." Thus he is always stretching his desire into the future, and this experience is indeed

---

162. In Pss 22, p. 225.   163. In Job, ch. 7, p. 29.

common for each person living on earth. But people perceive this to a greater or lesser degree depending on whether they are affected by a greater or lesser degree of joy or of sadness. But Job shows this desire to be strong within himself when he adds: "and I will be filled with grief until the dawn." He means that because of this sadness, if the present time is irksome to me, I will desire the future more than the present.[164]

FOX: You seem to be advocating a journey into one's deepest feelings—including the dark and painful ones. Yet there are those who say the spiritual journey is all about detachment from feelings or indifference to them.

AQUINAS: We are told that "Job opened his mouth and cursed the day of his birth." In regard to the passions of the soul, the emotions, there were two opinions in antiquity. The Stoics said that sadness did not happen to the wise person. The Peripatetics, however, said that the wise person could be sad, but that in sadness such a person would act moderately and in accord with reason. This latter opinion is the correct one. For reason cannot take away a natural condition. It is natural for a feeling nature to take delight in what is pleasing and to be sad about what is harmful. This cannot then be taken away by reason, but is guided in such a way that reason does not through sadness go off course. This opinion agrees with Sacred Scripture, which shows Christ, in whom is all fullness of virtue and wisdom, being sad.[165]

FOX: And what about Job?

AQUINAS: Job, because of his adversities, indeed felt sadness— otherwise the virtue of patience would have no place in him. However, the sadness did not cause his reason to fall away from its course, rather it was in control of the sadness. To show this it is said, "after this Job opened his mouth," that is, after seven days of silence. From this it is clear that the words that follow were spoken by reason undisturbed by sadness. For, if they had been spoken from a disturbed mind, they would have been expressed sooner when the power of the sadness was stronger. Sadness of any kind is diminished by the passage of time and is felt more strongly in the beginning. Thus it seems that Job was

---

164. Ibid.   165. In Job, ch. 3, p. 12.

silent so long lest he be judged to be speaking from a disturbed mind. This is also shown by the words, "he opened his mouth." When anyone speaks under the impulse of emotion, they do not open their mouth but are driven by emotion to speak. For we are not in control of our actions by emotion but by reason. By speaking, Job expressed the sadness he was feeling. It is customary among wise persons to speak from reason of the movements of emotion that they feel, as Christ did when he said, "my soul is sad even unto death."[166]

FOX: And so sorrow is a virtue when properly dealt with?

AQUINAS: Moderated sorrow for an object that ought to make us sorrowful is a mark of virtue.[167] Immoderate sorrow is a disease of the mind, but moderate sorrow is the mark of a well-conditioned mind, according to the present state of life.[168]

FOX: How do you recommend that we deal with deep sadness?

AQUINAS: While pleasure can be entire and perfect, sadness is always partial.[169]

FOX: Sadness passes, you are saying, and pleasure is more powerful than sorrow?

AQUINAS: The desire for pleasure is of itself more eager than the shunning of sorrow.[170] We never do that which we do with sorrow as well as that which we do with pleasure or without sorrow.[171]

FOX: Sorrow also interferes with work, does it not?

AQUINAS: Sorrow hinders work that makes us sorrowful. But it helps us to do more readily whatever banishes sorrow.[172]

FOX: What causes sorrow?

AQUINAS: In the movements of the appetite, sorrow is a kind of flight or withdrawal, while pleasure is a kind of pursuit or approach. Love is the cause of both pleasure and sorrow.[173] Sorrow arises from love, either through the absence of the thing loved, or because the loved object to which we wish well is deprived of its good or afflicted with some evil.[174] Sorrow also arises from the prospect of or the recollection of evil things.[175]

---

166. Ibid.   167. ST I-II, q. 59, a. 3.   168. Ibid., ad 3.   169. ST I-II, q. 35, a. 6.   170. Ibid.   171. Ibid., q. 37, a. 3.   172. Ibid., q. 59, a. 3, ad 2.   173. Ibid., q. 36, a. 1.   174. Ibid. II-II, q. 28, a. 1.   175. Ibid., q. 30, a. 1, ad 3.

FOX: Thus a journey into the heart opens up both issues of delight and issues of sadness—the Via Positiva and the Via Negativa—since love causes both. What happens when we fall into the dark night of sorrow and can't get out of it?

AQUINAS: If inward sorrow be very intense, it draws one's attention so that a person is unable to learn anything for the first time.[176]

FOX: Thus we are not able to learn new things, and depression preoccupies us?

AQUINAS: Sorrow depresses the soul . . . inasmuch as it hinders it from enjoying that which it wishes to enjoy.[177] As far as the movement of the appetite is concerned, contraction and depression amount to the same thing because the soul, when it is depressed so as to be unable to attend freely to outward things, withdraws to itself, closing itself up as it were.[178] Sorrow is said to consume a person when the force of the afflicting evil is such as to shut out all hope of evasion. Thus sorrow both depresses and consumes at the same time.[179]

FOX: So sadness can indeed lead to despair?

AQUINAS: Those who are sorrowful fall the more easily into despair. . . . Despair is born of sorrow.[180] Despair implies a movement of withdrawal. Consequently, it is contrary to hope, just as withdrawal is contrary to openness.[181]

FOX: You are saying that joy leads to hope and sorrow to despair?

AQUINAS: A person who is joyful has greater hope.[182]

FOX: Despair can actually lead to death, can it not?

AQUINAS: The weakness of the vital spirit shortens the days of life.[183] If the strength of the evil be such as to exclude the hope of evasion, then even the interior movement of the afflicted soul is absolutely hindered, so that it cannot turn aside either this way or that. Sometimes even the external movement of the body is paralyzed, so that one becomes completely stupefied.[184]

FOX: There seems to be so much suffering in our journeys but also so many ways of dealing with that suffering.

---

176. Ibid. I-II, q. 37, a. 1.   177. Ibid., a. 2.   178. Ibid., ad 2.   179. Ibid., ad 3.   180. Ibid. II-II, q. 20, a. 4, ad 2.   181. Ibid. I-II, q. 40, a. 4. 182. Ibid. II-II, q. 20, a. 4, ad 2.   183. In Job, ch. 17, p. 69.   184. ST I-II, q. 37, a. 2.

AQUINAS: "Lamentation" comes from the words expressing pain; "crying" has to do with the shedding of tears; "grief" with regard to a certain behavior in the expression of pain, as is shown in the changing of garments and the like. As Jeremiah says, "A voice has been heard in the streets, crying and wailing for the children of Israel, since they have behaved unjustly and have forgotten the Lord their God."[185]

FOX: Why is it that the Scriptures advocate so much lamentation and grieving, as we have seen above? What is the role of grief in the Via Negativa? Is this one way of buttressing this "vital spirit" of which you speak?

AQUINAS: Isaiah sets forth the compunction of one who prays in chapter 38. And Matthew's gospel says (5): "Blessed are those who grieve, since they will be consoled."[186]

FOX: And so our expressions of grief are important for our healing process?

AQUINAS: Tears and groans naturally assuage sorrow because a hurtful thing hurts yet more if we keep it shut up, because the soul is more preoccupied with it. Whereas, if we allow it to escape, the soul's intention is dispersed as it were on outward things, so that the inward sorrow is lessened. This is why people burdened with sorrow make outward show of their sadness by tears or groans or even by words—thus their sorrow is assuaged.[187]

FOX: You seem to be advocating art as meditation as a way to deal with sadness and despair—no doubt we will explore this in greater depth when we discuss the Via Creativa. Can sadness also interfere with our experience of contemplation?

AQUINAS: Physical pain more than sadness can prevent contemplation, which demands a quiet heart. Yet mental duress, if protracted, can drain our attention to such an extent that we can discover nothing further that is fresh. It was because of sadness that Gregory quit writing his Commentary on Ezechiel.[188]

FOX: "Discovering nothing that is fresh"—it seems that sadness shuns the Via Positiva, so full of fresh things that render the spirit "vital," as you put it.

---

185. In Jer 31, p. 649.   186. In Is 38, p. 524.   187. ST I-II, q. 38, a. 2.
188. Ibid., q. 37, a. 1, ad 3.

AQUINAS: The very neglect to consider the divine favors arises from acedia. For when anyone is influenced by a certain passion they consider chiefly the things that pertain to that passion. Thus anyone who is full of sorrow does not easily think of great and joyful things, but only sad things, unless by a great effort they turn their thoughts away from sadness.[189]

FOX: Then acedia kills the spirit in a sense?

AQUINAS: The life of the body happens through vital spirits that are spread from the heart to all the limbs. As long as these remain in the body, the body lives; but when the quality of the natural heat begins to be weakened in the heart, the spirit of this kind is diminished. Job designates this diminishing and weakness as the attenuation of the spirit. And he names the effect of this cause by saying, "my days are shortened."[190]

FOX: Yet awe banishes acedia, for as you said in our previous conversation, "acedia comes from a shrinking of the mind."

AQUINAS: Prayer has a double effect. One is the expulsion of sadness; the other is the increase of hope. The first effect comes about because the mind of a person ascends through prayer to God. And since God is the highest good, when the soul clings to God, it feels the greatest pleasure, and the delight drives out sadness or at least diminishes it. The other effect is that of growing in hope. For if a king admits someone to familiar company and conversation, that person assumes a trust of seeking and obtaining. But in prayer a person especially speaks with God. As the psalmist says (28): "In God my heart has hope."[191]

FOX: How is hope different from denial or pretending we do not experience despair? How is hope a help in our "bottoming out" of our experiences of despair? I ask these questions because I believe that our civilization, hanging on the brink of ecological disaster and nuclear annihilation, is deeply in despair. But we cover this up with a lot of happy talk and smiling politicians and by burying our heads in sands of consumerism and jingoism and misplaced patriotism.

AQUINAS: Hope is about the possible; despair is about the impossible.[192]

---

189. Ibid. II-II, q. 20, a. 4, ad 3.   190. In Job, ch. 17, p. 69.   191. In Pss 41, p. 312.   192. DS, 1, ad 1.

FOX: Hope seems to be a rare commodity today, especially among the young. Elaborate on hope.

AQUINAS: Hope is for a difficult good and is prompted by that part of us that is prepared to tackle opposition. Hope is excited by a good that can be secured. It wears an air of confidence. What makes hope different from fear is that it seeks something good. What distinguishes it from joy is that it seeks something future and not yet possessed. It is different from desire because it seeks something difficult. And, as I said, it is different from despair because it seeks something possible.[193]

FOX: In the depths of the dark night of the soul, where do we look for hope?

AQUINAS: It is true that when we are in adversities, it seems like we are repulsed by God.[194] Yet, you can never hope in God too much.[195] The first lesson learned from Christ's descent into hell is a firm hope in God. The deeper we are sunk in misery, the more we should trust and have confidence. Nothing could be more depressing than being in hell, and yet, if Christ freed people there, how firmly should we who are his friends rely on him to rescue us whatever our predicament.[196]

FOX: You alluded to Christ's descent into hell. What is hell?

AQUINAS: Hell is separation from God.[197]

FOX: We even have experiences of nothingness in our dark nights, do we not?

AQUINAS: Job says (14): "Human beings have a short life . . . their days are measured out, since one's tale of months depend on you." But although life is short and can be so precious that it is to be meditated on deeply, still it is nothing. For my substance and my nature and my life are nothing before you, that is, in comparison with you, though they seem to be something in comparison with weak creatures. Isaiah (40) says: "All peoples are as nothing before God." But nothingness can be understood in this way: "My substance," that is, I think of my substance as nothing when I consider that which is before you, that is, the eternal goods that you will give the saints. Or it can

---

193. Ibid.   194. In Pss 42, p. 313.   195. DS 1, ad 1.   196. AC, p. 48.
197. In Mt 4, p. 43.

mean that those who consider the things of the world before you, that is, from a divine viewpoint, consider them as nothing.[198]

FOX: So we do experience the nothingness of things at times in our lives. I think it is important to name nothingness for what it is—part of the reality of things.

AQUINAS: Ecclesiastes says (1): "All things are vanity." And they are called vanity because vanity is opposed to solidity and stability: for all things that are in the world are subject to change, and so are vain. And even among these, "every living being" is subject to change, and this is vanity. Romans 8 says: "For a creature," that is, the human being, "is not subject to vanity willingly." People are called vain because they pursue changeable things, as Jeremiah puts it (2): "They walked after vanities, and became vain."[199]

FOX: You have said that we are by no means alone in our deepest pain and darkness, even when it feels like we are dwelling in hell.

AQUINAS: The Holy Spirit itself is grieved when a person in whom the Spirit dwells is saddened.[200] The prophet Jeremiah makes imminent the remedy of consolation when he says: "The Lord says these things: The voice is quiet"—he means the voice of lamentation; "and the eyes"—he means in regard to crying the eyes are dried up. Thus the Book of Revelation says (21): "The Lord will wipe away all tears from the eyes of the saints: there will be no more death, and no more mourning or sadness. The world of the past has gone."[201]

FOX: It would seem that our darknesses and sufferings, although all-encompassing at times, do not represent the last word of God or of the universe.

AQUINAS: No person is in such darkness as to be completely devoid of divine light. The divine light shines in the darkness and radiates upon all.[202]

FOX: You say the divine light never leaves us, no matter how dark it seems to be?

---

198. In Pss 38, p. 297.   199. Ibid.   200. In Eph 4.30, p. 487.   201. In Jer 31, p. 649.   202. In Jn 1.5, n. 103.

AQUINAS: That life that is the light of human beings "shines in the darkness" (John. 1:5), that is, in created souls and minds, by always shedding its light on all.[203]

FOX: That the divine light is "always" with us is a statement that calls forth immense trust.

AQUINAS: Good is more powerful than evil. As long as we are living, we can never be so stuck in evil that divine grace cannot get us out.[204] Part of the goodness of human nature is that it is always capable of being restored from evil to justice. This goodness remains in spite of any fall from grace.[205]

FOX: I sense the reentrance of the Via Positiva here—that the delight we experience in creation and the Creator sustains our struggle in darkness.

AQUINAS: Happiness arms some people against the devil, as Proverbs (17) says: "A glad heart is excellent medicine, a spirit depressed wastes the bones away." And then the psalmist adds, "I will sing to the Lord," that is, I will praise God. Consider Psalm 22: "You who fear the Lord, praise God." For praise of God is very strong in assailing the devil.[206]

FOX: Life is about both light and darkness, joy and emptiness, pain and praise.

AQUINAS: The phrase "day and night" stands for prosperity and adversity. "I will praise you day and night," the psalmist promises.[207] The psalmist (Psalm 16) talks about our being enlightened by God. This can be understood in two ways: first, that prosperity is understood through the lamp; adversity through the shadows. Just as when anyone is happy, all things seem clear to them; but when one is sad, all things seem dark to that one. Therefore the psalmist says, "since you light my lamp, Lord," meaning you have given me prosperity, and you give it continuously: "enlighten my darkness," that is, if any adversity remains in me, drive and remove it from me.[208]

FOX: It seems that in times of darkness—more than ever—we need to remember the joyful times.

AQUINAS: The psalmist asks the question: "Why are you sad, my soul?" when you ought to take joy, since you are going to

---

203. Ibid., n. 102.   204. CG IV, ch. 71 n. 3.   205. Ibid., n. 5.   206. In Pss 12, p. 183.   207. In Pss 41, p. 310.   208. In Pss 17, p. 202.

the tabernacle, to the house of the Lord. So why are you sad? For small evils must not be regarded in the consideration of eternal goods. As the Book of Ecclesiasticus says (30): "Sadness," namely, of the world, "chase it far away." And Paul says (2 Cor. 7): "The sadness of the world brings death." The effect of sadness is disturbance, since from the disorder of the emotions reason itself is confused.[209]

FOX: Grief and joy, darkness and light, are not always exclusive of one another.

AQUINAS: There is a certain order in the penitential psalms in which they begin in grief and end in joy, since penitence accomplishes this. In the conclusion to Psalm 32 the psalmist urges the just and righteous on to good works and good intention by saying, "Rejoice in the Lord and exult."[210]

FOX: It seems that trust is learned in our struggle with adversity and darkness.

AQUINAS: The psalmist says, "Reach down your hand from above, save me, rescue me from deep waters, from the power of strangers who tell nothing but lies" (Ps. 144). It should be noted that there is a certain hand of divine guidance, as in Wisdom 7: "We are indeed in God's hand, we ourselves and our words, with all our understanding too, and technical knowledge." There is also a hand of divine generosity, as in Psalm 104: "All creatures depend on you . . . with generous hand you satisfy their hunger." And a hand of divine protection, as in Isaiah 49: "Under the covering of God's hand, the divine One protected me." There is also a hand of correction, as in Psalm 39: "Your hand has pressed down on me." And a hand of divine deliverance, as in Job 5: "God strikes, and the divine hand will heal." There is a hand of divine working, as in Ecclesiasticus 36: "Glorify the hand and the right arm." And a hand of divine condemnation, as in Hebrews 10: "It is terrible to fall into the hand of the living God."[211]

FOX: Your image of the hand of God as a healing hand is a rich one.

AQUINAS: God is the nourisher and the doctor. But a doctor withdraws nourishment from the sick, and makes them hungry

---

209. In Pss 41, p. 310.   210. In Pss 31, p. 259.   211. In Jer 16, p. 619.

and thirsty, since it is advantageous for health. So God, to the extent that it is advantageous to our salvation, sometimes introduces poverty, sometimes confers wealth, sometimes gives length of days, sometimes cuts them short.[212]

FOX: Your equating health with salvation and Divinity with a healer or doctor is well taken. You are reassuring us that God brings a healing peace to us whether we live in joy or in sorrow.

AQUINAS: By patience we obtain peace whether times be good or evil. For this reason, peacemakers are called the children of God—because they are like God: Just as nothing can hurt God, so nothing can harm them, whether they prosper or suffer. Therefore we read: "Blessed are the peacemakers, for they shall be called children of God" (Matt. 5:9).[213]

FOX: There seems to be another way in which grief and delight are related in our mystical experience as well as in the way we have been discussing.

AQUINAS: The greater the love, so much the greater is the grief as well.[214]

FOX: Can you give an example of this truism?

AQUINAS: Part of Job's adversity consisted in the outward signs of sadness into which the signs of joy had been changed. These were his musical instruments, and about this he says, "my lute has been turned into grief," as if to say: grief follows my lute, which I had been using for joy. Or as regards songs of the human voice, Job adds: "and my pipe"—which I had been using for joy—"has been turned into the voice of weeping."[215]

FOX: I see so much interplay between the Via Positiva and the Via Negativa motifs, so much dance between light and darkness, that I wonder if we are speaking of a kind of cosmic pattern when we speak of this interplay?

AQUINAS: Production of one thing spells destruction for another. Consequently, in human as in animal evolution, when the more perfect arrives the less perfect departs, yet in such a manner that the supervening form keeps the endowment of the preceding, and has much more besides.[216]

---

212. In Pss 33, p. 266.   213. OF, p. 157.   214. In Pss 37, p. 292.   215. In Job, ch. 30, p. 104.   216. ST I, q. 118, a. 2, ad 2.

FOX: You have spoken of the Holy Spirit wanting to rescue us from depression and darkness. What about Christ—what roles, in addition to those we have discussed above, does Christ play in the Via Negativa?

AQUINAS: The phrase in John's gospel, "that life was the light of human beings," can be explained in another way by the influx of grace, since we are illuminated by Christ. After the Evangelist considered the restoration of things through the Word, here he considers the restoration of the rational creature through Christ, saying, "and that life" of the Word "was the light of human beings," that is, of all human beings in general, and not only of the Jews. For the Son of God assumed flesh and came into the world to illumine all human beings with grace and truth.[217]

FOX: And so Christ assists us with light in the deep darkness of the Via Negativa path?

AQUINAS: By dying Christ destroyed our death. By the pains he underwent he freed us from pain. That was why he chose to suffer a painful death.[218]

FOX: You are saying that Christ's cross is evidence that he has suffered what we suffer?

AQUINAS: Our hearts have been washed by the wine of divine love, as in Genesis (49): "He will wash his cloak in wine, and his garment in the blood of the grape."[219] Our hearts have also been washed in the blood of the Lord's passion, as the Book of Revelation says (7): "They have washed their garments and made them white in the blood of the Lamb."[220] Christ suffered in his members from the beginning of the world. He suffered on the cross in his own person.[221]

FOX: The mystery of the cross takes on more meaning in this context.

AQUINAS: The cross is upheld by its depth, which lies concealed beneath the ground. It is not seen because the depth of the divine love that sustains us is not visible.[222]

FOX: So our entire discussion on the Via Negativa represents your theology of the Cross! You name the mystery of the divine

---

217. In Jn 1.5, n. 104.   218. ST III, q. 35, a. 6, ad 2.   219. In Jer 4, p. 590.   220. Ibid.   221. In Heb, ch. 12, p. 774.   222. In Eph 3.18, p. 474.

love sustaining us underground as something invisible to us. And you name Christ as one who, on the one hand, communicates with the unnameable mystery of the Godhead, and who, on the other hand, underwent the dark night of the soul and so tasted of the suffering dimension of the Via Negativa. Would you care to elaborate on the matter of the suffering of Christ?

AQUINAS: In the passion of Christ humanity ought first to recognize love, for the purpose of loving again. The Song of Songs (8) says: "Set me like a seal on your heart." Second, bitterness, for the purpose of empathizing, as in Lamentations (3): "Brooding on my anguish and affliction is gall and wormwood." Third, courage, for the purpose of suffering bravely. Hebrews 12 says: "Think of the way Jesus stood such opposition from sinners and then you will not give up for want of courage." Fourth, usefulness, for the purpose of acting with grace. The Song of Songs (7) says: "I will climb up into the palm tree, I will seize its dates."[223]

FOX: You call Christ the person of "perfect virtue" who shows us how to live. We will no doubt explore more of what you mean by "the virtuous person" in the next two conversations when we deal with the Via Creativa and the Via Transformativa. How does Jesus' experience on the cross teach us to live well?

AQUINAS: It is clear how profitable Christ's passion was as a remedy, but it is not less profitable as an example. . . . There is no virtue an example of which we do not find on the cross. *Charity.* If you seek an example of charity, "greater love has no person than to lay down one's life for one's friends" (John. 15:13), and Christ did this on the cross. If he laid down his life for us, we should not consider it a hardship to suffer any evils whatever for his sake: "What shall I render unto the Lord for all the things which God has rendered to me?" (Ps. 116:12).

Patience. If you seek an example of patience, you will find a most perfect example on the cross. For a person's patience is proved to be great on two counts: either when one suffers great evils patiently or when one suffers that which one is able to avoid yet does not avoid.

223. In Is, ch. 57, p. 560.

Now Christ suffered greatly on the cross: "O all you that pass this way, look and see: is any sorrow like unto my sorrow" (Lam. 1:12). And he suffered patiently inasmuch as "when he suffered he threatened not" (1 Pet. 2:23). "He shall be led as a sheep to the slaughter, and shall be dumb as a lamb before his shearer" (Isa. 53:7).

Moreover, he could have escaped but did not escape: "Do you not think that I can ask my Father and he will give me presently more than twelve legions of angels?" (Matt. 26:53). Great therefore was Christ's patience on the cross.[224]

FOX: Are there other virtues we learn from Jesus' experience on the cross?

AQUINAS: If you seek an example of humility, look on the crucified one. Although he was God, he chose to be judged by Pontius Pilate and to suffer death: "Your cause has been judged as that of the wicked" (Job 36:17). Truly "as that of the wicked," because: "Let us condemn him to a most shameful death" (Wis. 2:20). The master chose to die for his servant; (he who was) the life of the angels suffered death for humans: "Made obedient unto death" (Phil. 2:8).

Obedience. If you seek an example of obedience, follow him who was made obedient to the Creator even unto death: "As by the disobedience of one person, many were made sinners, so also by the obedience of one, many shall be made just" (Rom. 5:19).

Contempt for earthly things. If you seek an example of contempt for earthly things, follow him, the King of kings and Lord of lords, in whom are the treasures of wisdom; and see him on the cross, despoiled, derided, spat upon, scourged, crowned with thorns, served with gall and hyssop, dead. Therefore, take no account of your apparel or possessions, since "they parted my garments amongst them" (Ps. 22:18); nor of honors, since I suffered myself to be jeered at and scourged; nor of rank, since they plaited a crown of thorns and placed it on my head; nor of pleasures, since "in my thirst they gave me vinegar to drink" (Ps. 69:21).[225]

FOX: Might we say that Christ teaches us that the way of living virtuously is to dance the dance of the Via Positiva and the Via Negativa?

---

224. AC, 41–42.   225. Ibid., 43–44.

AQUINAS: Paul teaches that we are to stand firm in both adversity and prosperity.[226]

FOX: And would you say that this teaching from Paul and from the example of Christ's life is salvific?

AQUINAS: Salvation implies a freedom from dangers.[227] It is more important in a dangerous situation to be able to remain steady than to take the offensive.[228]

FOX: It sounds like you are providing us with practical advice about how a healthy Via Negativa allows us to endure struggle—it almost sounds like Aikido, this emphasis you give to remaining grounded rather than being offensive. The person who has learned to let go and let be has developed a way of freedom from danger—the danger of success *and* the danger of failure.

AQUINAS: Magnanimous people are not uplifted by great honors, because they do not deem them above them. Rather, they despise them—and even more so ordinary or little honors. Similarly, they are not cast down by dishonor, but despise it, since magnanimous persons recognize that they do not deserve it.[229]

FOX: You are saying that a person who has learned to let go endures through times of ecstasy and of emptiness?

AQUINAS: Since magnanimous people do not think much of external goods, that is, goods of fortune, they are neither uplifted by them if they have them, nor cast down by their loss.[230]

FOX: What are some additional practical consequences of this capacity to let go?

AQUINAS: The reign of God does not consist in eating and drinking, but in resignation to either lot. The apostles were neither elated by abundance nor depressed by want.[231]

FOX: Asceticism as such does not seem a part of your grasp of the Via Negativa.

AQUINAS: Abstinence as such has no essential bearing on salvation.[232] Fastings, vigils, meditations on the scriptures, nakedness, mortification in every faculty—these are not perfection,

---

226. In Eph 6.13, p. 502.   227. Ibid., 2.8, p. 459.   228. ST II-II, q. 123, a. 6.   229. Ibid., q. 129, a. 2, ad 3.   230. Ibid., a. 8, ad 3.   231. Ibid. III, q. 40, a. 2, ad 1.   232. Ibid.

but some instruments of perfection. We discipline ourselves by working through them, not by staying with them.[233]

FOX: Can you identify another practical consequence of our learning the art of letting go?

AQUINAS: It belongs to the generous person to let go of things. Thus generosity is also called openhandedness (*largitas*) because that which is open does not withhold things but parts with them. The word for generosity (*liberalitas*) also seems to allude to the fact that when anyone lets go of something they free it (*liberat*) so to speak from their keeping and ownership and show their intention to be free of attachment to it.[234]

FOX: And so, as you say, we free ourselves by practices of letting go that in turn lead to generosity. This would seem to be a matter we will want to pursue more fully in our discussion on the Via Transformativa—but an important lesson emerges here regarding the relation of the Via Negativa to the Via Transformativa. Our personal emptying makes for justice to happen in society.

Your life story seems an especially powerful parable of the letting go you are counseling. It is well known that the last year of your life you were struck dumb. You, the champion of Western intellectual life, lived your final year in silence, unable to talk or write. You left your greatest work and most prodigious effort, your *Summa theologiae,* unfinished. And all this happened because you experienced some kind of ineffable moment during worship. How do you explain this?

AQUINAS: [As I said then,] in the light of what I have seen, all my work is like straw.[235]

FOX: One wonders why you had to live out so literally your lesson of silence and letting go and the Via Negativa. Of course Jesus and Francis had similar experiences at the end of their lives. You must have been utterly exhausted from your intellectual labors and your constant battles with the anti-intellectual, fundamentalist Christians on the one hand; and with the secularist thinkers like Siger of Brabant on the other.

---

233. Ibid. II-II, q. 184, a. 3.   234. Ibid., q. 117, a. 2.   235. See Josef Pieper, *The Silence of Saint Thomas* (Chicago: Henry Regnery, 1965), 40.

AQUINAS: Wisdom cannot become a person's possession—it is given only as a loan.[236]

FOX: And your year of silence, the final year of your life, was that a kind of return on the loan? I am reminded of what Otto Rank says: life is a loan and death is its repayment.

AQUINAS: To anyone who sees the Creator, all creation seems puny. . . . No matter how little people see of the light of the Creator, all that is created becomes small for them.[237]

FOX: As a final statement on the Via Negativa, I am going to reproduce here a passage from a document attributed to you by ancient manuscripts. It is the document of a theologian of the Middle Ages going through a kind of breakdown while offering a commentary on one of your favorite books, The Song of Songs. We are not sure if it is yours or not, but we do know that as you lay dying the monks demanded that you speak some words about the Song of Songs, and, given the state you were in that final year, these may indeed be your words. Whether they are your words or not, they certainly do represent a certain experience of the Via Negativa. The person who brought this book, *Aurora consurgens,* to my attention was Louise von Franz, a disciple of Carl Jung. She says about this text: "I think our author had such an indescribable and overwhelming experience of the unconscious and that he tried, in a rather chaotic way, through a potpourri of biblical and alchemical quotations, to catch and describe what had happened to him."[238] She concluded that the book was written by a person who was "overwhelmed by the unconscious" at this moment in his life and that it was the text of a dying person. Because we are not sure these are your words we will reproduce them in italics. We know that you died at the small monastery of Santa Maria di Fossa Nuova in the middle of giving a seminar on the Song of Songs—at the words, "Come, my beloved, let us go forth into the field." This is in fact exactly where the text of *Aurora consurgens* concludes. Interestingly enough, these final hours of your life were not part of the canonization process in 1312, but that may be explained by the forces marshalled on behalf of your canonization not wanting to endanger their cause. (After all, your colleague

---

236. In Meta I, L. 3 n. 64.   237. ST II-II, q. 180, a. 5, ad 3.
238. Marie-Louise von Franz, *Alchemy* (Toronto: Inner City Books, 1980), 192.

Bonaventure tampered considerably with Francis of Assisi's biography in the process of procuring his canonization a century earlier.)

AQUINAS: All that I had written was straw.

FOX: While we are not certain the words that follow are your words, we are sure that the last months of your life were a deep letting go, a being taken over by dumbness and silence. And so there is a kind of parable in your life story which parallels your teaching about letting go.

Looking from afar, I saw a big cloud which, having been absorbed by the earth, covered it with blackness, and covered my soul, which the waters had entered so that they became corrupted, from the aspect of the deepest hell and the shadow of death because the flood has drowned me.

Then the Ethiopians will fall down on their knees before me and my enemies will lick my dust. Nothing healthy is in my body any more, and from the sight of my sins my bones tremble. I have cried the whole night, my throat has become hoarse. Who is the human being who lives, understanding and knowing, who can save my soul from the underworld?

Turn towards me with your whole heart and do not reject me because I am black, for the sun has taken my color away and the abyss has covered my face. The earth is polluted by my work, darkness has spread over the earth, I am at the bottom of the abyss and my substance has not yet been opened.

I cry from the depth and from the abyss of the earth, I raise my voice to all you who pass by, attend to me and look at me if there be anybody like unto me. To him I will give the morning star. Behold I have waited on my couch the whole night for someone to comfort me and have not found any. I called and none answered me.[239]

---

239. Ibid., 203, 266.

Third Conversation:

ON THE VIA CREATIVA

*Although a created being tends to the divine likeness in
many ways, this one whereby it seeks the divine likeness
by being the cause of others takes the ultimate place.
Hence Dionysius says, that "of all things, it is more
divine to become a co-worker with God" in accord
with the statement of the Apostle:
"We are God's co-workers" (I Cor. 3:9).*

(CG III, ch. 21 n. 8)

*Human virtue is a participation
in the divine power.*

(ST II-II, q. 129, a.1)

FOX: Brother Thomas, toward the end of our discussion on the Via Positiva you spoke of gratitude. In thinking about creativity I am reminded of how Otto Rank defines the artist: the artist is one who wants to leave behind a gift. How do you understand gratitude?

AQUINAS: Gratitude tries to return more than has been received.[1]

FOX: We have been discussing the Via Positiva and the Via Negativa. In the first two paths we are receptive of awe, wonder, darkness, and suffering; in the next two paths we are active as we respond to the godliness we have encountered.

AQUINAS: It is necessary to be aware that there exists in us a double composition of intellect: one that pertains to the discovery of truth; and another that pertains to its judgment.[2] The intellect exercises a twofold act—one of perception and another of judgment. The gift of understanding regards the former; the gift of wisdom regards the latter according to divine ideas, the gift of knowledge according to human ideas.[3]

FOX: The first two paths pertain to discovery, while the second two pertain more to judgment and action. The first two paths are about understanding—taking in, standing under, undergoing; the second two paths, those of the Via Creativa and the Via Transformativa, are about giving birth and being prophetic in our work. Would you agree with this?

AQUINAS: By discovering we collect from many and proceed toward one, whether the many things are called diverse objects of sense from which, through experiencing, we receive universal knowledge; or whether the many things are called diverse signs from which, by using reason, we arrive at universal truth.[4]

---

1. ST II-II, q. 106, a. 6.   2. DDN, n. 711, p. 266.   3. ST II-II, q. 45, a. 2, ad 3.   4. DDN, n. 711, p. 266.

FOX: In the Via Negativa we dealt with emptiness and silence and letting go—do you sense an inner logic in our moving now from the Via Negativa to the Via Creativa?

AQUINAS: [In the creation story] mention is made of several kinds of formlessness as regards the corporeal creature. One is where we read that "the earth was void and empty"; and another where it is said that "darkness was upon the face of the deep."[5]

FOX: And so emptiness, darkness, nothingness, formlessness pave the way for new birth and creation itself?

AQUINAS: The formlessness of darkness was removed by the production of light.[6]

FOX: The production of light—that is, the first creature created was light itself! Indeed, out of the darkness, that is, the Via Negativa, light is born. Birth happens. The Via Creativa is launched. And so we are now talking about the creativity of God.

AQUINAS: God's spirit is said to move over the waters as the will of artists moves over the material to be shaped by their art.[7]

FOX: God as artist. Let us pursue this theme more deeply. This very phrase of "moving over the waters" is such a fetal image; it conjures up deep resonance with the act of birthing as we know it in our species: water, fetal waters, wet communing that results in birth.

AQUINAS: "The Spirit of God moved over the waters"—this means over the formless matter, signified by water, just as the love of artists moves over the materials of their art, in order that out of them artists might form their work. "God saw that it was good" signifies that the things that God had made were to endure because they express a certain satisfaction taken by God in the divine works. Just as all artists take satisfaction in their art.[8]

FOX: And so God is pregnant with creativity, as every artist is?

AQUINAS: There is in God perfect fecundity.[9]

FOX: "Perfect fecundity"—elaborate on this rich phrase.

---

5. ST I, q. 67, a. 4.   6. Ibid.   7. Ibid., q. 66, a. 1, ad 3.   8. Ibid., q. 74, a. 3, ad 3.   9. Ibid., q. 27, a. 5, ad 3.

AQUINAS: Since it is the Godhead who grants generation to others, there is no way that God could be said to be sterile. The Scriptures have not been silent about the very name of "divine generation."[10]

FOX: Offer us an example from Scripture of the divine fecundity.

AQUINAS: The Scriptures say: "I, wisdom, have poured out rivers; I, like a channel out of a river of mighty water; I, like a brook from a river, and like a water channel came out of paradise. I said, 'I will water my garden of plants, and I will water abundantly my flower-beds.'" (Eccles. 24:40). . . . All things flow from God but without diminishing God. As brooks and irrigation canals are led from great rivers, so all the motions of creatures derive from the eternal activity of the divine Persons. . . . The Creator floods the creature, but the level of the main stream does not fall; the creature is distinct from the Creator, but the divine might is not diminished.[11]

FOX: So Divinity's "perfect fecundity" is part of God's very being?

AQUINAS: The generative power is really identical with the divine nature, so that the nature is essentially included in it.[12]

FOX: "Generative power." What is generation?

AQUINAS: Now, generation signifies something in the process of being made.[13] In another sense it properly belongs to living things for whom it means the origin of a living being from a conjoined living principle. This is properly called *birth*.[14]

FOX: So birthing or generation is a process—it is fecundity actually going on. How is this different from parenthood itself?

AQUINAS: Paternity, in contrast, signifies the completion of generation.[15]

FOX: But maternity does not, for it seems that the maternal act of birthing continues. Earlier you used the phrase the "generative *power*." How are birthing and creating and generating a kind of power?

AQUINAS: One thing we know about the Godhead is its power (*virtus*). It is through this power that things come forth from

---

10. CG IV, ch. 2 n. 5. See Ps. 2:7; Prov. 8:24–25; Isa. 66:9; John 1:14, 18; Heb. 1:6.   11. In I Sent, Prologue.   12. DP, q. 2, a. 2, ad 6.   13. ST I, q. 33, a. 2, ad 2.   14. Ibid., q. 27, a. 2.   15. Ibid., q. 33, a. 2, ad 2.

God as from their principle. The psalmist says (147:5): "Great is the Lord and great is God's power."[16]

FOX: And so to talk about the Via Creativa is to talk about power and empowerment?

AQUINAS: Power is twofold—namely, passive, which does not exist at all in God; and active, which we must assign to God in the fullest degree.[17]

FOX: Let us now discuss in more depth the active power that creativity represents.

AQUINAS: It is clear that all things—insofar as they are in act and are perfect—are the active principle of something. Whereas things are passive insofar as they are deficient and imperfect.[18]

FOX: And God?

AQUINAS: In God there is active power to the fullest degree.[19] Power of action is a consequence of perfection of nature. In creatures, for instance, we see that the more perfect the nature, the greater power is there for action.[20]

FOX: Why is it that you assign such preeminent power to God as generator?

AQUINAS: There is no lack of power in God. . . . In God is the generative power. For it is in the nature of every act to communicate itself as far as possible. Wherefore every agent acts to the extent that it is in act: while to act is nothing else than to communicate as far as possible that whereby the agent is in act. Now the divine nature is supreme and most pure act. . . . Given that in God there is generation, a term that is significative of action, it follows that we must grant God the power to beget, or a generative power.[21]

FOX: You seem perfectly at ease with the concept of power in God, and yet you seem to ground it first of all in the power to give birth.

AQUINAS: All operation proceeds from power. Now operation is supremely attributable to God. Therefore, power is most becoming to God.[22]

FOX: God then would seem to be the primary source of empowerment. And God's ultimate power is that of the artist?

---

16. In Rom, ch. 1, p. 16.   17. ST I, q. 25, a. 1.   18. Ibid.   19. Ibid.
20. Ibid., a. 6.   21. DP, q. 2, a. 1.   22. Ibid., q. 1, a. 1.

AQUINAS: Although every effect of God proceeds from each attribute, each effect is reduced to that attribute with which it is naturally connected. . . . Creation, which is the production of the very substance of a thing, is reduced to power.[23] One of the functions of divine wisdom is to create. God's wisdom is that of artists, whose knowledge of what they make is practical as well as theoretical: "Thou hast made all things in wisdom" (Ps. 104:24). It is Wisdom in person who speaks, "I was with God forming all things."[24]

FOX: So God is artist, even the Artist of artists, who is, we might say, fully communicative?

AQUINAS: Art, the idea of a thing to be made in the mind of the maker, is possessed most authentically by God. "Wisdom, which is the fashioner of all things, taught me," say the Scriptures (Wis. 7:21).[25] To give, not for any return, but from the very excellence and consonance of giving, is an act of generosity. God is supremely generous.[26]

FOX: Would you say that God's work as artist is a work that is without a why?

AQUINAS: The first cause, who is purely active and without passivity, does not work to acquire an end, but intends solely to communicate the divine excellence.[27]

FOX: If God is artist, then all of creation is God's art?

AQUINAS: All natural things were produced by the divine art, and so they may be called God's works of art.[28] God may be compared to created things as the architect is to things that are designed.[29]

FOX: Things are willed by God as art is willed by the artist?

AQUINAS: Things that proceed from the will are either things-to-be-done, such as acts of the virtues, which are perfections of the doer; or things-to-be-made, which pass into matter outside the agent. So it is clear that creatures proceed from God as things made. Now, as Aristotle says, "art is the reason concerned with things to be made." All created things, therefore, stand in relation to God as artifacts to the artist. But artists bring

---

23. ST I, q. 45, a. 6, ad 3. 24. In I Sent, Prologue. 25. CG I, ch. 93 n. 4. 26. Ibid., n. 7. 27. ST I, q. 44, a. 4. 28. Ibid., q. 91, a. 3. 29. Ibid., q. 27, a. 1, ad 3.

their works into being by the ordering of their wisdom and intellect. So, too, did God make all things by the ordering of the divine intellect.[30]

FOX: All things are then God's works of art?

AQUINAS: This truth is confirmed by divine authority. For we read in the Psalm (104:24): "You have made all things in wisdom"; and in the Book of Proverbs (3:19): "The Lord by wisdom has founded the earth."[31] As the maker is the cause of the thing made, so God is the cause of celestial bodies—though in a different fashion. For artists construct their work from preexisting matter, but celestial bodies cannot be made from preexisting matter, but along with their production matter was produced with its form.[32]

FOX: And God, as you said in our Via Positiva conversation, loves the divine work of art, even if it seems imperfect?

AQUINAS: Now all artists intend to give to their work the best disposition possible—not absolutely the best, but the best as regards the proposed end. Even if this entails some defect, the artist does not care. Thus, for example, when anyone makes a saw for the purpose of cutting, they make it of iron, which is suitable for the objective; they do not prefer to make it of glass, though this is a more beautiful material, because this very beauty would be an obstacle to the end in view. For this reason God gave to each natural being the best disposition—not absolutely speaking, but in view of its proper end.[33]

FOX: Does God as artist produce things in the same mysterious way that artists do?

AQUINAS: God is the cause of things by the divine intellect and will, just as artists are cause of the things made by their art. Now artists work through the word conceived in their mind, and through the love of their will toward some object. Hence also God the Creator made the creature through the divine Word, which is God's Son; and through the divine Love, which is the Holy Spirit. And so the processions of the Persons are the type of the productions of creatures inasmuch as they include the essential attributes of knowledge and will.[34]

---

30. CG II, ch. 24 n. 5.   31. Ibid., n. 6.   32. In Job, ch. 37, p. 125.
33. ST I, q. 91, a. 3.   34. Ibid., q. 45, a. 6.

FOX: And so we might say the Word of God is God's work of art as well?

AQUINAS: The Word's going forth from the Father is by mode of the interior procession whereby the word emerges from the heart and remains therein.[35]

FOX: And so what is deep within us creatively both emerges from the heart but also remains within the heart?

AQUINAS: Love in us is something that abides in the lover, and the word of the heart is something abiding in the speaker, yet with a relation to the object loved or the thing expressed by word. But in God, in whom there is nothing accidental, there is more than this because both Word and Love are subsistent.[36]

FOX: And so art comes from heart as well as from intellect and will. And it never leaves the heart, even when it emerges in communicative expression. This seems to argue for art as meditation, namely, that art can expand the heart because it challenges the heart to express its beloved. You say that our art and God's is different insofar as Word and Love are subsistent in God. How else do we differ as artists, God and us?

AQUINAS: Human beings are not the author of nature. But they use natural things in applying art and virtue to their own use.[37] Because the power of the human maker is confined to the form only, their causality is confined to the production of this or that form. On the other hand, God is the universal cause of all things, and creates not only the form, but also the matter.[38]

FOX: This is an important point you are making—that all our human creativity presupposes existing matter and that our true artistry is in birthing form for the already divinely made matter. You are stressing how interdependent we human beings are with the processes of nature even in our deepest acts of creativity and technology—we ought not take matter for granted.

AQUINAS: The principle of artifacts is the human intellect, which is derived by some sort of likeness from the divine intellect, and this latter is the principle of all natural things. Hence, not only must artistic operations imitate nature but also artifacts must imitate things that exist in nature.[39]

---

35. Ibid., q. 42, a. 5, ad 2.   36. Ibid., q. 37, a. 1, ad 2.   37. Ibid., q. 22, a. 2, ad 3.   38. AC, p. 16.   39. In Pol I, lect. 1, p. 566.

FOX: And yet art is not restricted to what is in nature—except, certainly, insofar as human imagination is also "in nature" and is natural?

AQUINAS: Of course, nature does not completely produce artifacts; it merely provides certain principles and offers some sort of working model. In fact, art can observe things in nature and use them to complete its own work; of course, it cannot completely produce these natural things. It is clear from this that human reason is merely cognitive in regard to things that exist in nature, but in regard to those which are artifacts it is both cognitive and productive.[40]

FOX: Will you give an example of art imitating nature?

AQUINAS: In its work, nature proceeds from simple things to complex ones; so, in the case of things made by the working of nature, that which is most complex is perfect and whole and the end of the others, as is clear in the relation of all whole things to their parts. So, too, human reason as operative proceeds from simple things to complex, going as it were from the imperfect to the perfect.[41]

FOX: And so human beings depend on nature and the author of nature for their own creativity?

AQUINAS: Just as art presupposes nature, so does nature presuppose God. Now, nature operates in the operations of art, since art does not work without the concurrence of nature. Thus fire softens the iron so as to render it malleable under the stroke of the blacksmith. It follows that God also works in the operation of nature.[42]

FOX: You are saying that, since it is natural to give birth and be creative, God operates in our operations of creativity?

AQUINAS: According to Aristotle, human beings and the sun generate another human being. Now, just as the generative act in the human being depends on the action of the sun, so does the action of nature depend on the action of God, and even more so. Therefore in every action of nature God operates also.[43]

FOX: This idea that we *and* the sun accomplish our creative work together is a very contemporary one in light of the discovery of photosynthesis and the fact that sun energy provides

---

40. Ibid.   41. Ibid.   42. DP, q. 3, a. 7.   43. Ibid.

the food that in turn provides for the energy in our bodies and minds with which we humans make things. It follows from what you are saying that we and God generate together—we are cocreators?

AQUINAS: God's power is in every natural thing, since God is in all things by the divine essence, presence, and power.[44]

FOX: I remember you stressing this point when we discussed panentheism in the Via Positiva.

AQUINAS: We must admit without any qualification that God operates in the operations of nature and will. Some, however, through failing to understand this correctly, fell into error, and ascribed to God every operation of nature in the sense that nature does nothing at all by its own power.[45]

FOX: I take it you are ill at ease with this ignoring of the power of secondary causes.

AQUINAS: This notion is opposed to reason, which convinces us that nothing in nature is void of purpose. Now, unless natural things had an action of their own, the forms and forces with which they are endowed would be to no purpose. Thus if a knife does not cut, its sharpness is useless. It would also be useless to set fire to the coal, if God ignites the coal without fire.[46] To exclude proximate causes, attributing solely to first causes all effects that happen in lower natures, is to derogate from the order of the universe, which is made up of the order and connection of causes, since the first cause, by the preeminence of its goodness, gives other beings not only their existence, but also their existence as causes.[47]

FOX: It is telling how you put the issue of our being causes and our need to honor that within the cosmic context of the "order of the universe" as well as within the context of blessing or the "preeminent goodness" of God. I hear you saying that the likeness that things have to God is a likeness not only in being but also in the power of generating.

AQUINAS: Things were made like God not only in being but also in acting.[48] Whatever causes God assigns to certain effects, God gives them the power to produce those effects. . . . The dignity of causality is imparted even to creatures.[49]

---

44. Ibid. 45. Ibid. 46. Ibid. 47. DV, q. 11, a. 1. 48. DP, q. 3, a. 7. 49. ST I, q. 22, a. 3.

FOX: I like your phrase "the dignity of causality." Every creature has dignity not only in its existence but in its power to cause.

AQUINAS: Secondary causes are the executors of divine providence.[50] The world is governed through secondary causes.[51]

FOX: That is a powerful statement—that the world is governed through secondary causes. Again, it puts tremendous responsibility on our work as agents of the divine will.

AQUINAS: It is not from weakness that God has shared the government of the universe with creatures, but from an abundance of divine goodness have creatures been endowed with the dignity of causality.[52]

FOX: Perhaps this phrase, "the dignity of causality," is another term for "cocreation." All things have this dignity of causality, it seems.

AQUINAS: Every creature strives, by its activity, to communicate its own perfect being, in its own fashion, to another; and in this it tends toward an imitation of the divine causality.[53]

FOX: So all creation participates in an effort to imitate God?

AQUINAS: All secondary causes, by the fact of being causes, attain the divine likeness.[54] If no creature had any active role in the production of any effect, much would be detracted from the perfection of the creature. Indeed, it is part of the fullness of perfection to be able to communicate to another being the perfection that one possesses.[55]

FOX: Some people, by ignoring the theme of cocreation and the path of the Via Creativa, seem to be ascribing all causality to God and seem to disempower creatures as cocreators.

AQUINAS: The argument that ascribes to God every operation of nature in the sense that nature does nothing at all by its own power . . . is altogether frivolous.[56]

FOX: Why is it frivolous?

AQUINAS: A deep embarrassment results from the idea that no creatures take an active part in the production of natural effects.

---

50. CG III, ch. 77 n. 2.   51. CT I, ch. 131.   52. ST I, q. 22, a. 3.
53. CT I, ch. 103.   54. CG III, ch. 75 n. 4.   55. Ibid., ch. 69 n. 15.
56. DP, q. 3, a. 7.

First of all, if only God operated and no creatures and no bodies in particular caused anything, then there would be no diversity among the apparent effects of creation. For God is not modified by working at producing variety. Does anyone expect fire to freeze or anything but a baby to be born from human parents? What causes everyday things to happen should not be so attributed to divine power that the power of everyday things is abolished.[57] To do this is to destroy all natural science, for if creatures played no real role in producing natural effects, we could never learn about them from their effects or offspring.[58]

FOX: I hear you passionately defending the power of things and the right of every creature to its divinely given empowerment.

AQUINAS: To detract from the proper actions of things is to disparage the divine goodness itself.[59] God works in every natural thing not as though the natural thing were altogether inert, but because God works in both nature and will when they work.[60]

FOX: How is this so?

AQUINAS: God acts in all things from within, because God acts by creating.[61] Since God is the proper cause of existence and existence is innermost to all things, it follows that God works at the heart of all activity.[62] One thing may be the cause of another's actions in several ways. First, by giving it the power to act. . . . In this way God causes all the actions of nature, because God gave natural things the forces whereby they are able to act, not only as the generator gives power to heavy and light bodies yet does not preserve it, but also as upholding its very being, forasmuch as God is the cause of the power bestowed, not only like the generator in its becoming, but also in its being. Thus God may be said to be the cause of an action by both causing and upholding the natural power in its being. Second, the preserver of a power is said to cause the action. Thus a remedy that preserves the sight is said to make a person see. Third, a thing is said to cause another's action by moving it to act.[63]

FOX: God then is involved as a principle of action in our creative moments?

AQUINAS: The end, the agent, and the form are principles of action, but in a certain order. The first principle of action is the

---

57. CG III, ch. 69 n. 12. 58. Ibid., n. 18. 59. Ibid., n. 15. 60. DP, q. 3, a. 7. 61. In Jn 1.10, n. 133. 62. ST I, q. 105, a. 5. 63. DP, q. 3, a. 7.

end that moves the agent; the second is the agent; the third is the form of that which the agent applies to action (although the agent also acts through its own form). This can be clearly seen in things made by art: for artists are moved to action by the end, which is the thing made, for instance, a chest or a bed; they put to action the axe, which cuts because it is sharp. In the same way, God works in every worker, according to these three things. First, as an end. Since every operation is for the sake of something good, real or apparent, and nothing is good either really or apparently except to the extent that it participates in a likeness to the Supreme Good, which is God, it follows that God is the cause of every operation as its end.

It is also to be observed that where there are several agents in order, the second always acts in virtue of the first, for the first agent moves the second to act. And thus all agents act in virtue of God. Therefore God is the cause of action in every agent. . . .

Third, God gives created agents their forms and preserves them in being, . . . preserving the forms and powers of things. . . . It follows that in all things God works intimately.[64]

FOX: Let us pursue more deeply how God shares the generative powers with other creatures.

AQUINAS: Some people presume that because God works in every active thing it is God alone who does the work and that no created power produces anything real. For example, that fire does not burn, but that God does. This is impossible, however. For such a situation would destroy the causal structure and interplay of the universe. And it would lead to positing a weakness in God, since it is from strength that any cause gives the power of causing to its offspring. Furthermore, if causal powers in fact did nothing and God did it all, then things would simply not have any power. They would be shams if you took away their proper activity, for they exist for their work. Thus, when speaking of God's universal causality, we must be careful to safeguard the proper activity of creatures.[65] God attributes power of action to created things, and this is not out of a weakness on God's part, but rather out of God's most perfect fullness, which is sufficient for sharing with all beings.[66]

---

64. ST I, q. 105, a. 5.   65. Ibid.   66. SC, a. 10, ad 16.

FOX: You say that all beings share in this power of sharing their power and in the power of doing their work.

AQUINAS: Providence is extended even to brute animals, which work diverse works at diverse times by a certain natural instinct. Thus Job says that "the beast will enter its lair," namely, in the rainy season, "and will remain in its cave," namely, when the time is right.[67]

FOX: What else do human and animal power of generation have in common?

AQUINAS: We find one thing in common among causes that produce something: they take care of what they produce. Thus, animals naturally take care of their young. And so too does God take care of the things of which God is the cause.[68]

FOX: And so the artists cherish what they give birth to. Yet human creativity and animal generativity differ, no doubt?

AQUINAS: That work which is fitting for any time human beings discern according to their divinely given reason (instead of according to animal instinct). This is evidence that God has placed in the hand or the operative power of all human beings, the fact that they know how to fittingly distribute their works over diverse times.[69] Horns and claws, which are the weapons of some animals, and toughness of hide and quantity of hair or feathers, which are the clothing of animals, are signs of an abundance of the earthly element. This does not agree with the equability and gentleness of the human temperament. Therefore, such things do not suit the nature of human beings. Instead of these, human beings have reason and hands whereby they can make themselves weapons and clothing and other necessities of life, of an infinite variety. Wherefore the hand is called by Aristotle the "organ of organs." Moreover, this was more becoming to the rational nature, which is capable of conceiving an infinite number of things, so as to make for itself an infinite number of instruments.[70]

FOX: I am struck by your repetition of the word "infinite" in this context. Just as in the Via Positiva you celebrated our "infinite" capacity to know, here you seem to be celebrating our infinite capacity to give birth.

---

67. In Job, ch. 37, p. 123.　68. CG III, ch. 75 n. 4.　69. Ibid.　70. ST I, q. 91, a. 3, ad 2.

AQUINAS: The rational creature tends, by its activity, toward the divine likeness in a special way that exceeds the capacities of all other creatures, as it also has a nobler existence as compared with other creatures. The existence of other creatures is finite, since it is hemmed in by matter, and so lacks infinity both in act and in potency. But every rational nature has infinity either in act or in potency, according to the way its intellect contains ideas. Thus our intellectual nature, considered in its first state, is in potency to its ideas; since these are infinite, they have a certain potential infinity. Hence the intellect is the form of forms, because it has a form that is not determined to one thing alone, as is the case with a stone, but has a capacity for all forms.[71]

FOX: So our minds are indeed unique in their capacity for the infinite?

AQUINAS: The end of the intellectual creature, to be achieved by its activity, is the complete actuation of its intellect by all the ideas for which it has a potency. In this respect it will become like God.[72]

FOX: So our creative capacity is what most makes us godlike?

AQUINAS: A thing is not called divine only because it comes from God but also because it makes us like God in goodness.[73]

FOX: Indeed, creativity is an original blessing. Can you elaborate?

AQUINAS: What the mind knows is properly described as a conception of the mind.[74]

FOX: I think it is telling that you use a sexual analogy to name the process of our knowing. This surely highlights the creative process that our knowing is about.

AQUINAS: What is formed in the mind is also conceived. The thing understood gives, as it were, and the understanding receives, and what is apprehended in and by the mind agrees with the quickening object, of which it is a kind of likeness, and with the mind, because there it has intelligible reality. Consequently what the mind knows is described as a conception of the mind quite simply.[75]

---

71. CT I, ch. 103.   72. Ibid.   73. In Ethics I, L. 14, p. 74.   74. CT I, ch. 38.   75. Ibid.

FOX: Of course the act of knowledge, creative as it is, also awakens pleasure and the will, does it not?

AQUINAS: The highest appetite is that which goes with knowledge and free choice, for this appetite moves itself somehow. So too the love pertaining to this is the most perfect and is called *delight* insofar as what is to be loved is discerned by free choice.[76]

FOX: And it is this capacity for free choice, as opposed to what you called "natural instinct," that most distinguishes human generativity from that of other animals?

AQUINAS: Children and other animals share in voluntary actions, in the sense that they operate by their own spontaneous motion. Yet they do not share in the act of choice, because their actions are not performed as a result of deliberation, which is a prerequisite for choice.[77]

FOX: And so you are distinguishing between a voluntary act and an act of choice—the former takes some rational deliberation, as you say.

AQUINAS: We call those actions that we perform suddenly voluntary, because their source lies within us; but they are not said to occur by choice, because they are not done deliberately.[78]

FOX: Of course sometimes things happen suddenly to us, and these would be neither voluntary nor deliberate.

AQUINAS: Violence is from an extrinsic principle. . . . It is directly opposed to the voluntary, as likewise to the natural.[79]

FOX: And yet human beings—by reason of our power of choice and creativity—can actually contribute mightily to violence and evil in the world. In fact, it seems, more than any other animal.

AQUINAS: The unjust person is worse than injustice and the evil person worse than a brute, because an evil person can do ten thousand times more harm than a beast, because we can use our reason to devise many diverse evils.[80]

FOX: And so deliberation and choice are key elements of the Via Creativa and of art itself. We will no doubt be returning to this theme later in this conversation. But as long as we touched

---

76. DDN, n. 402, p. 134.   77. In Ethics III, L. 5, p. 194.   78. Ibid.
79. ST I-II, q. 6, a. 5.   80. In Ethics VII, L. 6, p. 650.

on the differences between human and other animals' generativity, what other contrasts can you name between the two?

AQUINAS: Other animals take delight in the objects of the senses only as ordered to food and to sex; human beings alone take pleasure in the beauty of sense objects for its own sake. It is for this reason, since the senses are situated chiefly in the face, that other animals have their face turned to the ground, as it were for the purpose of seeking food and procuring a livelihood. Human beings, on the other hand, have their face erect in order that by the senses, and chiefly by sight, which is more subtle and penetrates further into the differences of things, they may freely survey the sense objects around them, both heavenly and earthly, so as to gather intelligible truth from all things.[81]

FOX: What do you think would be the result if humans did not stand upright surveying objects "both heavenly and earthly," as you say?

AQUINAS: If human stature were prone to the ground, they would need to use their hands as forefeet and thus their utility for other purposes would cease. Besides, if . . . human beings had to use their hands as forefeet, they would be obliged to take hold of their food with their mouth. As a result, they would have a protruding mouth, with thick and hard lips and also a hard tongue, so as to keep it from being injured by exterior things, as is the case with other animals. Furthermore, such a posture would tend to hinder speech, which is reason's proper function.[82]

FOX: To say that speech is reason's "proper function" is again to celebrate humanity's capacity for creativity, the creativity of language making. I hear you celebrating how the human being seems to be generative in many respects as God is.

AQUINAS: The higher a nature, the more intimate is what comes from it, for its inwardness of activity corresponds to its rank in being.[83] The supreme and perfect grade of life is found in mind, which can reflect on itself and understand itself. But there are different grades of intelligence. The human intellect, though able to know itself, must start from outside objects and

---

81. ST I, q. 91, a. 3, ad 3.   82. Ibid.   83. CG IV, ch. 11 n. 1.

cannot know these without sense-images. . . . The highest perfection of life is in God, where acting is not distinct from being,
and where the concept *is* the divine essence.[84]

FOX: You speak of "intimacy" and "inwardness of activity."
Let us probe more deeply the source of human creativity and
art, which is so like God as the Artist of artists.

AQUINAS: Where the word stops, there the song begins. The
song is the exultation of the mind bursting forth into voice.[85]

FOX: And where does this "bursting forth" come from?

AQUINAS: The psalmist says (44): "My heart overflowed with
a good word." Vomiting proceeds from too much fullness or
overflowing in which is meant an abundance of devotion or
wisdom. Consider Matthew (12): "From an abundance of the
heart the mouth speaks." We should note that the psalms attribute this production to the heart. From the great devotion in
the heart the abundance is composed. This is the opposite of
those of whom Isaiah speaks when he says (29): "This people
honor me with their lips, but their heart is far from me." In
contrast, the praise of Christ one proclaims from the heart: "I
will sing with the spirit, and I will sing with the mind" (1 Cor.
14).[86]

FOX: And so you attribute the passion of our creativity to the
heart, but you see prayer itself as this self-expression or "exultation" of what is in us. Indeed, I hear you speaking of art as
meditation.

AQUINAS: Prayer consists in two things: namely, in the interior
action of the heart, and in exterior works. As for the interior,
since God is spirit, it is fitting for those worshiping God to be
spiritual. John says (4): "True worshipers will adore the Creator
in spirit and in truth." And so the psalmist says (28): "Hear my
prayer when I pray to you." But we ought also to show respect
in our effects and exterior signs. For this reason the psalmist
says: "When I raise my hands to your holy temple." This can
be read in two ways—literally, in accord with the gloss, that the
Jewish people, wherever they were, were ordered to pray in the
direction that they knew Jerusalem to be. Or it can mean "when
I raise," that is, lift, "my hands toward the temple," that is, to

---

84. Ibid., n. 5.   85. In Pss, Prologue, p. 148.   86. In Pss 44, p. 319.

the sky. Psalm 11 says: "The Lord in his holy temple, etc." Therefore not only will I pray in devotion of heart, but also in exterior signs I will pray toward the sky and show some devotion. But the other way to interpret this text about "when my hands" means "my works" that "I raise to the temple," that is, I direct toward God. Psalm 141 says; "Let my speech be directed," that is, my works, "as incense, etc." This is what Christ did who lifted his hands toward the temple when he drove out those selling and buying in it. And also when he raised his hands on the cross.[87]

FOX: So our work—if it comes from the heart—can indeed be prayer—even if it is the work of driving money-lenders from temples. But again it seems that the "heart" is key. We need to return to our hearts to examine what is there and what motivates us and moves us.

AQUINAS: Good people love themselves by loving their inner person, because they wish the preservation of this inward self in its integrity. They desire good things for the inner self, namely, spiritual goods, and they do their best to obtain them. They take pleasure in entering into their own hearts, because they find there good thoughts in the present, the memory of past good, and the hope of future good—all of which are sources of pleasure. Likewise they experience no clashing of wills, for their whole soul tends to one thing.[88]

FOX: Are you saying that some people are incapable of art as meditation?

AQUINAS: Wicked persons have no wish to be preserved in the integrity of the inward self, nor do they desire spiritual goods for the self, nor do they work for that end, nor do they take pleasure in their own company by entering into their own hearts. The reason for this is that whatever they find there, present, past, or future, is evil and horrible. Nor are they able to find harmony with themselves because of the gnawings of conscience.[89]

FOX: And so it takes some effort to enter into heart-knowledge and undergo heart-work. Once again, as in the Via Positiva, you are connecting spirituality and joy.

---

87. In Pss 27, p. 241. 88. ST II-II, q. 25, a. 7. 89. Ibid.

AQUINAS: Matthew's gospel says: "Enter into the joy of your master" (Matt. 25:21). Joy is the reward, as John says (John 16:22): "I will see you and your hearts shall rejoice." Someone might ask, "Is not the vision the reward or some other good?" I say that, although something else may be called a reward, joy is, in fact, the final reward. Why does he say "enter into the joy" and not "receive the joy"? In answer I say that there are two kinds of joy: one is in interior things and the other in exterior things. Those who have joy in exterior things do not enter into joy—rather joy enters into them. The one who has joy in spiritual things enters into joy. "The king has brought me into his chambers" (Song of Songs 1:4). Or we could say that what is in something is contained by it and the thing containing is the greater. Therefore, when the joy is about something smaller than your heart, then the joy enters into your heart. God, however, is greater than the heart, and thus one who rejoices in God enters into joy.[90]

FOX: When we return to our hearts we make room for entertaining the spiritual guest there.

AQUINAS: Jesus says in John's gospel (15:7): "My words have remained in you." This happens in four ways: by loving, by believing, by contemplating, and by fulfilling. As Proverbs says (4:20): "Son, listen to what I have to say (namely, by believing) and incline your ear to my utterances (namely, by obeying or fulfilling), let them not depart from your eyes (by contemplating), and guard them within your heart"—that is, by loving.[91]

FOX: What are some results that flow from this return to the heart?

AQUINAS: The Holy Spirit ennobles us and makes us leaders. Galatians (4) says: "Since you are children of God, God sent the spirit of the divine Son into your hearts."[92]

FOX: Leadership comes from a return to our hearts? You seem to be saying that the artist is a leader, that true authority is about authorship and creativity. Can you elaborate on this notion?

AQUINAS: When the psalmist speaks of "the fruit-bearing olive" he is speaking of the sanctity of good people.[93] The same Holy Spirit that inspired the prophets and the other authors of

---

90. In Mt 25, p. 233. 91. In Jn 15.7, n. 1995. 92. In Pss 50, p. 349.
93. In Pss 51, p. 353.

Sacred Scripture moved the saints to work. For, as 2 Peter (1:21) says: "The holy ones of God have spoken inspired by the Holy Spirit." And Romans says (8:14): "Those who are led by the spirit of God, these are the children of God."[94] The apostles, who are the chiefs and leaders of Christian wisdom and were motivated every day by truth, witnessed, as is appropriate, not only in word but also in work.[95]

FOX: And so true art and true leadership and true work comes from the heart?

AQUINAS: In Matthew's gospel (25:12), to those who say "Lord, Lord, open the door for us," Jesus answers: "I say to you, I do not know you," because they did not speak from the heart but only from their mouths. The apostles, however, were authentic because their words were consistent with their actions.[96]

FOX: And this is how the prophets led as well?

AQUINAS: Take note of what Isaiah says, "who has announced?" since what moves in order to announce and proclaim, first of all, is the instinct of faith. Psalm 115 says: "I believed, because I have spoken." Second, the goad of zeal, as Jeremiah says (20): "And the word was shut up in my heart, like a burning fire." Third, the greatness of the reward, as in Matthew (5): "One who has acted and taught, this one will be called great in the kingdom of heaven."[97]

FOX: How do the prophets express themselves from the heart?

AQUINAS: Isaiah speaks of crying, which is the first characteristic of a devoted prayer. Consider Hebrews 5: "With loud crying and tears he was heard for his reverence." A second motive for crying is to intend to proclaim, as in John (7): "On the last day of the festival he cried out." A third motive is to make one's intention firm.[98]

FOX: Do the prophets do more than cry?

AQUINAS: When Isaiah says, "Sing to the Lord a new song," he invites us to thanksgiving. First, he speaks of praise (24): "We have heard the praise of the just." All that is full praises God, as Psalm 107 says: "Those who go down to the sea in ships,

---

94. In Jn 18.23, n. 2321.   95. DDN, n. 740, p. 278.   96. In Jn 13.13, n. 1776.   97. In Is 41, p. 531.   98. Ibid. 42, p. 532.

doing their business in many waters, themselves have seen the works of God and God's wonders in the deep." Also, those dwelling in the desert may "lift up their voice" in praise of God. The "desert" means its inhabitants, especially the Israelites; "in their houses" means in the custom of other nations. These were the first to wander through the desert. "The desert and pathless way will rejoice and the solitude will exult" (Isa. 35). Also, those who dwell in the mountains: "Praise the inhabitants of the rock" of that city in Palestine, which is placed among the rocks. Or any mountain at all, as in Isaiah (55): "The mountains and all the hills will sing to the Lord."[99]

FOX: Where does all this shouting and singing, this deep expression that is art, come from?

AQUINAS: The psalmist says (39): "My heart grew warm within me," meaning, the heat of charity was stirred up in my heart. Proverbs asks the question (6): "Is one able to hide a fire in one's breast, without setting one's clothes on fire?" Thus it is impossible that anyone hide the words of God, when their heart is inflamed by love. Psalm 118 speaks of "your word is aflame, etc." But the cause of one's excitement is the meditation on divine things; whence he says: "And the fire burned in my meditation."[100]

FOX: And so our hearts are moved to give birth because of love?

AQUINAS: If you wish to arrive at spiritual things your heart must be inflamed with love of God. The effect of the excitement is that one who preferred to be silent is moved to speak. And so the psalmist says, "I have spoken." And Acts (2) says: "All were filled with the Holy Spirit, and they began to speak." Gregory says: "Those whom the Spirit fills, it causes both to burn and speak." And Job says (4): "Who is able to keep from speaking once begun?"[101]

FOX: You speak of "spiritual goods" in the heart and that this comes about from meditation.

AQUINAS: From frequent meditation the fire of charity is enkindled in the heart. And from this a spiritual joy is born within

---

99. Ibid., 533.   100. In Pss 38, p. 296.   101. Ibid.

the heart, and thus Paul mentions "singing and making melody" so that our will would be stirred by spiritual joys to undertake good works.[102]

FOX: How do we move from heart to mouth, from heart to art, or sharing of what is in the heart?

AQUINAS: Spiritual goods consist in two things: namely, in proportion as they are in the mouth and in proportion as they are in the heart. In the mouth of the just there is nothing but good and truth—Ephesians (4) says: "Putting off lying, speak the truth." The psalmist also says, "The mouth of the just will contemplate wisdom."[103]

FOX: "The mouth": What does contemplation have to do with the mouth?

AQUINAS: The psalmist does not seem to be speaking correctly because to contemplate is an act of the heart, not the mouth. I respond, however, that that must be spoken which one meditates on, that is, one will speak or sing the things one has meditated on. Some meditate the increase of wisdom; others meditate Christ, who is the wisdom of God the Father, at least by believing. Deuteronomy says (4): "This is your wisdom and understanding before the peoples." Others meditate by bending down to intelligent creatures, as in Ecclesiasticus (6): "If you choose to hear, you will be wise." Certain people sing what they meditate: Colossians (3): "Singing in your hearts to the Lord." Proverbs says (at the end): "The law of wisdom has opened its mouth, with compassion on its tongue." But the mouth of the just contemplates wisdom by teaching. Paul says (1 Cor. 2): "We speak wisdom among the perfect."[104]

FOX: You say that we "must speak" that which we meditate on. By doing so you are naming the demand that the artists feel to express their truth. And so our sharing of truth is our prayer, our art as meditation.

AQUINAS: Human beings are given understanding and reason by which they can both discern and investigate the truth. They are given sensory powers, both internal and external, whereby they are helped to seek the truth. And they are also given the use

---

102. In Eph 5.19, p. 494.   103. In Pss 36, p. 287.   104. Ibid.

of speech, and it is through this function that they are empowered to convey to another person the truth that they conceive in their mind. In this way, people may help themselves in this process of knowing the truth, just as they may in regard to the other needs of life, for the human being is "a naturally social animal," as Aristotle says (*Politics* I, 2).[105]

FOX: I sense a passion for truth that compels the artist you are speaking of to give birth. Just how deeply are we to love truth?

AQUINAS: Unless one prefers truth to one's friends, it follows that one will make false judgments and bear false witness in their defense. This is contrary to virtue. While reason prescribes that all people should prefer truth to their friends, this holds in a special way for the philosophers that study wisdom, which is knowledge of truth.[106]

FOX: If there is a conflict between our human relationships and truth, truth comes first?

AQUINAS: Although we should have friendship for both truth and our fellow human beings, we ought rather to love truth, because we should love our fellow human beings especially on account of truth and virtue. . . . Now truth is a most excellent friend of the sort to whom homage is due. Besides, truth is a divine thing, for it is found first and chiefly in God.[107]

FOX: Earlier you compared our creativity to conception—you see it as a generative act.

AQUINAS: When the mind understands something other than itself, the thing understood is like the father of the word conceived in the mind, while the mind plays the part of the mother, in whose womb conception takes place.[108]

FOX: Creativity is a motherly process—we are all mothers when we give birth to our images.

AQUINAS: A mother is one who conceives within herself and by another.[109]

FOX: The mind is radically creative, then. To think is to give birth.

AQUINAS: Knower and known are not agent and patient to one another, they are two things from which one principle of knowledge results.[110] There is an inward procession corre-

---

105. CG III, ch. 147 n. 2.   106. In Ethics I, L. 6, p. 34.   107. Ibid.
108. CT I, ch. 39.   109. ST II-II, q. 23, a. 8, ad 3.   110. DV, q. 8, a. 7, ad 2.

sponding to the act remaining within the agent. This applies most obviously to the intellect, the action of which remains in the intelligent agent. For whenever we understand something, by the very fact of understanding, there proceeds something within us. This is a conception of the object understood, a conception issuing from our intellectual power and proceeding from our knowledge of that object. This conception is signified by the spoken word; and it is called "the word of the heart signified by the word of the voice."[111]

FOX: The terms "generation" and "procession" as you use them strike me as dynamic equivalents of our word "creativity" today. A voice that comes from the heart—what a fine definition of creativity you offer here! This must be what you imply when you say the "voice" remains within the agent or subject—that what we give birth to never really leaves our hearts—it actually expands them to reach others by way of our "voice" or work of art.

AQUINAS: Procession is to be understood by way of an intelligible emanation, for example, of the intelligible word, which proceeds from the speaker, yet remains within him or her. It is in this sense that the catholic faith understands procession as existing in God.[112]

FOX: You speak of the word of the voice emanating from the word of the heart, and you praise the apostles and prophets for that kind of preaching. Do mystery and silence such as we spoke of in the Via Negativa also play a role in our creativity?

AQUINAS: Conceptions of heart and mind come forth in silence and without sound, but by audible words the silence of the heart is manifested.[113]

FOX: So our self-expression is meant to be a manifestation of the silence of our hearts. And the Via Creativa flows from the Via Negativa and our letting go. I appreciate the nonelitist nature of the creativity we have been discussing, namely, the birthing of our own thoughts and words—something we can all do, provided we birth from the heart. I also sense in this discussion a playing out of your own vocation as a member of the Order of Preachers—the basic theme of "sharing the fruits

---

111. ST I, q. 27, a. 1.   112. Ibid.   113. DDN, n. 288, p. 90.

of your contemplation" that is a motto in your order. Your preaching movement scandalized some of the monks of your day, and it seems precisely around this theme of the Via Creativa that so much scandal occurred.

AQUINAS: It is better to light up than merely to shine, to deliver to others contemplated truths than merely to contemplate.[114] The creature approaches more perfectly to God's likeness if it is not only good, but can also act for the good of other beings, than if it were good only in itself. That which both shines and casts light is more like the sun than that which only shines.[115]

FOX: Why is that?

AQUINAS: Light is given to the sun not to shine alone on itself but also on the whole earth. So too, God wills that all our gifts of wealth, power, knowledge should benefit others.[116]

FOX: And so we are here to spread light, to illuminate, from our heartfelt wisdom?

AQUINAS: In Matthew's gospel teaching is prescribed to the disciples with the words, "let your light shine before people." . . . Among visible things, nothing is brighter than the light.[117] The word "you" means you who have been derived from me who am the first light, as in John's gospel (8:12): "I am the light of the world." When Jesus says "you are," he means you ought to be [lights of the world]. Behold the stability visible in the substantive word in which the deficiency of light is excluded, against those who proclaim falsehood; and the forming of the light against those who have transformed themselves into the angel of light (2 Cor. 11:14); and the diminution of light, against those who out of fear or flattery have not put an end to their vices.[118]

FOX: And so good preaching—or good art of any kind, I would imagine—is in some way illuminating or light bearing.

AQUINAS: Light heaps up delight. Scripture says (Eccl. 11:7): "The light is pleasing, and it is delightful for the eyes to see the sun." Likewise, it aids the fertility of the earth. Ecclesiasticus says (43:4): "It breathes out fiery rays, etc." Likewise light is knowledge for the living. The Philosopher says, "the human

---

114. ST II-II, q. 188, a. 6.   115. CG II, ch. 45 n. 4.   116. In 2 Cor, ch. 1, p. 301.   117. In Mt 5, p. 55.   118. Ibid., p. 56.

being and the sun generate the human." Besides these things, according to Basil, when the light of day comes, illnesses are alleviated, people are stirred from sleep, birds chatter, beasts depart from their lairs. So by the light of the apostles the world has been built by example, set on fire by teaching, fertilized by good works, liberated from sins, awakened from acts of negligence, animated toward the contemplation of heavenly things, snatched away from the power of the devil. Usefulness is made note of when Christ says "you are the light of the world." By this he means universally. As the psalmist says (19:4): "Their sound has gone out into every land."[119]

FOX: Is anything else implied in this image of the light-bearing artist or preacher?

AQUINAS: In a lamp there is fire and light. So in proclaiming there ought to be the fervor of the interior spirit and externally the light of good example. In this way it is said that John "was a lamp burning and shining" (John 5:35). Jesus says "do not put your light under a bushel," that is, in hiding; "but on a lampstand," that is, let it be out in the open.[120] Jesus says: "Where your treasure is, there your heart is also." . . . The light that is in you is heart and mind.[121]

FOX: How do we attain this treasure and make contact with this light?

AQUINAS: The saints flourish through the contemplation of wisdom. Ecclesiasticus says (6): "Like the one who plows or plants, approach wisdom and wait for her good harvest." They also flourish through the fervor of charity: Song of Songs (5): "Let my beloved come into his garden, in order that he may eat the fruit of his own orchard." They flourish through the profession of praise. Hebrews (13): "Through this very one let us always offer a sacrifice of praise to God, that is the fruit of lips that confess God's name." And they flourish through meritorious work. Psalm 84: "For the Lord will give what is good, and our earth will yield its fruit." They also flourish through the conversion of neighbors. John 15: "That you may go and bear fruit, and your fruit may remain."[122]

---

119. Ibid.   120. Ibid.   121. Ibid. 6, p. 73.   122. In Jer 17, p. 621.

FOX: I sense a great passion in you whenever you speak of work and bearing fruit, fruit that will remain. All this strikes me as the passion that accompanies the love artists have for what they give birth to.

AQUINAS: Jesus says (Matt. 7:2): "From their fruits you will know them." This phrase, "from their fruits," means "from their works."[123] In John's gospel Jesus says (15:2) "that it bring forth more fruit." This means that one grows in virtue so that one may be more productive as one is more pure. Consider Colossians (1:6): "The word of the Gospel bears fruit and grows."[124] And when Christ says "as the branch cannot bear fruit on its own unless it has remained on the vine, so neither can you unless you remain in me," he is showing that clinging to Christ is necessary for bearing fruit. He also shows that it is effective when he says, "those who remain in me and I in them, are going to bear much fruit."[125] It is effective because "those who remain in me" [do so] by believing, obeying, and persevering, "and I in them" occurs by illuminating, helping, and giving perseverance. "This very person will bear much fruit" and not another. I say they are going to bear triple fruit in this life. The first is to abstain from sins, as in Isaiah (27:4): "I will guard its fruit, that sin may be taken away." The second is to be free for the works of holiness, as in Romans (6:22): "You have your fruit in holiness. . . ." The third fruit is to be free for edifying others, as in Psalm 104:13: "With the fruit of your works the earth will be satisfied." One will even bear a fourth fruit in eternal life, as in John 4:36: "He gathers fruit for eternal life." This is the last and perfect fruit of our works, as Wisdom says (3:15): "The fruit of good works is glorious."[126]

FOX: And so those who do good work are fruitful or creative persons?

AQUINAS: The saints bring about a double good in the present church. First is this, that they are well disposed to their neighbor by bearing fruit in them; and so the just person is compared to an olive tree in Psalm 52, as if to say: The sinner without fruit is rooted out; but I am like a fruitbearing olive in the house of God. Such a person is compared to an olive tree on account of its richness, for an olive always has rich fruit. Compare Judith

---

123. In Mt 7, p. 79.   124. In Jn 15.2, n. 1985.   125. In Jn 15.4, n. 1989.
126. In Jn 15.5, n. 1992.

(9): "I cannot forsake my richness." And Jeremiah (11): "A fruitful olive tree bearing goodly fruit, the Lord has called your name." But the psalmist compares this person to an olive tree especially on account of its fruit. For oil comes from olives, by which compassion is signified, from which the just provide for others and do a fruitful thing in the church, as John 15 puts it: "I sent you so that you may go and bear fruit."[127]

FOX: And so the church is meant to be a place where fruits of creativity are shared and especially the oil of compassion?

AQUINAS: The church is a garden: "My sister, my spouse, is a garden enclosed" (Song of Songs 4:12). Here are many plots, all different according to our callings, but all planted by God, and the whole is watered by the streams of Christ's sacraments flowing from his side. Holy Scripture proclaims its loveliness: "How beautiful are your tabernacles, O Jacob, and your tents, O Israel; as wooded valleys, as watered gardens near the river" (Num. 24:5). Hence, also, the church's ministers are like gardeners: "I have preached, Apollo has watered," says Paul (1 Cor. 3:6).[128]

FOX: The image of church as garden and ministers as gardeners I find fresh and attractive—the whole imagery of making wet and watering and keeping moist reminds me of Hildegard of Bingen's admonition to be "green and juicy" and resist drying up.

AQUINAS: No good branch has any of the greenness (*viriditatem*) of good works if it does not remain in the root of love.[129] Some people remain in Christ only by faith—they do not share in the wetness of the vine because they do not dwell in love. . . . Bad Christians seem to have a certain greenness (*viriditatem*), but when they are separated from the saints and Christ, their dryness becomes apparent.[130]

FOX: I am excited at how you share Hildegard's language of *viriditas* or "greening power" and its opposite, the sin of drying up.

AQUINAS: Of course, for planting there is need of land moistened by water, otherwise it would grow dry. Therefore the psalmist (Ps. 1) says: "That which has been planted by streams

---

127. In Pss 51, p. 353.   128. In I Sent, Prologue.   129. In Jn 15.12, n. 2006.   130. In Jn 15.6, n. 1994.

of water," that is, near the currents of grace. And John says (ch. 7): "Those who believe in me, rivers of living water will flow from their breast." One who has roots near this living water will flourish by doing good works, and this follows, "it will give its fruit." Consider Galatians (ch. 5): "But the fruit of the Spirit is charity, joy, peace, patience, forbearance, goodness, kindness, etc." "In this time" means when it is the time of working, as in Galatians (at the end): "While we have time, let us work good for all." The ground does not grow dry—rather it is preserved.[131]

FOX: I get the impression that church for you is primarily a fertile garden where the gifts of the spirit are alive and well.

AQUINAS: Everything that is virtually in Christ is, as it were, filled out in some way in the members of the Church. For all spiritual understanding, gifts, and whatever can be present in the church—all of which Christ possesses superabundantly—flow from him into the members of the church, and they are perfected in them. Paul says "who is filled all in all," since Christ makes this member of the church wise with the perfect wisdom present in himself, and he makes another just with his perfect justice, and so on with the others.[132]

FOX: I feel more at home with your use of earth imagery vis-à-vis the church than I do with most institution-based ecclesiologies.

AQUINAS: The apostles are that land which has brought forth much fruit, as is said in John 15. "And you may become my disciples," through adherence to and fervor of charity. . . . They are made fit to bring forth the fruit of doctrine. And second, the observing of love. John 13:35: "In this all will recognize that you are my disciples, if you have love for one another." And from this they are made fit for bearing the fruit of good works, as Paul says (1 Cor. 13:2): "If I have prophecy, and know all the mysteries and all knowledge, etc." Knowledge in that passage is supposed to profit nothing without charity.[133]

FOX: It is interesting how you associate being an apostle with creativity—an apostle is the land that bears fruit, you say. You are getting to the true notion of "authority"—one who authors.

---

131. In Pss 1, p. 151.　132. In Eph, ch. 1, pp. 82–83.　133. In Jn 15.8, n. 1996.

What else is implied in the "fruits" that we give birth to when properly rooted?

AQUINAS: First the planting, then the harvest. . . . The fruits that wisdom has abundantly watered are the harvest. It is Christ who brings us to glory, Christ who brings to birth the church's faithful. . . . The fruits are the saints in glory: "Let my beloved come into his garden and eat the fruit of his apple trees" (Song of Songs 5:1). What abundance and ripeness is here! "They shall be inebriated with the vineyards of thy house" (Ps. 36:9). For indeed, they are drunk, their joy surpassing all measure of reason and desire.[134]

FOX: You wax so ecstatic when you celebrate our fruit bearing.

AQUINAS: We are in Christ when we bear fruit from him, and the Creator is glorified from our bearing fruit. Christ shows this when he says: "In this my Father has been glorified," that is, it redounds to the glory of the Father, "that you bring forth much fruit."[135]

FOX: You use strong language when you say we "glorify" God by the fruits we give birth to. You frequently use the imperative when you talk of bearing fruit—as if creativity were a necessary and even natural part of our lives. Where do you get this conviction about the creative imperative?

AQUINAS: The position of the hearers [of the word of good news] is symbolized in the metaphor of the earth. . . . Now the earth is fertile: "Let the earth bring forth" (Gen. 1:11). And so the hearers of this teaching . . . must be fertile, so that the words of wisdom that they receive will be fruitful in them, as Jesus said (Luke 8:15): "The seed that fell on good ground. . . ."[136]

FOX: Much earlier in this discussion you praised God as being eminently fertile. Now it is humanity's time to be godlike and earthlike and therefore fertile. What does fertility mean in this context?

AQUINAS: People need fertility in the sense of that capacity to discover things, which enables good students to explain a lot on the basis of a few things that they have heard. "Give wise people

---

134. In I Sent, Prologue.   135. In Jn 15.8, n. 1996.   136. IL.

the opportunity, and they will obtain more wisdom" (Prov. 9:9).[137]

FOX: "The ability to discover things"—this too is a nonelitist invitation. I hear you urging workers to be fruitful and ground their work in waters of wisdom. What happens if we fail to follow this law of nature, that of being fruitful and creative?

AQUINAS: What will come from a bad tree? "Every tree which does not bear fruit will be cut down," Jesus says in Matthew (7:2). For if the tree does not bear fruit or fails to do so when it can, it will be cut down. Thus John says (15:6): "If someone does not abide in me, he will be thrown away like a branch and will dry up." And Luke (13:7) talks about the fig tree and how the Lord ordered it to be cut down and destroyed: "Let the impious one be destroyed so that he may not see the glory of God." Therefore Jesus concludes in Matthew, "therefore from their fruits you will know them. Not all who call to me, 'Lord, Lord,' etc."[138]

FOX: This is strong language addressed to the squelching of creativity and the repression of the artist in us—language of destruction.

AQUINAS: God does not give grace to anyone unless they use it. And so, when anyone through negligence does not use the grace given to them, God takes it away from them in order to make the talent accessible [to another]. Consider Luke (19): "Take the talent from him, and give it to the one who has ten talents."[139]

FOX: Then our failure to be fertile is sinful?

AQUINAS: A tree that does not make good fruit will be cut down and thrown into the fire, as Matthew says (3). But a fruitful tree is pruned so that it is purified, according to John 15: "Every vine sprout which does not bear fruit he will cleanse so that it brings more fruit." So the impious are punished to destruction, but the just to perfection. But why we compare this to fruitless trees is shown in two ways: first, because someone consumes their goods in useless things, as Job says: "He strikes the sterile and the one who does not produce." . . . Second, because the sterile person does not assist the poor on account of his not being fruitful. And so Job adds, "he did not do good to

---

137. Ibid. 138. In Mt 7, p. 79. 139. In Pss 38, p. 296.

the widow." By "widow" he means the poor. Not only was this man fruitless, but he was even harmful, like a tree putting forth poisonous fruit.[140]

FOX: And so the poor are cheated if we fail to bear fruit. Your use of the parable of the talents seems especially apt in a discussion of creativity. If we all have images to share, it seems important to share them.

AQUINAS: The parable says that the one who had talents "made five more." How did he do it? There are two ways in which one can make progress: in oneself and in another. In oneself, if one has an understanding of the Scriptures; in another if one has love. He set out to benefit another so that what he received he might give. "As each has received a gift, employ it for one another" (1 Pet. 4:10). Therefore, if you receive anything, share it and you will gain just as much. This is why the Lord says "he made five talents more," because no one can give to another what one does not have. "For I have received from the Lord what I also delivered to you" (1 Cor. 11:23). A person makes progress in that which he or she possesses. This apostle says in 1 Corinthians 15:10, "his grace toward me was not in vain."[141]

FOX: And so we are not to bury our creativity?

AQUINAS: The effects of love should be displayed as well as felt.[142]

FOX: I remember you saying in our Via Positiva discussion that beauty ought to be in some way "conspicuous." A certain display is required, a giving of blessing to the community.

AQUINAS: According to Origen, if anyone has a gift of understanding and yet desires to live religiously but only for themselves when they could be benefiting many people, they hide their gift in the ground. "The gifts of God are to be acknowledged and made known" (Tob. 12:7). For this kind of wealth is to be multiplied and not hidden.[143]

FOX: There is a kind of wealth or treasure hidden inside each one of us that must not be buried.

AQUINAS: Note that to have wealth as a master is one thing and to have it as a slave is another. One has wealth as a master who

---

140. In Job, ch. 24, p. 90.   141. In Mt 25, p. 231.   142. In Rom, ch. 12, p. 124.   143. In Mt 25, p. 232.

uses it well, and creates a product from it. But that person is a slave to wealth who does not accept the product from it. Ecclesiasticus says (5:12): "That is an evil thing which I have seen under the sun: Wealth kept for the evil of the master himself."[144]

FOX: I hear you saying that to hold our creativity back is sinful.

AQUINAS: Omission signifies the nonfulfillment of a good—not indeed of any good, but of a good that is due. . . . Omission is a special sin distinct from the sins that are opposed to the other virtues.[145] The sin of omission is opposed to affirmative precepts, which regard the doing of good.[146]

FOX: It is an act of injustice, then, not to create?

AQUINAS: Nonaction is a kind of action.[147] Omission is directly opposed to justice . . . because it is nonfulfillment of a good of virtue but only under the aspect of what is due, which pertains to justice.[148]

FOX: And so it is a serious wrong—indeed an act of injustice—if our culture puts down the creativity in others or if we do so in ourselves.

AQUINAS: It is clear that not only those who do evil are cut off from Christ, but also those who neglect to do good.[149]

FOX: Why do you think many people ignore their creativity?

AQUINAS: Just as presumption makes people exceed what is proportionate to their power by striving to do more than they can, so pusillanimity makes people fall short of what is proportionate to their power by refusing to tend to that which is commensurate with it. Wherefore, just as presumption is a sin, so too is pusillanimity. Hence it is said that the servant who buried the money he had received from his master in the earth and did not trade with it through fainthearted fear was punished by his master (Matt. 25; Luke 19).[150]

FOX: It seems that you see pusillanimity as a serious sin of omission.

AQUINAS: It is possible for people, by reason of the virtue that they have, to be worthy of doing certain great things that are worthy of great honor, and yet through not trying to make use

---

144. In Mt 6, p. 73.   145. ST II-II, q. 79, a. 3.   146. Ibid., ad 3.   147. Ibid., ad 1.   148. Ibid., ad 4.   149. In Jn 15.2, n. 1984.   150. ST II-II, q. 133, a. 1.

of their virtue, a person sins sometimes venially, sometimes mortally. . . . If one fails to use the ability that one derives either from a good natural disposition, or from science, or from external fortune, for virtue, then one becomes guilty of pusillanimity.[151]

FOX: So we are asked to share the gifts we have been given, and to hold back our gifts out of pusillanimity is a sin?

AQUINAS: More is required for an act to be virtuous and meritorious than for it to be sinful and demeritorious, because good results from an entire cause, whereas evil arises from each single defect.[152]

FOX: I hear you saying that it can be sinful to resist our own creativity.

AQUINAS: It should be noted that sin is called cold by the prophet Jeremiah (6) because it extinguishes the heat of love. Matthew's gospel says (24): "Since iniquity has abounded, the charity of many has grown cold." Sin is also cold because it congeals the humor of devotion, as Ecclesiasticus says (43): "The cold wind has blown from the north and the ice freezes on the water." Sin is cold because the movement of good work is slowed down, as Proverbs puts it (20): "On account of the cold the lazy person did not want to plow, so he will beg in the summer and it will not be given to him."[153]

FOX: Some people who hear you might accuse you of advising presumption on the part of persons who want to be creative.

AQUINAS: Pusillanimity is a graver sin than presumption, since thereby a person withdraws from good things, which is a very great evil.[154]

FOX: This "very great evil" of holding back our creativity seems to me to apply to institutions and social structures as well as to individuals. The institutional church too sins gravely when it fails to act or create out of pusillanimity. Or when it attacks those who do work to create anew. What do you think about silencing people who are speaking from the conviction of their heart?

AQUINAS: Take note of the saying in Isaiah, "On account of Sion I will not be silent." The saints are not silent—first, because

---

151. Ibid., ad 2.   152. Ibid, q. 79, a. 3, ad 4.   153. In Jer 6, p. 595.
154. ST II-II, q. 133, a. 2, ad 4.

of their burning desire, as Jeremiah says (20): "And the word of the Lord was shut up in my heart, like a seething fire." Second, on account of evident truth, as Acts says (4): "For we cannot speak of the things we do not see." Third, because of required duty, as in 1 Corinthians (9): "Necessity lies upon me: for woe is me if I do not preach the good news." Fourth, because of an expected reward, as in Galatians (6:9): "Let us not be deficient in doing good; for if we do not give up, we shall have our harvest at the proper time."[155]

FOX: What kind of things cause pusillanimity, in your opinion?

AQUINAS: Even pusillanimity may in some way be the result of pride: when, for example, one clings too much to one's own opinion, whereby one thinks oneself incompetent for those things for which one is competent.[156]

FOX: And so letting go is necessary for creativity to happen. Perhaps a fear of letting go is behind some refusal to create.

AQUINAS: In the case of bodily things, what is given is not kept; give a horse away, and it is no longer yours. But reality may be both given and kept in the world of spirit, as when you communicate knowledge or when the Father gives the divine substance to the Son.[157]

FOX: Some spiritualities would say that the sin of pride urges one on to creativity and that humility requires that we keep our images to ourselves.

AQUINAS: If anyone despises the good things they have received from God, this—far from being a proof of humility—shows them to be ungrateful. And from this contempt acedia results, because we sorrow for things that we reckon are evil and worthless. Accordingly, we ought to think much of the goods of others, in such a way as not to disparage those we have received ourselves, because if we did disparage them, that would give us sorrow.[158]

FOX: Yes—the disparagement of our own gifts also leads to our projecting onto others the power that is within ourselves. What else brings on pusillanimity besides our putting ourselves down?

---

155. In Is 62, p. 568.   156. ST II-II, q. 133, a. 1, ad 3.   157. In Dec II, p. 309.   158. ST II-II, q. 35, a. 1, ad 3.

AQUINAS: Just as the magnanimous person tends to great things out of greatness of soul, so the pusillanimous person shrinks from great things out of littleness of soul.[159]

FOX: To speak of a "littleness of soul" suggests that magnanimity or greatness of soul is the opposite of pusillanimity.

AQUINAS: Pusillanimity is directly opposed to magnanimity.[160]

FOX: What is the essence of pusillanimity?

AQUINAS: Those who think themselves worthy of lesser things than they are worthy of are called pusillanimous. This is so, whether in fact they are worthy of great, mediocre, or small things. However, small-souled people are those who refuse to strive after great accomplishments and aim at certain petty undertakings when they are truly capable of what is great.[161]

FOX: It seems that true humility and self-knowledge would allow creativity to flow.

AQUINAS: Ignorance of self proceeds from laziness in considering one's own ability or in accomplishing what is within one's power.[162]

FOX: Laziness about our gifts and talents—that is not a sin that religion preaches much about, I must say! Should we fear the sin of presumption when we give birth to ourselves and our images?

AQUINAS: It is more characteristic of virtue to perform a good action than to refrain from an evil one.[163]

FOX: I feel that what you are saying is very important, because so often religion teaches the commandments as negative things —what *not* to do—but you are stressing what we *ought* to do, namely, to give birth. And you are saying that our sins of omission are very serious. Do you think fear contributes to our refusal to give birth?

AQUINAS: Pusillanimity may be considered in reference to its cause, which on the part of the intellect is ignorance of one's own qualifications, and on the part of the appetite is the fear of failure in what one falsely deems to exceed one's ability.[164]

---

159. Ibid., q. 133, a. 2.   160. Ibid.   161. In Ethics IV, L. 8, p. 324.
162. ST II-II, q. 133, a. 2, ad 1.   163. In Ethics IV, L. I, p. 289.   164.
ST II-II, q. 133, a. 2.

FOX: Fear of failure. That is a reality in our lives. Are there other obstacles to our creativity besides the ones we have been discussing?

AQUINAS: In Matthew's gospel the Lord speaks of the impediments to bearing fruit, which sometimes come from prosperity and sometimes from adversity. . . . The thorns are the cares of the world. For just as thorns prick people and do not allow them to be at ease, so do these cares. St. Paul says to Timothy, "as for the rich in this world, charge them not to be haughty nor to set their hopes on uncertain riches" (1 Tim. 6:17).[165]

FOX: You are underlying the importance of the Via Negativa for our creativity—we need to be able to let go of fear and of laziness as well as of both prosperity and adversity. And perhaps the prosperity is the greatest obstacle to creativity. Creativity is about bringing forth new things. Should newness disturb people?

AQUINAS: Christ is the primary source of newness and renovation.[166] And Paul prohibits what is characteristic of the old person, thereby expounding what he has said: "Put on the new person" (Eph. 4:24).[167]

FOX: The Via Creativa celebrates fertility in all its aspects. Perhaps it is the sexual energy behind creativity that disturbs people.

AQUINAS: Certainly all the power to procreate present in us is from God.[168] The blessing of God [around reproduction] in Genesis is repeated in the case of the human race . . . to prevent anyone from saying that there was any sin whatever in the act of begetting children.[169]

FOX: And so our generative instincts are a deep blessing?

AQUINAS: One is not evil because of one's desire and delight in bodily goods, for everyone enjoys food and sex to some degree. On the contrary, some people are blamed for not enjoying pleasures as they should. From this it is obvious that bodily pleasure is good up to a certain point, but its excess is bad.[170] For all the good things that we do, God works in us.[171]

---

165. In Mt 3, p. 52.   166. In Eph 4.24, p. 485.   167. Ibid. 4.25, p. 485.
168. Ibid. 3.15, p. 472.   169. ST I, q. 72, a. 1, ad 4.   170. In Ethics VII, L. 14, p. 695.   171. In Jn 15.15, n. 2015.

FOX: I get the impression, based on the passion with which you discuss work and creativity, that your own work is very important to you and that it is a work of deep creativity.

AQUINAS: The grace of the word is given to a person for the benefit of others.[172] Now, the knowledge one receives from God cannot be turned to another's profit, except by means of speech. And since the Holy Spirit does not fail in anything that pertains to the profit of the church, the Spirit provides also the members of the church with speech. The result is that one not only speaks so as to be understood by different people, which pertains to the gift of tongues, but also speaks with effect. And this pertains to the grace of the word.

This happens in three ways. First, in order to instruct the intellect, and this is the case when one speaks so as to *teach.* Second, in order to move the affections, so that a person willingly hearkens to the word of God. This is the case when one speaks so as to *please* one's hearers, not indeed with a view to one's own reputation, but in order to draw them to listen to God's word. Third, in order that people may love that which is signified by the word, and desire to fulfill it, and this is the case when one so speaks as to *sway* one's listeners. In order to bring this about the Holy Spirit makes use of the human tongue as an instrument. But it is the Spirit who perfects the work within.[173]

FOX: And so you enjoy your work as teacher and preacher?

AQUINAS: Doctrinal instruction and preaching are nobler than chant as methods of arousing people to devotion.[174]

FOX: That is a strong endorsement of the power of teaching to reach the hearts and minds of people!

AQUINAS: The act of teaching has two objects. Teaching takes place by way of talking, and talking is an audible sign of an inner thought. And from this point of view teaching sometimes concerns the active life and sometimes the contemplative life. It concerns the active life when you conceive some truth inwardly in your mind with a view to being guided by it in what you do outwardly. It concerns the contemplative life when you conceive some speculative truth that you enjoy looking at and derive pleasure from your love of it.[175]

---

172. ST II-II, q. 177, a. 1, ad 3.   173. Ibid., a. 1.   174. Ibid, q. 91, a. 2, ad 3.   175. Ibid, q. 181, a. 3.

FOX: And so you see your work as a teacher as one of "conceiving" or birthing both for others and for your own delight?

AQUINAS: A teacher must not be pictured as pouring one's knowledge into the learner, as though particles of the same knowledge could pass from one subject to another.[176] Teachers cause knowledge in their learners by reducing the student from potentiality to act.[177]

FOX: This sounds like midwifing, the bringing of another from potentiality to act. Is teaching an art for you?

AQUINAS: The teacher does not cause knowledge in the student in the same way as fire generates fire. For things are not in the same fashion generated by nature as by art; fire generates fire naturally, by making actual the form of fire potentially present in the matter, whereas teachers cause knowledge in their students by way of art, since this is the aim of the art of demonstration.[178]

FOX: And so teaching is a generative activity for you, and the teacher is indeed an artist.

AQUINAS: A sign of knowledge is the ability to teach, and this is so because each thing is perfect in its activity when it can produce another thing similar to itself. Therefore, just as the possession of heat is indicated by the fact that a thing can heat something else, in a similar way the possession of knowledge is indicated by the fact that one can teach, that is, cause knowledge in another. But people who have an art can teach, for since they know causes they can demonstrate from these, and demonstration is a syllogism that produces knowledge.[179] The teacher moves students by teaching so that they, by the power of their own intellect, form intelligible concepts, the signs of which are proposed to them from without.[180]

FOX: The teacher as artist—I like that.

AQUINAS: Knowledge is caused by a teacher in a pupil . . . as health in a sick person by a doctor, who causes health inasmuch as he or she furnishes some remedies that nature makes use of to cause health. In this way doctors proceed in the same order, in their curing, as nature would cure. For just as the principal

---

176. DV, q. 11, a. 1, ad 6.   177. ST I, q. 117, a. 1.   178. CG II, ch. 75 n. 14.   179. In Meta I, L. 1, p. 15.   180. ST I, q. 117, a. 1, ad 3.

healing force is one's interior nature, so the principle that chiefly causes knowledge is something intrinsic, namely, the light of the agent intellect, whereby knowledge is caused in us, when we descend through the application of universal principles to some special points, which we gain through experience in discovery. And similarly, the teacher draws universal principles down to special conclusions.[181]

FOX: I like the emphasis you put on the active role of the learner, who also creates in the teacher/student relationship. What makes for the best kind of teacher?

AQUINAS: The ability to teach belongs to people who are wise and who know something inasmuch as they can express their inner thought in words, so that they can lead somebody else to an understanding of truth.[182]

FOX: It is evident that for you experience is not as valuable as art when it comes to teaching.

AQUINAS: Persons who have experience [only] cannot teach; for since they do not know the causes, they cannot cause knowledge in someone else. And if they do teach others the things that they know by experience, these things are not learned after the manner of scientific knowledge, but after the manner of opinion or belief. Hence it is clear that persons who have an art are wiser and more knowing than those who have experience.[183]

FOX: The teacher is also a learner—is that not so? And this too adds to the creative energy in teaching.

AQUINAS: Intellectual virtue is both generated and increased for the most part by teaching. The reason is that intellectual virtue is ordered to knowledge, which we acquire more readily from teaching than from discovery. More people can know the truth by learning from others than by ascertaining it themselves. Everyone indeed who finds out from others will learn more than one can discover by oneself. But because we cannot proceed to infinity in the process of learning, people must learn many truths by discovery.[184]

FOX: When you speak about these matters it is not just theory, for we know how many battles you had to fight with William

---

181. SC, a. 9, ad 7.   182. ST II-II, q. 181, a. 3, ad 2.   183. In Meta I, L. 1, p. 15.   184. In Ethics II, L. I, p. 114.

of St. Amour and others who despised your work and that of other friars of your day.

AQUINAS: Teachers of theology are a kind of "architect." They investigate and teach how others ought to further the salvation of souls. So teaching theology, as such, is better and more meritorious, provided it is done with a good intention, than caring for the salvation of this or that person in particular. This is why the Apostle says of himself, "Christ did not send me to baptize, but to preach the gospel" (1 Cor. 1:17), in spite of the fact that baptizing is a work that is supremely useful for the salvation of souls. Again, in 2 Timothy (2:2) the same apostle says: "Entrust these things to faithful people who will be capable of teaching others too." Reason itself shows that it is better to give an education in the things that pertain to salvation to people who can derive benefit from it for themselves and for others than it is to give instruction to simple people who can only benefit from it for themselves.[185]

FOX: You seem to have a great respect for your calling and work.

AQUINAS: The active life has two different kinds of work. One kind flows from the fullness of contemplation, such as teaching and preaching. This is why Gregory says that Psalm 145:7, "they will celebrate your generous kindness," applies to the perfect returning from contemplation. And this is better than mere contemplation. It is a greater thing to give light than simply to have light, and in the same way it is a greater thing to pass on to others what you have contemplated than just to contemplate. The other kind of active work consists entirely in external business, like almsgiving, hospitality, and the like. These are inferior to the works of contemplation, except in an emergency.[186]

FOX: You appear committed to a spirituality of work.

AQUINAS: The error of the Eutichians is destroyed, who said that apostolic men ought not to work. Paul refutes them saying (2 Thess. 3:10): "Anyone who does not wish to work, should not eat." So all are bound to work, according to the Apostle. But I ask, is this a counsel or a command? If a command, then all are bound; but if a counsel, then not all, for only perfect

---

185. QQ I, q. 7, a. 2.   186. ST II-II, q. 188, a. 6.

persons are bound by counsel. . . . Since all are bound to preserve their own life, it follows that they are bound to all things
that act toward that end. Thus whoever does not have the
wherewithal to preserve life is bound to work to preserve it.[187]

FOX: How do we get everybody to work?

AQUINAS: Love often stimulates even lazy minds to work.[188]

FOX: It seems that we have returned to our beginning—to the
Via Positiva—for if we could get one another to "fall in love"
with existence, then creative work would be available, provided
social structures did not interfere or indeed misdefine work
for us.

AQUINAS: Intellectual pleasures are really better [because] such
pleasures lack an opposite pain, which they drive out; they have
consequently no excess to render them vicious. These pleasures
deal with things that are pleasurable naturally and not inciden-
tally.[189]

FOX: Yes. There are no hangovers with creativity. And there
are no limits to what we can and ought to give birth to that is
good, beautiful, and just, or what you would call "pleasurable
naturally." What is the basis and root of your own work?

AQUINAS: As artists delight in their work when the materials
are prepared, so a priest delights in prophesying when he sees
the people assembled.[190]

FOX: I like your comparing the priest to an artist and to the
prophet. For you delight comes from the heart?

AQUINAS: What I have in my heart, I will confess with my
mouth.[191] It can happen that people lack in their heart what they
speak with their mouth, as Matthew's gospel puts it (15): "This
people honors me with their lips, but their heart is far from
me." Not so concerning the just: what they speak, they hold in
their hearts. Such people have the law of God fixed in their
memory through contemplation, and in their will through love.
On account of this the psalmist says (37): "The law of God is
in their heart," meaning that they speak and meditate on the law
and justice. And he adds, "their reward will not be taken away."
He posits here the fruit of good works, since they will not be

---

187. In Mt 6, p. 74.   188. ST II-II, q. 182, a. 4, ad 3.   189. In Ethics
VII, L. 14, p. 697.   190. In Mt 5, p. 48.   191. In Pss 50, p. 349.

deficient or fraudulent, since they who have Sacred Scripture and the law of God in their heart are not deceived by the devil. Psalm 119 says: "I have hidden your words of truth in my heart so that I do not sin against you."[192]

FOX: Our work, then, must come from our heart?

AQUINAS: One who knows the cause knows the effect. But the cause of all human effects is the heart.[193]

FOX: Now we are truly speaking of art as meditation—of our returning to our hearts to give birth by centering there. And we encounter the divine in this return to the heart to give birth.

AQUINAS: God, who makes the heart, knows it. . . . God knows the heart. Therefore, also its works.[194]

FOX: And we encounter the truth of our experience when we return to our inner self as well?

AQUINAS: Contemplation is nothing else than the consideration of truth.[195]

FOX: Thus art as meditation brings forth the deepest desires of our hearts.

AQUINAS: The psalmist (37) says: "God will give you the desires of your heart." According to Origen, the petitions of the heart are what the heart desires, for according to him, if the eye could seek, it would desire pretty colors; and if the ears could seek, they would desire sweet sounds. But the object of the heart—those things that are desired by it—are truth and justice. "And these things," the psalmist says, "God will give to you." As in Matthew (7): "Seek and it will be given to you." The phrase "of the heart" also means when they will be of the heart, God will hear before you cry out. Isaiah (65) says: "Before they cry, I will hear."[196]

FOX: Your point that the heart desires truth and justice is an important one. Why is it that art is so powerful a way of eliciting the divine in us?

AQUINAS: Through good works one puts forth the image of the heavenly person in themselves.[197]

---

192. In Pss 36, p. 287.   193. In Pss 32, p. 263.   194. Ibid.   195. ST I-II, q. 35, a. 5, ad 2.   196. In Pss 36, p. 286.   197. In Pss 38, p. 297.

FOX: And so our work is our expression of the image of God that we are?

AQUINAS: Ezekiel writes (ch. 2): "Lo, a hand was there, stretching out to me and holding a scroll. He unrolled it in front of me. There was written on the back and front of it lamentations, wailings, moanings." When he says, "Lo, a hand was stretched out," he is talking about this hand as the wisdom of God by which all things have been made, as Psalm 104 says: "You have made all things in your wisdom." That very thing is what opens the intellect to seeing, as Ezekiel says (40): "The hand of God came on me, and led me there in visions of God." That very thing is what frees the tongue for speaking, as Jeremiah says (1): "God put forth his hand, and touched my mouth, and the Lord said to me: 'Behold I have given my words into your mouth.'" That very thing is what directs the hand in writing, as Daniel puts it (5): "Fingers appeared like those of one writing." These "fingers" are the prophets and other teachers among whom the gifts of wisdom are divided. By wisdom's authority, she brings about internally all that one does externally by one's sharing of divine wisdom through service. Isaiah says (ch. 26): "All our works have been done within us." And 2 Corinthians 3 says: "Not that we are sufficient to think something of ourselves, as if of ourselves alone, but our sufficiency comes from God." This wisdom indeed is so high, that while we are in the depths, we can receive nothing from it, save that it is sent to us.[198]

FOX: Truly an experience of being a channel for something greater than ourselves.

AQUINAS: This is why the Creator's kindness is signified in the sending of the hand. Romans says (11): "O the height of the riches of the wisdom and the knowledge of God!"

This wisdom is sent as if brought forth to us in three ways: first, in the creation of things, by which it is measured. Romans 1: "The invisible things of God are seen as understood through the things which have been made." Wisdom 13: "Since through the grandeur and beauty of the creatures we may, by analogy, contemplate their Author." Second, it is sent by internal inspiration. Wisdom 7: "In each generation she passes into holy souls,

---

198. In Lam, Preamble, 668.

she makes them friends of God and prophets." It has been sent most preeminently in the incarnation, when before corporeal eyes, invisible wisdom appeared, Wisdom 9: "Dispatch her from the holy heavens, send her forth from your throne of glory to help me and to toil with me and teach me what is pleasing to you."[199]

FOX: And so teachers and other artists are instruments of the creative Spirit just like the prophets were?

AQUINAS: The psalmist says that it should not be understood that he did this work on his own, but with the aid of the Holy Spirit, which uses his tongue as a scribe uses a pen (Ps. 45). And so the principal author of this psalm is the Holy Spirit. 2 Kings 23: "The Spirit of the Lord has spoken through me," as if through an instrument. 2 Peter 1: "Wisdom does not come from human will but by the Holy Spirit." And whose pen is it? "Of a scribe writing quickly," the psalmist says, meaning of the Holy Spirit, which writes quickly on the heart of human beings. For those who seek wisdom through study are eager to get it piece by piece and over a long time. But those who possess it from the Holy Spirit receive it quickly. Acts 2: "Suddenly there was a sound from heaven, etc."[200]

FOX: I like your image that the Holy Spirit writes on the hearts of human beings. And so the creative spirit of God works through our creativity, whether of speech or writing or song?

AQUINAS: The Holy Spirit enlightens our mind, because whatever we know, it is through the Holy Spirit that we know it.[201]

FOX: You see creativity as the work of the Spirit?

AQUINAS: The Holy Spirit moves the heart to work.[202]

FOX: How does it do that?

AQUINAS: The Holy Spirit is said to "move over the waters," not indeed in bodily shape but as the craftsperson's will may be said to move over the material to which he or she intends to give a form.[203]

FOX: Why the waters?

AQUINAS: A river signifies grace on account of the flooding of water, since in grace there is an abundance of gifts, as the psalmist says (65): "The river of God is full of water." In addition, the

---

199. Ibid.   200. In Pss 44, p. 319.   201. AC, pp. 72–73.   202. In Pss 45, p. 327.   203. ST I, q. 66, a. 1.

Holy Spirit is derived from the source, namely, from a spring
—a spring, however is not derived from a river, since a spring
is in its own beginning, and the Holy Spirit is from the Father
and the Son. Likewise, just as a river moves sand and stones, so
the Holy Spirit moves the heart to work. But there are some
rivers that move slowly, but this one is not of that ilk, for it
moves swiftly, as the psalmist says, "the force of the river."
There are two reasons for this, first because the grace of the
Holy Spirit flows suddenly through the heart—Acts 2 says:
"suddenly a sound was made from heaven"; and in another way
because it is by the force of love that the Holy Spirit moves the
heart. Isaiah says: "He came like a violent river"(56).[204]

FOX: Who came like a violent river?

AQUINAS: Christ is a violent river, first because of the multitude of waters. Psalm 65 says: "God's rivers brim with water."
Second, because of the fervor of love—Daniel 7 says: "A stream
of fire poured out from his face." Third, because of the velocity
of the course, as in Psalm 46: "There is a river whose streams
refresh the city of God." Fourth, on account of the height of its
origin, as in Revelation 22: "He showed me a river of living
water, rising from the throne of God and of the Lamb and flowing crystal-clear."[205]

FOX: Your imagery of the spring as its own source or beginning strikes me as important to the artist, for in a way our art
is a return to our origins. Can you comment on that and on your
reference to "living water"?

AQUINAS: There are two kinds of water—living and nonliving.
Nonliving water is water that is not connected or united with
the source from which it springs, but is collected from the rain
or in other ways into ponds and cisterns, and there it stands,
separated from its source. But living water is connected with its
source and flows from it. So, according to this understanding,
the grace of the Holy Spirit is correctly called living water, because the grace of the Holy Spirit is given to human beings in
such a way that the source itself of the grace is also given, that
is, the Holy Spirit. Indeed, grace is given by the Holy Spirit:
"The love of God is poured out into our hearts by the Holy

204. In Pss 45, p. 327.   205. In Is 59, p. 564.

Spirit who has been given to us" (Rom. 5:5). For the Holy Spirit is the unfailing fountain from whom all gifts of grace flow. . . . If anyone has a gift of the Holy Spirit without having the Spirit, the water is not united with its source, and so is not living but dead: "Faith without works is dead" (James 2:20).[206]

FOX: And so our works that truly come from within have the Holy Spirit as their origin. We might even say that they are graces and not works.

AQUINAS: An invisible mission takes place chiefly as regards anyone's proficiency in the performance of a new act, or in the acquisition of a new state of grace. Thus, for example, the proficiency in reference to the gift of miracles or of prophecy, or in the acquisition of a new state of grace; or, for example, the proficiency in reference to the fervor of charity leading a person to expose oneself to the danger of martyrdom, or to renounce one's possessions or to undertake any arduous work.[207]

FOX: And so our undertaking of arduous tasks is a graced event. Elaborate, please, on how the Holy Spirit moves us in our creative moments.

AQUINAS: Sometimes the images in the human imagination are divinely formed, so as to express divine things better than those do that we receive from sense objects. Prophetic visions would be an example of this.[208] In Sacred Scripture operations are meant metaphorically. . . . The operation of the tongue indicates that through the wisdom of the heart it is communicated to others; but the operation of the pen indicates that through the pen the wisdom that is in the heart is poured out onto sensible matter, namely, onto the paper. But God both speaks and writes: God speaks when God pours the divine wisdom into rational minds, as the psalmist puts it (85): "I am listening. What is God saying?" And this is called the Word, since all illumination is through it, as John says (1): "And his life was the light of humanity." God writes because God is pressing the judgments of the divine wisdom upon rational creatures. . . . Ecclesiasticus 1: "God pours wisdom forth over all the divine works." For as someone looking at a book knows the wisdom of the writer, so when we see creatures, we know the wisdom of God. Therefore the pen is the word of God.[209]

---

206. In Jn 4.10, n. 577.   207. ST I, q. 43, a. 6, ad 2.   208. Ibid., q. 12, a. 13.   209. In Pss 44, p. 319.

FOX: Once again I hear you talking about the "illumination" that our work entails. Can you develop this idea?

AQUINAS: The word of God is called fire because it illuminates, as in psalm 119: "Your word is a lamp for my feet." And also because it shines, as in psalm 104: "The word of the Lord has shined on him." And because it penetrates the innermost parts (Jer. 20): "And the word of the Lord became in my heart like a seething fire, and impressed itself on my bones." And Hebrews (4): "The word of God is alive, and effective, and more piercing than any two-edged sword, and reaching even to the division of soul and spirit, of the joints and marrows, and more able to judge the thoughts and intentions of the heart." Also, the word is fire because it melts things—thus psalm 147 says: "God utters the divine word, and make things melt; God's spirit blows, and the waters flow." Also, the word consumes the disobedient, as in Isaiah 30: "His lips are full of indignation, and his tongue like a devouring fire."[210]

FOX: We have pretty well established why you love your work. But let us turn to other kinds of work that other workers are involved in. Is pleasure in one's work possible for all workers?

AQUINAS: It is a fact that natural desires fit in harmoniously with actions that need to be performed.[211] In Matthew's gospel we read: "This is my beloved son in whom I am well pleased" (3:2). Now whenever the good of something is reflected, in that object there is something pleasing for the thing reflected. Thus artists please themselves through their beautiful art, and those who see their beautiful image in a mirror are pleased.[212]

FOX: And so love of work goes along with the creative act?

AQUINAS: Everything gives pleasure to the extent that it is loved.[213] It is natural for people to love their own work (thus it is to be observed that poets love their own poems): and the reason is that we love *to be* and *to live,* and these are made manifest in our *action.* Second, because we all naturally love that in which we see our own good.[214]

FOX: An added pleasure in creativity, it seems, is the joy of sharing our inner work with others.

---

210. In Jer 5, p. 593.   211. In Eph 5.31, p. 497.   212. In Mt 3, p. 36.
213. ST I-II, q. 31, a. 6.   214. Ibid. II-II, q. 26, a. 12.

AQUINAS: Doing good to another becomes a pleasure insofar as it arouses in people an imagination of abundant good existing in them and they are able to give others a share of this abundance. This is one reason why parents take pleasure in their children and in their own works as being things on which they bestow a share of their own good.[215]

FOX: It would seem too that if the Holy Spirit is involved in our creative work, that alone is reason for enjoying one's work.

AQUINAS: God is powerful enough to make every grace of the Holy Spirit abundant, and for this reason you should always rejoice in the good work that you do.[216]

FOX: Good things follow, no doubt, from the pleasure we can take in our work.

AQUINAS: In fact, we see that in any field of rational activity, those who enjoy their work are better able to judge detailed matters, and to make a precise investigation into those things that are accomplished with pleasure. Thus, geometricians, who take pleasure in the considerations proper to geometry, are better able to understand the detailed points in this kind of thinking, because the mind is more attentive to that in which pleasure is found. And the same argument goes for all the others; for instance, for those who like musical performances and take pleasure in them, and for those who enjoy the art of building, and for all others—because, by the fact that they take pleasure in such work, they make a great contribution to their kind of work. So, it is clear that pleasure increases activity.[217]

FOX: Of course there are pleasures and there are pleasures . . . even in work!

AQUINAS: It is quite apparent that pleasures are of different kinds, in view of the discovery that an appropriate pleasure increases activity while a foreign one impedes it. Indeed, we see that lovers of organ music cannot pay attention to the sermons addressed to them when they are listening to organ playing, for the very reason that they take more pleasure in the working of the art of the pipes than in the present work, that is, in the hearing of the words spoken to them. So, it is evident that the

---

215. Ibid. I-II, q. 32, a. 6. 216. In 2 Cor, ch. 9, p. 350. 217. In Ethics X, L. 7, pp. 892–893.

pleasure that accompanies the working of the art of organ playing is destructive of the activity of speech.[218]

FOX: I hear you saying that people are most motivated by pleasure and that it is by pleasure that we create good work, which
is, in fact, itself pleasurable precisely because it honors the inner
person, that hidden treasure yearning to express itself inside.

AQUINAS: It is obvious that the more enjoyable activity excludes the other, to the extent that if there be a great difference
in the amount of pleasure, one may entirely give up doing the
work that brings one less pleasure. That is why we can do nothing else when we keenly enjoy any one thing.[219]

FOX: Yes! Concentration in work comes with our ecstasy at
it—every artist knows this. "Where did the time go?" we ask
when we are loving our work deeply. In connecting creative
work and pleasure you seem to be saying that part of the artist's
task is indeed to give pleasure.

AQUINAS: Representations of things, even of those that are not
pleasant in themselves, give rise to pleasure. For the soul rejoices in comparing one thing with another, because comparison of one thing with another is the proper and connatural act
of the reason.[220]

FOX: To marvel at anything—and certainly at the work of human hands and imagination—is a great pleasure.

AQUINAS: Wonder gives pleasure . . . insofar as the wonderer
learns something new, in other words, that the cause is other
than one had thought it to be, or that those who wonder are
other than they thought themselves to be.[221]

FOX: Surprises give pleasure. And this seizes us. But what
about lesser pleasures?

AQUINAS: When some things give us moderate pleasure, that is
mild or small, we can do other things at the same time. This is
evident in the case of people who enjoy shows and games. In
fact, those who take little enjoyment in what they see there can
turn their attention to munching corn—which is not very enjoyable. This is especially true of people watching performers
who fail to put on a good show, with the result that the watching of this kind of performance is not enjoyable to them.[222]

---

218. Ibid., 892.   219. Ibid.   220. ST I-II, q. 32, a. 8.   221. Ibid., ad 1.
222. In Ethics X, L. 7, p. 892.

FOX: So you are not impressed by eating popcorn, even though we know you loved to eat! Well, maybe popcorn has improved over the centuries since you made this statement. You have spoken of yourself as a priest, preacher, and teacher and of other workers, including entertainers and organ players. I sense that you are fascinated by the diversity of work in our lives.

AQUINAS: Although there is naturally present in the human a desire to gather the things necessary for life, it is not such that everyone must be occupied with this work. Indeed, not even among the bees do all have the same function. Rather, some gather honey, others build their homes out of wax, while the rulers are not occupied with these tasks. And the same should hold in the case of human beings.[223]

FOX: Yet all have their contribution to make through work to the destiny of the whole?

AQUINAS: The more noble things are in the universe, the more must they participate in the order in which the good of the universe consists.[224]

FOX: And so we all have different tasks to do in the universe?

AQUINAS: Since many things are needed for the human beings' life, for which one person could not suffice of themselves, it is necessary for different jobs to be done by different people. For some should be farmers, some have care of animals, some are builders, and so on for the other tasks. And since human life requires not only corporeal but, even more, spiritual goods, it is also necessary that some people devote their time to spiritual things, for the betterment of others; and these must be freed from concern over temporal matters. Now, this division of various tasks among different persons is done by divine providence, inasmuch as some people are more inclined to one kind of work than to another.[225]

FOX: It is interesting how you see the various callings of work and art as being a providential arrangement. In some respects I feel we are returning to a theme that dominated in the Via Positiva: that of beauty. I have always maintained that a special relationship exists between the Via Positiva and the Via Creativa:

---

223. CG III, ch. 134 n. 2.   224. Ibid., ch. 90 n. 4.   225. Ibid.

our creativity, we might say, brings even more awe and more beauty into the universe.

AQUINAS: The beauty of the artwork proceeds from the beauty of the artist.[226]

FOX: Can you give an example of this?

AQUINAS: The beauty conceived in the heart of the Father is the Word. So the formation of everything is attributed to the Word, and for this reason the psalmist (33) says: "The heavens were established by the word of the Lord."[227]

FOX: It seems there is a special relationship between the artists and their art.

AQUINAS: When one thing makes and another is made, the making stands between them.[228]

FOX: And so beauty plays a big role in our creativity, you say?

AQUINAS: The psalmist shows the feeling he has for divine worship, which, in order that it be harmonious, ought to be an expression of love. For this reason he says, "Lord, I have loved the beauty of your house." Dionysius says: "The good and the beautiful is lovable to all." Thus every person loves beauty: carnal people love carnal beauty, spiritual ones love spiritual beauty, and this is the beauty of the house of God, as it says in Numbers (24): "How beautiful your tabernacle, Jacob, and your tents Israel, like a wooded valley, like irrigated gardens near streams, like tabernacles which the Lord has made." But this beauty is of good works, or of divine gifts, or of the saints themselves—for all these things are like the kind of beauty of the house of God.[229]

FOX: You are saying that our work is beautiful like the house of God, a temple for con-templing?

AQUINAS: "Therefore I have loved all these things, so that they have made me fit for the beauty of the house of God," the psalmist says. Therefore in this way the feeling is demonstrated since there is delight, and pulchritude, and comeliness. But one should know that this beauty comes from the dwelling of God; as a house is not beautiful unless it has been inhabited. Thus I have loved myself in order that you may dwell in me, or I have

---

226. In Pss 32, p. 260.   227. Ibid.   228. In Meta V, L. 20, p. 400.
229. In Pss 25, p. 235.

loved my native land in order that I may dwell there, or direct my course toward it. And for this reason the psalmist says, "And the place of the dwelling of your glory." And all these things, that is, good works, gifts of God, and the saints themselves, are the beauty of the house of God, inasmuch as divine grace shines in them. This grace beautifies like a light, as Ambrose says, because without light all things are ugly.[230]

FOX: Beauty, you say, is the indwelling of God. What else is beauty, what is ugly?

AQUINAS: There are three conditions of beauty—first, integrity or completeness, for broken things are ugly; second, due proportion and harmony; third, brightness and color.[231] Variety belongs to beauty, as the Apostle says (2 Tim. 2:20): "In a great house there are not only vessels of gold and silver, but also of wood and clay."[232] Beauty establishes the integrity of things in themselves, and also their participation in the whole, each in its own style, not with uniformity. The higher are shared and the lower are ennobled by this exchange.[233]

FOX: Is beauty an end in itself?

AQUINAS: Contemplation can be delightful both as a function and for its content. The activity itself is congenial to human nature and instinct, and especially when anyone thereby holds a thing they love. Thus seeing is enjoyable itself, and more so when it gazes on the form of the beloved.[234] The human being enjoys the scent of lilies and roses through smell and finds them pleasing in themselves. In contrast, other animals take pleasure in smells—dogs, for instance—and colors only because they point to something else.[235]

FOX: You are saying that beauty plays a different role in human life than it does in the lives of other animals, that for us it is more an end in itself?

AQUINAS: Senses are appointed to humans not only for procuring the necessities of life, as is the case with the other animals, but also for the sake of knowledge itself. Other animals take no pleasure in sense-objects unless they be related to food or to sex, but humans can delight in their very beauty.[236]

---

230. Ibid. 231. ST I, q. 39, a. 8. 232. Ibid. II-II, q. 183, a. 2. 233. DDN, n. 364, p. 118. 234. ST II-II, q. 180, a. 7. 235. C et M II, lect. 14. 236. ST I, q. 91, a. 3, ad 3.

FOX: I hear you saying that knowledge and beauty go together—perhaps another instance of how your culture's word
for "reason" might well be translated in our time as "creativity"
or that which births beauty.

AQUINAS: The senses most charged with knowledge are those
most set on beauty. The beautiful is the same as the good, but
with a difference of accent. Good is what all desire; therefore it
is of the essence of beauty that at the knowledge and sight of it
the desire is stilled. [237]

FOX: Beauty stills us, it catches us up short, it moves us to silence like ecstasy itself.

AQUINAS: The senses closest to the mind, namely, sight and
hearing, are most engaged by beauty. We speak about beautiful
sights and sounds, but not about beautiful tastes and smells.
And so beauty adds to the meaning of goodness a relationship
to the power of knowledge. The good is that which simply
pleases desire, the beautiful that which pleases on being perceived. [238] Clearness and proportion are both rooted in mind,
whose function it is to order and light up a symmetry. Hence,
beauty, pure and essential, dwells in the contemplative life,
wherefore it is said of the contemplation of wisdom, "and I became a lover of her beauty." [239]

FOX: And so beauty touches us with sights and sounds—color
and music, for example. Can you give us a concrete instance of
this?

AQUINAS: Musical harmonies change the feelings of people.
This is why Pythagoras, seeing that a youth was mad about
Phrygian sound, changed the mode. Thereby he tempered the
mind of the passionate boy according to the state of the most
diseased mind, as Boethius explains in the prologue to his book
on music. . . . In every culture some musical harmonies are
used to excite the mind of humans toward God. But this kind
of harmony is accustomed to be employed in two ways—sometimes in musical instruments and sometimes indeed in songs.
The psalmist (33) speaks of the first way when he talks about the
zither; and he speaks about the second way when he talks about
"singing for God." For the feelings of human beings are directed through instruments and musical harmonies in three

---

237. Ibid. I-II, q. 27, a. 1, ad 3.   238. Ibid.   239. Ibid. II-II, q. 180, a.
2, ad 3.

ways: sometimes it is set up in a certain rectitude and strength of mind; sometimes it is snatched up on high; and sometimes it turns into a sweetness and delight. And for this purpose, as the Philosopher [Aristotle] puts it in his *Politics* (Book 8, ch. 7), three kinds of song have been invented. For the first there is the Doric song, which is of the first and second tone, as some have it. For the second, there is the Phrygian song, which is of the third tone. For the third there is the Hippolydian song, which is of the fifth and sixth tone. Others are invented later. And these are played on instruments, since certain instruments make the first, like the tibia and the trumpet; certain make the second, like the organ; and certain the third, like the Psalter and the zither.[240]

FOX: The artist is one who gives birth to images and thereby awakens the imagination. How important are images to our lives?

AQUINAS: The image is a principle of our knowledge. It is that from which our intellectual activity begins, not as a passing stimulus, but as an enduring foundation.[241]

FOX: So without images and our own imaging there would be no intellectual life? Images are the source of that life?

AQUINAS: When the imagination is choked, so also is our theological knowledge.[242]

FOX: That is so true; the banishment of the artist from theological education has been a disaster. Rationalism has rendered theology without passion or compassion.

AQUINAS: Human contemplation in the present life cannot function without images, for to see meaning in the play of fancy is connatural to us. The purity of intelligible being is contemplated there, though intellectual knowledge does not consist in these images. This applies to the truths of revelation as well as to those of natural knowledge.[243]

FOX: And so we never escape our need for images?

AQUINAS: An image implies the idea of origin.[244] Imagining goes with thinking so long as we are in this present life, no matter how spiritual the knowledge. Even God is known through the images of the divine effects.[245]

---

240. In Pss 32, p. 260.   241. DT vi, 2, ad 5.   242. Ibid.   243. ST II-II, q. 180, a. 5, ad 2.   244. Ibid. I, q. 35, a. 1.   245. xvi De malo 8, ad 3.

FOX: Why is it that images and therefore the birthing of appropriate images are so important to our knowing?

AQUINAS: In its present condition the mind cannot actually understand anything except by reference to images. . . . In understanding, either freshly or summoning knowledge already gained, the mind's activity must be accompanied by activity of imagination and of other sense-powers. When the imagination is warped, as in madness, or the memory is lost, as in amnesia—either condition may result from bodily injury—one is prevented from understanding even those things one previously knew.

In addition, everyone experiences in themselves that when they attempt to understand a subject they must picture it and use images as examples to hold one's attention.[246]

FOX: Given your understanding of the necessity of images, it would seem that artists would never be without work. And neither would the artist inside each one of us. We have not yet talked about freedom and the artist, but it seems, from what we have discussed up to now, that artists need to be true to their images and to the Spirit who births these images in us.

AQUINAS: One reaches one's ultimate end by acts of the virtues, for happiness is assigned as a reward for virtue. Now, forced acts are not acts of the virtues, since the main thing in virtue is choice, which cannot be present without voluntariness, which is the opposite of violence.[247]

FOX: Yes! The Via Creativa is clearly the path of election and choice. We choose which images to go with and which ones to leave behind. Every artist has to do this.

AQUINAS: The exterior acts of virtue proceed from interior choice.[248]

FOX: Choice seems to lie at the core of the creative process.

AQUINAS: It says in Deuteronomy (30:15): "Consider that the Lord has set before you this day life and good, and on the other hand, death and evil."[249] . . . The proper object of choice is the means to an end. . . . Choice is the final acceptance of something to be carried out. This is not the business of reason but of

---

246. ST I, q. 84, a. 7.   247. CG III, ch. 148 n. 5.   248. In Ethics II, L. 5, p. 136.   249. CG III, ch. 148 n. 7.

will; for however much reason sets the one ahead of the other, there is not yet the acceptance of one in preference to the other as something to be done until the will inclines to the one rather than to the other.[250]

FOX: But you say that not to be able to choose one's images is an act of violence.

AQUINAS: The violent is incompatible with the voluntary. So it is impossible for the will to be moved by an extrinsic principle as by an agent; rather, every movement of the will must proceed from within.[251] Both natural and voluntary movement must arise from an intrinsic source.[252]

FOX: Is this what we mean by freedom?

AQUINAS: The free is that which is its own cause. Hence that which is not the cause of its own acting is not free in acting.[253] Slaves are those who do not act as cause of their own action, but as though moved from without.[254]

FOX: But it seems that woundedness and lack of privilege and opportunity all mitigate against a person's freedom to act and express themselves.

AQUINAS: In human activity two elements are to be found: First, the choice of a course of action. Now this is always in a person's power. Second, the carrying out or execution of the course of action. And this is not always within a person's power. . . . Thus one is not said to be free in one's actions, but free in one's choice, which is a judgment about what is to be done. This is what the term "free choice" refers to.[255]

FOX: It would seem from our discussion above that the artist who truly gives birth from his or her heart, from what you are now calling the "interior source," is anything but a slave—in fact such a person is expressing his or her deepest freedom.

AQUINAS: Anyone who does a thing through love does it of themselves, so to speak, because it is by their own inclination that they are moved to act. Thus it is contrary to the very notion of slavery that one should act from love.[256]

FOX: There seems to be a kind of responsibility that we must take when we give birth as well.

---

250. DV, q. 22, a. 15.   251. CG III, ch. 88 n. 5.   252. Ibid., n. 6.
253. Ibid. II, ch. 48 n. 3.   254. ST II-II, q. 19, a. 4.   255. DV, q. 24, a. 1, ad 1.   256. ST II-II, q. 19, a. 4.

AQUINAS: What we do of our own accord surpasses what we do through another.[257]

FOX: Artists seem to be touching divine powers when they give birth.

AQUINAS: One does not possess from oneself the thing in which one excels, for this is as it were something divine in one. For this reason honor is due principally not to the individual but to God. . . . The thing in which a person excels is given to that person by God in order that they may profit others thereby.[258]

FOX: Thus our creativity is a divine gift. One dimension that makes our creativity so awesome is its capacity for the infinite. You have spoken about our intellect's infinite capacities and of our hands' capacity to devise an infinite number of objects. Somehow I feel the artist faces an infinity of choices at times, and this makes the act of *electio* or choice all the more amazing in our creative works.

AQUINAS: The origin of works of art is the human mind, which is the image and offspring of the divine mind, which is the origin of natural things.[259] Intellectual apprehension is not limited to certain things, but reaches out to them all. This is why Aristotle in *De anima* III says of the possible intellect that it is "that by which we become all things." Hence, the appetite of an intellectual substance has relationship to all things . . . both possible and impossible.[260]

FOX: So our wills too are infinite in scope and possibility?

AQUINAS: Our will can reach out to all the things that we can understand, at least our will to know them. And the act of the will is clearly directed to the universal, as Aristotle says in the *Rhetoric,* "we hate robbers in general, but are angry only with individual ones."[261]

FOX: Such a responsibility! Such a divine power resides in our capacity for the infinite!

AQUINAS: Everything that brings something into actual being does so because it acts through God's power.[262] God so communicates the divine goodness to created beings that one thing that receives it can transfer it to another.[263]

---

257. Ibid., q. 26, a. 12, ad 1.   258. Ibid., q. 131, a.1.   259. In I Pol, lect. 1.   260. CG II, ch. 47 n. 5.   261. Ibid., ch. 60 n. 5.   262. Ibid. III, ch. 67 n. 7.   263. Ibid., ch. 69 n. 16.

FOX: God delights to have made us all artists, it seems.

AQUINAS: God loves us more than we love God, and parents love their children more than children love their parents.[264]

FOX: So God loves us as artists—which is what God is. As artists we are God's offspring and even works of art. And this pleases God.

AQUINAS: It is not superfluous, even if God can by the Godhead alone produce all natural effects, for them to be produced by certain other causes. For this is not a result of the inadequacy of divine power, but of the immensity of the divine goodness, whereby God has willed to communicate the divine likeness to things, not only so that they might exist, but also that they might be causes for other things. Indeed, all creatures generally attain the divine likeness in these two ways.[265]

FOX: Now I hear you putting our capacity to create or cause things on par with our existence itself as a radical likeness we share with Divinity.

AQUINAS: Things tend toward the divine likeness by the fact that they are the cause of other things.[266] In fact, a created being tends toward the divine likeness through its operation. Now, through its operation, one thing becomes the cause of another. Therefore, in this way, also, do things tend toward the divine likeness, in that they are the causes of other things.[267]

FOX: When I listen to you expound on the power of generation in things, I sense a great nobility in the act of generativity.

AQUINAS: Of these three powers—augmentative, nutritive, and generative—the generative has the greater finality, nobility, and perfection. . . . For it belongs to a being that is already perfect to produce another like itself. Furthermore, the generative power is served by the augmentative and nutritive powers.[268]

FOX: And this is a special power?

AQUINAS: The more perfect creatures cannot make anything like themselves. The sun, for example, cannot produce another sun, nor an angel another angel. It is true only among corruptible creatures, which have been divinely provided with a

264. ST II-II, q. 26, a. 12, ad 3.   265. CG III, ch. 70 n. 7.   266. Ibid., ch. 21 n. 1.   267. Ibid., n. 2.   268. ST I, q. 78, a. 3.

generative power in order that what cannot perdure as an individual may perdure in the species.[269]

FOX: It seems to be a great privilege to be a cause of other things, as God is.

AQUINAS: To be the cause of other things is good.[270] Each being is perfect when it can make something like itself . . . and for this reason Dionysius says about God that God is called perfect insofar as God pours forth the divine perfection from above on all creatures and this not as a result of diverse offerings, on the part of God who makes the offering, but as a result of one offering: this offering is indeed not deficient, but is ceaselessly giving forth the same things. Nor is it modest, for God gives "lavishly to all" (James 1).[271]

FOX: So to speak of our capacity to give birth is to speak of our likeness to God?

AQUINAS: Although a created being tends to the divine likeness in many ways, this one whereby it seeks the divine likeness by being the cause of others takes the ultimate place. Hence Dionysius says, in the third chapter of *On the Celestial Hierarchy,* that "of all things, it is more divine to become a co-worker with God" in accord with the statement of the Apostle: "We are God's co-workers" (I Cor. 3:9).[272]

FOX: Indeed, our creativity is our divinity expressing itself, as you say when you say it is the "ultimate" expression of our divinity, and how it is "more divine" to become God's co-worker. Cocreation indeed! I think our species should spend more time than it does just wondering at and celebrating our divine capacity to be creative. Sometimes I think we take it all for granted.

AQUINAS: Among the higher creatures, the closest to God are those rational ones that exist, live, and understand in the likeness of God. Consequently, God in the divine goodness gives them the power not only of pouring out upon other things but also of having the same manner of outpouring that the Godhead has—that is, according to their will, and not according to any necessity of their nature.[273]

---

269. DV, q. 27, a. 3, ad 24.   270. CG III, ch. 21 n. 4.   271. DDN, n. 968, p. 360.   272. CG III, ch. 21 n. 8.   273. DV, q. 5, a. 8.

FOX: So it is in our will or choices that we especially reflect the godlikeness that is ours. And we have the "same manner of out-pouring" that God has. What an immense power we possess in our powers of creativity! Say more about how it is that we work with God as cocreators.

AQUINAS: The same effect is not attributed to a natural cause and to divine power in such a way that it is partly done by God, and partly by the natural agent. Rather, it is wholly done by both, according to a different way, just as the same effect is wholly attributed to the instrument and also wholly to the principal agent.[274] Just as art presupposes a work of nature, so does a work of nature presuppose the work of God the Creator. In fact, the material for art products comes from nature, while that of natural products comes through creation by God. Moreover, art objects are preserved in being by the power of natural things; a house, for instance, by the solidity of its stones.[275]

FOX: You have spoken about our being cocreators with God. What about God's cocreating with us?

AQUINAS: The Scriptures say, "Lord, you have wrought all our works for us" (Isa. 26:12); and: "Without me, you can do nothing" (John 15:5); and: "It is God who works in us both to will and to accomplish according to the divine good will" (Phil. 2:13). And for this reason, the products of nature are often attributed in Scripture to divine working, because it is God who works in every agent operating naturally or voluntarily, as the text has it: "Did you not pour me out like milk, and curdle me then like cheese?; clothe me with skin and flesh, and weave me with bones and sinews?" (Job 10:10–11); and in the psalm (18:14): "God thundered from heaven, the Most High made the divine voice heard, launched the lightnings and routed them."[276]

FOX: Can you elaborate more on how it is that God works in every agent that acts?

AQUINAS: God applies active forces to effects, as does any artist. But God does more than that—God also makes the tools with which the artist works. God gives things their active forms and keeps them in being. Consequently God is the cause, not

---

274. CG III, ch. 70 n. 8.   275. Ibid., ch. 65 n. 6.   276. Ibid., ch. 67 n. 7.

merely as providing the active form (like an engineer who makes a machine that works on the force of gravity), but also as sustaining the form and power of everything (like the sun, which lights color). Because the form is inside a thing, and because the more profound and pervasive it is the more intimate it is, and because God is the proper cause of existence, which is innermost to all things, it follows that God works at the heart of all activity. "You have clothed me with skin and flesh, you have weaved me with bones and sinews" (Job 10:11).[277]

FOX: The artist, it seems, depends on God and nature in the common act of cocreating?

AQUINAS: Grace and virtue imitate the order of nature, which is established by divine wisdom.[278] Humanity is not the founder of nature. By art and virtue human beings make use of natural things for their own benefit.[279]

FOX: "Art and virtue," you say. One element of your theology of creativity that strikes me as very important is your calling art a virtue.

AQUINAS: There are five habits by which the soul always expresses the truth by either affirming or denying, namely, art, science, prudence, wisdom, and understanding. Clearly these are the five intellectual virtues.[280]

FOX: You get to the heart of the power of the praxis of art as meditation when you say art always expresses the truth. How do you actually define this virtue you call art?

AQUINAS: Art is nothing else but the right reason about certain works to be made. And yet the good of these things depends, not on a person's appetitive faculty being affected in this or that way, but on the goodness of the work done. For artists as such are commendable, not for the will with which they do a work, but for the quality of the work. Art, therefore, properly speaking is an operative habit.[281]

FOX: You mentioned the "good" of the things that the artist makes.

AQUINAS: The good of an art is to be found, not in the artist, but in the product of the art, since art is right reason about

---

277. ST I, q. 105, a. 5.   278. Ibid. II-II, q. 31, a. 3.   279. Ibid. I, q. 22, a. 2, ad 3.   280. In Ethics VI, L. 3, p. 553.   281. ST I-II, q. 57, a. 3.

things to be made. Since the making of a thing passes into external matter, it is a perfection not of the maker, but of the thing made, even as movement is the act of the thing moved; and art is concerned with the making of things.[282]

FOX: And so there is a difference between our being good and our work being good?

AQUINAS: Art does not require of artists that their act be a good act, but that their work be good. Rather it would be necessary for the thing made to act well (for example, that a knife should carve well or that a saw should cut well), if it were proper to such things to act, rather than to be acted on, because they do not have dominion over their actions. Wherefore artists need art, not that they may live well, but that they may produce a good work of art, and have it in good keeping. In contrast, prudence is necessary to human beings that they may lead good lives, and not merely that they may be good people.[283]

FOX: You mention prudence. How do art and prudence differ?

AQUINAS: Art confers the mere aptness for good work since it does not consider the appetite; whereas prudence confers not only aptness for a good work, but also the use, for it concerns the appetite since it presupposes the rectitude of it. The reason for this difference is that art is the right reason of things to be made while prudence is the right reason of things to be done. Now making and doing differ, in that making is an action passing into outward matter, for example to build, to saw, and so forth. Whereas doing is an action abiding in the agent, for example to see, to will, and the like. . . . For these reasons it is evident that prudence is a virtue distinct from art.[284] Things to be done differ from things to be made because the latter start from an agent and terminate in some extrinsic matters, as for example, a bench and a house. The reasoned plan of making them is called art. On the other hand, things to be done are actions that do not go outside the agent, but, instead, are acts that perfect one, as for example, chaste living, patient endurance, and the like. The reasoned plan for doing these things is called prudence.[285]

FOX: You call our creativity a virtue. What exactly is a virtue?

---

282. Ibid., a. 5, ad 1.   283. Ibid.   284. Ibid., a. 4.   285. DV, q. 5, a. 1.

AQUINAS: Virtue denotes a certain perfection of a power.[286] By its very name virtue means the completion of an active power.[287]

FOX: I am struck that you define virtue as "power" or "strength," which is indeed its root meaning in Latin. How would you define power?

AQUINAS: Power signifies a principle that puts into execution what knowledge directs and will commands.[288]

FOX: This certainly helps to explain how creativity is indeed a great power. You seem to be encouraging human beings to find their power and not to run from it.

AQUINAS: Active power belongs to the perfection of a thing; for the more perfect anything is, so much the greater is its power found to be.[289]

FOX: You see God as powerful, do you not?

AQUINAS: God is powerful, and strength of action is justly ascribed to God.[290] Divine power is God's very substance.[291] The divine power is not different from God's action.[292] One thing we know about God is God's power (*virtus*). According to this, things proceed from God as from a principle. "Great is the Lord, and great is God's power (*virtus*)" (Ps. 145). Philosophers judge this power to be perpetual. Accordingly, it is said that God's power (*virtus*) is also eternal.[293]

FOX: But didn't we determine that all beings have power?

AQUINAS: The distribution of divine virtue, on account of its own boundlessness, proceeds to all existing things and there is no existing thing that does not have some virtue. But it is necessary that it have either intellectual virtue, like the angels; or rational virtue, like human beings; or sensible virtue, like animals; or livening virtue, like plants; or substantial, like the others. And not only existing things, but even being itself possesses virtue in addition to that which it is from the supersubstantial virtue of God.[294]

FOX: Then it is right to speak of the virtue of all beings.

---

286. ST I-II, q. 55, a. 1.   287. DV, q. 14, a. 3.   288. ST I, q. 25, a. 1, ad 4.   289. CG II, ch. 7 n. 4.   290. Ibid., n. 1.   291. Ibid., ch. 8 n. 1. 292. Ibid., ch. 9 n. 1.   293. In Rom, ch. 1, p. 22.   294. DDN, n. 751, p. 283.

AQUINAS: The effects of the unfailing virtue of God proceed both to human beings and to animals and to plants and to all natural things.[295]

FOX: Your understanding of power and virtue is so cosmic! Our anthropocentric view of power has gotten our species into a lot of trouble lately. One of our mistakes is to have diminished the meaning of virtue—somehow equating it with "being righteous" for example, rather than being powerful.

AQUINAS: There arc some powers that of themselves are determined in their acts, for instance, the active natural powers. And therefore these natural powers are in themselves called virtues. But the rational powers, which are proper to the human, are not determinate to one particular action, but are inclined indifferently to many. They are determinate to acts by means of habits. Therefore human virtues are habits.[296]

FOX: Virtue is a habit that makes us strong, apparently, an act of empowerment.

AQUINAS: Virtues are the strength (*fortitudo*) of a person.[297]

FOX: I think this is a supremely important point—not that virtues are about being righteous but that they are about our *strength,* our empowerment. A virtuous person is a strong person.

AQUINAS: The very essence of virtue implies perfection of a power. . . . Virtue disposes to that which is best. . . . A power of the soul is the subject of virtue.[298] Divine virtue strengthensall things that are united in a certain friendship and communion with itself.[299]

FOX: Perhaps prayer is basically a strengthening exercise, then, that is meant to make us strong vis-à-vis God and our life in the world.

AQUINAS: Divine virtue firmly upholds the substantial and natural powers of all things, and of whatever thing it strengthens, as an indissoluble permanence insofar as all things preserve their status for themselves as fixed beforehand by God.[300]

FOX: And building our strength means building our virtue.

---

295. Ibid., n. 755, p. 285.   296. ST I-II, q. 55, a. 1.   297. In Pss 6, p. 164.   298. ST I-II, q. 56, a. 1.   299. DDN, n. 756, p. 285.   300. Ibid., n. 760, p. 286.

AQUINAS: In Matthew's gospel it says "the man who had received the five talents went away." Progress in virtue is demonstrated here. Psalm 84:7 says: "They go from strength to strength," and Genesis (26:13) says of Isaac that "he gained more and more," for virtue increases by being exercised. If it is not exercised it grows weak.[301]

FOX: And so it is necessary to practice virtue in order to strengthen it and develop it as a habit.

AQUINAS: As the sight of a single swallow on one clear day does not prove that spring is here, so a single good deed is not enough to make a person happy. It arises rather from the continued performance of good deeds throughout one's whole life.[302]

FOX: I find the idea that virtue is strength and empowerment refreshing!

AQUINAS: In us love is set in order by virtue.[303] Virtue is the art of right conduct.[304]

FOX: Not only is art a virtue but virtue is an art! You say virtue is about building up strength and authentic power and that for creative creatures like the human race this means a habit.

AQUINAS: Human virtue is essentially an operative habit.[305] Human virtue, which is an operative habit, is a good habit, productive of good works.[306] Virtue is a habit by which we work well. . . . Virtue is that which makes its possessor good, and their work good as well.[307]

FOX: Does art, then, make a person good?

AQUINAS: Through being gifted in science or art a person is said to be good not simply, but relatively. For instance, a "good" grammarian or a "good" blacksmith. . . . The subject of a habit that is called a virtue simply can only be the will or some power insofar as it is moved by the will.[308]

FOX: What is a habit?

AQUINAS: A habit is a state of potentiality in respect to operation. Thus habit is called "first act" and operation is called

---

301. In Mt 25, p. 232.   302. In Ethics I, L. 10, p. 55.   303. ST I-II, q. 55, a. 1, ad 4.   304. Ibid., q. 58, a. 2, ad 1.   305. Ibid., q. 55, a. 2. 306. Ibid., a. 3.   307. Ibid., q. 56, a. 3.   308. Ibid.

"second act."[309] Habit is a disposition of a subject that is in a state of potentiality to form or to operation.[310]

FOX: How does habit relate to power?

AQUINAS: Habit takes precedence over power as the complete takes precedence over the incomplete, and as act takes precedence over potentiality.[311] Habits are necessary in order that powers be determined to good.[312]

FOX: And there is something unique to the human being in our virtues being grounded in habit?

AQUINAS: Natural forces do not perform their operations by means of habits, because they are of themselves determined to one mode of operation.[313]

FOX: Thus it is because of our power of choice that our virtues are rooted in habits?

AQUINAS: Habit is that which one uses when one wills.[314] The image of God is the human being insofar as we are the principle of our actions as having free will and control of our actions.[315] A rational creature does not have determined actions but is in a state of indifference in regard to innumerable actions. A rational nature endowed with free choice is, however, different in its action from every other agent in nature.[316]

FOX: It is interesting to me that your use of the term "rational nature" includes will and free choice and action. "Rational" for you is not just about knowing abstractions but is about will as well.

AQUINAS: Reason, we must remember, is both speculative and practical.[317] The act of the will is to will, to choose, and to intend.[318]

FOX: And in the human species we have a special gift of will and of intellect that we apply to our creativity?

AQUINAS: The complete perfection of the universe required the existence of some creatures that return to God not only regarding likeness of nature, but also by their action. And such a return to God cannot be made except by the act of the intellect and will, because God has no other operation in respect to itself than

---

309. Ibid., q. 49, a. 3, ad 1.   310. Ibid., q. 50, a. 1.   311. Ibid., a. 2, ad 3.   312. Ibid., q. 49, a. 4, ad 3.   313. Ibid., ad 2.   314. Ibid., q. 50, a. 5.   315. Ibid., prologue to I-II.   316. DV, q. 24, a. 7.   317. In Ethics I, L. 5, p. 29.   318. DV, q. 22, a. 15.

these. The greatest perfection of the universe therefore demanded the existence of some intellectual creatures.[319]

FOX: So you see humanity as possessed with a quasi-divine way
of acting, namely, our immense creativity that comes with our
intellect and will?

AQUINAS: In order that creatures might perfectly represent the
divine goodness, it was necessary not only that good things
should be made, but also that they should by their actions contribute to the goodness of other things. But a thing is perfectly
likened to another in its operation when not only the action is
of the same specific nature, but also the mode of acting is the
same. Consequently, the highest perfection of things required
the existence of some creatures that act in the same way as God.
But it has already been shown that God acts by intellect and
will. It was therefore necessary for some creatures to have intellect and will.[320]

FOX: And so it is our use of choice in generating and creating
that distinguishes us from other species, and by it we can "perfectly represent the divine goodness." What a challenge!

AQUINAS: There is a perfection and dignity in human life because it is intellectual or rational. For although other things are
moved by themselves through an inner principle, that inner
principle is nevertheless not open to opposite alternatives; hence
they are not moved freely but from necessity. These are said
more truly to be made to act than to act themselves. But human
beings, since they are the masters of their acts, move themselves
freely to all that they will. Consequently, human beings have
perfect life, as does every intellectual nature.[321]

FOX: You are saying that only human beings have will. But
surely all animals follow their desires?

AQUINAS: There is in all things appetite for the good, since, as
the philosophers teach, the good is what all desire. In things
devoid of knowledge this desire is called "natural appetite."
Thus it is said that a stone desires to be below. In things having
sense knowledge this desire is called "animal appetite," which
is divided into concupiscible [desire] and irascible [anger]. In

---

319. CG II, ch. 46 n. 3.   320. Ibid., n. 4.   321. In Jn 1.4b, n. 99.

things possessed of understanding, it is called intellectual or rational appetite, and this is *will*. Created intellectual substances, therefore, are endowed with will.[322]

FOX: And so, in your opinion, our capacity to choose is unique among all the species?

AQUINAS: Intellectual substances are endowed with freedom of choice in acting.[323]

FOX: I believe that this emphasis on choice is critical for our grasp of the Via Creativa, for it is in our creativity that we humans opt for good or for evil, "for life or for death," as Deuteronomy puts it.

AQUINAS: That intellectual beings act by judgment is evident from the fact that through their intellectual cognition they judge of things to be done. And they must have freedom if, as just shown, they have control over their own action. Therefore, these substances in acting have freedom of choice.[324]

FOX: And other animals lack the freedom of choice that our creativity demands?

AQUINAS: Choice belongs properly to the will, and not to the sensitive appetite, which is all that irrational animals have. Wherefore irrational animals are not competent to choose.[325]

FOX: And yet nonhuman animals do demonstrate amazing accomplishments at times.

AQUINAS: In the works of irrational animals we notice certain marks of sagacity, insofar as they have a natural inclination to set about their actions in a most orderly manner through being ordained by the supreme art.[326]

FOX: As a lover and respecter of science I am sure that you would be thrilled with how today's science has been able to reveal how some of the "supreme art" works through other animals.

AQUINAS: By the divine wisdom God is the cause of diverse things, produced according to the diversity of things as known by God. This is like an artist who produces diverse works of art by apprehending diverse forms.[327]

---

322. CG II, ch. 47 n. 2.　323. Ibid., ch. 48 n. 1.　324. CG II, ch. 48 n. 2.　325. ST I-II, q. 13, a. 2.　326. Ibid., ad 3.　327. Ibid. I, q. 65, a. 3, ad 2.

FOX: Your celebration of diversity is admirable and seems key to a consciousness of creativity's value. How do we human beings develop our habits of empowerment for doing good things?

AQUINAS: A habit of virtue cannot be caused by one act, but only by many.[328] When we act repeatedly according to reason, a modification is impressed on the appetite by the power of reason. This impression is nothing else but moral virtue.[329]

FOX: Virtue takes discipline; it is harder work than just wishing for something or being inclined toward something.

AQUINAS: The word "habit" implies a certain lastingness while the word "disposition" does not.[330]

FOX: I hear you saying we have to practice. Practice makes perfect, so to speak.

AQUINAS: People become builders by building, and harpists by playing the harp. Likewise people become just or temperate or courageous by doing just actions or temperate actions or courageous actions. Therefore, virtues of this kind are not in us by nature.[331]

FOX: One thing that amazes me as I read your works is how many expressions of human work you call "art." I sense that all work flowing deeply from the heart is artwork for you. Speak to us of some of the jobs you call art.

AQUINAS: The military art commands the art of horse riding.[332] Some arts admit of conjecture, such as medicine, commerce, and the like.[333] There is an art of making what is pleasant, namely, the art of cooking and the art of making perfumes.[334] The habits of building and weaving and making music are in the soul and from the soul. But it is more accurate to say that the builder builds, and not that his art builds, though he builds through his art.[335] An art that is concerned with the end commands and makes the laws for an art concerned with means to the end. Thus, the art of civil government commands that of the military; the military commands the equestrian; and the art of navigation commands that of shipbuilding.[336]

FOX: I think your broad understanding of art and its relation to human work is very critical in our time, when work has been

---

328. Ibid. I-II, q. 51, a. 3.   329. In Ethics II, L. 1, p. 115.   330. ST I-II, q. 49, a. 2, ad 3.   331. In Ethics II, L. 1, p. 115.   332. ST II-II, q. 23, a. 4, ad 2.   333. Ibid. I-II, q. 14, a. 4.   334. Ibid., q. 34, a. 1.   335. In DA I, L. 10, p. 29.   336. CG III, ch. 64 n. 2.

so narrowly defined and when art has often become a kind of professional specialty. Does art itself bring ultimate happiness to people?

AQUINAS: Felicity does not consist in the operation of art, for the knowledge that pertains to art is also practical knowledge. And so, it is ordered to an end, and is not itself the ultimate end.[337] The ends of art operations are artifacts. These cannot be the ultimate end of human life, for we ourselves are, rather, the ends for all artificial things. Indeed, they are all made for humanity's use. Therefore felicity cannot lie in the operation of art.[338]

FOX: Your talking about artifacts and their purpose is especially useful to us today, when there has been such an explosion of technology. I hear you saying that we ought to measure the effects of artifacts on our lives if we are to use technology instead of it using us. Can you speak more about the artifacts we humans create?

AQUINAS: An arrow through the motion of the archer goes straight toward the target, as though it were endowed with reason to direct its course. The same may be seen in the movements of clocks and all devices put together by the art of human beings. Now as artificial things are in comparison to human art, so are all natural things in comparison to the divine art.[339]

FOX: What do you think of the statement that "art imitates nature"?

AQUINAS: There are some arts wherein the matter is not an active principle productive of the art's effect. The art of building is a case in point, since in wood and stone there is no active force tending to the construction of a house, but only a passive aptitude. On the other hand, there exists an art whose matter is an active principle tending to produce the effect of that art. Such is the art of medicine, for in the sick body there is an active principle conducive to health. Thus, the effect of an art of the first kind is never produced by nature, but is always the result of the art; every house is an artifact. But the effect of an art of the second kind is the result both of art and of nature without art, for many are healed by the action of nature without the art of

---

337. Ibid., ch. 36 n. 2.   338. Ibid., n. 3.   339. ST I-II, q. 13, a. 2, ad 3.

medicine. Now, in those things that can be done both by art and by nature, art imitates nature.[340]

FOX: In our culture medicine has become less of an art that respects nature's inclination to health than a technological intervention that presumably rescues the body with drugs, surgery, and other external interventions. Please elaborate on your notion of the art of medicine—it sounds very holistic to me.

AQUINAS: If the cause of a person's illness is something cold, nature cures him by heating; and that is why physicians, if their services are needed in order to cure the patient, do so by applying heat. Now the art of teaching resembles this art.[341]

FOX: How so?

AQUINAS: In the person taught there is an active principle conducive to knowledge, namely, the intellect, and there are also those things that are naturally understood, namely, first principles. Knowledge, then, is acquired in two ways: by discovery without teaching, and by teaching. So, the teacher begins to teach in the same way as the discoverer begins to discover, that is, by offering to the disciples' consideration principles known by them, since "all learning results from pre-existent knowledge" (Aristotle); by drawing conclusions from those principles; and by proposing sense examples, from which the images necessary for the learners' understanding are formed in the soul. And since the outward action of the teacher would have no effect without the inward principle of knowledge, whose presence in us we owe to God, the theologians remark that "human beings teach by outward ministration, but God by inward operation." So, too, are physicians said to minister to nature in the practice of their art of healing. Thus, knowledge is caused in students by their teacher, not by way of natural action, but of art, as was said.[342]

FOX: I like that phrase that the physician "ministers to nature." It puts our work into a cosmic context and thus underscores its dignity.

AQUINAS: The sun, moon, and stars cooperate in the work of production by their movements, as farmers cooperate by their labor, as Chrysostom remarks.[343]

---

340. CG II, ch. 75 n. 15.   341. Ibid.   342. Ibid.   343. ST I, q. 70, a. 1, ad 4.

FOX: Sometimes I feel that you sense only one work in the universe—that of God and of all creatures.

AQUINAS: Dionysius demonstrates the effect of divine power by the example of the [four] elements and says that divine power "makes the powers of fire inextinguishable," for a particular fire may be able to be extinguished, but fire taken universally is inextinguishable. Divine power also makes the currents of water flow continually because of, as he puts it, the perpetual flowing of rivers and the stirrings of the sea, which appear in the waves and the ebb and flow of the sea. God's power is also said to regulate the loss of air, because the property of humidity is especially suitable to the air, so that it will not come to a proper regulation on its own. For this reason, insofar as it is of itself, air possesses every mode of effusion, but by divine power it is curtailed within the limits of its own natural place. Divine power also places the earth in space, for the earth is continually placed by divine power in the middle of the universe and there is nothing to sustain it. Divine power also preserves the offspring generated by the earth itself, such as plants and other things that are born from the earth, "without distinction," that is, abiding uniformly in their own nature so that out of the seeds entrusted to the earth, similar plants are born.[344]

FOX: While our cosmology today is slightly different from that of your day, what moves me in your statement is the effort you and others of our ancestors took to apply your astrophysics (that of the four elements) to your understanding of God at work in the world. Previously you spoke about the teacher who proposes sensible examples to students "from which the images necessary for the disciple's understanding are formed in the soul." This seems to put considerable emphasis on our imagination, and this creative process of forming images "in the soul," as you say. Please elaborate on the role of imagination in learning.

AQUINAS: In the present state of life human contemplation is impossible without images, for it is connatural to the human to see intelligible forms in images.[345]

FOX: And for human beings our contemplation is a spiritual work?

---

344. DDN, n. 758, p. 286.   345. ST II-II, q. 180, a. 5, ad 2.

AQUINAS: Three spirits are discernible in the human person: one is the Holy Spirit; another is one's spiritual reason; and the final one is the human being's imaginative spirit.[346]

FOX: It would seem that these "three spirits" work together in some amazing ways in the act of creativity.

AQUINAS: Fantasy or imagination is as it were a storehouse of forms received through the senses.[347] The imagination's function is to retain those things that have been received from the senses and represent them again to understanding.[348]

FOX: In some ways your understanding of "imagination" includes what we would call memory as well.

AQUINAS: When the organ of the imaginative power is injured, the operation of the intellect is also hampered, because the intellect has need of images in its own operation.[349]

FOX: Thus our reason depends upon our images and imaginations — this explains why you say the teacher needs to elicit these from the learner.

AQUINAS: We cannot imagine what we have never perceived by the senses, either wholly or in part.[350]

FOX: This underscores the importance of sense-knowledge in our lives. Reason depends on it, our creativity depends on it.

AQUINAS: The first principle of the imagination is from the sense in act.[351]

FOX: What does reason do with the images it receives from the senses?

AQUINAS: By means of the imagination reason lays a particular thing before the sensual nature under the aspect of the pleasurable or the disagreeable as it appears to reason; in this way our sensual nature is moved to joy or to sorrow.[352]

FOX: And so reason together with imagination awakens our sensitive powers. Can you describe the artistic act for us?

AQUINAS: Artists first intend their work of art; next they shape it in their mind and imagination; and then shape it in their

---

346. In Eph 4.23, pp. 484–85. 347. ST I, q. 78, a. 4. 348. DV, q. 15, a. 2, ad 7. 349. Ibid., q. 26, a. 3. 350. ST I, q. 111, a. 3, ad 1. 351. Ibid. 352. DV, q. 25, a. 4.

material. Likewise, speakers first conceive the meaning they intend to convey; afterward they find a sign for it; and finally they pronounce it.[353]

FOX: In today's parlance, we would probably ascribe to our imagination this act of "intending" the work of art. I sense that you put great stock in the human's ability to "intend" a work.

AQUINAS: A chest made by an artisan is in itself neither alive nor life, yet the exemplar of the chest in the artisan's mind prior to the existence of the chest is in some sense living, insofar as it has an intellectual existence in the mind of the artisan.[354]

FOX: So the artist brings life, so to speak—new life—to the world, first of all in one's own mind or imagination.

AQUINAS: The forms of things inferior to the soul, such as corporeal things, are more noble in the soul than in the things themselves.[355]

FOX: But in addition to "intending" this form, our amazing minds can also give birth to the new forms we imagine.

AQUINAS: First the form, through which the intellectual substance acts, is grasped; it then proceeds from the intellect itself as something conceived, and in a way contrived by it. We see this in the case of the artistic form that artists conceive and contrive, and through which they accomplish their works.[356]

FOX: Here you are using such motherly language—that of conceiving—to name the creative process.

AQUINAS: A mother is one who conceives within herself and by another.[357]

FOX: I also hear you stressing here, as previously when you emphasized the role of making choices, how creativity is something we are all ultimately responsible for. It comes from inside us in a unique way.

AQUINAS: The most perfect agent operates according to its own form and is not moved by another.[358]

FOX: When we birth new forms we also have to employ our judgment in responding to them.

---

353. Ibid., q. 4, a. 1. 354. In Jn 1.4a, n. 91. 355. DV, q. 22, a. 11.
356. CG II, ch. 47 n. 4. 357. ST II-II, q. 23, a. 8, ad 3. 358. In Ethics
I, L. 9, p. 48.

AQUINAS: Intellectual habits render one ready to judge aright of those things that are pictured by one's imagination. Hence when one ceases to make use of one's intellectual habits, strange fancies, sometimes in opposition to them, arise in one's imagination.[359]

FOX: This is one more argument for art as meditation. Without a centering discipline our imaginations can run away with us! How important it is to be grounded and centered. Paranoia and much projection happen otherwise. We have been talking about art as a virtue and about a broader concept, that of the generative or creative process that is so powerful in the human being because it includes infinite reason, infinite options and powers of will and choice, and the reality of freedom of choice. And you have said that this power is a godlike power. All this deepens our understanding of the *process* that art as meditation is about, the process of cocreation in the cosmic evolution of the world.

I want to turn now to your moral teaching, for I am convinced that your moral teaching is very special and belongs in the Via Creativa and ultimately in the Via Transformativa. In a real sense the Via Positiva and Via Negativa are premoral. We undergo them. We undergo awe and we undergo darkness. But, as you said early in this conversation on the Via Creativa, judgment follows wonder and awe.

What I find most important in your moral teaching is that you do not center it around precepts or laws but around *building up of virtue.*

AQUINAS: God's commandments are about virtues.[360] In God's law, the necessity for various affirmative and negative precepts was that people might be gradually led to virtue, first by abstaining from evil, being induced to this by the negative precepts; and afterward by doing good, to which we are induced by the affirmative precepts.[361]

FOX: Yet we have already defined virtue as "power." You said above that "virtue denotes a certain perfection of a power." And so for you morality is about becoming empowered, joining the powers of the universe, becoming strong in order to participate in the work and cocreation of the universe. Am I correct about that?

---

359. ST I-II, q. 53, a. 3.   360. DC, 2.   361. ST I-II, q. 72, a. 6, ad 2.

AQUINAS: In God, virtue and power are identical. Virtue is the ultimate of power and as it were the perfection of power.[362]

FOX: This seems to be especially the case with God, who is a great power. I sense in this discussion of creativity and virtue as creative power a kind of redemption of the term "omnipotent" used of Divinity.

AQUINAS: That is called a great power that can produce many things, as a root is called powerful that produces many buds. In regard to this Dionysius says that the divine dwelling place produces all things from its own power, just as from a certain kind of omnipotent root. He shows the reason for omnipotence that is due to attraction. For that is called a great power that can draw or turn some things to itself, and with regard to this Dionysius says that God turns "all things toward" the Godhead, as toward a kind of "all-containing planting." For in God all things are planted, just as in the first beginning.[363]

FOX: By establishing your entire morality on the building up of virtue, you are inviting us to be empowered. In addition, you are inviting us, by stressing the responsibility we have to ground or "plant" ourselves in virtue, to be godlike.

AQUINAS: The virtues of all things exist primordially and supereminently in God, just as it has also been said concerning life and wisdom. . . . God is the cause of all virtue.[364]

FOX: But you are also inviting us to be creative, for we have to give birth to our virtue, that is, to our power. And this might well be the ultimate in acts of creativity—to birth oneself. Of course our capacity to give birth is also godlike, isn't it?

AQUINAS: Between God and the creature there can be a certain likeness of analogy. . . . This is true in one example insofar as creatures reproduce in their own way the idea of the divine mind, just as the work of artists is a reproduction of the form in their mind. In another way it is true in that creatures are somewhat likened to the very nature of God, forasmuch as they derive their being from the first being, their goodness from the sovereign good, and so on.[365]

---

362. In Eph 6.10, p. 500. 363. DDN, n. 852, p. 321. 364. Ibid., n. 748, p. 282. 365. ST I, q. 3, a. 4, ad 9.

FOX: And our capacity to birth—including the birthing of virtue—derives from the very Creator and artist of all things, including the human being.

AQUINAS: God is said to "make the soul" of humans, because making is characteristic of potters who impress beautiful form upon base matter. Thus God by creating pours souls into the earthy body, as Paul says (2 Cor. 4): "We have that treasure in earthen vessels." And Romans (9): "Can the thing that is made in the image of the one who made it, say: 'why did you make me thus?'"[366]

FOX: So God is the ultimate potter. And our dignity as artists is derived from the divine creative power.

AQUINAS: Pupils who would learn something should watch how their instructor sets about making something, so that in their turn they may work with the same skill. So should the human mind be enlightened by the divine mind when it sets about making things. In this way it should study natural processes, so that it may be in harmony with them.[367]

FOX: One more argument for studying nature and listening to scientists who do so. Our work of creativity is itself part of the unfolding of the divine mind, is it not? It is as if the Holy Spirit employed us, so to speak, in the work of cocreation. We truly are cocreators with the creative Spirit of God.

AQUINAS: Now art is in the reason.[368] The light of reason is nothing other than a certain participation in the divine light.[369]

FOX: And so we participate in the light of God when we create?

AQUINAS: God is light; and one who approaches this light is illuminated, as Isaiah says (60): "Rise, in love, and be enlightened."[370]

FOX: The artist experiences a kind of illumination in the work of creating. Art is a kind of prayer.

AQUINAS: By loving God a person is on fire to gaze on the divine beauty.[371] Prayer is an act of reason.[372]

FOX: So creating is both a contemplative and an active act, one flowing from the other. And both are from our reason and both

---

366. In Pss 32, p. 263.   367. In I Pol, lect. 1.   368. ST II-II, q. 134, a. 4, ad 3.   369. In Pss 30, p. 253.   370. In Pss 33, p. 266.   371. ST II-II, q. 180, a. 1.   372. In Pss 21, p. 219.

are our prayer. By emphasizing how prayer itself is an "act of reason," you are demonstrating that for you "reason" includes far more than analytic activity—it is essentially our capacity for creativity.

AQUINAS: Concerning natural things the mind is contemplative; concerning works of art it is productive as well.[373]

FOX: In spite of our being cocreators, instruments of the spirit, and enlightened co-workers with Divinity, there are limits to our creativity.

AQUINAS: Human art is not so powerful as the natural action able to produce a substantial form. Human art cannot go so far as that, for forms of art are the structures composed of accidental wholes. Yet art may apply a proper cause to its proper matter and so effect the alteration of substances, as for instance when heat is used in smelting or distilling.[374] Aristotle remarks that if art could make natural things it would act like nature, and conversely, if nature could make artificial things it would act like art.[375]

FOX: So our creativity contributes to the coming into being of things, but we depend on being itself in order to create.

AQUINAS: A cook dresses the food by applying the natural activity of fire; thus a builder constructs a house, by making use of cement stones and wood, which can be put together in a certain order to preserve that order. Therefore the being of a house depends on the nature of these materials, just as its becoming depends on the action of the builder. . . . The builder causes the house in its becoming, but he is not the direct cause of its being.[376]

FOX: What we give birth to itself needs to be critiqued. Not all birthing is indifferent morally or aesthetically speaking.

AQUINAS: Fault is a deviation from good purpose. A crime is perpetrated against art when the artist intends to make a good work but produces a bad one, or intends to make a bad thing but produces a good one. Here the artist is blamed.[377] When anyone gifted with an art produces bad workmanship, this is not the work of that art, in fact, it is contrary to the art.[378]

---

373. In I Pol, lect. 1.   374. ST III, q. 66, a. 4.   375. In I Pol, lect. 1.
376. ST I, q. 104, a. 1.   377. Ibid. I-II, q. 21, a. 2, ad 2.   378. Ibid., q. 57, a. 3, ad 1.

FOX: Artists, in other words, are to be held accountable for the value of their art?

AQUINAS: Reason stands in different relations to the production of art, and to moral actions. In matters of art, reason is directed to a particular end, which is something devised by reason; whereas in moral matters it is directed to the general end of all human life. . . . For some sins an artist is blamed as an artist; while for others they are blamed as a man or woman.[379]

FOX: In the broad sense, art and creativity are indeed virtues.

AQUINAS: Intellectual virtues may indeed be called virtues insofar as they confer aptness for a good work, for example, the conservation of truth. . . . That one makes use of the knowledge that one possesses is due to the motion of one's will.[380] The Philosopher says that art is a virtue (*Ethics* vi., 3, 4).[381] Art is called a virtue. Yet it falls short of being a perfect virtue, because it does not make its possessor to use it well. For this purpose something additional is required.[382]

FOX: And this something is the moral virtues we give birth to in birthing our character and our relationships in this world. Even our moral virtues are something we give birth to. Indeed, our whole being is something we give birth to. Thus, our art is a virtue and our moral virtue is an art. All of it is integral to the Via Creativa and to our responsibility for giving birth.

AQUINAS: It is a great thing to do miracles, but it is a greater thing to live virtuously.[383]

FOX: You say that to live virtuously is a greater thing than to perform miracles! That certainly puts our creativity as birthers of virtue into a grand context. Once again the underlying theme of power—the real meaning of "virtue"—is coming through in your teaching.

AQUINAS: Virtue by its very name means the completion of an active power. Now, there are two kinds of active powers, one whose action terminates in something performed outside the agent, as the action of the power of building terminates in the edifice. And the other, whose action does not terminate outside of the agent, but remains within them, as sight remains within

---

379. Ibid., q. 21, a. 2, ad 2.   380. Ibid., q. 57, a. 1.   381. Ibid., a. 3.
382. Ibid., ad 1.   383. In Mt 10, p. 97.

one who sees. . . . The power of one who builds consists in this, that they make a very good house. The completion of that other type of power is conceived according to its mode of acting, namely, that it act well and fittingly. And it is because of this that its act is called good. And so it is that in this type of power we call virtue that which makes the action good.[384]

FOX: Our virtue is our power for good.

AQUINAS: Virtue renders good both the power and the agent.[385] Virtue always works for good, indeed for good well performed, that is, voluntarily, readily, pleasurably, and firmly —these are the characteristics of virtuous activity, and they cannot be present unless you love what you are aiming at.[386]

FOX: Let us now turn to this vast empowerment you are advocating—one that is greater than doing miracles—to explore it in greater depth. Tell us about moral virtue and the art of birthing moral strength in ourselves.

AQUINAS: As temporal poverty causes exterior (or physical) weakness, so spiritual poverty causes spiritual weakness. "Virtue" may be used of corporeal strength, which is in the sinews and bones. The psalmist (31) talks about "my bones" as if to say that all on which his fortitude was based had been weakened. Consider Psalm 22: "My bones are altogether dried up."[387]

FOX: Once again you are equating virtue and strength.

AQUINAS: As sight is in the eye, so in the bones and sinews there is strength. And so, as sight is signified through the eyes, so strength and virtue are signified through the bones. For just as the body is sustained through the bones, so human life is sustained through the virtues. Therefore in the future God will totally free the bones, that is, the virtues, but meanwhile he guards them, as the psalmist says (34): "The Lord guards all their bones."[388]

FOX: Your analogy of our psyches as being like our bodies and virtues being like bones that support the body because they support our moral lives is very appealing to today's way of thinking. What other tasks does virtue perform besides supporting us and thereby making us strong?

---

384. DV, q. 14, a. 3. 385. DVV, q. 2. 386. DC, 2. 387. In Pss 30, p. 252. 388. In Pss 33, p. 268.

AQUINAS: Virtue does three things: it removes one from evils; it is occupied with and makes one be occupied with the good; and it disposes one toward the best.[389]

FOX: I hear you saying that virtue is a kind of spiritual path that assures a life of quality and purpose.

AQUINAS: The pathway is virtue and especially perfect virtue. For this reason the one in whom perfect virtue appears can be called happy because of hope. Just like a richly flowering tree can be called fruit-bearing.[390]

FOX: I like the way you link virtue with the art of bearing fruit and with the path to happiness. Healthy creativity leads to happiness, you are saying, and among the healthiest of creative acts is that of birthing virtue itself.

AQUINAS: Happiness is a virtue-oriented activity proper to humans in a complete life.[391] Every virtue shares the nature of goodness by bestowing its own act.[392]

FOX: We have talked a lot about "goodness" and blessing in our conversations, but now you are introducing it again. Why is virtue so great a good and so great a happiness (goodness of all kinds surrounds us)?

AQUINAS: [Divide] human goods into three classes. Of these (a) some are external, as riches, honors, friends, and such like. (b) Others are internal, and these again are of two kinds: 1. Some concern the body, as physical strength, beauty, and health. 2. Others concern the soul, as knowledge, virtue, and the like. These are the chief goods, for external things are for the sake of the body, and the body for the sake of the soul, as matter for form and as an instrument for a principal agent. Now the common view of all philosophers is that the goods of the soul are the most important.[393]

FOX: It sounds as if creativity were actually built into the power that virtue is—to be virtuous is to be creative, endowed with a power to "give forth," just as goodness itself does.

AQUINAS: The virtues are nothing but those perfections whereby reason is directed to God, and the inferior powers regulated according to the dictate of reason.[394]

---

389. In Mt 5, p. 50.   390. In Pss 31, p. 256.   391. In Ethics I, L. 10, p. 55.   392. ST II-II, q. 117, a. 6, ad 2.   393. In Ethics I, L. 12, p. 63. 394. ST I, q. 95, a. 3.

FOX: The first part of your definition—the directing of our reason or creativity to God—we discussed at some length above when we discussed the act of creativity. But the second part— the regulating of "inferior powers"—What do you have in mind by that phraseology?

AQUINAS: There are four principal passions of the soul: sadness, joy, hope, and fear.[395]

FOX: And the work of virtue is to steer these passions toward our desired goals, which—it's to be hoped—are good ones?

AQUINAS: The passions of the soul can stand in either of two relationships to the will, either as preceding it or as consequent upon it: as preceding it, inasmuch as the passions spur the will to will something; as consequent upon it, inasmuch as the lower appetite is stirred up with these passions as a result of the vehemence of the will through a sort of overflow, or even inasmuch as the will itself brings them about and arouses them of its own accord.[396]

FOX: And so the empowerment that virtue gives is an empowerment directed to our passions?

AQUINAS: Moral virtue is in the powers of the passions, anger and desire.[397]

FOX: So often we hear morality taught in terms of willpower or in terms of guilt and power-over. But I hear you saying a totally different thing when you say that moral virtue is actually found *in the passions*.

AQUINAS: Perfection of moral virtue does not wholly take away the passions, but regulates them. Thus the temperate person desires as one ought to desire, and what one ought to desire.[398]

FOX: Give an example of a passion that is virtuous in this sense. Take anger, for example.

AQUINAS: The praiseworthy person is the one who is angry about the right things, at the right people, and in due moderation, since they are angry as they should be, when they should be, and as long as they should be.[399]

---

395. DV, q. 26, a. 5.   396. Ibid., a. 7.   397. Ibid., q. 25, a. 5.   398. ST I, q. 95, a. 2, ad 3.   399. In Ethics IV, L. 13, p. 349.

FOX: So passion need not be a problem to the virtuous person?

AQUINAS: The movement of virtue, which consists in a perfect act of the will, cannot be had without any passion, not because the act of will depends upon the passion, but because in a nature subject to passion a passion necessarily follows upon a perfect act of will.[400]

FOX: But the heart of our birthing of moral virtue is like the heart of our birthing of any art, isn't it, namely, our act of choice?

AQUINAS: The principal act of moral virtue is *electio,* which is the act of the rational appetite.[401] Choice is said to be the principal element in moral virtue both from the point of view of the role of reason in it, and from that of the role of the will. Both are necessary for the essential character of moral virtue. Choice is called the principal element with reference to external acts.[402]

FOX: And so morality includes reason, will, and choice. You have already said how reason and will and choice carry an aspect of the "infinite" to them. No wonder we need some discipline for assisting in our choice making, which is so central to our creativity. Will you elaborate more on the deliberation that is integral to the act of creativity?

AQUINAS: Choosing and wishing are not the same. . . . A person's wish can center on actions that are not performed by oneself. An example is the person who is watching a duel; he may wish that one of the contestants will win, by identifying himself with this contestant. . . . But no one chooses actions that are accomplished by another person; one can choose only actions that one thinks one can do oneself. Therefore choice is different from wishing.[403]

FOX: Wishing seems more vague than choosing.

AQUINAS: Choice is solely concerned with the means to the end and not with the end itself. . . . For example, we chiefly wish health as the end of medical treatment; but we choose the medicines by means of which we may be made healthy.[404]

FOX: Choice seems like a considerable empowerment that our species possesses.

---

400. DV, q. 26, a. 7, ad 2.   401. DVC, a. 4, ad 13.   402. DV, q. 22, a. 15, ad 3.   403. In Ethics III, L. 5, p. 194.   404. Ibid.

AQUINAS: Choice may be seen to deal with things that are within our power. This is the reason why it applies neither to impossibilities, nor to actions performed by others, nor to the end, which for the most part is preestablished for us by nature.[405]

FOX: And you feel that this creative choice is unique to our species on this earth?

AQUINAS: Of course, irrational animated things know their end and move themselves locally toward that end, as possessors of judgment concerning the end; but the appetite for the end, and for the means to this end, are determined for them as a result of natural inclination. For this reason, they are things acted upon rather than agents. In their case, also, there is no free decision. However, rational agents, in whom alone is choice found, do know their end, and they know the proper relationship of means to the end itself. So, just as they move themselves toward their end, so also do they toward the desiring of the end, or of the means that are for the sake of the end; and due to this fact, free choice is present in them.[406]

FOX: Our God-given capacities for infinite creative possibilities seem to require some steering. Do you see our passions as enemies in this process of creativity, or as allies?

AQUINAS: Virtue overcomes inordinate passion; it produces ordinate passion.[407]

FOX: Passion then is actually a product of our creativity?

AQUINAS: The passion itself consequent in the lower appetite is a sign that the movement of the will is intense. For in a nature subject to passion it is impossible for the will to be strongly moved to anything without some passion following in the lower part.[408]

FOX: You speak of the "intensity" of the will and our being "strongly moved" as being a plus in our moral lives. Passions don't seem to threaten you at all. I hear you telling us to embrace them and nurture them.

AQUINAS: Acting from passion lessens praise and blame, but acting with passion can increase both of them.[409]

---

405. Ibid.   406. In Meta V, L. 16, p. 381.   407. ST I-II, q. 59, a. 5, ad 1.   408. DV, q. 26, a. 7.   409. Ibid., ad 1.

FOX: How so?

AQUINAS: When the passions are consequent upon the will they do not lessen the praiseworthiness of the act or its goodness, because they will be moderated in conformity with the judgment of reason upon which the act of will follows; but they will rather add to the goodness of the act. . . . When by a judgment of reason the will chooses anything, it does so more promptly and easily if in addition a passion is aroused in the lower part, since the lower appetitive power is closely connected with a change in the body.[410]

FOX: Can you give us an example, please?

AQUINAS: This is what the Philosopher also says, bringing in the verse of Homer: "Stir up your courage and rage," because when a person is virtuous with the virtue of courage, the passion of anger following upon the choice of virtue makes for greater alacrity in the act.[411]

FOX: And so anger—and other passions—actually assist us in the carrying out of our moral choices. We do them with more "alacrity," with greater "cheerful eagerness" that way.

AQUINAS: Both choice and execution are necessary in a virtuous deed. Discernment is required for choice. For the execution of what has been decided upon, alacrity is required. It is not, however, highly necessary that a person actually engaged in the execution of the deed deliberate very much about the deed. This would rather stand in the way than be of help, as Avicenna points out. Take the case of the lute player, who would be greatly handicapped if he had to give thought to each touch of the strings; or that of a scribe if he had to stop and think in the formation of each letter. This is why a passion that precedes choice hinders the act of virtue by hampering the judgment of reason necessary in choosing. But after the choice has already been made purely by a rational judgment, a passion that follows helps more than it hurts, because even if it should disturb rational judgment somewhat, it does make for greater alacrity in execution.[412]

FOX: But you are saying that passion should follow will and not the other way around?

---

410. Ibid., a. 7.   411. Ibid.   412. Ibid., ad 3.

AQUINAS: If it preceded, however, it would disturb the manner requisite for virtue.[413]

FOX: What about the idea that holiness is about detachment from passions?

AQUINAS: The passions of the soul, insofar as they are contrary to the order of reason, incline us to sin: but insofar as they are controlled by reason, they pertain to virtue.[414] Those who have the virtues of a purified soul are in some sense free from passions that incline us to the contrary of that which virtue chooses, and likewise from passions that influence the will, but not from those consequent upon the will.[415]

FOX: You used the example of the passion of anger. I sense that you are recommending a proper and creative expression of anger as a virtue; whereas repressing it can be a vice.

AQUINAS: People who are bitter retain their anger for a long time.[416]

FOX: What about the passion of lust—is that virtuous, too?

AQUINAS: There is question of the carnality of spiritual affection only if the passion of love precedes the affection of the will, but not if it follows. For in the latter event there would be question of the fervor of charity, which consists in the fact that the spiritual affection, which is in the higher part, by reason of its vehemence, overflows to the extent of altering the lower part.[417]

FOX: And so virtues are regulatory habits that keep our will, reason, choices, and passions interacting so that they all take us toward the good we desire to attain or to share.

AQUINAS: Habits are defined as that "by reason of which we are well or ill disposed with regard to actions and passions" (Aristotle, *Ethics,* 2.5).[418] A habit is a kind of medium between mere power and mere act.[419] A habit is the perfection of a power.[420] Habits incline persons like a second nature to particular kinds of operations, so that the operations become sources of pleasure. Thus, as by a similitude, any kind of work in which a person takes delight, so that one's bent is toward it, one's time spent in it, and one's whole life ordered with a view toward it, is said to

413. Ibid., a. 7.   414. ST I-II, q. 23, a. 2, ad 3.   415. DV, q. 26, a. 7, ad 6.   416. ST I-II, q. 46, a. 8.   417. DV, q. 26, a. 7, ad 7.   418. ST I, q. 83, a. 2.   419. Ibid., q. 87, a. 2.   420. DVV, 2.

be the "life" of that person. Hence some are said to live a life of self-indulgence, others a life of virtue.[421]

FOX: You are saying that virtue and pleasure go together?

AQUINAS: Works of virtue afford pleasure in themselves.[422] A person is reckoned to be good or bad chiefly according to the pleasure of the human will, since that person is good and virtuous who takes pleasure in the works of virtue. And that person is evil who takes pleasure in evil works.[423]

FOX: The idea that virtue and pleasure go together takes us beyond guilt and fear and duty as a motive for moral action.

AQUINAS: The more pleasurably something is done out of a virtuous habit, the more pleasurable and meritorious is its action.[424] Pleasure is the perfection of activity.[425] Happiness is activity flowing from virtue.[426]

FOX: What activity, in your opinion, affords human beings the greatest happiness?

AQUINAS: The most delightful of all virtuous activities is the contemplation of wisdom—an evident fact conceded by everyone.[427] Those who gives themselves to the contemplation of truth are the happiest anyone can be in this life.[428]

FOX: You rather surprise me when you speak of virtue as pleasurable and delectable.

AQUINAS: Activities in accord with virtue are not only pleasurable but also beautiful and good. They are pleasurable in relation to the agent to whom they are agreeable by virtue of a proper habit. They are beautiful because of a due order of circumstances, as of certain parts. For beauty consists in a due composition of parts. They are good because of an order to the end.[429]

FOX: The idea that both pleasure and beauty are tests of our moral actions is very appealing to me.

AQUINAS: To act virtuously is to do what one ought spontaneously and readily.[430] It is a condition of virtue that the virtuous person must act with firmness and joy. But love is the

421. ST I, q. 18, a. 3, ad 2.   422. Ibid. II-II, q. 136, a. 1, ad 3.   423. Ibid. I-II, q. 34, a. 4.   424. In III Sent 23.1.1, ad 4.   425. In Ethics X, L. 6, p. 886.   426. Ibid. I, L. 4, p. 23.   427. Ibid. X, L. 10, p. 908.   428. Ibid., L. 11, p. 914.   429. Ibid. I, L. 13, p. 69.   430. ST II-II, q. 58, a. 3, ad 1.

chief producer of this result, for we do a thing firmly, and with joy, as a result of love. Therefore, love of the good is the ultimate object intended in divine law.[431]

FOX: It is striking that you use the imperative when you speak of the need to act with joy. How important is joy?

AQUINAS: Joy and sadness are the most important among the passions.[432]

FOX: And they are related to each other, obviously.

AQUINAS: Keen joy drives out all sadness, even that which is not contrary.[433] The delight of virtue overcomes spiritual sorrow.[434]

FOX: I hear you underlying an important connection between the Via Positiva and the Via Creativa: both involve joy and pleasure, beauty and goodness. What we give birth to increases the delight of creation itself. We are indeed cocreators. Another implication of what you are saying is that the joy of creating can overcome sadness and depression in our lives. Creativity is an antidote to acedia. Empowerment results in happiness.

AQUINAS: Some happiness might consist in the good use of power, which is by way of virtue, rather than in power for its own sake.[435]

FOX: We are back to the etymological meaning of virtue as "power." The Via Creativa seems to be a path of discovering our power and birthing it.

AQUINAS: The word "virtue" refers to the extreme limit of a power. Now a natural power is, in one sense, the power of resisting corruptions, and in another sense is a principle of action. . . . This latter meaning is the more common.[436]

FOX: Virtue touches the "extreme limit of a power." Can you elaborate on this?

AQUINAS: It belongs to the notion of virtue that it should regard something extreme.[437] The utmost or best to which the power of anything extends is called its achievement of excellence. It belongs to the virtue of everything, therefore, to achieve excellence. Because a perfect operation proceeds from a

---

431. CG III, ch. 116 n. 4.   432. DV, q. 26, a. 5, ad 6.   433. Ibid., a. 10, ad 2.   434. ST II-II, q. 123, a. 8.   435. Ibid. I-II, q. 2, a. 4.   436. Ibid. II-II, q. 123, a. 2, ad 1.   437. Ibid., a. 4.

perfect agent, it follows that everything is both good and operates well according to its virtue.[438]

FOX: You are celebrating our striving for excellence as an urge
of our power and virtue. But virtue is also about finding the
mean between unpalatable extremes, is it not?

AQUINAS: It is difficult to be good or virtuous, because we see
that in every case it is difficult to discover the mean, but easy to
deviate from the mean. Thus not everyone—only an informed
person who is a geometrician—can find the center of a circle.
On the other hand, anyone can easily deviate from the center.
Likewise anyone can hand out money and waste it. But not everyone (for it is not easy) can give to the right person the right
amount, at the right time, for the right purpose, in the right
manner—all of which belongs to virtuous giving. Indeed because of the difficulty it is a rare and a difficult thing, but praiseworthy and virtuous precisely as conforming to reason.[439]

FOX: You say that virtue can be difficult to come by. What
really is the bottom line when it comes to virtue—it cannot be
laws, since laws are made by human beings and evolve as culture evolves. Where do we go ultimately to learn virtue?

AQUINAS: The good person is the norm in humankind.[440]

FOX: And so we ultimately learn to be good from good people?
This would seem to endorse the importance of good parenting
as well as the value of mentors in our lives.

AQUINAS: Those actions are really excellent and pleasant that
are judged such by a good person who is the norm of human
acts.[441]

FOX: We have spoken of the joy that our work can bring about,
but of course we are fully capable of bringing about sadness,
too, are we not? What about the evil we commit in our capacity
for creativity?

AQUINAS: It sometimes happens that we do certain things deserving of admiration for which we are responsible, but not all
the things which we do are admirable. For we sometimes do evil
and defective acts.[442]

FOX: How are you defining evil in the context of our actions?

---

438. In Ethics II, L. 6, p. 140.   439. Ibid., L. 11, p. 166.   440. Ibid. IX,
L. 11, p. 841.   441. Ibid. X, L. 9, p. 904.   442. DDN, n. 440, p. 144.

AQUINAS: Every action has goodness, insofar as it has being. Whereas it is lacking in goodness, insofar as it is lacking in something that is due to its fullness of being: and thus it is said to be evil.[443]

FOX: How is sin different from evil?

AQUINAS: Evil is more comprehensive than sin, just as good is more comprehensive than right. For every privation of good in whatever subject is an evil; whereas sin consists properly in an action done for a certain end, and lacking due order to that end.[444] Good or evil, in voluntary action alone, renders them worthy of praise or blame. And in actions like these, evil, sin, and guilt are one and the same thing.[445]

FOX: Judging from our previous conversation about passion, it seems that virtue wrestles with making sure that passion contributes to what is good and not what is evil.

AQUINAS: It is inordinate passion, not ordinate passion, that leads to sin.[446]

FOX: It is telling that we are only now—after dozens of pages of discussion on the Via Creativa—getting around to talking about sin. Your approach to morality emphasizes the building up of virtue and thus is a totally different starting point from a sin-oriented approach.

AQUINAS: While the negative precepts of the Law forbid sinful acts, the positive precepts inculcate acts of virtue.[447] Precepts are about acts of virtue.[448] God's commandments are about virtues. Without doubt love is a virtue.[449]

FOX: Earlier you said that all law has to do with love.

AQUINAS: Love is the most potent of virtues.[450] Love is the root and end of all the virtues. Indeed, a root, because from love established in the heart of a person one is moved to fulfill all other precepts. Romans 13:8 says: "One who loves one's fellow human beings has fulfilled the law." Therefore all precepts as it were are ordered so that persons may show kindness toward others in their relationships, and not harass them: this indeed comes most powerfully from love. But we say charity is "the

---

443. ST I-II, q. 18, a. 1.   444. Ibid., q. 21, a. 1.   445. Ibid., a. 2.
446. Ibid., q. 59, a. 5, ad 2.   447. Ibid. II-II, q. 33, a. 2.   448. Ibid., q. 32, a. 5.   449. DC, 2.   450. Ibid.

end" because all precepts are ordered to it, and in charity alone they are made firm.[451]

FOX: Can you elaborate on the relation between law and virtue?

AQUINAS: We are made virtuous by means of laws.[452] The purpose of human law is to lead people to virtue—not suddenly, but gradually. Wherefore law does not lay upon the multitude of imperfect people the burdens of those who are already virtuous, that is, that they should abstain from all evil. Otherwise these imperfect ones, being unable to bear such precepts, would break out into yet greater evils.[453] The proper effect of law is to lead its subjects to their proper virtue. . . . It is to make those to whom it is given good, either simply or in some particular respect.[454]

FOX: How can law make people good?

AQUINAS: So far as human acts conduce to virtue, so far does law make people good.[455]

FOX: By emphasizing the Via Creativa as a building up of virtue, you are offering a much more positive and challenging understanding of morality. You are urging us to undergo the challenge to be responsible for creating ourselves.

AQUINAS: To do good is more than to avoid evil, and therefore the positive precepts virtually include the negative ones.[456] Virtue is not in all people; it is cast out by sin.[457]

FOX: Speaking of sin, I wonder whether it is not time to inquire about an issue that is particularly pertinent to a discussion on creativity—namely, fear. The topic of fear has come up several times, and certainly it is integral to any discussion of passion, since fear is a passion. But I am particularly struck by the relation of fear to the inability to be creative. Otto Rank, a psychologist of our century whose entire life of healing was dedicated to working with creative people, concluded that the primary obstacle to creativity is fear: the fear of death and its counterpart, the fear of life.

AQUINAS: Those who are in great fear are so intent on their own passion that they pay no attention to the suffering of others.[458]

---

451. In Jn 15.12, n. 2006.   452. In Ethics X, L. 15, p. 936.   453. ST I-II, q. 96, a. 2, ad 2.   454. Ibid., q. 92, a. 1.   455. Ibid., ad 1.
456. Ibid. II-II, q. 44, a. 3, ad 3.   457. Ibid. I-II, q. 63, a. 1.   458. Ibid. II-II, q. 30, a. 2, ad 2.

FOX: That is quite a grave observation, and it helps to explain fundamentalism, which strikes me as a religion built on fear. I find it very difficult to penetrate the wall of fear that surrounds fundamentalists, and the evidence that the wall is impenetrable is the fact that the suffering of others is never alluded to. I never hear them talk of injustice, of racism or sexism or ecocide or the militarism that causes so much suffering in the world. They are, as you say, so wrapped up in their own passion of fear that all else is subservient to that passion. Are you saying that fear is sinful?

AQUINAS: Fear is a sin through being inordinate, that is to say, through shunning what ought not to be shunned according to reason.[459]

FOX: But of course we all feel afraid at times, do we not?

AQUINAS: Passions call for neither praise nor blame, because we neither praise nor blame those who are angry or those who are afraid, but only those who behave thus in an ordinate or inordinate manner.[460]

FOX: Thus fear is not always sinful.

AQUINAS: A human act is said to be a sin on account of its being inordinate, because the good of a human act lies in due order. And due order dictates that certain things should be shunned and some sought after. . . . Accordingly, when the appetite shuns what the reason dictates we should endure, so that we may not abandon other objectives that we should pursue, fear is inordinate and sinful.[461]

FOX: And the suffering of others, as you say, is one of those things that reason indicates we ought to respond to. I think it is important to be able to call fear a sin when it qualifies as such in our time. For much suffering comes from our fear, our inability to give birth, and our sins of omission that result from this lack of creativity. You spoke eloquently of that above when you talked about the burying of our talents. Where do you suppose our fear comes from?

AQUINAS: All fear arises from love, since no one fears something unless it threatens something one loves.[462]

---

459. Ibid., q. 125, a. 3.   460. Ibid., a. 1, ad 1.   461. Ibid., a. 1.
462. Ibid., a. 2.

FOX: Yet love also saves us from fear, doesn't it?

AQUINAS: Perfect love drives out servile fear, which is fear that expects punishment before everything else.[463]

FOX: What are other causes of fear?

AQUINAS: There is an intrinsic double cause of fear, namely, ignorance and weakness. Thus one will be more fearful in the dark. Against the second cause of fear, which is weakness, there is a remedy from God. Against the first there is illumination, whence the psalmist (27) says: "Lord my light" and Micah says (8): "When I sit in darkness, the Lord is my light." Against the second cause of fear, which is weakness, there is salvation, whence there follows [in Psalm 27]: "The Lord is my light and my salvation." Compare Psalm 62, which reads: "In God is my strength and my glory, God is my help, and my hope is in God." And therefore the psalmist shows confidence. "Whom will I fear," being so enlightened? Romans 8 says: "If God is for us, who is against us?" The exterior cause is human beings, who oppose us. And before them one must not fear, since the Lord opposes like a shield, whence the psalmist says, "the Lord is the protector of my life."[464]

FOX: Thus salvation can mean salvation from fear. Do you think one reason for fear is our making an idol of security?

AQUINAS: The overriding consideration of an admiral is not to keep his ships undamaged, for his fleet is meant to serve a purpose outside itself, as that is entrusted to him. So a person is commissioned by their reason and will, and since people are not themselves the supreme good, their business is to serve another end. Consequently one's own safety is not one's ultimate end.[465]

FOX: Your point is well taken—that we are here for purposes bigger than ourselves and that we are all "captains of fleets" with tasks to accomplish. What would be the opposite of fear?

AQUINAS: Confidence, which here is accounted a part of fortitude or courage, gives people hope in themselves, yet under God.[466]

FOX: Thus trust (or faith) is the opposite of fear?

---

463. Ibid. III, q. 7, a. 6, ad 3.   464. In Pss 26, p. 237.   465. ST I-II, q. 2, a. 5.   466. Ibid. II-II, q. 128, a. 1, ad 2.

AQUINAS: The Holy Spirit is called the "Spirit of Fortitude" (Isa. 11:2). . . . This gift of fortitude prevents a person's heart from fainting through fear of lacking necessities, and makes one trust without wavering that God will provide one with whatever one needs.[467]

FOX: And so the Spirit builds confidence and we are to build up self-confidence in order to combat fear—and to build it up in one another?

AQUINAS: Fear is repugnant to a magnanimous person.[468] Insofar as one's own ability goes, it belongs to the magnanimous to have self-confidence.[469]

FOX: This is one problem I have with an ideology of original sin—that it displaces self-confidence. Your teaching also has great implications for our approach to education, especially that of the young. We are to assist them to build up the kind of confidence that makes for their growing into large-souled persons.

AQUINAS: To venture on anything great seems to involve danger, since to fail in such a thing is very disastrous. Confidence relates to fortitude in the face of imminent danger.[470]

FOX: I like the invitation to greatness that you extend to all people willing to give birth to themselves.

AQUINAS: The greatest virtues must necessarily be those that are most profitable to other people, because virtue is a faculty of doing good to others. . . . For this reason the greatest honors are accorded the brave and the just, since bravery is useful to others in warfare, and justice is useful to others both in warfare and in time of peace.[471]

FOX: I like your point about how virtue is for others. You are also saying that fortitude is that virtue that takes us beyond fear.

AQUINAS: Fortitude is about fear and daring.[472]

FOX: And fortitude and justice making are related.

AQUINAS: The fact that anyone behaves justly pertains to fortitude.[473]

---

467. OF, 137.   468. In Ethics IV, L. 10, p. 337.   469. ST II-II, q. 129, a. 6, ad 1.   470. Ibid., q. 128, a. 1, ad 3.   471. Ibid., q. 58, a. 12. 472. Ibid. I-II, q. 60, a. 4.   473. In Mt 5, p. 52.

FOX: This is an important point: that where justice is lacking fear takes over and courage is rare. We shall want to pursue the justice issue in greater depth when we discuss the Via Transformativa. But for now, speak to us more about this important virtue of courage or fortitude.

AQUINAS: Bravery serves to strengthen the mind, lest anyone withdraw from the good on account of the threat of difficulties. But the psalmist (18) shows how courageous he is. One needs courage for two things: first in good things, that one be stable in them; therefore the psalmist says, "The Lord is my support," that is, my strong foundation. Compare 2 Kings 22: "The Lord is my rock." And Matthew 7: "Everyone who hears my words and does them, is like someone building their house on a rock." Likewise, one needs courage in the midst of evil things, and this in two ways: In one way, before it comes, in order to flee it. Thus the psalmist says: "You are my refuge." And Proverbs (14) says: "There is strong confidence in the name of the Lord." And Psalm 104 says: "Rock, a refuge for rabbits." In a second way one needs courage after evil has come in order to liberate oneself. Thus the psalmist says, "You are my liberator."[474]

FOX: How do we learn courage or fortitude?

AQUINAS: We receive strength from God in two ways: sometimes we draw near to God, as Psalm 32:6 says: "Draw near to God and be radiant, and your face will not be ashamed." At other times we draw others to God, as 1 Cor. 3 says: "For we are co-workers of God."[475]

FOX: It is striking to me that you talk of becoming strong both by approaching God and by approaching others. I hear echoes of the action/contemplation dialectic in your response, or what I prefer to call the mystical/prophetic dialectic. I like your emphasis on prayer as a source of strength, our going to God and our leading others to God as a kind of strength.

AQUINAS: A person ought to take strength in God as in the final end.[476] Jeremiah proposes a likeness taken from the tree, first with regard to the strength of its roots: "And he will be like wood," in which there is the image of the strength of divine protection. Psalm 1 says: "And he will be like the tree which has

---

474. In Pss 17, p. 194.   475. In Mt 4, p. 41.   476. Ibid.

been planted near streams of water, for it will produce fruit in its own time." Second, with regard to the vigor of its leaves: "And he will be like a leaf," in which temporal prosperity is signified, and spiritual strength. Proverbs 11 says: "Just people will flourish like green leaves." Third, with regard to the richness of the fruits, in which the abundance of good works is signified: "Nor does it cease to make fruit in season." The Book of Revelation says (21): "Producing its fruit month after month."[477]

FOX: So our strength comes from being grounded and rooted in God.

AQUINAS: The Holy Spirit strengthens in two ways: in one way against evils, as Isaiah (8) says: "I have raised you up with a strong hand." In another way among good things, as Isaiah says (40): "Those who hope in the Lord will acquire their courage." This courage is kept through the Holy Spirit, for just as the body is not strong for sustaining or doing unless on account of the strength of the spirit, so a person is not strong without the Holy Spirit.[478]

FOX: I like your emphasis on the work of the Spirit as the work of making us strong. Prayer as strengthening us instead of prayer as piety or feeling religious comfort. Prayer as the building up of courage or a big heart. What exactly does courage do for us?

AQUINAS: The principal act of fortitude is endurance, that is, to stand immovable in the midst of dangers rather than to attack them.[479]

FOX: You are talking like Gandhi and Dr. King—the courage of nonviolence, standing for something without attacking others.

AQUINAS: Endurance is more difficult than aggression.[480]

FOX: An obvious question that follows on this building up of fortitude is the following: What should we fear?

AQUINAS: Nothing should be feared—not human beings and not any other thing.[481] One must fear nothing save sin, since no adversity will harm if iniquity does not dominate. Proverbs (28) says: "The impious person flees when no one pursues."[482]

---

477. In Jer 17, p. 620.   478. In Pss 50, p. 348.   479. ST II-II, q. 123, a. 6.   480. Ibid., ad 6.   481. In Pss 26, p. 237.   482. In Pss 48, p. 335.

FOX: What about God? Should people fear God?

AQUINAS: Job talks about "the fear of God that is wisdom," because through reverence for God human beings cling to God, in whom there is true wisdom as in the highest cause of all things.[483] Ecclesiasticus (1) says: "the fear of the Lord is the beginning of wisdom." Initial and chaste fear is properly called reverence.[484]

FOX: And so the awe and wonder we spoke of in the Via Positiva contains a kind of "chaste" fear, a sense of reverence.

AQUINAS: "I meditate on all your works, I muse on the work of your hands" (Ps. 143:5). . . . We are led to wonder at God's power, and so to hold God in reverence. The maker is nobler than the things they make. We gaze at the heavens and the earth, "Why then, how much greater must the One be who formed them!" (Wis. 13:4). "For the invisible things of God from the creation of the world are clearly seen, being understood by the things which are made, even God's eternal power and godhead" (Rom. 1:20). From wonderment we come to fear and reverence: "Your name is great in might; who would not fear you, O King of nations!" (Jer. 10:6–7).[485]

FOX: Elaborate, please, on what you have called "chaste fear."

AQUINAS: Servitude properly comes from fear. But there is a double fear, namely, servile, which charity expels: 1 John 4:18: "There is no fear in charity." Another kind of fear is filial, which originates from charity, when someone fears to lose that which one loves. This fear is good and chaste, concerning which it is said in Psalm 19:9: "Fear of the Lord remains holy forever." And according to this there are two servitudes: one that proceeds from filial fear, and with respect to this all just persons are servants and children of God, as was said above. The second servitude is that which proceeds from the fear of punishment, and is contrary to love. About this Jesus says: "Now I do not call you servants."[486]

FOX: You say that Jesus freed us from fear based on servitude.

AQUINAS: Jesus says, "I have called you friends." Servitude is contrary to friendship. Therefore first Jesus excludes servitude,

---

483. In Job 28, p. 155.   484. In Pss 34, p. 276.   485. CG II, ch. 2 n. 3.
486. In Jn 15.15, n. 2015.

saying, "now I do not call you servants," as if to say: "Although once you were like slaves under the law, now you are like free persons under grace" (Rom. 8:15). "You have not accepted the spirit of servitude again in fear, but you have accepted the spirit of the adoption of children of God."[487]

FOX: You speak of friendship being opposed to fear and servitude. What is friendship?

AQUINAS: Friendship is love simply speaking.[488] Jesus teaches the true sign of friendship to his own when he says, "whatever I have heard from my Father, I have made known to you." For it is a true sign of friendship that a friend reveal the secrets of one's heart to a friend. For when the heart and soul of friends are one, they do not seem to separate what they reveal to their friend from their own heart.[489]

FOX: One more endorsement of art as meditation—the act of creativity as the act of revelation of one's heart to friends. How important is the creative act of friendship, in your opinion?

AQUINAS: Happy people need friends in order that they act well and in order that they may do good to them; in order that they may delight in seeing them do good; and also in order that they may be helped by them in their good work. For in order that one may do well, whether in the works of the active life or in those of the contemplative life, one needs the fellowship of friends.[490]

FOX: Delight and conviviality are a part of friendship, then?

AQUINAS: You cannot make friends with people whose company and conversation you do not enjoy. Those who are not truly friendly do not share their lives and rejoice together in the company of friends.[491]

FOX: I conclude from this discussion that for you God is a friend who is to be loved more than feared.

AQUINAS: People have more desire for what they will because of love than for what they will because of fear only, for what one loves only from a motive of fear is called an object of a divided will.[492]

---

487. In Jn 15.15, n. 2014.   488. ST I-II, q. 26, a. 4.   489. In Jn 15.15, n. 2016.   490. ST I-II, q. 4, a. 8.   491. In Ethics VIII, L. 6, p. 731. 492. CG III, ch. 116 n. 3.

FOX: And for you to "do the will of God" is not a matter of fear so much as of love.

AQUINAS: The will adheres to a thing, either because of love or because of fear, but not in the same way. For, if one clings to something because of fear, one clings because of something else, for instance, to avoid an evil that threatens unless one clings to that thing. But if one clings to a thing because of love, one does so for the sake of that thing. Now, what is valued for its own sake is of greater importance than what is for the sake of something else. Therefore, the adherence to God in love is the best possible way of clinging to God. So, this is what is chiefly intended in the divine law.[493]

FOX: I hear you saying that all law is about love, not fear.

AQUINAS: Worldly fear is that which arises from worldly love as from an evil root, for which reason worldly fear is always evil.[494]

FOX: You seem to be saying that love and fear are incompatible.

AQUINAS: Servile fear, insofar as it is servile, is contrary to charity.[495] Servile fear, as regards its servility, is entirely cast out when charity comes, although the fear of punishment remains as to its substance. This fear decreases as charity increases, chiefly as regards its act, since the more anyone loves God, the less they fear punishment. First, because one thinks less of one's own good, to which punishment is opposed; second, because the more strongly one clings, the more confident one is of the reward, and consequently the less fearful of punishment.[496]

FOX: So love is to be preferred to fear.

AQUINAS: Love and hope, to which the Scriptures are constantly calling us, are to be preferred to being afraid. Thus when Peter said, "Leave me, Lord, for I am a sinner," Jesus responded: "Do not be afraid."[497]

FOX: I like your observation that the Scriptures are "constantly calling us" to love and hope.

AQUINAS: Christ had no servile fear.[498]

---

493. Ibid., n. 2.   494. ST II-II, q. 19, a. 4.   495. Ibid.   496. Ibid., a. 10.   497. Ibid. III, q. 80, a. 10, ad 3.   498. Ibid. III, q. 7, a. 6, ad 3.

FOX: If Christ had no servile fear, it is particularly disturbing to find his followers who do. It does not work to mix fear with love, does it?

AQUINAS: Fear has a greater tendency than desire to cause involuntariness.[499]

FOX: Then a religion of fear is hardly true religion?

AQUINAS: What is done through fear is less voluntary, because when fear lays hold of anyone they are under a certain necessity of doing a certain thing. Hence the Philosopher says (*Ethics,* iii) that those things that are done through fear are not simply voluntary, but a mixture of voluntary and involuntary.[500]

FOX: Fear remains a sin, then?

AQUINAS: Fear excuses, not because of its sinfulness, but because of its involuntariness.[501] Fear . . . is the cause of despair, which withdraws from good. Aristotle says, therefore, that cowards are people who despair inasmuch as they fear their deficiency in everything. On the contrary, brave people have great hope because they are courageous.[502]

FOX: Don't we talk about "the fear of God" as being a gift of the Holy Spirit?

AQUINAS: The fear of God, which is numbered among the seven gifts of the Holy Spirit, is filial or chaste fear. The gifts of the Holy Spirit are certain habitual perfections of the soul's powers, whereby these are disposed to the movement of the Holy Spirit.[503]

FOX: And among these movements of the Spirit are strength and courage, as we saw above. What brings about fear, would you say?

AQUINAS: Love causes fear, since it is through one's loving a certain good that whatever deprives one of that good is an evil to one. Consequently one fears that as an evil.[504]

FOX: Is fear the same thing as sorrow, then?

AQUINAS: Fear has less passion than sorrow, which concerns present evil, because fear concerns future evil and this is not so strong a motive as present evil.[505]

---

499. Ibid. I-II, q. 6, a. 7, ad 1.   500. Ibid. II-II, q. 125, a. 4.   501. Ibid., ad 1.   502. In Ethics III, L. 15, p. 243.   503. ST II-II, q. 19, a. 9.   504. Ibid. I-II, q. 43, a. 1.   505. Ibid., q. 41, a. 1.

FOX: It seems to me that fear renders our soul smaller. When we are fearful we sort of shrink up.

AQUINAS: From the very imagination that causes fear there ensues a certain contraction in the appetite. . . . When fear happens a contraction of heat and vital spirits toward the inner parts takes place in the body itself.[506]

FOX: Yes, you are right. There are certainly chemical changes that take place in our bodies when we are afraid. But when I hear you speak of how fear "contracts," I am reminded of a point you made earlier—that sorrow contracts and that joy expands.

AQUINAS: External obstacles to persistence in good are especially those that cause sorrow.[507]

FOX: One more argument for opening our hearts up by way of the wonder and awe of the Via Positiva.

AQUINAS: Fear is the beginning of despair even as hope is the beginning of daring. Thus, just as fortitude, which employs daring in moderation, presupposes hope, so on the other hand, despair proceeds from some kind of fear.[508]

FOX: This is an important point—that despair (which you earlier called the most dangerous of sins) proceeds from fear. It underscores the extreme troubles into which fear leads us.

AQUINAS: If anyone through fear of the danger of death or of any other temporal evil is so disposed as to do what is forbidden, or to omit what is commanded by the divine law, such fear is a mortal sin.[509] Just as ordinate love is included in every virtue, . . . so inordinate fear is included in every sin. Thus the covetous person fears the loss of money, the intemperate person the loss of pleasure, and so on.[510]

FOX: This helps to explain a society that is overly invested in outward expressions of security. When I think of the mortal sin of fear I think of the timidity of church officials, who at times seem afraid to preach good news and who fall back so readily on pusillanimous shibboleths. I think this discussion of fear applies to institutions as much as to individuals. What they do and fail to do often brings about despair instead of hope.

---

506. Ibid., q. 44, a. 1.   507. Ibid. II-II, q. 137, a. 3, ad 1.   508. Ibid., q. 125, a. 2, ad 3.   509. Ibid., a. 3.   510. Ibid., a. 2.

AQUINAS: Fear in its generic sense denotes avoidance in general.[511]

FOX: Somehow I find lack of hope, a contraction of the spirit, in tired people and their institutions, a kind of cynicism, a power of the negative *senex,* that in growing old projects its despair and pessimism onto others.

AQUINAS: Youths, on account of the heat of their nature, are full of spirit; so that their heart expands. And it is owing to the heart being expanded that one tends to that which is arduous. For this reason youths are spirited and hopeful.[512]

FOX: Being young or being in touch with our own youthfulness seems to be a necessary part of being creative, then.

AQUINAS: Youth is the cause of hope on these three counts, namely, because the object of hope is future, is difficult, and is possible. For the young live in the future and not in the past; they are not lost in memories but full of confidence. Second, their warmth of nature, high spirits, and expansive heart embolden them to reach out to difficult projects; therefore they are mettlesome and of good hope. Third, they have not been thwarted in their plans, and their lack of experience encourages them to think that where there's a will there's a way. The last two factors, namely, good spirits and a certain recklessness, are also at work in people who are drunk.[513]

FOX: I am amused when you compare young people to drunken people.

AQUINAS: Because of their growth young people have many disturbances of spirits and humors, such as occur in intoxicated persons. So, on account of activity of this sort, young people especially seek pleasure.[514]

FOX: I sense that you feel that we should all be youthful in some regards if we are to have the "expansive hearts" necessary for creativity and the vulnerability to being "intoxicated" by life itself.

AQUINAS: Youth and age can be in the soul both at once, though not in the body.[515] The immortal soul can have a spiritual birth and spiritual maturity; bodily age is no prejudice to

---

511. Ibid., a. 1, ad 1.   512. Ibid. I-II, q. 40, a. 6.   513. Ibid.   514. In Ethics VII, L. 14, p. 697.   515. ST III, q. 1, a. 6, ad 1.

its life. It can attain a perfect age when the body is young, and be born again when the body is old.[516]

FOX: Your point that youths have something in common with people who are drunk parallels the point you made in the Via Positiva about our becoming "intoxicated" by the universe. I hear you saying that with expanded hearts (that is, courage or a big heart) we can and should take on arduous tasks.

AQUINAS: It is essential to virtue to be about the difficult and the good.[517] Virtue is about the difficult and the good.[518]

FOX: And so life is an adventure for the virtuous person! I find this point important, because acedia and pusillanimity both seem to render our souls so small and our work so meager. Trust seems necessary for magnanimity as well.

AQUINAS: The trust that is part of fortitude signifies the hope that one puts in oneself—a hope naturally in subordination to God as well.[519]

FOX: So hope is essential in order to do great things?

AQUINAS: In the object of hope four notes are struck: that it is good, future, arduous, possible. Hence, respectively, hope differs from fear, joy, simple desire, and despair.[520]

FOX: I think that many people yearn to do something bigger with their lives than they feel invited to do.

AQUINAS: Magnanimity is the expansion of the soul to great things.[521] To do something great—whence magnificence takes its name—belongs properly to the very notion of virtue.[522] Magnificence directs the use of art to something great.[523]

FOX: If magnificence belongs to the very notion of virtue and indeed of all art, then all people—because we are all called to virtue and to creativity—are called to greatness.

AQUINAS: Human virtue is a participation in divine power. But magnificence belongs to divine power, according to Psalm 136:35: "God's magnificence and power reach to the clouds."[524]

FOX: How important it is that we hear this today—that our human virtue is a participation in divine power! The very word "magnanimity" or "big-souled" means the opposite of pusillanimity or "puny-souled."

---

516. Ibid. III, q. 72, a. 8.   517. Ibid. II-II, q. 129, a. 2.   518. Ibid., q. 137, a. 1.   519. Ibid., q. 123, a. 10, ad 3.   520. DS, 1.   521. ST II-II, q. 129, a. 1.   522. Ibid., q. 134, a. 1.   523. Ibid., a. 4, ad 3.   524. Ibid., a. 1.

AQUINAS: It pertains to magnanimity to have a great soul.[525] People are said to be magnanimous chiefly because they are minded to do some great act.[526]

FOX: What makes an act a great act?

AQUINAS: An act is simply and absolutely great when it consists in the best use of the greatest thing.[527] It belongs to magnanimity not only to tend to something great, but also to do great works in all the virtues, whether by making, or by any kind of action.[528]

FOX: In all the virtues, you say?

AQUINAS: Magnanimity makes all virtues greater.[529]

FOX: Talk to me more about this virtue of great-souledness or magnanimity. I think we need to hear more of this in our time and culture.

AQUINAS: Magnanimous people do not expose themselves to dangers for trifles, nor are they lovers of danger, as it were exposing themselves to dangers hastily or lightly. However, magnanimous people brave great dangers for great things because they put themselves in all kinds of danger for great things, for instance, the common welfare, justice, divine worship, and so forth.[530]

FOX: I am struck by how you categorize justice making, the common good, and also divine worship as "great things" demanding courage. What other characteristics delineate a magnanimous person?

AQUINAS: It is characteristic of magnanimous people to be more solicitous about the truth than about the opinions of others. They do not depart from what they ought to do according to virtue because of what people think.[531] It is a mark of magnanimous people to speak and work openly, because they pay little attention to others. Consequently, they publicly divulge their words and deed. That people hide what they do and say arises from the fear of others.[532] Magnanimous people deliberately determine to forget injuries they have suffered.[533]

FOX: There seems to be a special relationship between magnanimity and courage.

---

525. Ibid., q. 129, a. 3.   526. Ibid., a. 1.   527. Ibid.   528. Ibid., q. 134, a. 2, ad 2.   529. Ibid., q. 129, a. 4, ad 3.   530. In Ethics IV, L. 10, p. 335.   531. Ibid., p. 337.   532. Ibid.   533. Ibid.

AQUINAS: Magnanimity is a part of the virtue of courage or fortitude.[534] Magnanimity goes with courage insofar as it establishes the soul when arduous tasks arise.[535] Magnanimity is properly about hope in some arduous task. Therefore, ... trust pertains to magnanimity.[536] Trust furnishes a certain vigor to hope. For this reason it is the opposite of fear, as is hope. But because courage properly speaking strengthens a person against evil, magnanimity strengthens a person to take on good tasks. That is why trust pertains more properly to magnanimity than to courage.[537]

FOX: It sounds like magnanimity is rather rare.

AQUINAS: It is difficult for anyone to be magnanimous.[538] No evil person is able to be magnanimous.[539]

FOX: Aren't all people called to greatness, that is, to use the best they can of the greatest gifts they have been given? And isn't this call a lot like the call to holiness itself?

AQUINAS: It pertains to every perfect virtue to do something great in the genus of that virtue, if "doing" be taken in the broadest sense.[540] Magnificence is connected with holiness, since its chief effect is directed to religion or holiness.[541]

FOX: How do you arrive at this conclusion?

AQUINAS: The intention of magnificence is the production of a great work. Now, works done by human beings are directed to an end: and no end of human work is so great as the honor of God. Thus magnificence does a great work especially in reference to the divine honor.[542]

FOX: It seems to me that it is important to understand this kind of teaching insofar as it applies to a community of persons and not just as it applies to an individual. Communities have the potential to undertake "great works," such as feeding the hungry and educating the ignorant and healing the wounded. No doubt we will treat this aspect of community virtue in the Via Transformativa. But it concerns me here because I get the impression that you or Aristotle or both put too much emphasis on the "magnificent individual" without asking where so-and-so's wealth came from and at whose expense. I return to an

---

534. ST II-II, q. 129, Preamble.   535. Ibid., a. 5.   536. Ibid., a. 6.
537. Ibid., ad 2.   538. In Ethics IV, L. 8, p. 326.   539. Ibid.   540. ST II-II, q. 134, a. 2, ad 1.   541. Ibid., ad 3.   542. Ibid.

earlier question: Are all persons called to this virtue of magnificence?

AQUINAS: Not every free person is magnificent as regards their actions, because they lack the wherewithal to perform magnificent deeds. Nevertheless, every free person has the habit of magnificence, either actually or in respect of a proximate disposition to it.[543] It is possible to have a habit of virtue without performing the act: thus a poor person has the habit of magnificence without exercising the act. Sometimes, however, a person who has the habit begins to perform the act yet does not finish it. For instance, a builder begins to build a house, but does not complete it.[544]

FOX: Is every person capable of being magnanimous as well?

AQUINAS: Since magnanimous people tend to great things, it follows that they tend chiefly to things that involve a certain excellence, and shun those that imply defect. Now it savors of excellence that a person is beneficent, generous, and grateful.[545]

FOX: And yet, as we have said earlier in this conversation, all creativity is a kind of "thank-you." It seems that ingratitude and acedia go together.

AQUINAS: Acedia is indeed a flight from a spiritual good[546] [in which] human beings regret having to do something for God's sake.[547]

FOX: It seems that acedia is the parent of many other kinds of troubling attitudes in our lives.

AQUINAS: According to the Philosopher (*Ethics* viii, 5.6), "No one can be a long time in company with what is painful and unpleasant." It follows that something arises from sorrow in two ways: first, that people shun whatever causes sorrow; second, that they pass to other things that give them pleasure.[548]

FOX: This might explain the many addictions common in our culture today.

AQUINAS: Spiritual goods, which are the object of the sorrow of acedia, are both end and means. Avoidance of the end is the result of *despair,* while avoidance of those goods that are the means to the end, in matters of difficulty that come under the

---

543. Ibid., a. 1, ad 1.   544. Ibid., q. 137, a. 1, ad 2.   545. Ibid., q. 129, a. 4, ad 2.   546. viii De malo 1, ad 7.   547. ST II-II, q. 35, a. 3, ad 2. 548. Ibid., a. 4, ad 2.

counsels, is the effect of *pusillanimity,* and in matters of common justice, is the effect of *boredom with precepts.* The struggle against spiritual goods that cause sorrow is sometimes with people who lead others to spiritual goods, and this is called *spite;* and sometimes it extends to the spiritual goods themselves, when a person goes so far as to detest them, and this is properly called *malice.* Insofar as a person has recourse to external objects of pleasure, the daughter of acedia is called *wandering after unlawful things.*[549]

FOX: There seems in our consumer society to be a lot of distraction, a lot of wandering after unnecessary things.

AQUINAS: This tendency to wander, if it reside in the mind itself that is desirous of rushing after various things without rhyme or reason, is called *uneasiness of the mind,* but if it pertains to the imaginative power, it is called *curiosity;* if it affect the speech it is called *loquacity;* and insofar as it affects the body that changes place, it is called *restlessness of the body,* when for example anyone demonstrates the unsteadiness of their mind by the inordinate movements of limbs of their body; while if it causes the body to move from one place to another, it is called *instability;* or instability may denote changeableness of purpose.[550]

FOX: You seem to have named much that is going on in our society and psyches today by your deep analysis of the sin of acedia and its many offspring. The insatiable curiosity of which you speak helps explain the titillating dimension of so much modern-day media, for example.

AQUINAS: There is a roaming unrest of the spirit, an unbridled desire to break out of the citadel of the spirit into diversity.[551]

FOX: You are naming what happens when our spirits wander aimlessly and without roots. Our very capacity for the infinite and for the divine becomes a burden to us all and to all of creation when it knows no home. If, as you said above, the "chief act of virtue is the inward choice," then the many outward choices that an addictive society that references itself externally calls upon us to make destroy virtue. I see in this rich phrase of yours, "our inward choice," a complete naming of the essence

---

549. Ibid.   550. Ibid., ad 3.   551. xi De malo, 4.

of creativity—that it be from inside out. We choose our lives, we make them, we cocreate them, we give birth to them by the "inward" choices we make. Our creativity lies at the heart of who we are. Of course it is our divine or "infinite" capacity for creativity, as you call it, that explains our species' capacity for evil, does it not?

AQUINAS: The higher one's nature is, the more terrible and pernicious it is when one turns to evil. An evil person is worse than all the bad animals.[552] The Philosopher says that a bad man is worse than a bad beast; since, when his intelligence is accompanied by an ill-will, he invents diverse evils.[553]

FOX: It seems then that our divine capacity for creativity also constitutes our demonic capacity for evil.

AQUINAS: Despair comes from the flight from spiritual goods that can be enjoyed and the withdrawal from the divine good that is hoped for. . . . When it comes to undertaking arduous tasks that fall under the counsels to perform, pusillanimity enters in.[554]

FOX: And so acedia opens the door to despair and to pusillanimity? No wonder it is considered a mortal sin and a capital sin.

AQUINAS: The fact that pusillanimity and despair pertain to the instinct of anger does not prevent them from being caused by acedia, for the passions of anger are all caused by the passions of desire.[555]

FOX: Acedia names the ultimate, we might say, in the loss of desire. And when acedia takes over, so do despair and pusillanimity. Let us turn to another issue that arises when one plunges into the Via Creativa: that of worship. You analyze worship as a creative act, therefore a virtue. Indeed, you analyze worship as being part of the virtue of religion.

AQUINAS: It belongs to religion to do certain things through reverence for God.[556] Every good act belongs to a virtue. Now, it is evident that to render anyone their due has the aspect of good, since by rendering a person their due, one becomes properly related to that person, through being ordered to them in a becoming manner. . . . Since it belongs to religion to pay due

---

552. In Eph 6.12, p. 501.   553. In Pss 48, p. 337.   554. xi De malo, 4.
555. Ibid., ad 3.   556. ST II-II, q. 81, a. 2, ad 1.

honor to someone—namely, to God—it is evident that religion is a virtue.[557]

FOX: It seems that worship and ritual are an important part of humanity's relationship to the Divine, an important act of our collective Via Creativa.

AQUINAS: We pay God honor and reverence, not for God's sake (because the Godhead is of itself full of glory to which no creature can add anything), but for our own sake. For by the very fact that we revere and honor God, our mind is subject to Godself.[558]

FOX: This is a very important point you are making—that worship is for humanity's sake more than for God's sake.

AQUINAS: We praise God, not for God's benefit, but for ours.[559]

FOX: How does ritual effectively bring about this benefit that worship brings our species?

AQUINAS: The human mind, in order to be united to God, needs to be guided by the sense world, since "invisible things . . . are clearly seen, being understood by the things that are made," as the Apostle says (Rom. 1:20). Wherefore in divine worship it is necessary to make use of corporeal things, in order that the minds of people may be aroused thereby, as by signs, to the spiritual acts by means of which human beings are united to God.[560]

FOX: And so our bodily rituals are a pathway to awakening human consciousness to praise and thanks?

AQUINAS: Certain bodily actions are performed by human beings, not to stimulate God by such things, but to awaken people themselves to divine matters by these actions—for example, such things as prostrations, genuflections, chants, and hymns.[561]

FOX: What is the deep purpose of these varied forms of worship?

AQUINAS: It profits one nothing to praise with the lips if one does not praise with the heart.[562]

---

557. Ibid., a. 2.   558. Ibid., a. 7.   559. Ibid., q. 91, a. 1, ad 3.   560. Ibid., q. 81, a. 7.   561. CG III, ch. 119 n. 4.   562. ST II-II, q. 91, a. 1, ad 2.

FOX: Once again you are underscoring the essence of all prayer and all art as meditation: that we give expression from our hearts. Our artwork is our heart-work. This includes the artwork that ritual and worship is meant to elicit.

AQUINAS: Gratitude depends chiefly on the heart.[563]

FOX: The praise from the heart that true worship elicits seems to arise from awe, reverence, and gratitude for being.

AQUINAS: Human beings feel that they are obliged by some sort of natural prompting to pay, in their own way, reverence to God, from whom comes the source of humanity's being and of all goodness.[564] Honor is rendered to God who is the Parent of all beings.[565] People offer material sacrifices to God, not because God needs them, but so that people may be reminded that they ought to refer both their own being and all their possessions to God as end, and thus to the Creator, Governor, and Lord of all.[566]

FOX: I am struck by how cosmic your language is when you speak of the God whom we worship—the "Parent of all being," the "Governor of all," the "Source of all goodness." Clearly worship for you is meant to be a microcosmic expression of a macrocosmic wonder.

AQUINAS: It belongs to religion to show reverence to one God under a single aspect, namely, as the first principle of the creation and government of things.[567]

FOX: An implication of what you say is that a cosmology or creation perspective is necessary for worship. Religion is not primarily about redemption. You also say that the forms that ritual requires of us assist to "awaken us." This would seem to imply that when forms are not awakening us we ought to find deeper and more effective ones.

AQUINAS: These bodily acts of worship are done not because God needs them, for God knows all things, and God's will is immutable, and the disposition of the divine mind does not admit of movement from a body for God's own sake. Rather, we do these things for our sakes, so that our attention may be directed to God by these bodily actions and that our love may be

---

563. Ibid., q. 106, a. 3, ad 5.   564. CG III, ch. 119 n. 7.   565. Ibid., n. 8.   566. Ibid., n. 2.   567. ST II-II, q. 81, a. 3.

aroused. At the same time, then, we confess by these actions that God is the author of soul and body, to whom we offer both spiritual and bodily acts of homage.[568]

FOX: You seem to put great emphasis on the bodily dimension of ritual or worship.

AQUINAS: It is not astonishing if heretics who deny that God is the author of our body condemn such manifestations [as bodily acts of homage]. This condemnation shows that they have not remembered that they are human beings when they judge that the representation of sense objects to themselves is not necessary for inner knowledge and for love. For it is evident from experience that the soul is stimulated to an act of knowledge or of love by bodily acts. Hence, it is obvious that we may quite appropriately use even bodily things to elevate our mind to God.[569]

FOX: And so the interior act of the heart and the exterior acts of our bodies at prayer together constitute healthy worship?

AQUINAS: The *cult* of God is said to consist in these bodily expressions to God. For we are said to *cultivate* those things to which we devote effort through our works. Indeed, we show our zeal in regard to God by our activity—not, of course, to benefit God (as we are said to do, when we cultivate other things by our actions), but because we approach more closely to God by such acts. And since we directly tend toward God though interior acts, we therefore properly give cult to God by interior acts. Yet exterior acts also pertain to the cult of God, to the extent that our mind is lifted up to God by such acts, as we have said.[570]

FOX: Your language when speaking of worship is very sensual—you talk of "arousal," of being "awakened," of "attention directed by bodily actions," of being "stimulated," of demonstrating our "zeal" in this way.

AQUINAS: God's name is expressed in external words.[571]

FOX: And the purpose of all worship is rest, repose, or delight with the beloved?

AQUINAS: Rest is prescribed at certain times from outward works, so that the mind may be devoted to divine contempla-

---

568. CG III, ch. 119 n. 4.   569. Ibid., n. 5.   570. Ibid., n. 6.   571. Ibid., n. 3.

tion; and thus it is stated: "Remember to keep holy the sabbath day" (Exod. 20:8).[572] Movement cannot be called completed till it comes to rest, for rest denotes consummation of movement. . . . By the fact that God ceased making creatures on the seventh day, God is said on that day to have completed the divine work.[573]

FOX: So to say that God rested really means that God enjoyed creation on the seventh day. Worship also seems to be about gratitude. After all, the word "Eucharist" is from the Greek word meaning "to give thanks."

AQUINAS: Religion is supreme thankfulness or gratitude.[574]

FOX: I like that definition of religion as "supreme gratitude." What else can you say about gratitude?

AQUINAS: Gratitude is paid spontaneously. Thanking is less thankful when it is compelled.[575] The debt of gratitude flows from charity.[576]

FOX: What about our refusal to say thank-you or to give back more for what we have received?

AQUINAS: Every ingratitude is a sin.[577] The supreme degree of ingratitude is when anyone fails to recognize the reception of a favor.[578]

FOX: This would seem to be the essence of failure in worship: our inability to recognize the gift of our existence and therefore our refusal to give thanks. This would almost seem to constitute the essence of our being asleep. People who are asleep are not giving thanks; they are in no way zealous. Do you see waking up as one of the themes of the Via Creativa?

AQUINAS: A gloss interprets that in order that light might prevail the Holy Spirit says: "Rise you who sleep! Arise from the dead and Christ shall enlighten you." The Apostle Paul introduces the image found in Isaiah 60 (1): "Arise, be enlightened, O Jerusalem; for your light is come, and the glory of the Lord is risen upon you." Rise from a neglect of good works, you who sleep. "How long will you sleep, O sluggard?" (Prov. 6:9). "Shall he that sleep rise again no more?" (Ps. 41:9).[579]

---

572. Ibid., ch. 120 n. 25.   573. ST I, q. 73, a. 1.   574. Ibid. II-II, q. 106, a. 1, ad 1.   575. Ibid., ad 2.   576. Ibid., a. 6, ad 2.   577. Ibid., q. 107, a. 1.   578. Ibid., a. 2.   579. In Eph 5.14, p. 492.

FOX: You seem to be equating our waking up with the theme of the resurrection of Christ.

AQUINAS: "And arise from the dead" means from dead or destructive actions. Christ "will cleanse our conscience from dead works" (Heb. 9:14). "Your dead men shall live, the slain shall rise again" (Isa. 26:19). Rise therefore "and Christ will enlighten you."[580]

FOX: Are we capable of rising from our sleepiness and sin ourselves, since Paul says, "Rise and Christ shall enlighten you"?

AQUINAS: Two things are requisite for the justification of a sinner, namely, a free decision cooperating in the act of rising from sin and grace itself.[581]

FOX: For you, then, Christ's resurrection prefigures our own. Yet our own begins in this life.

AQUINAS: We can learn four things from this article of faith, that "on the third day Christ rose again from the dead." First, let us try to rise spiritually from the soul's death, brought on by our sins, to that life of justice obtained through penitence: "Rise, you who sleep, and rise from the dead; and Christ shall enlighten you" (Eph. 5:14). This is the first resurrection: "Blessed and holy is one who has part in the first resurrection" (John 20:6).

Second, let us not put off rising until our death, but do so now, since Christ arose on the third day: "Delay not to be converted to the Lord; and defer it not from day to day" (Eccles. 5.8). When overcome by illness you will not be able to attend to what is involved in salvation, and in addition you will by persevering in sin be unable to participate in all the good accomplished in the church, and you will bring about many evils.

Third, let us arise again to an incorruptible life so as never to die again, resolving to sin no more. "Knowing that Christ, being raised from the dead, dies now no more. Death shall no more have dominion over him" (Rom. 6:9).

Fourth, let us again rise to a new and glorious life by avoiding everything that formerly was an occasion and cause of our death and sin: "As Christ is risen from the dead by the glory of the

---

580. Ibid.   581. Ibid., pp. 492–93.

Father, so we also must walk in newness of life" (Rom. 6:4). This new life is the life of justice renewing the soul and leading it to the life of glory.[582]

FOX: I like your phrase "the first resurrection." That pertains to the issue of our sleepiness as a people and as a church at times in history. Yet you see Christ as assisting our awakening.

AQUINAS: Christ's resurrection was the first in the order of all resurrection. Christ's resurrection must be the cause of ours, and this the Apostle says (1 Cor. 15:20): "Christ is risen from the dead, the first fruits of them that sleep; for by a human came death, and by a human came the resurrection of the dead." [583]

FOX: So you see resurrection as applying to souls as well as bodies?

AQUINAS: Christ's resurrection acts in virtue of the Divinity. Now, this power extends not only to the resurrection of bodies, but also to that of souls; for from God it comes about that the soul lives by grace and that the body lives by the soul. Therefore, Christ's resurrection is instrumentally effective not only with respect to the resurrection of bodies, but also with respect to the resurrection of souls.[584]

FOX: This is an exciting idea and a practical one—that of a resurrection before we die.

AQUINAS: There is a double resurrection, one of the body, when soul rejoins body, the other spiritual, when soul reunites to God. Christ's bodily resurrection produces both in us— though he himself never rose again spiritually, for he had never been separated from God.[585]

FOX: I seldom hear Western theologians speaking of this "first resurrection"—that of the awakening of the soul of the person— that you see as an important dimension to the meaning of Jesus' resurrection.

AQUINAS: Christ's resurrection is an exemplary cause with respect to the resurrection of souls, since even in our souls we must be conformed with the risen Christ; as the Apostle says (Rom. 6:4–11): "Christ is risen from the dead by the glory of the Father, so we also must walk in the newness of life; and as

---

582. LAP, a. 5. See also: AC, pp. 54–55.   583. ST III, q. 56, a. 1.
584. Ibid., a. 2.   585. CT I, 239.

he, rising again from the dead, dies now no more, so let us reckon that we are dead to sin, that we may live together with him."[586]

FOX: So Jesus helps us overcome our fear of death—and therefore to get on with living?

AQUINAS: By willing to become a human being, God clearly displayed the immensity of the divine love for humanity, so that henceforth human beings might serve God, no longer out of fear of death, . . . but out of the love of charity.[587] In not refusing to die for truth, Christ overcame the fear of dying, which is the reason human beings for the most part are subject to the slavery of sin.[588]

FOX: Do you believe that Jesus taught about both the first and the second resurrections?

AQUINAS: Our Lord promises both resurrections, for he says: "Amen, Amen, I say to you that the hour is coming, and now is when the dead shall hear the voice of the Son of God and they that hear shall live." And this seems to pertain to the spiritual resurrection of souls. . . . But later, it is the bodily resurrection he expresses, saying: "The hour is coming when all that are in the graves shall hear the voice of the Son of God" (John 5:25, 28). For, clearly, souls are not in the graves, but bodies. Therefore, this foretells the bodily resurrection.[589]

FOX: No doubt there are more dimensions to resurrection than those we have been able to enumerate so far.

AQUINAS: On that day on which the resurrection took place a kind of new creation, as it were, began. As the psalmist says (104:30): "Send forth your spirit, and they will be created, and you will renew the face of the earth." And as Galatians puts it (6:15): "In Christ Jesus neither does circumcision nor uncircumcision have any value, but a new creation does."[590]

FOX: And so resurrection is a kind of new creation for us all.

AQUINAS: The life of the risen Christ is spread to all humanity in common resurrection.[591] Christ's resurrection is the cause of newness of life, which comes through grace or justice.[592]

---

586. ST III, q. 56, a. 2.   587. CT I, 201.   588. Ibid., 227.   589. CG IV, ch. 79 n. 8.   590. In Jn 20.1, n. 2471.   591. In Job, ch. 19, p. 76. 592. ST III, q. 56, a. 2, ad 4.

FOX: Your sense of the Cosmic Christ seems to come through when you speak of the universality of resurrection.

AQUINAS: The primordial cause of human resurrection is the life of the Son of God, which does not take its beginning from Mary, as the Ebionites have said, but always was, according to the Apostle in the Letter to the Hebrews near the end: "Jesus Christ yesterday and today, and forever." For this reason Job does not say symbolically "the redeemer will live" but "lives." And from this perspective he proclaims future resurrection, determining its time, when he adds: "And on the last day I will be raised up from the earth."[593]

FOX: Sometimes our work exhausts us and we need some of the "first resurrection" just to recover from it.

AQUINAS: Sensitive nature is always under tension while at work, and work is wearisome, as the statements of the natural scientists attest.[594]

FOX: The first resurrection, you say, is a resurrection of soul; what about this "second resurrection"?

AQUINAS: Since the soul is immortal the body should be joined to it again. This is to rise again. The immortality of the soul, then, would seem to demand the future resurrection of the body.[595] When the body is resumed, bliss will grow, not in depth, but in extent.[596]

FOX: And so the second resurrection for you includes both soul and body?

AQUINAS: Job does not say "not only will my soul stand upon the earth" but "I myself" will. This self consists of soul and body. And that Job might show that the body too will be a sharer of that vision in its own way, he adds, "and my eyes will see God all together." Not that the eyes of the body are going to see divine essence, but because the eyes of the body are going to see God made human and will also see the glory of God shining in creation, according to Augustine in his *City of God*.[597]

FOX: Hope, then, is one of the gifts of the resurrection to us.

AQUINAS: Christ's resurrection raises our hope, because by seeing Christ our head rise again we hope that we also shall rise

---

593. In Job, ch. 19, p. 76. 594. In Ethics VII, L. 14, p. 697. 595. CG IV, ch. 79 n. 10. 596. ST I-II, q. 4, a. 5. 597. In Job, ch. 19, p. 76.

again. Thus it is written (1 Cor. 15:12): "Now, if Christ be
preached that he rose from the dead, how do some among you
say that there is no resurrection of the dead?"[598] Job says, "My
hope has been renewed in my breast" in order to show that he
does not only have this hope in words, but hidden in his heart.
His hope is not doubtful, but very firm; not base, as it were, but
precious-like. For that which is hidden in the breast is held in
secret and firmly preserved and considered dear.[599]

FOX: Your hope sounds very deep.

AQUINAS: If God made something out of nothing we must believe that God can remake all things if they happen to be destroyed: God can give sight to the blind, raise the dead to life,
and work other similar miracles.[600]

FOX: I am struck by how your hope is related to your sense of
God as Creator or Maker of things from nothing. How else do
you see Christ's role in the resurrection?

AQUINAS: Christ raised us up first as a victor in order to free his
captive. Second, like a doctor to heal the sick. Third, like a law-
yer to acquit a defendant. Fourth, like a brave person who de-
fends the weak. Fifth, as a husband to take pleasure with his
spouse, as it says in Hosea 2: "I will wed myself to you in justice
and in faith."[601]

FOX: In addition to his act of resurrection and his life that frees
people for resurrection, what other role do you attribute to
Christ in the Via Creativa?

AQUINAS: Since the grace of Christ was most perfect, there
flowed from it, in consequence, the virtues that perfect the several powers of the soul for all the soul's acts. Thus Christ had
all the virtues.[602]

FOX: Then it follows that Jesus gave birth to his own virtues or
power most fully, demonstrating to us our responsibility to do
the same. How else does Christ enter the Via Creativa?

AQUINAS: Note the fourfold beauty in Christ. First, according
to divine beauty or form, as Philippians says (2): "Though he
was in the form of God." According to this he was visible to the
sons and daughters of the human race. For all people only have

---

598. ST III, q. 53, a. 1.   599. In Job, ch. 19, p. 76.   600. AC, p. 16.
601. In Is 41, p. 531.   602. ST III, q. 7, a. 2.

grace as a result of overflowing and sharing; but he has it through himself and fully. As Colossians says (2): "In his body dwells all the fullness of divinity." And Hebrews (1) says: "He is the splendor of God's glory and the image of God's substance." And Wisdom (7) says: "She [Wisdom] is a reflection of eternal light and a spotless mirror of God's glory."

A second beauty is the beauty of justice and truth, as Jeremiah puts it (31): "Lord, may the beauty of justice bring blessing to you." John 1 says: "Full of grace and of truth." A third beauty is the beauty of honest conversation. And concerning this 1 Peter speaks of "being made an example to the flock." And by this example Christ was visible to the children of the human race, since his conversation was more honest and virtuous than anyone else's. As 1 Peter (2) puts it: "He did not sin, nor was deceit found in his mouth."[603]

FOX: What do you have in mind when you speak of the "conversation" that emanated from Jesus?

AQUINAS: Christ alone is the master teaching within each of us.[604]

FOX: And so Christ, like yourself, was an artist insofar as he was a great teacher. We might say that teaching was his "art as meditation." Indeed, his parable-telling was the work of a unique artist. What made him such a great teacher?

AQUINAS: Jesus says, "And you are right for what you say is true, it applies to me, I am Teacher and Lord, teacher because of the wisdom. I teach by words and am Lord because of the power I show by miraculous signs." . . . So Jesus said to the disciples, "You are right. I am your teacher and Lord because you hear me as teacher and follow me as Lord." Thus we read in John 6:69: "To whom shall we go? You have the words of eternal life" and in Matthew (19:27): "Behold, we have left all things and followed you."[605]

FOX: And so you attribute Jesus' creative vocation as teacher to his wisdom?

AQUINAS: In 1 Corinthians 1 the Apostle says of Christ that he is the power of God and the wisdom of God; he is Lord of all,

---

603. In Pss 44, p. 320.   604. In Jn 13.13, n. 1775.   605. In Jn 13.13, n. 1776.

for as Ambrose says, "Lord is a word of power." Insofar as he is the wisdom of God, he teaches all people, and therefore his disciples called him "Lord," as in John 6:69, "Lord, to whom shall we go?" and also teacher, as in John 4:51. Rightly so, for he is the one Lord creating and re-creating.[606]

FOX: Christ, then, is surely the Cosmic Christ for you, for both titles you are dealing with—that of wisdom and that of Lord—are cosmic titles.

AQUINAS: Jeremiah says that with regard to the wisdom of the heart, "he will be wise," indeed, he will be wisdom itself, as Corinthians 1 has it: "Christ, the power of God and the wisdom of God."[607]

FOX: So Christ for you not only possesses all wisdom but is wisdom or Sophia; and Christ not only possesses all virtue and power but is the "virtue or power of God." This must be the ultimate in morality: to become virtue itself; the ultimate in empowerment: to become one with the divine power. Will you please elaborate on Christ as the wisdom of God?

AQUINAS: Whoever makes something must preconceive it in their wisdom, which is the form and pattern of the thing made: as the form preconceived in the mind of an artisan is the pattern of the cabinet to be made. So God makes nothing except through the conception of the divine intellect, which is an eternally conceived wisdom, that is, the Word of God and the Son of God.[608]

FOX: For you creativity and wisdom go together. I am reminded of Hildegard of Bingen's words, "there is wisdom in all creative works." And you understand the Word of God, the Cosmic Christ, as a great act of creativity on Divinity's part—a true generation of the Father/Mother God?

AQUINAS: Wisdom is personified in the Son, of whom it is written, "I, wisdom, have poured forth rivers." These rivers I interpret to mean the ineffable flow of the everlasting streams, of Son from Father and of Holy Spirit from them both. These are the streams that once seemed underground, and so lost to sight in the confusion of creatures, that the wisest of people could hardly come to know the mystery of the Trinity. But

---

606. In Jn 13.13, n. 1775.   607. In Jer 23, p. 632.   608. In Jn 1.3, n. 77.

now, "the depths of the rivers he has searched, and the hidden things he has brought to light (Job 28:11)." Now the Son has come, he has brought us good tidings and opened their courses to us. "Teach you all nations, baptizing them in the name of the Father and of the Son and of the Holy Spirit."[609]

FOX: Your imagery of Christ as wisdom is very wet.

AQUINAS: Christ is a dew for cooling—consider Isaiah 18: "Like a cloud of dew on the day of the harvest." He is rain for making fruitful, as in Psalm 71: "He will descend like rain upon the fleece." He is like a seed for bringing forth fruit, as Jeremiah says (23): "I will raise the just seed of David." The fruit spoken of is justice, which arises with him in three ways: He has fulfilled justice by his labor, as in Matthew 3: "Thus it is fitting for us to fulfill all justice." He has taught justice in his speaking, as in Isaiah 63: "I who announce justice, and am a defender with power to save." And he gave justice as a gift, as in 1 Corinthians (1): "He has been made wisdom and holiness and justice for us."[610]

FOX: The words the Word gave birth to are indeed powerful ones.

AQUINAS: The psalmist (45) calls the words of Christ "arrows" for three reasons: First, since the arrow penetrates to the heart with its sharpness, as Hosea puts it (2): "I will lead her into solitude, and speak to her heart." So the words of Christ, as Hebrews puts it (4): "The word of God is living and effective and is more able to penetrate than any two-edged sword." Likewise, the arrow moves rapidly. So the word of Christ suddenly filled the whole world, since the word of Christ was spread nearly through the whole world before the destruction of Jerusalem. Consider Psalm 147: "His word runs quickly." Likewise, the arrow reaches things far away—so too does the word of Christ, as Psalm 19 puts it: "Into every land the sound went forth."[611]

FOX: How do you image the Word of God?

AQUINAS: The beauty conceived in the heart of the Father is the Word.[612]

---

609. In I Sent, Prologue.   610. In Is 45, p. 540.   611. In Pss 44, p. 322.
612. In Pss 32, p. 260.

FOX: When you call Christ "beauty" you are celebrating another aspect of the Via Creativa of the Godhead: Christ the word is the "art as meditation" of God the Father, one might say.

AQUINAS: The Incarnate Word is like a word of speech. Just as physical sounds express what we think, so too Christ's body expresses the Eternal Word.[613]

FOX: And this Word of God is a very creative word.

AQUINAS: God knows the self of God. But God both knows and makes creatures. Thus the Word is expressive of God the Creator; yet it is both expressive and creative of the universe.[614]

FOX: This Word is truly a cosmic word, then.

AQUINAS: The formation of everything is attributed to the Word; thus the psalmist says (33): "The skies have been formed by the word of the Lord."[615] The Word is the source, as it were, from which realities stream, flowing into the very being that things have within themselves.[616]

FOX: For you the Word is clearly cosmic Wisdom as well. All this discussion is about the creativity of the Cosmic Christ.

AQUINAS: One of divine wisdom's functions is to create. . . . It is Wisdom in person who speaks: "I was with him forming all things" (Prov. 8:30). So we think of the Son when calling him the image of God invisible and the pattern to which all things are made, "The first-born of every creature, for in him were all things created in heaven and on earth" (Col. 1:15–16). Since "all things were made through him" (John 1:3) rightly do we think of the Son when it is written, "I am like a stream flowing from the waters of a great river." . . . Aristotle declares that the original that comes first is the cause of its copies that come after.[617]

FOX: What other functions does wisdom perform?

AQUINAS: The one who makes a thing is the one who can repair it, and so the restoration of creation is the third function of wisdom: "by wisdom were they healed" (Wis. 9:19). This especially was the work of the Son, who was made human in order to change the very state of our nature and restore everything human: "Through him reconciling all things unto himself, both

---

613. DV, q. 4, a. 1, ad 6.   614. ST I, q. 34, a. 3.   615. In Pss 32, p. 260.   616. ST I, q. 58, a. 6.   617. In I Sent, Prologue.

what is on earth and what is in heaven" (Col. 1:20). Justly then do we read these lines of the Son "I, like the stream of a river, and like a channel of a river came out of Paradise." This Paradise is the glory of God the Father, and from this paradise the Son descended into our vale of tears, not losing glory, but hiding it: "I came forth from the Father, and am come into the world" (John 16:28). Here let us pause to reflect how he came, and what was the fruit. How water rushes down! How Christ was urged by love of us throughout the mystery of his life! "A pent up stream, which the Spirit of the Lord drives on!" (Isa. 59:19).[618]

FOX: It is telling to me how your grasp of a theology of the Cosmic Christ and of Christ as Sophia or Wisdom puts the redemption, what you have just called the "restoration of creation," into a much broader context than is offered in a fall/redemption ideology. For you, redemption is the third work of wisdom, following on creation, which in turn follows on revelation of the nature of the Godhead.

AQUINAS: This is what the highest wisdom does: it manifests the hidden truths of Divinity; it produces the works of creation, and furthermore restores them at need; it brings them to the completion of achieving their own proper and perfect purpose.[619]

FOX: Please elaborate on the first work of wisdom: revealing the mystery of the Godhead.

AQUINAS: God alone knows the depths and riches of the Godhead, and divine wisdom alone can declare its secrets. Our knowledge of God, whatsoever it may be, comes from God, for imperfection is the shadow cast by perfection, and what is partial originates from what is complete. "Who shall know your thoughts if you do not give wisdom?" (Wis. 9:27). Above all the revelation of the Blessed Trinity is found in the deeds of the Son, who is the Word of God, uttered by the Father. "No one knows the Father but the Son, and those to whom it shall please the Son to reveal the Father" (Matt. 11:27).[620]

FOX: You said above that Christ came to earth from the "glory" of the Father. Would you elaborate on this?

AQUINAS: Christ is splendid first from the image of the Father, as Hebrews 1 puts it: "He is the splendor of God's glory, and

---

618. Ibid. 619. Ibid. 620. Ibid.

the image of God's substance." Second, by the light of the saints, as in Psalm 109: "From the womb of the morning I begot you in the splendor of the saints." Third, from a fullness of glory, as Matthew 7 puts it: "His face was resplendent like the sun." Fourth, by the rightness of his teaching, as in Isaiah 60: "The people will walk in your light, and the kings in the splendor of your rising."[621]

FOX: The words "glory" and "splendor" are always words denoting the Cosmic Christ in the Scriptures, and I am struck by how often you invoke them.

AQUINAS: In order for anyone to go straight along a road one must have some knowledge of the end. Thus an archer will not shoot the arrow straight unless he see the target first. Above all this is necessary when the road is hard and rough and the going is heavy, though the end is delightful. Now by his passion Christ achieved glory, not only of his soul, which he had from the first moment of his conception, but also of his body. Luke says: "Ought not Christ to have suffered these things, and so to enter into his glory?" (Luke 24:26). Christ brings those who follow the footsteps of his passion into this same glory.[622]

FOX: You link Christ's glory with his passion — what about the Transfiguration experience, was that not a moment of revelation of the glory of the Cosmic Christ as well?

AQUINAS: The clarity that Christ assumed in his Transfiguration was the clarity of glory as to its essence.[623] It was fitting that Christ should show his disciples the glory of his clarity, which is what it means to be transfigured. He will configure those who are his into this glory.[624] Christ wished to be transfigured in order to show human beings his glory and to arouse them to a desire for it themselves.[625]

FOX: Is this glory we are promised an awesome thing?

AQUINAS: It was fitting that the disciples were afraid and fell down when they heard the voice of the Father [at the Transfiguration], to show that the glory that was then being revealed surpasses in excellence the sense and faculty of all mortal beings, as in Exodus 33:20: "No one shall see me and live." . . . But human beings are healed of this weakness by Christ when he

---

621. In Is 62, p. 568.   622. ST III, q. 45, a. 1.   623. Ibid., a. 2.   624. Ibid., a. 1.   625. Ibid., a. 3.

brings them into glory. And this is meant by what Christ says to the disciples: "Arise, and fear not."[626]

FOX: I was moved above when you applied Jesus' attraction as teacher to this walking in the light, this allurement to his glory or splendor. Can you elaborate on Jesus as teacher?

AQUINAS: Take note of the saying in Isaiah (32): "Happy those who sow beside the waters," for the teaching of the Lord is water. First, because it is abundant. Ecclesiasticus 24 says: "I have poured forth rivers of my wisdom." Second, because it makes things cool, as Proverbs puts it (25): "Cold water for the thirsty soul." Third, because it makes fruitful, as in Isaiah 55: "As the rain descends from the sky and does not return there on its own, but soaks the earth, and makes it sprout, so will the word be that goes out of my mouth." Fourth, because it moves quickly, as John 4 says: "In him there will be a spring of running water gushing up to eternal life." Fifth, because it shapes itself for individuals, as Proverbs puts it (5): "Divide your waters into channels."[627]

FOX: And so a disciple is one who follows Christ the teacher?

AQUINAS: It should be noted that some people follow Christ through the integrity of the flesh, as in Revelation 14: "For these are virgins, and they follow the lamb wherever it goes." Others follow Christ through the intention of the heart, as Philippians 3 puts it: "I press on so that I may understand in some way." Others through the suffering of tribulation, as in 1 Peter 2: "Christ suffered for us leaving an example for you, so that you may follow in his footsteps." Others, through the observation of the commandments. Job says (23): "My foot followed in his footsteps, I kept to his path and did not turn aside from it." Others, through the reception of glory, as Ecclesiasticus puts it (23): "To follow the Lord is great glory; for a long span of days will be given them."[628]

FOX: Yet Christ as wisdom is not only the teacher but the thing taught—wisdom itself.

AQUINAS: Christ is the book. A book is an instrument in which there are conceptions of the heart—but in Christ there are conceptions of the divine intellect. Colossians (2) says: "In him are

---

626. Ibid., a. 4, ad 4.   627. In Is 32, p. 515.   628. In Jer 17, p. 621.

hidden all the treasures of the wisdom and knowledge of God."
The heading of the book is God the Creator (1 Cor. 11): "The
head of Christ is God." And in the heading of the book, that is,
in the will of God the Father it has been written, that means
ordained, concerning me, that I will come.[629]

FOX: The following of Christ, who is the Wisdom, the Word,
and the Child of God, would seem to be part of our creative
response to hearing Christ preach Good News.

AQUINAS: The reason Paul says (Phil. 1:21), "for to me to live
is Christ and to die is gain," is based on the fact that he is entirely
dedicated to the service of Christ. . . . Now, life produces activity, for that seems to be at the root of one's life which is the
principle of one's activity. Hence some call that by which they
are roused to activity their "life." Hunters, for example, call
hunting their life, and friends their friend. So, Christ is our life,
because the whole principle of our life and activity is Christ.[630]

FOX: And so the activity and creativity of preaching Christ was
Paul's response to his spiritual calling; it was Paul's power or
virtue and work?

AQUINAS: Paul talks about his confidence when he says that
"with full courage now as always Christ will be honored in my
body." As if to say, many persecute me, but I put my trust in
the Lord: "I will trust, and will not be afraid" (Isa. 12:2). He
shows his intention is right because "Christ will be honored."
Since Christ is God, he cannot be honored (increased) or diminished in himself, but in us, that is, in our knowledge. For
one honors Christ when one increases one's knowledge of him:
"Who can extol him as he is?" (Eccles. 43:31). And this in word
and deed when the greatness of Christ's effects shows Christ's
greatness.[631]

FOX: And so when we birth our response to Christ, we both
honor Christ and display the greatness of Christ?

AQUINAS: As long as the marvelous effects of Christ lie hidden
in anyone's heart, Christ is not honored by it, except in that
heart, but not in regard to others, until it breaks out into external, visible actions. This is why Paul says "in my body."

---

629. In Pss 39, p. 302.   630. In Phil 1.21, p. 509.   631. Ibid.

Christ is honored in our body in two ways: in one way, inasmuch as we dedicate our body to his service by employing our bodies in his service: "Glorify God in your body" (1 Cor. 6:20); in another way by risking our body for Christ: "If I deliver my body to be burned" (1 Cor. 13:3). The first is accomplished by life, the second by death.[632]

FOX: I like this idea that our work and creativity is an expression of our "glorifying God" in our bodies, for all art and creativity are so bodily; in some ways we sacrifice our bodies in our work of generating. We do pay a bodily price for what we give birth to.

AQUINAS: Paul says, "if it is to be life in the flesh, that means fruitful labor for me;" as if to say, if Christ is glorified in my body as long as I am alive, my life in the flesh will bear fruit, that is, if life brings me as its fruit that Christ is honored, life in the flesh is good and fruitful: "The return [fruit] you get is sanctification and its end, eternal life" (Rom. 6:22).[633]

FOX: So our work is fruitful when it is in Christ or with Christ.

AQUINAS: Isaiah says (7:2) that "his name will be called Emmanuel," that is, God-with-us, because Christ is with us in many ways. First, like a brother, through natural kinship. Song of Songs (8) says: "Who will give you to me as a brother nursed at the breasts of my mother, so that I may find you beside me, and kiss you?" Second, like a husband, through the bonds of love. John 14 says: "If someone loves me, he will keep my word." Third, like a shepherd, through the solace of a maternal comfort. Revelation (3) says: "Behold, I am standing at the door and knocking. If anyone hears my voice and opens the door, I will enter their house, and dine with them." Fourth, like a savior, through the help of protection. Jeremiah (30) says: "So do not fear, my servant Jacob, says the Lord, and Israel do not be afraid, since lo I will save you from a faraway land." Fifth, like a leader, through the example of work. Exodus says (32): "The Lord alone was his leader."[634]

FOX: Doesn't Christ also promise us the Holy Spirit?

AQUINAS: The Holy Spirit is promised to those who believe: "I will put a new spirit within you . . . and I will give you a new

---

632. Ibid. 1.20, p. 509   633. Ibid. 1.22, p. 510.   634. In Is 7, p. 462.

Spirit" (Isa. 37:7). By the very fact that this Spirit is given to us we become the children of God.[635]

FOX: What are some implications of Christ's sending the Holy Spirit?

AQUINAS: In Psalm 45 the Holy Spirit is called "oil," since oil surpasses all liquids, so the Holy Spirit surpasses all creatures. Genesis 1 says: "The Spirit of the Lord hovered over the waters," that is, it ought to hover over all in the hearts of human beings, since it is the love of God. Second, because of its sweetness. Compassion and all sweetness of mind is from the Holy Spirit. 2 Corinthians (6) says: "In sweetness, in gentleness, in the Holy Spirit." Third, because oil is diffusive, as the Holy Spirit is communicative. Consider 2 Corinthians, at the end: "May the fellowship of the Holy Spirit be with you all, amen." And Romans 5: "The love of God is in your hearts through the Holy Spirit." Likewise oil is the lotion of fire and heat, and the Holy Spirit fosters and nourishes the heat of love in us. The Song of Songs says: "His lamps are lamps of fire." Likewise, oil illuminates, just like the Holy Spirit, as Job puts it (32): "The inspiration of the Almighty gives understanding."[636]

FOX: Why does Psalm 45 speak of "the oil of happiness"? How does this relate to the creative process of the Holy Spirit enlightening us?

AQUINAS: It is called the oil of happiness because in the time of happiness Easterners anoint themselves with oil. Isaiah (61) says: "The oil of joy instead of grief." The Holy Spirit is the cause of joy, as Romans says (14): "And joy in the Holy Spirit." Galatians (5) says: "Love, joy, peace" because the Holy Spirit cannot be in anyone without their rejoicing in the good and in the hope of future good.[637]

FOX: You seem to be addressing the disease of acedia once again when you celebrate the Holy Spirit as the "oil of joy." It would seem that part of the "restoration" or redemption that Christ brought us was this ability to once again experience joy and goodness, hope and a future.

AQUINAS: Christ was the ointment above all the other saints. John 1 says: "We saw him full of grace and of truth." His co-workers are said to be anointed, since whatever of that oil is

---

635. In Eph 1.13, p. 451.   636. In Pss 44, p. 323.   637. Ibid.

kept, that is, of the grace of the Holy Spirit, is from the over-flowing of Christ. John 1 says: "Of his fullness we have all received." And Psalm 133 says, "like an ointment on the head," etc.[638]

FOX: It is interesting to hear you play with the theme of "oil" and "anointing" in the context of the Cosmic Christ, since the word "Christ" simply signifies "the anointed one."

AQUINAS: "Christ" is a Greek word that means "anointed." Kings and priests were anointed. Thus Jesus is a king and a priest. As the angel says in Luke 2:11, "There is born to us today a savior who is Christ the Lord." He is the Christ in a singular way because others are anointed with visible oil, he with invisible oil, that is, the Holy Spirit, and more abundantly than all the others. Psalm 45:7 has, "God your God has anointed you with the oil of gladness above your fellows." It is above your fellows because, as is stated above in John 3:34, "It is not by measure that he gives the Spirit."[639]

FOX: So Jesus truly fulfills his name as "the Christ," the "anointed one."

AQUINAS: God the Father anointed Christ with the oil of sacerdotal dignity, like a priest with the purpose of offering sacrifices. Ecclesiasticus 45 says: "He anointed him with holy oil." Second, [it was an oil] of regal power, like a king for the purpose of governing. 2 Kings 12 says: "I anointed you king and leader of my people." Third, an oil of boundless courage, like a fighter for the purpose of fighting. 2 Kings 1 says: "How has the shield of the brave been cast down, the shield of Saul and Jonathan, as if it had not been anointed with oil?" Fourth, an oil of outstanding delight, like a generous person for the purpose of showing compassion. Psalm 112 says: "A handsome man who shows compassion and is kind." Psalm 45 says: "God your God anointed me with the oil of joy above your companions." Likewise the devoted servant anointed Christ first with the tears of compunction. Matthew 6 says: "Anoint your head and wash your face." Second, with the ointment of devotion. Luke 7 says: "But this one anointed my feet with an ointment." Third, with the oil of pure intention. Ecclesiastes 9 says: "Wear white all the

---

638. Ibid.   639. In Jn 11.27, n. 1520.

time, do not stint your head of oil." Fourth, with the oil of praise and thanksgiving, as in Genesis 28: "Rising up in the morning, Jacob took a stone . . . and set it up it as a sign, pouring oil upon it."[640]

FOX: You said above that there was a fourth function that wisdom performs. Please elaborate on that, and on Christ's role in performing that function.

AQUINAS: A fourth function of divine wisdom is the fostering of things to the fulfillment of their purpose. Otherwise, what is left but vanity? Vanity, which wisdom will not abide, for wisdom "reaches from end to end mightily and orders all things sweetly" (Wis. 8:1). And when are we at ease but when we have arrived and rest where we desire to be? This is the doing of the Son, the true natural son of the Father, who brings us into the glory of his birthright: "for it became him for whom are all things and by whom are all things, who has brought many children to glory" (Heb. 2:10).[641]

FOX: And so Christ has brought about our own sonship and daughtership in the glory of God?

AQUINAS: When Paul says (Rom. 8) "through whom we cry out," he shows that we are children of God by our own testimony. For we profess to have God as our father by God's own instruction when we say in prayer, "Our father who art in heaven." This is true of both Jews and Gentiles, and so he writes two words meaning the same thing, "Abba," which is Hebrew, and "Pater," which is Greek or Latin. Thus the Lord says in Mark 14:36, "Abba, Father, everything is possible to you." Jeremiah says, "You will call me father" (3:19). This we say not so much with the sound of our voices as with the intention of our hearts, which because of its greatness is called a "cry," as it was said to a silent Moses in Exodus 19:15, "Why do you cry to me?" This powerful intention proceeds from filial love, which the Spirit produces in us, and therefore Paul says "through which" (meaning the Holy Spirit) "we cry Abba, Father."[642]

FOX: And Christ, by sending the Spirit, has made this filial relationship possible—or at least known to us?

---

640. In Is 61, p. 567.   641. In 1 Sent, Prologue.   642. In Rom, ch. 8, p. 80.

AQUINAS: When Paul says, "the Spirit himself gives witness," he shows that we are sons and daughters through the testimony of the Spirit, lest someone say that we were deceived in our witnessing. Thus he is saying that in the Spirit we cry "Abba, Father." For the Spirit gives testimony that we are children of God. He gives this testimony, not with an exterior voice to human ears, as the Father declared about the Son in Matthew 3; rather, he gives testimony through the effects of filial love, which he produces in us. Therefore Paul says "he gives testimony" not to human ears but "to our spirit that we are children of God."[643]

FOX: Being children of God is also being heirs of a divine inheritance.

AQUINAS: Someone is said to be an heir who receives or acquires the principal goods of another—not when they receive only a small amount. For we read in Genesis (25:5) that Abraham "gave everything he owned to Isaac, to the sons of his concubines, he gave gifts." The principal good by which God is rich is God's very self. God is not rich through something else, because God does not need extrinsic goods, as is stated in Psalm 16: Thus the children of God obtain God's self as an inheritance.[644]

FOX: But a child does not gain the inheritance unless the parent dies. It would seem then that human beings cannot be heirs of God, because God never dies.

AQUINAS: This is true in regard to material things, which cannot be possessed by many at the same time, and therefore it is necessary that one die so that another may take possession. Spiritual goods, however, can be possessed by many at the same time. Therefore, it is not necessary that the father die so that the children may be heirs. Paul also describes this inheritance in relation to Christ. He, as the principal son, in whom we all participate in sonship, is the principal heir to whom we are all united in the inheritance.[645]

FOX: In other words we also become Cosmic Christs. Does that mean we also become bearers of cosmic wisdom?

AQUINAS: John 1:12 says: "He gave them the power to become the children of God" and 1 John 4:16 says: "Those who abide

---

643. Ibid.   644. Ibid.   645. Ibid.

in love abide in God and God in them."[646] In using the phrase "the children of God" we are touching on the reward of Wisdom. For we are called God's children by taking on the likeness of God's natural and only-begotten Son—"chosen especially long ago and intended to become true images of God's Son" (Rom. 8:29). This Son is begotten Wisdom.[647]

FOX: It sounds as if we also became bearers of wisdom with Christ's support.

AQUINAS: Wisdom as a gift is more excellent than wisdom as an intellectual virtue, for it touches God more intimately by a kind of union of the soul with God. Wisdom is able to direct us not only in contemplation but also in action.[648]

FOX: Once again I hear you celebrating how our work (what you just called our "action") flows from our hearts (contemplation).

AQUINAS: To wisdom belongs first of all contemplation, which is the vision of the Beginning; following this comes the direction of human acts according to the divine order. The direction of wisdom does not result in any bitterness or toil in human acts; on the contrary, the result of wisdom is to make the bitter sweet, and labor a rest.[649]

FOX: How would you name the opposite of wisdom?

AQUINAS: Isidore says that "a fool is one who through dullness (*stuporem*) remains unmoved." Folly implies apathy in the heart and dullness in the senses. . . . For *sapiens* (wise) as Isidore says "is so named from *sapor* (savor), because just as the taste is quick to distinguish between savors of meats, so too a wise person is quick in discerning things and causes." Thus it is clear that folly is opposed to wisdom as its contrary . . . the fool has the sense, though dulled, whereas the wise person has the sense acute and penetrating.[650]

FOX: Your speaking of dullness and apathy speaks to me deeply of our need today for wisdom, as opposed to mere knowledge. Our knowledge has multiplied rapidly but our wisdom has not kept pace.

AQUINAS: Through the spirit of wisdom one has the eyes of one's heart enlightened in a clearer knowledge of God.[651]

---

646. In Jn 17.24, n. 2258.   647. ST II-II, q. 45, a. 6.   648. Ibid., a. 3, ad 1.   649. Ibid., ad 3.   650. Ibid., q. 46, a. 1.   651. In Eph 1.18, p. 452.

FOX: If we share in Christ's "Sophia" work as Wisdom, no doubt we also share in Christ's "Logos" work as a kind of word of God?

AQUINAS: Creatures manifest God's mind as effects manifest their causes. Thus creatures can be called God's words.[652] Just as by the work of creation the divine goodness is communicated to all creatures in a certain likeness, so by the work of adoption the likeness of natural sonship or daughtership is communicated to human beings, according to Romans 8:29.[653]

FOX: So we are God's sons and daughters, too.

AQUINAS: By adoption we are made brothers and sisters to Christ, as having with him the same Father, who is, nevertheless, Christ's Father in one way and ours in another.[654]

FOX: Why do we have to be adopted by God if we are the images of God already?

AQUINAS: Considered in its nature humanity is not a stranger in respect to God, as to the natural gifts bestowed on them. But as to the gifts of grace and glory, humanity is a stranger. It is in regard to these that human beings are adopted.[655]

FOX: Once again you are celebrating our divinization, since to be God's child is to participate in Divinity.

AQUINAS: Truly there is only one God, "although there are those who are called gods" by a genuine participation in Divinity, such as the saints. Psalm 82:6 says: "I have called you gods" whether in heaven, as the saints who possess heavenly glory, or on earth, as the saints still on the journey.[656]

FOX: And so we are participants in the divine nature by what you call "grace and glory"?

AQUINAS: Virtues dispose people in a higher manner and toward a higher end, and consequently in relation to some higher nature, that is, in relation to a participation in the divine nature according to 2 Peter 1:4. And it is in respect to receiving this nature that we are said to be born again as children of God.[657]

FOX: And so grace renders us still more godlike.

---

652. DV, q. 4, a. 1.   653. ST III, q. 23, a. 1, ad 2.   654. Ibid., a. 2, ad 2.   655. Ibid., a. 1, ad 1.   656. In 1 Cor, ch. 8, p. 214.   657. ST I-II, q. 110, a. 3.

AQUINAS: The light of grace . . . is a participation in the divine nature.[658] The gift of grace surpasses every capability of created nature, since it is nothing short of a partaking of the divine nature, which exceeds every other nature. . . . It is as necessary that God alone should deify, bestowing a partaking of the divine nature by a participated likeness, as it is that only fire can enkindle.[659]

FOX: You talk about God "deifying" us and about our participation in the divine nature—this is not familiar talk to most Christians of the Western church. Do you get this from the Scriptures?

AQUINAS: The Father loved the disciples . . . in order that they be gods through a sharing of grace. Psalm 82:5 says: "I have said, you are gods." And 2 Peter 1:4 says: "Through whom he has given great and precious promises to us, in order that through this we be made the divine consorts of nature." Likewise in order that they be taken up into a unity of feeling since "one who clings to God is one spirit" (1 Cor. 6:17). Romans 8:39 says: "The ones whom God has already known have become like in form to the image of his Son, in order that he himself may be only begotten among many brothers and sisters." So thus God the Father has manifested in the divine Son a greater good according to each of his natures, than the Son has manifested in his disciples. But nonetheless it is similar.[660]

FOX: Christ got himself in deep trouble for proclaiming his sonship, did he not? Can we expect the same difficulties?

AQUINAS: Everywhere people said, "he made himself the Son of God," as if he were not. But this is not against the law, as he proved to them in John 10:34, through Psalm 82:5: "I have said, you are gods." For if other people, who are adopted children, say that they are children of God without blasphemy, by how much more does Christ, who is through his nature the Son of God, say this without blasphemy? But since they did not understand eternal generation, therefore they considered it both false and blasphemous.[661]

FOX: It is telling that you credit the misunderstanding of Jesus' mission with a failure to grasp the Via Creativa—the "eternal generation"—of Divinity.

---

658. Ibid.   659. Ibid., q. 112, a.1.   660. In Jn 15.9, n. 1999.   661. In Jn 19.7, n. 2387.

AQUINAS: Divine good exists in every particular creature, but never totally perfect except in the Son and the Holy Spirit. Therefore it is not wholly pleasing to itself except in the Son, who has as much good as the Father. John 3:35: "The Father loves the Son, and has given all things into his hand."[662]

FOX: And so we are *truly* divine but not *fully* divine to the extent that Jesus is. Your Christology is so rich in this path of the Via Creativa—you don't see Christ as just the redeemer. But you have called him our brother, our teacher, our wisdom—Sophia, virtue incarnate, splendid and beautiful and full of glory, Son of God, cocreator and restorer of creation, Logos, revealer of the mystery of God, artist, a mighty water, dew, a sender of the Spirit of oil and compassion, justice and a teacher of justice whose words pierce like arrows, our husband, our shepherd, our leader, as well as our savior and brother who renders us participants in the divine nature. When I listen to you I feel that a fall/redemption theology that calls Christ exclusively "savior" has left us with a deeply impoverished Christology. Christ brings so many and varied gifts to us.

AQUINAS: Christ was given to us in the role of a doctor. Joel says (2): "Children of Sion exult, and take joy in the Lord your God, since he has given a doctor of justice to you." He is given us as a watchman also. Ezekiel (33) says: "Sons of man, I have given you as a watchman to the house of Israel." Also, as a defender. Isaiah 19 says: "He will send them a savior and defender to deliver them." Also, as a shepherd, as in Ezekiel 34: "And I will raise up for them a shepherd, to feed them." He is given us in the example of his labor, as in John 13: "For I have given an example to you, in order that you also may do as I have done." He is also given us in the food of a traveler, as in John 6: "The bread which I will give you is my flesh for the life of the world." Also, in the price of redemption, as in Matthew 20: "The son of man did not come to be served, but to serve, and to give his life as a ransom for many." Also, in the reward of recompense, as in Revelation 2: "I will give to the one who conquers to eat of the hidden manna."[663]

FOX: All those images are rich indeed—Christ as doctor of justice; as watchman; as a defender; as a shepherd; as a worker; as

---

662. In Mt 3, p. 36.   663. In Is 9, p. 469.

food for the traveler; as well as the price of redemption. And Christ also brings us glory, is that not so?

AQUINAS: It is Christ who brings us to glory, Christ who brings to birth the Church's faithful: "Shall not I that make others to bring forth children myself bring forth, says the Lord; shall I, that give birth to others, be barren, says the Lord your God?" (Isa. 66:9).[664]

FOX: How telling that you and Scripture both utilize the birthing imagery when speaking of Christ's work. You leave us with the image of Christ as mother, an appropriate way to conclude a discussion on the Via Creativa.

AQUINAS: By his human nature Christ is like a mother (*similis matri*).[665]

---

664. In I Sent, Prologue.   665. In Pss 41, p. 311.

Fourth Conversation:

ON THE
VIA TRANSFORMATIVA

Through compassion human beings imitate God.

(In Pss 40, p. 305)

*We find these two things, compassion and justice,
in all the works of God.*

(In Pss 24, p. 231)

FOX: Brother Thomas, we have been discussing the first three paths in creation spirituality: that of the Via Positiva, the way of delight, awe, and wonder; that of the Via Negativa, the way of silence, letting go, darkness, and suffering; and that of the Via Creativa, the way of birthing, imagination, creativity, and art as meditation. Now let us talk about Path Four, the Via Transformativa, wherein we take the energy of our creativity and apply it compassionately to the task of social transformation.

AQUINAS: The deepest changes according to the laws of nature are transformations.[1]

FOX: Indeed! There is nothing superficial about the Four Paths we are examining, and especially their culmination as found in the Via Transformativa. Let us begin at the heart of the matter: What role should compassion play in our spirituality?

AQUINAS: Through compassion human beings imitate God.[2]

FOX: "Imitation of God"—that would seem to be what a spiritual path is all about, the living out of our divinity.

AQUINAS: To be compassionate is proper to God the Father. . . . God is compassion itself.[3] God's holy name is the name of the divine compassion.[4]

FOX: If compassion comprises our imitation of God, then we really need to delve deeply into the meaning and practice of compassion, don't we? What do we mean when we say to imitate God is to be compassionate?

AQUINAS: In every work of God, viewed at its primary source, there appears compassion. In all that follows, the power of compassion remains, and works indeed with even greater force.[5]

---

1. ST III, q. 75, a. 4.   2. In Pss 40, p. 305.   3. In 2 Cor, ch. 1, p. 301.
4. In Pss 32, p. 264.   5. ST I, q. 21, a. 4.

FOX: You are saying that the first source of all God's work is compassion?

AQUINAS: The effect of the divine compassion is the foundation of all the divine works.[6]

FOX: Why is this so?

AQUINAS: Compassion is especially to be attributed to God, as seen in its effect, but not as an affection of passion. The proof of this is that one is said to be compassionate (*misericors*) because one has a sorrowful heart (*miserum cor*); being affected with sorrow at the misery of another as though it were one's own. This urges one to try to dispel the misery of the other as if it were one's own. And this is the *effect* of compassion. It does not belong to God to sorrow over the misery of others, but it does belong to God most properly to dispel that misery, whatever be the defect we call by that name. Now defects are not removed except by the perfection of some kind of goodness: and the primary source of goodness is God. . . . Insofar as perfections given to things by God expel defects, it belongs to compassion.[7]

FOX: I have to say that I am not at home with the idea that God does not undergo sorrow of heart. Your argument seems to be almost a linguistic one—that in Latin the word for compassion means a sorrowful heart; but in our language the word for compassion means "passion with." I think that this word gets closer to your emphasis on responding to another "as if it were one's own."

AQUINAS: God is compassionate.[8] God is "rich in compassion because of the abundant charity by which God loved us." (Eph. 2.4) . . . We can think of a fourfold goodness and efficacy of the divine love. First, it brought us into existence: "For you love all things that are, and hate none of the things which you have made" (Wis. 11:25). Second, God made us according to the divine image, capable of enjoying God's own beatitude: "You who have such love for our ancestors, in your hand are all the holy ones" (Deut. 33:3). Third, God restored some corrupted by sin. "Yes, I have loved you with an everlasting love, therefore have I drawn you, taking pity on you" (Jer. 31:8). Fourth, for our salvation God gave up God's own Son: "For God so loved the world, as to give the only begotten Son" (John 3:16).[9]

---

6. Ibid., q. 25, a. 3, ad 3.   7. Ibid., q. 21, a. 3.   8. Ibid., ad 2.   9. In Eph, 2.4, p. 458.

FOX: Explain more how we can say that God is "rich in compassion."

AQUINAS: When love brings forth goodness in the beloved, then it is a love springing from compassion. The love with which God loves us produces goodness in us; hence compassion is presented here as the root of the divine love: "I will remember the tender mercies of the Lord, the praise of the Lord for all the things that the Lord has bestowed upon us . . . which God has given them according to the divine kindness and according to the multitude of the divine mercies" (Isa. 63:7).[10]

FOX: It is telling that you link compassion with goodness or the Via Positiva. You seem to celebrate goodness and compassion as almost identical.

AQUINAS: Compassion and goodness are in God as in a subject, but they differ in reason. For in God goodness is considered as the sharing of goods among creatures, since goodness diffuses itself. Compassion in fact means a special outpouring of goodness for removing misery. Therefore the psalmist sings: "remember me according to your compassion," and not according to my sins.[11]

FOX: So God's compassion is very great?

AQUINAS: Joel says (2): "Turn to the Lord your God since God is kind and compassionate, rich in compassion and ready to relent."[12]

FOX: How is God's compassion different from our own?

AQUINAS: Isaiah says that the fruit of returning [to God] is compassion, "And let him return to the Lord . . . since God is full of a manifold compassion." . . . The impediments to compassion are excluded when God says: "My thoughts are not your thoughts," as if to say, "You are impious, I pious; you meditate revenge; I, compassion."[13] God is said to be rich in compassion because God possesses an infinite and unfailing compassion, which human beings do not. For humanity has a compassion that is bounded or limited in three ways. First, in bestowing temporal benefits, humanity's compassion is restricted by the amount of one's own possessions. "According to

---

10. Ibid.   11. In Pss 24, p. 231.   12. In Is 55, p. 556.   13. Ibid.

your ability be compassionate" (Tob. 4:8); whereas God is "rich unto all who call upon God" (Rom. 10:12). Second, the compassion of human beings is limited since they can only pardon offenses against themselves. Even with these there ought to be a certain qualification, for one should not forgive so indiscriminately that whoever is pardoned becomes more bold, prone and ready to offend again. "For, because sentence is not speedily pronounced against the evil, the children of men commit evils without any fear" (Eccles. 8:11). But nothing can harm God and hence God can forgive every offense: "If you sin, how will you hurt him?" . . . Third, one shows compassion in remitting punishment; yet here too a qualification must be observed: one must not contravene the justice of a higher law. God, on the other hand, can remit all punishment, since God is not bound by any higher law: "Who gave God charge over the earth? Or who set God over the world which God made?" (Job 34:13). Thus the compassion of God is infinite because it is not limited by a scarcity of wealth, nor is it restricted through a fear of injury, nor by a higher law.[14]

FOX: God's compassion is infinite, you say.

AQUINAS: Divine compassion does not have a measurement, and always exceeds judgment.[15]

FOX: Is it also eternal?

AQUINAS: God's compassion is forever.[16] The compassion of God is peaceful in prosperity and in adversity. As regards prosperity, the psalmist says (42): "By day the Lord ordered the divine compassion," that is, in the time of prosperity, as if to say, "whatever prosperity I have, I impute to divine compassion." Lamentations says (3): "The compassion of the Lord never ceases." As regards adversity, the psalmist says, "and at night"—that is, in the time of adversity—"God put the divine song on my lips,"—that is, joy, which is the greatest consolation. This comes from divine compassion.[17]

FOX: And so compassion is present in the dark and in the light—in the Via Negativa and in the Via Positiva.

AQUINAS: Whatever God makes in us is either from justice or from compassion or from truth. From justice when one gives

---

14. In Eph 2.4, pp. 458–59.   15. In Is 2, p. 439.   16. In Pss 51, p. 353.
17. In Pss 41, p. 312.

back what is due. From truth, when one gives back what has been promised. From compassion, when one surpasses what was due or promised. Let us prove these three things. The justice of God is great, since nothing so great is merited but that God returns more. Truth is greater, since God promises and gives what we never merited, like the incarnation and other things that pertain to the mystery of redemption. But compassion is the greatest: for God bestows things that we cannot even conceive. As 1 Corinthians 2 says: "The eye has not seen, etc." And so the psalmist compares justice to the mountains, truth to clouds, which are higher, and compassion to the skies, which are over all things. He says, "Lord, your compassion is in the sky," that which is cause of all my goods is in the sky.[18]

FOX: It is striking indeed that you talk of compassion as the "greatest" of the mysteries of God, a power that envelops all things, like the sky itself.

AQUINAS: Psalm 33 says: "The earth is full of the compassion of God." And in all things compassion has a place. For just people have preserved innocence on account of the compassion of God. Likewise sinners have been turned toward justice on account of the compassion of God. 1 Timothy 1 says: "I have received compassion." Likewise those living in sin have experienced the compassion of God, and Lamentations says (3): "The compassion of the Lord is manifold, so that we have not been consumed."[19]

FOX: To picture the divine compassion as like the sky is to image how omnipresent compassion is. It fills the earth *and* the universe.

AQUINAS: God's pitying is over all the divine works; for compassion does not signify a passion of the mind in God, but the divine goodness for overcoming misery.[20]

FOX: One feels hope when hearing about this omnipresent compassion of God.

AQUINAS: God's compassion is of great duration, as Isaiah says (54): "In eternal compassion I will have pity on you." Likewise it is with great power, for when God made the divine human, God brought the divine down from heaven to earth, and made

---

18. In Pss 35, p. 278. 19. In Pss 50, p. 345. 20. Ibid.

the immortal die. God's compassion has great effect, for the human being can be raised up from every misery through the divine compassion. Psalm 86 says: "Your compassion towards me is great, and you have forgiven the impiety of my sin." . . . In all things from the beginning of the world I have found the effects of your compassion.[21]

FOX: Now I better understand your insistence on our imitating God's compassion, for you see it as so powerful and so inclusive. Once again I sense a cosmic dimension—a deeply nonanthropocentric dimension—to your understanding of the divine love of things.

AQUINAS: The psalmist says that "the earth is full of the compassion of the Lord." Lo, he shows it through a sign, for all the fullness of the Earth proceeds from the compassion of God, since the Earth is not full with temporal but with spiritual goods; and this is especially true after the coming of Christ, as Acts says (2): "All were filled with the Holy Spirit." For all these come from the compassion of God. As Romans says (9): "It is not from human will or exertions, but from God having compassion." But the psalmist talks of "the Earth" and not the sky. Why? Because there is no misery in the sky, and therefore it does not need compassion. But the Earth—where human beings are filled with many miseries—needs the fullness of compassion.[22]

FOX: God's compassion is extended to all things on this earth.

AQUINAS: The hand of God is a hand of compassion in three ways. First, it is one of healing, as in Job 5: "The Godself makes the wound, and heals it; God's hands strike the blow, and they will heal it." Second, it is a hand of feeding, as in Psalm 95: "God's people, and the sheep of God's pasture." Third, it is a hand of crowning, as in Wisdom 5: "They will receive the crown of beauty and the jewels of splendor from the hand of the Lord."[23]

FOX: It seems that our path to God is necessarily a path of compassion, as you indicate. To find God is to find compassion, and vice versa.

AQUINAS: Among all the things that cause enjoyment concerning the Lord, there are two—namely, compassion and justice.

---

21. Ibid.   22. In Pss 32, p. 260.   23. In Is 8, p. 466.

Proverbs says (20): "Compassion and truth guard a king." For through justice subjects are defended. Take justice away, and no one will be secure and happy. Likewise without compassion, all are fearful and do not love. The psalmist shows this to be understood about God, when he says, "The Lord loves compassion and justice." For God loves them in themselves, since these things are in the work. As Psalm 25 puts it, "all the ways of the Lord [are] compassion and truth." Likewise, God loves them in each person, as Micah puts it (6): "I will show you, O people, what is good , and what the Lord requires of you." And so the psalmist says, "exult," for truly God "loves compassion."[24]

FOX: It is telling, I believe, how you link justice and compassion as both bringing joy in our experience of God.

AQUINAS: Justice without compassion is cruel, and compassion without justice is the mother of weakness. And therefore it is necessary that they be joined together according to Proverbs 3:3: "Compassion and truth will not forsake you, etc." And Psalm 85:10 says: "Compassion and truth have met, etc."[25]

FOX: Compassion, then, seems to be the path we need to take.

AQUINAS: Micah (6) says: "I will show you, O people, what is good, and what the Lord requires of you. Especially to do justice, to cherish compassion, and to walk humbly with your God."[26]

FOX: We will want to examine the relation between compassion and justice at greater length, for, as you point out, without justice, compassion can be sentimental or what you call the "mother of weakness."

AQUINAS: The progress of the Lord in the Lord's works refers to two things, namely, to compassion and to justice. For if something is said about God and humanity, it is understood according to the standard of each. Therefore, when compassion is said of God, it is understood according to the standard of God, and of humanity according to the standard of human beings. . . . We find these two things, compassion and justice, in all the works of God. . . . Compassion comes first, and after it follows justice. Therefore the psalmist says, "all the ways of the Lord [are] compassion and truth." And Tobias (3) says: "All

---

24. In Pss 32, p. 260.   25. In Mt 5, p. 52.   26. In Is 56, p. 557.

your ways [are] compassion and truth." And Psalm 145 says: "God's compassion over all the divine works."[27]

FOX: And so there is no compassion without justice?

AQUINAS: God is compassionate. God does not work in opposition to divine justice, but transcends it. Compassion is the fulfillment of justice, not its abolition.[28]

FOX: Please elaborate on the meaning of this path of compassion that we are called to travel.

AQUINAS: In Matthew's gospel we read: "Blessed are the compassionate for they themselves shall attain compassion." To be compassionate is to have a heart that suffers from the misfortune of others because we think of it as our own. But we are pained by our own misfortune and are eager to repel it, so you are truly compassionate when you are eager to repel the misfortune of others.[29]

FOX: So compassion is our capacity to treat others as ourselves—a sign of our radical interdependence.

AQUINAS: Compassion is the fullness of all graces.[30]

FOX: But I thought charity or love was the fulfillment of all grace, the entire law of God in two commandments of love.

AQUINAS: One must first of all love one's neighbor in order to love God worthily.[31] Job teaches that "he who robs his friend of compassion in the time of misery leaves fear of the Lord behind," that is, the reverence that he ought to have for God, on account of whom and in whom his neighbor must be loved. "He who does not love his brother whom he sees, how can he love God whom he does not see?" as is said in the first letter of John.[32]

FOX: I am struck by how you have just interpreted the phrase, "fear of the Lord"—namely, as the *reverence* we have for God and a reverence from which our compassion for our neighbor flows.

AQUINAS: We are truly compassionate when we work to remove the misfortune of others.[33]

---

27. In Pss 24, p. 231.   28. ST I, q. 21, a. 3, ad 2.   29. In Mt 5, p. 52.
30. In Jn 1.14b, n. 189.   31. Sermo, p. 101.   32. In Job, ch. 6, pp. 27–28.   33. In Mt 5, p. 52.

FOX: Several times you have alluded to the fact that when we relieve the misfortune of others we are truly relieving our own. Thus I hear you alluding to compassion as a consciousness of interdependence—that we truly are one with one another in our shared misery.

AQUINAS: Since sorrow or grief is about one's own ills, one grieves or sorrows for another's distress, insofar as one looks upon another's distress as one's own.[34] If all things are united with all things, it is necessary that all things come together into one whole. And thus, all things will share in one thing, as parts share in the shape of the whole.[35] Anything whose nature as such consists in being part of another is intent first and above all on that to which it belongs, rather than on itself. Instinctive manifestations are a pointer to this natural inclination; we observe that a member naturally exposes itself for the safety of the whole, as when without hesitation up goes the arm to ward off a blow.

Now, since reason imitates nature, a similar tendency is displayed in the political virtues, as when the good citizen risks death for the safety of the commonwealth: this is a natural motion if we suppose that people are born to belong to a state. God is the universal good, embracing pure spirits and humanity and all creatures. Every creature is entirely of God.[36]

FOX: You mention "political virtues." We are truly talking about political virtues in the Via Transformativa when we speak of justice and compassion, and these seem to be a further step in the development of virtue that we discussed in the Via Creativa.

AQUINAS: The human being is a social animal, and one's desire is not satisfied in providing for oneself, but one wants to be in a position to take care of others. This, however, must be understood within limits.[37]

FOX: And so political virtue is part of our moral behavior and decision making?

AQUINAS: Aristotle's work on the *Politics* [is] a conclusion to the whole work of the *Ethics*.[38]

---

34. ST II-II, q. 30, a. 2.   35. DDN, n. 979, p. 364.   36. ST I, q. 60, a. 5.   37. In Ethics I, L. 9, p. 49.   38. Ibid. X, L. 16, p. 942.

FOX: And what you call our "taking care of others" falls under the "political virtues," as you call them.

AQUINAS: Political science [is] the practical knowledge concerning human affairs.[39] Certainly it is a part of that love which should exist among people that a person preserve the good even of a single human being. But it is much better and more divine that this be done for a whole people and for states. . . . It is much more divine that it be done for a whole people that includes many states.[40]

FOX: And so to discuss the things we are discussing is a quasi-divine task.

AQUINAS: The end of political science is the good of humanity, that is, the supreme end of human affairs.[41] But we should note that Aristotle says political science is the most important, not simply, but in that division of practical sciences that are concerned with human affairs, the ultimate end of which political science considers. The ultimate end of the whole universe is considered in theology, which is the most important without qualification. He says that it belongs to political science to treat the ultimate end of human life.[42]

FOX: And yet to treat ultimate ends in human life such as justice and compassion, it seems that one must also have a deep grasp of human nature and the human soul.

AQUINAS: The political leader must know to some extent the things belonging to the soul, as the physician who treats the eyes and the whole body must study something about the eyes and the whole body. The obligation of a political leader to study the soul whose virtue he or she seeks is greater, because political science is more important than the science of medicine.[43]

FOX: When we speak of compassion we are truly including passion.

AQUINAS: Jeremiah demonstrates compassion when he says, "on account of this my inner being is crushed." He demonstrates a sense of humanity in which there is interior compassion and of "commiserating" in which there is interior aid. Hosea says (11): "My heart recoils within me, my compassion grows

---

39. Ibid.   40. Ibid. I, L. 2, p. 15.   41. Ibid., 14–15.   42. Ibid., 15.
43. Ibid. I, L. 19, p. 98.

warm and strong."[44] Compassion means grief for another's distress. Now this grief may denote, in one way, a movement of the sensitive appetite, in which case compassion is not a virtue but a passion.[45]

FOX: And so, with us human beings, compassion is indeed a passion. But it need not stop there. It is also a virtue in the fullest sense of the word.

AQUINAS: Compassion, considered as a virtue, is a moral virtue having relation to the passions. . . . Even as passions, these powers [of compassion] are praiseworthy. Yet nothing prevents them from proceeding from some habit of choice, in which case they assume the character of virtue.[46] Since it is essential to human virtue that the movements of the soul should be regulated by reason, it follows that compassion is a virtue.[47]

FOX: How does compassion compare to love?

AQUINAS: Compassion is a virtue and an effect proper to love.[48] What does Jesus mean when he says that the great commandment is to love "with all your heart and all your soul and all your mind?" There are in loving two things, the principle or source and the effect or result. The source of love can be either from passion or from the judgment of reason. It comes from passion when anyone does not know how to live without someone they love. It comes from reason insofar as one loves as reason dictates. The Lord says that one loves with all the heart when one loves bodily (*carnaliter*) and with all the soul when one loves from the judgment of reason. And we should love God in both ways. "Bodily" means that the heart is moved in regard to God, as in Psalm 84:2, "My heart and my flesh sing for joy to the living God." The third command, that is, "with the whole mind," is the result of loving because I freely see, think about, and do what pleases the one I love. "One who loves me will keep my words" (John 14:28). I refer everything to the one I love. "How lovely is your dwelling place, Oh Lord of hosts. My soul longs, and sighs, for the courts of the Lord" (Ps. 84:1).[49]

FOX: How does compassion compare to the other virtues?

AQUINAS: In itself compassion takes precedence over the other virtues, for it belongs to compassion to be bountiful to others,

---

44. In Jer 31, p. 649.   45. ST II-II, q. 30, a. 3.   46. Ibid., ad 4.   47. Ibid., a. 3.   48. Ibid., q. 36, a. 3, ad 3.   49. In Mt 22, p. 204.

and, what is more, to succor others in their wants, which pertains chiefly to one who is superior. Hence compassion is accounted as being proper to God: and therein God's omnipotence is declared to be chiefly manifest.[50]

FOX: What you say is most striking—that God's omnipotence is not to be understood as "power-over" or in terms of "judgment" but that it is expressed precisely in compassion. You touch on a great mystery here.

AQUINAS: God's compassion can be neither understood nor analyzed—it is unsearchable.[51]

FOX: What about compassion among us humans? Is that also our greatest "power," as it is for God?

AQUINAS: As regards human beings, who have God above them, charity, which unites them to God, is greater than compassion, whereby human beings supply the defects of their neighbor. But of all the virtues that relate to our neighbor, compassion is the greatest, even as its act surpasses all others. For it belongs to one who is higher and better to supply the defect of another, insofar as the latter is deficient.[52]

FOX: "Compassion is the greatest of the virtues," you say. That is quite a statement in light of our lengthy discussion in the Via Creativa on the power that the virtues are all about.

AQUINAS: Compassion likens us to God as regards similarity of works.[53] The sum total of the Christian religion consists of compassion as regards external works. But the inward love of charity, whereby we are united to God, takes precedence over both love and compassion for our neighbor.[54]

FOX: Compassion, then, is our way of expressing love of neighbor.

AQUINAS: In regard to the misfortune of our neighbors, we ought to have a heart that is suffering. 1 John 3:17 says: "Those who possess the substance of this world, and see their own brother or sister lacking, and close their own heart to them, how can God's charity remain in them?"[55] The love of neighbor requires that not only should we be our neighbor's well-wishers, but also their well-doers, according to 1 John 3:18: "Let us not

---

50. ST II-II, q. 30, a. 4.   51. In Eph 3.8, p. 469.   52. ST II-II, q. 30, a. 4.   53. Ibid., ad 3.   54. Ibid., ad 2.   55. In Mt 5, p. 52.

love in word, nor in speech, but in deed, and in truth." And in order to be a person's well-wisher and well-doer, we ought to succor their needs.[56]

FOX: "To succor their needs." Can you elaborate on these acts of compassion?

AQUINAS: The temporal goods that God grants us are ours as to the ownership; but as to the use of them, they belong not to us alone but also to those whom we are able to succor out of what we have over and above our needs.[57]

FOX: And so we owe it to others to assist them in this shared life of ours?

AQUINAS: The common good of many is more godlike than the good of an individual.[58] In a case of extreme necessity, all things are common property. Hence anyone who is in such dire straits may take another's goods in order to succor themselves, if they can find no one who is willing to give them something.[59]

FOX: This would seem to be fulfilling the law of compassion—in this case, toward oneself. When I hear you speak I feel that you are saying that compassion must happen one way or another. It is a law of the universe.

AQUINAS: The words of Ambrose apply, "feed him that is dying of hunger; if you have not fed him, you have slain him." [60]

FOX: Those are strong words from Ambrose—that our failure to be compassionate is at times tantamount to murder.

AQUINAS: The person who has gained riches is the one who should distribute them.[61] Matthew 5 says: "Blessed are the poor in spirit, since theirs is the kingdom of heaven." And Ecclesiasticus 31 says: "Blessed the rich person who is found blameless, etc." But a person may be rich in act, but not in attachment. And this situation can be healthy, as in the case of Abraham or King Louis of France. But another is rich both in act and in attachment—and this is not healthy. Concerning this it is discussed in Matthew 19 that "It is easier for a camel to enter etc." since as it is against nature for a camel to enter through the eye of a needle, so for a rich person to enter the kingdom of heaven

---

56. ST II-II, q. 32, a. 5.   57. Ibid., ad 2.   58. Ibid., q. 31, a. 3, ad 2.
59. Ibid., q. 32, a. 7, ad 3.   60. Ibid., a. 5.   61. CT I, 241.

is against divine justice. The latter persons are earth-born (*terrigemae*) while the former ones are the sons and daughters of the human race (*filii hominum*).[62]

FOX: And so it is what we do without wealth that determines whether we are compassionate or not according to the laws of divine justice?

AQUINAS: A person in hunger is to be fed rather than instructed; for a needy person money is better than philosophy, although philosophy is better simply speaking.[63] We are bound to give alms of our surplus, as also to give alms to one whose need is extreme.[64] Almsgiving is a matter of precept.[65]

FOX: And so our giving of alms is one expression of compassion?

AQUINAS: The works of mercy are properly speaking acts of compassion. . . . They are acts of love through the medium of compassion.[66]

FOX: What about other works of mercy?

AQUINAS: Corporal need occurs either during this life or afterward. If it occurs during this life. . . . The internal need is twofold: one need is relieved by solid food, namely, the need of the hungry. Thus we are told to "feed the hungry." While another is relieved by liquid food, namely, thirst, and thus we are told to "give drink to the thirsty." The common need with regard to external help is twofold: one concerns clothing, and for this we are told to "clothe the naked"; while the other concerns a dwelling place, and for this we are told to "shelter the homeless." If the need is a special one, it is either the result of an internal cause, like sickness, and so we are told to "visit the sick," or it results from an external cause, and then we are to "ransom the captive." After this life we "bury the dead."[67]

FOX: And what about the so-called spiritual works of mercy?

AQUINAS: Spiritual needs are relieved by spiritual acts in two ways, first, by asking for help from God, and in this respect we have *prayer,* whereby one person prays for others; second, by offering human assistance, and this happens in three ways. First, in order to relieve a deficiency on the part of the intellect, and

---

62. In Pss 48, p. 335.   63. ST II-II, q. 32, a. 3.   64. Ibid.   65. Ibid.
66. Ibid., a. 1.   67. Ibid., a. 2.

if this deficiency is in the speculative intellect, the remedy is applied by *teaching,* and if in the practical intellect, the remedy is applied by *counseling.* Second, there may be a deficiency on the part of the appetitive power, especially by way of sorrow, which is remedied by *comforting.* Third, the deficiency may be due to an inordinate act, . . . for example, the remedy for the sinner takes the form of *reproof.* . . . In respect of the person sinned against—if it is committed against ourselves—we apply the remedy by *pardoning the injury.* . . . If the sinner is an annoyance to those who live with him . . . the remedy is applied by *bearing with him.*[68]

FOX: What do you see to be the principal obstacles to compassion?

AQUINAS: The impediment to compassion is usually of two kinds. The first is a contempt for the wretched, whom some do not think worthy of compassion. Those are accustomed to be despised who are badly clothed, and to be honored who wear expensive clothing. Whence it is said in Ecclesiasticus 19: "What the clothing of the body reveals about the man." But Job excludes this impediment to compassion from himself when he adds, "If I looked down upon the passer-by," that is, any stranger going along the way, "and the poor person because he lacked clothing," I (Job) understand these or other things may befall me. Not only have I not looked down upon anyone in need of clothing, but I have even provided them with what they need. Thus he adds: "If his limbs have not blessed me," which of course when uncovered I have covered, and they were thus an occasion for blessing me. And he explains his reasoning, adding, "and he has been warmed by the wool of my sheep," namely, through the clothing given to him.

But a second impediment to compassion is assurance of one's own power, by which it seems to anyone that they can burden others with impunity and especially inferior persons. And this Job excludes from himself when he says, "If I had raised my hand against an orphan," namely, with the result that I have oppressed him, "especially when I had supporters at the gate," that is, in the place of judgment, "superior," that is, more powerful. But it is just that a person be deprived of those limbs that

---

68. Ibid.

he uses for injustice; and therefore he adds a loss as a punishment, not only of a hand but even of an arm, in which the hand is rooted, and of the shoulder, to which the arm is attached; whence he adds: "Let my shoulder fall from its joint and my arm be broken," namely, if I have debased my hand by the oppression of the poor.[69]

FOX: Are there other examples of obstacles to compassion that you could mention?

AQUINAS: Jesus explains the parable of the sower and, because he had spoken of two kinds of ground, he explains first the bad ground and then the good. He also divides the bad ground into three, that along the path, that among rocks, and that with thorns. Toward the understanding of all this, you should know that hearing the word of God should have as its first effect that it be implanted in the heart—"Blessed is anyone who meditates on the law of the Lord day and night" (Ps 1:2) and "I have laid up your word in my heart, that I may not sin against you" (Ps. 119:11). A second effect is that it should be carried into action. In some the first effect is blocked; in others, the second. . . . The latter effect is blocked by both prosperity and adversity.[70]

FOX: It is interesting to hear you explain the teachings of Jesus as lessons in compassion.

AQUINAS: The will of Christ is twofold, namely, of compassion and of justice. But it is first indeed concerned with compassion both of itself and in itself, since "God's compassion is over all God's works" (Ps. 145:9) and "God wants everyone to become free" (1 Tim. 2: 4).[71] As is said elsewhere, "all the ways of the Lord [are] compassion and truth." This is why thanksgiving pertains first to the effects of justice, as the psalmist puts it, "your right hand is full of justice." The psalmist lays out the perfection of divine compassion and the effect of this perfection.[72]

FOX: And you find this perfection of compassion in Jesus Christ?

AQUINAS: In a certain way compassion is Christ himself, who was given to us out of the compassion of God. As psalm 102 puts it, "Since the time for compassion has come." This can be

---

69. In Job, ch. 31, p. 107.   70. In Mt 13, p. 128.   71. In Jn 17.24, n. 2253.   72. In Pss 47, p. 333.

explained from the two forms of the temple and the two forms of undertaking—namely, the bodily (and the spiritual) temple. Thus these are the words of the just Simeon: "O God, we take your compassion, namely Christ, into our arms in the midst of your [material] temple." Likewise, these words can be understood concerning the reception of faith. Thus the sense is, "O God, we take Christ, given compassionately, into our arms through faith." James says (1): "In meekness receive the inborn word."[73] Proverbs (16) says: "The throne of the king is strengthened by justice" for the compassion of neighbors. Isaiah says (16): "And a throne of compassion will be made ready, and he will sit on it in truth in the tabernacle of David." And for the grace of humility, Ezekiel (43) says: "This is the place of my throne, and the place for the soles of my feet, where I dwell in the midst of the sons and daughters of Israel for ever."[74]

FOX: If "Christ is compassion," as you say, then there is little wonder that his teachings culminate in his teaching about compassion. Wisdom teaches wisdom and compassion teaches compassion.

AQUINAS: Compassion is the fire the Lord came to send on the earth (cf. Luke 12).[75]

FOX: Why "fire"?

AQUINAS: Compassion proceeds from love of God and neighbor, which is a consuming fire.[76]

FOX: Indeed! Compassion is a kind of *passion,* a fire in the belly.

AQUINAS: Take note of Isaiah's saying, "his tongue is like fire," because charity is called a fire primarily because it illuminates. Ecclesiasticus 2 says: "You who fear God love God, and your hearts will be enlightened." Second, because it warms. Song of Songs (2) says: "Support me with flowers, refresh me with apples, since I languish from love." Third, because God turns all things toward the Godhead, as Romans (8) puts it: "We know that for those who love God all things work together for good." Fourth, because it is made easy. John 14 says: "If anyone loves me, they will keep my word." Fifth, because it raises one up. Song of Songs (3) says: "Upon my bed I sought him whom my soul loves; I sought him, and did not find him."[77]

---

73. Ibid.   74. In Jer 14, p. 614.   75. In 2 Cor, ch. 11, p. 364.   76. Ibid.
77. In Is 30, p. 513.

FOX: The image of fire also conjures up sacrificial offerings, which were invariably burnt offerings.

AQUINAS: "I desire compassion and not sacrifice" is written in Hosea 6:6, and it is explained in two ways. First, so that one thing is understood to be preferred to another: since I wish for compassion more than for judgment. Thus compassion is preferred to sacrifice. Sacrifice is the lamb, and likewise compassion. For God pities such victims. What is better than those? Proverbs (21:3) says: "It is more pleasing to God to show compassion and justice than to offer sacrifice." . . . "I wish for compassion and not a sacrifice" also means that one wishes for that which one desires on account of itself and not for the sake of something else.[78]

FOX: And so compassion is the ultimate form of sacrifice to God?

AQUINAS: Certain things have been accepted by God in themselves, like the work of justice, charity, faith, and virtue. And this is spoken about in Deuteronomy 10: "Now, Israel, what does the Lord your God ask from you? Except that you serve the Lord your God with your heart and soul." But God does not accept an offering for what it is in itself, as Psalm 50 says: "What, will I eat flesh, etc." No. But what? In the same psalm God says: "Let thanksgiving be your sacrifice to God, etc."[79]

FOX: Now you are raising another dimension of compassion, that of praise, thanksgiving, and celebration. This seems to be the sacrifice God most wants from us.

AQUINAS: God prefers that we offer a sacrifice of the lips, that is, of praise of the works of God, rather than a sacrifice of animals. And so the psalmist talks about "ears, etc." as if to say: "You ask that of me which you gave me in the first place, namely, the virtue of seeking wisdom. And you ask this, that I show the wisdom which we receive for this purpose, that we may declare and prophesy." Isaiah 50 says: "The Lord has opened my ears."[80]

FOX: And this kind of offering is the best kind of worship, it would seem.

---

78. In Mt 9, p. 91.   79. In Pss 39, p. 302.   80. Ibid.

AQUINAS: We worship God by external sacrifices and gifts, not for God's own profit but for that of ourselves and our neighbor. For God does not need our sacrifices, but wishes them to be offered to God in order to arouse our devotion and to profit our neighbor. Hence compassion . . . is a sacrifice more acceptable to God because it leads us more directly to our neighbor's well-being, as Hebrews (13:16) says: "Do not forget to do good and to share what you have, for by such sacrifices God's favor is obtained."[81]

FOX: Will you comment more on how Christ is compassion and a teacher of compassion?

AQUINAS: When we admonish those who are falling away to come back, we are compassionate. Matthew (9:36) reports that "Jesus, seeing the crowds, was moved by compassion." So those who are compassionate are happy (see Matthew 5:2). And why? "Because they themselves will obtain compassion." And it should be known that the gifts of God always exceed our merits, as Ecclesiasticus (33:11) says: "When the Lord recompenses, God will recompense you seven times over." Therefore the compassion that the Lord bestows on us is far greater than that which we bestow on our neighbor.[82]

FOX: I sense a deep trust is necessary for compassion.

AQUINAS: Compassion is the cause of trust.[83] The actual counsel [in Matthew 5] is this: That amidst the afflictions of this world we will attain compassion.[84]

FOX: Hope indeed! Compassion is attainable in this life. We seem to be touching on a certain antidote to despair in our time when we can promise that compassion is possible.

AQUINAS: The reason why presumption is less a sin than despair is that it is more characteristic of God to have compassion and to spare than it is to punish. Compassion springs from God's very being; punishment is occasioned by our fault.[85]

FOX: On several occasions in this discussion on compassion you have connected justice and compassion. It seems appropriate now to pursue the topic of justice in greater depth. How do justice and compassion relate?

---

81. ST II-II, q. 30, a. 4, ad 1.   82. In Mt 5, p. 52.   83. In Pss 39, p. 50.
84. In Mt 5, p. 52.   85. ST II-II, q. 21, a. 2.

AQUINAS: The work of divine justice always presupposes the work of compassion and is founded upon it. . . . Why is it that we have human nature except for the divine generosity? And so compassion is the root in each and every divine work, and its virtue persists in everything that grows out of that, and even more vehemently flourishes there.[86]

FOX: Are you saying that compassion is more encompassing than justice—though by no means exclusive of it?

AQUINAS: The order of justice would be served by much less than that which is in fact granted by divine generosity. This far exceeds what is owing.[87] It is an act of justice to do what is just in the same way as a just person, in other words, with readiness and delight. . . . We ought to give alms on principle, that is, for God's sake and with delight and readiness.[88]

FOX: Do you see justice as a cosmic law, something common to the entire universe and all things in it?

AQUINAS: There are two kinds of justice, commutative and distributive justice. The former enters into the exchange of goods, and does not apply to God, since as the Apostle says, "Who has first given to God that a gift may be given in return?" (Rom. 11:35). The other enters when things are shared out, as when a ruler or steward gives to each according to his deserts. In a well-ordered state or household this kind of justice is displayed by the lord and master. So the order of the universe, embracing natural and voluntary things alike, manifests the justice of God.[89]

FOX: The idea that the order of the universe manifests the justice of God truly grounds our understanding of justice in a cosmic setting. It carries us beyond guilt-based or compulsive liberalism and beyond anthropocentric work-ethic philosophies.

AQUINAS: Why did John the Baptist not warn about justice in the beginning of his prophecy, but instead speak of penitence? It has to be said that the reason for this was that he first warned about justice through the law of nature and scripture, but the people had transgressed these laws. Isaiah 24:5 says: "They have transgressed the laws, they have violated the statutes, they have broken the eternal covenant." For in this he gives to understand

---

86. Ibid. I, q. 21, a. 4.   87. Ibid.   88. Ibid. II-II, q. 32, a. 1, ad 1.
89. Ibid. I, q. 21, a. 1.

that he finds all persons sinners. 1 Timothy 1:15 says: "Christ Jesus came into this world to save sinners." Romans 3:23 says: "For all have sinned, and fall short of the glory of God." And this is to "do penance."[90]

FOX: What you say is most interesting, for it implies that the primary sin of the human race is injustice and we are sinners because we are unjust. In addition to seeing justice as the cosmic order of things, do you also see justice as a local thing, common to individual beings?

AQUINAS: Whatever is done by God in created things is done according to proper order and proportion wherein consists the idea of justice. Thus justice must exist in all God's works.[91]

FOX: How does justice exist in all God's works?

AQUINAS: The idea of justice is preserved in creation by the production of beings in a manner that accords with the divine wisdom and goodness.[92] As the justice of human beings is to the community or household, so the justice of God is to the whole universe.[93]

FOX: Your point that creation itself holds and preserves the justice of God is a deeply important one for an ecological spirituality. Does God's compassion add something to God's justice?

AQUINAS: God acts compassionately not indeed by going against the divine justice, but by doing something more than justice; thus a person who pays another two hundred pieces of money, though owing him only one hundred, does nothing against justice, but acts generously or mercifully. The case is the same with one who pardons an offense committed against him, for in remitting it he may be said to bestow a gift. Hence the Apostle calls remission a forgiving: "Forgive one another, as Christ has forgiven you" (Eph. 4:32). Hence it is clear that compassion does not destroy justice, but in a sense is its fulfillment. And thus it is said, "compassion exalts itself above judgment" (James 2:13).[94]

FOX: You are implying that God is always compassionate toward things that exist.

AQUINAS: God out of the abundance of the divine goodness bestows upon creatures what is due to them more bountifully

---

90. In Mt 4, p. 43.   91. ST I, q. 21, a. 4.   92. Ibid., ad 4.   93. CG I, ch. 93 n. 12.   94. ST I, q. 21, a. 3, ad 2.

than is proportionate to their deserts, since less would suffice for preserving the order of justice than what the divine goodness confers. For between creatures and God's goodness there can be no proportion.[95]

FOX: There have been occasions in our conversation on the Via Transformativa when I have sensed you equating justice and truth. Am I correct in that perception?

AQUINAS: God's justice, which establishes things in the order conformable to the rule of the divine wisdom, which is the law of justice, is suitably called truth. Thus in human affairs we also speak of the truth of justice.[96] Whatever God does in us is either from justice or from compassion or from truth. . . . The psalmist compares justice to mountains, truth to clouds, which are higher, and compassion to the skies, which are higher than all things. . . . All these things are said according to the effect, since they are the same in essence.[97]

FOX: Justice, truth, and compassion are the same in essence, you say, and they have to do with whatever God makes in us. Thus truth and justice lie at the heart of the inner person. I also sense a connection to your understanding of beauty when I hear you equate justice and truth and compassion.

AQUINAS: Take note of the saying in Isaiah that "the work of justice will be peace," since the peace of the saints in the land of the Creator will be beautiful, primarily because it will not be false. Also, because it will not be broken, as Isaiah says (9): "And there will be no end to peace." Third, because it will be full.[98]

FOX: Peace and justice go together, then?

AQUINAS: Peace is caused by justice, which is about action, as Isaiah puts it (32:17): "The work of justice shall be peace." For one who refrains from wronging others lessens the occasions of quarrels and disturbances.[99]

FOX: And to walk in justice is to walk in peace and beauty?

AQUINAS: Take note of the saying in Isaiah (26:7): "The path of the just person [is straight]" because the way of justice is straight. First, on account of the shortness of the way. Wisdom

---

95. Ibid., a. 4.   96. Ibid., a. 2.   97. In Pss 35, p. 278.   98. In Is 32, p. 515.   99. ST II-II, q. 180, a. 2, ad 2.

(5) says: "We have crossed deserts where there were no tracks." Second, on account of the evenness of the ground, for what is straight is midway between the extremes. Third, on account of beauty, as Jeremiah (31) says: "May the Lord bless you, pasture of justice, sacred mountain."[100]

FOX: Is justice a matter of intellect or of will?

AQUINAS: Justice, as to the law that governs, resides in the reason or intellect. But as to the command whereby our actions are governed according to the law, it resides in the will.[101]

FOX: And God is just?

AQUINAS: There is justice in God, to whom it belongs to give to each one what belongs to them. Hence it says in Psalm 9:8: "The Lord is just and has loved justice."[102]

FOX: Will you elaborate on the relationship of God and justice?

AQUINAS: God is Wisdom and Justice.[103] God is just and God is justice. Consider Psalm 9: "Just is the Lord," etc.[104] God is the One who is the most just (*justissimus*).[105] God's being is identical with God's acting—therefore for God to be good and to be just are one and the same.[106] God is praised in Sacred Scripture as virtue and as justice and as salvation and as freedom.[107]

FOX: If God is justice itself and if God is the "most just," and if Justice is a biblical name for God, then clearly our efforts at creating justice and relieving injustice are tantamount to our imitation of God. Speak to us more about the virtue of justice.

AQUINAS: Justice is the chief of the moral virtues. By it one is directed in one's relations toward another.[108]

FOX: Why do you call justice the chief of the moral virtues?

AQUINAS: Simply speaking, a moral virtue is the nobler for the amount of reasonable goodness suffusing it. Accordingly, justice, as such, excels among the other moral virtues, and is called the brightest, outshining morning and evening star.[109]

FOX: You say that justice brings about the greatest suffusion of goodness.

AQUINAS: In a certain way all virtue is called justice.[110] Justice, by imitating the divine Mind, is united thereto by an everlasting

---

100. In Is 26, p. 503. 101. ST I, q. 21, a. 2, ad 1. 102. CG I, ch. 93 n. 6. 103. ST I-II, q. 79, a. 1. 104. In Pss 32, p. 259. 105. In Pss 7, p. 165. 106. CBH, 5. 107. DDN, n. 742, p. 281. 108. ST II-II, q. 181, a. 1, ad 1. 109. Ibid. I-II, q. 66, a. 4. 110. DDN, n. 777, p. 292.

covenant. [It is among those virtues] attributed in this life to some who are at the summit of perfection.[111]

FOX: By justice we "imitate the Divine Mind"—that is quite a high order! No wonder justice does not come easily to the human species.

AQUINAS: From the point of view of reason it is difficult to find and establish the rational means in some particular matter. This difficulty is found only in the act of intellectual virtues, and in the act of justice.[112]

FOX: How is it that the divine Mind is so closely allied with justice?

AQUINAS: Divine wisdom . . . is the first root of justice.[113] It is written (Wis. 8:7): "Divine wisdom teaches . . . justice and courage."[114]

FOX: Justice and other moral virtues concern our getting along with others, do they not?

AQUINAS: The moral virtues are practiced in matters pertaining to the life of the community.[115] Legal justice stands foremost among all the moral virtues, inasmuch as the common good transcends the individual good of one person.[116]

FOX: You say that legal justice excels other moral virtues— what is legal justice?

AQUINAS: There must be one supreme virtue essentially distinct from every other virtue, which directs all the virtues to the common good. And this virtue is legal justice.[117]

FOX: The "common good" seems like a very rich phrase by which to critique our efforts at virtue, power, and justice.

AQUINAS: The good of any virtue, whether such virtue directs one in relation to oneself or in relation to others, is referable to the common good, to which justice directs. Thus all acts of virtue can pertain to justice, insofar as it directs people to the common good. . . . In "legal justice" one is in harmony with the law, which directs the acts of all the virtues to the common good.[118]

---

111. ST I-II, q. 61, a. 5.   112. Ibid. II-II, q. 129, a. 2.   113. DV, q. 23, a. 6, ad 6.   114. ST I-II, q. 63, a. 3.   115. Ibid., q. 66, a. 3, ad 1. 116. Ibid. II-II, q. 58, a. 12.   117. Ibid., a. 6, ad 4.   118. Ibid., a. 5.

FOX: Thus goodness and justice go together in human beings just as you said above that they go together in God.

AQUINAS: Good people are so called chiefly from their justice.[119]

FOX: You say that law directs people to the common good.

AQUINAS: Political justice consists in a community of life that is ordered to a self-sufficiency of the things pertaining to human living. And the state-community should be such that everything sufficient for the needs of human life is found in it.[120] Since political justice exists among the free and equal, in people who do not have freedom and justice, there is not found political justice, which is unqualified justice. The justice of a master or father is a qualified justice inasmuch as it has some likeness to political justice.[121]

FOX: What is the relationship between law and justice?

AQUINAS: Because injustice consists in this, that one attributes to oneself too many of the benefits and too few of the burdens, it follows that in good government of the multitude we do not permit that people should rule according to whim and human passion, but that the law, which is a dictate of reason, should rule people, or that a person who acts according to reason should rule.[122]

FOX: And so law helps to curb human tendencies to injustice?

AQUINAS: A prince has been given the office to observe justice, and consequently equality, which he neglects when he usurps for himself too many beneficial and too few onerous things.[123] Since a prince—if he is just—assigns no more of the good things to himself than to others (unless perhaps according to a proper ration of distributive justice), it follows that he does not labor for the advantage of himself but of others. Because of this . . . legal justice, by which the prince rules the multitude of the people, is the good of another.[124]

FOX: In what other ways do law and justice connect?

AQUINAS: Justice has two parts: to withdraw from evil and to do good. And so the psalmist says, "Refrain from evil and do good." But these two parts of justice correspond to the precepts

---

119. Ibid., a. 3.   120. In Ethics V, L. 11, p. 436.   121. Ibid., 436–37.
122. Ibid., 437.   123. Ibid.   124. Ibid.

of law: for justice is regulated by law. In law there are certain affirmative precepts, which are fulfilled by doing good: and certain ones are negative, which are fulfilled by refraining from evil. Likewise through these two the natural inclination of appetite is fulfilled, of which there are two objects: namely, good and evil; since appetite naturally turns toward the good and flees from deceptive evil.[125]

FOX: I hear you saying that justice is our pathway to God.

AQUINAS: The way, prepared and straight, for receiving the Lord is the way of justice, according to Isaiah (26:7): "The way of the just is straight."[126]

FOX: How is justice different from other moral virtues?

AQUINAS: It is proper to justice, as compared with the other virtues, to direct people in their relations with others because it denotes a kind of equality, as its very name implies. Indeed, we are accustomed to say that things are adjusted when they are made equal, for equality is the relation of one thing to another. On the other hand, the other virtues perfect people only in those matters that befit them in relation to themselves.[127]

FOX: What then is justice?

AQUINAS: Isidore says, "One is said to be just because one respects the rights (*jus*) of others."[128] Justice is a habit whereby one renders to each one their due by a constant and perpetual will.[129] Justice is the most excellent of all the moral virtues, as being most akin to reason. . . . It is about actions, whereby one is to find balance not only in oneself, but also in relation to others.[130]

FOX: Can justice be a greater virtue than courage?

AQUINAS: Fortitude holds the first place among those moral virtues that are concerned with the passions, but it is subordinate to justice.[131] Although courage is about the most difficult things, it is not about the best, for it is only useful in warfare, whereas justice is useful both in war and in peace.[132]

FOX: Is justice different from compassion?

AQUINAS: Since justice is a cardinal virtue, other secondary virtues, such as compassion, generosity, and the like, are connected to it. Wherefore to succor the needy, which belongs to

---

125. In Pss 36, p. 287.   126. In Jn 1.23, n. 239.   127. ST II-II, q. 57, a. 1.   128. Ibid., q. 58, a. 1.   129. Ibid.   130. Ibid. I-II, q. 66, a. 4. 131. Ibid.   132. Ibid. II-II, q. 58, a. 12, ad 3.

compassion, is by a kind of reduction ascribed to justice as to its principal virtue.[133] Compassion is the fulfillment of justice, not its abolition.[134] The works of justice and compassion are like a sacrifice, as Hebrews says at the end, "Don't neglect to do good and share."[135]

FOX: Does God practice justice, then?

AQUINAS: Among the moral virtues, justice alone can be properly attributed to God. For other moral virtues are concerned with passions, which have no place in God, like temperance with respect to feelings of lust, bravery with respect to feelings of fear and rashness. But justice is concerned with actions such as distributions and retributions, which can be suitable for God.[136] Just as through the ordering of distributive justice in a city governed by a first citizen, the entire political order is preserved, so through this ordering of justice the entire universe is preserved by God. For when this is removed, all things become confused. And this indeed is an act that is "fitting for God." For it is fitting for God to preserve out of the divine goodness those whom God has made.[137]

FOX: You say that justice preserves the "whole universe." That certainly places justice and its opposite, injustice, in a cosmic context. To say that God's justice preserves things sounds like an understanding of salvation we seldom hear about: that of preserving things by justice.

AQUINAS: Justice preserves all existing things to the extent that the nature of each thing receives and upholds it according to its own particular kind.[138] Divine justice is praised as the "salvation" of all [by Dionysius] because it saves all things, insofar as it guards and preserves three things in each being: First, it preserves the "substance of each thing properly," that is, in the uniqueness of its own nature, "and purely," that is, without extraneous mixture. Second, similarly, it preserves "the order" of each thing, proper and pure. Third, it is the cause in all things of their proper and pure operation. And in this way the nature of salvation consists in things being preserved in the things that are in accord with their own uniqueness.[139]

FOX: I cannot imagine a definition of salvation more apt for an ecological era like ours than the one you have just uttered—

---

133. Ibid., a. 11, ad 1.   134. Ibid. I, q. 21, a. 3, ad 2.   135. In Pss 50, p. 350.   136. DDN, n. 771, p. 291.   137. Ibid., n. 22, p. 8.   138. Ibid., n. 796, p. 297.   139. Ibid., n. 786, p. 295.

"preserving things in the good." Now, a salvation theology can link up with a creation theology, for nature needs its goodness acknowledged and preserved. How does God preserve things by justice?

AQUINAS: Divine justice is for all things the cause of their proper activity.[140]

FOX: I think your teaching that salvation is not just our being freed from evil but that it is also the good work that goes on in things in their own right is a very important contribution to overcoming the distortion of the meaning of "salvation" that we inherit from a fall/redemption religious ideology.

AQUINAS: Salvation and freedom . . . are the effects of justice.[141] We ought to receive one who generously praises divine salvation not only with respect to preservation in God but also with respect to separation from evil.[142]

FOX: Yet it seems that the former kind of salvation precedes the latter, just as blessing precedes sin and goodness precedes oppression.

AQUINAS: The first meaning of salvation consists in the preservation of the good. This preservation takes place in the good in many ways.[143] For certain things are preserved in the good by God, who has established them as unchangeable in themselves, just as there are celestial bodies that are far from corruption and also the blessed ones who cannot sin. Second, as far as some things that are unchangeable are preserved so that they do not have any counter-action, just as sometimes God, seeing some to be weak, does not allow them to be tempted and thus saves them by preserving them in the good. Third, from the fact that God allows some to be attacked, but gives them the fortitude to be able to resist the attacks, just as the strong are preserved against what is worse, that is, against weaker things.[144]

FOX: I am so struck by your defining salvation in light of the preservation of blessing. This surely links up the Via Positiva and the Via Transformativa; the latter becomes a way to preserve the former and to extend it. It also honors our work and the work intrinsic to all beings in the universe as holy work with a salvific impact.

---

140. Ibid., n. 777, p. 292.   141. Ibid., n. 743, p. 282.   142. Ibid., n. 787, p. 295.   143. Ibid., n. 788, p. 295.   144. Ibid., n. 789, p. 295.

AQUINAS: The meaning of salvation consists first and principally in this, that something is preserved in the good.[145]

FOX: That is a very powerful and pertinent definition for an ecological era like ours: that salvation means to preserve things in the good, to preserve their blessing power. Is this one way that divine justice operates in the world?

AQUINAS: Concerning divine justice, it is necessary to consider that justice truly consists in this: that it gives to all things according to their proper worth and that it preserves the nature of each thing in its proper order and power, namely, that in the beings that are immortal according to their own nature, it preserves their immortality; and in mortals, their mortality.[146]

FOX: Thus divine justice respects the intrinsic nature of things. But divine justice also liberates, does it not?

AQUINAS: Dionysius says that the holy doctors call divine justice "liberation" and the cause of liberation, insofar as it saves one from evil, and this in many ways. First, inasmuch as it does not permit those who have true being to fall from their substances to the point where they are nothing, but always something of their substance remains in them. Second, with regard to the fact that if some truly existing being falls into some sin in action, into something inordinate by the inclination of the appetite and into some defect of its proper action, God "liberates" that which falls in this way from the passion that led toward sin, and also from the weakness that fails to maintain its requisite order, as well as from the privation that pertains to the loss of perfection.[147]

FOX: I am very struck by your identification of salvation with liberation—up to now many of us thought this concept was exclusively a Marxist one. You speak of liberation from privation—how are we liberated from privation?

AQUINAS: God liberates us from privation insofar as God makes up for our defects. God liberates us from weakness insofar as God supports us in our weakness with a paternal and compassionate affection. But God liberates us from the revival of passion, in other words, God calls us back from evil and, what is more, firmly establishes us in the very good that was

---

145. Ibid., n. 792, p. 296.   146. Ibid., n. 781, p. 292.   147. Ibid., n. 793, p. 296.

stricken or diminished and weakened. God fulfills things by restoring them. And that which had fallen into sin God has stood on its feet again, that is, God strengthens and adorns or disposes with a certain propriety. And thus God draws forth all lawlessness and disorder toward integrity and dissolves all the stains of sin.[148]

FOX: None of this liberation and healing is done in contradiction to our free will, is it?

AQUINAS: Those beings that fall are restored according to their free will, and this includes those things that fall as a result of their natural corruption.[149]

FOX: Salvation and creation, then, go together.

AQUINAS: When a thing attains the end for which it was made it is said to be saved, whereas when it fails to reach that end it is said to be lost. Now God made humans for eternal life; and consequently, when people attain eternal life they are saved, which is God's will.[150] When in truth out of sin God makes a being just, then God is said to create in the strict sense. Ephesians (2) says: "By God's own creation we have been created in Christ Jesus for good works" and James (1) says: "So that you are the first fruits of the creation of God," namely, of God's spirit.[151]

FOX: I think that many people have been confused about the words "justice" and "justification." Would you comment on their difference and their connection?

AQUINAS: Justice in the proper sense is always between different persons. Every sin is opposed to justice in the sense of metaphorical justice or right relation to God, neighbor, and self and lower to higher powers in the self, since some of the order mentioned is destroyed by every sin. Consequently it is from this sort of justice that justification gets its name.[152]

FOX: That is quite a statement—that every sin is opposed to justice in some way. And so "justification" refers to the harmony in our own psyches or souls?

AQUINAS: Justification is not so called from legal justice, which is all about virtue, but from the justice that means a general good order in the soul.[153]

---

148. Ibid.   149. Ibid., n. 792, p. 296.   150. OF, p. 131.   151. In Pss 50, p. 348.   152. DV, q. 28, a. 1, ad 3.   153. Ibid., ad 2.

FOX: What would constitute the opposite of justice?

AQUINAS: Injustice is twofold. First, there is illegal injustice, which is opposed to legal justice. And this is essentially a special vice, insofar as it regards a special object, namely, the common good, which it despises. . . . Contempt of the common good may lead to all kinds of sin. Thus too all vices, as being repugnant to the common good, have the character of injustice, as though they arose from injustice.

Second, we speak of injustice in reference to an inequality between one person and another, when one person wishes to have more goods, riches for example, or honors, and less evils such as toil and losses.[154]

FOX: Legal justice is about the common good?

AQUINAS: Justice directs people in their relation with other people. Now this may happen in two ways: first as regards one's relation with individuals, second as regards one's relations with others in general, insofar as a person who serves a community serves all those who are included in that community. Accordingly, justice in its proper meaning can be directed to another in both these senses. Now, it is evident that all who are included in a community stand in relation to that community as parts to a whole; while a part, as such, belongs to a whole, so that whatever is the good of a part can be directed to the good of the whole. . . . Since it belongs to the law to direct to the common good, it follows that the justice that is in this way styled general is called "legal justice," because thereby one is in harmony with the law, which directs the acts of all the virtues to the common good.[155]

FOX: You seem to be tying all the virtues that we dealt with in the Via Creativa into that of justice here in the Via Transformativa.

AQUINAS: The good of any virtue, whether such virtue directs one in relation to oneself, or in relation to certain other individuals, is referable to the common good, to which justice directs. Thus all acts of virtue can pertain to justice, insofar as it directs a person to the common good.[156]

---

154. ST II-II, q. 59, a. 1.   155. Ibid., a. 5.   156. Ibid.

FOX: It seems that justice is the most all-encompassing of the virtues for you.

AQUINAS: Temperance and fortitude are in the sensitive appetite, in regard to desire and anger. Now these powers are an appetite for certain particular goods, even as the senses are perceptive of particular things. On the other hand, justice is in the intellectual appetite as its subject, which can have the universal good as its object, knowledge of which belongs to the intellect. Hence justice can be a general virtue rather than temperance or fortitude.[157]

FOX: This shows how sentimentalism and other forms of anti-intellectualism destroy a consciousness of justice and distract from it. No wonder structures of injustice invest heavily in sentimental and titillating distractions from an intellectual life. For you, justice oversees all the other virtues.

AQUINAS: Legal justice directs the acts of all the virtues to the common good.[158] There must be one supreme virtue essentially distinct from every other virtue that directs all the virtues to the common good. And this virtue is called legal justice.[159]

FOX: Justice is not just about the common good, however.

AQUINAS: Just as in addition to legal justice there is a need for particular virtues to direct one in relation to oneself, such as temperance and fortitude, so too besides legal justice there is need for particular justice to direct people in their relations to other individuals.[160]

FOX: What, then, is the essence of the act of justice?

AQUINAS: The proper act of justice is nothing else than to render to each one what is their own.[161]

FOX: And what is "their own"?

AQUINAS: Their own is that which is due to them according to equality of proportion.[162]

FOX: Why is it that we symbolize justice by a woman with scales in her hand?

AQUINAS: The person who has too much exceeds the mean. . . . Therefore, we will know by this mean what we ought to

---

157. Ibid., ad 2.   158. ST II-II, q. 58, a. 6.   159. Ibid., ad 4.   160. Ibid., a. 7.   161. Ibid., a. 11.   162. Ibid.

take from those who have more and give to those who have less; besides we will know that we ought to take from the greater, that is, from those who have more, the amount by which they ought to give one who has less by which the mean exceeds.[163]

FOX: And so justice has an element of balance to it that we must constantly assess. To make clear what I have heard so far, I hear you saying that justice is the foremost of all the moral virtues.

AQUINAS: It is evident that legal justice stands foremost among all the moral virtues, because the common good transcends the individual good of one person.[164]

FOX: This phrase "the common good" can easily be lost sight of in our day—will you expound on it?

AQUINAS: The common good comprises many things because the community of the state is composed of many persons and its good is procured by many actions.[165] The common good of the state cannot flourish unless citizens are virtuous, at least those whose business it is to govern.[166]

FOX: Can you give an example of the opposite of the common good?

AQUINAS: The disregard of the common good is greater under an oligarchy than under a democracy, where, after all, the welfare of the majority has been attempted. But worst of all is a tyranny where the advantage of one man is sought. As the rule of the king is best, so the rule of a tyrant is worst.

Security is banished and everything is uncertain when people are cut off from law and depend on the will, I would even say the greed, of another. A tyrant oppresses the bodies of his subjects, but, what is more damnable, he threatens their spiritual growth, for he is set on his own power, not their progress. He is suspicious of any dignity that they may possess that will prejudice his own iniquitous domination. A tyrant is more fearful of good persons than of bad persons, for he dreads their strange virtue.

Fearful lest they grow strong and so stout of heart as no longer to brook his wicked despotism, but resolve in companionship to enjoy the fruits of peace, a tyrant is constrained to destroy good people's confidence in one another, lest they band together

---

163. In Ethics V, L. 7, p. 416.   164. ST II-II, q. 58, a. 12.   165. Ibid. I-II, q. 96, a. 1.   166. Ibid., q. 92, a. 1, ad 3.

to throw off his yoke. Therefore he sows discord among them, and encourages dissensions and litigation. He forbids celebrations that make for good fellowship, weddings and feasts and such events that are likely to promote familiarity and mutual loyalty.[167]

FOX: You see law and legal justice as encouraging virtue and the "common good" of the citizenry?

AQUINAS: So far as human acts conduce to virtue, so far does law make people good.[168] Human laws do not forbid all vices, from which the virtuous abstain, but only the more grievous vices, from which it is possible for the majority to abstain.[169] Human law does not forbid all vicious acts, by the obligation of precept; nor does it prescribe all acts of virtue.[170]

FOX: So law has its place but law cannot accomplish everything. Law is imperfect.

AQUINAS: Human reason cannot have a full participation of the dictate of the divine reason, but according to its own mode and imperfectly.[171]

FOX: Virtue goes deeper than law, then. Law is, as you say, imperfect. I find some groups in our country today operating out of a kind of fanaticism, trying to legislate virtue instead of basic legal justice. In your opinion, do other kinds of justice besides legal justice outrank the other moral virtues?

AQUINAS: Even if we speak of particular justice, it excels the other moral virtues for two reasons. First, . . . because justice is in the more excellent part of the soul, namely, the rational appetite or will, whereas the other moral virtues are in the sensitive appetite, where the passions are found that are the matter of the other moral virtues. The second reason is taken from the object, because the other virtues are commendable with regard to the sole good of virtuous people themselves, but justice is praiseworthy with regard to the virtuous person being well disposed toward another, so that justice is in a way the good of another person.[172]

FOX: I like that phrase of yours that justice is "the good of another person." Is justice greater than magnanimity and courage?

---

167. I DRP, 3.   168. ST I-II, q. 92, a. 1, ad 1.   169. Ibid., q. 96, a. 2.
170. Ibid., a. 3, ad 1.   171. Ibid., q. 91, a. 3, ad 1.   172. Ibid. II-II, q.
58, a. 12.

AQUINAS: When magnanimity is added to justice it increases the latter's goodness; and yet without justice, it would not even be a virtue.[173]

FOX: Now it becomes clearer why the kinds of justice you spoke about above—justice as preservation and justice as liberation—both constitute our deep experience of salvation.

AQUINAS: Justice leads to the reign of God, as Proverbs (8:20) says: "I walk in the way of virtue, in the paths of justice, enriching those who love me, filling their treasures," etc.[174]

FOX: Did Jesus teach this?

AQUINAS: Christ did not come to call the just to penitence, but to greater justice.[175]

FOX: Holiness and justice go together, then?

AQUINAS: The saints have a heart full of justice. . . . The saints have justice, charity, and effects of this kind, which are most like God—they know more than the others. As Psalm 34:8 says: "Taste, and see that the Lord is good."[176] Isaiah talks about two things—namely, justice, which he possesses, and a vision of God. And they follow one upon another. For the vision of God is arrived at through justice. Consider Psalm 15: "Who will dwell in your tabernacle, etc. One who walks without blemish and exercises justice." Another line says, "But I will see your face in justice, and therefore, I will appear in your sight," that is, "I will come to see you, and I will be sated when your glory has appeared," that is, when I see you. And I will be filled with all goods. Psalm 103 says: "The one who satisfies your desire for good," namely, your glory, in which all good things exist.[177]

FOX: You say that justice and a vision of God follow on one another and that this is a path to holiness. Can you elaborate on this, please?

AQUINAS: The soul is elevated toward God in four ways: namely, for the purpose of admiring the height of God's power, as Isaiah puts it (40): "Lift your eyes on high, and see who created these things." Psalm 104 says: "How wonderful are your works, O Lord." And this is the elevation of faith. Second, the mind is raised for the purpose of embracing the excellence of

---

173. Ibid., ad 2.   174. In Mt 6, p. 75.   175. In Mt 9, p. 91.   176. In Mt 5, p. 53.   177. In Pss 17, p. 193.

eternal Beauty. Job 2 says: "You can lift your face without stain, you will be stable and you will not fear. You will also forget misery, and a kind of noontime brightness will rise from you." And this is the elevation of hope. Third, the mind is raised to cling to divine good and sanctity, as Isaiah puts it (51): "Awake, rise up Jerusalem, etc." And this is the elevation of charity. Fourth, the mind is raised to work for the imitation of divine justice. Lamentations 5 says: "We will lift up our hearts with our hands to God in the heavens." And this is the elevation of justice. The fourth way is also indicated when he says, "To the holy and on high," since the two last ways of elevation pertain to his saying, "to the holy"; the first two ways pertain to when he says "to you on high."[178]

FOX: These four ways of prayer or "elevation" sound much like the Four Paths we have been discussing. Indeed, it all leads to holiness. I particularly appreciate your including our "work for the imitating of divine justice" as an integral example of deep prayer and spirituality. That is surely what the Via Transformativa is all about, after all.

AQUINAS: Proverbs 13 says: "If desire is fulfilled it delights the soul." If you cling to God, your desire will be fulfilled. But for this it is required that your desire be just, for God is not the originator of injustice. For this reason the psalmist first lays out the root of just desire—namely, that human beings be delighted in God through love. This is why he says, "to delight in God," that is, all your love is in God. Philippians 4 says: "Always take joy in God." In the Greek *delitiare* is used, as if he were saying, "May you not be content with what is necessary for welfare, but seek choice superabundance, just as pleasure-loving persons are not content with common foods." Job 22 says: "Then you will abound with delight with the all-powerful." And then, God will grant you the petitions of your heart. The author does not say "of the flesh," for the petitions of the heart, according to Origen, are what the heart desires. For example, according to him, if the eye could seek, it would desire pretty colors; but the ears would desire sweet sounds. So the object of the heart, when there is truth and justice—these are the things desired by

---

178. In Pss, Prologue, 148.

it. And these, he says, God will give to you. Consider Matthew 7: "Seek and it will be given to you."

Another understanding of the phrase "of the heart" is when they will be of the heart—God will hear before one calls. Isaiah 65 says: "Before they call, I will hear."[179]

FOX: What you have just spoken of is very rich indeed. You connect heart with truth and justice, and you seem to be connecting joy and justice making. I think that is a valuable thing to do since justice workers must avoid the dual temptations of sadness and self-righteousness.

AQUINAS: To the extent that the just love justice, they will take pleasure in doing just deeds.[180]

FOX: Why is this so?

AQUINAS: Everyone finds pleasure in what they are fond of. As lovers desire the thing that is absent, so they take pleasure in it when it is present. In this way a lover of horses finds pleasure in a horse, and a lover of shows in a show. Hence it is evident that the virtuous love the activities of their own virtue as something agreeable to them. To the extent that the just love justice, they will take pleasure in doing just deeds.[181] No one will call that person just who does not rejoice in doing just deeds.[182]

FOX: I feel you are recovering for us the sense of passion that is behind our compassion. For example, I sense that anger is a passion that plays for you a positive role in our acts of justice making or compassion.

AQUINAS: That which provokes anger is always something considered in the light of an injustice. . . . Those who do an injury on purpose seem to sin from contempt. For this reason we are angry with them most of all.[183] If we are angry with those who harm others and seek to be avenged on them, it is because those who are injured belong in some way to us: either by some kinship or by friendship, or at least because of the nature we share in common.[184]

FOX: The passion of anger is by no means a negative thing necessarily—in fact, moral outrage is a necessary part of compassion.

---

179. In Pss 36, p. 281.   180. In Ethics I, L. 13, p. 68.   181. Ibid.   182. Ibid., p. 69.   183. ST I-II, q. 47, a. 2.   184. Ibid., a. 1, ad 2.

AQUINAS: When a passion forestalls the judgment of reason so as to prevail on the mind to give its consent, it hinders counsel and the judgment of reason. But when it follows that judgment, as though being commanded by reason, it helps toward the execution of reason's command.[185]

FOX: And so our anger assists our struggle for justice. It seems that our very interconnectedness causes anger in us when we see what we love threatened by injustice.

AQUINAS: In saying "Our Father" [in the prayer "Our Father"], our feelings for our neighbors are set in order. "Is there not one Father of us all?" (Mal. 2:10). If we all have one Father, none of us ought to despise any of our neighbors on the grounds of their being different from us. Jesus says "our Father," not "my Father." . . . The Lord teaches us not to make private prayers, but to pray generally for the whole people; this kind of prayer is more acceptable to God. In Chrysostom's words, "In God's eyes a prayer is more pleasing if it comes from fraternal love rather than from need."[186]

FOX: And yet, because we all share one Creator, we are all brothers and sisters. You also connect justice with joy and delight of the heart. Here it seems we are moving into another dimension of compassion—that of the way of celebration. Our hearts are not just touched by one another's suffering but also by one another's joy. Our shared passion concerns celebration as well as brokenness.

AQUINAS: It can be said that there are two kinds of gates: certain ones that are evil, which close the entrance to life; others that are good, by which the way of life is opened. Psalm 118 says: "Open the gates of life," that is, of justice, etc. The evil gates are sins; but the good are virtues.[187]

FOX: And one might say that our radical response to life—which is what prayer is all about—concerns our response to both of these "gates."

AQUINAS: One is prepared for praying in two ways. Either through lifting the mind toward God, since as John Damascene says, "prayer is the ascent of the mind toward God;" or through the confidence one has from God. With regard to the first, the

---

185. Ibid., q. 59, a. 2, ad 3.   186. In Mt 6.9, p. 70. Portions of this text are from Simon Tugwell in *Albert & Thomas: Selected Writings* (New York: Paulist Press, 1988), 458.   187. In Pss 23, p. 228.

psalmist says: "O Lord, I have lifted my soul toward you, seeing your goodness in contemplation and in love." Lamentations 3 says: "Let us lift up our hearts with our hands toward God." With regard to the second, which no one obtains unless they pray confidently, James 1 says: "Let one ask in faith, not hesitating." Hebrews 4 says: "Let us approach in trust toward the throne of glory," or of God's grace. And therefore the psalmist says, "In you, I trust, my God." And 2 Corinthians (3) says: "We have such faith in God through Christ, not because we are sufficient to think something by ourselves."[188]

FOX: It would seem that in prayer our trust allows us access to our true selves and our hearts so that compassion as justice and joy can truly flow from heart to heart among us.

AQUINAS: Spiritual blindness and hardness of heart imply the movement of the human mind in cleaving to evil and turning away from the divine light.[189]

FOX: Compassion then challenges the hardness of our hearts?

AQUINAS: The Holy Spirit dissolves the hardness of hearts, as Luke 12 puts it: "I have come to send fire on the earth."[190]

FOX: The fire of compassion, then, can be said to melt hearts and minds that are cold and hard.

AQUINAS: Spiritual blindness refers to sight and discovery; and heaviness of the heart refers to hearing and teaching; and hardness of heart refers to the affections.[191]

FOX: I hear you speaking of something that religion rarely touches on—what we might call spiritual sins, closing the mind and hardening the heart.

AQUINAS: Spiritual sins are of greater guilt than carnal sins. . . . Spiritual sins are more grievous than carnal sins, other things being equal. . . . Carnal sin as such denotes a *turning toward* something, and for that reason implies a closer cleaving. Whereas spiritual sin denotes more of a *turning from* something, whence the notion of guilt arises. For this reason it involves a greater guilt.[192]

FOX: This reminds me of your distinction between venial and mortal sin. It is so telling to hear you speak of how "turning

---

188. In Pss 24, p. 229.   189. ST I-II, q. 79, a. 3.   190. In Pss 45, p. 329.
191. ST I-II, q. 79, a. 3.   192. Ibid., q. 73, a. 5.

from" is more grievous than "turning toward," because it seems to me that much of the institutional church's teaching on morality has been restricted to issues of "turning toward" and indeed of "carnal sin," whereas instruction on how to "turn from" and how to combat spiritual sin has been so sparse.

AQUINAS: When one sins without turning away from God, by the very nature of the sin, one's disorder can be repaired because the principle of the order is not destroyed. These sins are called venial.[193]

FOX: How alike are venial and mortal sins?

AQUINAS: Mortal and venial sins are infinitely apart as regards what they *turn away from,* but not as regards what they *turn to,* that is, the object that specifies them.[194]

FOX: What about opening up of the mind—is there a sin in remaining closed-minded?

AQUINAS: There is sin in the reason insofar as it errs in the knowledge of truth, which error is imputed to the reason as a sin when it is in ignorance or error about what it is able and ought to know.[195]

FOX: You are saying that ignorance itself can be sinful. I am thinking, for example, of the sins of the church when it becomes forgetful or even ignorant of, for example, its own mystical and prophetic heritage.

AQUINAS: Ignorance denotes privation of knowledge, that is, lack of knowledge of those things that one has a natural aptitude to know. Some of these things we are under an obligation to know, those, namely, without whose knowledge we are unable to accomplish a due act rightly.[196]

FOX: Anthropocentrism would be such a sin, I believe.

AQUINAS: If the reason is negligent, ignorance of what one is bound to know is a sin.[197]

FOX: And so we do sin against truth—not only as individuals but as communities and institutions as well. And for you the greatest sin is the sin of injustice?

---

193. Ibid., q. 72, a. 5.   194. Ibid., ad 1.   195. Ibid., q. 74, a. 5.   196. Ibid., q. 76, a. 2.   197. Ibid.

AQUINAS: The greatest sin must of necessity be directly opposed to the greatest virtue.[198]

FOX: Again, the institutional church has so often been unbalanced in its teaching about chastity, for example, that people never even hear its teaching about justice.

AQUINAS: Temperance without justice would not be a virtue.[199]

FOX: That is a strong affirmation indeed about the need for justice in our moral lives.

AQUINAS: Perfection consists in the pursuit of the very thing that comes from charity. 1 Corinthians 13:3 says: "If I distribute all my goods as food for the poor; and if I hand over my body so that I am burned, but I do not have charity, it benefits me nothing." For perfection does not consist in what is exterior to it, such as poverty, virginity, and the like, except when these are instruments of charity.[200]

FOX: There is no love without justice.

AQUINAS: Love alone is the special gift of the just, for "anyone who abides in charity abides in God and God in them," as is said in 1 John 4:16.[201]

FOX: You said above that God is justice and that justice is the one moral virtue we can attribute to God. But what if someone grows up in an abusive situation, for example, and never experiences the God of justice. Does that mean one can never know God?

AQUINAS: God is known not only in the works that proceed from justice, but also in God's other works. Hence, granted that someone does not know God as just, it does not follow that one does not know God at all. Nor is it possible for anyone to know none of God's works, since being in general, which cannot be unknown, is God's work.[202]

FOX: One more reason for including celebration in our grasp of compassion—God is known in the Via Positiva at the level of the marvel of being and in the Via Transformativa at the level of the liberation and transformation of being. Celebration and justice seem to go hand in hand.

---

198. Ibid., q. 73, a. 4.   199. Ibid., q. 68, a. 5, ad 3.   200. In Mt 4, p. 45.   201. CG III, ch. 154 n. 25.   202. DV, q. 10, a. 12, n. 10.

AQUINAS: The hand of God is a divine hand in three ways. First, it is a hand of divine power, and this is in three ways: first, it is one creating, as Job says (10): "Your hands have made me and fashioned me." Second, it is one governing, as Psalm 94 puts it, "In your hand, Lord, are all the ends of the earth." Third, it is one protecting, as in Isaiah 49: "In the shadow of the divine hand God protected me."

The second hand of God is the hand of justice, and this will be in three ways: first, it is a hand trying to test, as in Job 19: "The hand of the Lord has touched me." Second, it is a hand that chastises in order to cleanse, as in 2 Machabees 6: "For if in the present time I avoid the punishments of men, yet from the hand of the Almighty I will escape neither alive nor dead." Third, it is the hand of one who oppresses for the sake of condemning, as Hebrews 10 puts it: "One must shudder to fall into the hands of the living God."

The third hand is the hand of compassion and that also in three ways: first, of one healing, as in Job 5: "God makes the wound, and heals it; God's hands strike the blow, and they will heal it"; second, of one feeding, as in Psalm 95: "His people, and the sheep of his pasture." Third, of one crowning, as in Wisdom 5: "They will receive the crown of beauty and the jewels of splendor from the hand of the Lord."[203]

FOX: I appreciate your summarizing our conversation so far around the image of the "hand of God" being one of creating, justice making, and compassion—a challenge to us in our efforts at the "imitation of God." You have spoken about compassion and delight or celebration. I think it is important that we go more deeply into that aspect of compassion, now that we have spent as much time on the justice aspect as we have. Speak to us, if you will, about compassion as celebration. First, it seems that there is a connection between compassion as justice and compassion as joy.

AQUINAS: The psalmist urges on the just and righteous to do good works and to have the right intention when he says: "Rejoice in the Lord and exult, you just." It is as if he were saying, there are two things necessary for humanity, namely, right

---

203. In Is 8, p. 466.

work—and justice does this; and right intention—and joy does this. Therefore he says, "rejoice and exult, you just!"[204]

FOX: And so the fullest intention of our works is joy itself. One might even say that justice is a means toward joy, for we cannot celebrate without justice. There is also joy to be had in the experience of justice making.

AQUINAS: Joy results from the act of justice—at least in the will, in which case it is not a passion. And if this joy be increased through the perfection of justice, it will overflow into the sensitive appetite.[205] One is not just who does not take joy in justice. But God is just, and God is justice. Psalm 11 says: "Just [is] the Lord, etc." and so "the just exult in the Lord." And Habakkuk (3) says: "I will take joy in the Lord, and exult in God my savior."[206]

FOX: Joy is not the same thing as mere positivism. It does not come from denial of suffering or struggle.

AQUINAS: Exultation comes from interior joy. But in whom? . . . Philippians (4) says: "Take joy in the Lord, again I say take joy."[207] But those who wish to commit themselves to the will of God, these take joy in both prosperous things and adverse things. This is why the psalmist says, "great praise" for they give praise about all, not only about some things.[208]

FOX: That is an important point—that a consciousness of joy finds joy "in all things." And so joy and justice go together and together comprise compassion?

AQUINAS: Isaiah talks of "everlasting joy." This is true as long as one abides in justice, as Jeremiah explains (chapter 18). Isaiah (35) says: "With everlasting joy upon their heads, they will obtain joy and gladness." And he assigns a reason: "Since I am the Lord." And the sense is this: because the Lord cherishes justice, he will grant that you be just, so that you may please him, and he will make with you a pact of everlasting joy.[209]

FOX: Celebration and joy, then, are integral to the dimension of *passion* that is our compassion.

AQUINAS: It belongs to the perfection of moral good that people should be moved to good, not only regarding their will, but

---

204. In Pss 31, p. 259.   205. ST I-II, q. 59, a. 5.   206. In Pss 31, p. 259.
207. Ibid.   208. Ibid., 260.   209. In Is 61, p. 567.

also regarding their sensitive appetite. Psalm 84:3 says: "My heart and my flesh have rejoiced in the living God." By "heart" we are to understand the intellectual appetite, and by "flesh" the sensitive appetite.[210]

FOX: Joy is no obstacle to our just actions.

AQUINAS: Pleasure arising from virtuous activities will be more delightful than any other pleasures.[211] One may by the judgment of one's reason choose to be affected by a passion in order to work more promptly with the cooperation of the sensitive appetite. And thus a passion of the soul increases the goodness of an action.[212]

FOX: I hear you saying that an increase of virtue, for example, our love of justice, actually increases our passion.

AQUINAS: The more perfect a virtue is the more does it cause passion.[213]

FOX: And our joy comes in the Via Transformativa from participating in the realization of the reign of God?

AQUINAS: One who has charity loves God and possesses God; and one who has that which one loves is happy. So where there is charity, there is joy. Romans 14 says: "The reign of God is not in food and drink but in joy in the Spirit." This joy the psalmist had lost and so he seeks to have it restored to him, when he says: "Restore my happiness to me."[214]

FOX: Can you deepen our understanding of the word "joy" as you are using it?

AQUINAS: Spiritual joy has three levels. The first consists in the harmony of feeling; the second in the expansion of the heart; the third in the progress toward exterior things. Harmony through joy is spoken of when the psalmist says, "To my heart, etc." . . . When indeed the feeling rests in the beloved, then one's soul is expanded in order to experience greater expansion; and this even appears in sensible things. 2 Corinthians (6) says: "Our heart has been expanded." And so the psalmist speaks of "joy" that causes the expansion as a kind of joy. Furthermore, joy flows back into the body. Proverbs 17 says: "The mind full of joy makes the days of one's life to flower, the sad spirit dries up

---

210. ST I-II, q. 24, a. 3.   211. In Ethics I, L. 13, p. 69.   212. ST I-II, q. 24, a. 3, ad 1.   213. Ibid., q. 59, a. 5.   214. In Pss 50, p. 348.

its bones." And so in a vision of glory in the homeland after the resurrection, the body will be glorified from the joy of the mind. Isaiah says (at the end): "You will see, and your heart will rejoice, and your bones will flourish like grass." And so the psalmist says: "The bones of the humble will rejoice." And this applies to a present glorification, for the heart of people is worn down by the sadness of penitence. And so when people are happy, it is a sign that the bones that were worn down and afflicted have a share of joy.[215]

FOX: And so what you call our "present glorification" is real: We experience deep joy in this lifetime as part of the Via Transformativa?

AQUINAS: Jeremiah promises first the temporal pleasure of the people when he speaks of "the voice of joy." "From them I will banish the voice of joy and the voice of gladness, the voice of husband and the voice of wife, the sound of the mill, and the light of the lamp" (25). The spiritual pleasure is expressed by divine praises: "The voice of those saying: 'Confess to the Lord.'" Isaiah 51 says: "Joy and gladness will be found in it, and thanksgiving, and the voice of praise." Tobiah 13 says: "Through all its villages, the Alleluia will be sung." And in offerings, "And of those carrying offerings into the house of the Lord." Jeremiah assigns a reason for this, "For I will bring about a conversion of the earth." Lamentations (end) says: "Renew our days as from the beginning."[216]

FOX: The renewal begins now and is not something we experience only after death.

AQUINAS: All the rewards [of the beatitudes] will be fully consummated in the life to come; but meanwhile, they are, in a manner, begun even in this life. For the "reign of heaven," as Augustine says, can denote the beginning of perfect wisdom, insofar as the Spirit begins to reign in human life. The "possession" of the land denotes the well-ordered affections of the soul that rests, by its desire, on the solid foundation of the eternal inheritance, signified by "the land." They are "comforted" in this life by receiving the Holy Spirit, who is called the "Paraclete," that is, the Comforter. They "have their fill" even in

---

215. Ibid., 347.   216. In Jer 33, p. 654.

this life, of that food of which Our Lord said (John 4:34): "My meat is to do the will of the One that sent me." Again, in this life, people obtain God's compassion. Again, the eye being cleansed by the gift of understanding, we can, so to speak, "see God." Likewise, in this life, those who are the "peacemakers" of their own movements approach a likeness to God, and are called the "children of God."[217]

FOX: The renewal and the new beginnings that transformation brings signal joy to us.

AQUINAS: The psalmist says: "God makes my youth happy," that is, there will be renewal and youth, since as is said in Ephesians 4, "We will all attain to the measure of the stature of the fullness of Christ." And so he speaks of "Youth." Psalm 103 says: "Your youth will be renewed like an eagle's." And the priests say this psalm when they approach the altar ("I will go up to the altar of God, to God who gives joy to my youth") because these two things—namely, joy and renewal—are necessary for those who wish to approach the heavenly altar. Leviticus 10 says: "How is it possible to eat and please God in ceremonies with a sorrowful heart?" Likewise there is no old age in regard to sin. 1 John 2 says: "I write to you young ones."[218]

FOX: Worship, joy, renewal, justice—all seem to come together in the act of celebration.

AQUINAS: The custom [in Israel] was that when some went through the crowds to the tabernacle, they went with joy. Isaiah 30 says: "The song will be to you as a voice of holy solemnity and joy." So one who goes with a flute goes joyfully. And so the psalmist says, "I will go to the place of the tabernacle, etc." and with joy, since "in the voice of exultation and praise there is the sound of one feasting." In another sentence he has, "the sounds of banqueting," as if to say, I will listen to the voice of the sound of banqueting, since in banquets is the sound of joy. And this is much more clear in the light of other joys that are there. First there will be the joy of good habits. Isaiah 35 says: "They will have joy and happiness." Second, there will be praise and thanksgiving, since they know they have gotten

---

217. ST I-II q. 69, a. 2, ad 3.   218. In Pss 42, p. 314.

those things through the grace of God. And so they will confess the wonders of God and so there follows thanksgiving and the voice of praise. Third, there will be spiritual restoration. Isaiah, near the end, says: "My servants will eat, and you will be hungry; my servants will drink, and you will be thirsty, etc." Matthew 5 says: "Happy those who hunger and thirst for justice, etc." And so there will be the sound of feasting. Likewise of festivity, that is, continual exaltation.[219]

FOX: Feasting, exaltation, festivity—all mingled with the promise of justice making. This is compassion indeed. It seems that justice is necessary for celebration to happen.

AQUINAS: It pertains to justice to reduce unequal things to an equality. When equality exists the work of justice is done. For that reason equality is the goal of justice and the starting point of friendship.[220]

FOX: "Justice is the starting point of friendship": this explains why conviviality requires justice and why compassion includes both.

AQUINAS: The psalmist posits the fruits of exaltation when he says, "They will exult and be happy." But he places joy as the fruit of the saints, since happiness means the expansion of the heart, which signifies interior joy. Psalm 119 says: "You have expanded my heart." And this happiness is proper to the just. Psalm 97 says: "The light has risen for the just, and happiness for the righteous of heart." Exaltation means joy breaking forth externally from within; and this exaltation is fitting for the just. Psalm 32 says: "You just, exult in the Lord." And this is fitting for the righteous, whence he speaks of "those who desire my justice," namely, to imitate it. Or, if it is said about the person of David, "They desire my justice" that is, they take joy in my goodness, this is their joy of heart, and from this follows exultation of voice. Isaiah 51 says: "Joy and happiness will be found in this, the thanksgiving and the voice of praise." And so the psalmist adds, "Let them always say, the Lord will be magnified," that is, the saints will magnify God. Not, truly speaking, by making God great, but by announcing and proclaiming God great. Psalm 34 says: "Magnify the Lord with me, etc." Ecclesiasticus 43 says: "God's magnificence is wonderful."[221]

---

219. In Pss 41, p. 310.   220. In Ethics VIII, L. 7, pp. 737–38.   221. In Pss 34, p. 276.

FOX: Our joy and exaltation, our common celebration, is in some way an eschatological anticipation of the full reign of God.

AQUINAS: The kingdom is happiness. It is called kingdom from ruling, for one is ruled at the time when one is subject to the will of the one ruling. But this will be in heaven, whence Luke 14:15 says: "Happy is the one who eats bread in the kingdom of God." Likewise justice leads to the reign of God.[222]

FOX: We are promised an entrance into the joy of God.

AQUINAS: "Enter into the joy of your master" could mean, rejoice in that by which and in which your Lord rejoices, that is, in the enjoyment of God's very being. Then people will rejoice as the Lord when they have the same satisfaction as the Lord. Just as Jesus says to his apostles, "I appoint you that you may eat and drink at my table in my kingdom" (Luke 22:30). That is to say, that you may be happy in that in which I am happy.[223] By the table is meant the replenishment of joy that God has in the Godhead and that the saints have from God.[224]

FOX: Part of the fruits we enjoy is the fruit of our own labor for justice and compassion.

AQUINAS: The just eat well the fruit of their own creations.[225] "How beautiful on the mountains are the feet of those who announce and proclaim peace!" Here Isaiah indicates joy for those freed, and he first describes the joy in the light of the reception of the messengers who, coming from Chaldea, gave the message. "Beautiful" because to hear them announcing such things was beautiful and delightful to the people; "on the mountains" so that they might hear; "proclaiming" publicly the peace restored from Cyrus. The "good" is that of promised relief; "salvation" from captivity. Second he describes the joy from the perspective of the sentinels, who saw the Lord returning to Sion, raising their voice of exaltation: "The voice of joy will resound." Acts 4: "With one accord they lifted up their voice to God." And the reason for the joy, "since they will see eye to eye." As if they would see with their own eyes the captives coming. Isaiah 30 says: "Your eyes will see, Jerusalem, your teacher." Third, with regard to the coming of the captives, "take joy."[226]

---

222. In Mt 6, p. 75.   223. In Mt 25, p. 233.   224. CT II, ch. 9.   225. In Jer 17, p. 620.   226. In Is 52, p. 551.

FOX: Justice and liberation do indeed give us reasons to take joy. And God celebrates with us in this great act of cosmic compassion?

AQUINAS: Love is the cause of joy for everyone takes joy in their beloved. But God loves the Godhead and the divine creature, especially the rational one, with whom God has shared an infinite goodness.[227]

FOX: God has shared an "infinite goodness" with us, you say. I sense the Via Positiva coming to a fulfillment and a new beginning within the celebrative dimension to the Via Transformativa. It seems that the very act of celebration is itself a healing act where we can remember this "infinite goodness" with which God gifts us.

AQUINAS: One way to comfort others is by the example of our own happiness. You cannot know how to comfort another unless you are yourself at peace.[228]

FOX: And so another dimension to compassion as celebration is the dimension of peace.

AQUINAS: It is just like Jeremiah, who "found grace" in the past by traveling through the desert to the land of promise. The grace he found was compassion before God, because "he goes into calmness," that is, to his own land in which he rests peacefully. This is able to be explained mystically with regard to peace as they understood it in the time of Simon Machabeus (1 Mach. 14). Isaiah says (13): "My people will sit in the beauty of peace, and in the tabernacle of trust and in plenteous repose."[229]

FOX: Yet there is such a thing as false peace.

AQUINAS: It should be noted that there is a certain kind of false peace. Wisdom 14 says: "Those living in great strife due to ignorance call so many and such great evils peace." Certain fraudulent things such as Psalm 28 speaks of: "Those who speak peace with their neighbors, nonetheless have evil in their hearts." Certain transitory things also constitute false peace, as 1 Thessalonians says at the end of the letter: "For when they speak of peace and security, suddenly destruction will come upon them."[230]

---

227. In Jn 15.11, n. 2004.   228. In 2 Cor, ch. 1, p. 301.   229. In Jer 31, p. 648.   230. In Jer 14, p. 614.

FOX: What is true peace?

AQUINAS: Jesus says: "Peace I leave you, my peace I give you." Now, peace is nothing else than the tranquillity of order. For things are said to have peace when their order is undisturbed. Among human beings there is a threefold order, that is, of a person within himself or herself, of a person in relation to God, and of one person to another. Thus there is a threefold peace within a human person. There is an intrinsic kind by which one is at peace within oneself, "all one's powers undisturbed." Consider Psalm 119, "There is great peace for those who love your law."

There is another kind of peace by which a person is at peace with God, completely in tune with God's plan. Consider Romans 5:1, "Justified by faith we have peace with God." The third kind of peace is with one's neighbor. Consider Hebrews 12:14, "Strive for peace with all people." We should note that within us three things need to be put in order, the intellect, the will, and the appetite of the senses, so that the will is directed by the intellect, the appetite by the intellect and will. . . . This peace the holy have here, in this life, and will have in the future. Now, however, they have it imperfectly because neither within ourselves nor toward God, nor toward our neighbor can we have peace without some disturbance.[231]

FOX: Peace in the heart and celebration among the people are by no means exclusive of one another—together they make up authentic celebration—and with justice regulating our peace with our neighbor we have compassion at work.

AQUINAS: With regard to the pleasing of the heart Jeremiah says: "Virgin of Israel, you will go forth to the dance with your drums," that is, a dance playing to the sound of the drum. Isaiah 30 says: "The gladness of the heart, just like one who sets out to the sound of the flute, in order to enter into the mountain of the Lord, the rock of Israel." As concerns the tranquillity of peace: "Still you will plant vines in the mountains of Samaria," in reference to the three cities that have been added to the Jews. Isaiah 65: "They will plant vines, and they will eat their fruit."

Jeremiah marks out a reason for prosperity: "Since the day will come" in which is meant the return to the worship of God, on

231. In Jn 14.27, n. 1962.

which they encourage one another. . . . Consider Isaiah 2: "Come, let us ascend to the mountain of the Lord, and to the house of the God of Jacob; and God will teach us God's ways, and we will walk along God's paths."[232]

FOX: We bring our peace and joy with us when we worship or celebrate together—and this seems to increase the joy among us.

AQUINAS: It is natural for people to seek after pleasure, and they always seek after it and if it is lost through anxiety, then one immediately rushes into the pleasures of evil.[233]

FOX: This observation helps explain, I think, many of the addictions into which adults have fallen in our time: anxiety outweighs authentic pleasure, and so people turn to drugs and unhealthy pleasures. How important it is that adults rediscover our childlike ways of playing—that is, celebrating—in the universe!

AQUINAS: Children do not have anxieties, so they are free in regard to the things that they seek for themselves: this is playing.[234]

FOX: It seems to me that adults in our culture often feel guilty about playing.

AQUINAS: A game is not evil in and of itself; otherwise there could not be a virtue in games, which is called *eutrapelia* (playfulness). But depending on the diverse purposes by which a game is ordered and the diverse circumstances that define it, it can be an activity either of virtue or of vice. For since it is impossible to be always engaged in the active and contemplative life, therefore it is sometimes necessary to intersperse joys with cares, lest the mind be broken by too much severity. In this way a person may be more readily open to virtuous activity.[235]

FOX: Can adults retrieve the instinct for play that we once had as children?

AQUINAS: Human beings are naturally social, and on account of this, since one naturally needs another, they find pleasure in living together. Thus the Philosopher says in 1 *Politics:* "Every person who is solitary is either more than human and is a god;

---

232. In Jer 31, p. 648. 233. In Mt 11, p. 110. 234. Ibid. 235. In Is 3, p. 445.

or is worse than human and is a beast." Thus it is said in Matthew's gospel "for those sitting in the marketplace," because no one wishes to play by oneself, but in the forum or meeting place where many gather is where play takes place. Likewise it must be noted that it is natural for human beings that their delight be in some representation: thus if we see something well sculpted that represents well that which it should, then we are delighted. In the same way children who are delighted in games always play those games with some representation either of war or the like. It should also be noted that all affects of the mind end in one of two passions: namely, either joy or grief.

Matthew's gospel says: "Those who are calling, etc." This must be seen in the following way: Let us suppose that there are some boys on one side and others on another in such a way that some are going to sing, others dance; these do one thing, the others respond to them. If one group sang, and the other did not respond to them in accordance with their beauty, they would be treated unjustly by them. Thus the gospel says: "They say: we have sung for you, and you have not danced."[236]

FOX: How important this is—that our refusal to celebrate, to return blessing for blessing, or song for dance, if you will, is an issue of *justice and injustice*. Another instance where compassion brings together justice and celebration.

AQUINAS: Nothing alters the soul like a song: whence Boethius recounts in his *Musica* about a certain man who was arguing with another man in the presence of Pythagoras, and others were present who were singing in chant. Then Pythagoras made them change the mode, and the man calmed down. Thus all were trained in music. Therefore it should be noted that a certain song is for joy, as Ecclesiasticus 40:20 says: "Wine and music gladden the heart." Therefore it is said in the gospel, "We have sung," that is, we have uttered a song of joy, "and you have not danced." Likewise it is a custom that as some are influenced toward joy, so some are moved toward weeping. Whence Jeremiah 9:17 says: "Call the mourners, and let them mourn over us, etc." Therefore the gospel says: "We have wept," that is, we have made songs of mourning, "and you have not grieved."[237]

---

236. Ibid.   237. In Mt 5, p. 52.

FOX: You mentioned that our capacity for festivity and play is a kind of virtue.

AQUINAS: There can be a virtue about games. The Philosopher gives it the name of *eutrapelia* or playfulness, and a person is said to be playful or witty from having a happy turn of mind (from the Greek word *trepein,* to turn).[238]

FOX: I suspect that calling a virtue about celebration "turning" might also imply the ability to change gears, to see paradox, to fall into laughter and to move others, as well as to let go by suspending the busyness of our minds and bodies.

AQUINAS: Words or deeds wherein nothing further is sought than the soul's delight are called playful or humorous. Hence, it is necessary at times to make use of them, in order to give rest, so to speak, to the soul.[239]

FOX: Tell us more about this virtue of game playing—I think we adults need much more of it in our day. To teach and learn it would truly be part of a transformative process in an adultist and self-conscious society that takes itself too seriously.

AQUINAS: Just as people need bodily rest for the body's refreshment, because they cannot always be at work, since their power is finite and equal to a certain fixed amount of labor, so too is it with our soul, whose power is also finite and equal to a fixed amount of work. . . . Just as weariness of the body is dispelled by resting the body, so weariness of the soul must of necessity be remedied by resting the soul; and the soul's rest is pleasure.[240]

FOX: Pleasure brings rest to the soul, you say. I sense here some insight about the problem of acedia that we spoke of earlier: one remedy to a weariness of soul and body is the refreshment that celebration brings.

AQUINAS: It is related of Blessed John the Evangelist in the *Conferences of the Fathers* (24:21) that when some people were scandalized on finding him playing together with his disciples, he is said to have told one of them who carried a bow to shoot an arrow. And when the latter had done this several times, he asked him whether he could do it indefinitely, and the man answered that if he continued doing it, the bow would break.

---

238. ST II-II, q. 168, a. 2.   239. Ibid.   240. Ibid.

Whence Blessed John drew the inference that in like manner a person's mind would break if its tension were never relaxed.[241]

FOX: What kind of virtue is our art of playfulness?

AQUINAS: To be playful is part of the virtue of modesty.[242]

FOX: That is interesting—it helps explain why a playful person is more trustworthy than an overly serious one. Play has something to do with acknowledging our limits. If celebration is a virtue, then the refusal of people to be playful or of our institutions to teach us arts of celebration would seem to relate to pride or excessive self-consciousness.

AQUINAS: In human affairs whatever is against reason is a sin. Now it is against reason for anyone to be burdensome to others by offering no pleasure to them, and by hindering their enjoyment. . . . Now anyone who is without mirth is not only lacking in playful speech, but is also burdensome to others, since they are deaf to the moderate mirth of others. Consequently they are sinful and are said to be ungrateful boors.[243]

FOX: This discussion about compassion as celebration reminds me of our previous Via Creativa discussion of the contemplative life as also being a life of play and celebration.

AQUINAS: Contemplation concerns ends that serve no ulterior purpose. Play, too, is concerned with ends when you play for the fun of it, though with means to ends when you take exercise in order to keep fit.[244] The contemplative life is a kind of holiday. "Be still and see that I am the Lord" (Ps. 46:10). It is a life lived with divine things.[245]

FOX: And a great delight ensues from our contemplative experience?

AQUINAS: There may be delight in any particular contemplation in two ways. First, by reason of the operation itself, because everyone delights in the operation that befits them according to their own nature or habit. Now, contemplation of the truth befits one according to one's nature as a rational animal: the result being that all people naturally desire to know, so that consequently they delight in the knowledge of truth. And more delightful still does this become to those who have the habit of

---

241. Ibid.   242. Ibid.   243. Ibid., a. 4.   244. CG III, ch. 2 n. 9.   245. ST II-II, q. 182, a. 1.

wisdom and knowledge, the result of which is that they contemplate without difficulty.

Second, contemplation may be delightful in respect to its object, insofar as one contemplates that which one loves. Even as bodily vision gives pleasure, not only because to see is pleasurable in itself, but because one sees a person whom one loves. Since, then, the contemplative life consists chiefly in the contemplation of God, of which charity is the motive, it follows that there is delight in the contemplative life, not only by reason of the contemplation itself, but also by reason of divine love.[246]

FOX: And this pleasure is a very great one, you are saying?

AQUINAS: In both respects this delight surpasses all human delight, both because spiritual delight is greater than carnal pleasure . . . and because the love whereby God is loved out of charity surpasses all love. Hence it is written (Ps. 34:8): "O taste and see that the Lord is good."[247]

FOX: I hope when you contrast "spiritual delight" to "carnal pleasure" you are not creating an either/or. After all, lovemaking can surely qualify as a spiritual delight. This is what the "Song of Songs" celebrates in the Bible. Yet it is clear from your statement that contemplation for you is not a merely rational exercise.

AQUINAS: Although the contemplative life consists chiefly in an act of the intellect, it has its beginning in the appetite, since it is through charity that one is urged to the contemplation of God. And since the end corresponds to the beginning, it follows that the term also and the end of the contemplative life has its being in the appetite, since one delights in seeing the object loved, and the very delight in the object seen arouses a yet greater love. . . . This is the ultimate perfection of the contemplative life, namely, that the divine truth be not only seen but also loved.[248]

FOX: And this tasting and loving is of a deeply delightful mode.

AQUINAS: The love of the Holy Spirit overwhelms the soul like a torrent, as Isaiah puts it (59): "Like a violent river which the spirit of the Lord sets in motion." And it seems pleasurable,

---

246. Ibid., q. 180, a. 7.   247. Ibid.   248. Ibid., ad 1.

since it makes pleasure and sweetness in the soul, as Wisdom (12) says: "O how good and sweet, Lord, is your spirit in us!" And the good drink this drink, as in 1 Corinthians 10: "They drank the same spiritual drink." Or with the onrush of your pleasure, namely, of God, which is called an onrush. Proverbs 18 speaks of "a flowing torrent, a fountain of wisdom." Since God's will is so effective that it cannot be resisted as an onrush cannot. Romans 9: "Who can resist God's will?" . . . Jeremiah 2 says: "They left me the fountain of living water, etc." Which truly is the fountain of life, that is, of spiritual goods, from which all things are enlivened.[249]

FOX: In this entire discussion of compassion as justice making and as celebration I get the feeling that we are in fact involved in redefining—or, if you will, more fully defining—the very meaning of words like "salvation" and "redemption," which I fear we throw around too easily in our religious language. The Via Transformativa is surely that—a transformation of our ways and even of our words.

AQUINAS: Jeremiah announces deliverance and brings it forth. First he stirs the nations up to attention. "Hear!" he says in order that all may take confidence in the one who is able to liberate in the way he is doing. Isaiah 49 says: "Hear you islands, and pay attention, you people from far away." Second, Jeremiah proclaims the deliverance of the people, in spite of divine indignation, since "he who scatters Israel will bring it back together again." Isaiah 40 says: "As a shepherd gathers his lambs in his arms, he brings his lambs together and carries them in his lap and he himself will carry the newborn." The power of those who detain does not hinder: "He redeems them," namely, the Chaldeans. Psalm 72 says: "God has freed the poor ones from the powerful, and the needy from the one who was not his helper." Third, he promises prosperity to those who have been freed—first in regard to all he promises about the due observance of religion. Isaiah 51 says: "Those who have been redeemed by the Lord will return, and will come to Sion with praise and with eternal joy upon their heads." He also promises the abundance of temporal goods, proclaiming the fertility of good things with regard to the burgeoning elements of the earth

---

249. In Pss 35, p. 280.

that produce our food, and with regard to animals that furnish our food. "And they will flow together and they will praise" God "over grain and wine." Genesis 27: "I have established him with grain and wine and olive oil." And he promises the satiety of those possessing them: "And their soul will be like an irrigated garden" that does not wait for the rain. This can be understood from the spiritual goods brought together through Christ, which will be fulfilled now partially, but totally in the future. Revelation 7 says: "They will not be hungry, nor will they thirst any more, nor will the sun strike them, nor any burning heat." And Jeremiah promises the gladness of the heart, with regard to the signs of gladness, he says: "Israel will be gladdened." Chapter 30: "Praise will go forth from them, and the voice of those playing, and I will increase their numbers, etc." And with regard to the elimination of sadness, he says: "I will turn their grief into joy."[250]

FOX: Yes! In this passage from your commentary on Jeremiah's promise of a New Covenant you surely do seem to summarize beautifully the discussion we have had up to now about the Via Transformativa—Liberation and Celebration coming together. You also reintroduce the role of Christ. Earlier you spoke of Christ as being Compassion and the teacher of compassion. Who else is Jesus for you in light of the Via Transformativa? How does Christ enter further into this discussion on compassion, justice, and celebration?

AQUINAS: Jeremiah says: "In those days I will make the seed of David sprout justice." Christ is justice itself. Isaiah 11 says: "A sprout from the root of Jesse will come forth, and a flower will come up from its root."[251]

FOX: To say that "Christ is justice itself" is surely to put the struggle for justice at the heart of the Christian way of life.

AQUINAS: Jesus Christ was always wisdom and justice in himself, yet it can be said that he was newly made justice and wisdom for us.[252]

FOX: What does it mean to say Christ is justice itself?

AQUINAS: Christ makes judgment first by coming on behalf of the world, and second by teaching justice about the world when

---

250. In Jer 31, p. 648. 251. In Jer 33, p. 655. 252. In Jn 1.3, n. 92.

he teaches with the word, and by fulfilling it in himself by his deeds and in the gift of grace toward others. Psalm 119 says: "I have made judgment and justice."[253]

FOX: Is compassion part of the mystery of the Incarnation?

AQUINAS: To assume flesh was a sign of an incomprehensible compassion on God's part.[254]

FOX: And so the very existence of Christ and his life is a kind of teaching of compassion on God's part toward us?

AQUINAS: The life of Christ is the model and form of our justice.[255]

FOX: What would be an example of this?

AQUINAS: Peace is maintained by justice. "And the work of justice shall be peace" (Isa. 32:17).[256]

FOX: But isn't peace a fruit of love more than of justice?

AQUINAS: Peace is the work of justice indirectly, insofar as justice removes the obstacles to peace. But it is the work of charity directly, since love, according to its very nature, causes peace.[257]

FOX: I understand how justice, by removing injustice, makes peace possible. But how does love cause peace?

AQUINAS: Charity causes peace precisely because it is love of God and of our neighbor. . . . There is no other virtue except charity, whose proper act is peace. We have said the same thing about joy.[258]

FOX: How does Christ bring peace?

AQUINAS: Christ makes peace and gives peace, since "He himself is our peace, who makes all things one" (Eph. 2). "And in me you have peace" (John 17).[259]

FOX: Can you give us a concrete example of how Christ brought peace?

AQUINAS: The manner of convergence is revealed when Paul states in the letter to the Ephesians that Christ "breaks down the middle barrier of partition." The method, then, consists in removing what is divisive. To understand the text we should imagine a large field with many people gathered on it. But a

---

253. In Jer 33, p. 655.   254. In Jn 1.14a, n. 169.   255. In Eph 1.19b, p. 453.   256. Ibid. 4.3, p. 476.   257. ST II-II, q. 29, a. 3, ad 3.   258. Ibid., a. 4.   259. In Pss 34, p. 276.

high barrier was thrown across the middle of it, segregating the peoples so that they did not appear as one people but two. Whoever would remove the barrier would unite the crowds of people into one multitude, one people would be formed.[260]

FOX: Thus Christ destroys dualisms and thereby brings peace?

AQUINAS: Christ has put an end to this barrier, and since no division remained, the Jews and the Gentiles became one people. This is what Paul says: I affirm that Christ "has made both one" by the method of "breaking down the middle barrier." . . . To break down this barrier of partition is to destroy the hostility between the Jews and Gentiles. . . . But certainly Christ has abolished this animosity in his assumed flesh. For at his birth peace was immediately proclaimed to humans (cf. Luke 2:14). Or, in his immolated flesh since "he has delivered himself for us, an oblation and a sacrifice to God" (Eph. 5:2).[261]

FOX: Your description of Christ's redemption or liberation in terms of breaking down dualisms and barriers has many practical applications far beyond the Jew/Gentile issue. It would seem to be applicable to so many of our issues of war and peace; of earth/human; of male/female, poor/wealthy, black/white, and so on.

AQUINAS: Christ's coming has broken down the old barrier of damnation. The entire human race is now more open to receive grace than before. . . . Now the Gospel has been preached and all is set for every imperfection of our humanity to be cleared away.[262]

FOX: You certainly sound hopeful. Can you further describe the liberation that Christ brings?

AQUINAS: Isaiah foretells the liberation of the tribes from the servitude of sin, through the son born of God. First he describes their liberator with regard to the eminence of his grace: he will understand with regard to the fullness of his wisdom; [he will be] "servant" according to his assumed nature, the Christ. Philippians 2 says: "Taking the form of a servant." Proverbs 14 says: "He found favor with the king as a wise servant." "He will be exalted" says Isaiah, meaning with regard to the work of the virtues. Psalm 21 says: "Be exalted in your strength, O Lord!"

---

260. In Eph 2.14, p. 462.   261. Ibid.   262. In I Sent, 15.5.2 and ad 2.

Isaiah says he will be "lifted up," this applies to his ascension. Psalm 8 says: "Since your glory has been raised above the heavens." "And sublime," says Isaiah, sitting at the right hand of the Father. Isaiah 4 says: "The branch of the Lord shall be beautiful and glorious and the fruit of the earth shall be a source of pride." And with regard to the ignominy of his passion, for "just as they were astonished" by his example, miracles and teaching. Matthew 12 says: "All the crowds were astounded by his teaching, and by the miracles which he performed." He will be "inglorious" in his passion "and without beauty" regarding the comeliness of his spirit. Psalm 22 says: "I am a worm, not a man, scorned by men, and rejected by the people."

Isaiah also foretells liberation with regard to the forgiveness of sins: "That one will sprinkle"—by the sprinkling of his blood and the water of baptism. With regard to the veneration of that one, "Over that one kings will restrain their mouth, keeping silent," in order to hear, not presuming to handle the mysteries of that one. Job 29 says: "The nobles will stop speaking." And with regard to the knowledge of the truth: "Since to them," namely, to the people, "it has not been told," through the prophets, "they have seen," with their heart, "they have heard," that one proclaiming personally. Isaiah 65 says: "Behold, I go to the people who do not know me and who do not call on my name."[263]

FOX: Once again, as when we discussed Christ in the Via Creativa, I sense how rich your Christology is and how it is by no means limited to the cross/redemption motifs. You see Christ in so many modes, including that of teacher. It is obvious that Christ, who is, as you said, supremely virtuous, is compassionate and just—or even "justice itself" as you said above—but does he also instruct us in the celebrative dimension of compassion?

AQUINAS: Christ takes joy in eternity from two things: namely, from his good and from that of the Father. Proverbs 8:30 says: "I was God's delight playing on earth before God." Likewise Christ takes joy from the good of the rational creature, as in Proverbs 8:31: "My delight is to be with the sons and daughters of the human race." This means in that which I am

---

263. In Is 52, p. 552.

sharing with the children of the human race and from these things Christ takes joy in eternity. Isaiah (62:5) says: "Your God will rejoice over you."[264]

FOX: This lends a whole new dimension to our need to learn celebration—namely, that Divinity depends on us for its own joy and delight! Of course Christ calls us to share his joy as well.

AQUINAS: The Lord wishes that through observing his commands we are made sharers in his joy: whence he says, "That my joy"—namely, by which I take joy in my divinity and that of the Father—"be in you." This is nothing other than eternal life, which is joy in truth.[265]

FOX: So "eternal life" means joy. Christ's teaching also brings us joy.

AQUINAS: The doctrine of Christ is light in its effect among all persons, for it alters the heart and makes us love not temporal things but more spiritual things.[266]

FOX: And Christ's redemption also liberates us for compassion, that is, for justice and celebration?

AQUINAS: Even to the end of the world Christ's sons and daughters are regenerated by virtue of his death. John 12 says: "If the grain of wheat which falls on the earth does not die, it remains alone by itself; however, if it does die, it brings forth much fruit."[267] Against sin Isaiah promises the passion of Christ; against depression, he promises exaltation, as in chapter 54: "Sing, barren one, who did not beget." Against poverty, he promises the gratuitous fruition of things in this place, as in chapter 55: "All you who are thirsty, come to the waters."[268]

FOX: Was Christ a man of poverty?

AQUINAS: Christ was poor not only in his desire but also in fact.[269] Christ in his own person, living in this world, was both beggarly and poor. 2 Corinthians 8 says: "You know the grace of our Lord Jesus Christ who, although he was rich, became poor for us, so that by his poverty you might become rich." He is called beggarly who seeks food from another; indeed a pauper, who is not sufficient for himself. And these two things are said of Christ, as in Luke 9: "The son of man does not have a

---

264. In Jn 15.11, n. 2004. 265. Ibid. 266. In Mt 11, p. 114. 267. In Is 53, p. 554. 268. Ibid., p. 552. 269. CI ch. 6, p. 31.

place to lay his head." Or spiritually, I have need to depend on
God for the help of grace. "And I am a pauper," since what I
have is not sufficient.[270] By altogether despising all riches,
Christ showed the highest kind of generosity and magnificence.[271]

FOX: And yet Jesus' poverty was certainly less strict than that
of others, for example, that of John the Baptist in the desert.

AQUINAS: Since John was a pure man, he withdrew himself
from carnal desires; but Christ was God, so if he had led an
austere life, he would not have shown himself to be human;
therefore he undertook more of a human life. Likewise John was
the end of the Old Testament, upon whom heavy burdens were
placed; but Christ was the beginning of the new law, which
proceeds along the path of gentleness.[272]

FOX: We will no doubt want to go more deeply into Christ's
teaching about the New Law later, but I am struck by your
statement on the gentleness of that law.

AQUINAS: When anyone loves anyone else, whatever they suffer for their beloved does not burden them: whence love makes
all burdensome and impossible things light. Thus if anyone
loves Christ well, nothing is burdensome for them; and therefore the new law does not burden.[273]

FOX: Christ's teaching is also good news to the poor, is it not?

AQUINAS: Matthew says "The poor have the gospel preached
to them," that is, poverty has the gospel preached to it. Thus
Matthew 5:3 says: "Happy the poor in spirit, etc." And Luke
4:18 says: "The spirit of the Lord is upon me on account of
which God has anointed me and sent me to preach good news
to the poor."[274]

FOX: You are citing a text that speaks of Christ as prophet. Do
you understand Jesus as being part of the prophetic tradition of
Israel?

AQUINAS: Christ was a prophet, as is clear from "The Lord
your God will raise up a prophet among you, from your nation
and your brothers; he will be like me. You will listen to him"

---

270. In Pss 39, p. 304.   271. ST III, q. 7, a. 2, ad 3.   272. In Mt 11, p.
111.   273. Ibid., 114.   274. Ibid., 108.

(Deut. 18:15). This text is referred to Christ.[275] The greatest of the prophets is none other than Christ.[276]

FOX: Do you believe Christ calls us all to be prophets?

AQUINAS: It is characteristic of prophets to reveal what is not present but hidden. Although Christ was a prophet, he was more than a prophet because he produces prophets: "Wisdom produces friends of God and prophets" (Wis. 7:27).[277]

FOX: This saying of yours is very powerful. Previously in the Via Creativa you established Christ as Wisdom; now you celebrate Christ as prophet in the Via Transformativa. Let us pursue more deeply your understanding of prophecy, as this will shed light not only on Christ but on all of us who are, as you say, prophets that Christ "produces." What do we mean when we use the word "prophet"?

AQUINAS: The act of prophecy is to know hidden things and to announce them.[278] The prophet is said to be not only one who speaks from afar, that is, one who announces, but also one who sees from afar, from the Greek *phanos,* which is an appearing.[279]

FOX: One might say then that the prophet has vision and announces vision for the people.

AQUINAS: Prophecy has two acts: one is primary, namely, sight; and the other is secondary, namely, announcing. The prophet does the announcing either by words or even by deeds, as is clear in Jeremiah (13:5). . . . But in whichever of the two ways the prophetic announcing is made, it is always made by someone not transported out of their senses, for such an announcing takes place through certain outward signs. Hence, the prophets doing the announcing have to use their senses for their announcement to the perfect. Otherwise, the prophet would make the announcement like an insane person.[280]

FOX: Does prophecy deal with issues that we can know by ways other than inspiration, for example, by way of science?

AQUINAS: Many things that are proved in the sciences can be useful for instruction in the faith or for the formation of morals. For instance, that our understanding is incorruptible, and also

275. In Jn 4.44, n. 667.   276. In Jn 1.21, n. 233.   277. In Jn 4.19, n. 596.   278. DV, q. 12, a. 3, ad 15.   279. Ibid., a. 1.   280. Ibid., a. 9.

those things that when considered in creatures lead to admiration of the divine wisdom and power. Hence, we find that mention of these is made in Holy Scripture. . . . Thus, conclusions that are demonstrated in the sciences can belong to prophecy.[281]

FOX: Thus our scientific work and other professions all have a potential prophetic contribution to make. Do you see Jesus' role as prophet as fulfilling the two aspects of prophecy—vision and announcing?

AQUINAS: The prophet makes known, announces: Christ was a prophet in this sense for he made known the truth about God: "For this was I born, and for this I came into the world: to testify to the truth" (John 18:37). As for the seeing function of a prophet, we should note that Christ was at once both a "wayfarer" and a "comprehensor," or blessed. He was a wayfarer in the sufferings of his human nature and in all the things that related to this. He was blessed in his union with the Divinity, by which he enjoyed God in the most perfect way. There are two things in the vision or seeing of a prophet. First, the intellectual light of the mind; and regarding this Christ was not a prophet, because his light was not at all deficient; his light was that of the blessed. Second, an imaginary vision is also involved; and with respect to this Christ did have a likeness to the prophets insofar as he was a wayfarer and was able to form various images with his imagination.[282]

FOX: I am interested in the role of the imagination in our prophetic vocation, especially in light of the relationship between the Via Creativa, where imagination is awakened and trained, and the Via Transformativa, when we are, like Christ, anointed as prophets. Can you elaborate on the role imagination plays in prophecy?

AQUINAS: Now, prophecy has two acts: sight and declaration. For sight, however, two things are needed: judgment, which is in the understanding, and reception, which is sometimes in the understanding and sometimes in the imagination.[283] Perfection of the imagination is needed for prophecy, but it is not necessarily needed beforehand. For God, who infuses the gifts of prophecy, can improve the constitution of the organ of the imaginative powers, as God can make bleary eyes see clearly.[284]

---

281. Ibid., a. 2.   282. In Jn 4.44, n. 667.   283. DV, q. 12, a. 13.   284. Ibid., a. 4, ad 2.

FOX: You called prophecy a gift.

AQUINAS: Prophecy is classified among the greatest goods, since it is a free gift.[285]

FOX: And so if anyone has not trained their imagination—if the Via Creativa has not been undergone in some depth so that a disposition for imagination is present—then it seems the person can refuse the gift and abort their prophetic call.

AQUINAS: One can prevent oneself from using prophecy. And the proper disposition is a necessary requirement for the proper use of prophecy, since the use of prophecy proceeds from the created power of the prophet. Hence, a definite disposition is also required.[286]

FOX: Every potential prophet ought to exercise the artist within them if they are to be ready and disposed when the prophetic call comes. There is a very important lesson here in terms of theological pedagogy, it seems to me. Without art as meditation enabling our potential prophets to exercise their imaginations, we will have fewer prophets than we need. And yet, while we can acquire the disposition for prophecy by exercising our imaginations, still, prophecy is a gift beyond our human imaginations, is it not?

AQUINAS: Two things concur in effecting prophetic revelation: the illumination of the mind and the formation of the image in the imaginative power.[287] The prophet does not need a new infusion of the image of those things that they have seen, but only an orderly grouping of the images retained in the storehouse of the imaginative power, which can suitably designate the thing to be prophesied.[288] The formation of images in the sight of imagination takes place supernaturally in the prophet.[289]

FOX: And so the prophet's imagination is touched by God.

AQUINAS: The images preexisting in the imaginative power of the prophet, insofar as they exist there, are not capable of signifying future things. Therefore, they must be reshaped into something else by the divine power.[290] The images preexisting in the imagination of the prophet are, as it were, the elements of that vision of imagination which is revealed by the divine

---

285. Ibid., a. 3, ad 15.   286. Ibid., a. 4.   287. Ibid., a. 8.   288. Ibid., a. 7, ad 3.   289. Ibid., ad 5.   290. Ibid., ad 6.

power, since it is somehow made up of them. Thus it is that prophets use the likenesses of things with which they are familiar.[291]

FOX: What else is needed by the prophet besides understanding and imagination?

AQUINAS: There are two excellent gifts in the prophet, namely, prophecy, as Joel says (2:28): "I will pour forth my spirit upon all flesh, and your sons and daughters will prophesy." And also the gift of justice. 1 Corinthians 1:30 says: "But you are from the very one who has been made wisdom and justice for you."[292]

FOX: And so the prophet has a special relationship to the vision of justice and the criticism of injustice.

AQUINAS: The prophet hated the unjust, as such, and the object of the prophet's hate was their injustice, which was their evil. Such hatred is complete, of which God himself says (Ps. 139:22): "I have hated them with a perfect hatred." Now hatred of a person's evil is equivalent to love of a person's good. Hence also this perfect hatred belongs to charity.[293]

FOX: And so hatred of injustice—a passion for justice—lies in the belly of every prophet. Does this passion for justice not arouse enemies as well?

AQUINAS: John's gospel says that "Jesus himself had testified that a prophet has no honor in his own country." . . . Now what the Lord says was true with respect to most of the prophets, because in the Old Testament it is hard to find any prophet who did not suffer persecution, as stated in Acts (7:52): "Which of the prophets did your fathers not persecute?"; and in Matthew (23:37): "Jerusalem, Jerusalem, you kill the prophets and stone those who are sent to you." Further, this statement of our Lord holds true not only in the case of the prophets among the Jews, but also, as Origen says, with many among the Gentiles, because they were held in contempt by their fellow citizens and put to death: they lived among men in the usual way, and too much familiarity lessens respect and breeds contempt. So it is

---

291. Ibid., ad 7.   292. In Mt 10, p. 108.   293. ST II-II, q. 25, a. 6, ad 1.

that those with whom we are more familiar we come to reverence less, and those with whom we cannot become acquainted we regard more highly.[294]

FOX: It is interesting to me that you point out that the Gentiles too have their prophets.

AQUINAS: At no time have there ever been persons lacking the spirit of prophecy, not indeed for the declaration of any new doctrine of faith, but for the direction of human acts.[295] At all times humanity was divinely instructed about what they were to do, according as it was expedient for the spiritual welfare of the elect.[296]

FOX: Prophecy then is one way in which the Spirit guides us in our actions—in "what we are to do," as you put it.

AQUINAS: Prophecy is directed to the knowledge of divine truth, by the contemplation of which we are not only instructed in faith, but also guided in our actions.[297]

FOX: The prophet, then, wrestles with evil spirits, one might say.

AQUINAS: Evil results from a failure to act.[298] The need for prophecy comes from the multitude of evils, "since they have multiplied beyond the number of good things." And so for this—that evils be lessened and good things increased—it was necessary that an announcement be made to the people. Matthew 7 says: "Narrow is the way that leads to life, and wide is that way which leads to destruction." And Ecclesiastes 1 says: "The number of fools is infinite."[299]

FOX: If the prophet must wrestle with evil forces, it seems the sin of fear raises its head again here in the Via Transformativa as it did in the Via Creativa, for example. The prophet needs the virtue of courage.

AQUINAS: The prophet Jeremiah, in order to proclaim the word of God, exposed himself to the danger of death, left his home and fatherland, and endured the traps of his compatriots like those of lions, both cunning in their trickery and full of malice.[300]

---

294. In Jn 4.44, n. 666.   295. ST II-II, q. 174, a. 6, ad 3.   296. Ibid., a. 6.   297. Ibid.   298. DSS, 152.   299. In Pss 39, p. 301.   300. In Jer 12, p. 609.

FOX: And so the prophet needs courage to live as well as courage to speak out.

AQUINAS: For proclamation something is needed in those proclaiming, namely, a certain boldness so that they will not be afraid to speak the truth because of the opponents of the truth. In this sense the Lord said to Ezekiel (3:8–9): "Behold I have made your face stronger than their faces: and your forehead harder than their foreheads . . . fear them not, neither be you dismayed at their presence."[301]

FOX: The prophet is bold, you say. Can you give us an example of this boldness among the prophets?

AQUINAS: The occasion of the persecution of Jeremiah came from his proclaiming. Thus first he refers to the place of his proclaiming, "Stand in the doorway of the house of the Lord, and there proclaim an all-encompassing word" (Jer. 7:1).[302]

FOX: It would seem that the vocation to announce gets the prophet in a certain amount of trouble.

AQUINAS: Isaiah shows the strength of prophecy by comparison with the fragility of men: whence the Lord first indicates a shouting, which signifies a distinct and clear announcement. "Shout!" Isaiah 58 says: "Shout, do not stop. Raise your voice like a trumpet!"[303]

FOX: Please elaborate on the "announcing" that the prophet is called to do.

AQUINAS: Isaiah lays out who, for whom, and in what way he will announce. Who? The one who has the duty, "you who proclaim the gospel." Romans 10 says: "How will they proclaim, unless they are sent?" Isaiah designates the manner by three things: first, by the height of the place, in order that the one announcing the good things be heard from afar, "on the mountain." . . . Isaiah 2: "Come, let us ascend the mountain of the Lord." Isaiah 42: "From the top of the mountain, they will shout." Second, by the noise of their voice, "rise up in strength," so that many may hear, by praying clearly and steadfastly. Isaiah 58: "Shout, do not cease, raise your voice like a trumpet." Third, through the security of one's heart. "Rise up,

---

301. DV, q. 12, a. 13.   302. In Jer 26, p. 639.   303. In Is 40, p. 527.

do not fear." Jeremiah 1: "Do not fear facing them, since I am with you."[304]

FOX: Part of the prophet's task is to shout like a trumpet?

AQUINAS: Take note of the saying in Isaiah, "exalt like a trumpet." For the proclamation is a trumpet. First, because it stirs one up to the state of life, as in 1 Corinthians 15: "For the trumpet will sound, and the dead will arise incorruptible." Second, because it urges us on to war. 1 Corinthians 14: "If the trumpet gives an uncertain sound, who will prepare themselves for war?" Third, because it announces the waking of someone. Isaiah 27: "A trumpet will be blown." Fourth, because it calls one to a plan. Hosea 8 says: "Set a trumpet to your lips." Fifth, because it invites to a feast, as in Psalm 81: "Blow the horn in the ceremonies on the special day of your solemnity."[305]

FOX: Once again I am impressed—as I was in the Via Creativa—at your application of biblical texts usually invoked for the "second resurrection" or our death to what you called earlier the "first resurrection" or our waking up here and now. Truly prophets awaken us, and part of their trumpeting is telling us the bad news that we would rather deny or avoid. They dare to lead us into the Via Negativa, where we do not want to go.

AQUINAS: Jeremiah puts forth the greatness of fear and anxiety: "Woe, because of a great"—by a greatness of tribulation—"day"—that is, the taking of Jerusalem. Wisdom 1 says: "The sound of the day of the Lord is bitter; at that time the brave person will be troubled. That day is the day of wrath, the day of tribulation and perplexities; the day of calamity and of wretchedness; the day of shadows and of darkness, the day of cloud and whirlwind; the day of trumpet and of confusion, etc."[306]

FOX: No wonder the prophet is seldom popular! He or she names the fear of the times.

AQUINAS: Fear makes people slaves. Love sets them free.[307]

FOX: Sometimes I wonder what price humanity pays for fear.

AQUINAS: When they are brought up under a regime of fear people inevitably degenerate. They become mean-spirited and adverse to many and strenuous feats.[308]

---

304. Ibid. 305. In Is 58, p. 562. 306. In Jer 30, p. 645. 307. Sermo, p. 97. 308. I DRP 3.

FOX: And so fear discourages magnanimity and the expansion of the soul. Of course the prophet offers some good news too in the form of hope for liberation.

AQUINAS: Jeremiah also promises future salvation: and first he promises deliverance. "And by that very one he will be saved," namely, from time, as though from evil. Hosea 1 says: "I will save them by the Lord their God." Second, Jeremiah promises the manner and order of salvation, promising freedom from servitude excluding the power of enemies. "And it will be on that day . . . I will break the yoke," which is Nebuchanezar himself. "And they will not be dominated," . . . Or reference must be made to the freeing made through Christ from the power of demons. Isaiah 9 says: "For you have broken the yoke of his burden, and the bar upon his shoulder, and the rod of his oppressor."[309]

FOX: The prophet has enemies then and faces them.

AQUINAS: Christ had and has many enemies. Psalm 119 says: "They hated me without cause." And God has enemies: John 15 says: "They hated me and my Father." And other just people have enemies, who do not live without affliction. The psalmist says, "and they were much strengthened," that is, they have great power, in fact, they are too powerful. "And those who hate me wickedly were increased," that is, unjustly, since they persecute me on account of the justice that I was following.[310]

FOX: It is the prophets' trust in God that makes them strong.

AQUINAS: The psalmist says that other people are made weak on account of the fear of the world, since they waver; but fear of God makes us strong. Since, as is said in Ecclesiasticus 34: "One who fears the Lord will tremble at nothing."[311]

FOX: In spite of the struggle, the prophet experiences a deep peace.

AQUINAS: Take note of the saying in Isaiah, "the work of justice will be peace. . . ." The saints reckon three things in regard to the peace that they desire. First, the strength of divine power. Psalm 125 says: "Those who believe in the Lord are like Mount Sion which will never be shaken, those who live in Jerusalem."

---

309. In Jer 30, p. 645.   310. In Pss 37, p. 295.   311. In Pss 24, p. 232.

Second, the purity of one's own conscience, as in Proverbs 3: "You will walk confidently along your way, and your foot will not stumble." Third, the removal of hostile evil, as in John 16: "Be confident, I have overcome the world."[312]

FOX: A prophet is in some sense a warrior, then, who struggles with justice and injustice and who resists fear.

AQUINAS: Jeremiah excludes the fear of enemy persecution: "Do not fear." Isaiah 51 says: "Who are you that you fear mortal man, and the son of man, who will be consumed like straw?" And God promises the help of assistance: "Since I am with you" (Jer. 20). "The Lord is with me like a brave warrior. Therefore those who persecute me will fall, and become weak, and will be greatly ashamed, since they do not understand; their everlasting disgrace will never be forgotten." Isaiah 50 says: "The Lord God is my helper, and therefore I am not troubled."[313] Jeremiah even provides a deliverance from captivity, putting an end to the fear of the people. "So you may not fear me." Isaiah 43 says: "Don't fear, since I am with you. I will bring your offspring from the east, and will assemble you from the west." And putting forth the deliverance as a beginning point (*terminus a quo*): "Lo since I will save you from a faraway land." Zechariah 8 says: "Lo, I will save my people from the land of the east, and from the land of the setting sun, and I will lead them: and they will dwell in the midst of Jerusalem, and will be a people for me, and I will be God for them, in truth and in justice." And as an end point (*terminus ad quem*): "And he will be turned back and made quiet," as toward the tranquillity of peace, "and among all," as toward the fruitfulness of things. Isaiah 32 says: "My people will abide in the habitation of peace, and in a secure dwelling and in a quiet resting place."[314]

FOX: So part of the meaning of "savior" is assisting the "spiritual warrior" within us.

AQUINAS: Jeremiah shows the author of salvation: and first he brings forth the presence of the savior: "Since I am with you." Jeremiah 20 says: "The Lord is with me like a brave warrior." Second, he protects against enemies: "For I will make a consummation." He will lead them to the fulfillment of their purpose. Isaiah 10 says: "The Lord God will make a consummation

---

312. In Is 32, p. 515.   313. In Jer 42, p. 667.   314. In Jer 30, p. 645.

and cutting short of armies in the midst of all the earth." Third, he announces God's compassion in preserving [them]. "Of you I will not make a seed so that a remnant will remain." Jeremiah 5 says: "But in those days, the Lord does not say, 'I will make an end of you.' " Fourth, he brings in the moderate punishment for the purpose of chastising: "I will chastise you in justice." Jeremiah 10 says: "Snatch me away, Lord, but yet in justice, and not in your fury, lest perchance you reduce me to nothing, in just judgment."[315]

FOX: Jesus teaches his followers how their prophetic persecution will occur, doesn't he?

AQUINAS: Jesus says: "If they have persecuted you in one city, flee to another" (Matt. 10).[316] He says: "They have said every evil against you," that is, by harming your reputation in your absence by all kinds of evil words. And in this way there is a triple persecution: namely, of the heart, of the work, and of the mouth. . . . "For in this way they have persecuted the prophets." . . . They ought to suffer the passion by the example of the prophets. Whence, "thus"—that is, through insolence, injustices, and malicious words, "they have persecuted the prophets." James 5:10 says: "Take as an example, brothers, of suffering and endurance, of labor and patience, the prophets who have spoken in the name of the Lord" who "have been before you" and therefore their examples invite you.[317]

FOX: And so the communion of saints assists us in our need for endurance in our prophetic vocation and living out of the eighth beatitude.

AQUINAS: The eighth beatitude is a confirmation and declaration of all those that precede. Because from the fact that someone is confirmed in poverty of spirit, meekness, and the rest, it follows that no persecution will induce them to renounce them. Hence the eighth beatitude corresponds, in a way, to all the preceding seven.[318]

FOX: This is a powerful point you make that really underscores the centrality of the prophetic calling as Jesus teaches it: namely, that being a prophet and being treated like one summarizes the entire teaching of the Sermon on the Mount, which you have

---

315. Ibid., 646.   316. In Jer 26, p. 639.   317. In Mt 5, p. 54.   318. ST I-II, q. 69, a. 3, ad 5.

already labeled the "whole process of forming the life of a Christian." Why do you think prophets are so often hated?

AQUINAS: The apostles were chosen and elevated above the world to the extent that they were effective sharers in Divinity, and joined with God, and therefore the world considered them hateful. From this it follows that the world hated God in them rather than themselves. And the cause of this hatred was that the world did not have a true knowledge of God, namely, from true faith and devoted love. Otherwise, if they had known them as the friends of God, they would not have persecuted them.[319]

FOX: The prophet as warrior is also one who enters into the power of anger to get strength.

AQUINAS: To draw away from the harmful and to draw near to the pleasurable are both the business of the power of desire. But to fight against and overcome what can be harmful pertains to the power of anger.[320]

FOX: One might say, then, that our mysticism, which is our "Yes" to the beauty of life, is about the desire; and our prophecy, which is our "No" to that which interferes with life, is about the anger.

AQUINAS: The object of the power of anger is to resist the onslaught of what is opposed to us.[321] The anger is, as it were, the champion and defender of the desire, when it rises up against what hinders the acquisition of the attractive things that we desire or against what inflicts harm, from which the desire flees. And for this reason all the passions of the instinct of anger rise from the passions of the instinct of desire and terminate in them. For example, anger rises from sadness and, when it has wrought vengeance, terminates in joy. For this reason also the quarrels of animals are about objects of desire—namely, food and sex.[322]

FOX: I think it is important that you ground the anger, that is, the prophetic, in the desire, that is, the mystical. The Via Positiva precedes the Via Transformativa, after all.

AQUINAS: Prayer is the expression of desire.[323]

FOX: The prophet, it seems, practices a healthy anger.

---

319. In Jn 15.21, n. 2043.   320. DV, q. 25, a. 2, ad 3.   321. ST I, q. 81, a. 2, ad 1.   322. Ibid., a. 2.   323. OF, p. 103.

AQUINAS: Good and evil absolutely considered regard the instinct of desire, but insofar as the aspect of difficulty is added, they belong to the instinct of anger.[324] Jeremiah demonstrates zeal for justice: "I am full with the fury of the Lord," with fire— that is, with the zeal for the justice of the Lord. Numbers 25 says: "By zeal for me Phineas was moved against them, so that I did not destroy the sons of Israel in my zeal." Jeremiah also gives the command of destruction for his enemies: "Pour forth, on the Chaldean, your wrath," that is, abundantly, "abroad," on the plains and fields. Ecclesiasticus says (36): "Stir up fury, and pour forth wrath."[325]

FOX: Of course this zeal and fury and moral outrage that move the prophet are not the same as personal injury or not, as you say, "contrary to reason."

AQUINAS: The meek are so disposed first, that they are not disturbed internally in the judgment of reason by anger; second, they are not led by anger in external choice, for reason determines the objects of anger and the length of time within which anger should react.[326] Fury that is inordinate anger shares in the good to the extent that it is moved in a certain direction that appears good and just to it, namely, the vindication of an offense, and insofar as it desires to reduce and transform things, which by themselves appear evil, like harming a neighbor, into something appearing good and beautiful. For it is characteristic of anger always to strive toward that thing which seems to inflict punishment justly.[327]

FOX: The prophet's anger is not an end in itself, is it?

AQUINAS: The instinct of anger is, as it were, the champion of the instinct of desire, attacking what hinders pleasure or inflicts harm, which the instinct of desire both longs for and shrinks from. Anger starts from desire and leads to it.[328]

FOX: I think this is a very important point—that prophecy serves mysticism or what we desire and cherish. Too many people can let their anger run their lives, and that is not what prophecy is about. The irascible serves the concupiscible; anger is not a goal; rest in the objects of our desire is the goal. The prophet's response to anger also constitutes the work of the Spirit in transforming history, does it not?

---

324. ST II-II, q. 120, a. 1, ad 1.   325. In Jer 6, p. 594.   326. In Ethics IV, L. 13, p. 349.   327. DDN, n. 507, p. 177.   328. ST I, q. 81, a. 2.

AQUINAS: Sometimes the Spirit moves by disturbing the reason, sometimes by strengthening it. Whence comes this difference between the motion of the devil and that of the Holy Spirit. For one is not lord except through reason, through which one is free: for when anyone is not moved according to reason, then their motion is rather hasty. When with reason, then the motion is said to be from the Holy Spirit. For the motion of the devil disturbs reason. But in those who can speak from the Holy Spirit reason still remains; and therefore they even speak from reason, not as people who are too hasty. Whence Scripture leads them back to prophetic truth, as is said in 2 Peter 1:19: "And we have a stronger prophetic word."[329]

FOX: Prophets act with anger but not out of anger, we might say.

AQUINAS: They do this when on behalf of the good, that is, from love of God and for justice and virtue they strive standing up "manfully amidst adversities." And thus, if the saints of that age amidst their adversities pursued what they desired, namely, by despising temporal goods, to cling to spiritual ones, it was not done badly by them, but well. Whence truly it can be said that "it is proper for divine justice" that it does not destroy or soften spiritual virtue through a participation in prosperity. But if someone tried to do this, namely, to fight on behalf of the truth, the fact is that God does not let such things go without divine help. God strengthens those in beauty who stand firm in spiritual goods through which they are consoled in adverse conditions. And further, God repays such people in the future, according to the worthiness of their own merit.[330]

FOX: But shouldn't the prophet be virtuous, and isn't patience a virtue that fury and anger are opposed to?

AQUINAS: It is not inconsistent with patience that anyone should, when necessary, rise up against someone who inflicts evils on them.[331]

FOX: But isn't nonviolence also called for at times?

AQUINAS: The worth of virtue shines out when anyone readily bears many and grievous blows of misfortune: not that they are

---

329. In Mt 10, p. 101.   330. DDN, n. 783, p. 293.   331. ST II-II, q. 136, a. 4, ad 3.

insensitive to pain and sadness, as the Stoics urged, but that they remain strong and great-hearted, and upright in their reason.[332]

FOX: What about the teaching in the Sermon on the Mount, "I say unto you, resist not evil; if one strike you on the right cheek, offer him the other" (Matt. 5:39)?

AQUINAS: Holy Scripture must be understood in the light of what Christ and the saints have actually practiced. Christ did not offer his other cheek, nor Paul either. Thus to interpret the injunction of the Sermon on the Mount *literally* is to misunderstand it. This injunction signifies rather the readiness of the soul to bear, *if it be necessary,* such things and worse, without bitterness to the attacker. This readiness our Lord showed, when he gave up his body to be crucified. That response of the Lord was useful, therefore, for our instruction.[333]

FOX: Can you furnish another example of the advantages of nonviolence?

AQUINAS: When persons are afflicted, unless they bear it patiently, they are first moved in mind; then they unleash themselves in words. But the remedy, that one not be moved in mind, is that they be like a deaf person, not hearing the unjust words. And therefore the psalmist says, "But I am like a deaf person not hearing," that is, I would imagine that I heard. Ecclesiasticus 1 says: "Even to the right moment he will remain patient." Likewise, in the same book at chapter 28: "Surround your ears with a hedge, and don't listen to a worthless tongue." The remedy that one not unleash oneself in words is that one be like a mute. Psalm 38 says: "I am bowed down and prostrate, etc." Whence the psalmist says, "And like a dumb person not opening his mouth." And Christ especially did this, as is said in Matthew 27: "And he did not respond a word to him, so that the governor was amazed." Isaiah 53: "As the sheep is led to the slaughter, etc." This too a just person ought to do. Psalm 39 says; "I have placed a guard on my mouth, while a sinner takes his stand against me." "And I have become like a man not hearing." Here the effect of patience is posited; but this is against the opinion of evil persons, who think this is due to cowardice, not to virtue. . . . Hence it is said about Christ (Luke 23) that Herod treated him with contempt and looked down on him.[334]

---

332. In Ethics I, L. 16, p. 85.   333. In Jn 18.23, n. 2321.   334. In Pss 37, p. 293.

FOX: This kind of patience, which is nonviolent, sometimes makes friends of enemies, does it not?

AQUINAS: Sometimes it happens from the compassion of God that one who suffers some tribulation sustains evils that are brought upon them by others so that they may have peace with their enemies. Proverbs 16 says: "Since his ways are pleasing to God he turns his enemies to peace." Job 5 says: "The beasts of the earth will be peaceful to you." And this is even natural, since no one is so savage and cruel, that when he sees someone humiliated he harasses him further. Even a dog will not bite a man lying down.[335]

FOX: Prophets do not speak their own words, it seems, but are an instrument for God's word.

AQUINAS: Prophets do not speak of their own will.[336] Prophecy is given to people for the profit of the Church and not for themselves.[337]

FOX: It seems that the gift of prophecy is a kind of ongoing revelation for the Church.

AQUINAS: Gregory in Book One of his *Commentary on Ezekiel* says that if the voice of psalm-singing is raised with sincerity of heart, through it a way is prepared for Almighty God to the heart so that God pours into the earnest soul either the mysteries of prophecy or the grace of compunction. Therefore the end is that the soul is joined with God, as with the holy One on high.[338]

FOX: Are we saying that the inspiration of the prophet is like that of the biblical writers?

AQUINAS: It should be noted that there is one thing in Sacred Scripture and another in other kinds of knowledge. For other kinds of knowledge are produced through human reason, but Scripture itself through the instigation of divine inspiration. 2 Peter 1 says: "For prophecy is not bestowed by human will, but the inspired speak from the Holy Spirit, etc." And therefore the tongue of a human being is moved in Holy Scripture like the tongue of a body saying words that another furnishes. Psalm 45 says: "My tongue is as a pen," and 2 Kings 23 says: "The Spirit of the Lord has spoken through me, and God's word through

---

335. Ibid., 294.   336. In Pss 5, p. 162.   337. DV, q. 12, a. 5.   338. In Pss, Preamble, 148.

the Lord, and of glory," which are said through revelation. Thus 3 Kings 20 says: "Strike me in the word of the Lord," that is, in divine revelation.[339]

FOX: Let us go more deeply into how you understand our development as prophets. What more is required of a prophet?

AQUINAS: These three things are necessary for a prophet: prophetic dignity, communal charity, and compassionate piety. So when a prophet is set up as it were between God and people, as is said in Deuteronomy 5, "I have been a mediator and medium between God and you," it is fitting that they be joined to God through the gift of prophecy, as is said in Wisdom 7: "She passes herself in every generation into holy souls;" and through the bond of charity wisdom is joined to the people. Ephesians 4 says: "Those careful to preserve the unity of spirit in the bond of peace." And thus by praying for the cause of the people they make reference to God, and by proclaiming the cause of God they make reference to the people. For these three things, however, three other things immediately appear. For of necessity a way of speech is opened up that proceeds by way of metaphors and figures, which is the proper mode of prophets. Numbers 12 says: "If someone shall have been a prophet of the Lord among you, I will appear to them in a vision, and through dreams I will speak to them."[340]

FOX: Your point that metaphors and figures are the proper mode of prophets underscores the role of art and art as meditation in developing the prophet in us. It also serves to critique an educational model that excludes such modes of learning. You mention compassion—is the prophet especially knowledgeable about compassion?

AQUINAS: The prophet Jeremiah shows his compassion when he says, "I have pain in my belly," meaning that his feelings are afflicted; and "the sense of my heart," meaning his mind is perturbed. "I will not be silent,"—he will even lament outwardly, as Lamentations 2 says: "My eyes are spent with weeping, my stomach has been disturbed."[341]

FOX: You underscore here the special connection between the Via Negativa and the Via Transformativa—the prophet feels deeply in heart and gut the pain of the world.

---

339. Ibid.   340. In Jer, Preamble, 578.   341. In Jer 4, p. 589.

AQUINAS: Jeremiah expresses the compassion of the prophet, saying, "since if you have not heard, your soul will lament in secret," as if to say, let not victors be displeased. Isaiah 22 says: "Withdraw from me, I will weep bitterly. Don't come to console me about the destruction of the daughter of my people." Ezekiel 24 says: "You shall not wail or weep; but you shall put away your iniquities." And Jeremiah gives us the reason for compassion: "Lamenting he will lament, and your eyes will bring forth tears, since the flock of the Lord has been seized." And again (chapter 50): "The flock of my people has been lost, their shepherds have led them astray, and made them wander in the mountains."[342]

FOX: Compunction seems to result from the deep compassion of the prophet.

AQUINAS: Isaiah posits the consoling compassion of the prophet when he says, "Withdraw," you consoling prophets, "don't press on in the manner of those who console. Jeremiah (9) says: "Who will give water to my head, and a fountain of tears to my eyes, that I may weep over my people who have been killed?"[343] The prophets and other just persons, who by proclaiming Christ in advance and demanding him from God with their tears, have wept for him in a certain way. Psalm 72 says: "[Tears] will descend like rain upon the fleece."[344]

FOX: Yet, as we established above in our discussion on compassion, compassion is not only about pain and suffering and injustice—it is also about joy and celebration. The prophets announce good news as well as bad, do they not?

AQUINAS: Isaiah says: "You will call Sabbath a delight." That means you will celebrate a Sabbath of this kind, with regard to the performance of good works. Exodus 20 says: "Remember to keep holy the day of the Sabbath." Isaiah secondly lays down the fruits: "They will be pleased," with regard to spiritual goods. "I will raise you up" by lowering the earth to you, which is mountainous. "I will eat," with regard to the fruition of the goods of the earth. Job 22 says: "Then you will abound with delights in the Almighty."[345] Jeremiah promises the prosperity of humans that will please the heart. "And praise concerning them will go forth." Isaiah 51 says: "Joy and happiness

---

342. In Jer 13, p. 611.   343. In Is 22, p. 495.   344. In Is 47, p. 559.
345. In Is 58, p. 562.

will be found in it, and thanksgiving, and the voice of praise."
As for the multitude of people, "I will increase them and they
will not be diminished," as far as in me, and so long as they do
not come forward out of their sin. Psalm 139 says: "If I try to
count them, they are more than the sand."[346]

FOX: You said earlier that prophets "refuse to be silent." But it
seems that sometimes prophets prefer to be silent and often-
times—as in the case of Moses and Jeremiah—want to resist the
call to prophecy.

AQUINAS: Isaiah said, "Here I am, send me." This seems to be
presumptuous. Moses refused a call (Exod. 3) and Jeremiah also
demurred (Jer. 1:6). But, as Gregory says, both kinds of responses were rooted in love. Moses and Jeremiah because of the
love of God did not want to lose the consolation of contemplation, and Isaiah because of love of neighbor wished to be sent
in order to be of some help. Nevertheless, the first two, when
ordered, did not obstinately refuse, and the third did not present
himself until after he had been cleansed and a call had been
given.[347]

FOX: You understand prophecy as a call and as a gift. Obviously you have in mind a gift giver and a caller who is God.

AQUINAS: The gift of prophecy is touched on by Isaiah when
he says: "The spirit of the Lord is upon me because God has
anointed me," filling me with the gift of prophecy. 2 Peter 1
says: "For it is not by human will that prophecy has been announced, but the saints, men and women of God, have spoken
inspired by the holy Spirit." Or of Christ, concerning whom
Isaiah says (11): "The spirit of the Lord will rest upon him."
Psalm 45 says: "God your God anointed me with the oil of gladness beyond your companions."[348]

FOX: And so prophets are called to be such by God and indeed
the Spirit of God.

AQUINAS: One is called a prophet . . . on account of one's being deputed by God, as with Jeremiah (1:5), "And I made you
a prophet unto the nations."[349]

FOX: And yet you seem to have a sense of a nonelitist call to be
prophetic, as when you said above that all cultures and histori-

---

346. In Jer 30, p. 646.   347. In Is 6, p. 458.   348. In Is 61, pp. 566–67.
349. ST II-II, q. 171, a. 2, ad 2.

cal periods have their prophets. Apparently all cultures need prophets.

AQUINAS: The prophetic light extends even to the direction of human acts; and in this way prophecy is requisite for the government of a people, especially in relation to divine worship, since for this nature is not sufficient and grace is necessary.[350]

FOX: It seems that there are many more prophets in our midst than we knew.

AQUINAS: Saints are called prophets of God for three reasons. First, because they were inspired by God. Joel 2 says: "I will pour out my spirit over all flesh, and your sons and daughters shall prophesy." On the other hand, concerning false prophets, who speak from their own spirit, it is said in Ezekiel 13: "Woe to the foolish prophets who follow their own spirit, and see nothing." Second, because they were sent by God, Matthew 23 says: "Behold, I send to you prophets, and wise people, and scribes." Isaiah 29 says: "And now the Lord, and his spirit, have sent me." On the other hand, concerning false prophets, see Jeremiah 23: "I did not send them, and yet they ran; I did not speak to them, and yet they prophesied." Third, since they witnessed to God (Acts 10): "All the prophets give witness to God, etc." Isaiah 44 says: "You are my witnesses." But a fervent feeling is shown by their communal charity, of which he says: "Here is one who loves the brotherhood."[351]

FOX: Women too are prophets, as Joel mentions in the scriptural passage you just cited.

AQUINAS: The blessed virgin is a prophetess who prophesied saying, "My soul magnifies the Lord" (Luke 1). God approached her through prophetic intelligence and through faith. Also, the Holy Spirit is called a prophetess, who is the beginning of all prophecy. 2 Peter 1 says: "For it is not by human will that prophecy is brought forth, but inspired by the Holy Spirit the saints, men and women of God, have spoken." For among the Hebrews "spirit" is in the feminine gender, namely "Ruah," and respecting this, "Mary conceived," that is, the Spirit made her to conceive. For that which "has been born in her is from the Holy Spirit."[352]

---

350. Ibid., q. 172, a. 1, ad 4.   351. In Jer, Preamble, 577.   352. In Is 8, p. 464.

FOX: Do you recognize other women prophets besides Mary?

AQUINAS: A triple privilege was placed upon Mary Magdalene. First, prophecy, because she deserved to see the angels, for prophecy is between the angels and the people. Second, the dignity of the angels, because she saw Christ, upon whom the angels want to look. Third, the apostolic office to be sure. She became the Apostle of the apostles, because the announcing of the Lord's resurrection to the disciples was entrusted to her. Just as a woman first announced the words of death to man, so also woman first announced the words of life.[353]

FOX: And you esteem the courage the women demonstrate?

AQUINAS: Due to the fact that both women were standing near the cross and Jesus' disciples had fled leaving him behind, John commends the devoted constancy of the women. Job 19:20 applies: "My flesh having been eaten away, my bones cling to my skin." In other words, the disciples, who were signified by the flesh, had withdrawn, while the women, who are understood by the skin, hung on.[354]

FOX: You seem to admire Mary Magdalene as a prophet and a courageous individual.

AQUINAS: The boldness of the woman is amazing.[355]

FOX: Why do you say that?

AQUINAS: Mary says [to the gardener]: "Tell me where you have laid the body of Jesus and I will take him away." The boldness of the woman is amazing. It removes the fear of the sight of a dead person and impels her to try to do more than she is able, that is, to carry away the corpse. This is what Paul means in 1 Corinthians 13:7, "Love hopes all things." She wished to take him away and bring him to another, unknown place, so that the Jewish [leaders] would not harm the lifeless body.[356]

FOX: Do you understand the prophetic word to emerge from the divine word?

AQUINAS: Prophetic words are many in and of themselves, but they are one in their origin, since they originate from an uncreated word.[357]

---

353. In Jn 20.17, n. 2519.   354. In Jn 19.25, n. 2438.   355. In Jn 20.15, n. 2512.   356. Ibid.   357. In Jer 1, p. 579.

FOX: You make a powerful connection in what you have just said between the creative word of God and the prophet's word—between creation and liberation, between the Via Positiva and the Via Transformativa.

AQUINAS: The formal element in prophetic knowledge is the divine light.[358]

FOX: The prophetic word is almost like a new creation happening: "Let there be light" is the first act of creation—and in this instance, of re-creation. It is like the Spirit of God that "hovered over the waters" in Genesis to begin creation and that, through the prophet, brings a new creation.

AQUINAS: The Holy Spirit is the spirit of prophecy, as Joel says (2:28): "I shall pour out my spirit upon all flesh and your sons and your daughters shall prophesy."[359]

FOX: The prophetic word is often an unsettling one, yet transformative.

AQUINAS: Ecclesiasticus 49 says: "A prophet has been consecrated to overturn, root up, destroy, and again to build and renew."[360]

FOX: How do you understand the prophetic call touching the prophet's imagination?

AQUINAS: The supernatural reception proper to prophecy is in the vision of imagination, and in order to see the vision human power is enraptured by some spirit and transported out of the senses. . . . Hence, whenever prophecy takes place according to the vision of imagination, the prophet must be transported out of his or her senses. . . . Therefore, prophecy that takes place with the vision of imagination always comes either in a dream, when one is deprived of sense-consciousness through a properly disposed physical cause, or in a vision, when the transport comes from some cause in the soul.[361]

FOX: Your description of the prophet being touched by the spirit seems to parallel strikingly your descriptions of the artist being inspired—another correlation between the Via Creativa and the Via Transformativa.

---

358. ST II-II, q. 171, a. 3, ad 3.   359. In Heb, ch. 1, p. 678.   360. In Jer 1, p. 581.   361. DV, q. 12, a. 9.

AQUINAS: The prophet's mind thus enlightened may be called a mirror, insofar as a likeness of the truth of the divine fore-knowledge is formed therein, for which reason it is called the "mirror of eternity," as representing God's foreknowledge. For God in the divine eternity sees all things as present before the Godhead.[362]

FOX: Of course prophets are not prophets all the time. Individual persons are inspired about some moral insight for the people but never about all the needs of the people.

AQUINAS: The Lord reveals to the prophets all things that are necessary for the instruction of the faithful; yet not all to every one, but some to one, and some to another.[363] Since prophetic light is not something abiding in the prophet, but a kind of transient impression, it is not necessary for the prophet always to possess the same grade of prophecy. In fact, revelation comes to them sometimes according to one grade and sometimes according to another.[364]

FOX: Our prophetic consciousness waxes and wanes and needs constant instruction and inspiration.

AQUINAS: Otherwise a prophet would always be able to prophecy, which is clearly false. . . . Just as the air is ever in need of a fresh enlightening, so too the prophet's mind is always in need of a fresh revelation.[365] Prophecy is something imperfect in the genus of Divine revelation. Thus it is written (1 Cor. 13:8) that "prophecies shall be made void" and that "we prophesy in part," that is, imperfectly.[366]

FOX: In this sense too prophecy is not a virtue or a habit that one always possesses.

AQUINAS: The spirit of prophecy is not present to prophets all the time, but when their minds are illuminated by Divinity.[367] The prophetic light must not be a habit, but must exist in the soul of the prophet in the manner of a transient impression, as the light of the sun exists in the air. And, as the light remains in the air only when the sun is shining, so the previously mentioned light remains in the mind of the prophet only when it is actually being divinely inspired.[368]

---

362. ST II-II, q. 171, a. 2, ad 3. 363. Ibid., a. 4, ad 1. 364. DV, q. 12, a. 13, ad 3. 365. ST II-II, q. 171, a. 2. 366. Ibid., a. 4, ad 2. 367. In Heb, ch. 1, p. 669. 368. DV, q. 12, a. 1.

FOX: Prophets are indeed visionaries, receivers of the light.

AQUINAS: Hosea says (12): "I have multiplied visions among them."[369] In prophetic knowledge the human intellect is passive to the enlightening of the divine light.[370]

FOX: How is prophecy different from merely experiencing a vision?

AQUINAS: Prophecy supplies an act of exterior concern that goes beyond the vision. The vision will be the material cause in respect to prophecy.[371]

FOX: The native people of our land say that a vision is not a vision until it is shared with the people; that corresponds to your idea of the "exterior concern." In also underscores how the native people understood the role of vision as a preamble to prophecy "so that the people might live," as they say. When you say prophecy is receptive, you are not saying that a certain capacity to respond to the prophetic call manifested by responses in the past plays no role at all?

AQUINAS: Just as wood once ignited is more easily ignited again, so too in the prophet's intellect, after the actual enlightenment has ceased, there remains an aptitude to be enlightened anew. Thus when the mind has once been aroused to devotion, it is more easily recalled to its former devotion.[372]

FOX: And so the prophet does not receive prophecy altogether passively—he or she does have something to say about it?

AQUINAS: People have no foreknowledge of the future, but they can acquire it by means of experience, wherein they are helped by their natural disposition, which depends on the perfections of their imaginative powers and the clarity of their understanding.[373]

FOX: Once again I hear you connecting the Via Creativa—the development of our imaginations and clarity of understanding—and the Via Transformativa, our prophetic vocation.

AQUINAS: Prophecy strictly so-called cannot be from nature but only from divine revelation.[374]

FOX: Are there some visions that cannot be prophetic?

---

369. In Is 1, p. 430.   370. ST II-II, q. 171, a. 2, ad 1.   371. In Is 1, p. 430.   372. ST II-II, q. 171, a. 2, ad 2.   373. Ibid., q. 172, a. 1.   374. Ibid.

AQUINAS: Both the corporeal and spiritual or imaginative visions are something of a prophecy, but they cannot be called true prophecies unless there is added an intellectual vision in which the reason of the prophecy has been fulfilled. Daniel 10 says: "Intelligence is needed in a vision." And he goes on to say, "And he [namely, Daniel] understood the word." But vision is primarily said concerning corporeal vision.[375]

FOX: And so reason or intelligence plays an important role in the gift of prophecy.

AQUINAS: The intellect is lifted toward prophecy by the light of grace freely given, which is the gift of prophecy. For it does not attain to the sight of God to the extent that it is an object of happiness, but to the extent that it is the reason of the things that pertain to the placement of people in the world.[376]

FOX: Again I hear you saying that prophecy is for the people.

AQUINAS: Prophecy is given not for the prophet's sake but for the building up of the church.[377] Sometimes the gift of prophecy is given to people both for the good of others and in order to enlighten their own mind. Such are those whom divine wisdom, communicating itself by sanctifying grace to their minds, makes friends of God and of prophets. Others, however, receive the gift of prophecy merely for the good of others. (See Matthew 7:22.)[378]

FOX: The gift of prophecy, I take it, is not always given to the most perfect among us.

AQUINAS: God's gifts are not always bestowed on those who are simply the best, but sometimes are given to those who are best regarding the receipt of this or that gift. Accordingly, God grants the gift of prophecy to those whom God judges best to give it to.[379]

FOX: And so prophecy remains a gift freely given by the Gift giver for the sake of the people. Is God the only gift giver of prophecy?

AQUINAS: The gratuitous graces are ascribed to the Holy Spirit as their first principle: yet the Spirit works grace of this kind in people by means of the angels.[380]

---

375. In Is 1, p. 431.   376. Ibid.   377. DV, q. 12, a. 5.   378. ST II-II, q. 172, a. 4, ad 1.   379. Ibid., ad 4.   380. Ibid., a. 2, ad 2.

FOX: You spoke of angels earlier when you talked of the prophecy of Mary Magdalene. Why do you say that angels are involved in the prophetic work?

AQUINAS: The divine enlightenments and revelations are conveyed from God to humans by the angels. Now, prophetic knowledge is bestowed by divine enlightenment and revelation. Therefore it is evident that it is conveyed by the angels.[381] Prophecy is a perfection of the intellect, in which an angel also can form an impression.[382] Prophetic revelation, which is conveyed by the ministry of the angels, is said to be divine [revelation].[383]

FOX: What happens to the prophet surprises even the prophet, does it not?

AQUINAS: Since the prophet's mind is a defective instrument, even true prophets do not know all that the Holy Spirit means by the things they see, or speak, or even do.[384]

FOX: You mention *doing*. The prophet sees, speaks, and does things?

AQUINAS: The prophet's mind is moved not only to apprehend something, but also to speak or to do something; sometimes indeed to all these three together, sometimes to two, sometimes to one only.[385]

FOX: I am struck when I read in your work that prophecy and ecstasy or rapture often go together.

AQUINAS: Rapture is a degree of prophecy.[386] Paul's rapture (see 2 Cor. 12:2) pertains somewhat to prophecy.[387]

FOX: How are you defining "rapture"?

AQUINAS: In rapture a person is uplifted by the spirit of God to things supernatural, and withdrawn from the senses. According to Ezekiel (8:3): "The spirit lifted me up between the earth and the heaven, and brought me in the vision of God into Jerusalem."[388]

FOX: Is rapture the same as ecstasy?

---

381. Ibid., a. 2.   382. Ibid., ad 1.   383. Ibid., ad 3.   384. Ibid., q. 173, a. 4.   385. Ibid.   386. Ibid., q. 171, Preamble.   387. Ibid., q. 175, a. 3, ad 2.   388. Ibid., a. 1.

AQUINAS: Rapture adds something to ecstasy. For ecstasy means simply a going out of oneself by being placed outside one's proper order; while rapture denotes a certain violence in addition.[389]

FOX: What causes rapture?

AQUINAS: The divine assistance is bestowed on human beings in every gift of grace.[390] Love is the cause of rapture.[391]

FOX: From this rich discussion on the prophets and from your Christology wherein you celebrate Jesus as prophet, it seems to me that you place high priority on our prophetic vocations and on listening to prophets past and present in our midst.

AQUINAS: The doctrine of both apostles and prophets is necessary for salvation.[392]

FOX: I like your attributing "doctrine" to the prophets. It follows that doctrine is about justice and injustice, about boldness and the confrontation of the enemies of justice, about passion and compassion, and not merely about dogmas as such. I also appreciate your point that what the prophetic spirit brings us is "necessary for salvation." Prophecy is about adventure and the courage necessary for true moral adventure. I also appreciate your classifying prophets with apostles, since we have often been instructed by ecclesiastical hierarchies that the question of "apostolic succession" is what counts—but I seldom hear talk of "prophetic succession."

AQUINAS: The reign of Christ is a reign of fairness and justice. . . . For this reason when Scriptures say "you have loved justice" they are commending the goodness of the one who governs. For some people serve fairness not on account of their love of justice but more because of fear or for the sake of personal glory. Such a reign does not endure. But Christ serves fairness for the sake of the love of justice. Thus in saying "you have loved justice" it is as if Scripture were saying the rod that you use to measure with is fair and direct precisely because you have loved justice. As the book of Wisdom puts it (1:1): "Love justice you who judge on earth." Moreover there is no just person who does not love justice.[393]

---

389. Ibid., a. 2, ad 1.   390. Ibid., a. 1, ad 2.   391. Ibid., a. 2, ad 1.
392. In Eph 2.20, p. 465.   393. In Heb, ch. 1, p. 677.

FOX: There are examples in history of false prophets. Could you comment on this?

AQUINAS: In Jeremiah (chapter 12) we note that the leaders destroy the people on account of the perversity of their work. Jeremiah 10 says: "Since the shepherds have acted foolishly, and have not sought the Lord, therefore they have not understood, and their whole flock has been scattered" on account of the falsehood of their doctrine. Jeremiah 30 says: "The flock, my people has been lost, their shepherds led them astray, and made them wander in the mountains, etc.," on account of the cowardice of fear. Zechariah 11:17 says: "Trouble is coming to the worthless shepherd who deserts the flock! May the sword strike his arm and his right eye!" on account of the austerity of the Lord. Ezekiel 34 says: "You ruled with austerity, and with power, and my sheep have been scattered, etc.," on account of the slackening of care. Zechariah 11 says: "I am raising up a shepherd in the land who will not visit the abandoned, who will not seek the dispersed, and who will not heal the contrite, who will not nourish that which stands, and will eat the flesh of fattened creatures, and will tear off their claws."[394]

FOX: It is interesting that you cite Jeremiah in his criticism of religious leaders.

AQUINAS: Jeremiah talks about the faults of prelates, which is frequently the cause of fault in subordinates. Thus he says, "Since there have been found among my people scoundrels." First he charges their fault as a violation of justice; second as a perversion of doctrine, when he says, "there is bewilderment and many things have been done on the earth."[395]

FOX: Now I see why you place the act of judgment as being at the heart of the prophetic vocation. The prophets do indeed make a judgment.

AQUINAS: Jeremiah first shows the injustice of the prelates with regard to the unjust and fraudulent oppression of the poor, bringing forth trickery, when he calls them "scoundrels." Psalm 10 says: "They seize the poor and rob them." "Full of trickery" means being full of the riches that they have acquired by trickery. And the result of trickery is in the increase of riches: "Thus they are magnified," in honors, "endowed," with riches.

---

394. In Jer 12, p. 610.   395. In Jer 5, p. 592.

Jeremiah 17 says: "Like a partridge that nurtures that which she did not lay, they amass riches unjustly." And in the increase of sins. . . . Second, he shows their injustice with regard to the lack of just judgment, "the cause of the widow" [is neglected]. Isaiah 1: "They do not judge on the orphan's behalf, and the cause of the widow does not touch them."[396]

FOX: And so it is possible for anyone—prelates included—to abandon their prophetic responsibilities and also to be false prophets?

AQUINAS: Rabbi Moses [Maimonides] says that entanglement in the pleasures and cares of this world is a sign that one is a false prophet. And this agrees with what we read in the Gospel of Saint Matthew (7:15): "Beware of false prophets" and a little later (7:16): "By their fruits you shall know them."[397]

FOX: It seems that what we call conscience today was very dear to the prophets. For sometimes their inspiration urges them to criticize powers-that-be.

AQUINAS: Matthew's gospel says: "Therefore any good that causes a scandal for us or others, we ought to cut away from us." Likewise, "if your right eye," that is, a friend or adviser in divine matters, causes a scandal, by drawing into heresy, such a one should be rooted up by refutation, cast forth, by speaking clearly out in the open. Likewise if parents cause a scandal, by impeding the sanctity of life, such an eye should be rooted out by resisting it, cast forth by separating oneself from it. Likewise if the contemplative life causes a scandal, by turning one toward boredom and arrogance, it must be rooted out, sometimes by lessening it; cast it forth, by going over to the active life.[398]

FOX: I see that conscience played a big role in your own prophetic vocation. We all know of the story of your family kidnapping you when you chose the vocation of the revolutionary movement of Dominicans over the privileges guaranteed you by the Benedictine establishment of your day. Speak to us more about conscience. It seems that we can't be prophetic without one.

AQUINAS: It is a grievous matter for anyone to yield to another what ought to be one's own.[399]

---

396. Ibid.   397. DV, q. 12, a. 5.   398. In Mt 5, p. 61.   399. ST I, q. 96, a. 4.

FOX: And conscience, our own judgment of right and wrong, is one of those things we cannot surrender to another?

AQUINAS: Every judgment of conscience, be it right or wrong, be it about things evil in themselves or morally indifferent, is obligatory, in such a way that anyone who acts against their conscience always sins.[400]

FOX: That is a strong statement—that we must follow conscience even if it leads to what is evil.

AQUINAS: Conscience is more to be obeyed than authority imposed from the outside. By following a right conscience you not only do not incur sin but are also immune from sin, whatever superiors may say to the contrary. To act against one's conscience and to disobey a superior can both be sinful. Of the two, the first is the worse since the dictate of conscience is more binding than the decree of external authority.[401]

FOX: Why are you so adamant about the priority of conscience over what you call "external authority"?

AQUINAS: As long as such a conscience remains, one sins mortally by acting against it.[402]

FOX: Even if our conscience is mistaken, we must follow it?

AQUINAS: What is dictated by a mistaken conscience is not consonant with the law of God, nevertheless it is construed as the law of God, and therefore, simply speaking, if a person goes against it that person contravenes the law of God.[403]

FOX: What is conscience?

AQUINAS: Conscience is the dictate of reason. . . . Now, because the object of a volition is that which is proposed by the reason, if the will chooses to do what the reason considers to be wrong, then the will goes out to it in the guise of evil. Therefore it must be said flatly that the will that disobeys the reason, whether true or mistaken, is always in the wrong.[404]

FOX: You say conscience is a judgment and a dictate of reason; some people look on it as a little voice inside of us. But you emphasize that it is an act of decision making.

---

400. QQ 3, q. 12, a. 2.   401. DV, q. 17, a. 5.   402. Ibid., a. 4, ad 4.
403. Ibid., ad 1.   404. ST I-II, q. 19, a. 5.

AQUINAS: Strictly speaking, conscience is not a faculty, but an activity, namely, the actual application of moral science to conduct.[405]

FOX: You seem to take conscience out of the arena of will and more into the arena of reason and even law.

AQUINAS: The dictate of will should not be accounted the first rule of conduct, for will is directed by reason and mind, in God as well as in us.[406]

FOX: This underscores once again how basic justice is to conscience and moral decision making.

AQUINAS: To say that justice depends on mere will is to say that the divine will does not act according to the order of wisdom, and is blasphemous.[407]

FOX: You said above that conscience is like a law of God. Yet it often puts us in opposition to other laws in our lives. Crises of obedience often become crises of conscience—or is it vice versa?

AQUINAS: A correct conscience binds absolutely and perfectly against the command of a superior. . . . Conscience binds more than the precept of a superior.[408] Obedience is commanded within the limits of due observance. . . . St. Paul says, "let every soul be subject unto the higher powers, for there is no power but of God." Therefore a Christian should obey power that is from God, but not otherwise.[409]

FOX: When do we know when power is or is not from God?

AQUINAS: Power may not stem from God for two reasons: it may be defective either in its origins or in its exercise.

Concerning the first, the defect may lie either in the personal unworthiness of the person or in some flaw in the manner of obtaining high position—violence, bribery, or some other illicit practice. . . . The abuse of power may take two directions. Either the ruler imposes what is contrary to the purpose for which authority is instituted, for instance, if they command sin, contrary to the virtues authority is supposed to promote and sustain. In that event, not merely is one not bound to obey, one is also bound not to obey, following the martyrs, who suffered

---

405. Ibid. I, q. 79, a. 13.   406. DV, q. 23, a. 6.   407. Ibid.   408. Ibid., q. 17, a. 5.   409. In II Sent 44.2.2.

death rather than carry out the wicked decrees of tyrants. Or the ruler may make demands where his warrant does not run, for instance, in exacting tributes to which he has no title, or something of that sort. In such cases a subject is not bound to obey, neither are they bound not to obey.[410]

FOX: You are saying that there is a law higher than human law.

AQUINAS: One ought to obey God more than human beings.[411]

FOX: You are enunciating a principle that has many practical—though politically disturbing—implications.

AQUINAS: Those who obey kings rather than God, in matters where they ought not to obey them, make kings their gods: "We ought to obey God rather than humans" (Acts 5:29). Those who love their children or kindred more than God imply by their deeds that there are many gods.[412] Though a superior be higher than a subject, nevertheless God, in virtue of whose command conscience binds, is higher still.[413] Both subject and superior are bound to examine their actions according to the knowledge they have from God, whether natural, acquired, or infused. For every person should act according to reason.[414]

FOX: Now a further dimension emerges to your rich phrase of "acting according to reason"—that of following one's conscience.

AQUINAS: Since conscience is nothing else but the application of knowledge to an act, it is obvious that conscience is said to bind by the power of divine precept.[415]

FOX: It sounds that, while you respect law, you feel all have access to the light of God in their decisions of conscience.

AQUINAS: Among all other creatures, the rational creature is subject to divine providence in the most excellent way, insofar as it partakes of a share of providence, by being provident both for itself and for others. . . . The light of natural reason, whereby we discern what is good and what is evil, which is the function of the natural law, is nothing else than an imprint on us of the divine light.[416] God is the universal cause of the enlightening of souls (cf. John 1:9) just as the sun is the universal cause of the enlightenment of bodies, though not in the same

---

410. Ibid.   411. In Mt 4, p. 41.   412. AC, p. 13.   413. DV, q. 17, a. 5, ad 3.   414. Ibid., ad 4.   415. Ibid., a. 3.   416. ST I-II, q. 91, a. 2.

way. For the sun enlightens by necessity of nature, whereas God works freely through the order of the divine wisdom.[417]

FOX: And so everyone has a conscience they can follow?

AQUINAS: I say that a correct conscience binds absolutely because it binds without qualification and in every circumstance. . . . I also say that a correct conscience binds for an intrinsic reason, and a false conscience binds for an extrinsic reason.[418]

FOX: How does your teaching on conscience relate to the matter of proselytizing and religious conversions?

AQUINAS: Unbelievers who have never accepted the faith should be subject to no compulsion at all, for belief is an act of free will.[419] To punish unbelief in those who have never embraced the faith is not within the church's power.[420]

FOX: I wish the Inquisitions since your day had read the two sentences you just uttered. How does your teaching on conscience apply to our role as citizens?

AQUINAS: One who snatches power by force is not truly lord and master.[421] Tyrannical government is unjust because it is not directed to the common good but to the private good of the ruler, as is clear from the philosopher in *Politics* III and *Ethics* VIII. Therefore, the overthrow of such government is not strictly sedition, unless perhaps when accompanied by such disorder that the community suffers greater harm than from the tyrannical government. A tyrant is himself, moreover, far more seditious when he spreads discord and strife among the people subject to him so that he may dominate them more easily. For tyranny is the directing of affairs to the private benefit of the ruler with harm to the community.[422]

FOX: Do you consider it moral for persons to overthrow a tyrant even if they previously promised to obey him?

AQUINAS: A society of free persons is not to be regarded as acting unfaithfully in thus deposing the tyrant, even if it had previously sworn to him forever; for he deserved to be deserted, in not keeping faith in the ruling of his people, since this is an

---

417. Ibid., q. 79, a. 3.　418. DV, q. 17, a. 4.　419. ST II-II, q. 10, a. 8.
420. Ibid., q. 12, a. 2.　421. In II Sent 44.2.2.　422. ST II-II, q. 42, a. 2.

obligation on his part, if the compact made with him by the subjects is to be maintained.[423]

FOX: And so obligations run in two directions and leaders too are obliged to obey the compacts they make with the people. You seem, in your celebration of the inviolability of conscience, to be placing limits on obedience.

AQUINAS: The obedient person is moved to the command of the ruler by a certain necessity of justice, just as a natural thing is moved by some naturally necessitated motion. . . . Likewise, there can be two reasons why a subject is not obliged to obey one's superior in all things. First, on account of a command of a higher power. The gloss says in reference to the text of St. Paul, Romans 13: " . . . Therefore when the Emperor commands one thing and God another, one should ignore the former and obey the latter." Another way in which the inferior is not obliged to obey his superior occurs when the latter commands something in matters where he is without authority. . . . In those things depending upon the interior movement of the will, the human is not obliged to obey humans but only God. Humans, however, are obliged to obey humans in regard to external bodily actions; but even here in what regards the nature of the body one is not obliged to obey humans, but only God, for all persons are equal by nature.[424]

FOX: "All persons are equal by nature," you say—that sounds very modern; indeed, the American Declaration of Independence begins with that notion.

AQUINAS: By nature all persons are equal in liberty, but not in other endowments. One is not subordinate to another as though one were a utility.[425]

FOX: Can you give an example of how we are to obey only God in what you call issues that concern "the nature of the body"?

AQUINAS: For example, the sustaining of the body and the procreation of children. Hence in the contracting of matrimony or making a vow of chastity or such things servants are not obliged to obey their masters, nor children their parents.[426]

FOX: But you say we are obliged when it comes to "external bodily actions." Can you give examples of those?

---

423. I DRP, 6. 424. ST II-II, q. 104, a. 1. 425. In II Sent 44.1.3, ad 1.
426. ST II-II, q. 104, a. 1.

AQUINAS: In what has to do with the disposition of human actions and dealings, subjects are obliged to obey their superior, in the sectors of their superiority, just as a soldier obeys his general in matters of war; a servant his master in the tasks assigned to him; a son, his father in matters included in the discipline and management of family life, etc.[427]

FOX: What about slavery? Must slaves obey their master?

AQUINAS: Servitude by which one person is subject to another person belongs to the body; not to the soul, which remains free. . . . And so those who become sons and daughters of God through grace are free from the spiritual servitude to sin, but not however from bodily servitude, by which they are bound to temporal masters.[428]

FOX: I am disappointed to hear you invoke a body-soul dualism, since body and soul are thoroughly intermingled, as you insisted all your life. So there surely are times when we must resist servitude of body or soul. I think your position on slavery, based as it is on body-soul differences, is wrong and has probably contributed to human enslavement.

AQUINAS: One is bound to obey secular rulers to the extent that the order of justice requires. Therefore if rulers have no just title to power, but have usurped it; or if they command unjust things, their subject are not obliged to obey them, except perhaps in some cases in order to avoid scandal or danger.[429]

FOX: Justice rules—not necessarily law.

AQUINAS: Law is nothing else than an ordinance of reason for the common good, made by one who has care of the community and promulgated [to the community].[430] A tyrannical law, because it is not according to reason, is not a law strictly speaking, but rather a perversion of law.[431] Unjust laws . . . are acts of violence rather than laws. . . . Such laws do not bind in conscience. . . . Laws of this kind must in no way be observed.[432]

FOX: Are there other occasions when law need not be obeyed?

AQUINAS: In some cases it is bad to follow the law, and it is good to set aside the letter of the law and to follow the dictates

---

427. Ibid.   428. Ibid., ad 1.   429. Ibid., ad 3.   430. Ibid. I-II, q. 90, a. 4.   431. Ibid., q. 92, a. 1, ad 4.   432. Ibid., q. 96, a. 4.

of justice and the common good. This is the object of *epikeia,* which we call equity. Therefore it is evident that *epikeia* is a virtue.[433]

FOX: You are saying that it is a virtue to resist the letter of the law under certain circumstances?

AQUINAS: To follow the letter of the law when it ought not to be followed is sinful.[434] Necessity knows no law.[435]

FOX: What might be some operative rules for our moral obedience and disobedience?

AQUINAS: Human law cannot repeal any part of divine law or natural law.[436] All law is directed to the common well-being. From this it draws its force and meaning, and to the extent that it falls short of this it does not oblige in conscience.[437]

FOX: In your definition of law you talk about laws made for the common good. Who do you see as responsible for making laws?

AQUINAS: There can be two conditions of peoples. One is that of a free people, able to frame laws for themselves. Here the consent of the people to an observance, manifested by custom, is of greater force than the authority of the prince, who does not possess the power of framing laws except insofar as he is the public authority representing the people, for though no particular person can enact laws the whole people can. The other condition is that of a people who do not enjoy the unfettered power of making their own laws or of abrogating the laws of a higher ruler. Nevertheless, even here prevailing custom obtains the force of law so long as it is permitted, and therefore approved, by those whose business it is to legislate.[438]

FOX: I hear you critiquing the misuse of power by a few over the many.

AQUINAS: Human power is very imperfect; for it is rooted in the wills and opinions of people in which inconstancy is very considerable; and the greater the power, the greater the number of those on whom it depends.[439]

FOX: I hear you saying that the people are really the source of power in a community.

---

433. Ibid. II-II, q. 120, a. 1.   434. Ibid., ad 1.   435. Ibid. I-II, q. 46, a. 6.   436. Ibid. II-II, q. 66, a. 7.   437. Ibid. I-II, q. 96, a. 6.   438. Ibid., q. 47, a. 3, ad 3.   439. CG III, ch. 31 n. 5.

AQUINAS: If the head is higher than the human body, nevertheless the body is greater; the body is ruled by the head, but the head is carried by the body; no less does the head need the body than the body the head. . . . Thus the ruler has power from the subjects, and eminence; and in the event of his despising them, sometimes he loses both his power and his position.[440]

FOX: And sometimes he loses his head, I might add! Your notion that the ruler "has power from the subjects" is very modern. What working principles do you use to describe a leader's obligations?

AQUINAS: The unity of the people, called peace, is to be procured through the assiduity of the ruler. Three things are requisite to the good living of the people. First, that they be constituted as a harmonious whole; second, that, thus united in the bonds of peace, they may be directed to a fair existence. . . . Third, it is required that, through the endeavors of the ruler, a sufficiency of those things that are necessary to a good life be available.[441]

FOX: You are speaking of the peace that derives from justice, which you spoke of earlier in this conversation when you talked about a "fair existence" and the community aspect of being in harmony. But what do you mean when you talk about "those things necessary for a good life"?

AQUINAS: A good life for the people entails whatever particular goods are procurable by human effort—for example, wealth, profit, health, eloquence, learning.[442]

FOX: It is telling how you include the psychological, physical, economic, educational, and even aesthetic well-being of all in your understanding of the purpose of governing. I also hear the implicit criticism of systems where peace cannot be obtained because justice does not prevail. Let us talk more about the relationship of poverty and wealth and of injustice and justice. This subject often seems to be the basis of prophetic outrage.

AQUINAS: Because God hates evil, and the good is pleasing to God, God hears the oppressed shouting—God does not hear the oppressors. Thus Job says, "They will shout," namely, the oppressors and tyrants, as if seeking the fulfillment of their desires

---

440. I DRP, 6.   441. Ibid., 15.   442. Ibid.

from God, "and God will not hear them." This happens on account of the pride of evil persons, as Psalm 102 says: "God regards the speech of the humble."[443]

FOX: So you believe in a God who liberates the oppressed from injustice?

AQUINAS: The wealthy are strong: Proverbs 18 says: "The substance of the wealthy is a strong city, etc." But God frees the poor from them. For the wealthy first attack the poor, and then they despoil the weak. But God frees them from these. With regard to the poor, the psalmist says, "Snatching away the poor," who are without resource, "from the hand of the stronger." With regard to the wealthy, the psalmist says, "and the needy and poor from those who despoil them." Someone is called needy who lacks necessities.[444]

FOX: What is poverty?

AQUINAS: Poverty is manifold. There is a poverty of earthly possessions. James 2 says: "Didn't God choose the poor in this world to be rich in faith, to be heirs of the kingdom that God has promised to those who love God?" There is a poverty of humility, as in Matthew 5: "Blessed are the poor in spirit, since theirs is the kingdom of heaven." A poverty of affliction, as in Psalm 69: "I am poor and in distress: your salvation, Lord, sustains me." Of knowledge: Revelation 3: "You do not know since you are poor." Of imperfection: Lamentations 2 says: "I, a man, see my poverty in the rod of God's indignation."[445]

FOX: Let us discuss here the first kind of poverty you mention, that concerning earthly possessions. Discussions about the rich and the poor often break down because we don't pay enough attention to the basic point of having what you call "necessities." It seems to me that if all had necessities we could build communities of justice and joy.

AQUINAS: As a matter of fact, external riches are necessary for the good of virtue, since by them we support our body and give assistance to other people. Now, things that are means to an end must derive their goodness from the end. So, external riches must be a good for human beings—not of course, the principal

---

443. In Job, ch. 35, p. 119.   444. In Pss 34, p. 272.   445. In Jer 5, p. 593.

good, but a secondary good. For the end is the principal good, while other things are good because they are ordered to the end.[446]

FOX: You have touched on another issue—the confusion of means and ends. There is something about external riches—especially in a consumer society—that eliminates all other ends and therefore distorts the usefulness of goods.

AQUINAS: If the practice of virtue is hindered by riches, then they are not to be numbered among goods, but among evils. Hence it happens to be a good thing for some people to possess riches, for they use them for the sake of virtue, but for others it is a bad thing to have them, for these people are taken away from virtue by them, either through too much solicitude or affection for them, or also because of mental pride resulting from them.[447]

FOX: It seems that wealth is a relative term. I like to talk about the real wealth of our species being the basic health of the earth, its ecosystems, and its creatures. But my society talks about wealth as money and stocks and bonds and gold and property.

AQUINAS: Wealth is of two kinds, natural and artificial. Natural wealth, such as food, drink, clothing, and shelter, supplies natural needs. . . . Natural wealth ought to support human nature, and therefore cannot be ultimate since it is subservient to humanity itself.[448]

FOX: In the sense of natural wealth, then, we all need to be wealthy, for I hear you speaking here of our basic needs—what you call our natural needs. What about artificial wealth?

AQUINAS: Artificial wealth, such as money, does not directly serve nature, but is invented by art to facilitate the exchange of goods. . . . With much less reason (than with natural wealth) is artificial wealth humanity's last end, for it is but a means to natural wealth.[449]

FOX: "Artificial wealth is a means to natural wealth"—would that we could always keep that perspective about things. How can we further analyze this issue of wealth?

AQUINAS: External things may be looked at in two ways. First, as to their nature; and the nature of things is not subject to hu-

---

446. CG III, ch 133 n. 1.   447. Ibid.   448. ST I-II, q. 2, a. 1.   449. Ibid.

man power, but only to divine power, whose will all things obey. Second, as to the use of such things; and in this way humanity has a natural control over external things, because through human reason and will people can use external things for their own advantage.[450]

FOX: I fear that we tend to hurry over the first point you make—that all things are subject to divine power. It seems to me that we need to relearn a sense of reverence for all things. Then our compulsions to control things will lessen, for we will relate to them differently.

AQUINAS: People should consider two points with respect to external possessions. One of these is the power of acquiring and disposing. . . . The other point that concerns people with regard to external things is their use. And in respect to this, people should not hold external things for their own use but for the common benefit, so that each one should readily share material things with others in their need. Whence the Apostle Paul says (Tim. 1), "Charge the rich of this world to give easily, to communicate to others."[451]

FOX: I see a logic to your position. You seem to keep coming back to one point: that external goods are *means* and not ends.

AQUINAS: According to the natural order founded by divine providence, material things are ordered to the alleviation of human needs.[452]

FOX: Now I see why it takes prophets to remind us of these things. The distinction between need and desire and between rich and poor can be fiercely denied and resisted.

AQUINAS: When people have as their goal the gaining of wealth they will use any means—fraud or anything else—to this final end. Thus they become robbers and while they are robbing their wealth abounds. From this abundance follows contempt for God, and so Job adds that they "boldly provoke God." . . . Those who take as their ultimate end the gaining of wealth, from this very fact, consider as good whatever they do to gain this end. It is clear that when they gain wealth through robbery they provoke God by acting contrary to justice. Hence it follows that they boldly provoke God.[453]

---

450. Ibid. II-II, q. 66, a. 1.   451. Ibid., a. 2.   452. Ibid., a. 7.   453. In Job 12, p. 52.

FOX: Justice demands that the many have necessities before the few have luxuries?

AQUINAS: Whatever anyone has in superabundance is owed of natural right to the poor for their sustenance. So Ambrose says, and it is also found in Gratian's Decree XLVII: "The bread that you withhold belongs to the hungry; the clothing that you store away to the naked; and the money that you bury in the earth is the redemption and security of the penniless." But because there are many who suffer need, and they cannot all be assisted from the same source, it is entrusted to the will of the individuals to provide from their own wealth assistance to those suffering need. If, however, there is such urgent and obvious need that there is clearly an immediate emergency for sustenance, as when anyone is immediately endangered without means of alleviation, then one may legitimately take from another person's good what one needs, either openly or secretly. Nor is this, strictly speaking, fraud or robbery.[454]

FOX: I find your emphasis on the "will of the individuals" a bit privatistic; it seems that society itself may at times have to undertake the kind of assistance you speak of. But your last point, that the truly poor have a right to take from those who have more than enough, is strong medicine indeed.

AQUINAS: It is not theft, properly speaking, to take secretly and use another's property in a case of extreme need, because that which one takes for the support of one's life becomes one's own property by reason of that need.[455]

FOX: You say that it is of "natural right" or "natural law" that the poor must be assisted by those who have enough. Can you elaborate on that?

AQUINAS: A person is even entitled to take somebody else's property secretly in order to help another where that other is also in extreme need.[456]

FOX: Are you saying that one's property is not inviolable?

AQUINAS: There is no distinction of property according to natural law but rather according to human agreement, which belongs to positive law. Hence private property is not opposed to natural law but is an addition to natural law devised by human reason.[457]

---

454. ST II-II, q. 66, a. 7.   455. Ibid., ad 2.   456. Ibid., ad 3.   457. Ibid., a. 2, and 1.

FOX: You do see a place for private ownership of things?

AQUINAS: In our present state a division of possessions is necessary on account of the multiplicity of masters, inasmuch as community of possession is a source of strife. In the state of innocence, however, the will of the people would have been so ordered that without any danger or strife they would have used in common, according to each one's need, those things of which they were masters—this state of things is now to be observed even now among many good people.[458]

FOX: And so, while you criticize the wealthy's relationship to wealth and to the poor, you are not denying the usefulness and even the right to private property?

AQUINAS: Private possession is necessary for human life for three reasons: first, because people are more careful to procure something that concerns themselves alone than something that is common to all or to many others (for each one, escaping work, leaves for the other person any common task, as happens when there are a great many officials); second, because human affairs are handled in a more orderly fashion when every one goes about their own business—there would be complete confusion if everyone tried to do everything. Third, because this leads to a more peaceful condition for people, while everyone is content with what they have. Hence we see that among those possessing something in common, disputes arise more often.[459]

FOX: I hear you insisting on right relationship to wealth and to the poor. Wealth seems capable of totally distracting us from our true goals and indeed from our true relationships, including those with the poor.

AQUINAS: Jesus says: "Where your treasure is, there your heart is too." . . . If you love earthly things, there your heart will be, for where there is love, there the eye is: The eyes of the fool [extend] to the boundaries of the earth.[460]

FOX: Wealth then becomes an idol, an end instead of a means.

AQUINAS: Each thing that anyone makes his own end is that person's god. Thus those who place their end in wealth, that is their god, just as is said of those "whose God is the stomach" (Phil. 3:19).[461]

---

458. Ibid. I, q. 98, a. 1, ad 3.   459. Ibid. II-II, q. 66, a. 2.   460. In Mt 6, p. 73.   461. Ibid.

FOX: In this way the end justifies the means.

AQUINAS: People are made arrogant by wealth because they think that through their wealth they are self-sufficient, and therefore they boldly despise God while confiding in their wealth. "The beloved became fat and kicked" (Deut. 32:15).[462]

FOX: And greed follows.

AQUINAS: The greed for gain knows no limit and tends to infinity.[463]

FOX: It is almost as if material goods tap into our divinity, which is our capacity for spirit or the infinite. One more reason for developing a theology of our divinity, for if we do not have one, then all people are set up to be infinitely voracious consumers.

AQUINAS: Unnatural desire is altogether infinite. Because it follows from reason and it belongs to reason to proceed to infinity. Hence one who desires riches may desire to be rich, not up to a certain limit, but to be simply as rich as possible.[464]

FOX: You say that "unnatural desire" is infinite. What about desire for natural goods?

AQUINAS: Natural desire cannot be actually infinite because it is of that which nature requires, and nature always tends to something finite and fixed. Hence no one ever desires infinite meat, or infinite drink.[465] The desire for natural riches is not infinite because they suffice for nature in a certain measure. But the desire for artificial wealth is infinite, for it is the servant of disordered desire, which is not curbed. Yet this desire for wealth is infinite in a way different from the desire for the sovereign good. For the more perfectly the sovereign good is possessed, the more it is loved and other things despised, because the more we possess it, the more we know it. . . . On the other hand, in the desire for wealth and any kind of temporal good whatsoever, the contrary is the case: for when we already possess them we despise them, and seek others. . . . The reason for this is that we realize more their insufficiency when we possess them; and this very fact shows that they are imperfect and that the sovereign good does not consist therein.[466]

---

462. In Job 12, p. 52.   463. ST II-II, q. 77, a. 4.   464. Ibid. I-II, q. 30, a. 4.   465. Ibid.   466. Ibid., q. 2, a. 1, ad 3.

FOX: This talk of finite and infinite limits is very important in our time when the Earth shudders from so much greed and abuse.

AQUINAS: Those who place their end in riches have an infinite desire of riches; whereas those who desire riches on account of the necessities of life desire a finite measure of riches, sufficient for the necessities of life.[467] The multitude of fools, who know nothing other than material goods that can be obtained for money, [believe] that all material things obey money. But we should take our estimation of human goods not from the foolish but from the wise.[468]

FOX: The problem today is that the industry of advertising is so powerful that it seems to have the power to make us all into a "multitude of fools," that is, into consumers seeking an infinite amount of goods. What would be an alternative to avarice?

AQUINAS: Love itself considered as such has no limit to its increase, since it is a participation in the infinite love that is the Holy Spirit. In addition, the cause of the increase of love who is God is possessed of infinite power. Furthermore, on the part of its subject, no limit to this increase can be determined, because whenever love increases, there is a corresponding increased ability to receive a further increase. It is therefore evident that it is not possible to fix any limits to the increase of love in this life.[469]

FOX: It seems that when we put our quest for the infinite into an obsession with goods, compassion vanishes.

AQUINAS: The psalmist says: "Blessed are those who consider the poor and needy." Happy is the one who is compassionate, who cares for the needy and the poor. Proverbs 14 says: "One who pities the poor will be happy," and the psalmist says, "One who considers." He does not say, "one who helps" because, as has been said, one ought to be compassionate in the manner of God. But God does not wait until the Godself is always sought. God aids desire before God is sought. And so one is truly compassionate who helps not only any one who is seeking, but also any one needing before being asked to do so. Job 31 says: "If I denied the poor what they desired, if I made the eyes of the widow wait."[470]

---

467. Ibid., q. 30, a. 4.   468. Ibid., q. 2, a. 1, ad 1.   469. Ibid. II-II, q. 24, a. 7.   470. In Pss 40, p. 305.

FOX: What then is avarice or greed?

AQUINAS: Avarice is defined as immoderate love of possessions. . . . Avarice is a sin.[471]

FOX: Against whom is avarice a sin?

AQUINAS: Avarice may signify immoderation about external things in two ways: first, regarding the acquisition and keeping of such things, as for example when a person acquires or keeps them more than is due. In this way it is a sin directly against one's neighbor, since one person cannot overabound in external riches without another person lacking them, for temporal goods cannot be possessed by many at the same time.[472]

FOX: I think this is an extremely important point: one person's (or people's) excess is another's loss of necessities. Temporal goods are not possessable by many at once—yet spiritual goods, like ideas and creativity, music, and so forth, can indeed be possessed by many at once. You are saying that avarice feeds injustice.

AQUINAS: This [kind of] avarice is opposed to justice, and in this sense avarice is mentioned by Ezekiel (22:27): "Her princes in the midst of her are like wolves ravaging the prey, shedding blood . . . and running after gains through avarice."[473]

FOX: Why do you think injustice and avarice go together?

AQUINAS: Unjust persons are never satisfied. But persons who have justice itself as their end, do not overindulge. Proverbs (13:25) says: "The just person eats, and is satisfied."[474]

FOX: Who else is offended by the sin of avarice besides our neighbor?

AQUINAS: Second, avarice may signify immoderation in the internal affections that a person has for riches, when, for instance, a person loves them, desires them, or delights in them immoderately. In this way by avarice one sins against oneself, because it causes disorder in one's affections, though not in one's body as do the sins of the flesh. As a consequence, however, it is a sin against God, just as all mortal sins, inasmuch as people despise things eternal for the sake of temporal things.[475] In this sense

---

471. ST II-II, q. 118, a. 1.   472. Ibid., ad 2.   473. Ibid., a. 3.   474. In Mt 5, p. 52.   475. ST II-II, q. 118, a. 1, ad 2.

avarice is opposed to generosity, which moderates these affections.[476]

FOX: How serious a sin do you take avarice to be?

AQUINAS: [When] it is opposed to justice. . . . avarice consists in the unjust taking or retaining of another's property, and this belongs to theft or robbery, which are mortal sins. [When] it denotes inordinate love of riches, if the love of riches becomes so great as to be preferred to charity, in such a way that one, through love of riches, fears not to act counter to the love of God and one's neighbor, avarice will then be a mortal sin. If, on the other hand, . . . one is unwilling for the sake of riches to do anything in opposition to God or one's neighbor, then avarice is a venial sin.[477] Lust for riches, properly speaking, brings darkness on the soul, when it puts out the light of charity, by preferring the love of riches to the love of God.[478]

FOX: When you say that our greed can bring "darkness on the soul" I sense something quite ominous in our avarice. I also sense that greed can bring "darkness on the soul" of a culture and a people as well as on individuals.

AQUINAS: The degrees of sin may be considered in regard to the good to which the human appetite is inordinately subjected; and then the lesser the good, the more deformed is the sin. For it is more shameful to be subject to a lower than to a higher good. Now the good of external things is the lowest of human goods since it is less than the good of the body; and this is less than the good of the soul, which is less than the divine good. From this point of view, the sin of avarice, whereby the human appetite is subjected even to external things, has in a way a greater deformity.[479]

FOX: One wonders whether the industry of advertising is not rendering us all "deformed" because it subjects our appetite to the least important goods or blessings in life.

AQUINAS: Ecclesiasticus 10:9 says: "Nothing is more wicked than an avaricious person. There is not a more wicked thing than to love money: for such a person sets even his own soul up for sale." Hence it is given as a reason that the greedy person "sets his own soul up for sale" that he does so because he exposes his soul—that is, his life—to danger for the sake of

---

476. Ibid., a. 3.   477. Ibid., a. 4.   478. Ibid., ad 3.   479. Ibid., a. 5.

money. Hence the text continues, "Because while he lives he has cast away"—that is, despised, "his inner self" in order to make money. [The philosopher] Tully also adds that it is the mark of a "narrow mind," namely, that one be willing to be subject to money.[480]

FOX: I get the impression from listening to you that the cure to avarice is not really to rail about materialism. It seems that avarice is a quest to satisfy a spiritual need more than a material one, namely, our yearning for the infinite.

AQUINAS: Avaricious people take pleasure in the consideration of themselves as possessors of riches. Therefore avarice is a spiritual sin.[481]

FOX: Will you refresh my mind as to what you mean by this term "spiritual sin"?

AQUINAS: Every sin consists in the desire for some mutable good for which one has an inordinate desire. Spiritual sin concerns the soul; carnal sin concerns touch and bodily pleasure.[482] Adultery belongs not only to the sin of lust, but also to the sin of injustice . . . so that adultery is much more grievous than theft.[483]

FOX: I remember you saying earlier that a spiritual sin is greater than a carnal sin because the former turns the soul away from God while the latter turns one toward an experience of physical communion.

AQUINAS: Mortal sin cannot exist in our sensual nature but only in our reason,[484] and it is not our sensual nature that is held responsible for it but our reason.[485]

FOX: Yes, it is our reason after all that makes the *electio* or choices we make. The Christian church has tended to preach much more forcefully against sins of the flesh than against these sins of the soul, which you call "spiritual sins." Now, by calling avarice a spiritual sin you are emphasizing its gravity. In your allusion to adultery you are emphasizing once again how injustice arises from so-called spiritual sins and for this reason renders them serious. Please elaborate on how it is that avarice is a spiritual sin.

---

480. Ibid., ad 1.   481. Ibid., a. 6.   482. Ibid. I-II, q. 72, a. 2.   483. Ibid., q. 73, a. 5, ad 1.   484. Ibid., q. 74, a. 4.   485. Ibid., ad 1.

AQUINAS: Avarice with regard to a bodily object seeks the plea-sure, not of the body but only of the soul, forasmuch as anyone takes pleasure in the fact that they possess riches: wherefore it is not a sin of the flesh. Nevertheless by reason of its object it is a mean between purely spiritual sins, which seek spiritual pleasure by way of spiritual objects (thus pride is about excel-lence), and purely carnal sins, which seek a purely bodily plea-sure by way of a bodily object.[486]

FOX: What sort of consequences can we expect in a culture or economic system that is built on avarice?

AQUINAS: Avarice gives rise to insensibility to compassion, be-cause one's heart is not softened by compassion to assist the needy with one's riches. . . . It also gives rise to restlessness, by hindering one with excessive anxiety and care, for "an avari-cious man shall not be satisfied with money" (Ecclesiastes 5:9). . . . The avaricious, in acquiring other people's goods, sometimes employ force, which pertains to violence; sometimes deceit, and then if they have recourse to words, it is falsehood, if it be mere words; perjury if they confirm their statement by oath. If they have recourse to deeds, and the deceit affects things, we have fraud. If persons, then we have treachery, as in the case of Judas, who betrayed Christ through avarice.[487]

FOX: You certainly do seem to be naming some of the shadow spirits of our culture when you talk about these "daughters of avarice." I am especially struck by your explanation for "rest-lessness," which seems so prevalent in the West today, and for your allusion to the forgetfulness of compassion.

AQUINAS: Greed of filthy lucre belongs to restlessness. . . . In-humanity is the same as insensibility to compassion.[488]

FOX: Once again I have to say that your point that avarice is a spiritual sin gives us a clue as to where we will find its cure, namely, by going to its source. We need spiritual teaching and practice that, by offering ways to the truly infinite, can combat the avarice and its offspring that you so pointedly name for us.

Turning now to other subjects of injustice, it seems that eco-nomic injustice often deprives others of their rights, but we can get confused about where the rights of the "haves" end and those of the "have-nots" begin.

---

486. Ibid. II-II, q. 118, a. 6, ad 1.   487. Ibid., a. 8.   488. Ibid., ad 3.

AQUINAS: One would not act unfairly if one went beforehand to the theater in order to prepare the way for others; what is unfair is blocking the enjoyment of others by preventing them from going. Similarly, a rich person does not act unlawfully if they enclose what was common at the beginning and give others a share. But they sin if they indiscriminately exclude others from the benefit. Hence Basil says, "How can you abound in wealth while another begs?"[489]

FOX: One thing that complicates our economic lives today is the nature of capitalism, which makes the rich richer and the poor poorer. In other words, the system is such that those with wealth get more of it while those without wealth rarely get any. Granted that you did not live in so elaborate a capitalist system, nevertheless you did live at the birth of capitalism. Do you have any observation to make about the issue of making money on money?

AQUINAS: To take usury for money lent is unjust in itself, because this is to sell what does not exist, and this evidently leads to inequality, which is contrary to justice. . . . It is of its very nature unlawful to take payment for the use of money lent, which payment is known as usury. And just as one is bound to restore other ill-gotten goods, so is one bound to restore the money that one has taken in usury.[490]

FOX: Not everyone these days would say that usury is a serious sin.

AQUINAS: To lend money at usury is grave sin . . . because it is against natural justice. Consider its meaning. The word comes from *usus:* usury puts a price on a money-loan, and sells the use of money that is lent.

Reflect that different things have different uses. In some cases their use involves the consumption of their substance: the proper use of wine is to be drunk, of bread to be eaten, in both cases their substance is consumed. Similarly, the proper use of money is to be expended in return for other things; as Aristotle remarks, coins are minted to serve exchange. There are other things, however, whose use does not involve the consumption of their substance. The use of a house is to serve as a dwelling, and the nature of dwelling does not require that the house

---

489. Ibid., q. 66, a. 2.   490. Ibid., q. 78, a. 1.

should be pulled down. . . . Because such things are not necessarily consumed in their use, the thing itself and the use of it can be separately conveyed or sold. . . .

But in the case of things whose use is their consumption, wherever the use is granted so also is the thing itself, and conversely. When someone lends money, therefore, on the understanding that he will receive his money back and in addition demands a charge for the use of it, it is clear that he is selling separately the substance of the money and the use of it. In consequence he is selling something that does not exist, or he is selling the same thing twice, which is manifestly against the notion of natural justice. Therefore to lend money at usury is a grave kind of sin, and the same holds true with other things whose use is their consumption, such as wine and flour.[491]

FOX: Usury is about charging an excess of interest on a loan, I take it.

AQUINAS: Some people, like pimps, make profit from sordid and unlawful dealing, for example, prostitution and the like. Still others enrich themselves by unjust exaction, for instance, usurers and those who want at least a little gain from a large gift or loan. All these receive from reprehensible sources, that is, mean or shameful works, or they receive more than they should, like usurers who take more than the interest. All have profit, and this paltry, in common. Those who make enormous profits, and make them by shameful means—they are considered disgraceful for this reason—are not called ungenerous but rather wicked, unjust, and impious against God, as if they were criminals.[492]

FOX: And yet you are not condemning all commerce.

AQUINAS: Exchange of things is twofold: one, natural as it were, and necessary, whereby one commodity is exchanged for another, or money taken in exchange for a commodity, in order to satisfy the needs of life. . . . The other kind of exchange is either that of money for money, or of any commodity for money, not on account of the necessities of life, but for profit. . . . The former kind of exchange is commendable because it supplies a natural need: but the latter is justly deserving

---

491. xiii De malo, 4.   492. In Ethics IV, L. 5, p. 307.

of blame, because considered in itself, it satisfies the greed for gain, which knows no limit and tends to infinity.[493]

FOX: You are saying that trading with a purpose other than profit is justifiable?

AQUINAS: Nothing prevents gain from being directed to some necessary or even virtuous end, and thus trading becomes lawful. Thus, for instance, one may intend the moderate gain that one seeks to acquire by trading for the upkeep of one's household, or for the assistance of the needy: or again, a person may take to trade for some public advantage, for instance, lest one's country lack the necessities of life, and seek gain, not as an end, but as payment for his labor.[494] Not everyone who sells at a higher price than they bought is a merchant, but only one who buys in order to sell at a profit. If, on the contrary, one buys not for sale but for possession, and afterward, for some reason wishes to sell, it is not a trade transaction even if one sells at a profit. For one may lawfully do this, either because one has bettered the thing, or because the value of the things has changed with the change of place or time, or on account of the danger one incurs in transferring the thing from one place to another, or again in having it carried by another. In this sense neither buying nor selling is unjust.[495]

FOX: A bottom line to what you are saying seems to be that money is not the path to happiness.

AQUINAS: Money is acquired under coercion and is parted with under coercion. But this is not in keeping with happiness, which is the goal of voluntary operations.[496]

FOX: Money is a means and not an end.

AQUINAS: Money is sought for something beyond itself since it is by nature a useful good. Therefore happiness does not consist in money.[497]

FOX: Can there be happiness in the generous giving away of money?

AQUINAS: The generous person commendably spends more on others than on oneself.[498]

FOX: But generosity and justice are not the same thing, are they?

---

493. ST II-II, q. 77, a. 4.   494. Ibid.   495. Ibid., ad 2.   496. In Ethics I, L. 5, p. 31.   497. Ibid.   498. ST II-II, q. 117, a. 1, ad 1.

AQUINAS: It belongs to generosity to make good use of riches as such, because riches are the proper matter of generosity. On the other hand, it belongs to justice to make use of riches under another aspect, namely, that of debt, insofar as an external thing is due to another.[499] Generosity is not a kind of justice, since justice pays another what belongs to them, while generosity gives another what is one's own.[500] Justice establishes equality in external things, but has nothing to do properly speaking with the regulation of internal passions.[501]

FOX: And generosity is about our inner attitudes toward money?

AQUINAS: It is proper to a generous person to use money. Now the use of money consists in parting with it. For the acquisition of money is like generation rather than use; while the keeping of money, insofar as it is directed to facilitate the use of money, is like a habit. . . . Parting with money by giving it to others proceeds from a greater virtue than when we spend it on ourselves. . . . Therefore we praise a generous person chiefly for giving.[502]

FOX: And this giving comes from an inner place?

AQUINAS: The desire and delight in money is not referable to the body but rather to the soul.[503] It belongs to prudence to keep money, lest it be stolen or spent uselessly. But to spend it usefully is not less but more prudent than to keep it usefully since more things have to be considered in money's use, which is likened to movement, than in its keeping, which is likened to rest.[504]

FOX: We have been talking of some practical applications of the principle of justice in our lives and society. Now let us return to another aspect of the Via Transformativa, that of the transformation that Christ brings. We have spoken of Christ as prophet and as justice and teacher of justice and of Christ as compassion and teacher of compassion. But is there more that Christ brings in assisting us to be instruments of transformation and prophets of liberation—our own and others'?

AQUINAS: [There is] a new mode of liberation. Hebrews 9 says: "Through his own blood, Christ entered first into the sacred

---

499. Ibid., a. 3, ad 1.   500. Ibid., a. 5.   501. Ibid., a. 2, ad 3.   502. Ibid., a. 4.   503. Ibid., a. 5, ad 2.   504. Ibid., a. 4, ad 1.

place, having won an eternal redemption for us." "And the Lord placed a new song into my mouth." A new song means the New Testament. Isaiah 55 says: "I will make an everlasting covenant with you, my steadfast love for David." Revelation 14 says: "No one could sing the song, except those 144,000," since there is a new king, new law, new joys. . . . All people are singing a new song of a new law that Christ the new man has brought. Revelation 21 says: "Lo, I am doing new things." So a new people sings new things: namely, of the Incarnation of the Lord, of his resurrection, his ascension, his nativity, and other things of the like. Whence in these special ceremonies the ministers of the Church, clothed in white or silk garments, sing and read, so no one except the renewed person presumes to sing a new song. I say "song," not of vanity, not of sins, but of that which pleases God. Whence the psalmist says, "hymn" or ode, which pleases our God, that is, praise to God. Psalm 114 says: "A hymn is pleasing to you, God, in Sion." Ephesians 5 says: "Singing and making hymns in your hearts to God."[505]

FOX: You call Christ "the new man" and you speak of the "new law" that he brings that urges us to "sing new songs."

AQUINAS: In the Letter to the Ephesians Christ himself is called a "new man" on account of the new manner of his conception: "For the Lord has created a new thing upon the earth: a woman shall compass a man" (Jer. 31:22). Another factor is the novelty of the grace he bestows: "For in Christ Jesus neither circumcision avails any thing, nor uncircumcision; but a new creature" (Gal. 6:15); "and be renewed in the spirit of your mind, and put on the new person who is created according to God" (Eph. 4:23). [Christ is also a new man] on account of the new commands he sets forth: "A new commandment I give you: that you love one another as I have loved you" (John 13:34).[506]

FOX: Can you elaborate on the "new law" that Christ brings us?

AQUINAS: The teaching of Christ is called the New Testament because in it a new pact has been made between us and God concerning the kingdom of heaven.[507] Christ says, "Don't think" . . . that I shall have come, "to dissolve the law or the

---

505. In Pss 39, p. 300.   506. In Eph 2.15, p. 463.   507. In Mt 4, p. 43.

prophets." Through these two things he understands the entire continuity of the whole law, since the law was principally for the purpose of refusing evil and prophecy was for the purpose of doing good. The former was for those who do works, the latter for those who believe. . . . Christ did not come to dissolve, since it is fulfilled spiritually. For this reason he says, "I have not come to dissolve" the law, "but to complete it," that is, to fill it to perfection.[508]

FOX: How did Christ fill the law to perfection?

AQUINAS: First he filled it morally, with the sweetness of charity, by seasoning it, since the fullness of the law is delight (Rom. 13:10). John 15:11 says: "This is my command, that you love one another, just as I have loved you." Second, he fulfilled it ceremonially, by removing the veil of figures. Matthew 27:51 says: "The curtains of the temple have been torn in two." Revelation 5:9 says: "Worthy is the lamb to open the book, and solve its riddles," that is, the observations of the figures in the law. Third, Christ fulfilled the law by showing the prophecies are complete in himself. Luke (chapter 24) says: "It is necessary that the things written in the prophecies be fulfilled concerning me." Fourth, by strengthening the promises. In Galatians 3:16 it says, "The promises were made to Abraham." Fifth, by tempering judgments with compassion. John 8:11 talks about adultery: "Nor will I condemn you." Sixth, by adding counsels. Matthew 19:21 says: "Go and sell all things, etc." Seventh, by fulfilling all the promises made to them by the sending of the Holy Spirit and the Incarnation of the Son, etc. Hebrews 8:8 says: "It has been consummated."[509]

FOX: Previously in our conversation you alluded to the New Law as being one that is light and not burdensome.

AQUINAS: When anyone is in love they do not feel overburdened with the sufferings they endure for the sake of the beloved. One makes light of them. In this way the New Law is no burden.[510] It is lighter because it is the law of love, and love makes all things light.[511]

FOX: This new law certainly sounds like good news! Where do we find it?

---

508. In Mt 5, p. 57.   509. Ibid.   510. In Mt 11, p. 114.   511. In Mt 5, p. 58.

AQUINAS: The New Law is in the first place a law that is inscribed on our hearts; only secondarily is it a written law.[512]

FOX: Since you said above that "all people" are singing this new law and new song, it follows that it is available to all.

AQUINAS: When a circumference is placed in a gyre, its center is in the middle. The people of the Jews were in the middle of the tribes who stood around Judea, where praises were made to God, sacrifices were offered, and prophets did not cease. But now the compassion of God has been spread among all the peoples standing around. At the end of Mark's gospel it says: "Going into the whole world, proclaim the gospel to all creation." Therefore the psalmist says, "in the city surrounding," meaning among all the peoples of the tribes [of the earth].[513]

FOX: You say that the New Law is only secondarily a written law. But is it not written in the gospels?

AQUINAS: The letter, even of the Gospel, would kill, unless there were the inward presence of the healing grace of faith.[514] The gospel writings contain only such things as pertain to the grace of the Holy Spirit, either by disposing us to it or by directing us to the use of it.[515]

FOX: How do the gospels direct us to the use of the grace of the Holy Spirit?

AQUINAS: As to the use of spiritual grace, this consists in works of virtue to which the writings of the New Testament exhort people in diverse ways.[516] The New Law is instilled into people, not only by indicating to them what they should do, but also by helping them to accomplish it.[517]

FOX: You have spoken of the New Law as a law of love that is light to bear. How else would you characterize the New Law?

AQUINAS: The New Law is called the "law of perfect liberty" (James 1:25).[518]

FOX: What does this mean?

AQUINAS: The Gospel is called the "Law of Liberty" because the Old Law decided many points and left few to people to decide as they chose.[519] The New Law had nothing to add as regards external action.[520]

---

512. ST I-II, q. 106, a. 1.   513. In Pss 30, p. 255.   514. ST I-II, q. 106, a. 2.   515. Ibid., a. 1, ad 1.   516. Ibid.   517. Ibid., ad 2.   518. Ibid., q. 108, a. 1, ad 3.   519. Ibid., a. 1.   520. Ibid., ad 2.

FOX: That is an interesting point. The New Law adds nothing externally. Thus it is a simplification of our lives that comes about from living at a great depth and from a spiritual conversion. How would you characterize this living out of the New Law?

AQUINAS: The reign of God consists chiefly in internal acts. As a consequence all things that are essential to internal acts belong also to the reign of God. Thus, if the reign of God is internal righteousness, peace, and spiritual joy, all external acts that are incompatible with righteousness, peace, and spiritual joy are in opposition to the reign of God.[521]

FOX: Do you envision the reign of God evolving in different times, cultures, and historical periods?

AQUINAS: The state of the New Law is subject to change with regard to various places, times, and persons, according as the grace of the Holy Spirit dwells in people more or less perfectly. Nevertheless we are not to look forward to a state wherein humanity is to possess the grace of the Holy Spirit more perfectly than they possessed it in the past, especially the apostles.[522]

FOX: In other words, spiritual "progress" is not necessarily linear?

AQUINAS: The ultimate consummation of grace was effected by Christ, wherefore the time of His coming is called *the time of fullness* (Gal. 4:4). Hence those who were nearest to Christ, whether before him such as John the Baptist, or after him such as the apostles, had a fuller knowledge of the mysteries of faith. For even with regard to humanity's state we find that the perfection of human life comes in youth, and that a person's state is all the more perfect, whether before or after, the nearer it is to the time of one's youth.[523]

FOX: You certainly give youthfulness its due in the opinion you have just stated. You make a good argument against adultism. Do you see Jesus teaching us something about this need to be young or childlike?

AQUINAS: Isaiah says "a child has been born," because Christ is called a child. First, in his nativity on account of his age. Matthew 2 says: "Entering into the house, they came upon a child

---

521. Ibid., ad 1. 522. Ibid., q. 106, a. 4. 523. Ibid. II-II, q. 1, a. 7, ad 4.

with Mary his mother." Second, by possession, on account of Jesus' poverty. 2 Corinthians 8 says: "You know the grace of our Lord Jesus Christ, since on your account he became poor, although he was rich." Third, by his heart, through his humility. Matthew 11 says: "Learn from me, since I am gentle and humble of heart." Fourth, by his death, on account of the vileness of the death. Wisdom 2 says: "Let us condemn him to a shameful death."[524]

FOX: Thus you see the Jesus story as an affirmation of the *puer* side of Divinity and indeed of us. You seem to celebrate the child inside each of us.

AQUINAS: The "old person" (spoken of in the Letter to the Ephesians) is enslaved by a senility in the soul. Anything will corrupt when it deviates from the order of its inner being.[525]

FOX: And our inner being is youthful and open to the New. You earlier spoke of the New Law as being about "righteousness, peace, and spiritual joy" and as a gift of the spirit in these matters. Can you elaborate on these dimensions to the New Law?

AQUINAS: Christ was the beginning of the New Law, which proceeds along the path of gentleness.[526] The sermon that our Lord delivered on the mountain contains the whole process of forming the life of a Christian. Therein persons' interior movements are ordered. For after declaring that the human being's end is beatitude, . . . Jesus orders one's interior movements, first in regard to oneself, second in regard to one's neighbor.[527]

FOX: And so you see the Sermon on the Mount as the laying out of the New Law in which all Christians should be formed?

AQUINAS: In that sermon of the Lord the whole perfection of our life is contained. And Matthew demonstrates this through that which the Lord . . . promises. But that which human beings most desire is happiness (or "beatitude").[528]

FOX: It seems, then, that you see the Sermon on the Mount as a treatise on blessing or happiness?

AQUINAS: One must know that in those words all happiness is fully included, for everyone seeks happiness, but they differ in judging about happiness. Therefore some seek this and some

---

524. In Is 9, p. 469.   525. In Eph 4.22, p. 484.   526. In Mt 11, p. 111.
527. ST I-II, q. 108, a. 3.   528. In Mt 5, p. 49.

seek that. But we have found a fourfold opinion concerning happiness. For certain people believe that it consists only in exterior things, namely, the affluence of those temporal things. Psalm 144:15 says: "They have called the people happy who have these things." Others, that perfect happiness consists in that by which one satisfies one's own desires: whence we say: happy is one who lives as they wish. Ecclesiastes 3:12 says: "And I know that there is nothing better than to be happy, etc." Others say that perfect happiness consists in the virtues of an active life. Others, in the virtues of a contemplative life, namely, of divine and intelligible things. Aristotle is of this opinion. But all those opinions are false, but not in the same way. Whence the Lord reproves all of them.

The opinion of those who said that it consists in the affluence of exteriors, Jesus reproves when he says, "Happy the poor," namely, as it were, "unhappy the affluent." In truth the opinion of those who placed happiness in the satisfying of the appetite he reproves when he says, "Happy those who mourn." But it must be known that the appetite in a person is threefold: One is prone to anger who seeks vindication from his enemies, and this he reproves when he says, "Happy the meek." One is lustful whose good is to enjoy and take delight. This he reproves when he says, "Happy those who mourn." The third appetite is that of the will, which is twofold according to the two things it seeks. First, that no will may be coerced by a higher law; second, that it can restrict others as subjects and thus it desires to be in charge and not to be submissive. But the Lord shows the contrary in each case: according to the first, he says, "Happy those who hunger and thirst for justice;" but according to the second, he says, "Happy those who are compassionate." Therefore those who place happiness in exterior affluence and in the satisfaction of the appetite also err.

But those who place happiness in the acts of the active life, namely, in moral acts, err, but less so, since that is the way to happiness. Thus the Lord does not reprove it as an evil, but shows it ordered toward happiness, either because it is ordered toward itself, such as temperance and the like, and their end is purity of heart, since they make it overcome the passions. Or it is ordered toward another thing, and thus their end is peace and the like. For the work of justice is peace. And therefore these virtues are paths to happiness, and not happiness itself. And there is the statement: "Happy those with a clean heart, for they will see God." He does not say, "they see," since this would be happiness itself. And again, "Happy the peacemakers"—not because they are peacemakers, but because they tend toward another thing, "since they will be called the children of God."

But the opinion of those who say that happiness consists in the contemplation of divine things, the Lord reproves in regard to the temporal situation, because otherwise it is true: since ultimate happiness consists in a vision of the best intelligible being, namely, God. This is why he says, "They will see."[529]

FOX: One thing I hear you saying is that the Via Creativa, which among other things marks the birthing of virtue in us, is not the endpoint of our spiritual journey. We go beyond it; we put it to use for compassion's sake in the Via Transformativa.

AQUINAS: It is very difficult, merely to do virtuous deeds that receive the common designation of justice, but to go even further and to do them with an unsatiable desire. This is signified by hunger and thirst after justice. . . . There is a definite connection between the fourth beatitude, "Blessed are those who hunger and thirst after justice," and the gift of fortitude.[530]

FOX: And so for true beatitude we need more than virtue, we need the gifts of the Spirit.

AQUINAS: The active life consists chiefly in one's relations with one's neighbor, either by way of duty or by way of spontaneous gratuity. To the former we are disposed by a virtue, so that we do not refuse to do our duty to our neighbor, and this virtue is justice. But we are also disposed by a gift, so that we do the same much more heartily, by accomplishing works of justice with an ardent desire, even as a hungry and thirsty person eats and drinks with eager appetite. Hence the fourth beatitude is: "Blessed are they that hunger and thirst after justice."[531]

FOX: Even in the Via Transformativa, justice is not the whole journey. Rather peace and the celebration it brings is closer to the goal. But are you saying that contemplative acts do not make one happy?

---

529. Ibid.   530. ST II-II, q. 139, a. 2.   531. Ibid. I-II, q. 69, a. 3.

AQUINAS: With regard to the point that contemplative acts make one happy, two things are required. One with regard to substance, namely, that it be an act with the highest intelligible being, which is God. The other with regard to form, namely, love and delight. For delight is the perfection of happiness, as beauty is that of youth. And therefore the Lord puts forth two points: "They will see God" and "They will be called children of God." For this pertains to the nature of love. 1 John 3:1 says: "See what sort of love the Creator has given, that we are called and are the children of God."[532]

FOX: What follows from the fact of our being sons and daughters of God?

AQUINAS: We owe God imitation, since God is our Father: "Thou shalt call me Father and shall not cease to walk after me" (Jer. 3:19).[533]

FOX: How do we imitate God and walk in God's footsteps?

AQUINAS: This is done in three ways: first, by loving God. We imitate God by loving God. "Be you imitators of God as most dear children and walk in love" (Eph. 5:1–2). And this must be in the heart. Second, by showing compassion. We imitate God by being compassionate because compassion is bound to accompany love. "Be you compassionate as your Creator in heaven is compassionate" (Luke 6:36). And this must be in deed. Third, by being "perfect" (Matt. 5:48).[534]

FOX: Of course, that word "perfect" is not about perfectionism but about coming to our fullness and maturity like a ripe piece of fruit.

AQUINAS: The word "perfection" means completeness of being. . . . The terms "perfect" and "whole" have the same or nearly the same meaning.[535]

FOX: In addition to the points you have just made, is it not also true that the good news of our divinization is news that delights us and renders us blessed or happy?

AQUINAS: The virtues that dispose one toward the best dispose toward two things, namely, toward a vision of God, and toward delight. And just as purity of heart disposes toward the vision of God, so peace disposes toward the delight of God by

532. In Mt 5, p. 49. 533. OF, p. 109. 534. Ibid. 535. In Meta V, L. 18, p. 391.

which we are called and are the children of God; and thus it disposes toward delight in one's neighbor since, as is said in 1 John 14:20, "he who does not love his brother whom he sees, how can he love God whom he does not see?"[536]

FOX: It seems that you are putting a lot of emphasis on Jesus' teaching about peacemaking—that this work of the Via Trans-formativa is what brings authentic happiness in our lives.

AQUINAS: It should be noted that the two rewards of happiness are put forth in the following statements: "Happy the peace-makers" and "Happy those who suffer persecution on account of justice." All the preceding points are reduced to those two, and are the effects of all the preceding. For what happens through poverty of spirit, through grief, through gentleness, except that the heart be kept clean?[537]

FOX: Another way of saying this is that the Via Negativa, wherein we learn poverty of spirit and gentleness and undergo grief, is a path to a pure heart. But what is a pure heart?

AQUINAS: Just as an eye seeing a color ought to be pure, so the mind seeing God. Wisdom 1:1 says: "Seek God in the simplicity of the heart since God is found by those who do not test God but the Godhead manifests itself to those who have faith in it." For the heart is purified by faith. Acts 15:9 says: "By faith purifying their hearts." And since the vision follows upon faith, therefore Jesus says: "For they themselves will see God. Happy those with a pure heart," namely, those who have a general purity from the thoughts of others, by which their heart is a holy temple of God in which they see God contemplated. For a temple seems to be named from contemplating. . . . "Happy those with a pure heart" can be understood from the vision of the way. For the saints have a heart full of justice, they see more splendidly than those who see through bodily effects. For, to the extent that the effects are closer, to that extent is God more known through them. Whence the saints have justice, love, and effects of this kind, which are most like God, they know more than others. Psalm 34:8 says: "Taste, and see that the Lord is good."[538]

FOX: You said, in effect, that the heart is made pure through the Via Negativa. I am struck by your phrase, that "the saints have

---

536. In Mt 5, p. 53.   537. Ibid.   538. Ibid.

a heart full of justice." Can you elaborate more on the path to justice?

AQUINAS: What happens through justice and compassion, except that we have peace? Isaiah 32:17 says: "For the fruit of justice is peace, and the cultivation of justice is quiet and security forever." "Happy," therefore, "are the peacemakers."[539]

FOX: I hear you speaking of peace as a fruit of our work for justice, which in turn renders us delighted. How do you define peace and how do you understand Jesus' teaching assisting us to arrive at it?

AQUINAS: What peace is must be seen, and how we can arrive at it. Peace is the tranquillity of order. But order is a disposition bestowing its place on every thing unequally. Therefore peace consists in the fact that every thing has its own place. Whence the mind of the human ought to be subjected to God. Second, motion and inferior powers, which are shared by us and the animals, are subject to human beings, for humanity through its reason has charge over animals. Genesis 1:26 says: "Let us make humankind in our own image and likeness, and let them preside over the fish of the sea and the birds of the skies, and the animals of the earth, and each reptile which moves in the earth."[540]

FOX: I like the word you use—"preside" (*praesit*)—as opposed to lording over or being master of.

AQUINAS: Third, human beings may have peace with others and thus it will have been totally ordained. But that ordaining cannot be except among holy people. Psalm 119 says: "Your name is peace for those who are troubled by many things." Isaiah 48:22 says: "There is no peace for the impious." For they cannot have interior peace. Wisdom 14:22 says: "Those living in great conflict due to ignorance call so many and such great evils peace." Such a peace the world cannot give. John 14:27 says: "In a way the world cannot give, I give to you." Likewise this whole does not suffice, but they ought to make peace instead of discord. Proverbs 12:20 says: "Joy follows those who enter into the counsels of peace."[541]

FOX: But peace, even though a fruit of the spirit and of justice, is only partial and imperfect in this life.

---

539. Ibid.   540. Ibid.   541. Ibid.

AQUINAS: It should be known that peace here is incomplete, and it is not perfect, since no one can totally have their animal instincts subjected to reason. Romans 7:23 says: "I see another law in my limbs repudiating the law of my mind, and making me captive to the law of sin, which is in my limbs." Whence peace will be true peace in eternal life. Psalm 4:8 says: "In peace itself I will sleep and rest." Philippians 4:7 says: "The peace of God surpasses all understanding."[542]

FOX: Can you elaborate on Jesus' promise of our divinity when he says that we shall be called the children of God?

AQUINAS: "For they will be called the children of God" has a threefold meaning. The first is that they have the function of the Son of God for this reason: the Son of God is said to have come into the world to assemble those who have been scattered. Ephesians 2:14 says: "For he himself is our peace." Colossians 1:20 says: "Making peace with the blood of his cross both with that which is on earth and that which is in heaven." Second, through peace with love the eternal kingdom is reached in which all are called children of God. Wisdom 5:5 says: "Behold how they have been numbered among the children of God, and their lot is among the saints." Ephesians 4:3 says: "Those anxious to preserve the unity of the spirit in the bonds of peace." Third, because through this person there is a likeness to God, since where there is peace, there is no resistance. But no one can resist God. Job 9:4 says: "Who resists him, and has peace?"[543]

FOX: The beatitudes promise a fullness of joy even in this life.

AQUINAS: All these rewards [of the beatitudes] will be fully consummated in the life to come. But meanwhile they are, in a manner, begun even in this life. Because the "reign of heaven" . . . can denote the beginning of perfect wisdom, insofar as "the spirit" begins to reign in human beings.[544]

FOX: We are back to a point you made earlier: that eternal life begins here and now. Can you describe more about the blessing of eternal life?

AQUINAS: Eternal life consists in the pleasant companionship of all the blessed, a companionship that is replete with delight, since each one will possess all good things together with the

---

542. Ibid.   543. Ibid.   544. ST I-II, q. 69, a. 2, ad 3.

blessed. They will all love one another as themselves, and therefore will rejoice in the happiness of others' goods as their own. Consequently, the joy and gladness of one will be as great as the joy of all: "The dwelling in you is as it were of all rejoicing" (Ps. 85:7).[545]

FOX: You certainly name well here the celebrative side to compassion, that of rejoicing in one another's joys as one's own!

AQUINAS: These forms of happiness add to one another reciprocally, for to attain compassion is more than to be satisfied, for to be satisfied is to be filled with that which is in proportion to itself. But compassion is superabundant. Likewise not all those who receive compassion are given an audience from one king to another living king. Likewise, to be the son of a king is more than to see the king.[546]

FOX: To know that we are children of the "king" or the Creator is to experience joy?

AQUINAS: Wisdom makes us the children of God.[547]

FOX: Just as it made Christ the son of God?

AQUINAS: Wisdom 10:2 says: "Wisdom has opened the mouth of the mute, and made the tongues of infants eloquent." For Jesus himself is the wisdom of the Father.[548] Now people are called the children of God insofar as they participate in the likeness of the only-begotten and natural Son of God, according to Romans 8:29, "whom God foreknew . . . to be made conformable to the image of the divine Son." This Son is Wisdom begotten. Hence by participating in the gift of wisdom, humans attain the sonship and daughtership of God.[549]

FOX: You sense a connection between the promise of the reign of God and wisdom?

AQUINAS: The seventh beatitude is fittingly ascribed to the gift of wisdom, both as to the merit and as to the reward. The merit is denoted in the words, "Blessed are the peacemakers." Now a peacemaker is one who makes peace, either in oneself or in others: and in both cases this is the result of setting in due order those things in which peace is established, for "peace is the tranquillity of order," according to Augustine. Now it belongs to wisdom to set things in order. . . . The reward is expressed in the words, "they shall be called the children of God."[550]

---

545. AC, p. 96. 546. In Mt 5, p. 53. 547. Ibid., p. 54. 548. Ibid., p. 48. 549. ST II-II, q. 45, a. 6. 550. Ibid.

FOX: A big part of our happiness is our coming to the realization of our divinity.

AQUINAS: The Holy Spirit is called the "Spirit of adoption" insofar as we receive from the Spirit the likeness of the natural Son, who is the begotten Wisdom.[551]

FOX: So peace and happiness seem to accompany the gift of wisdom.

AQUINAS: To wisdom belongs first of all contemplation that is the vision of the Beginning, and afterward the directing of human acts to the divine law. From the direction of wisdom there does not result any bitterness or toil in human acts; on the contrary, the result of wisdom is to make the bitter sweet, and labor a rest.[552]

FOX: You say that the promises of happiness build one on the other. How do you reconcile that with the final beatitude, which is one of suffering?

AQUINAS: The eighth beatitude signifies the perfection of all the preceding ones. For humanity has been perfected in all those things at the time when people abandon none because of tribulations. Ecclesiasticus 27:5 says: "A furnace puts a potter's vessels to the test, tribulation puts just people to the test." "Happy," therefore, "are those who suffer persecution, etc."[553]

FOX: But how is persecution compatible with peace that makes us happy?

AQUINAS: Some will say that these people are not happy due to their persecution since persecution disturbs their peace or totally destroys it. But surely not their interior peace but only their exterior peace is harmed. Psalm 119 says: "Peace is your law for those who are burdened by many cares, etc."[554]

FOX: I hear you saying that the culmination of the beatitudes is that we become prophets, since prophets all undergo trials and tribulations in their struggle for justice and compassion. Are you saying that prophets are blessed and happy in spite of their trials?

AQUINAS: The persecution itself does not make people happy, but its cause does. This is why Jesus says "on account of justice." 1 Peter 3:14 says: "If you suffer anything on account of

---

551. Ibid., ad 1.   552. Ibid., a. 3, ad 3.   553. In Mt 5, p. 54.   554. Ibid.

justice, you are happy." Chrysostom says: "He did not say on account of the pagans, or on account of faith, but on account of justice."[555] Therefore Jesus says: "Happy are you," that is, the cause of acquiring happiness is present to you, "when people have cursed you," that is, when sinners have cursed you.[556]

FOX: The New Law that you find summarized in the beatitudes truly seems to be a spiritual path and one that, perhaps not so surprisingly, follows the four paths of creation spirituality.

AQUINAS: The Lord promises a kingdom that embraces each person. But he says one must arrive at this kingdom through the path of poverty, not of riches. Whence, "Happy are the poor." Others arrive at those honors through wars; but the Lord says, "Happy are the meek, etc." Others seek their consolations in pleasures, but the Lord says, "Happy those who hunger and thirst for justice." Some wish to avoid their misfortune by oppressing their subjects; the Lord says, "Happy the compassionate, etc." Some place the vision of God in the contemplation of truth along the way, but the Lord promises it in his own land; whence, "Happy those with a clean heart, etc."[557]

FOX: The kingdom of which you speak and that the New Law promises and that is under way even in this lifetime seems to include not only the beatitudes but also the fruits and the gifts of the Spirit. Can you say more about the nature of these fruits and gifts?

AQUINAS: The fruits of the Spirit are so called because they are something ultimate and delightful, produced in us by the power of the Holy Spirit.[558] The notion of fruit implies two things: first, that it should come last; second, that it should calm the appetite with a certain sweetness and delight.[559]

FOX: When I think of fruit I think of something delicious.

AQUINAS: Romans 14 says: "The kingdom of God is not food and drink, but justice and peace and joy in the Holy Spirit." Galatians 5 says: "The fruit of the spirit is peace, joy, etc." And this because it makes us love God. And in this love there is always enjoyment, since anyone is delighted in the presence of the beloved and those who love God have God present to them.[560] Proverbs 3 says that "the acquisition of wisdom is

---

555. Ibid.   556. Ibid.   557. Ibid., 49.   558. ST II-II, q. 8, a. 8.   559. Ibid. I-II, q. 11, a. 3.   560. In Pss 45, p. 327.

more rewarding than gold and silver." . . . Song of Songs 2 says: "Its fruit is sweet to my taste." . . . Ezekiel 36 says: "May you cause the mountains of Israel to shoot out like your branches, and offer your fruit to the people of Israel." . . . And Song of Songs 4 says: "Your scents are like a garden of pomegranates with all kinds of fruit."[561]

FOX: What you are saying certainly sounds delicious.

AQUINAS: Among material things fruit is the product of a plant when it comes to fruition, and it has a twofold sweetness. It has a twofold relation—to the tree that produces it and to the person who gathers the fruit from the tree. Accordingly, in spiritual matters we may take the word "fruit" in two ways: first, insofar as the fruit of anyone, who is likened to a tree, is that which they produce; second, insofar as a person's fruit is what one gathers. Yet not all that a person gathers is fruit, but only that which is last and gives pleasure.[562] The fruits are any virtuous deeds in which one delights.[563]

FOX: You say that fruit denotes something ultimate?

AQUINAS: Now the ultimate in practical matters consists not in knowledge but in an action that is the end. Hence nothing pertaining to practical knowledge is numbered among the fruits, but only such things as pertain to action, in which practical knowledge is the guide. Among these we find *goodness* and *kindness,* which correspond to compassion.[564]

FOX: And so the fruits assist our work of compassion and transformation and seem to flow from these activities. What would be another example?

AQUINAS: Peace is placed among the beatitudes, which are acts of perfect virtues. It is also numbered among the fruits insofar as it is a final good, having spiritual sweetness.[565]

FOX: And so peace comes from justice but it is not a virtue itself.

AQUINAS: Peace is not a virtue, but the fruit of virtue.[566] Peace is indirectly the work of justice, which removes the obstacles, but directly it is the work of friendship.[567] By peace one is single-minded in oneself and of one mind with others.[568] Peace is

561. In Is 3, p. 443.   562. ST I-II, q. 70, a. 1.   563. Ibid., a. 2.   564. Ibid. II-II, q. 52, a. 4, ad 3.   565. Ibid., q. 29, a. 4.   566. Ibid.   567. Ibid., a. 3, ad 3.   568. In 2 Thess, p. 584.

opposed to conflict within oneself, as well as to conflict with others outside.[569]

FOX: How about the gifts: What are they and what do they do?

AQUINAS: The gifts of the Holy Spirit are habitual dispositions of the soul, rendering it open to the movement of the Holy Spirit.[570] The gifts perfect the soul's powers, inasmuch as they are moved by the Holy Spirit.[571]

FOX: But don't the virtues we discussed in the Via Creativa perfect the soul?

AQUINAS: The virtues, which do perfect the powers of the soul as they are controlled by reason, no matter how perfect they are, need to be helped by the gifts, which perfect the soul's powers inasmuch as these are moved by the Holy Spirit.[572] In order to differentiate the gifts from the virtues, we must be guided by the way in which Scripture expresses itself, for we find there that the term employed is "spirit" rather than "gift." For thus it is written (Isa. 11:2–3): "The spirit . . . of wisdom and of understanding . . . shall rest upon him, etc." From these words we are clearly given to understand that these seven [gifts] are set down here as being in us by divine inspiration.[573]

FOX: It is telling that you find the scriptural basis for the gifts in the prophet Isaiah and you see them as applicable to Jesus. Thus they fill out a true "imitation of Christ" because, as you say, Christ was a prophet as well. Since the gifts are special divine inspirations, they would seem to relate to the reality of our divinization.

AQUINAS: These gifts have something over and above the virtues, understood in the broad way, insofar as they are divine virtues, perfecting human beings as moved by God. Hence the Philosopher [in *Ethics* vii. 1] places a kind of "heroic" or "divine virtue" above virtue commonly so called. Regarding this virtue some people are called "divine."[574] The movement of the human reason receives . . . the prompting or motion of the Holy Spirit, according to Romans 8:14, 17: "Whosoever are led by the Spirit of God, they are the children of God . . . and if children, heirs also."[575]

---

569. ST II-II, q. 29, a. 1, ad 2.   570. Ibid., q. 121, a. 1.   571. Ibid. III, q. 7, a. 5.   572. Ibid., ad 1.   573. Ibid. I-II, q. 68, a. 1.   574. Ibid., ad 1.   575. Ibid., a. 2.

FOX: And so the gifts round out the naming of our own divinity as sons and daughters of God. How would you name the origin of these gifts?

AQUINAS: All the gifts, considered as such, are attributed to the Holy Spirit forasmuch as the Spirit is by its nature the first Gift, since the Holy Spirit is Love.[576]

FOX: Will you please name these gifts of which we speak?

AQUINAS: For the apprehension of truth, the speculative reason is perfected by *understanding;* the practical reason by *counsel.* In order to judge aright, the speculative reason is perfected by *wisdom;* the practical reason by *knowledge.* The instinct of desire, in matters touching a person's relations to another, is perfected by *piety;* in matters touching oneself, it is perfected by *fortitude* against the fear of dangers. And against inordinate lust for pleasures, by *fear.* . . . Hence it is clear that these gifts extend to all those things to which the virtues, both intellectual and moral, extend.[577]

FOX: Do you consider the gifts more excellent than virtues?

AQUINAS: The gifts of the Holy Spirit are the origin of the intellectual and moral virtues, while the theological virtues are the origin of the gifts.[578] The gifts are more perfect than the moral and intellectual virtues, but they are not more perfect than the theological virtues. Rather, all the gifts are ordained to the perfection of the theological virtues as to their end.[579]

FOX: Did Christ have these gifts?

AQUINAS: The gifts properly understood are certain perfections of the soul's powers, inasmuch as these have a natural aptitude to be moved by the Holy Spirit, according to Luke 4:1: "And Jesus, being full of the Holy Spirit, returned from the Jordan, and was led by the Spirit into the desert." Hence it is manifest that in Christ the gifts existed in a preeminent degree.[580]

FOX: Now I feel I understand your spirituality much more profoundly. For I see that your entire teaching culminates as Jesus' did in his Sermon on the Mount—in preaching the coming of the reign of God. You even delineate what the reign of God is all about, namely, the beatitudes with their attendant fruits and

576. Ibid. I, q. 43, a. 5, ad 1.   577. Ibid. I-II, q. 68, a. 4.   578. Ibid. II-II, q. 19, a. 9, ad 4.   579. Ibid., q. 9, a. 1, ad 3.   580. Ibid. III, q. 7, a. 5.

gifts, and also how we get there, the "path" we take, as you call it. This path does seem to me, more than ever, to correspond to the Four Paths of creation spirituality, culminating as they do in the way of compassion. But it also takes us back to where we started, for we began with blessing (the Via Positiva) and we are ending with blessing (the beatitudes of the reign of God in the Via Transformativa). This in turn leads back to the Via Positiva. You have spoken earlier about contemplation being about the Beginning. The beginning and the end seem to be about blessing, goodness, and ultimately what you call "sheer joy."

AQUINAS: It is a mark of a good person to look for the achievement of good.[581] Sheer joy is God's and this demands companionship.[582]

FOX: And I guess that "explains," if anything does, the mystery of our existence—that we be companions to the "sheer joy" of God. I thank you for these conversations and I go away feeling a deeper connection with you than ever before. Perhaps we can conclude with some shared silence, for in a real sense it seems that silence was your final word to us—not only the silence imposed by that mysterious final year of your life, but also the silence that precedes the word and creation and that follows on our awe at creation; that underlies our letting go and that accompanies our being emptied; that emerges when we give birth ecstatically; and that occurs when transformation comes about so that we can return to the silence behind creation once again. Thank you for your words and thoughts. And also for the deep silence from which they come and to which they point.

---

581. In Ethics IX, L. 4, p. 805.   582. 1 Sent 2.1.4.

Toward the end of the last century there was a movement sponsored by Rome to revive the study of St. Thomas Aquinas and to establish his theology as the norm for Catholic seminaries throughout the world. The revival of biblical and Patristic studies later in this century and the opening of the Liturgy to the vernacular, thus displacing the dominance of Latin in the church, had the effect of moving Aquinas from the center, and his philosophy lost most of its importance for the church as a whole. It is true that Gilson with his study in the spirit of Medieval philosophy and Maritain with his attempt to show the significance of Aquinas for science, art, and politics, as well as metaphysics, had a profound effect on Catholic thought, and Garrigou Lagranace with his work on contemplation and contemplative life was able to give the mystical theology of Aquinas a central place in the doctrine of spiritual life, but the outlook of the Thomist revival was too confined to be an adequate basis for theology as a whole.

In this book Matthew Fox, in the light of his creation spirituality and his theology of the Cosmic Christ, has succeeded in restoring Aquinas to a central place in theology today. By placing the theology of Aquinas in the context of the Four Ways of the spiritual life, Positive, Negative, Creative, and Transformative, he has given it new meaning for the world today. This paradigm of the Four Ways is a deliberate shift from that of the purgative, illuminative, and unitive way of Catholic tradition. By placing the purgative ways first, this tradition gave a negative turn to the spiritual life with its emphasis on sin and redemption, while rejecting the positive values of the present world, of nature, the body, and the senses.

By placing the Positive Way first, Matthew Fox has been able to show how the theology of Aquinas is first of all a cosmology, which recognizes the revelation of God in creation as a "book" of revelation, paralleled to the revelation of the scriptures, and revealing God above all as one who pours out the divine goodness on all creatures and above all on humankind, which in Christ God assumes into God's own divine life. Aquinas's insistence on the immanence of God in creation, as he understood it, in the light of Aristotle's philosophy, actually led to his condemnation after his death by the orthodox theologians of his day. But today it can be seen as a vindication of the method of modern science in the attempt to explore the mystery of the created universe.

But the Positive Way of Aquinas is balanced by the Negative Way, in which he shows how, though God is revealed in all creatures, the Godhead yet remains in itself beyond all created beings and so far transcends our human understanding that we have to say that the universe rather tells us what God is not than what God is. The divine nature remains in itself an unfathomable mystery.

Nevertheless, because we recognize the presence of God in all creation, we are led to thank and praise God for the creation and to celebrate it as our life and work. This leads to the Creative Way. The sense of the presence of God in the world around us and in our own hearts awakens the creative powers in our nature and calls us to express our joy in art and poetry, music, and dance, and to order our lives in justice and truth.

This in turn leads to the Transformative Way, in which an inner transformation takes place. The mind and the will are transformed by the indwelling presence of God, particularly by the gifts of the Holy Spirit. This leads to social transformation as justice and compassion are seen to be the expression of the inner response to God's grace and love in human affairs. Thus, Aquinas leads us through all the stages of the spiritual life, until we reach the final transformation of our human life and of humanity and the universe as a whole in the vision of God.

Matthew Fox's method of expounding the teaching of Aquinas is by way of a dialogue between himself and the saint, in which he asks questions relevant to our present understanding of the world and elicits replies from Aquinas, all of which are taken from his own writings. He draws not only on the *Summa theologiae* and his other philosophical and theological works, but also on his commentaries on the scriptures, many of which have never been translated into English before, and also his commentary on the works of Dionysius the Areopagite, whose work he was exposed to in his youth, which reveals the depth of his mystical theology.

We have therefore in this book a compendium of the spiritual theology of Aquinas, in which his teaching comes through with a fullness and an insight that has never been presented in English before, and that moreover is shown to have a vital message for the world today. It is, therefore, a work of major importance not only for the church and the Dominican order but also for the wider world, which is looking for a philosophy that can act as a guide in the moral, social, and political problems of the world today.

It should be added that there is an unexpected personal drama in the life of the saint. In the last year of his life he was literally struck dumb. He was unable to speak or to write anymore. He himself is reported to have said that all that he had written seemed to him like straw in comparison with what he had seen. This suggests that he underwent a mystical experience that transformed his being. But it also appears that after a passionate intellectual life, in which he experienced much opposition, his human nature suffered a psychological shock. Thus Aquinas does not seem so remote from other men and women of genius who have experienced similar psychological traumas. He remains a model of a philosopher who, after devoting his whole life to the study of the ultimate meaning of nature and the human world, had at the end to surrender himself to the divine mystery that transcends the world.

BEDE GRIFFITHS

Aquinas on Cosmology

In reproducing this passage from Aquinas in which, among
other things, he corrects Aristotle's astronomy, I do not expect
the reader to follow his entire argument, since I do not myself.
The purpose of reproducing it is to demonstrate how indeed
Aquinas did understand this ancient cosmology. And to read it
is to appreciate how passionate Aquinas was about the issues of
science. One can imagine on reading this how closely Aquinas
would be studying the story of the universe as scientists are
teaching it today. Rare has been the theologian since Aquinas
who was as committed to science (what was called "philosophy
of nature" in his day) as Aquinas was.[1]

> Aristotle states the opinions which the astronomers of his time
> held about the number of planetary motions. First, he gives
> the opinion of Eudoxus; and second, that of Callipus.
>
> Now, in regard to the first opinion it must be understood
> that Plato, in attributing unfailing circularity and order to the
> celestial motions, made mathematical hypotheses by which the
> apparent irregular motions of the planets can be explained; for
> he claimed that the motions of the planets are circular and ar-
> ranged in an orderly way. And the Pythagoreans, with a view
> to putting into due order the irregularity which appears in the
> planetary motions on account of their standing still and mov-
> ing backwards, and their rapidity and slowness, and their ap-
> parent differences in size, claimed that the motions of the
> planets involve eccentric spheres and small circles, which they
> called epicycles; and Ptolemy also subscribes to this view.
>
> However, something contrary to the points demonstrated in
> the philosophy of nature seems to follow from this hypothe-

sis; for not every motion will be either towards or away from or around the center of the world. Furthermore it follows that a sphere containing an eccentric sphere either is not of equal density, or there is a vacuum between one sphere and another, or there is some body besides the substance of the spheres that lies between them which will not be a circular body and will have no motion of its own.

Further, from the hypothesis of epicycles it follows either that the sphere by which the epicycle is moved is not whole and continuous, or that it is divisible, expansible and compressible in the way in which air is divided, expanded and compressed when a body is moved. It also follows that the body itself of a star is moved by itself and not merely by the motion of an orb; and that from the motion of the celestial bodies there will arise the sound about which the Pythagoreans agreed.

Yet all conclusions of this kind are contrary to the truths established in the philosophy of nature. Therefore Euxodus, seeing this and seeking to avoid it, claimed that for each planet in the world there are many concentric spheres, each of which has its proper motion, and that as a result of all these motions the observable motion of the planets is accounted for. Hence Euxodus held that the motion of the sun as well as that of the moon involves three spheres.

For the first motion of the sun as well as that of the moon, which is the daily motion, is that by which they are moved from east to west; and he calls this motion "that of the stars whose positions remain unchanged," i.e., of the stars that do not wander, namely, the fixed stars; for, as was said above, since the motion of the fixed stars, which is from east to west, was not yet discovered to be contrary to the first motion, it was thought that the daily motion was proper to the eighth sphere, which is the sphere of the fixed stars. It was not thought, however, that the first sphere alone might be sufficient to move all the spheres of the planets by a daily motion, as Ptolemy assumed; but he thought that each planet had its own sphere which would move it by a daily motion. Therefore with a view to explaining this motion he posited a first sphere for both the sun and the moon.

He also posited a second sphere to account for the motion of the sun and the moon. This passes through the middle of the zodiac with what is called "longitudinal motion," according to which both the sun and the moon are moved from east to west in an opposite direction to the motion of the firmament.

He posited a third sphere to account for the oblique motion across the latitude of the animals symbolized in the zodiac, inasmuch as a planet sometimes seems to be farther south and sometimes farther north of the middle line of the zodiac. But this motion is more apparent and has a broader spread in the case of the moon than in that of the sun. Hence he adds that the motion by which the moon is carried along is inclined at a greater angle than the sun's motion. And Ptolemy attributed latitudinal motion to the moon but not to the sun. Hence Euxodus posited a third motion, as Simplicius says, because he thought that the sun also deviated from the middle line of the zodiac towards the two poles; and he made this assumption because the sun does not always rise in the same place during the summer solstice and during the winter solstice. But if it returned in latitude and in longitude at the same time by means of the declination of the great circle [i.e., the ecliptic] along which the sun travels, one sphere would suffice for this. Since this is not the case, however, but it passes through its course in longitude at one time and returns in latitude at another time, for this reason it was necessary to posit a third sphere. And he claimed that this third sphere of the sun is moved in the same direction as the second sphere, but about a different axis and on different poles. He also claimed that this third sphere of the moon is moved in the same direction as the first sphere. But in each case he claimed that the motion of this third sphere was slower than that of the second.

And he claimed that the motion of each of the other five planets involves four spheres, with the first and second sphere of each planet having the same function as the first and second sphere of the sun and of the moon; because the first motion, which he assumed to be that of the fixed stars, and the second motion, which passes in longitude through the middle line of the zodiac, appear to be common to all the planets.

Next he posited a third sphere for all of the planets in order to account for their latitudinal motion, and he assumed that the poles about which it is revolved were located in the middle line of the zodiac. But since he claimed that all spheres are concentric, it would follow from this that the zodiac would pass through the poles of the great circle of the third sphere, and it would follow in the opposite way that the great circle of the third sphere would pass through the poles of the zodiac. Hence it would follow that the motion of the third sphere would carry a planet right up to the poles of the zodiac, which is never seen to occur.

Therefore he had to posit a fourth sphere, which is the one that would carry the planet, and it would revolve in an opposite direction to the third sphere, namely, from east to west, in equal time, so as to prevent the planet from being diverted farther in latitude from the zodiac. This is what Aristotle means when he says that Eudoxus claimed that the fourth motion of the star is in a circle inclined at an angle to the middle of the third sphere, i.e., to its great circle.

Therefore, if he posited four spheres for each of the five planets, it follows there would be twenty spheres for these five planets. And if the three spheres of the sun and the three spheres of the moon are added to this number, there will be twenty-six spheres in all, granted that the body of each planet is understood to be fastened to the last of its own spheres.

Then Aristotle gives the opinion of Callipus about the number of spheres. Now Callipus, as Simplicius tells us, was associated with Aristotle at Athens when the discoveries of Eudoxus were corrected and supplemented by him. Hence Callipus maintained the same theory of the spheres as Eudoxus did; and he explained the positions of the spheres by the arrangement of their distances, because he gave to the planets and to their motions and spheres the same order as Eudoxus did.

And he agreed with Eudoxus as to the number of spheres of Jupiter and Saturn, because he assigned four spheres to each of these; but Callipus thought that two spheres must be added both to the sun and to the moon, if one wants to adopt a theory about them which accords with their motions. He seems to have added these two spheres in order to account for the rapidity and slowness which appears in their motions. The sun would then have five spheres, and the moon likewise would have five. He also added one sphere to each of the remaining planets—Mars, Venus and Mercury—thus giving each of them also five spheres. Perhaps they added this fifth sphere to account for the backward motion and the standing still which appear in these stars. These spheres are called different spheres, then, because the body of a planet is carried along by them.

But in addition to these spheres they posited others, which they called revolving spheres. It would appear that they were led to posit these because the last sphere of a higher planet, for example, of Saturn, must share in the motion of all the higher planets, so that its motion gets away somewhat from that of the first sphere. Hence the first sphere of Jupiter, whose poles are fastened in some way to the highest sphere of Saturn, shared to some extent in the motion of the spheres of Saturn, and thus it was not moved uniformly by the daily motion like the first sphere of Saturn. Therefore it seemed necessary to posit another sphere which revolves this first sphere in order to restore the speed which it loses because of the higher planets. And by the same reasoning it was necessary to posit another sphere which revolves the second sphere of Jupiter, and a third sphere which revolves the third sphere of Jupiter. But it was unnecessary to posit another sphere which revolves the fourth sphere, because the motion of the first sphere, to which the star is fixed, must be composed of all the higher motions. Hence Jupiter has four deferent spheres and three revolving spheres. And in a similar way the other planets have as many revolving spheres, minus one, as deferent spheres.

Therefore he says that, if all spheres taken together must account for and explain the apparent motion of the planets, it is necessary to posit, in addition to the deferent spheres mentioned above, other spheres, one less in number, which revolve and restore to the same place the first sphere of the star next in order below; for only in this way can the motions of the planets accord with all appearances.

Therefore, since the deferent spheres which belong to Saturn and to Jupiter are eight in number, because each is assumed to have four spheres; and since those which belong to the other five planets are twenty-five in number, because each of these only has five spheres, and of those at the end, which carry and regulate the star are not revolved, it follows that the revolving spheres of the first two planets, i.e., of Saturn and Jupiter, are six in number, and that those of the last four planets are sixteen in number. But since after Saturn and Jupiter there are five other planets, he evidently omits one of them, i.e., either Mars or Mercury, so that his statement regarding the last four refers to the four lowest; or he omits the moon, so that he refers to the four planets immediately following. Now he omits this either by error, which sometimes happens in the case of numbers, or for some reason which is unknown to us; because the writings of Callipus are not extant, as Simplicius tells us. Hence the total number of deferent spheres and of revolving spheres together is fifty-five.

But because the difficulty could arise whether it is necessary to add two spheres to the sun and two to the moon, as Callipus did, or whether only two spheres must be given to each, as Eudoxus claimed, he therefore says that, if one does not add two motions to the sun and two to the moon, as Callipus did, it follows that the total number of spheres will be forty-seven; for four deferent spheres would then be subtracted from the above number—two for the sun and two for the moon—and also the same number of revolving spheres; and when eight is subtracted from fifty-five, forty-seven remains.

But it must be noted that, if above when he said that the revolving spheres of the last four planets are sixteen in number, he omitted the moon, then if two deferent spheres are subtracted from the moon and two from the sun, four revolving spheres are not subtracted but only two, granted that the spheres of the moon do not have revolving spheres, i.e., four deferent and two revolving spheres; and then it follows that the total number of spheres is forty-nine. Hence it seems that Aristotle did not wish to omit the moon but rather Mars, unless one says that Aristotle had forgotten that he had assigned revolving spheres to the moon, and that this is the reason the mistake was made, which does not seem likely.

Last, he draws his conclusion that the number of spheres is that mentioned.

Then Aristotle infers the number of immaterial substances from the number of celestial motions; and in regard to this he does three things. First, he draws the conclusion at which he aims. Second, he rejects certain suppositions which could weaken the foregoing inference ("However, if there can be"). Third, he compares the points demonstrated about separate substance with the opinions of the ancients and with the common opinions held about these things during his own time ("Now traditions have").

He says, first, that, since the number of celestial spheres and the number of celestial motions is as has been stated, it is reasonable to suppose that there are the same number of immaterial substances and immobile principles and even the same number of "perceptible principles," i.e., celestial bodies. He uses the term "reasonable" in order to imply that this conclusion is a probable one and not one that is necessary. Hence he adds that he is leaving the necessity of this to those who are stronger and more capable of discovering it than he is.

Here the Philosopher rejects those suppositions by which the conclusion given above could be weakened; and there are three of these. The first is that one could say that there are certain separate substances to which no celestial motion corresponds.

In order to reject this he says that, if there can be no celestial motions which are not connected with the motion of some star, and again if every immutable substance which has reached "in itself the highest good," i.e., which has reached its own perfection without motion, must be considered an end of some motion, there will be no immutable and immaterial nature besides those substances which are the ends of celestial motions; but the number of separate substances which correspond necessarily to the number of celestial motions.

Yet the first assumption is not necessary, namely, that every immaterial and immutable substance is the end of some celestial motion. For it can be said that there are separate substances too high to be proportioned to the celestial motions as their ends. And this is not an absurd supposition. For immaterial substances do not exist for the sake of corporeal things, but rather the other way around.

Then he rejects the second supposition which could weaken the inference mentioned above. For one could say that there are many more motions in the heavens than have been counted, but that these cannot be perceived because they produce no diversity in the motion of one of the celestial bodies which are perceived by the sense of sight and are called stars.

And in order to reject this he had already equivalently said that there can be no celestial motion which is not connected with the motion of some star. His words here are that there cannot be other motions in the heavens besides those which produce the diversity in the motions of the stars, whether they be the motions mentioned or others, either the same in number or more or fewer.

This can be taken as a probable conclusion from the bodies which are moved; for if every mover exists for the sake of something moved, and every motion belongs to something which is moved, there can be no motion which exists for itself or merely for the sake of another motion, but all motions must exist for the sake of the stars. For otherwise, if one motion exists for the sake of another, then for the same reason this motion also must exist for the sake of another. Now since an infinite regress is impossible, it follows that the end of every motion is one of the celestial bodies which are moved, as the stars. Hence there cannot be any celestial motion as a result of which some diversity in a star cannot be perceived.

Then he rejects a third supposition by which the above inference could be weakened. For someone might say that there are many worlds, and that in each of these there are as many spheres and motions as there are in this world, or even more, and thus it is necessary to posit many immaterial substances.

He rejects this position by saying that there is evidently only one heaven. If there were many numerically and the same specifically, as there are many human beings, a similar judgment would also have to be made about the first principle of each heaven, which is an immovable mover, as has been stated. For there would have to be many first principles which are specifically one and numerically many.

But this view is impossible, because all things which are specifically one and numerically many contain matter. For they are not differentiated from the viewpoint of their intelligible structure or form, because all the individuals have a common intelligible structure, for example, a human being. It follows, then, that they are distinguished by their matter. Thus Socrates is one not only in his intelligible structure, as a human being, but also in number.

However, the first principle, "since it is a quiddity," i.e., since it is its own essence and intelligible structure, does not contain matter, because its substance is "complete reality," i.e., actuality, whereas matter is in potentiality. It remains, then, that the first unmoved mover is one not only in number. Hence the first eternal motion, which is caused by it, must be unique. It therefore follows that there is only one heaven.

Aristotle shows how the points discovered about an immaterial substance compare with both ancient and common opinions. He says that certain traditions about the separate substances have been handed down from the ancient philosophers, and these have been bequeathed to posterity in the form of a myth, to the effect that these substances are gods, and that the divine encompasses the whole of nature. This follows from the above points, granted that all immaterial substances are called gods. But if only the first principle is called God, there is only one God, as is clear from what has been said. The rest of the tradition has been introduced in the form of a myth in order to persuade the multitude, who cannot grasp intelligible things, and inasmuch as it was expedient for the passing of laws and for the benefit of society, that by inventions of this kind the multitude might be persuaded to aim at virtuous acts and avoid evil ones. He explains the mythological part of this tradition by adding that they said that the gods have the form of men and of certain other animals. For they concocted the fables that certain men as well as other animals have been turned into gods; and they added certain statements consequent upon these and similar to the ones which have just been mentioned. Now if among these traditions someone wishes to accept only the one which was first noted above, namely, that the gods are immaterial substances, this will be considered a divine statement, and one that is probably true. And it is so because every art and every philosophy has often been discovered by human power and again lost, either because of wars, which prevent study, or because of floods or other catastrophes of this kind.

It was also necessary for Aristotle to maintain this view in order to save the eternity of the world. For it was evident that at one time human beings began to philosophize and to discover the arts; and it would seem absurd that the human race should be without these for an infinite period of time. Hence he says that philosophy and the various arts were often discovered and lost, and that the opinions of those ancient thinkers are preserved as relics up to the present day.

Last, he concludes that "the opinion of our forefathers," i.e., the one received from those who philosophized and after whom philosophy was lost, is evident to us only in this way, i.e., in the form of a myth, as has been stated above.

NOTES

1. This passage is from In Meta XII, L. 10, pp. 904–910. It comprises the entire tenth lesson. The only alterations in the text have been the dropping of brief phrases from Aristotle in order to render the text more readable. For more on Aquinas's cosmology see his *De coelo et mundo* and also "A Note on St. Thomas' Cosmology" in Matthew Lamb, trans., *St. Thomas' Commentary on St. Paul's Epistle to the Ephesians* (Albany, NY: Magi Books, 1966), 306–309.

BIBLIOGRAPHY

Latin Editions Used as the Primary Texts of Aquinas

Aquinatis, Sancti Thomae. *Opera omnia*. Parma: Fiaccadori, 1852–1873. 25-folio vol. Reprinted New York: Masurgia, 1948–1950. [All translations from this edition contain page numbers in the footnote references.]

———. *Expositio in librum beati Dionysii de divinis nominibus*. Rome: Marietti, 1950.

———. *Super evangelium S. Joannis lectura*. Rome: Marietti, 1952.

———. *Summa theologiae*, I-III. Rome: Marietti, 1952.

———. *Quaestiones disputatae*, I-I. Rome: Marietti, 1949.

———. *Quaestiones quodlibetales*. Rome: Marietti, 1949

English Translations Consulted or Employed

Aquinas, St. Thomas. *Commentary on the Gospel of St. John*. Part I. Translated by James Weisheipl, F. R. Larcher. Albany, NY: Magi Books, 1980. (This translation ends with Aquinas's commentary up through Jn 7:53. References to his commentary beyond Jn 7:53 are from the Latin edition.)

———. *Commentary on the Metaphysics of Aristotle*. 2 vols. Translated by John P. Rowan. Chicago: Henry Regnery, 1961.

———. *Commentary on the Nicomachean Ethics*. 2 vols. Translated by C. I. Litzinger. Chicago: Henry Regnery, 1964.

———. *Commentary on Saint Paul's Epistle to the Galatians*. Translated by James Weisheipl, F. R. Larcher. Albany, NY: Magi Books, 1966.

———. *Commentary on St. Paul's Epistle to the Ephesians*. Translated by M. L. Lamb. Albany, NY: Magi Books, 1966.

———. *Commentary on Saint Paul's Epistle to the Philippians and First Thessalonians*. Translated by F. R. Larcher and Michael Duffy. Albany, NY: Magi Books, 1969.

———. *Compendium theologiae*. Translated by Cyril Vollert. Saint Louis: B. Herder, 1947.

———. *The Division and Methods of the Sciences*. Translated by Armand Maurer. Toronto: The Pontifical Institute of Mediaeval Studies, 1963.

——. *The Literal Exposition on Job*. Translated by Anthony Damico. Atlanta, GA: Scholars Press, 1989. (I did not use this text, but since it is based on the Leonine version, I recommend it.)

——. *On the Power of God*. 3 vols. Translated by the English Dominican Fathers. Westminster, MD: Newman Press, 1952.

——. *On Spiritual Creatures*. Translated by Mary C. FitzPatrick. Milwaukee, WI: Marquette University Press, 1949.

——. *On Truth*. 3 vols. Translated by R. W. Mulligan, James V. McGlynn, and Robert W. Schmidt. Chicago: Henry Regnery, 1952–1954.

——. *Summa contra Gentiles*. 4 vols. Translated by Anton C. Pegis, Vernon J. Bourke, and James F. Anderson. Notre Dame, IN: University of Notre Dame Press, 1975.

——. *Summa theologica*. 3 vols. Translated by Fathers of the English Dominican Province. NY: Benziger Brothers, 1947.

——. *Three Greatest Prayers*. Translated by Ralph McInerny. Manchester, NH: Sophia Institute Press, 1990.

——. *The Trinity and the Unity of the Intellect*. Translated by Sister Rose Emmanuella Brennan. St. Louis: B. Herder Book Co., 1946.

Source Works in English that Contain Selections from Aquinas's Writings

Bourke, Vernon J. *The Pocket Aquinas*. New York: Pocket Books, 1973.

Clark, Mary T. *An Aquinas Reader*. Garden City, NY: Doubleday, 1972.

E'Entreves, A. P., ed. *Aquinas' Selected Political Writings*. Oxford: Basil Blackwell, 1948.

Gilby, Thomas. *St. Thomas Aquinas: Philosophical Texts*. Durham, NC: The Labyrinth Press, 1982.

——. *St. Thomas Aquinas: Theological Texts*. Durham, NC: The Labyrinth Press, 1982.

Tugwell, Simon. *Albert and Thomas Selected Writings*. New York: Paulist Press, 1988.